Computational Approaches to Emotion in Artificial Psychology

Edited by

Nataša Kovač, Hojjatollah Farahani,
and Peter Watson

Routledge
Taylor & Francis Group
LONDON AND NEW YORK

Designed cover image: Getty Images

First published 2027
by Routledge
4 Park Square, Milton Park, Abingdon, Oxon OX14 4RN

and by Routledge
605 Third Avenue, New York, NY 10158

Routledge is an imprint of the Taylor & Francis Group, an informa business

British Library Cataloguing-in-Publication Data
A catalogue record for this book is available from the British Library

ISBN: 9781032800363 (hbk)
ISBN: 9781032795867 (pbk)
ISBN: 9781003495123 (ebk)

DOI: 10.4324/9781003495123

Typeset in Sabon
by Deanta Global Publishing Services, Chennai, India

Contents

Computational Approaches to Emotion in Artificial Psychology

Computational Approaches to Emotion in Artificial Psychology provides readers with a comprehensive introduction to how emotions can be processed by AI systems. It offers theoretical and practical guidance on data preprocessing and emotion analysis techniques, explores diverse real-world applications, and bridges the gap between AI and psychology.

Beginning with an introduction to the emerging field of artificial psychology, it explores the study, understanding, and recognition of emotions in various bodily signals, including facial expressions, voice, heart rate, and neural mechanisms. The book delves into data preprocessing for embodied emotion analysis, encompassing multiple data modalities like text, audio, visual, and gaze data, with a focus on Python basics for emotional AI. Additionally, it discusses EEG-based emotion decoding, emotional insights from medical imaging, affective image analysis, text-based emotion recognition, multimodal data integration, unsupervised learning for embodied emotion discovery, reinforcement learning, emotion elicitation, and predicting personality and emotional abilities using machine learning. The book concludes by examining the close relationship between cognition and emotion from the perspective of the universal structure of language and describing the use of deep fuzzy cognitive maps in diagnosing coronary artery disease.

By promoting research and innovation through case studies and experiments, the book addresses the current lack of comprehensive resources in this interdisciplinary field, making it an essential reference for researchers, practitioners, students, and professionals seeking to navigate the intersection of AI and emotions.

Nataša Kovač is an Associate Professor at the Faculty of Applied Sciences, University of Donja Gorica.

Hojjatollah Farahani is an Associate Professor at Tarbiat Modares University, Iran.

Peter Watson is a statistician at the Cognition and Brain Sciences Unit, University of Cambridge.

About the Editors

Nataša Kovač is Associate Professor at the Faculty of Applied Sciences, University of Donja Gorica. She defended her PhD thesis entitled "Metaheuristic approach to solving a class of optimization problems in transport" in 2018 at the Faculty of Mathematics, University of Belgrade, and at the same time acquired the title of Doctor of Mathematics. She was employed as an assistant at the Faculty of Technical Sciences in Novi Sad and the Faculty of Maritime Studies in Kotor. She worked as a lecturer at the Mediterranean University in Podgorica, and she also taught as a professor at the Gymnasium in Kotor. She is currently employed at the Faculty of Applied Sciences in Podgorica where she teaches euclidean and analytical geometry, stochastic processes and probability and mathematical statistics. Her research interests are statistical analysis, metaheuristics, optimization, algorithm development and applied mathematics in engineering sciences. She has specializations in data science and was awarded the following certifications: Certified Data Collection and Processing with Python (University of Michigan), Statistics with Python specialization (University of Michigan), Introduction to Data Science specialization (IBM), Applied Data Science specialization (IBM), and IBM Data Science specialization (IBM). She has published more than 60 scientific papers and has been involved in more than 10 international projects. She is one of the founders of the SME "MoDrone" supported by the Montenegrin government, which is dedicated to the development and promotion of innovative solutions. She is a full member of the Scientific Research Honor Society Sigma Xi.

Hojjatollah Farahani is Associate Professor at the Tarbiat Modares University (TMU), Iran. He received his PhD from Isfahan University in 2009, and he was a postdoctoral researcher in Fuzzy inference at the Victoria University in Australia (2014–2015), where he started working on Fuzzy Cognitive Maps (FCMs) under the supervision of Professor Yuan Miao. He is the author or co-author of more than 200 research papers and a reviewer in numerous scientific journals. He has supervised and advised many theses and dissertations in psychological sciences. His research interests and directions include psychometrics, advanced behavioral statistics, fuzzy psychology, artificial intelligence and machine learning algorithms in psychology. His recent book entitled *An Introduction to Artificial Psychology: Application Fuzzy Set Theory and Deep Machine Learning in Psychological Research using R* was published in 2023.

Peter Watson holds three degrees in Mathematical Statistics, including a PhD (Manchester). He has been providing statistical support to the research at CBSU, the Cognition and Brain Sciences Unit in Cambridge (and its predecessor, the Applied Psychology Unit) since 1994 (and prior to that fulfilling a similar role at the MRC Age and Cognitive Performance Research Centre in Manchester). He is the co-author of over 100 papers and lectures at the University of Cambridge. He is a statistical referee for several journals including *BMJ Open* and the *Journal of Affective Disorders*. He has also been a major contributor to the online CBSU statswiki web pages which receive upwards of 100,000 visits annually. He has also been Secretary of the Cambridge Statistics Discussion Group and chair since 1996 and has been a meeting organiser for the SPSS users' group (ASSESS) since 2001 and has also been a member of the Clinical Trials Advisory Panel for Alzheimer's Research UK.

Contributors

Dimitrios J. Apostolopoulos is a Greek electrical and computer engineer and researcher, born on 6 April 1980, in Athens, Greece. He holds a degree in Electrical and Computer Engineering from the National Technical University of Athens (NTUA) and has been a research associate since 2004. He is an Assistant Professor at NTUA, focusing on all-optical broadband communication systems and has authored over 150 publications in leading scientific journals. Apostolopoulos has also received the Dimitris N. Chorafas Foundation Award for his doctoral research and has served on technical program committees for various conferences.

Ioannis D. Apostolopoulos, born in Athens, Greece, in 1991, is a distinguished academic and researcher with a strong background in artificial intelligence, deep learning and data analytics. He holds degrees from the University of Patras, with a focus on Biomedical Engineering and a Doctorate in Medical Sciences. His research spans medical imaging, nuclear medicine, and air quality sensors, with a focus on developing innovative solutions using AI and machine learning. Apostolopoulos has co-authored 14 scientific papers and has been involved in multiple research projects, showcasing his commitment to advancing technology and healthcare through research.

Teresa Baggio is a prominent researcher at the University of Trento, known for her contributions to the field of neuroscience. Her work focuses on understanding the neural underpinnings of anxiety and its impact on individuals, particularly in young populations. Baggio's research has been published in prestigious journals such as the European Journal of Neuroscience and Scientific Reports, highlighting her expertise and influence in the academic community.

Richard Bakiaj has a PhD in Cognitive Science from the Università di Trento. He has a strong academic background, having double majored in Psychology and Sociology with an emphasis in Criminal Justice. Bakiaj has been involved in various extracurricular activities, including playing for the Baker men's soccer team and being a member of the Kappa Sigma fraternity. He has also served as a writing tutor and teaching assistant for Research Methods in Psychology and Human Development. Bakiaj is recognized for his contributions to the field of cognitive science and his involvement in the academic community at Baker University.

Carlo Cattani is recognized as one of the top Italian scientists in the field of mathematics. His academic contributions span various subfields, including wavelets, fractals, fractional calculus and nonlinear dynamics. Cattani has authored over 150 scientific articles and has co-authored multiple books. His research has been published in prestigious journals and has been recognized with an H-Index of 59 and 11,377 citations. He is affiliated with the University of Tuscia in Italy and has held various academic positions, including honorary professorships in Russia. Cattani's work has been influential in advancing the understanding of complex systems and has been recognized with numerous awards and honours.

Anna Feleki is a researcher with a strong background in deep learning and artificial intelligence. She has contributed to various fields, including coronary artery disease, image classification and medical decision support systems. Her work has been recognized by the European University Institute and the University of Thessaly, where she has held positions in the Department of Energy Systems and the Department of Nuclear Medicine. Anna Feleki's expertise and contributions to these fields are reflected in her publications and research activities.

Parisa Ahmadi Ghomroudi has made significant contributions to the field of neuroscience through her research publications. Her work focuses on understanding emotional processes in health and disease, utilizing MRI, fMRI and EEG to investigate various emotion regulation strategies such as acceptance, reappraisal and suppression. The full-text PDF files of her publications are available only when deposited as Open Access files, allowing for broader dissemination of her research findings.

Alessandro Grecucci is a prominent figure in the field of affective neuroscience and neurotechnology. He received his PhD in Neuroscience from the International School for Advanced Studies (I.S.A.S. - S.I.S.S.A.) and is currently the Principal Investigator of the Clinical and Affective Neuroscience Lab (www.alessandrogrecucci.it), within the Department of Education, Psychology and Communication Sciences (For.Psi.Com.), University of Bari, Italy. His research focuses on the psychological and neural mechanisms of normal emotion generation and regulation, as well as the development of biomarkers of psychological syndromes. Grecucci's work has been recognized with various awards and has been presented at international conferences, showcasing his significant contributions to the field.

Khanitin Jornkokgoud is a Lecturer in Psychology at department of Educational Psychology and Guidance, Faculty of Education, Mahasarakham University, Thailand. His research focuses on the intersection of psychology, cognitive, social and affective neuroscience, as well as machine learning. With over 9 years of experience in the technology field, he has advanced from programming and software development to system analysis and consulting. His expertise includes database design, object-oriented programming, ETL processes and data warehouse management. He has also conducted visiting research under the supervision of Prof. Remo Job and Prof. Alessandro Grecucci at the Clinical and Affective Neuroscience Lab, University of Trento. Jornkokgoud has contributed to various projects, including developing automated speech-language-based remote neuropsychological tests and creating cognitive interventions using virtual reality and augmented reality.

Miriam Langerbeck graduated from the Psychology Master's programme, specializing in Cognitive Neuroscience, at Maastricht University (Tum). She then obtained a diploma with the distinction Cum Laude. Miriam then took up a research internship at the Knolle lab at the university under the supervision of Dr Franziska Knolle, investigating changes in white matter tracts in individuals with schizotypal traits. More recently whilst at the Knolle lab Miriam has undertaken a PhD with Dr Gerard Derosiere from the Neuroscience Research Center in Lyon.

Irene Messina is a professor at Mercatorum University known for her research on attachment orientations and emotion regulation, contributing significantly to the field of psychotherapy and psychology. Her academic contributions include studies on mindfulness, psychopathological symptoms, and the relationship between attachment insecurity and depression. Messina's research has been published in reputable journals such as Research in Psychotherapy: Psychopathology, Process and Outcome, and Cognitive Therapy and Research.

Dionéia Motta Monte-Serrat is a distinguished researcher with a diverse academic background. Collaborating Researcher at the Department of Physics of the University of Sao Paulo, USP (2025–), having previously collaborated with the Department of Computing and Mathematics at USP and the Language Institute of the University of Campinas, UNICAMP, Brazil. She holds a Direct Doctoral degree in Psychology from FFCLRP-USP, Brazil, and has completed a doctoral degree programme partly at Université Paris III, Sorbonne Nouvelle. Her research interests span across various fields, including Neuroscience, Neurolinguistics, Brain Impairment, Artificial Intelligence, Neurophysiology and Natural Language. She has contributed to the National Science Network for Education (Brazil), is a member of the British Wittgenstein Society, member of the Center for Artificial Intelligence, C4AI-USP-IBM-FAPESP, leader of a research group registered with the Ministry of Science and Technology, CNPq, Brazil, to promote best practices and evidence-based educational policies. Her work has been recognized with an ORCID iD and a ResearcherID, reflecting her significant contributions to the field of research.

Serafeim Moustakidis is a distinguished AI researcher and entrepreneur with over 15 years of experience in various AI fields. He holds a PhD in Computational Intelligence and Machine Learning from Aristotle University of Thessaloniki, Greece. His research interests include signal processing, machine learning, fuzzy logic systems, support vector machines, wavelet analysis and genetic algorithms. Dr Moustakidis has published over 100 scientific papers and led more than 30 high-impact R&D projects, focusing on innovative solutions in healthcare, energy and manufacturing. He is also the founder and Chief Technology Officer of AIDEAS OU, where he leads a team creating cutting-edge AI solutions.

Elpiniki Papageorgiou is a distinguished academic and researcher with a PhD in Electrical Engineering and Computer Science from the University of Patras. She has been involved in numerous research projects and has authored several publications in the field of artificial intelligence and decision support systems. Her work has been recognized with multiple citations and she has been involved in various European and Greek projects.

For six consecutive years (2020–2025), she has been ranked among the world's top 2% most influential scientists in the field of Artificial Intelligence, according to the Stanford University study by Prof. John Ioannidis. In addition, she has been listed among the top Computer Science researchers by Guide2Research.

Papageorgiou is also the Editor of the book *Fuzzy Cognitive Maps for Applied Sciences and Engineering: From Fundamentals to Extensions and Learning Algorithms*.

Dr Nikolaos Papandrianos is an accomplished academic and researcher in the field of nuclear medicine and medical imaging. He has a strong educational background, having graduated from the Medical School of the University of Patras in 2000 and completing his PhD in Nuclear Medicine in 2011. His career includes various roles such as Consultant in the Nuclear Medicine Department of University Hospital, Larissa, Greece and Director of the Nuclear Medicine Laboratory at "Diagnostico Medicine Ltd", Larissa, Greece. Dr Papandrianos has authored numerous publications and has participated in numerous national and international conferences and seminars. His research interests span nuclear medicine, nuclear imaging, decision-making, myocardial perfusion scintigraphy, SPECT/CT imaging and medical informatics with applications in artificial intelligence techniques.

Nikolaos D. Papathanasiou is an Assistant Professor in Nuclear Medicine-Hybrid Imaging at the Patras Hospital University, where he focuses on clinical duties related to the PET/CT Unit of the Nuclear Medicine Department. He graduated from the Medical School of the National Kapodistrian University of Athens in 1999 and completed his PhD thesis.

Mirela C. C. Ramacciotti is a distinguished professional with a rich academic background and extensive experience in education, particularly in neuroscience, language acquisition and pedagogical practices. She holds multiple advanced degrees, including two PhDs, and specializes in the transdisciplinary area of Mind, Brain and Education. Her professional experience spans decades, and she is recognized for her contributions to the field through her research and publications. Ramacciotti is also involved in various educational initiatives and has been a consultant and trainer for schools in learning and education management. She is an Adjunct Coordinator for the National Science for Education Network (CpE Network) that promotes best practices and evidence-based educational policies.

Rudolfo Rizzi holds a master's degree in Cognitive Science from the University of Trento with a thesis in precision psychiatry titled "Detecting Major Depressive Disorder from rs-fMRI and sMRI features: a data fusion machine learning approach".

Preface

There is a growing intersection of artificial intelligence, psychology and human emotion. As AI systems become more integrated into our lives, understanding and recognizing emotions becomes crucial for enhancing human-computer interaction, mental health monitoring and personalized user experiences. Although science has comprehensive resources, they do not bridge the gap between AI and emotions. In this regard, it is important to set the stage for computational approaches to emotion in artificial psychology with the goal of propelling the development of new cognitive and behavioral models and theories with higher predictive power. This book seeks to fill this gap, making it essential for researchers, professionals and students looking to explore this cutting-edge field.

We aim to offer practical guidance on data preprocessing and emotion analysis techniques, exploring diverse real-world applications, bridging the gap between AI and psychology, promoting research and innovation through case studies and experiments, and addressing the current lack of comprehensive resources in this interdisciplinary field. In doing so, we hope that this text becomes an essential reference for researchers, practitioners, students and professionals seeking to navigate the intersection of AI and emotions, equipping readers with practical tools, including Python-based techniques, to study, analyze, understand and recognize emotions with artificial intelligence.

Acknowledgement

We would like to thank the team at Taylor & Francis for their support in bringing this book to fruition. Our thanks go to Tori Sharpe for supporting our ideas at the outset and suggesting further topics to explore, Ceri McLardy for facilitating publication and Ilma Warsi for reviewing the content and commenting about the layout of the book.

1 Introduction to Emotions

An Ideological, Historical, and Transactional Overview

Mirela C. C. Ramacciotti

1.1 Introduction

In the Western world, around the 16th century, the word "emotions" entered our vocabulary. Based on the Latin word *emovere*, from *e-* (variant of *ex-*) meaning "out" joined with *movere* meaning "move", the term was used to refer to a public disturbance, as literature in the French language attests (Dixon, 2012). However, in the Eastern world, in China more specifically, origins date back to the early sixth to fifth centuries BCE (Seok, 2021). Interestingly, Chinese origins of emotions are linked to that of *qing* (情), an ideogram that semantically encompasses – among other uses and transformations over time – ontological meanings of essence, nature, reality *on a par* with psychological meanings of disposition, desire, and feelings that emerge *genuinely* (Seok, 2021). From its inception, *emotions* in Chinese philosophy are fundamentally based on interactive dispositions, thus involving genuine perceptions, motivations and affections of the self in relation to others (Seok, 2021).

Back in the western world, the spelling in French – *émotion* – derived from the word *émouvoir* meaning "excite". The French philosopher Descartes tried to incorporate the term into his works as a substitute for the term passion (Dixon, 2012). However, it took more than a century, and other contributors – David Hume and Adam Smith – for emotions to figure as a general term denoting mental agitation (Dixon, 2003, 2012). In the 17th century, the term entered the English language through a translation of Michel de Montaigne's essays (Dixon, 2012).

In both (English and French) linguistic traditions, the term "emotion" historically denoted a form of physical perturbation – manifesting as public commotion, bodily agitation of organic matter, and the animation of entities, whether human or non-human (Dixon, 2012). During the 18th century, emotion denoted a combination of bodily agitation and mental feelings (Dixon, 2012). It was in the 19th century, though, that emotions definitely entered our language as referring to appetites, desires (or passions) and affections (or sentiments) in humans. This feat was achieved by the moral philosopher and professor, Thomas Brown, during his lectures on the science of the mind

DOI: 10.4324/9781003495123-1

(Dixon, 2003, 2012). Since then, emotions have designated all-encompassing feelings (and their states), sentiments, pleasures, pains and affections in a term that went from folk usage to the scientific realm (Dixon, 2012). This turned the work of those involved in understanding and researching emotions into a herculean task. Arguably, hitherto have come the multitude of theories and conceptions that have populated the field ever since.

Emotion as a keyword became known through the works of William James due to his usage of the term in the article "What Is an Emotion?" (Dixon, 2012; James, 1884). James brought to the fore the idea that emotions as feelings are not static states but rather dynamic, i.e., subject to change. This happens according to changes in perceptions of physiological conditions, meaning autonomic and motor functions (Scarantino & de Souza, 2021). Perhaps the following phrase best summarises this key notion: "our feeling of [bodily] changes as they occur is the emotion" (James, 1884, pp. 189–190).

Hence from the Western tradition, it carries a lot of weight, semantically speaking, in thinking that emotions are what make us connect to the outside world – the moving outwardly of our initial quest – generating some disturbance or change thereby denoting certain excitement. In that sense, it is not dissociated from the Chinese philosophical conceptualisation of emotions for they are taken as holistic affects that include senses, thinking, and feelings in constant interaction with the outside world (Seok, 2021). In short, emotions constitute communication heuristics;[1] they provide shortcuts for internally generated messages that are channelled out via facial configurations. If there is universality in them, it should be taken as genuine expressions of individualised, constantly reconstructed messages which depend on others to be construed at each moment in time.

Thus, emotion expressions communicate instances, states, and experiences, much like language does (Kalateh et al., 2024). Henceforth, emotions should not be taken as universally pre-set, deterministic phenomena, as many still believe, and most perpetrate, based on identification of standardised facial expressions. In addition, the notion that emotions communicate bodily states without the need for words does not mean that words should not be considered when emotions are created and/or communicated (Barrett, 2017a, 2020). Emotions, by virtue of their communicative function, serve to convey internal states both to oneself and to others. In doing so, they integrate elements of creation – understood as the recombination of fundamental components – and of communication, which presupposes the transmission of meaning between a sender and a receiver grounded in shared conceptual frameworks (Berlo, 1960 in the communication model known as source-message-channel-receiver, or SMCR).

Therefore, language – meaning the use of words – becomes a crucial element when the concept of emotion is formed in one's mind (Barrett, 2017a, 2020). Further, language is also necessary to enable recognition by another mind that sits at the receiver end and has to construe what a certain emotion entails in the social reality shared by the sender and receiver (see Figure 1.1).

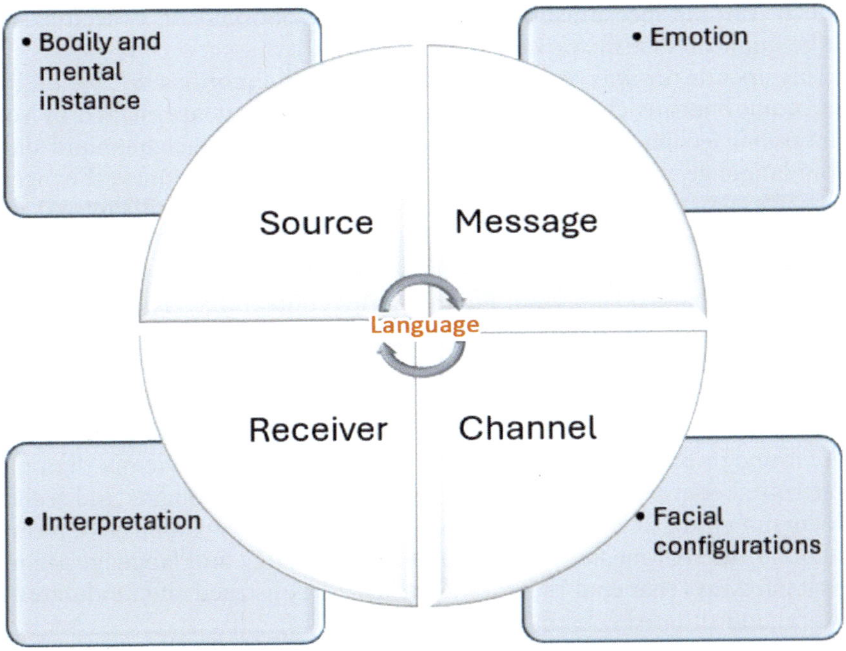

Figure 1.1 The SMCR model (Berlo, 1960) applied to an overarching understanding of emotions based on meaning-making dependent on language. Source: Author.

Of note, emotions imply mutual understanding and carry with them a repertoire of words that generate widely shared concepts. Such concepts allow for categorizations underlying constructs that become shared. These constructs enable interpretations which tend to be shared, reinforced and reiterated. When considering universality that emotions entail, appreciation should be turned not to their end means, i.e., their expression, but rather to their origins, i.e., how emotions got to be what we understand them to be. This process happened through constructs and concepts acquired over time as individuals developed and interacted with the contexts in which they found themselves. As we shall later appreciate in greater detail, recent research on brain encoding of emotion concepts showed how representations of emotion concepts find stability by late childhood and synchronization between individuals in adolescence (Camacho et al., 2023). This stability is intrinsically related to statistical learning. As perceptions shift over time, the way emotions develop and are learned since infancy happens through extraction of environmental patterns that are subject to change (LoBue & Ogren, 2022). These patterns sustain the regularities of emotion display in different social contexts (Wang et al., 2025). Critically, this extraction is regarded as an implicit learning mechanism, meaning that consciousness or awareness may not be implicated in the process (Conway, 2020).

This upends the way that we discuss emotions. Emotions do rely on biological mechanisms engendered in our species, but they are shaped by socioemotional feedback, which is enhanced by words that change and differ (from language to language). Words enable us to form the mental concepts that are externalised – sometimes via facial configurations – in cultural contexts. Such are the shared spaces where emotions acquire a transactional nature due to the co-construction that shapes our realities from time to time (Barrett, 2017a, 2017b, 2020). Enlarging this context in geographical terms, as in westernised-only versus other-worldly reports of shared constructs, may shift how emotions are configured. Cultural differentiation also matters in how physiological aspects are viewed and narrated. For instance, in studying an African tribe's account of emotionally laden experiences, participants were found to rely much more on concrete and contextual factors than their westernised counterparts, who relied more heavily on thoughts and feelings (Hoemann et al., 2023). There is more to emotions than subjective feelings and other internal mental states. In summary, biology and language are universal pathways that enable emotions which are construed and modulated by cultural and situated constraints.

Thus, taking emotions for expressions that are universal and have an evolutionary significance to justify automation for emotion detection might conflate ideas that deserve a more careful treatment. For instance, pushing forward the notion that emotions are universal to justify shortcuts in emotion recognition means overlooking important differences that cultures hold in making facts out of the meaning that emotions carry (Mesquita et al., 2017; Mesquita & Walker, 2003). Further, culture shapes perceptions to the point of running counter to the evolutionary perspective of emotions as universal features impervious to cultural modulation (Crivelli et al., 2016, 2017; Gendron et al., 2018, 2020) or to the situation or goal one may hold from time to time (Hoemann et al., 2023).

Treating emotions in a careful way implies digging into their basic foundations, those that take us from the simple – yet prescient – semantically rhetorical question asked in the beginning – to the cardinal points in the study of emotions as definitions that are very hard to come by (Adolphs et al., 2019; de Waal & Andrews, 2022; Dixon, 2012; Izard, 2010a, 2010b; LeDoux, 2021). Treating emotions this way may prevent us from misconstruing concepts, such as smiles equating joy and tears equating sadness.

Emotion, as an area of knowledge, undergoes constant progress to account, for example, for physiological activity (Hoemann et al., 2023) and multiplicity in facial movements (Dúran & Fernández-Dols, 2021) that point towards the importance of embodiment, culture, and language (the cardinal points mentioned in the previous paragraph). Both topics – physiology and facial movements – signal endeavours to uncover bodily and mental events that exemplify and reflect neural representations in more ways than one (Westlin et al., 2023). They also encompass physical and bodily properties that enable cellular ensembles – in a many-to-one fashion (Westlin et al., 2023) – of neural patterns. For these collections to become meaningful prescriptions for actions – or emotions – we need a brain that detects and interprets interoceptive signals; a mind that develops them into concepts; and other people that co-construct a social reality where emotions become "sources of wisdom" when displayed (Barrett, 2017a, p. 246). Doing so may allow us to comprehend what emotions entail.

And while we have opted for the use of "humans" focusing attention on our species, it does not follow that other animals do not have emotions. It is just a necessary resource to limit this overview to the inherent complexity – originating from multiple causality and implying variable instead of normative treatments – that contemplating emotions in our species entails. It also entails treating emotions as conscious precepts that allow for differentiated assessment (Malezieux et al., 2023).

1.2 Emotions: Notions That Steered Taxonomies

In the first half of the 20th century, Donald O. Hebb (1946) ascertained that emotions could be referenced as "summary descriptions and predictions of behavior" (op. cit, p. 89). He also advanced that emotions are "inferred special states...of changed responsiveness" (Hebb, 1946, p. 104). Presciently, Hebb touched on some aspects that have proved relevant to how the study of emotions has developed, especially in the present century. Let us examine them in turn.

A summary, as stated by Hebb, presupposes a combination of primary elements, those that provide the main facts or ideas about something (as stated by the Cambridge Dictionary, online version[2]). To pave our understanding, emotions may be constituted of distinct affects, the primary elements, that combine to give a main idea about an emotional state. This indeed seems to be the current direction in the field (Hoemann et al., 2023). An inference, as stated by Hebb, presupposes that a given result comes from a most probable (inferred) cause. Hence, emotional states may be regarded by each individual subjectively based on the most likely cause(s) available (Barrett et al., 2019). According to Hebb, a special physiological state arises in organisms striving for constancy or homeostasis within dynamic environments. This state presupposes that the brain continuously regulates metabolic states by integrating signals that indicate changes requiring intervention (Barrett, 2017a, 2020). Thus, emotions may be taken as concepts formed over time that attribute meaning to interoceptive, sensory, and musculoskeletal signals (Barrett, 2017a, 2020). According to this viewpoint, these concepts emerge as an integrative experience that spans over sensory modalities, i.e., it is supramodal (Barrett, 2017b). Another viewpoint attributes such meaning as independent of the sensation evoked, i.e., an amodal experience (Kryklywy et al., 2020). In section 1.4 we further explore what these different viewpoints mean to emotions. Returning to Hebb's influential work, he discussed the prediction of behaviours as contingent upon contextual factors. Therefore, the specific situation, cultural background, and manner of emotional expression should be incorporated into a comprehensive understanding of emotions and the discourse surrounding them (Barrett, 2017a, 2020; Hoemann et al., 2023; Immordino-Yang, Yang & Damasio, 2016; Saxbe et al., 2013).

Defining a construct is necessary for the application of a scientific treatment. This is especially relevant for emotions, a field with a long-suffering history of a lack of consensus (Gendron, 2010; Gendron & Barrett, 2009). Over time, different strands have merged into clusters based on how characteristics were combined. Gendron and Barrett (2009) presented distinct researchers whose work can be understood in the following succinct way: (i) The *basic emotions approach* combines theories and works that have taken emotions to be innate and universal, reflexive and homologous, composing a fixed set of recognisable facial expressions largely independent of culture and language; (ii) The *appraisal approach* combines theories and works that claim emotions are intentional states that presuppose a cognitive mechanism which emerges via meaningful interpretation of situational events; and (iii) The *psychological constructionist approach* takes emotions as subjective, individual experiences constructed or inferred based on psychical compounds pertaining to different mental states which are combined and generated in varied ways dependent on cultural, contextual, and linguistic influences. Figure 1.2 summarizes how these approaches share an evolving interrelatedness yet preserve their distinctness focused on how emotions are characterized.

Given such a definition, emotions have been distinguished over time based on their independent qualities. This had a precursor in the works by Wilhelm Wundt, as related by Gendron and Barrett (2009). According to them, emotions are distinct from simple feelings or momentary affective states. This is a relevant distinction and can exemplify how emotions become a complex area. Whereas some authors take emotions to be synonymous with *affect* (*e.g.*. Kuppens, 2015), others distinguish them (*e.g.*, Barrett, 2017a, 2020) by the point of complexity (Reitsema et al., 2022). Concerning affect, operationally defined as the conscious feeling of experiences lived, core elements are (i) valence (pleasant and unpleasant); (ii) arousal (arousing and subduing);

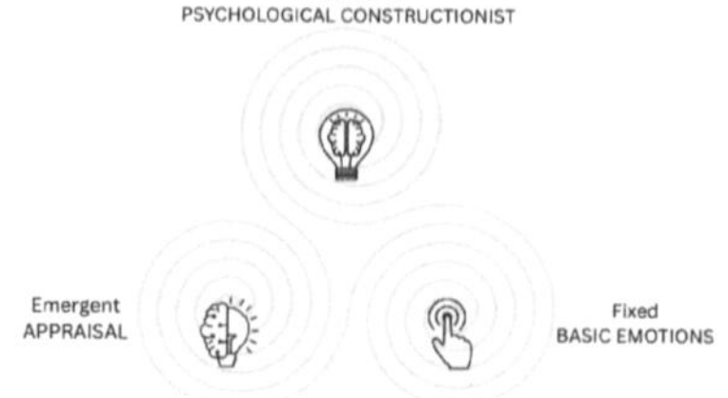

Figure 1.2 Main approaches to how emotions are characterised. Source: Author based on Gendron & Barrett (2009).

and (iii) intensity (straining and relaxing). But it was with appraisal, meaning how one interprets a situation, that feelings of attraction or aversion as distinctive processes underlying emotions came to the fore (Arnold, 1960). Recognizing that the same stimulus can evoke different emotions in the same person depending on timing and context, the field advanced by understanding that actions such as withdrawal or approach are driven not by events themselves, but by how individuals appraise these events and the emotions that result. Arnold (1960) devised a three-dimensional structure for appraisal depending on an internal, individualised analysis of the ensuing circumstances that could be ascertained as good or bad, present or absent, and easy to attain or avoid (Scarantino & de Souza, 2021).

Further, when emotions were taken as constructs based on affective states, patterns began to emerge. Such patterns can be different between individuals (Barrett, 2017a, 2020) for reasons like culture and language as referenced before, but also within the same individual (Fisher, Medaglia, & Jeronimus, 2018) in any single day. Understanding how emotions change means conceptualising them in terms of dynamics that fluctuate over different time periods (as in hours, days, years, and developmental periods) over the life course (Barrett et al., 2016; Houben et al., 2015; Reitsema et al., 2022). Emotional dynamics encompass the intensity (strength), variability (dispersion), inertia (temporal persistence) and instability (temporal dependent fluctuations) that a single emotional concept may have and also the augmentation (increase) and/or blunting (decrease) together with differentiation or granularity (specificity) multiple emotion concepts may display over time (Reitsema et al., 2022).

In the face of the inherent complexity of tackling a topic that has failed to reach a consensus and that has so many variables to account for, here we will proceed with an analysis of attributes considering that: (i) emotions may be positive or negative; and while some have taken them to vary along a continuum with paired opposites, such as ecstasy and grief (Plutchik, 2001), others have taken them to be discrete, distinctive – although interrelated – elements in a contained set, such as Ekman's seven basic emotions (Ekman, 2012); and (ii) emotions are the precursors of motivated behaviours, such as when one runs away because they get afraid of unusual sounds like the roar of a bear (James, 1884). Taken together, those two attributes have given rise to various theoretical taxonomies of emotions, a few of which we have singled out to be succinctly analysed next.

When emotions are considered in a continuum, dimensional circumplex models have been created to organise them. Russell (1980) laid out emotion/affect in a bidimensional activation model where arousal (high or low levels of physiological excitation on a *y axis*) and valence (positive and negative activation on a hedonic scale or *x axis*) are used to map emotions in a cartesian plane which vary in intensity according to how far they are from the centre (see Figure 1.3).

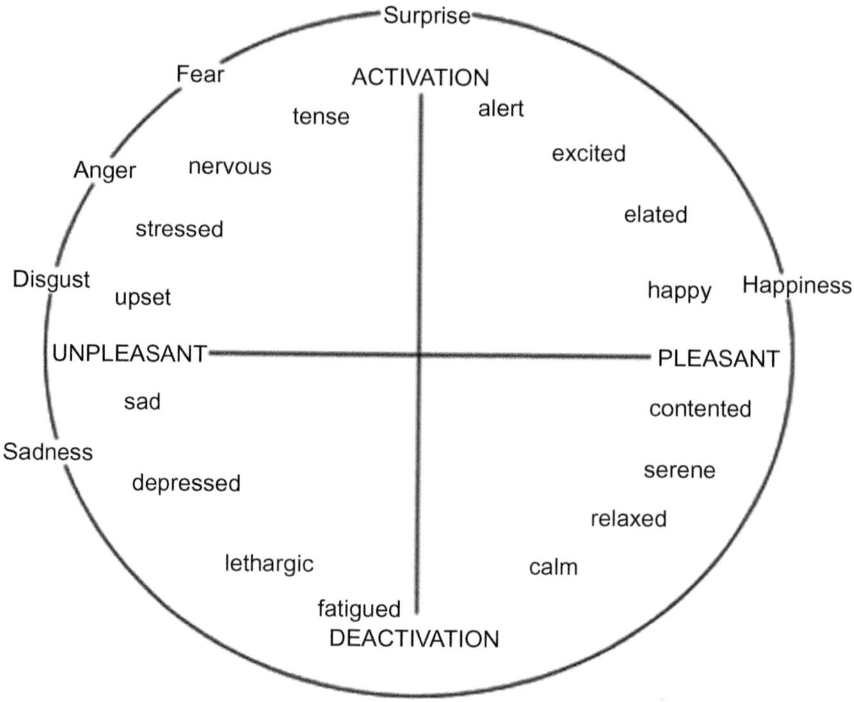

Figure 1.3 Russell's (1980) circumplex model.

Since then, the model has been further developed by Watson and Tellegen (1985) who rotated the original circumplex model by 45 degrees (see Figure 1.4). That allowed them to add two new dimensions termed High Positive Affect and High Negative Affect. The result was a set of eight octants spread out over four dimensions: (i) pleasantness/unpleasantness; (ii) engagement/disengagement; (iii) positive affect; and (iv) negative affect. Later Watson et al. (1999) termed Positive Affect and Negative Affect as Positive Activation and Negative Activation. This was done to emphasise that such terms represent highly activating emotions.

In 1999, Russell and Barrett defined core affect as a conscious process that can be reached via pleasant/unpleasant feelings (x axis) and activation (y axis). The novelty of their model lay with "prototypical emotional episodes" that could happen longitudinally and might be categorised (as anger, fear, shame, etc.).

In 2001, Plutchik presented a three-dimensional model based on a coloured wheel. The vertical axis of the cone-shaped model accounts for intensity while the circular dimension represents similarity and builds on four opposing pairs – ecstasy-grief; admiration-loathing; terror-rage; amazement-vigilance

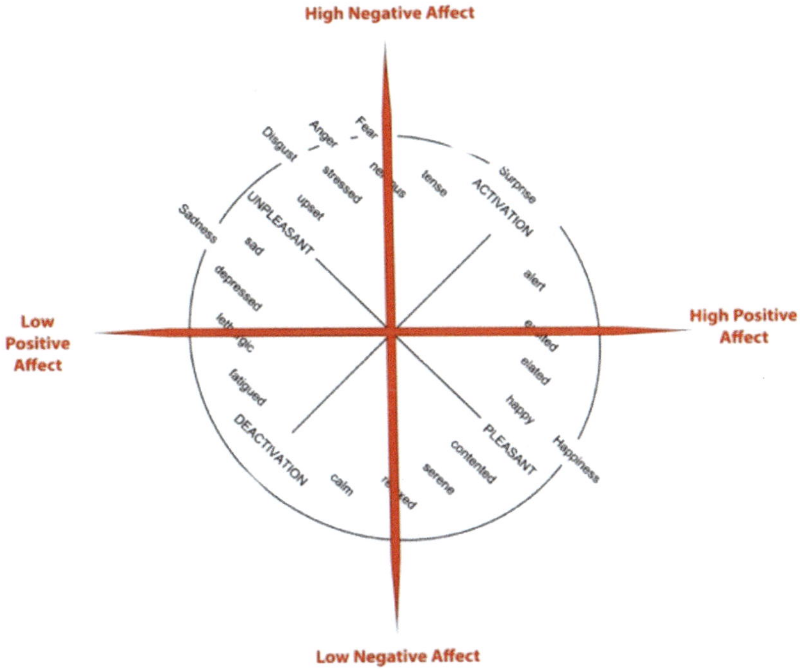

Figure 1.4 Watson and Tellegen's (1985) 45° rotation of Russell's (1980) circumplex model.

– of the eight primary emotion dimensions that vary in degree of arousal (see Figure 1.5).

Opposing a Cartesian view, Barrett proposed in 2006 that emotions are constructed concepts. Such concepts would be steered by core affects, or neurophysiological states, which build upon valence (pleasure or displeasure) representing subjectivity, and upon arousal (or the amount of uncertainty when brains try to predict the meaning of the signals they get from metabolic states). Affects would activate or deactivate concepts in instances rather than categorically. That would explain why emotions could vary according to the situation and the individual as they are dependent on the context one is in. We will come back to this notion in greater depth in Section 1.4.

When emotions are taken as discrete categories – or labels – they tend to be considered as innate and universal, therefore serving an evolutionary purpose that builds on primary elements. These elements, in turn, may be combined to give rise to more elaborate states. Paul Ekman (2012) is credited with work on a set of seven basic emotions, although stating that "no emotion exists as a single affective or psychological state" (https://www.paulekman.com/universal-emotions/). Together with other colleagues, Ekman theoretically and experimentally developed, along two decades of research,

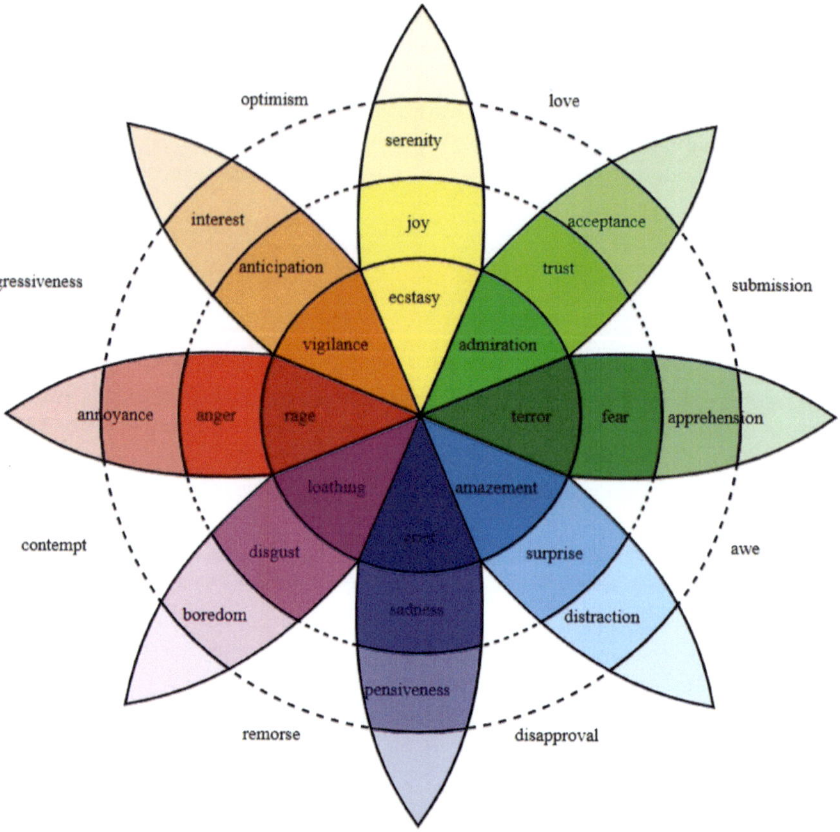

Figure 1.5 Plutchik's wheel of emotions. Source: Created by Machine Elf 1735 - Own work, Public Domain, https://commons.wikimedia.org/w/index.php ?curid=13285286

the notion of seven core emotions (joy, anger, fear, surprise, sadness, disgust, and contempt) taken as automatic appraisals that transcend cultural differences. Most of these discrete categories were also taken as innate, but termed "affects" by Sylvan Solomon Tomkins, a mentor to Ekman. Tomkins, in a series of four volumes (1962, 1963, 1991, 1992), defined the affect system as consisting of dyads (interest-excitement, enjoyment-joy, surprise-startle, distress-anguish, anger-rage, fear-terror, shame-humiliation), disgust [to noxious tastes] and revulsion [to noxious odours] to account for possible variations. Another disciple of Sylvan Tomkins, Carroll Izard, provided an enlarged set of ten discrete emotions (fear, anger, shame, contempt, disgust, guilt, distress, interest, surprise, and joy) which he insisted were distinct and innate (Izard, 1977). At a time when emotions were indiscriminate, Izard defended the idea that emotions served the purpose of adaptation and could be expressed distinctively via facial feedback.

Except for the notion developed by Barrett (2006), theories developed under both models – discrete or dimensional – subscribe to the idea that emotions are bound to, or emerge from, a primary and innate set, recognisable across the human species, i.e., they are not culturally responsive. This leads to the notion that they have developed alongside our evolution as mammalians. Hence, we proceed now to a brief exploration of historical beginnings with ideas put forth over time.

1.3 Emotions: Brief Overview of Main Contributions Across Time

In recollecting some milestones for the understanding of emotions, we intend to give their main ideas spread over the past couple of centuries in tandem with the objectives of their work. For a dedicated historical account, we recommend readers to the works of Dalgleish (2004), Barrett and Lindquist (2008), Gendron and Barrett (2009) and Gendron and Barrett (2017, especially for faces).

The field of affective neuroscience began over 150 years ago (Graeff, 2018). It is taken generally as initiating with Charles Darwin's book *The Expression of Emotions in Man and Animals* (Darwin, 1872). In this publication, initially conceived as a chapter of a previous book (*Descent of Man* published in 1871), Charles Darwin proposed a biological, evolutionary trait untethered from culture and learning (Castilho, 2021). In this proposition, basic emotions would be constituted into modules generating specific behaviours manifested as joy, fear, sorrow, and anger (Darwin, 1872). Darwin's theoretical proposal was based on the observation of animals, in general, and on the correlation of these observations with human behaviours (Graeff, 2018). In his proposal, Darwin generated a postulate; that emotions would have an adaptive value, contributing to a natural selection of the best set of emotions, understood as reactions, which would allow humans to better adapt to environments – therefore preserving the individual and the species – in order to lead to better social communication. Darwin also postulated that such evolutionary sets of reactions would be homologous, i.e., bear correspondence between species (Graeff, 2018).

Darwin's theory inspired several followers such as Walter Rudolf Hess, Nobel laureate in Physiology or Medicine in 1949 for having made the link between pre-organised neural networks in the central nervous system (CNS) and basic emotions, such as fear. By working with animal models, Hess stimulated the medial hypothalamus of cats, the subcortical area of the diencephalon, and observed defence responses similar to those presented to natural threats (Hess & Brügger, 1981). In the experimental paradigm, the cat manifested the same behaviour (fear) as if it were facing an aggressive dog. Through this paradigm, Hess claimed to have furnished evidence of the Darwinian theory of the expression of emotions, emphasising the role of the hypothalamus in coordinating the functions of internal organs. Hess shared the Nobel Prize that year with neurosurgeon Antônio Egas Moniz for the surgery he had performed – a lobotomy of the prefrontal cortex – in order to deal with certain psychoses or mental disorders. Dr Moniz was the preceptor for the neuroscientist Antonio Rosa Damasio, an important researcher in our current knowledge of emotions who we will return to, in greater depth, in the next section.

In the last quarter of the 19th century, William James (1884), in the United States, and Carl G. Lange (1885), in Denmark, held coincidental – yet separately proposed – theories about how emotions evolve. To both of them, organic sensations were responsible for physiological responses – vasomotor or circulatory according to Lange (1885) and visceral according to James (1884) – and behavioural responses. Their views were so contingent on physiological manifestations that, should they be removed from the emotional experience, nothing would remain according to their propositions (Cannon, 1927).

Thus, to James and Lange, sensations – or bodily changes – came before the individual perception experienced subjectively as an emotion. Their joint views of emotions as organic processes were shaped into, and named, a theory of emotions by John Dewey (1895). As the saying goes, whoever tells a tale adds a tail, and Dewey seems to have done that because he claimed that James assigned a distinct biological state to each category of emotion (Barrett, 2017a, 2020). However, what James postulated was that each instance of an emotion might be linked to a distinct biological state (Barrett, 2017a, 2020). As instances are different from categories, the tail seems to have become a tale and interpretations led to some confusion.

However, important caveats to the so-called James-Lange proposition soon emerged. By the end of the first quarter of the 20th century, Cannon (1927) pointed out that physiological changes – by being more stable and slower in processing stimuli – occurred independently of behaviours deemed emotional. In a later development of experimental findings derived from visceral phenomena, Cannon, together with Philip Bard (his doctoral student at the time), postulated a theory of emotions based on an uncoupling of the emotional expression, processed by the hypothalamus, and the emotional feeling, processed by the dorsal portion of the thalamus. Cannon (1927) contested the notion that visceral processes underlie emotions, stating that: "responses in the viscera seem too uniform to offer a satisfactory means of distinguishing emotions which are very different in subjective quality" (1927, p. 110). Importantly, Cannon pointed out that afferent impulses from viscera were not the total picture and that subcortical centres, such as the thalamic complex, were the driving forces of emotional expressions. Of note, Cannon encouraged the notion that subjectivity did play a part in emotions.

In 1962, Stanley Schachter and Jerome E. Singer published a paper entitled "The Cognitive, Social, and Physiological Determinants of Emotional State" relating findings obtained from an experiment conducted at the University of

Minnesota as part of a research programme based at Columbia University. Findings confirmed the authors' hypothesis that cognitions may explain physiological arousals and, should they be lacking, i.e., in the absence of an appropriate explanation, the sympathetic activation (physiological arousal) may give rise to a variety of emotional states. Theirs was a two-component model (general arousal and pertaining cognitive interpretations resulting in an emotion) that paved the way for psychological constructionist views. Their conclusions were crucial in spreading the notion that "cognitive factors appear to be indispensable factors in any formulation of emotion" (Schachter & Singer, 1962, p. 398).

Following these theories, there were great efforts in explaining emotions. Most, however, have arisen from central tenets of each theory. Pribram (1970) and Nauta (1971), for instance, built on the ideas of James and Lange on physiological arousal. Specifically, in investigating the role of the prefrontal cortex, Nauta (1971) explored interoceptive information, i.e., that information whose "pre-setting could be thought to establish a temporal sequence of affective reference points serving as 'navigational markers' and providing, by their sequential order, at once the general course and the temporal stability of complex goal-directed forms of behaviour" (1971, p. 183). Pribram (1970) defined emotions as "neural programs which are engaged when the organism is disequilibrated" (op. cit., p. 43). To Pribram, emotions should be conceived as "plans" engaged to provide for the arousal, or reaction, that the organism experiences when a reason emerges. Both notions, i.e., *interoceptive information* (Nauta, 1971) and *emotions as plans of neural programmes engaged in an unbalanced state* (Pribram, 1970) – have grounded subsequent works by Damasio and colleagues (Damasio, 1994; Damasio, 1996; Damasio et al., 1991) who developed the notion of *somatic markers*, i.e., physiological modifications in visceral and musculoskeletal systems that signal the brain to release neurotransmitters, cause changes in somatosensory maps, and modify signalling from the body to somatosensory areas. As much as Pribram (1970) distinguished emotions from feelings, Damasio (1999, 2003) proposed that responses from the body (or "soma" in Greek) and the brain compose an *emotion* while signals in somatosensory regions constitute an individually accrued perception of a *feeling* (Bechara & Damasio, 2005). In the next section, we will turn our attention to what that distinction implies.

1.4 Emotions: Different Viewpoints

Current understanding of the brain takes it to be an apparatus of metabolic efficiency that regulates the interfaces of the organism's internal and external environments in ways that are optimally conducive to its constancy and reproduction (Barrett, 2017a, 2020). This is attributed to its primary function of managing metabolic resources (e.g., enzymes, neurotransmitters, hormones) via their designated cells (neurons and glia) in an efficient way to keep our bodies alive and active and thus ensure the reproduction of the species

(Barrett, 2017a, 2020). Doing this requires resources, such as glucose uptake, to be used as long as there is a need, such as reacting to a stimulus perceived as threatening. What follows is that there must be a reason for resources to be directed to one action (to the detriment of another) or to one decision (and not to another). Indeed, the brain, as part and parcel of a biological system, seems to optimise cost functions (Marblestone et al., 2016).

Our brain seems to construe meaning in several ways – via internal information (such as the burning of the stomach denouncing a possible inflammatory state or anxiety) and external information (such as the smell of burning that can mean a fire) and its interaction (in the previous examples, burning is a common denominator with differing meanings leading to diverse interpretations). That's why context – both internal and external – needs to be appraised. This means that each brain needs to interpret information from its internal and external world. When information comes from external sources (captured by our senses), the brain interprets sensations and performs the same interpretative process with regard to information from internal sources (interoceptively meaning using autonomic, hormonal, visceral and/or immunological signals, Barrett & Simmons, 2015). That is the underlying reason for the concept of 'burning' being distinct to designate an interoceptive state, like the burning in one's stomach, from a sensorial perception, like the burning smell. Both refer to instances that generate conceptual knowledge.

For the perception that we are feeling something to arise, however, it is necessary for the brain to pair the new stimulus (whether internal or external) with some previous information that allows its recognition. This information is prior knowledge, or *priors*. These *priors* form the internal model of the world that each brain builds and that allows the brain to make an inference based on an inverse probability. This means that the same effect/pattern of stimulation can have many different causes. Such inference – starting from what is known to infer probabilities about what this new stimulus means – is an *a posteriori* probability. This way of treating variables by assigning them a value in a probabilistic distribution was first described mathematically by Thomas Bayes in the eighteenth century. Later, this probabilistic distribution came to be known as *inverse probability* – because of the inference made in reverse, i.e., from the effect to the cause – until, in the middle of the 20th century, it became known as Bayesian statistics (Fienberg, 2006).

Currently we have a set of possible explanations, which have become a theoretical framework – with elaborations still being refined – that manages to account for how experience, in the form of memories, and salience, in the form of attention, compose a scenario of sensory anticipation that allows us to perceive the stimuli present in our context – internal or external – at each moment (Gardner & Gardner, 2023). This is the framework of the Bayesian Brain which we will further discuss below.

The Bayesian Brain – a name among others that designates a predictive process – accounts for a theoretical framework for how the brain operates, in neurobiological terms, to process information. In general, the theory presupposes the existence of an internal model of the world embodied in each brain that generates predictions at all times about the causes of what we perceive (Friston, 2003, 2005; Rao & Ballard, 1999). This is accomplished through information we get from our environment, whether external (such as sensory stimuli) or internal (such as visceral information). This framework is based on the idea that the brain makes an inference (Friston, 2003, 2005), that is, we have the result (such as the burning sensation in our gut) but we still don't know what exactly is causing that sensory information. In the example above, the symptom could be physical, such as heartburn, which requires prompt attention to prevent discomfort. It could also indicate a mental state, such as anxiety, which likewise deserves immediate consideration as it directly affects our emotional well-being (Barret & Bar, 2009).

It is through the experiences we collect, in the various environments in which we live and through the succession of experiences with similar results (a burning sensation is not so easily forgotten) that we achieve an internal repertoire (i.e., our internal model of the world) that prepares us to receive information from external sources (such as an upcoming test that may cause some anxiety) or internal sources (such as the restlessness that ensues from a burning gut, which leads us to reason that something is not all right). Depending on the intensity of the stimulus (such as whether the burning is too strong and accompanied by nausea), we make a decision based on information we have (such as the need to look for professional help), and thus, we recalibrate our internal model, generating one that contemplates different possibilities for the same originating source.

It is at this point that the theoretical framework lives up to its designation – that of a probabilistic processing – which receives several denominations according to components and viewpoints (see Table 1.1 below). Basically, the designations refer to how the brain makes an inference based on an *a posteriori* distribution of probabilities (all the possibilities and their expectations of becoming reality listed above for the example of the burning gut). The designation is justifiable as it presupposes the weighing of probabilities to make inferences. In this framework, the brain recognises and categorises information allocating attention and mobilising resources where action is needed. For a more detailed account involving algorithmic rendition of diverse models of predictive coding, readers are referred to Spratling (2017).

Note that what is described above occurs from the inside (in this case, from the brain) to the outside (operating on the stimulus received) and not the other way around. In this sense, beliefs and explanations are not taken as conscious mental states, but rather as probabilistic distributions that are encoded in our neurons in an unconscious processing (Seth & Friston, 2016). In addition, what is noted is that the representations – here understood as the dynamical pattern used in neural networks that encodes processes such as attention (e.g., to list the visceral stimulus of burning as relevant to be attended); memory (e.g., of the feeling of previous episodes of anxiety); and reasoning (e.g., thinking that if it is an inflammatory condition, it is necessary

Table 1.1 Denominations, selected examples sources, and theoretical frameworks used to designate probabilistic inference performed by the brain

Denomination	*Example sources*	*Theoretical framework*
Bayesian Brain	Clark, 2016; Doya, 2007; Friston, 2012; Hohwy, 2016; Parr et al., 2022; Seth & Friston, 2016	The nomenclature is based on Bayes' model (*a posteriori* probability) to explain the prediction mechanism (i.e., inference) about the possible cause(s) of new information based on *priors*. This process is deemed to update our internal model of the world.
Predictive Coding	Clark, 2016; Friston, 2009, 2010; Huang & Rao, 2011; Rao & Ballard, 1999	The nomenclature deals with how neural responses are encoded (in algorithmic terms conceptualized as data compression) based on prediction error. The denomination accounts for a simplified version of the free-energy minimization scheme (Spratling, 2017).
Predictive Processing	Clark, 2013, 2016; Friston, 2005, 2014; 2019; Friston et al., 2013 Hohwy, 2012; Keller & Mrsic-Flogel, 2018 Seth, 2014	The nomenclature designates action instantiated by motor and autonomic reflexes that obey Bayesian filtering. The process implies *active inference* centred on prediction error.
Bayesian Predictive Coding	Aitchison & Lengyel, 2017	The nomenclature indicates neural responses represented by both prediction error and Bayesian inference. This latter element represents behaviour. The use of both terms aims at encompassing restrictive uses of the terms in *Predictive Coding* and the *Bayesian Brain.*

to call for competent help) – operate based on the information received (by visceral afferent pathways) and determine the execution of a motor action (to be performed by our body), denoting one of the organisational principles of the brain: its hierarchy (Friston, 2008).

It is important to emphasise that the processing of all the operations exemplified above represents a joint probabilistic inference, one in which "best guesses" (such as assuming that the burning sensation may signal a medical condition requiring quick action) about what we experience (the information that reaches us at each moment) act as *priors* for our perception and attention – and vice versa, because when we attend to and perceive something it is because there was an internal model that allowed the identification and relevance of the information received – in a continuous process where attention works to optimise inferences (Clark, 2016; Feldman & Friston, 2010; Hohwy, 2016, 2020).

In summary, our effort in this section so far has been to provide an understanding of a theoretical framework with possible explanations of phenomena evidenced about how the brain processes information to generate perceptions[3] and emotions. This framework, based on predictive processing, offers models for information processing in the brain. Such information, consisting of sensory and interoceptive signals, is the source of emotions. Understanding how this has been conceived in cortical layers may benefit machine learning tasks (Tscshantz et al., 2023).

We adopted the nomenclature of Bayesian Brain, although there are several denominations and possible understandings with different nuances that imply algorithmic adjustments (as explained in Table 1). In general, this understanding regards the brain as an organ capable of an active inferential process that generates predictions based on sensory (proprioceptive), interoceptive and external (exteroceptive) information. This perspective entails conceptualising the brain as an entity capable of constructing and continuously refining a generative model of the external environment, utilising probabilistic inference to assign likelihoods to the potential causes underlying incoming data (Friston, 2010; Hobson & Friston, 2012; Picard & Friston, 2014; Friston & Frith, 2015). In this sense, active inference translates into how the brain interprets sensory prediction errors, i.e., actively (Seth & Friston, 2016). Importantly, each brain, when managing resources economically, seeks the most likely explanation for causes/information that may remain inaccessible (Palmer et al., 2015). That is why emotions stand a greater chance of being better understood as heuristics in communicating internally generated instances demanding actions.

We know that the understanding of "what" happens in the brain for emotional processes to have full development implies using a scientific model to understand a certain phenomenon, i.e., the *map* of the neural territory that encompasses representations, distributions and transformations. We also know that this understanding differs from the understanding of "how" these emotional processes operate and enable the full functioning of the cognition that underlies the individual's performance. This implies a neural system that specifies implementation, i.e., the *territory*[4]. Such understanding permeates, for example, the notion that evidence on neural activation patterns consists of datasets with probabilistic treatment whose nominal values can reflect enormous variation (Barrett, 2017a, 2017b; Reitsema et al., 2022). In other words, it is one thing to map the functional layout (Van Essen et al, 2017) and another to account for how each brain processes information (Kriegeskorte & Douglas, 2018). Caveat made, we proceed with an effort to pave understanding starting with a theoretical framework for the functional layout.

Based on evolving evidence from sensory systems, such as vision (Peelen et al., 2024; Perrinet, 2020; Rao & Ballard, 1999), we now know that perception occurs via an active inferencing process (involving enaction or embodiment), predictive by nature, where affective valence seems to play a key entry role (Barrett & Bar, 2009; Shenhav et al., 2013; Lebrechet et al., 2012) but where more nuanced aspects (such as brightness in relation to visual perception) still require deeper analysis (Jacobson et al., 2024) .

For perception to occur, iteration is required. As stated by Miskovic and collaborators (2016): "perception is more properly conceptualised as a dynamically reverberating loop rather than encapsulated bottom-up and top-down streams." (Miskovic et al., 2016, p. 41). In this sense, context is constantly informing predictions and neurons operate differently according to the task involved (Hackel et al., 2016). That is why a view from the brain and the mind might unite what history has biasedly separated. Clear-cut definitions between perceptual, cognitive and emotional processes stem from more theoretically driven experimental studies about how brain and mind operate that have been criticised (Hackel et al., 2016; Miskovic et al., 2016). However, earlier notions of affect's role in perception, steered by Wundt in the late nineteenth century (as stated in the first section), seem to have found traction in recent studies. These propose that neural substrates that code for affective dimensions also work for physical properties of the stimuli (Miskovic et al., 2016). In summary, brain states that reflect subjective experiences are observable and overlap with those that have been associated with cognition (Todd et al., 2020) and also with perception, action and motivation (Pessoa, 2022) making emotions a whole-brain state (Malezieux, Klein, & Gogolla, 2023).

To elucidate the emergence of dynamic loops from the processing of information streams, we now present a concise and foundational overview of information processing mechanisms. This may be considered elementary by individuals possessing prior knowledge of brain mechanisms. To those, please feel free to skip to the next paragraph. Inside the brain, primary areas, or areas lower in the hierarchy, are those that mostly receive sensory afferents while associative areas, or higher areas in the hierarchy, mostly process multiple modalities related to the same stimulus. In neurobiological terms, the underlying reason resides in the direction of the connections between neurons – the nerve cells responsible for signalling in the nervous system. This signalling happens in the brain when electrical signals (or action potentials) propagate between a set (or network) of neurons that connect (or synapse). For information to be communicated, primary or afferent sensory neurons carry data to the Central Nervous System (CNS). In order for data to inform actions, information is communicated from the CNS to motor organs by efferent or motor neurons.

Hence, diverse patterns of interconnection between neurons allow the transmission of different information – for perception or action – according to the anatomy or functioning of the system in demand. In general, ascending projections of primary neurons to the CNS are called *feedforward*, as their axons project from lower to higher areas of the hierarchy. Neurons whose axons have descending projections, usually modulating motor commands, are called *feedback* (Amaral, 2023; Berezovskii et al., 2011).

A growing research body, based on experimental studies in differing mammalians, makes evident that feedback connections take more time to mature than feedforward ones (Berezovskii et al., 2011). While hypotheses of cost functions that change across development and areas in the brain lend more recent support to the idea (Marblestone et al., 2016), a prolonged maturational process supports the notion of feedback as predictive because it relies on a mature feedforward circuitry possibly aligned with visual experience (Berezovskii et al., 2011). The same kind of support justifies a certain vulnerability that nature and nurture selectively impose on feedback connections generating auditory hallucinations and visual illusions, such as that regarding the size-weight distortion or the hollow-mask illusion (Berezovskii et al., 2011).

In the cerebral cortex, the portion closest to the surface – the neocortex to many, also referred to as isocortex by some (e.g., Pessoa, 2022) – contains layers and columns on its extensive surface that were made possible evolutionarily by the number of grooves and gyres present in mammalian brains (see Figure 1.6). This had a relevant consequence: there was an increase in computational efficiency between afferents and efferents in each of the six cortical layers composing the brain's grey matter. The neural organisation

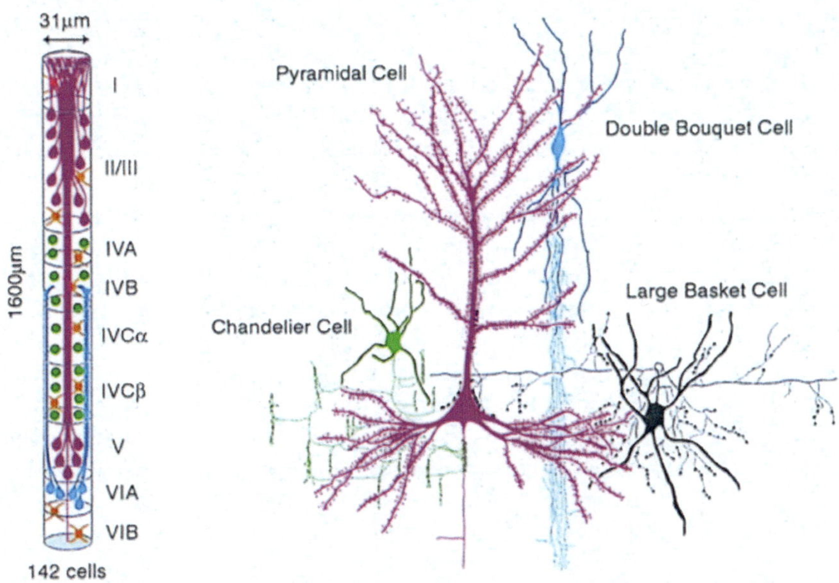

Figure 1.6 Illustration of a column (left) and types of cells (right) illustrative of the composition of the six-layered mammalian cortex from Jones (2000). [authorisation for reproduction granted]

regarding brain functioning occurs in columns, and each column – which runs through the six cortical layers – makes up a computational module that aggregates neurons with a similar functioning pattern thus forming a specific and local processing network. To get an idea of the specificity of brain functioning, the primary somatosensory cortex, which processes the sensation of touch in fingers, encompasses many cortical columns and contains four somatotopic maps, or neural representations, of the skin that are connected in a distinct, as in each map is responsible for processing specific information, and dedicated way, as in each map is responsible for a certain function (Amaral, 2023).

In summary, each sensory modality maps onto a specific cortical area with a dedicated set of cortical columns, whose processing occurs through a series of circuits, with increasing complexity, in areas of unimodal association to later converge to areas of multimodal association. Of note, specialisation becomes a central tenet for the brain's efficiency. From what has been evidenced so far, patterns of information flow differently across brain areas to provide an efficient solution to computational problems (Marblestone et al., 2016).

Essentially, there are two-way processes that seem to be happening in the brain regarding stimuli. For stimuli captured by the sensory organs to become perception, there need to be certain regularities. Those are obtained via statistical computations that are performed from birth in sensory-motor patterns. These patterns, formed across time and in multiple interactions, constitute internal representations that are stored in the brain. They become prior knowledge. When stimulated by incoming information, the brain predicts what this new information might be based on priors. Priors act like signposts that allow for the recognition of stimuli to be processed by dedicated neural networks (Barrett & Bar, 2009). Regarding the incoming stimuli that may be proprioceptive, interoceptive, and exteroceptive, which are being continuously captured, the path will feature: (i) stimulation of receptor cells in specific parts of the body; (ii) transformation of the captured stimulus into neural representation via fragmentation of the stimulus into components encoded by dedicated projection neurons; (iii) serial and parallel upstream uptake of neural representations; (iv) modification and regulation of the signals received via feedforward and feedback projections; (v) integration of the representation of the input (such as an object, person or scene) by neural networks; (vi) selection of abstract features based on detailed input; (vii) salience of features according to temporal/spatial importance (Gardner & Gardner, 2023). Interestingly, such features form the internal representations that compose sensory-motor patterns. They have been referred to as affective (Barrett & Bar, 2009) as they affect how we perceive something. Affective value – the percept's characteristic of being experienced as good or bad – imbues perception, even for faces in the absence of valence configurations (Siegel et al., 2018). That absence is noteworthy.

Compounding and converging evidence from sensorial afferents seems to indicate that sensory afferents that carry affective-valence information are processed by different nerve fibres from those that carry valence-independent information (for a review, see Kryklywy et al., 2020). According to this viewpoint, abstract cognitive states, i.e., emotions, are the accrued result of "the perceptual experience of specific exteroceptive sensation of objectively valence objects" (Kryklywy et al., 2020, p. 926). In the end, we have perception as an affective, mental/cognitive construction that uses environmental – either internal or external – stimuli. Not the other way around.

Integral to this view is the issue of valence-coding. In tandem with psychological viewpoints, current neuroscientific evidence points towards the relevance of valence for survival mechanisms that maximise resources and minimise threats (Kryklywy et al., 2020). Valence-coded information, those denoting affective states, is crucial not because they are endpoints in a dimension but rather because they operate as superordinates, i.e., they organise one's behaviour and experience (Kryklywy et al., 2020). A recent review (Malezieux et al., 2023) highlights that neural underpinnings in the processing of emotions should be uppermost in future studies. This is because semantic hyperordination, such as the broad categorisation of emotions, fails to account for distinct aspects that require more precise nomenclature. Greater specificity would facilitate deeper understanding of features, interpretations, contextual evaluation, and adaptive expression (Malezieux et al., 2023). An essential part of how such distinctiveness might unravel lies with understanding the performance of each set of neurons, that is, the character of the transmitted and sustained signal.

Most of the neurons that relay sensory information in the thalamic nuclei receive excitatory signals in a convergent manner – as in many to one. In information integration, relay hubs combine inhibitory signals at the layers and columns before passing the information on to multimodal association areas. This means that we indeed have an efficient encoding by sensory neurons; efficient because it is able to reduce redundancy without losing the essence (Gardner & Gardner, 2023). This process occurs laterally, that is, relay neurons within the same layer transmit excitatory signals, forming recurrent networks capable of amplifying the signals of the stimulus being processed. Meanwhile, interneurons are designed in such a way as to contain – via an inhibitory signal – the amount of sensory information that is relayed to the upper layers. This inhibition is important because it reduces irrelevant information by focusing attention on neural pathways that effectively lead to the achievement of the task (Gardner & Gardner, 2023). It is throughout the processing, via excitation and inhibition, in a parallel and serial way, that the spatial arrangement, i.e., the dedicated and specific processing of the stimulus components, lays the groundwork for relevant features that the stimulus might have for behaviour (Gardner & Gardner, 2023).

It is important to note that each of the primary sensory areas is endowed with more feedback axons than feedforward ones (Gardner & Gardner, 2023). This means that higher areas modulate sensory receptor responses. If a form of comparison could capture – however faintly – this processing from sensation to perception, the process would not be like a standard relay race where the baton is passed from one [neuronal assembly] to another till the finish line. Rather, what we have is a process of constant restructuring, as if in order to add more value and produce with more quality, the runners [connecting neurons] had to redistribute roles and reorganise to speed up the process, as in "The Amazing Race"[5]. In this way, perceptions and affective states are subjective because they depend on the capacity for continuous reorganisation of each brain.

Circling back to the brain as an optimiser of cost functions, evolution seems to have forged a way for unsupervised learning to conjure up relatively limited input with the right output, that is, an individually weighted, adequate behaviour that sometimes demands recruitment of selective variables, over long timescales for coherent action (Marblestone et al., 2016). This seems possible via an internal bootstrapping process whereby one template is used to generate different goal-targets that attend to skill development (Marblestone et al., 2016). Whether it may be taken today as amodal due to an evolutionary refinement of specific sensory events in our interaction with the outside world (Kryklywy et al., 2020) still requires more concerted efforts. However, the similarities between what the brain does – and neuroscience may reveal – and machine learning operations regarding cost functions should not be equated (Bengio et al., 2009). There is much more that the brain does regarding supervised, unsupervised and reinforcement learning to account for the adaptability and suitability of core processes, like facial movements, to convey individual needs within their ecology.

1.5 Interfaces Between Neuroscience and Emotions: What Have We Learned

In science that caters for how humans evolve and develop, sound reasoning and research should draw the line between where consensus and dissensus lie and show assertions through documentation (Bornstein & Lamb, 2011). On the topic of emotions, that documentation finds in neuroscience a major thoroughfare as it confers legitimacy and explanatory depth to neural correlates (Busso & Pollack, 2015), i.e., biological tissue, of emotional substrates.

The biological tissue in the brain shows excitability when neurons fire. Their spikes may be registered in terms of (i) frequency, measured in hertz (Hz) accounting for how many times neurons fire, i.e., metabolise oxygen and glucose, at each time interval; (ii) amplitude, measured in microvolts (μV) accounting for how many different sets of neurons fire at each frequency; and (iii) potency, obtained by the amplitude squared (measured in microvolts or mV, where 1 mV = 1,000 μV) accounting for the relative size of the neuronal set firing at each frequency. That is how measurements are obtained. Let us turn to what those measurements are tracking.

As described in the previous section, neurons in cortical layers interact, via association and projection fibres, to enable network formation from which ensues mental states and activity. The highly dynamic nature of such neural networks produces oscillations that can be recorded via electroencephalography (EEG). Circuits within cortical columns and those encompassing different brain regions characterise complex neural networks that enable sensory, motor, and cognitive functions with distinct oscillatory frequencies and amplitudes. Different sets of neurons synapsing into a network can represent the same category of information, such as an emotion category, creating a spatiotemporal pattern. That is called "degeneracy" (Barrett, 2017 after Edelman & Gally, 2001) where different forms come to shape the same pattern. In general, local networks operate in fast frequencies while more diffuse networks, covering large distances, present slower frequencies justified by the delay implicated in their distancing (Aboitiz, 2024). The same has been noted in relation to emotionally salient facial features (Symons et al., 2016).

Understanding the "what" and the "how" of neuronal coding measurements opens up a window into the mechanisms underlying energy patterns, or the amplitude of neuronal modulations taken at many rates simultaneously (Buzsáki et al., 2013; Doelling & Assaneo, 2021). Brain waves, or oscillations, encode rhythms entrained in patterns. When many neurons fire at rhythmic patterns, they encode oscillating networks – triggered by internal and/or external ongoing activity – that together generate perception (Calderone et al., 2014). Of note, research has highlighted how ongoing, or internally generated, oscillations are capable of modulating responses that shape perceptual, motoric, and cognitive processes (Alamia & VanRullen, 2019; Calderone et al., 2014; Thut et al., 2012) underlying emotions. Oscillatory phenomena have reshaped our understanding of some aspects of emotions, such as memory (Headley & Paré, 2013), regulation (Popov et al., 2012) and expression (Symons et al., 2016).

The takeaway for emotion research is twofold: (i) Degeneracy, which refers to the phenomenon whereby similar emotional experiences can arise from distinct spatiotemporal neural configurations, challenges the notion that facial expressions are fixed, universally recognisable indicators of emotion, as this view is not substantiated by contemporary neuroscientific evidence (Barrett, 2017b); (ii) Ongoing neural activity, encompassing more than discrete stimuli derived from sensory or interoceptive inputs, undermines the stimulus-response paradigm traditionally used to conceptualise emotions. Rather than being elicited by isolated stimuli, emotional experiences emerge from the continuous engagement of neural systems with contextual information (Barrett, 2017b). What follows is that there does not seem to be a dedicated brain region or system for how we feel, think or act (Barrett, 2017b). In other words, emotion, cognition and perception share neuronal networks devoted to entraining patterns that make efficient use of the metabolic resources that the brain manages to keep us alive, developing and reproducing[6], i.e., keep us active in the world (Barrett, 2017b).

Pezzulo et al. (2021) posit that, to achieve adaptive control, organisms must reduce the number of possible states to align with the specific demands of their environmental context and ensure survival. Whatever lies outside the boundaries of such states constitutes a surprise, i.e., anything that may threaten adaptive survival computed via sampled sensory data combined with their internally generated predictions (Barrett & Simmon, 2015; Barrett, 2017b; Holmes & Nolte, 2019). Thus, the brain – in experiencing different bodily states when combining internal prediction with incoming evidence – is constantly comparing experiences with expectations. Ensuing perceptions may contain prediction errors which are, in typical conditions, expertly used to modify future behaviour as an emotional display (Platt & Spelke, 2009). A caveat is necessary, though, and that has to do with the free-energy principle.

According to the free-energy principle, living organisms continuously engage in inferential processes to counteract their inherent tendency toward entropy (Friston, 2011). This is achieved through the construction and iterative refinement of an internal generative model that represents the structure of the external world. Through sustained interaction with the environment and the accumulation of sensory evidence, this model is progressively updated. Consequently, each organism, by enacting behaviours through its bodily interface with the environment, contributes to the emergence of an adaptive phenotype optimally attuned to its ecological niche (Friston, 2011). Reaching optimal levels of adaptation means reducing the amount of free energy; therefore, embodiment becomes an integral part of the statistical process that allows for an internal model of the agent in that environment (Friston, 2011). That means, for the brain to generate inferences, the context is important (Friston, 2011).

When the context holds more novelty potential, expectation increases, i.e., the more surprises the context offers, the less accurate the inference is likely to be (Piekarski, 2021). In other words, inferences with low accuracy upgrade our level of surprise (or novelty expectation) and make our senses more open to new information, i.e., senses tend to get more tuned in, more precise, as they become more necessary to update one's own generative model of the world (Piekarski, 2021). On the other hand, inferences with high accuracy are used to represent the causal structure of the world and of one's own bodily states (Piekarski, 2021). This means that they become heuristics, i.e., perceptual shortcuts, that are engaged frequently to make sense of information. This may engender a vicious circle that tends to fixate a mechanism – of perceptual inference – that should never be fixed, to allow one to maintain a healthy perspective and stance in the world. For example, when you see a snake, even living in an urban environment where snakes are not prevalent, you may get goosebumps, thus you infer – either consciously or not – that you must be afraid. Consider now an encounter with a piece of rope; you may take it for a snake, get goosebumps and feel afraid. In this case, if you use a mechanism that allows you to balance your former experience (of seeing a snake) against the latter experience (with a rope), you will confer a value that renders each experience in a precise way. The mechanism would mean that, when your brain notices that the information looks the same but behaves differently (in the example above, realising that a rope does not slither), it would be performing a weighted precision balancing act (Clark, 2013, 2017; Seth, 2014). In this act, the brain generates an error signal (e.g., realising the information is a rope and not a snake) resulting in a prediction error (Hohwy, 2012; Seth, 2014). This error is sent forward and sideways via distinct networks, i.e., in serial and parallel processing pathways, that will probably improve the perception you have of future input that looks like a snake, but that is most likely a rope and thus will not give cause to a feeling of fear. Learning has taken place and the error that has been previously made (e.g., of thinking that the rope you saw was a snake) is taken as a model of neural responsivity (Heilbron & Chait, 2018). In this example, the fixed mechanism would be taking every rope encountered as being a snake. Most likely, that would imply the agent is not coming close to, nor interacting with, the environment where the object (rope, most probably) lies. That would perpetuate the assumption and reinforce the fear that could be reasonably justified (in case of a snake) but not in case of a rope, especially considering the urban context where the agent is. The takeaway message here is to understand that perceptions are inferred based on constructed sensorial and interoceptive stimuli placed in a context so that interaction with that input happens as a constant, ongoing activity, forging ways of forming knowledge representations in the brain.

Let us turn now to how formed knowledge is represented in the brain through our motor cortices or via action. To think of action related to emotions and sensations, one must consider that the body has to be factored into the equation, i.e., taking some level of action – either using one's own bodily parts or imagining their use when physical action is not feasible. This account challenges the classical views of cognitive psychology where mental representations get entrained irrespective of their sensorimotor afferences (Macrine & Fugate, 2022).

Sometime before and throughout the 20th century, philosophers like Gilbert Ryle and Maurice Merleau-Ponty together with psychologists like John Dewey, William James, and James Gibson severed this notion by pointing out that mental and physical worlds merge into bodily perceptions of information to generate knowledge and states (Macrine & Fugate, 2022). In the present century, Clark (2013, 2016, 2019) emphasizes the role that active inference plays for the brain to generate predictions about the world. This is seen when one's own senses, i.e., bodily mechanisms, are actively engaged in interactions with contextual information or input.

Historically, the idea that body and mind converse in transactional, recursive patterns emerged in this century based on the tenets of (i) embodied realism; where the body grounds mental knowledge; (ii) sensorimotor simulations; where perceptual symbols arise based on sensorial afferents; and (iii) situated cognition, where context matters for the representation of abstract, mental concepts (Barrett & Lindquist, 2008). Therefore, all forms of cognition and emotion come from an embodiment where experience becomes the product of model-based predictions that are flexible, i.e., not fixed or immutable, as the same elements may yield different experiences over time (Barrett, 2017b; Clark et al., 2019).

As one's knowledge depends on structures shaped by experiences that one has, and as experiences may vary according to culture, norms, and language one adopts (Macrine & Fugate, 2022), it follows that embodiment offers the possibility of forging patterns that serve as heuristics when interacting with the world (Clark, 2016). This may be taken, at the surface level, to explain why smiles are taken as symbols for happiness at a rate that is more often than chance but, at a deeper level, it makes more plausible the reasoning that smiling may communicate different instances of emotion, such as surprise and even sadness, or a combination of both, when cultural values and constraints are factored in (Barrett et al., 2019).

Taken together, perception from sensory and somatosensory cortices together with action involving motor cortices are entrained along multiple space and time scales and interactions shaping how the brain simulates emotions and forms conceptual knowledge (Barrett, 2017a, 2017b). In this framework, and as we have seen before, language plays a constitutive role in emotional experience (Gendron et al., 2012; Lindquist & Gendron, 2013; Satpute & Lindquist, 2021). This derives from the notion that language drives the acquisition of categorical patterns (see the Chapter on Language by Monte-Serrat & Cattani in this book) formed via automatic (largely sensorial and visceral), behavioural (how we display our emotions in the world) and experiential (how action enables experiencing emotions) information that forms the building blocks of individualised conceptual emotional knowledge (Barrett, 2017a, 2017b).

From the neuroscientific input we have laid out here, emotions may be taken as the compilation of affect – that are innate and biologically driven – and conceptual knowledge – formed through inferences – forming patterns, or categories, that imply changes in states for the emergence of a behaviour, i.e., instances of emotions that we perceive in others, via facial configurations. These configurations are made or constructed internally via inferences which make them highly flexible (Barrett, 2017a). Language is a means – a culturally shaped cognitive tool – that enables one to categorise emotions (Barrett et al., 2001) parsing them into specifics that allow us to differentiate between them (Tugade, Fredrickson, & Feldmann Barrett, 2004). In other words, the highly flexible system that configures emotions is the product of affects (innate, biological, and basic) and conceptual knowledge (acquired from prior experience and language). Given its exposure to diverse cultural contexts and individual-specific factors, this adaptive system exhibits considerable variability, thereby challenging the notion of emotions as invariant signatures and positioning variation as a fundamental characteristic (Barrett, 2017a, 2017b).

Further, because emotions are formed by conceptual knowledge derived from probabilistic estimations, they cannot be construed as reactions.

Instead, they become simulations, here taken to be constructed internal representations of long-term prospections (i.e., predictions) that are formed by deterministic short-term processes (i.e., inferences) (Barrett, 2017a, 2017b; Brown & Brune, 2012). As Barrett (2017b) posits, there is a "lesson here, for the science of emotion, [in] that the brain does not process individual stimuli—it processes events across temporal windows. Emotion perception is event perception, not object perception" (2017b, p. 12).

1.6 The Search for Biomarkers: Breakthroughs and Thresholds

As previously seen, understanding emotions requires a dive into the seat of its processing – the brain – here understood as the set of structures and networks, in and among cortical and subcortical regions, that underlie behaviours and that are part of the central nervous system. By dive we mean an incursion into how processes develop to underlie networks and enable neural systems. To address processes, we have opted in the present work to restrict explanations to encompassing terms, like cortical and subcortical regions, and have used underlying structures, like the amygdala – which, incidentally, should receive a more thorough treatment given its status as a complex of distinct nuclei (Freese & Amaral, 2009) – only when strictly necessary. This approach was developed with careful consideration of the intended audience bearing in mind the implications of an accurate neurobiological analysis of structures and their associated terminology. Another choice concerns theories that inform how data is treated.

As previously discussed, the field of emotion research is characterised by a proliferation of theoretical perspectives, with limited integrative efforts aimed at synthesising these viewpoints to advance the discipline. Notable exceptions exist (e.g., Barrett et al., 2019), though some attempts remain insufficiently informative (e.g., Dukes et al., 2021). Consequently, this section concentrates on examining three prominent theoretical frameworks – affective feelings, homeostatic feelings, and constructed emotions – highlighting proponents and their foundational contributions to the understanding of emotional phenomena.

Affective neuroscience has emerged as a discipline to address the need for a comprehensive examination of emotional information processing and the mechanisms underlying expressive behavior (Davidson & Sutton, 1995). At the time, it was seen as a field that merited a separate treatment from cognitive neuroscience, perhaps mirroring the siloed treatment that emotions received. Back then, it was attributed mainly to a persistent view of independent and/or non-related treatment of subcortical substrates (e.g., the amygdala) as an apt way to investigate emotional phenomena. Also, the siloed treatment was observed in the consideration given to processing sites (e.g., the prefrontal cortex) as sets of "pure" cognitive phenomena (Davidson, 2000). Fortunately, this siloed route soon took a turn to convey research that addressed the pertaining and inextricably related cognitive processing of emotional substrates (Davidson, 2000).

A more contemporary view addresses emotional science based on neurobiological substrates that consider the dangers of regarding affect and cognition as (i) present in distinct parts of the body; (ii) independent from each other; (iii) in the realm of siloed perspectives; (iv) species-specific; and (v) comprising totally conscious phenomena (Davidson, 2003). That said, and perhaps to show how emotional science progresses much like the nonlinear way that the brain operates (Vignesh et al., 2024), we proceed in this section with an examination of the breakthroughs provided by three key exponents of affective neuroscience. After each contribution, we summarise their main ideas and weave them into the great tapestry of understanding that such breakthroughs represented. Lastly, we look at the most recent findings that unfold the possibilities of research in the field of emotions.

1.6.1 Some Breakthroughs

Similarly to most specific fields of study, affective neuroscience has an exponent regarded by many as its "father" (Spektrum der Wissenschaft, 2012), in the late psychobiologist and neuroscientist Jaak Panksepp, a first proponent of the [then] emerging field of studies (Panksepp, 2003, p. 2), who gained some fame for tickling rats. Through his experimental work, Panksepp discovered that rats emitted ultrasonic vocalizations – inaudible to the human ear – when subjected to tickling, indicating a form of laughter. Utilising animal models, Panksepp established the biological underpinnings of affective neuroscience by identifying a set of primary affective systems, which he conceptualised as fundamental categories of emotional consciousness that influence behaviour. These *affective feelings* involve distinct neurobiological processes – different from emotional and motivational feelings – driving organisms towards cognitive choices, as in what to eat when hungry (Panksepp, 2003).

To Panksepp, affective systems would be localized subcortically and bear an evolutionary – therefore homologous to other mammals – root as they satisfied basic needs, either biological, social, or concerning safety (Panksepp, 1998; Toronchuk & Ellis, 2013). According to Panksepp, affective systems have two valences: positive and negative. Those of positive valence provide some kind of reward to our brain and the negative ones are aggressive to our brain. Among the rewarding systems we have (i) seeking, generating enthusiasm; (ii) play, generating fun and joy; (iii) care, generating parental affective vigilance and nurturing; and (iv) lust, linked to sexual desire itself and relevant for the reproduction of the species, and also reproductive desire, focused on maternal behaviour related to the desire to protect offspring. Among the negative valence systems, Panksepp identified (v) fear, generating anxiety; (vi) rage, generating anger; and (vii) panic, generating loneliness and sadness ensuing from separation and the unmet need to be cared for (Panksepp, 1998; Panksepp & Watt, 2011).

Panksepp (2001) stressed the importance of understanding the basic emotional drivers, i.e., *affective feelings*, humans share with other animals, even considering how their expression might be different in the face of our larger repertoire of cognitive abilities. He defended his position based on the similarity of a neurobiological makeup – emotions are in the brain – common across species. Panksepp emphasised the distinction between evolutionarily older affective states – mediated by subcortical and limbic structures and governed by action–perception mechanisms – and more recently evolved, cognitively mediated emotional processes, which involve cortical regions and operate through perception–action dynamics. It is at this point that another neuroscientist, Antonio R. Damasio, stands out and joins Panksepp in teasing apart ideas that often received a unique label. Damasio did this by studying patients whose emotions displayed incongruent patterns.

Damasio, as seen in Section 1.1, makes a clear distinction between emotions, taken as reactions and belonging to the body, and feelings. In his own words (Damasio, 2001) Damasio states:

> An emotion, be it happiness or sadness, embarrassment or pride, is a patterned collection of chemical and neural responses that is produced by the brain when it detects the presence of an emotionally competent stimulus — an object or situation, for example. The processing of the stimulus may be conscious, but it need not be, as the responses are engendered automatically. Emotional responses are a mode of reaction of brains that are prepared by evolution to respond to certain classes of objects and events with certain repertoires of action. Eventually, the brain associates other objects and events that occur in individual experience with those that are innately set to cause emotions, so that another set of emotionally competent stimuli arises. (...) Thus, emotions are not subjective, private, elusive or undefinable.

To Damasio, emotions taken as action plans would implicate a three-stage processing of (i) what external or internal stimulus triggers the system; (ii) what neural correlates put the plan into action; and (iii) the action itself (Damasio, 2011). In assuming emotions as an evolutionary trait, i.e., part of a species' genome, the processing described above would eventually lead to a perception. Following in Darwin's steps, Damasio (2011) posits that emotions as action programmes form a set – like the set of emotions that conceptualise fear, disgust, sadness, joy, anger, and surprise – with enthusiasm and its counterpart (discouragement) regarded as simpler programmes. Social emotions, which include embarrassment, shame, guilt, contempt, compassion, and admiration, would be part of a more complex set (Damasio, 2011).

In 2003, Damasio put forward the notion that a feeling would be "an idea of a certain aspect of the body, its interior, in certain circumstances"

(Damasio, 2011, p. 88). Such ideas, in Damasio's conception, would represent the message contained in internal maps of the body-sensing regions. Of note, feelings would not accrue from actual bodily states, but rather from their representations in the brain (Damasio, 2003).

A central tenet for Damasio is that emotions are distinct from feelings of emotions – a distinction that he proclaimed had been intended originally by William James, but which found confusion in the elaboration of his thinking (Damasio, 2011). Thus, to Damasio (2011), "feelings of emotions are the perceptions of the action program that constitutes an emotion as it unfolds together with the salient representation of the causative object and with thoughts related to the situation" (Damasio, 2011). Feelings would be elaborations by the mind based on emotions, i.e., the mental representation of our bodily state identified through reactions to stimuli present in the internal or external environment (Damasio, 2011, 2021).

In Damasio's theory, emotions are automatic and feelings, being their consequence, get conditioned as they pass through the filter of our cognition and may have interference from several other neural and non-neural substrates (Damasio & Damasio, 2023). Hence, feelings derive from reactions (emotions) understood as a response to contextual demands, whether internal or external. Further, feelings are modulated by mechanisms that take place in the CNS but involve mental elaboration that integrates stimuli (of an afferent, sensory nature) and responses (of an efferent, motor nature). Thus, feelings emerge as critical mental constructions that imply some level of consciousness in order to be elaborated. Consciousness means our feelings are rooted in the body, which possesses an inherent biological intelligence. This intelligence maintains internal balance, allowing us to function effectively in our environment (Damasio, 2021). In other words, the emergence of consciousness from perceptions and thoughts in an individual organism means that experiences are registered as mental events. This happens due to feelings that regulate our living needs (e.g., hunger, thirst, pain) and metabolic expenditure (e.g., breathing and thermoregulation), and are thus regarded as *homeostatic feelings* (Damasio, 2021; Damasio & Damasio, 2023).

The importance of homeostatic feelings lies in setting a cornerstone of biological evolution as they provided organisms with consciousness which, in turn, gave organisms knowledge about how life could be regulated (Damasio & Damasio, 2023). By allowing the mental inspection of consciousness over life, feelings as sentinels operate under interactive mechanisms, of (i) interoceptive elements regulated by the nervous system, and (ii) viscera and related chemical elements of a non-neural nature, in an ongoing fashion (Damasio & Damasio, 2023). Therefore, feelings as hybrid constructs with organic origin (from viscera) and neural processing (by brain-dedicated networks) would remain dependent on interoception, since they require a notion of what happens within the organism through sensory and mental inspection. It is such inspection that would provide information of a positive or negative valence and of different gradients (Damasio, 2021).

To recap, in Damasio's framework, feelings are disturbances that exist for a purpose: they are sentinels of our internal states. Therefore, they demand attention and involvement and depend on a physiology that is elaborated, with gradients of quantity and quality that bring imprecision. Feelings become conscious by way of interactive perceptions. This means that they are (i) hybrids; they manifest themselves in the body and depend on mental work; (ii) internalised; they are inherent to oneself, so much so that the reactions and consequences they trigger become individually perceived; and (iii) emotionally modulated; they affect mood states in a positive way (with enthusiasm) or in a negative way (with discouragement), which, in turn, affects motivation. Homeostasis confers biological parameters that impact perception based on emotions. In this construction, perception means inferring mental states based on experiences of the tripartite state that organisms may hold: (i) internal, represented by interoception; (ii) of one's own body in a physical environment, represented by proprioception; and (iii) of the environment, represented by exteroception. Therefore, emotions are understood as *involuntary internal responses* initiated by certain perceptions that contribute to maintaining homeostasis. These responses generate feelings, which are considered mental phenomena primarily associated with bodily states and secondarily with emotional states, and are continuously influenced by the central nervous system.

Lisa Feldman Barrett also makes a very strong point about how the brain is involved in emotions but not by following the same line of experimentation and reasoning that Damasio has done. To Barrett (2016, 2020), – whose initial efforts relied on trying to reproduce earlier findings, compiling evidence and critically reviewing the literature – brains run bodily systems and aim at metabolic efficiency. This means being frugal in spending resources, i.e., the body is efficient not when dynamically balancing needs (homeostasis), but rather when predicting where needs will be felt (allostasis). Thus, for efficiency, the brain regulates the body based on signals that the body sends to the brain. Such signals are the information that sensory organs (e.g., eyes, ears, nose) and internal organs (e.g., viscera) send to the brain via afferent pathways. Upon receiving such signals, the brain processes them to produce a general summary, one that provides affects (or moods). These are effective results of how metabolic states are experienced.

However, to interpret what such results (or internal states) mean, the brain "backtracks" to infer the most probable cause for the results (or affects). As we have stated before (in Section 1.1), Barrett calls this a reverse inference (Barrett, 2017a). In inferring the cause, the brain attributes mental states that seek to identify, explain and predict behaviours. Thus, emotions are taken as generated by the combination of affect, that is a transient alteration in a neurophysiological state, combined with the knowledge that we obtain in extracting information based on a distributional computation of their value. In this perspective, Barrett (2006, 2012, 2016, 2017a, 2017b, 2020) posits that emotions (i) emerge as mental states that make use of biological substrates also employed in cognitive and perceptual instances; (ii) are formed according to the situation one is in; varying individually depending on the context and demands of each situation; and (iii) generate a highly flexible system that encompasses variation due to the diversity of cultures, languages, and expressions.

In 2015, Barrett and Simmons (2015) proposed the Embodied Predictive Interoception Coding (EPIC) model to show how active inference (see Section 1.4) gets implemented in interoception[7]. According to the EPIC model, the cingulate cortex, the posterior ventral medial prefrontal cortex, the posterior orbitofrontal cortex, and the most ventral portions of the anterior insula are jointly responsible for the process of allostasis. Further, Barrett and Simmons (2015) posit visceromotor cortices as drivers of active interoceptive perception. They also diverted the focus for consciousness or emotional awareness away from the anterior insula by redirecting concerted efforts into understanding how interoceptive perceptions get shaped via multiple pathways in a cortical interoceptive network and via ascending pathways in a finding that points towards degeneracy (see Section 1.5).

In summary, Barrett has largely evidenced that individual brains construct their concept of emotions over time as categories of meaning that enable plans for action to attain preferred states. Such states are expressed in behaviours, like facial configurations. In so doing, emotions may hold different definitions as people and places vary. Therefore, *emotions are constructed* by each individual according to the inferences made relative to the internal, such as sensorial and interoceptive input, and external information, such as culture and language, available to them at different instances represented in diverse temporal patterns[8] (Singh et al., 2021). In that framework, variation becomes the norm. And to realise and truly invest in this notion, the field would do well to acknowledge that:

> It will never be possible to measure an emotion by merely measuring facial muscle movements, changes in autonomic nervous system signals, or neural firing within the periaqueductal gray or the amygdala. To understand the nature of emotion, we must also model the brain systems that are necessary for making meaning of physical changes in the body and in the world. (Barrett, 2017b, p. 16)

1.6.2 Interim Summary

Thus far we have offered a closer examination of three exponents in affective neuroscience and their breakthroughs. Panksepp and Damasio provided experimental basis for distinguishing between affects, emotions, and feelings while Barrett's concerted efforts went towards evidencing how emotions are constructed. Departing from the reference viewpoints established in Section 1.1, we offered in this section exemplary trajectories of distinct ideological, theoretical and experimental fronts that were instrumental in advancing our understanding of what emotions are. With their work and those of many others, the field presently recognises that emotions demand a more complex, refined thinking that should encompass bodily and mental states represented by neural substrates. To move the field forward, their concerted efforts involved a more intensive and directed investigation of neural substrates – the topic we explore next.

The notion that cognition and emotional feelings are inextricably tied (Damasio, 2003) was a breakthrough that needs acknowledging as it was taken as radical when initially proposed (Panksepp, 2003). Of note, Damasio centred his work on the distinction between emotions and feelings. This has been consistently evidenced through an emphasis on the externally consequential nature of the first and the privately experienced consequences that configure the latter (Dolan, 2003). Damasio has made significant and influential contributions to the identification of brain regions associated with emotional processing. Starting with the somatosensory cortex (Damasio, 1994), Damasio moved on to incorporate the hypothalamus, basal forebrain and brainstem (Damasio, 2001) and insular and cingulate cortices (Damasio, 2001, 2003), regarding subcortical regions as the first site for neural representations of feeling later repeated in cortical regions (Damasio et al., 2013).

Another important breakthrough was Panksepp's notion that affects guide our actions and perceptions, being precursors and propellers of other states. As stated in 2001, "our feelings still remain like centres of gravity around which our cognitive apparatus tends to revolve—unless, of course, all our needs are satisfied". (Panksepp, 2001, p. 139). In relation to neural substrates, Panksepp postulated that affective feelings originate from lower regions (subcortical areas), the processing site of emotional responses (Panksepp, 2003). He was also adamant in drawing attention to the highly inflated role attributed to the amygdala in recent years (Panksepp, 2003). That position, albeit not fully in sync, has also been observed by Gendron and Barrett (2017), in positioning the amygdala as engaged in fear poses (rather than in pure fear) and also in positive stimuli and novelty. This extended an earlier notion of the amygdala as a gating, modulatory substrate of emotional input, like facial expressions (Morris et al., 1998).

Barrett's work represents a significant advancement in challenging established beliefs about emotions and examining their implications for the identification of biomarkers. In an authoritative, largely evidenced study shared with eminent subscribers to different theories, Barrett et al. (2019) held two hypotheses to scrutiny: (i) that emotion categories, like fear, anger, disgust, joy, sadness, and surprise, can be expressed by unique facial configurations; and (ii) that such categories could be inferred solely from their corresponding facial expressions. Their study pointed to three key insights on how emotional expressions could not be regarded as a valid path for academic, social, commercial, and computational pursuits. As stated, the limits imposed concern their reliability, specificity, and generalisability. In other words, emotion categories are not all the same; they do not hold a unique facial configuration; and they are impacted by cultural and contextual factors (Barrett et al., 2019).

As posited by Barrett (2017a, 2017b), when one experiences an emotion, the process becomes one where first a core affect, taken as a transient alteration in a neurophysiological state, guides basic behavioural displays, such as hunger or sleep. How one perceives that affect is shaped by a probabilistic computation of value, that is, emotions become a situated, contextualised concept that is in line with the view of cognition as socially situated. Therein lies the reason for heterogeneity in concept formation; individuals construct their conceptual knowledge based on their context and the demands at hand. This means that the situation one is in determines how the emotion enacted is represented; it ties together meaning, context, and experience that eventually becomes highly flexible. Therefore, emotions become situational constructs (Barrett, 2006, 2017a, 2017b).

Taken as situated concepts, emotions can be understood as perceptual symbols that simulate sensorimotor states. Those cannot be reduced into pattern classification as they represent conceptual categories that vary individually, thereby not sharing universal or patterned features (Barrett, 2020) as postulated herein in Section 1.1. However, we recognise that it takes many instances for such notions to become acquired knowledge. Therefore, let us pause here and make use of some analogies with our senses to illustrate how this comes to fruition.

Take colour for instance; it is presently acknowledged as the way that the brain interprets and labels light when it refracts from artefacts and is captured by our retina (Kandel et al., 2023). Light, in turn, is measured in wavelengths and each band yields a different colour. Let us turn now to emotions. For emotions to form, stimuli are expressed through the coupling of affect and conceptual knowledge as different categories or patterns to yield different emotions. In a similar way, for colour vision to ensue, light is measured in wavelengths that yield different colours. Taking the analogy a little further to illustrate how situational constraints matter, in the same way as birds can capture ultraviolet rays that the human retina cannot transduce due to lacking the specialised photoreceptor, different species may hold a diverse set of receptors – automatic, behavioural or experiential – that confer them with different abilities for emotion detection and treatment thus rendering emotions as dependent on specialised processes within each organism as it interacts with contextual variables.

Let us turn now to taste. For taste to exist, there needs to be gustation (the process), and tastants (the stimuli) transduced into molecules that are captured by specialised receptors. A tastant is a chemical, soluble in water, that activates taste receptor cells to produce a taste sensation via activity in dedicated brain pathways (Di Lorenzo et al., 2019). A taste sensation is then conferred by basic tastants whereas flavour, which is multisensory, is how the brain experiences taste in combination with other senses (like smell and vision). An affect, like taste, is generated by basic stimuli (a disturbance) in a neurophysiological state, but it needs to be coupled with conceptual knowledge to yield emotion, as much as taste needs coupling with other senses to give flavour.

A final analogy is the sense of touch, which has several different receptors that form the somatosensory system. There are receptors for pressure and vibrations (mechanoreceptors), for changes in temperature (thermoreceptors), for pain (nociceptors), and for the body in space (proprioceptors). Likewise, emotions have different categories that are all part of emotional systems that get set into motion by different contextual stimuli; that is, they are culture-specific and highly individualised (value driven). Those categories are triggered via affective regulation (as in anxious states), bodily regulation (as in different heartbeats), sensations (as in physical pain), and cognition (as in the executive control) so that emotions become rudders (Cantor et al., 2021; Fischer & Bidell, 2006) that impact academic performance, confidence, motivation, persistence, self-control, and curiosity (Immordino-Yang & Damasio, 2007; Meyer & Turner, 2006).

Taken together, these analogies – made solely to gain a better understanding – illustrate how emotions, taken as organisers of prior knowledge formation and conceptualisations, steer processes that drive automatic actions, beliefs and attributions in conscious and unconscious ways. Therefore, emotions are not different from cognition and perception as brain-related processing mechanisms in that they hold no specific locations and should be rather taken as whole-brain states (Barrett, 2006, 2017a; Barrett & Satpute, 2013). This is an important caveat in the search for biomarkers as it calls for novel approaches in finding biological substrates involved in emotion generation.

Further, studies have shown that feelings do not come from interoceptive information directly and the reason for this rests on attention (Barrett et al., 2004). It is only when internal information is perceived – because it was attended to – that attribution of emotional feelings is possible. However, this is not straightforward; it varies, both among people and even for the same person (Barrett et al., 2004). Thus, biomarkers should not be taken as a silver bullet in the quest for emotions.

1.6.3 Some Thresholds

Having briefly addressed the role of biomarkers for emotions and finding that the term is inappropriate as there are no single structures, patterns nor regions that could altogether represent shared instances (Barrett, 2016), let us turn our attention to new research areas, i.e., thresholds. To that end, we need to refer to two crucial actions that are employed when we process an emotion: reverse inference and conditional probability (Barrett et al., 2019). As previously explained in this chapter, the first refers to what we assume based on the best available evidence, e.g., we see a scowl and assume the scowler is angry. The second refers to what we attribute as most likely resulting from a given stimulus, e.g., the scowler is most probably angry because of their scowl (Barrett et al., 2019).

Taking emotions as categories of a highly flexible system seems a promising way to understand depressive states, a specially relevant threshold for clinical perspectives. The Bayesian Predictive Coding framework (see Section 1.4) has shown how we are constantly making inferences about incoming input to predict, inform and update, via the generating of models, our knowledge of the world and of ourselves. Doing that is possible via perceptual inference, that feeds into mechanisms of inference as a necessary component (Hohwy, 2016), or via active inference, that relies on the body being present, involved in the constant updating of internal models (Clark, 2013). However, if one detaches oneself from such instances, what may unfold is a vicious circle of self-predictions that lock oneself in a confirmation bias akin to a self-fulfilling prophecy generating disengagement and lack of interest (Smith at al., 2020). Also, if one feels overwhelmed and lacking in cognitive appraisal capacity, a negative feedback loop may take hold and lock one in further depressive states (Hutchinson-Wong et al., 2025). What follows is that the depressed individual tends to steer further away from instances of active engagement with stimuli – objects, events, other people and their own perceptions of emotions – thereby closing in on themselves and their appetite for social contact (Giurgi-Oncu et al., 2021).

Another possibility to be explored concerning emotions within the Predictive Processing framework is how emotions seem to change once one is able to talk and, by talking, reframe thinking about bodily states, such as emotional pain (Solms, 2021). It is by making use of words – an investment in identifying and communicating emotional granularity (Barrett et al., 2004; Tugade et al., 2004) – that people may find new pathways to comprehend themselves and their states as well as their transience in the face of newer, updated versions of previous processes.

Yet another possibility to explore emotions, in their nature and flexibility, offered by the Bayesian Brain approach, lies with attention in relation to meditation. It is outside the scope of this work to define, characterise and debate the concept of meditation; however, suffice it to say that attention, a cognitive capacity influenced by emotions (Taylor & Fragopanagos, 2005; Yiend, 2010), is impacted by meditation practices (Lippelt et al., 2014; Lutz et al., 2008; Raffone & Srinivasan, 2010; Sumantry & Stewart, 2021), which relies on a mechanism of balancing acts in the brain (Feldman & Friston, 2010). Attention in a Bayesian framework is taken as the inference about the precision of sensory signals and their causes (Feldman & Friston, 2010). Interestingly, attention in this framework is related to precision and not to the primary cause of sensory input. This leads to a possible exploration of ways to modulate – or balance – the process of synaptic gain that is encoded in precision. As stated in clear terms by Feldman and Friston (2010): "Things get more interesting if we consider that the precision of sensory signals depend on states of the world. This means that optimizing precision entails optimizing inferred states of the world that affect the precision or uncertainty about our sensations." (2010, p. 2). Some stimuli that hold emotional salience can bias attention. This is a bottom-up process – in this case biased – that captures attention and may determine a change in precision (Feldman & Friston, 2010). An exploration of emotional modulation, in turn, may lead to a greater understanding of possible differences in how we experience emotions by relying on mechanisms that encode stimulus based on predictions, errors and balancing acts.

1.7 Closing Remarks

In this chapter dedicated to emotions, we have proceeded with a tripartite analysis. In the first section, we have delineated, in three parts, different directions to explore emotions. First, we introduced defining ideas that have steered notions about what emotions are. Next, we provided a description of different views of emotions across time and showed how research in the area began by considering emotions as innate and homologous. Findings stemming from the early works of Darwin spurred a series of ideas, experiments, and models by Hess, Tomkins, Ekman, and Izard. In considering emotions from a physiological perspective, James and Lange presented ideas that found counterpoints in Cannon and Bard and moved the field forward with later models by Schachter and Singer. Ideas put forth by Nauta and Pribram ignited modern notions and models that emphasised the transactional, recursive nature of emotions in body and mind. In a field that deals with dynamical changes of bodily states – or emotions, in short – there is much more to be analysed and considered than facial expressions. Emotions may be common and shared with other species, but that does not turn them into simple concepts or plain, immutable states to be recognised,categorised or mimicked, by artificial intelligence. Care and depth should be the first considerations in how we may explore emotions in different perspectives and for diverse outcomes.

In the later sections, we strived to show how recent years have seen a focus on networks in neuroscience – rather than modules – that operationalise how brains perform their tasks in a metabolically efficient way: they predict bodily states, simulate emotional states, infer actions, and develop heuristics to optimise pathways. In that sense, the constructed theory of emotions stands at the forefront of what evolving research that concerns emotions may reveal. Considering future implications, any field that may come to work with emotions should pay close heed to what this line of research unveils.

In the last section, we brought to attention exponential gains in understanding neurobiological substrates of emotion processing through the works of three contemporary researchers, Jaak Panksepp, Antonio R. Damasio, and Lisa Feldman Barrett. Rather than pointing towards a single substrate, complex, or region that would be akin to a biomarker, their work jointly leads us to regard emotions as whole brain states which, in all their complexity, clearly bind emotions to many substrates, rather than just the one. Underlying the elusive quest for biomarkers, we stressed how understanding the neuronal coding that the brain performs represents a more robust basis upon which thresholds in research on emotional distress, such as in depressive states, and on possible treatments, such as psychoanalysis and meditation, could be found. Stronger efforts to advance integrative methods and models will continue to lead us towards new ways to improve understanding of emotional states and brain function.

Acknowledgements

Thanks to Caroline Handley and two anonymous readers for very helpful feedback on earlier drafts of this chapter.

Notes

1 Heuristics are herein referred to as priors (prior knowledge) used at large as a way to simplify motor planning and control (using the same example found in McLeod & Dienes, 1996) provided in Marblestone et al., 2016)
2 The Cambridge Dictionary definition of "summary" is "a short, clear description that gives the main facts or ideas about something". Available at https://dictionary.cambridge.org/dictionary/english/summary. Accessed on 7 August 2025.
3 Of note, we take perception in this work as different from behaviour according to the process of active inferencing where "perception can be understood as resolving (exteroceptive) prediction errors by selecting predictions that best explain sensations, while behaviour suppresses (proprioceptive) prediction error by changing (proprioceptive) sensations". (Seth & Friston, 2016, p. 3)
4 In 1933, Alfred Korzybski (1958) wrote the book "Science and Sanity: An Introduction to Non-Aristotelian Systems and General Semantics". The work presents his reasoning and logical constructions on the "maps" that encompass all the formulations that humans make. On p. 58 (5th edition), he wrote: "A map is not the territory it represents, but, if correct, it has a *structure similar* to the territory, which explains its usefulness". It is to this reasoning and intended usefulness that we allude to when referring to *map* and *territory* in the present work.
5 *The Amazing Race* is an adventure competition formatted as a reality show. Teams of two people race other teams in tasks where they have to deduce clues, navigate foreign terrain, interact with local people, and accomplish challenges. Many means of transportation lead teams in a progressive elimination route until only a few remain. The first team to get to the finish line is granted the grand prize. Source: https://en.wikipedia.org/wiki/The_Amazing_Race
6 Barrett (2017b) refers to this mechanism as *allostasis*. For the purposes of general understanding of the present work, *allostasis*, together with its counterpart *homeostasis*, may be better understood as two sides of the same construct: physiological regulation, albeit research in the area does not show total assent (Ramsay & Woods, 2014). While homeostasis refers to how organisms maintain internal balance dynamically, allostasis refers to how an organism's internal parameters vary when change – brought about by internal or external demands – happens (McEwen & Wingfield, 2010).

7 Fermin, Friston and Yamawaki (2022) propose a role for the insular cortex in interoceptive self-modelling aligned with the Active Inference framework. They explain how insular interoceptive predictive functions consider the parallel connections of the insular cortex with dorsolateral and ventromedial PFC together with the supplementary motor area (SMA) and the striatum-dopaminergic system for (i) interoceptive habit; or supervised interoceptive control; (ii) interoceptive model-based inference; for categorical and episodic interoception; and (iii) interoception exploration; for Pavlovian and innate interoception responses. Their model highlights the forward connections involving (from lower to higher systems): visceral, subcortical, insula, and PFC (with SMA) to represent interoceptive prediction errors, and the backward connections; aligning the same systems in descending order (from higher to lower), to code for interoceptive predictions.

8 According to Barrett (2017b), the study of patterns in emotions can be misguided if not attentive to what patterns mean, as in "(...) A pattern that diagnoses sadness is not the brain state for sadness but merely a statistical summary of a highly variable set of instances." (2017b, p. 15)

References

Aboitiz, F. (2024). *A history of bodies, brains, and minds: The evolution of life and consciousness*. MIT Press.

Adolphs, R., Mlodinow, L., & Barrett, L. F. (2019). What is an emotion? *Current Biology*, *29*(20), R1060–R1064.

Aitchison, L., & Lengyel, M. (2017). With or without you: Predictive coding and Bayesian inference in the brain. *Current Opinion in Neurobiology*, *46*, 219–227.

Alamia, A., & VanRullen, R. (2019). Alpha oscillations and traveling waves: Signatures of predictive coding?. *PLoS Biology*, *17*(10), e3000487.

Amaral, D. G. (2023). Bases Neuroanatômicas pelas quais os Circuitos Neurais Medeiam o Comportamento. In E. R. Kandel, et al. (org.). *Princípios de Neurociências* (6th ed., pp. 64–83). AMGH.

Arnold, M. B. (1960). *Emotion and personality*. Columbia University Press.

Barrett, L. F. (2006). Solving the emotion paradox: Categorization and the experience of emotion. *Personality and Social Psychology Review*, *10*(1), 20–46.

Barrett, L. F. (2012). Emotions are real. *Emotion*, *12*(3), 413–429.

Barrett, L. F. (2016). Navigating the science of emotion. In H. L. Meiselman (Ed.), *Emotion measurement* (pp. 39–84). Woodhead Publishing.

Barrett, L. F. (2017a). *How emotions are made: The secret life of the brain*. Pan Macmillan.

Barrett, L. F. (2017b). The theory of constructed emotion: An active inference account of interoception and categorization. *Social Cognitive and Affective Neuroscience*, *12*(1), 1–23.

Barrett, L. F. (2020). *Seven and a half lessons about the brain*. Picador.

Barrett, L. F., & Bar, M. (2009). See it with feeling: Affective predictions during object perception. *Philosophical Transactions of the Royal Society B: Biological Sciences*, *364*(1521), 1325–1334.

Barrett, L. F., & Lindquist, K. A. (2008). The embodiment of emotion. In G. R. Semin & E. R. Smith (Eds.), *Embodied grounding: Social, cognitive, affective, and neuroscientific approaches* (pp. 237–262). Cambridge University Press.

Barrett, L. F., & Satpute, A. B. (2013). Large-scale brain networks in affective and social neuroscience: Towards an integrative functional architecture of the brain. *Current Opinion in Neurobiology*, *23*(3), 361–372.

Barrett, L. F., & Simmons, W. K. (2015). Interoceptive predictions in the brain. *Nature Reviews Neuroscience*, *16*(7), 419–429. https://doi.org/10.1038/nrn3950

Barrett, L. F., Adolphs, R., Marsella, S., Martinez, A. M., & Pollak, S. D. (2019). Emotional expressions reconsidered: Challenges to inferring emotion from human facial movements. *Psychological Science in the Public Interest*, *20*, 1–68. https://doi.org/10.1177/1529100619832930

Barrett, L. F., Gross, J., Christensen, T. C., & Benvenuto, M. (2001). Knowing what you're feeling and knowing what to do about it: Mapping the relation between emotion differentiation and emotion regulation. *Cognition & Emotion*, *15*(6), 713–724.

Barrett, L. F., Lewis, M., & Haviland-Jones, J. M. (2016). *Handbook of emotions* (4th ed.). Guilford Publications, Inc.

Barrett, L. F., Quigley, K. S., Bliss-Moreau, E., & Aronson, K. R. (2004). Interoceptive sensitivity and self-reports of emotional experience. *Journal of Personality and Social Psychology*, *87*(5), 684–697. https://doi.org/10.1037/0022-3514.87.5.684

Bechara, A., & Damasio, A. R. (2005). The somatic marker hypothesis: A neural theory of economic decision. *Games and Economic Behavior*, *52*(2), 336–372.

Bengio, Y., Louradour, J., Collobert, R., & Weston, J. (2009). Curriculum learning. In *Proceedings of the 26th Annual International Conference on Machine Learning* (pp. 41–48). Montreal, QC.

Berezovskii, V. K., Nassi, J. J., & Born, R. T. (2011). Segregation of feedforward and feedback projections in mouse visual cortex. *The Journal of comparative neurology*, *519*(18), 3672–3683. https://doi.org/10.1002/cne.22675

Berlo, D. K. (1960). *The process of communication: An introduction to theory and practice*. Holt, Rinehart and Winston.

Bornstein, M. H., & Lamb, M. E. (2011). *Cognitive development: An advanced textbook*. Psychology Press.

Brown, E. C., & Brüne, M. (2012). The role of prediction in social neuroscience. *Frontiers in Human Neuroscience*, *6*, 147.

Busso, D. S., & Pollack, C. (2015). No brain left behind: Consequences of neuroscience discourse for education. *Learning, Media and Technology*, *40*(2), 168–186.

Buzsáki, G., Logothetis, N., & Singer, W. (2013). Scaling brain size, keeping timing: Evolutionary preservation of brain rhythms. *Neuron*, *80*(3), 751–764.

Calderone, D. J., Lakatos, P., Butler, P. D., & Castellanos, F. X. (2014). Entrainment of neural oscillations as a modifiable substrate of attention. *Trends in Cognitive Sciences*, *18*(6), 300–309. https://doi.org/10.1016/j.tics.2014.02.005

Camacho, M. C., Nielsen, A. N., Balser, D., Furtado, E., Steinberger, D. C., Fruchtman, L., Culver, J. P., Sylvester, C. M., & Barch, D. M. (2023). Large-scale encoding of emotion concepts becomes increasingly similar between individuals from childhood to adolescence. *Nature Neuroscience*, *26*(7), 1256–1266. https://doi.org/10.1038/s41593-023-01358-9

Cannon, W. B. (1927). The James-Lange theory of emotions: A critical examination and an alternative theory. *The American journal of psychology*, *39*(1/4), 106-124.

Cantor, P., Osher, D., Berg, J., Steyer, L., & Rose, T. (2021). Malleability, plasticity, and individuality: How children learn and develop in context 1. In P. Cantor & D. Osher (Eds.), *The science of learning and development* (pp. 3–54). Routledge.

Castilho, F. M. (2021). A expressão das emoções no homem e nos animais, de Charles Darwin: algumas considerações. *Filosofia e História da Biologia*, *16*(2), 173–207.

Clark, A. (2013). The many faces of precision (Replies to commentaries on "Whatever next? Neural prediction, situated agents, and the future of cognitive science"). *Frontiers in Psychology*, *4*, 270.

Clark, A. (2016). *Surfing uncertainty: Prediction, action, and the embodied mind*. Oxford University Press.

Clark, A. (2017). Busting out: Predictive brains, embodied minds, and the puzzle of the evidentiary veil. *Noûs*, *51*(4), 727–753.

Clark, A. (2019). Consciousness as generative entanglement. *The Journal of Philosophy*, *116*(12), 645–662.
Clark, A., Friston, K., & Wilkinson, S. (2019). Bayesing qualia: Consciousness as inference, not raw datum. *Journal of Consciousness Studies*, *26*(9–10), 19–33.
Conway, C. M. (2020). How does the brain learn environmental structure? Ten core principles for understanding the neurocognitive mechanisms of statistical learning. *Neuroscience and Biobehavioral Reviews*, *112*, 279–299. https://doi.org/10.1016/j.neubiorev.2020.01.032, PubMed: 32018038
Crivelli, C., Jarillo, S., Russell, J. A., & Fernandez-Dols, J. M. (2016). Reading emotions from faces in two indigenous societies. *Journal of Experimental Psychology: General*, *145*(7), 830–843.
Crivelli, C., Russell, J. A., Jarillo, S., & Fernández-Dols, J.-M. (2017). Recognizing spontaneous facial expressions of emotion in a small-scale society of Papua New Guinea. *Emotion*, *17*(2), 337–347.
Dalgleish, T. (2004). The emotional brain. *Nature Reviews Neuroscience*, *5*, 582–585.
Damasio, A. R. (1994). *Descartes' error: Emotion, reason, and the human brain*. Putnam.
Damasio, A. R. (1996). The somatic marker hypothesis and the possible functions of the prefrontal cortex. *Philosophical Transactions of the Royal Society of London. Series B: Biological Sciences*, *351*(1346), 1413–1420.
Damasio, A. R. (1999). *The feeling of what happens: Body and emotion in the making of consciousness*. Houghton Mifflin Harcourt.
Damasio, A. R. (2001). Fundamental feelings. *Nature*, *413*(6858), 781–781.
Damasio, A. R. (2003). *Looking for Spinoza: Joy, sorrow, and the feeling brain*. Houghton Mifflin Harcourt.
Damasio, A. R. (2011). Neural basis of emotions. *Scholarpedia*, *6*(3), 1804.
Damasio, A. R. (2021). *Saber e sentir*. Companhia das Letras.
Damasio, A. R., & Damasio, H. (2023). Feelings are the source of consciousness. *Neural Computation*, *35*(3), 277–286.
Damasio, A. R., Damasio, H., & Tranel, D. (2013). Persistence of feelings and sentience after bilateral damage of the insula. *Cerebral Cortex*, *23*(4), 833–846.
Damasio, A. R., Tranel, D., & Damasio, H. (1991). Somatic markers and the guidance of behavior: Theory and preliminary testing. In H. S. Levin, H. M. Eisenberg, & A. L. Benton (Eds.), *Frontal Lobe function and dysfunction* (pp. 217–229). Oxford University Press.
Darwin, C. R. (1872). *The expression of the emotions in man and animals*. John Murray.
Davidson, R. J. (2000). Cognitive neuroscience needs affective neuroscience (and vice versa). *Brain and Cognition*, *42*(1), 89–92.
Davidson, R. J. (2003). Seven sins in the study of emotion: Correctives from affective neuroscience. *Brain and Cognition*, *52*(1), 129–132.
Davidson, R. J., & Sutton, S. K. (1995). Affective neuroscience: The emergence of a discipline. *Current Opinion in Neurobiology*, *5*(2), 217–224.
de Waal, F. B. M., & Andrews, K. (2022). The question of animal emotions: Do animals, including invertebrates, have felt emotions and does this morally matter? *Science*, *375*, 1351–1352.
Dewey, J. (1895). The theory of emotion. II. The significance of emotions. *Psychological Review*, *2*, 13–32. doi:10.1037/h0070927
Di Lorenzo, P. M., Chen, J. Y., Rosen, A. M., & Roussin, A. T. (2009). Tastant. In M. D. Binder, N. Hirokawa, & U. Windhorst (Eds.), *Encyclopedia of neuroscience*. Springer. https://doi.org/10.1007/978-3-540-29678-2_5888
Dixon, T. (2003). *From passions to emotions: The creation of a secular psychological category*. Cambridge University Press.

Dixon, T. (2012). "Emotion": The history of a keyword in crisis. *Emotion Review*, *4*(4), 338–344.
Doelling, K. B., & Assaneo, M. F. (2021). Neural oscillations are a start toward understanding brain activity rather than the end. *PLoS Biology*, *19*(5), e3001234.
Dolan, R. (2003). Feeling emotional. *Nature*, *421*, 893–894.
Doya, K. (Ed.). (2007). *Bayesian brain: Probabilistic approaches to neural coding*. MIT Press.
Dukes, D., Abrams, K., Adolphs, R., Ahmed, M. E., Beatty, A., Berridge, K. C., & Sander, D. (2021). The rise of affectivism. *Nature Human Behaviour*, *5*(7), 816–820.
Durán, J. I., & Fernández-Dols, J. M. (2021). Do emotions result in their predicted facial expressions? A meta-analysis of studies on the co-occurrence of expression and emotion. *Emotion*, *21*(7), 1550.
Edelman, G. M., & Gally, J. A. (2001). Degeneracy and complexity in biological systems. *Proceedings of the National Academy of Sciences*, *98*(24), 13763–13768.
Ekman, P. (2012). *Emotions revealed: Understanding faces and feelings*. Hachette.
Feldman, H., & Friston, K. J. (2010). Attention, uncertainty, and free-energy. *Frontiers in Human Neuroscience*, *4*, 215.
Fermin, A. S., Friston, K., & Yamawaki, S. (2022). An insula hierarchical network architecture for active interoceptive inference. *Royal Society Open Science*, *9*(6), 220226.
Fienberg, S. E. (2006). When did Bayesian inference become "Bayesian"? *Bayesian Analysis*, *1*(1), 1–40.
Fischer, K. W., & Bidell, T. R. (2006). Dynamic development of action and thought. *Handbook of Child Psychology*, *1*, 313–399.
Fisher, A. J., Medaglia, J. D., & Jeronimus, B. F. (2018). Lack of group-to-individual generalizability is a threat to human subjects research. *Proceedings of the National Academy of Sciences*, *115*(27), E6106–E6115.
Freese, J. L., & Amaral, D. G. (2009). Neuroanatomy of the primate amygdala. In P. J. Whalen & E. A. Phelps (Eds.), *The human amygdala* (pp. 3–42). Guilford Press.
Friston, K. (2003). Learning and inference in the brain. *Neural Networks*, *16*(9), 1325–1352.
Friston, K. (2005). A theory of cortical responses. *Philosophical transactions of the Royal Society of London. Series B, Biological Sciences*, *360*(1456), 815–36.
Friston, K. (2008). Hierarchical models in the brain. *PLoS Computational Biology*, *4*(11), e1000211.
Friston, K. (2009). The free-energy principle: A rough guide to the brain? *Trends in Cognitive Sciences*, *13*(7), 293–301.
Friston, K. (2010). The free-energy principle: A unified brain theory? *Nature Reviews. Neuroscience*, *11*(2), 127–138.
Friston, K. (2011). Embodied inference: Or I think therefore I am, if I am what I think. In W. Tschacher & C. Bergomi (Eds.), *The implications of embodiment (Cognition and Communication)* (pp. 89–125). Imprint Academic.
Friston, K. (2012). The history of the future of the Bayesian brain. *NeuroImage*, *62*(2), 1230–1233.
Friston, K. (2014). Active inference and agency. *Cognitive Neuroscience*, *5*(2), 119–121.
Friston, K. (2019). Waves of prediction. *PLoS Biology*, *17*(10), e3000426.
Friston, K., & Frith, C. D. (2015). Active inference, communication and hermeneutics. *Cortex*, *68*, 129–143.
Friston, K., Schwartenbeck, P., FitzGerald, T., Moutoussis, M., Behrens, T., & Dolan, R. J. (2013). The anatomy of choice: Active inference and agency. *Frontiers in Human Neuroscience*, *7*, 598.

Gardner, E. P., & Gardner, D. (2023). Codificação Sensorial. In E. R. Kandel, et al. (org.). *Princípios de Neurociências* (6th ed., pp. 346–365). AMGH.
Gendron, M. (2010). Defining emotion: A brief history. *Emotion Review*, *2*(4), 371–372.
Gendron, M., & Barrett, L. F. (2017). Facing the past: A history of the face in psychological research on emotion perception. In J.-M. Fernández-Dols & J. A. Russell (Eds.), *The science of facial expression* (pp. 15–36). Oxford University Press.
Gendron, M., & Feldman Barrett, L. (2009). Reconstructing the past: A century of ideas about emotion in psychology. *Emotion Review*, *1*(4), 316–339.
Gendron, M., Lindquist, K. A., Barsalou, L., & Barrett, L. F. (2012). Emotion words shape emotion percepts. *Emotion*, *12*(2), 314.
Gendron M., Crivelli C., Barrett L. F. (2018). Universality reconsidered: Diversity in making meaning of facial expressions. *Current Directions in Psychological Science*, *27*(4), 211–219.
Gendron M., Hoemann K., Crittenden A. N., Mangola S. M., Ruark G. A., Barrett L. F. (2020). Emotion perception in Hadza hunter-gatherers. *Scientific Reports*, *10*(1), Article 3867.
Giurgi-Oncu, C., Bredicean, C., Frandeş, M., Enătescu, V., Papavă, I., Riviş, I., & Ursoniu, S. (2021). Social inferences as mediators of wellbeing in depression. *Neuropsychiatric Disease and Treatment*, *17*, 1679–1687.
Graeff, F. G. (2018). Evolução da neurociência comportamental nos últimos 50 anos. Foco no sistema de defesa e na neurotransmissão. *Medicina (Ribeirão Preto)*, *51*(2), 89–111.
Hackel, L. M., Larson, G. M., Bowen, J. D., Ehrlich, G. A., Mann, T. C., Middlewood, B., Roberts, I. D., Eyink, J., Fetterolf, J. C., Gonzalez, F., Garrido, C. O., Kim, J., O'Brien, T. C., O'Malley, E. E., Mesquita, B., & Barrett, L. F. (2016). On the neural implausibility of the modular mind: Evidence for distributed construction dissolves boundaries between perception, cognition, and emotion. *The Behavioral and Brain Sciences*, *39*, e246. https://doi.org/10.1017/S0140525X15002770
Headley, D. B., & Paré, D. (2013). In sync: Gamma oscillations and emotional memory. *Frontiers in Behavioral Neuroscience*, *7*, 170.
Hebb, D. O. (1946). Emotion in man and animal: an analysis of the intuitive processes of recognition. *Psychological Review*, *53*(2), 88–106.
Heilbron, M., & Chait, M. (2018). Great expectations: Is there evidence for predictive coding in auditory cortex?. *Neuroscience*, *389*, 54–73.
Hess, W. R., & Brügger, M. (1981). The subcortical center of the affective defense reaction. In W. R. Hess (Ed.), *Biological order and brain organization: Selected works of WR Hess* (pp. 183–202). Springer Berlin Heidelberg.
Hobson, J. A., & Friston, K. J. (2012). Waking and dreaming consciousness: Neurobiological and functional considerations. *Progress in Neurobiology*, *98*(1), 82–98.
Hoemann, K., Gendron, M., Crittenden, A. N., Mangola, S. M., Endeko, E. S., Dussault, É., Barrett, L. F., & Mesquita, B. (2023). What we can learn about emotion by talking with the Hadza. *Perspectives on Psychological Science*, *19*(1), 173–200. https://doi.org/10.1177/17456916231178555 (Original work published 2024).
Hoemann, K., Wormwood, J. B., Barrett, L. F., & Quigley, K. S. (2023). Multimodal, idiographic ambulatory sensing will transform our understanding of emotion. *Affective Science*, *4*(3), 480–486.
Hohwy, J. (2012). Attention and conscious perception in the hypothesis testing brain. *Frontiers in Psychology*, *3*, 96.
Hohwy, J. (2016). The self-evidencing brain. *Noûs*, *50*(2), 259–285.

Hohwy, J. (2020). New directions in predictive processing. *Mind & Language*, *35*(2), 209–223.

Holmes, J., & Nolte, T. (2019). "Surprise" and the Bayesian brain: implications for psychotherapy theory and practice. *Frontiers in Psychology*, *10*, 592.

Houben, M., Van Den Noortgate, W., & Kuppens, P. (2015). The relation between short-term emotion dynamics and psychological well-being: A meta-analysis. *Psychological Bulletin*, *141*(4), 901.

Huang, Y., & Rao, R. P. (2011). Predictive coding. *Wiley Interdisciplinary Reviews: Cognitive Science*, *2*(5), 580–593.

Hutchinson-Wong, N., Glue, P., Adhia, D., & de Ridder, D. (2025). How does depressive cognition develop? A state-dependent network model of predictive processing. *Psychological Review*, *132*(2), 442–469. https://doi.org/10.1037/rev0000512

Immordino-Yang, M. H., & Damasio, A. (2007). We feel, therefore we learn: The relevance of affective and social neuroscience to education. *Mind, Brain, and Education*, *1*(1), 3–10.

Immordino-Yang, M. H., Yang, X. F., & Damasio, H. (2016). Cultural modes of expressing emotions influence how emotions are experienced. *Emotion*, *16*(7), 1033.

Izard, C. E. (1977). *Human emotions*. Plenum Press. https://doi.org/10.1007/978-1-4899-2209-0

Izard, C. E. (2010a). The many meanings/aspects of emotion: Definitions, functions, activation, and regulation. *Emotion Review*, *2*, 363–370.

Izard, C. E. (2010b). More meanings and more questions for the term "emotion." *Emotion Review*, *2*, 383–385.

Jacobson, H., Ongil, Z., Algom, D., & Usher, M. (2024). Valence in perception: Are affective valence and visual brightness integral dimensions in visual experience?. *Consciousness and Cognition*, *126*, 103783.

James, W. (1884). What is an emotion? *Mind*, *9*, 188–205.

Jones, E. G. (2000). Microcolumns in the cerebral cortex. *Proceedings of the National Academy of Sciences*, *97*(10), 5019–5021.

Kalateh, S., Estrada-Jimenez, L. A., Hojjati, S. N., & Barata, J. (2024). A systematic review on multimodal emotion recognition: building blocks, current state, applications, and challenges. *IEEE Access*. https://doi.org/10.1109/ACCESS.2024.3430850

Kandel, E. R., Koester, J. D., Mack, S. H., & Siegelbaum, S. A. (2023). *Princípios de Neurociências*, 6e. McGraw Hill.

Keller, G. B., & Mrsic-Flogel, T. D. (2018). Predictive processing: A canonical cortical computation. *Neuron*, *100*(2), 424–435.

Korzybski, A. (1958). *Science and sanity: An introduction to non-Aristotelian systems and general semantics*. Institute of GS.

Kriegeskorte, N., & Douglas, P. K. (2018). Cognitive computational neuroscience. *Nature Neuroscience*, *21*(9), 1148–1160.

Kryklywy, J. H., Ehlers, M. R., Anderson, A. K., & Todd, R. M. (2020). From architecture to evolution: multisensory evidence of decentralized emotion. *Trends in Cognitive Sciences*, *24*(11), 916–929.

Kuppens, P. (2015). It's about time: A special section on affect dynamics. *Emotion Review*, *7*(4), 297–300.

Lange, C. G. (1885). The mechanism of the emotions. *The classical psychologists*, 672-684.

Lebrecht, S., Bar, M., Barrett, L. F., & Tarr, M. J. (2012). Micro-valences: Perceiving affective valence in everyday objects. *Frontiers in Psychology*, *3*, 107.

LeDoux J. 2021. What emotions might be like in other animals. *Current Biology*, *31*(13), R824–R829.
Lindquist, K. A., & Gendron, M. (2013). What's in a word? Language constructs emotion perception. *Emotion Review*, *5*(1), 66–71.
Lippelt, D. P., Hommel, B., & Colzato, L. S. (2014). Focused attention, open monitoring and loving kindness meditation: Effects on attention, conflict monitoring, and creativity–A review. *Frontiers in Psychology*, *5*, 1083.
LoBue, V., & Ogren, M. (2022). How the emotional environment shapes the emotional life of the child. *Policy Insights from the Behavioral and Brain Sciences*, *9*, 137–144. https://doi.org/10.1177/23727322211067264
Lutz, A., Slagter, H. A., Dunne, J. D., & Davidson, R. J. (2008). Attention regulation and monitoring in meditation. *Trends in Cognitive Sciences*, *12*(4), 163–169.
Macrine, S. L., & Fugate, J. M. (2022). Embodied cognition and its educational significance. In S. L. Macrine & J. M. B. Fugate (Eds.), *Movement matters: How embodied cognition informs teaching and learning* (pp. 13–24). The MIT Press.
Malezieux, M., Klein, A. S., & Gogolla, N. (2023). Neural circuits for emotion. *Annual Review of Neuroscience*, *46*(1), 211–231.
Marblestone, A. H., Wayne, G., & Kording, K. P. (2016). Toward an integration of deep learning and neuroscience. *Frontiers in Computational Neuroscience*, *10*, 215943.
McEwen, B. S., & Wingfield, J. C. (2010). What is in a name? Integrating homeostasis, allostasis and stress. *Hormones and Behavior*, *57*(2), 105–111. https://doi.org/10.1016/j.yhbeh.2009.09.011
McLeod, P., & Dienes, Z. (1996). Do fielders know where to go to catch the ball or only how to get there? *Journal of Experimental Psychology: Human Perception and Performance*, *22*, 531.
Mesquita, B., & Walker, R. (2003). Cultural differences in emotions: A context for interpreting emotional experiences. *Behaviour Research and Therapy*, *41*(7), 777–793.
Mesquita, B., Boiger, M., & De Leersnyder, J. (2017). Doing emotions: The role of culture in everyday emotions. *European Review of Social Psychology*, *28*(1), 95–133.
Meyer, D. K., & Turner, J. C. (2006). Re-conceptualizing emotion and motivation to learn in classroom contexts. *Educational Psychology Review*, *18*, 377–390.
Miskovic, V., Kuntzelman, K., Chikazoe, J., & Anderson, A. K. (2016). Representation of affect in sensory cortex. *Behavioral and Brain Sciences*, *39*, e252.
Morris, J. S., Friston, K. J., Büchel, C., Frith, C. D., Young, A. W., Calder, A. J., & Dolan, R. J. (1998). A neuromodulatory role for the human amygdala in processing emotional facial expressions. *Brain: A Journal of Neurology*, *121*(1), 47–57.
Nauta, W. J. H. (1971). The problem of the frontal lobe: A reinterpretation. *Journal of Psychiatric Research*, *8*, 167-187.
Palmer, C. J., Seth, A. K., & Hohwy, J. (2015). The felt presence of other minds: Predictive processing, counterfactual predictions, and mentalising in autism. *Consciousness and Cognition*, *36*, 376–389.
Panksepp, J. (1998). *Affective neuroscience*. Oxford University Press.
Panksepp, J. (2001). On the subcortical sources of basic human emotions and the primacy of emotional–affective (action–perception) processes in human consciousness. *Evolution and Cognition*, *7*(2), 134–140.
Panksepp, J. (2003). Damasio's error?. *Consciousness and Emotion*, *4*(1), 111–134.
Panksepp, J., & Watt, D. (2011). What is basic about basic emotions? Lasting lessons from affective neuroscience. *Emotion Review*, *3*(4), 387–396.
Parr, T., Pezzulo, G., & Friston, K. J. (2022). *Active inference: The free energy principle in mind, brain, and behavior*. MIT Press.

Peelen, M. V., Berlot, E., & de Lange, F. P. (2024). Predictive processing of scenes and objects. *Nature Reviews Psychology*, *3*(1), 13–26.
Perrinet, L. U. (2020). From the retina to action: Dynamics of predictive processing in the visual system. In D. Mendonça, M. Curado, & S. S. Gouveia (Eds.), *The philosophy and science of predictive processing* (pp. 85–104). Bloomsbury Academic.
Pessoa, L. (2022). *The entangled brain: How perception, cognition, and emotion are woven together*. MIT Press. https://doi.org/10.7551/mitpress/14636.001.0001
Pezzulo, G., Parr, T., & Friston, K. (2022). The evolution of brain architectures for predictive coding and active inference. *Philosophical Transactions of the Royal Society B*, *377*(1844), 20200531.
Picard, F., & Friston, K. (2014). Predictions, perception, and a sense of self. *Neurology*, *83*(12), 1112–1118.
Piekarski, M. (2021). Understanding predictive processing. A review. *AVANT. Pismo Awangardy Filozoficzno-Naukowej*, *1*, 1–48.
Platt, M. L., & Spelke, E. S. (2009). What can developmental and comparative cognitive neuroscience tell us about the adult human brain? *Current Opinion in Neurobiology*, *19*(1), 1–5
Plutchik, R. (2001). The nature of emotions: Human emotions have deep evolutionary roots, a fact that may explain their complexity and provide tools for clinical practice. *American Scientist*, *89*(4), 344–350.
Popov, T., Steffen, A., Weisz, N., Miller, G. A., & Rockstroh, B. (2012). Cross-frequency dynamics of neuromagnetic oscillatory activity: two mechanisms of emotion regulation. *Psychophysiology*, *49*(12), 1545–1557.
Pribram, K. H. (1970). Feelings as monitors. *Feelings and emotions*, *41*, 53.
Raffone, A., & Srinivasan, N. (2010). The exploration of meditation in the neuroscience of attention and consciousness. *Cognitive Processing*, *11*, 1–7.
Ramsay, D. S., & Woods, S. C. (2014). Clarifying the roles of homeostasis and allostasis in physiological regulation. *Psychological Review*, *121*(2), 225–247. https://doi.org/10.1037/a0035942
Rao, R. P., & Ballard, D. H. (1999). Predictive coding in the visual cortex: A functional interpretation of some extra-classical receptive-field effects. *Nature Neuroscience*, *2*(1), 79–87.
Reitsema, A. M., Jeronimus, B. F., van Dijk, M., & de Jonge, P. (2022). Emotion dynamics in children and adolescents: A meta-analytic and descriptive review. *Emotion*, *22*(2), 374.
Russell, J. A. (1980). A circumplex model of affect. *Journal of Personality and Social Psychology*, *39*(6), 1161.
Russell, J. A., & Barrett, L. F. (1999). Core affect, prototypical emotional episodes, and other things called emotion: Dissecting the elephant. *Journal of Personality and Social Psychology*, *76*(5), 805.
Satpute, A. B., & Lindquist, K. A. (2021). At the neural intersection between language and emotion. *Affective Science*, *2*(2), 207–220.
Saxbe, D. E., Yang, X. F., Borofsky, L. A., & Immordino-Yang, M. H. (2013). The embodiment of emotion: Language use during the feeling of social emotions predicts cortical somatosensory activity. *Social Cognitive and Affective Neuroscience*, *8*(7), 806–812.
Scarantino, A., & de Sousa, R. (2021). Emotion. In E. N. Zalta (Ed.), *The Stanford encyclopedia of philosophy* (Summer 2021 ed.). https://plato.stanford.edu/archives/sum2021/entries/emotion/
Schachter, S., & Singer, J. (1962). Cognitive, social, and physiological determinants of emotional state. *Psychological Review*, *69*(5), 379.

Seok, B. (2021).The emotions in early Chinese philosophy. In E. N. Zalta (Ed.), *The Stanford encyclopedia of philosophy* (Winter 2021 ed.). https://plato.stanford.edu/archives/win2021/entries/emotions-chinese/

Seth, A. K. (2014). A predictive processing theory of sensorimotor contingencies: Explaining the puzzle of perceptual presence and its absence in synesthesia. *Cognitive Neuroscience*, *5*(2), 97–118.

Seth, A. K., & Friston, K. J. (2016). Active interoceptive inference and the emotional brain. *Philosophical Transactions of the Royal Society B: Biological Sciences*, *371*(1708), 20160007.

Shenhav, A., Barrett, L. F., & Bar, M. (2013). Affective value and associative processing share a cortical substrate. *Cognitive, Affective, & Behavioral Neuroscience*, *13*(1), 46–59.

Siegel, E. H., Wormwood, J. B., Quigley, K. S., & Barrett, L. F. (2018). Seeing what you feel: Affect drives visual perception of structurally neutral faces. *Psychological Science*, *29*(4), 496–503.

Singh, A., Westlin, C., Eisenbarth, H., Losin, E. A. R., Andrews-Hanna, J. R., Wager, T. D., & Erdogmus, D. (2021, November). Variation is the norm: Brain state dynamics evoked by emotional video clips. In *2021 43rd Annual International Conference of the IEEE Engineering in Medicine & Biology Society (EMBC)* (pp. 6003–6007). IEEE.

Smith, R., Kuplicki, R., Feinstein, J., Forthman, K. L., Stewart, J. L., Paulus, M. P., & Khalsa, S. S. (2020). A Bayesian computational model reveals a failure to adapt interoceptive precision estimates across depression, anxiety, eating, and substance use disorders. *PLoS Computational Biology*, *16*(12), e1008484.

Solms, M. (2021). *The hidden spring: A journey to the source of consciousness*. Profile Books.

Spektrum der Wissenschaft. (2012). A 1-hour interview with Jaak Panksepp, the father of affective Neuroscience [video]. https://youtube.com/watch?v=u4ICY6-7hJo%3Fcolor%3Dred%26modestbranding%3D1%26showinfo%3D0%26origin%3Dhttps%3A

Spratling, M. W. (2017). A review of predictive coding algorithms. *Brain and Cognition*, *112*, 92–97.

Sumantry, D., & Stewart, K. E. (2021). Meditation, mindfulness, and attention: A meta-analysis. *Mindfulness*, *12*, 1332–1349.

Symons, A. E., El-Deredy, W., Schwartze, M., & Kotz, S. A. (2016). The functional role of neural oscillations in non-verbal emotional communication. *Frontiers in Human Neuroscience*, *10*, 239.

Taylor, J. G., & Fragopanagos, N. F. (2005). The interaction of attention and emotion. *Neural Networks, 18*(4), 353–369.

Thut, G., Miniussi, C., & Gross, J. (2012). The functional importance of rhythmic activity in the brain. *Current Biology*, 22(16), R658–R663.

Todd, R. M., Miskovic, V., Chikazoe, J., & Anderson, A. K. (2020). Emotional objectivity: Neural representations of emotions and their interaction with cognition. *Annual Review of Psychology*, *71*(1), 25–48.

Tomkins, S. S. (1962). *Affect imagery consciousness: Vol. I. The positive affects*. Springer.

Tomkins, S. S. (1963). *Affect imagery consciousness: Vol. II. The negative affects*. Springer.

Tomkins, S. S. (1991). *Affect imagery consciousness: Vol. III. The negative affects: Anger and fear*. Springer.

Tomkins, S. S. (1992). *Affect imagery consciousness: Vol. IV. Cognition: Duplication and transformation of information*. Springer.

Toronchuk, J. A., & Ellis, G. F. (2013). Affective neuronal selection: The nature of the primordial emotion systems. *Frontiers in Psychology, 3*, 589.
Tscshantz, A., Millidge, B., Seth, A. K., & Buckley, C. L. (2023). Hybrid predictive coding: Inferring, fast and slow. *PLOS Computational Biology, 19*(8), e1011280. https://doi.org/10.1371/journal.pcbi.1011280
Tugade, M. M., Fredrickson, B. L., & Feldman Barrett, L. (2004). Psychological resilience and positive emotional granularity: Examining the benefits of positive emotions on coping and health. *Journal of Personality, 72*(6), 1161–1190.
Van Essen, D. C., Smith, J., Glasser, M. F., Elam, J., Donahue, C. J., Dierker, D. L., & Harwell, J. (2017). The brain analysis library of spatial maps and atlases (BALSA) database. *Neuroimage, 144*, 270–274.
Vignesh, D., He, S., & Banerjee, S. (2024). A review on the complexities of brain activity: Insights from nonlinear dynamics in neuroscience. *Nonlinear Dynamics, 112*(24), 29443–29464.
Wang, Y., Lu, L., & Wu, M. (2025). Statistical learning across cognitive and affective domains: a multidimensional review. *Frontiers in Integrative Neuroscience, 19*, 1460471.
Watson, D., & Tellegen, A. (1985). Toward a consensual structure of mood. *Psychological bulletin, 98*(2), 219.
Watson, D., Wiese, D., Vaidya, J., & Tellegen, A. (1999). The two general activation systems of affect: Structural findings, evolutionary considerations, and psychobiological evidence. *Journal of Personality and Social Psychology, 76*(5), 820.
Westlin, C., Theriault, J. E., Katsumi, Y., Nieto-Castanon, A., Kucyi, A., Ruf, S. F., & Barrett, L. F. (2023). Improving the study of brain-behavior relationships by revisiting basic assumptions. *Trends in Cognitive Sciences, 27*(3), 246–257.
Yiend, J. (2010). The effects of emotion on attention: A review of attentional processing of emotional information. *Cognition and Emotion, 24*(1), 3–47.

2 Analysing Embodied Emotions through Artificial Psychology

Nataša Kovač, Hojjatollah Farahani, and Peter Watson

2.1 Introduction

Every emotion begins with a signal but that signal, whether a flicker in an EEG trace, a shift in gaze, a subtle muscular tension, or a whisper in the voice, is rarely clean. It arrives tangled in noise, in missing fragments, in the idiosyncrasies of bodies and machines alike. To extract meaning from this cacophony, we must first prepare the data to hear what the emotion might be saying.

Over recent years, the study of human emotion has undergone a profound conceptual transformation. Rather than treating affect as a purely cognitive or physiological phenomenon, researchers are increasingly viewing it as an embodied process, an inseparable interplay between brain, body, and environment. The past five years (2020–2025) have seen the scientific community definitively move past traditional boundaries of cognition and physiology, embracing an embodied perspective that grounds emotion in the dynamic interchange between the brain, the body, and the environment (Pinna & Edwards, 2020). This transformation establishes the foundation of Artificial Psychology (AP), a discipline dedicated to modelling and replicating human emotional processes through computational mechanisms that account for the body's active role.

Central to this paradigm is interoception, the brain's continuous sensing and interpretation of internal bodily states, such as heart rate and respiration. A synthesis of systematic reviews confirms that interoception provides the pre-reflective ground for affective awareness (Klein et al., 2025). High interoceptive accuracy correlates with greater emotional intensity and improved regulatory control, while deficits are commonly implicated in psychological challenges, underscoring the body's role as an emotional generator, not merely a vessel for expression (Pinna & Edwards, 2020).

Complementing internal sensing, the external bodily expression of emotion, posture, gesture, and movement is confirmed as a universal channel for social communication. Systematic analyses of kinematic data show that specific, measurable patterns, such as expansive postures associated with joy or rigid postures linked to fear, reliably predict emotional valence across diverse groups (Lin & Zhang, 2022; Dael et al., 2012). These findings confirm that the emotional state is readable through the entire physical form, reinforcing the adage that we feel with our bodies as much as with our minds.

DOI: 10.4324/9781003495123-2

This holistic understanding provides the operational blueprint for contemporary AP and Affective Computing (AC). Multimodal deep learning systems now achieve superior accuracy by directly integrating physiological signals, posture, and facial expressions, successfully mimicking the human brain's own integrative, embodied processing of affect (Lin & Zhang, 2022; Wu et al., 2025). This fusion of data streams goes beyond simple facial recognition to include the subtle cues from the entire physical self. It allows artificial systems to interact with humans with unprecedented nuance and contextual awareness (Wu et al., 2025).

The clinical applications of this framework are already transformative. Systematic reviews of AI-driven mental health interventions, such as conversational agents and Extended Reality (XR) therapies, show promising results in achieving symptom reduction (Botes, 2025). The next generation of these tools is moving towards true Embodied AI (EAI), leveraging virtual agents and immersive environments that respond not just to user dialogue, but to their posture and psychophysiological state, thereby creating more emotionally resonant and therapeutically effective interactions.

Despite these technical advances, the integrative reviews identify persistent, human-centred challenges that define the next phase of research. A primary concern is the potential for algorithmic bias stemming from a lack of cross-cultural diversity in the datasets used to train emotion recognition systems (Barker et al., 2025). Suppose EAI is to realise its potential in diverse global contexts. In that case, researchers must prioritise cultural inclusivity and ethical development to prevent the misinterpretation or misrepresentation of embodied emotional cues in non-Western populations (Lin & Zhang, 2022). Furthermore, clinical reviews call for increased methodological rigour and long-term clinical validation to ensure the sustained effectiveness and ethical sustainability of these EAI interventions (Botes, 2025). The future of AP rests not just on perfecting the technical replication of emotion, but on ensuring that its models are scientifically sound and genuinely reflective of the full, diverse spectrum of human embodied experience.

2.2 Python Basics for Emotional Artificial Intelligence

We are beginning to recognise that artificial intelligence (AI) significantly impacts the study of human emotion by enabling the interpretation of complex physiological signals, facial expressions, vocal cues, and text data, a crossover often described as Artificial Psychology (PsAIchology) (Farahani et al., 2024). Analysing this embodied emotional information requires equally advanced computer tools for researchers and practitioners. To fully unlock the potential of emotional artificial intelligence, robust computing tools capable of managing, analysing, and visualising emotionally rich data are essential. Due to its simplicity, readability, and comprehensive libraries, Python has become the dominant programming language in this interdisciplinary field (VanderPlas, 2016). Python has become a leading language in emotional AI applications for several convincing reasons. Its straightforward syntax closely resembles English, making it accessible even for newcomers from psychology, neuroscience, or other non-technical fields. Beneath its simplicity, Python offers advanced computational capabilities, from statistical analysis and signal processing to sophisticated machine learning and deep learning techniques (Kovač et al., 2024).

Python offers a broad array of open-source libraries that enable researchers to rapidly prototype, analyse, visualise, and deploy advanced emotional models. These libraries manage various aspects of the emotional AI pipeline, from initial data management and preprocessing to emotional feature extraction and visualisation, culminating in the deployment of robust predictive models. Consequently, the successful implementation of Emotional AI with Python requires understanding and effective utilisation of its key libraries:

1. NumPy provides robust support for numerical computation and managing arrays of physiological and behavioural data. Its ability to handle large-scale numeric data makes it suitable for emotional analysis tasks involving EEG, heart rate, and other biometric signals:

```
import numpy as np
eeg_data = np.random.normal(0, 1, 5000)
mean_eeg = np.mean(eeg_data)
print("Mean EEG signal:", mean_eeg)
```

2. *Pandas* simplifies data cleaning and preprocessing, which are vital steps in ensuring data quality. Researchers frequently handle datasets from multiple emotional modalities, requiring structured dataframes to simplify complex analysis pipelines:

```
import pandas as pd
emotions_df = pd.DataFrame({
    "Subject": [1, 2, 3],
    "Emotion": ["happy", "sad", "neutral"],
    "Intensity": [7, 5, 3]
})
print(emotions_df)
```

3. Visualisation is essential for intuitively interpreting emotional data. *Matplotlib* and *Seaborn* convert raw numerical data into meaningful visuals, such as graphs or heatmaps, making it easier to understand emotional patterns:

```
import seaborn as sns
import matplotlib.pyplot as plt
intensity = np.random.rand(100)
sns.histplot(intensity, kde=True, color="green")
plt.title("Distribution of Emotional Intensity")
plt.show()
```

4. Voice carries rich emotional signals. *Librosa* enables easy extraction of emotional audio features like pitch, rhythm, and timbre, essential for understanding affective vocal characteristics:

```
import librosa
y, sr = librosa.load("voice_emotion.wav")
tempo, _ = librosa.beat.beat_track(y, sr=sr)
print("Detected tempo:", tempo, "BPM")
```

5. Facial expression analysis involves detecting and interpreting subtle movements. Libraries such as *OpenCV* and *dlib* offer powerful tools to detect faces, track facial landmarks, and extract emotion-sensitive features:

```
import cv2
import dlib
detector = dlib.get_frontal_face_detector()
image = cv2.imread("face.jpg")
gray = cv2.cvtColor(image, cv2.COLOR_BGR2GRAY)
faces = detector(gray)
print("Number of faces detected:", len(faces))
```

6. Emotion recognition and prediction rely heavily on machine learning, and similar supervised pipelines are increasingly used across psychological health domains, including the prediction of chronic pain severity (Kovač et al., 2025). *Scikit-learn* provides an easy-to-use toolkit for traditional machine learning, while *TensorFlow* supports sophisticated deep learning methods. A complementary line of work uses calibrated regression to predict internal shame, with XGBoost performing best and distress tolerance emerging as the strongest predictor (Kovač et al., 2025b).

```
from sklearn.ensemble import RandomForestClassifier
X = np.random.rand(50, 10)
y = np.random.randint(0, 2, 50)
model = RandomForestClassifier()
model.fit(X, y)
accuracy = model.score(X, y)
print("Emotion classification accuracy:", accuracy)
```

These libraries create a cohesive framework, enabling researchers to move from raw emotional data collection through advanced analysis to meaningful emotional insights. By mastering these core tools, readers will be well prepared to navigate and apply powerful emotional AI applications effectively.

In addition to technical knowledge of Python, it is important to note that ethical considerations are equally important. Emotional AI often deals with sensitive and personal data, which requires careful handling to protect the privacy and dignity of individuals. Python's transparent and readable code, as well as its commitment to open source, encourages ethical clarity, transparency, and accountability in research and applications (Jobin et al., 2019). We believe that researchers, in addition to regularly documenting Python code, should also maintain data privacy protocols, secure consent, and implement strict anonymisation procedures to respect participant confidentiality.

Embarking on Python programming for emotional AI might seem daunting initially. Yet, the supportive community, abundance of tutorials, and accessible documentation dramatically reduce entry barriers. Beginners should start by mastering basic Python syntax, then gradually explore libraries, and eventually move into specialised emotion-focused tools (Librosa, OpenCV, dlib), and machine learning libraries (Scikit-learn, TensorFlow). Through consistent practice and incremental learning, even those without prior technical backgrounds can achieve proficiency, enabling sophisticated analyses of complex emotional phenomena.

2.3 From Data to Embodied Emotion

Emotion is not stored in a single variable. It pulses through muscle tensions, breath rhythms, glance trajectories, and vocal microfluctuations. Each of these signals can be digitised, sampled, measured, annotated, and transformed into features that AI systems can understand. The journey from unstructured signals to computational representations is neither trivial nor purely technical. It demands sensitivity to the psychological context, to the nature of embodiment, and to the epistemological assumptions we make when we convert movement into numbers.

At its core, data preprocessing for embodied emotion begins with a commitment to *integrity*, not just of the data, but of its meaning. This involves:

- *Retaining affective variance* while removing irrelevant noise.
- *Aligning multimodal sources* without distorting temporal dynamics.
- *Extracting features* that have interpretive resonance in both psychological theory and algorithmic performance.

Figure 2.1 encapsulates the logic of embodiment. Every arrow hides hundreds of decisions: how to threshold noise, what interpolation strategy to use, how to respect time when aligning sources.

What we call preprocessing is, in essence, a filtering of the world. The data we collect is always partial, always noisy, always filtered through human design choices. As Gendron and Barrett (2009) have argued, *emotion data is not found; it is made*. The act of preprocessing is therefore both statistical and philosophical: it frames which aspects of human experience are legible to machines.

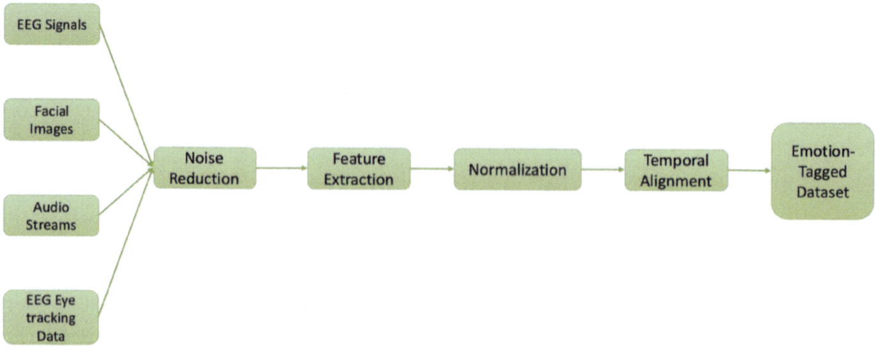

Figure 2.1 From data to embodied emotion.

Recent work in embodied AI (Calvo & D'Mello, 2010; Schuller & Batliner, 2013) has emphasised the need for *context-aware data pipelines, w*here preprocessing is guided by the psychological properties of the emotion under study. For example, preprocessing gaze data for disgust differs vastly from preprocessing voice data for sadness, not just in technique, but in what counts as a meaningful signal.

Capturing embodied emotion is more than placing sensors on a participant's body or turning on a camera. It is a philosophical commitment, a methodological stance, and a technical operation wrapped into one. The data we acquire defines the boundaries of what we can know, what we can model, and what we are willing to assume about the nature of emotion itself. If we record only facial expressions, we risk privileging visible emotion while ignoring the body's internal story. If we focus only on brain signals, we may interpret affect as neurological when it is equally social, physiological, and behavioural.

No single sensor can fully capture the complexity of an emotional experience. That complexity unfolds across multiple dimensions, such as facial muscle movements, vocal inflections, gaze shifts, heart rhythms, and even the electrical patterns of cortical oscillations. Each of these dimensions offers a different window into emotional processing, and each requires a distinct mode of capture. The question, then, is not whether one should use EEG or voice data or eye tracking. Rather, it is how one chooses from these modalities based on the *psychological construct under investigation*. For example, if the research focuses on emotional reactivity in social contexts, gaze data might reveal patterns of approach or avoidance. In contrast, if one is examining affect regulation, heart rate variability, or frontal alpha asymmetry could provide more meaningful insight. Before data collection, researchers have to recognise the nature of the emotion signal and the limitations each sensor brings. Sensors do not simply record; they interpret. Physiological signals have long been central in emotion research, largely due to their involuntary nature. Unlike self-report or facial expressions, bodily reactions often escape conscious modulation, offering a more reliable path to affective truth. At least in theory.

Electroencephalography (EEG) remains one of the most frequently used methods for investigating the brain's dynamic response to emotional stimuli. Capable of capturing millisecond-level changes in electrical activity across the scalp, EEG provides a lens into attentional focus, affective valence, and cognitive engagement. For example, the asymmetry of alpha band power over the frontal cortex has been repeatedly associated with the direction of affect. Greater left-side activity is often interpreted as indicative of approach-related emotions, while right-side activity may signal avoidance or withdrawal tendencies (Davidson, 2004; Coan & Allen, 2004).

However, EEG is sensitive to a wide range of artefacts, including eye movements, muscle contractions, and environmental electrical interference. This sensitivity demands careful preparation: high-conductivity electrodes, proper placement using the 10–20 system, and often a quiet, shielded room. While dry electrode systems like OpenBCI allow for greater mobility, they may sacrifice some signal quality when compared to gel-based systems such as the *g.HIamp* from *g.tec*.

Another commonly used physiological modality is *electrodermal activity (EDA)*, sometimes referred to as galvanic skin response (GSR). This signal measures the skin's ability to conduct electricity, which varies with sweat gland activity and is linked to sympathetic nervous system arousal. Emotional stimuli typically provoke transient spikes in skin conductance. These can be used to detect engagement, stress, or fear. Devices such as the Empatica E4 or Shimmer GSR+ make real-time measurement of EDA feasible, even in ambulatory contexts.

Cardiac activity provides deeper insight into the regulation and pacing of emotional states. Standard metrics include heart rate (HR) and heart rate variability (HRV), which are typically recorded using electrocardiography (ECG) or photoplethysmography (PPG). HRV in particular has gained attention as an index of emotional resilience and self-regulation, where greater variability is linked to flexible adaptation in emotionally challenging scenarios. While ECG remains the gold standard for capturing precise interbeat intervals, wearable PPG devices (e.g., Polar H10, Biopac, or Empatica's wrist-worn monitors) offer a reasonable compromise between accuracy and ecological practicality.

Each of these physiological signals carries a temporal footprint that shapes how it must be collected. EEG, with its high temporal resolution, demands high sampling rates (256–1024 Hz), while EDA and HRV are often sampled more modestly (10–100 Hz). Understanding these constraints is essential for multimodal integration, which we discuss later.

Where physiology speaks in rhythms, *behavioural signals speak in patterns*. These include overt facial expressions, vocal prosody, gestures, and gaze dynamics. They are often the most visible aspects of emotion, and also the most culturally and contextually mediated.

Facial expressions are frequently treated as the canonical medium of emotional communication. Decades of work, especially from Ekman and Friesen (1978), have led to standardised coding systems such as the Facial Action Coding System (FACS). However, manual FACS annotation is time-consuming and often inconsistent across annotators. As a result, automated systems like OpenFace or commercial solutions like FaceReader have become popular. These systems analyse video data frame-by-frame to extract facial action units (AUs) and head pose metrics, providing continuous estimates of expression intensity. The accuracy of these tools is influenced by camera placement, lighting conditions, frame rate, and even the participant's facial morphology. Thus, researchers must attend not just to the software they use but also to the physical design of the recording environment.

In parallel, *voice* has emerged as a powerful channel for emotion recognition. Unlike facial expressions, vocal emotion may be detectable even in the absence of visual cues. Acoustic features such as pitch (fundamental frequency), jitter, shimmer, formant structure, and Mel-frequency cepstral coefficients (MFCCs) form the backbone of most vocal affect models. Python libraries like librosa enable researchers to extract these features and visualise affective contours in speech.

The *gaze* offers another entry point into the affective state. Eye-tracking systems such as Tobii Pro or Pupil Labs record where and for how long a person fixates during a task. Metrics like fixation duration, saccade velocity, and blink rate can signal arousal, cognitive load, and social interest. Importantly, gaze also reflects the structure of attention, a process tightly intertwined with emotional appraisal.

Emotion-aware research paradigms often benefit from combining these behavioural modalities. A spoken word paired with a gaze aversion may imply sarcasm, discomfort, or shame. Facial tension combined with a flat voice may reveal suppressed anger. Without multimodal capture, such subtleties remain invisible. When capturing multiple emotion signals, the challenge becomes *integration*. This doesn't mean simply recording everything at once, but ensuring that all data streams are meaningfully aligned. A multimodal setup might include an EEG system, a video camera for facial tracking, a microphone for voice capture, a wristband for skin conductance, and a wearable for HRV. But if these devices are not synchronised in time, their combined interpretive power collapses. There are three principal methods used to synchronise emotion data streams. The first involves *hardware triggers*, where physical signals such as TTL pulses are sent to each device at known timepoints. These serve as temporal anchors, allowing all recorded signals to align with precision down to the millisecond. Though highly accurate, this approach demands technical expertise and device compatibility, making it best suited for lab-based studies.

A more adaptable method relies on a shared timing protocol implemented via *middleware,* such as the *Lab Streaming Layer (LSL)*. LSL offers a software-based infrastructure to time-align data streams from different hardware sources. It does so by synchronising each data source to a master clock, usually the host computer's system time, and then recording precise timestamps for every sample. This allows researchers to collect EEG, EDA, eye tracking, audio, and video within the same experimental timeline. Unlike TTL triggers, LSL is scalable and device-agnostic, making it especially valuable for real-time applications and mobile research environments.

In cases where neither hardware triggers nor shared clocks are available, researchers may resort to *software-based post hoc alignment.* This method involves identifying shared events and then interpolating timestamps across devices. While less precise, this approach allows for flexible integration of heterogeneous data sources, particularly when using commercial tools with limited interoperability. Each synchronisation method embodies a different perspective on what emotion research prioritises: precision, scalability, or adaptability. The essential task is to choose an integration strategy that aligns with both the scientific question and the practical constraints of the data collection environment.

No matter how advanced a multimodal system becomes, it remains an artificial construct unless designed to honour the *ecological validity* of emotion. Emotions are not confined to sterile labs. They occur while navigating a street, receiving a text, standing before an audience, or lying awake at night. Capturing them authentically requires extending our sensors into these lived contexts. Wearable EEG caps, smartwatches, smartphone microphones, and unobtrusive video recording can bring emotion research into the wild. But doing so comes at a cost: more noise, more missing data, more unpredictable behaviour. At the same time, this data is *truer*, messier, yes, but closer to how emotion is experienced and expressed in natural life.

With this ecological expansion comes *ethical responsibility*. Data collected from the body must be handled with exceptional care. Participants should be informed not only about what is recorded, but also what may be inferred. Researchers must ensure that the data pipeline respects privacy and avoids reductionist or pathologising interpretations.

Emotion is not a biometric. It is a lived, layered, socially negotiated experience. Any attempt to capture it must do justice to this complexity. To acquire emotion is not to extract it; it is to *co-create a setting* where the body speaks, and the machine listens. The setup, sensors, and protocols we choose shape what counts as emotion in our datasets. They shape what AI will learn as emotion. This responsibility cannot be offloaded to the hardware engineer or outsourced to a software package. It is the ethical, epistemological, and psychological foundation of every model we build.

2.4 Data Cleaning and Feature Extraction for Emotion Analysis

Once the raw emotional data has been collected through multimodal sensors, the next vital step involves transforming these raw, often chaotic streams of information into meaningful inputs for computational models. This stage, known as data cleaning and feature extraction, greatly affects the quality and accuracy of emotional insights obtained from computational analyses. Figure 2.2 shows a high-level schematic of how physiological signals (EEG, EDA, HRV) and behavioural signals (voice, facial expressions, gaze) flow into the preprocessing stack: noise reduction/filtering, feature engineering grounded in theory, and ethical compliance checks that govern every stage.

Real-world emotion data, whether recorded in a controlled laboratory or collected via mobile sensors, inevitably contains noise and artefacts. These disturbances can result from sensor limitations, environmental interferences, human movements, or even physiological activities unrelated to the emotion of interest. Ignoring such contamination not only diminishes the accuracy of subsequent analyses but may also lead to fundamentally incorrect emotional interpretations (Soleymani et al., 2017; Aguilera et al., 2023).

Data cleaning, therefore, serves as an essential safeguard which can carefully discriminate between authentic emotional signals and unwanted artefacts. Such processes include filtering, artefact removal, baseline correction, and temporal synchronisation, each performed with careful attention to retaining genuine emotional variability (Calvo & D'Mello, 2010). Physiological signals require particularly meticulous cleaning strategies due to their high susceptibility to noise and artefacts. EEG signals (Figure 2.3), for example, typically undergo preprocessing steps such as band-pass filtering, artefact detection (eye-blinks, muscle movements), and epoch segmentation (Davidson, 2004; Delorme & Makeig, 2004).

Light Blue Line contains electrical noise: spikes, irregular patterns, and other disruptions that are not from the brain. After signal cleaning (orange line), the waves are more stable and clearer. This makes it easier to detect patterns associated with different emotional or cognitive states. Just like a

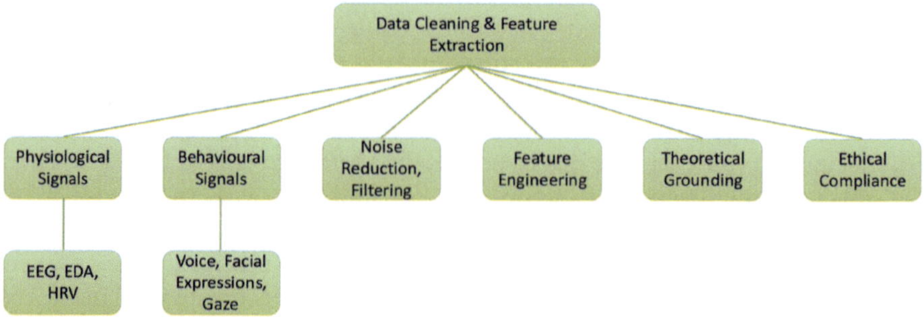

Figure 2.2 Data cleaning and feature extraction for embodied emotion

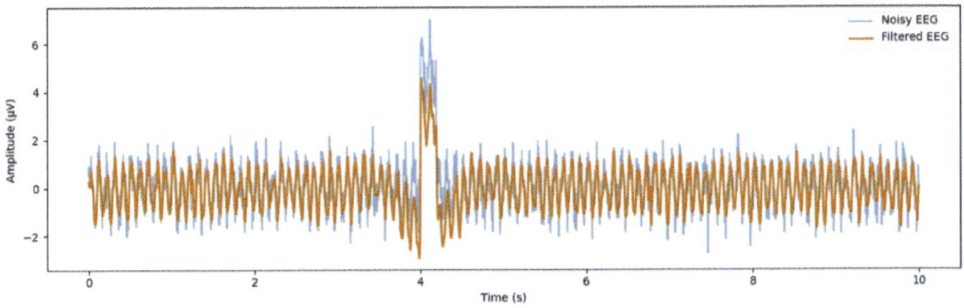

Figure 2.3 EEG signal cleaning: before and after filtering.

blurry photo needs sharpening, an EEG needs cleaning before we can extract meaningful features like alpha power or emotional arousal indicators.

Similarly, EDA or GSR data cleaning typically includes smoothing (Figure 2.4) and baseline removal, aimed at isolating event-related peaks from noise (Boucsein, 2012). Figure 2.4 shows the original recording as a blue line, which contains electrical noise and other spikes not related to real physiological changes. After applying filters, the signal is smoother, and the peaks (which indicate moments of arousal) become clearer. Cleaning ensures that we're not misinterpreting noise as emotional arousal. Only cleaned data should be used in modelling real emotional responses.

After ensuring the cleanliness of the data, the next step is feature extraction, performed to select and calculate attributes that meaningfully represent emotional states. Effective feature extraction bridges raw data and theoretical emotion models, allowing computational methods to more accurately infer affective states (Scherer, 2009). Key strategies for feature extraction include:

- *Temporal features* (mean, variance, peaks, valleys).
- *Spectral features* (power in EEG bands, MFCCs for voice).
- *Event-based features* (latency and amplitude of emotion-relevant events).

For instance, EEG-based features commonly include alpha-band asymmetry (Figure 2.5), known to be indicative of emotional valence (Davidson, 2004), and event-related potentials (ERPs) reflecting attention and cognitive-emotional appraisal.

This plot displays how much *power* (signal strength) exists in various frequency ranges of EEG data. Power Spectral Density (PSD) measures how strong each brainwave frequency is. Frequency (Hz) ranges from slow waves (e.g., delta) to fast waves (e.g., gamma). The highlighted region (orange band) focuses on Alpha waves (8–13 Hz), often linked to relaxation and calm attention. Different emotions can shift the balance between these frequencies. For example, increased beta power might suggest tension, while strong alpha may suggest serenity. Extracting frequency-domain features is a core task in emotional state classification from EEG.

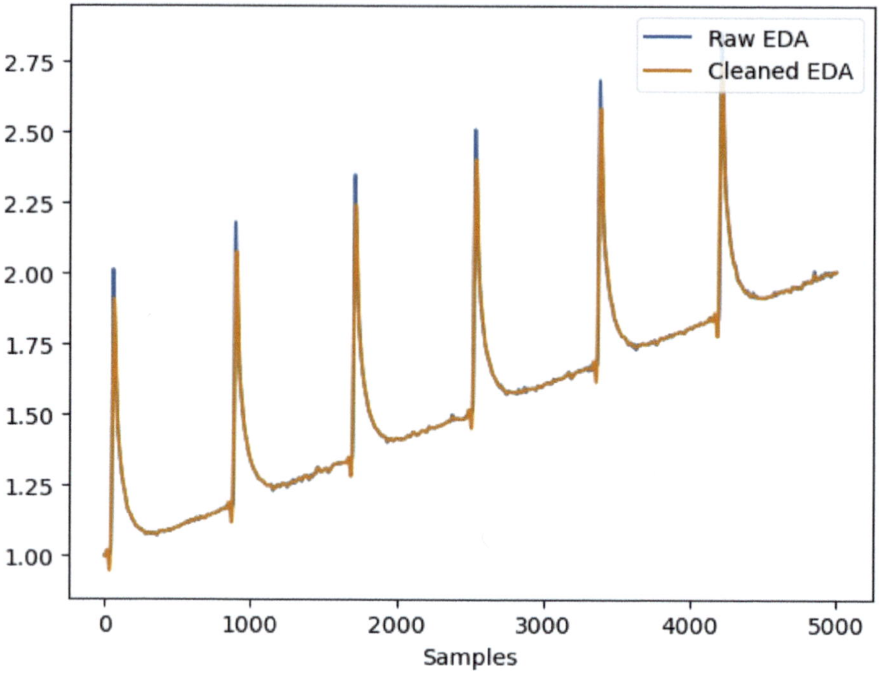

Figure 2.4 Raw vs. cleaned EDA signal.

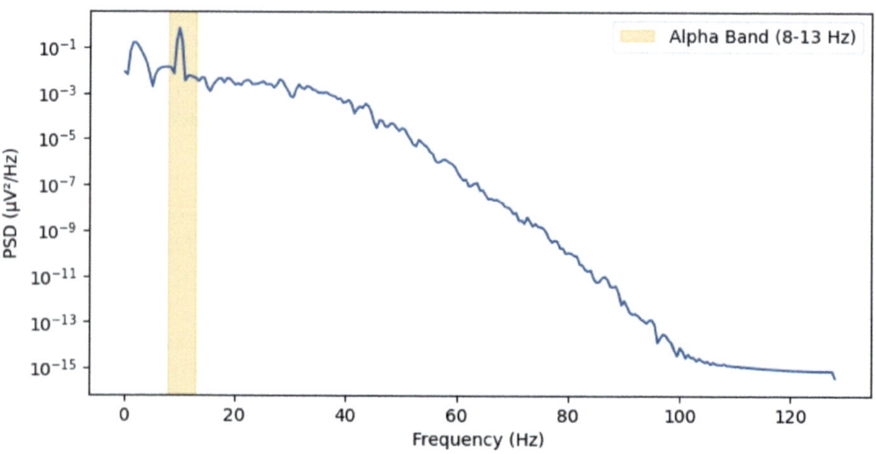

Figure 2.5 EEG spectral power for alpha band extraction.

Voice data offers rich emotional information, embedded in pitch variations, loudness fluctuations, and spectral contours. Features such as Mel-frequency cepstral coefficients (MFCCs) (see Figure 2.6), pitch (fundamental frequency), and speech rate are robust predictors of emotional states (Schuller & Batliner, 2013).

The plot in Figure 2.6 may look abstract, but it's a powerful way to visualise how the sound of a person's voice carries emotional meaning. MFCC Values Over Time are features extracted from the voice recording and are sensitive to pitch, tone, and other properties that convey affect. Blue areas show lower energy, while red areas show higher energy. Emotions like anger, fear, or calmness change how we speak. MFCCs are used by computers to *hear* emotions even if they don't understand language. They're widely used in speech emotion recognition models.

The moment we choose features, we decide what kind of *listener* our model will be. A raw EEG trace or an audio waveform is too unruly to reason with directly; features translate those messy biographies of the body into compact, comparable descriptors. But in affective computing, features are never just arithmetic. They crystallise a theory about how appraisal unfolds in time, how regulation shows up across channels, and how context reshapes display. Put differently: a feature set is a set of commitments (Can et al., 2023).

A good place to begin is by imagining the kinds of stories we want our system to understand. Some are *temporal*: a quick spike in sympathetic arousal, a slow return to the baseline after a social stressor, an episode that flickers more than it roars. Others are *spectral*: a shift in EEG alpha, a change in voice fundamental frequency (F0) and spectral tilt, a modulation in the low–high balance of heart-rate variability. Some are *event-related*: the way a skin-conductance response blooms a second or two after an appraisal, or the way an ERP component indicates attention. Still others are *spatial or kinematic:* the micro-geometry of facial action units (AUs), head pitch when a person leans in, the peculiar rhythm of a hurried gait. What makes this more than taxonomy is that each family of features embodies a different

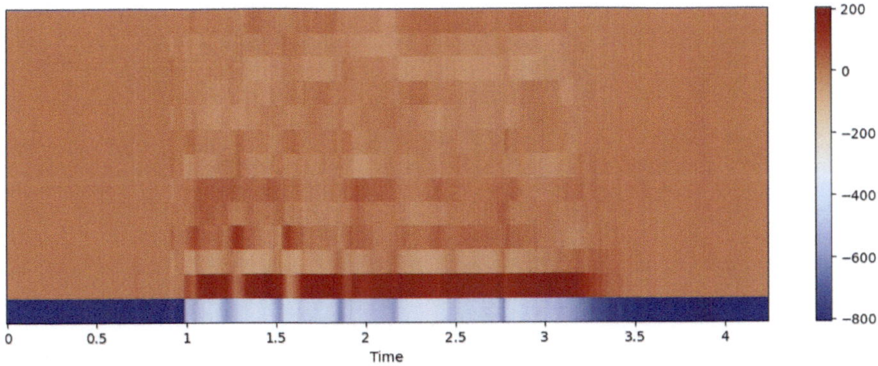

Figure 2.6 MFCCs for vocal emotion analysis.

psychological hypothesis: arousal occurs in rapid sympathetic bursts and parasympathetic withdrawal; approach withdrawal appears as frontal EEG asymmetry; valence often influences prosody and facial expression; regulation modifies how much the face *tells* compared to the body or the autonomic system (Gross, 2015; Can et al., 2023).

Figure 2.7 visualises this landscape. It is deliberately compact: one view, many pathways. You can read it in any direction. Start at *Feature Space* and move toward *Temporal* if your phenomena are short and phasic; follow *Spectral* if your signal-to-noise is better in frequency than in time; walk the *Cross-modal* edge if you expect divergence between what people show and what they feel.

The question that follows is not *which features are best?* but *which features are faithful to this study's assumptions and ecology?* In a lab study with clean stimulus onsets, event-locked windows can support ERP-like EEG features and precise skin-conductance response (SCR) metrics. In the wild,

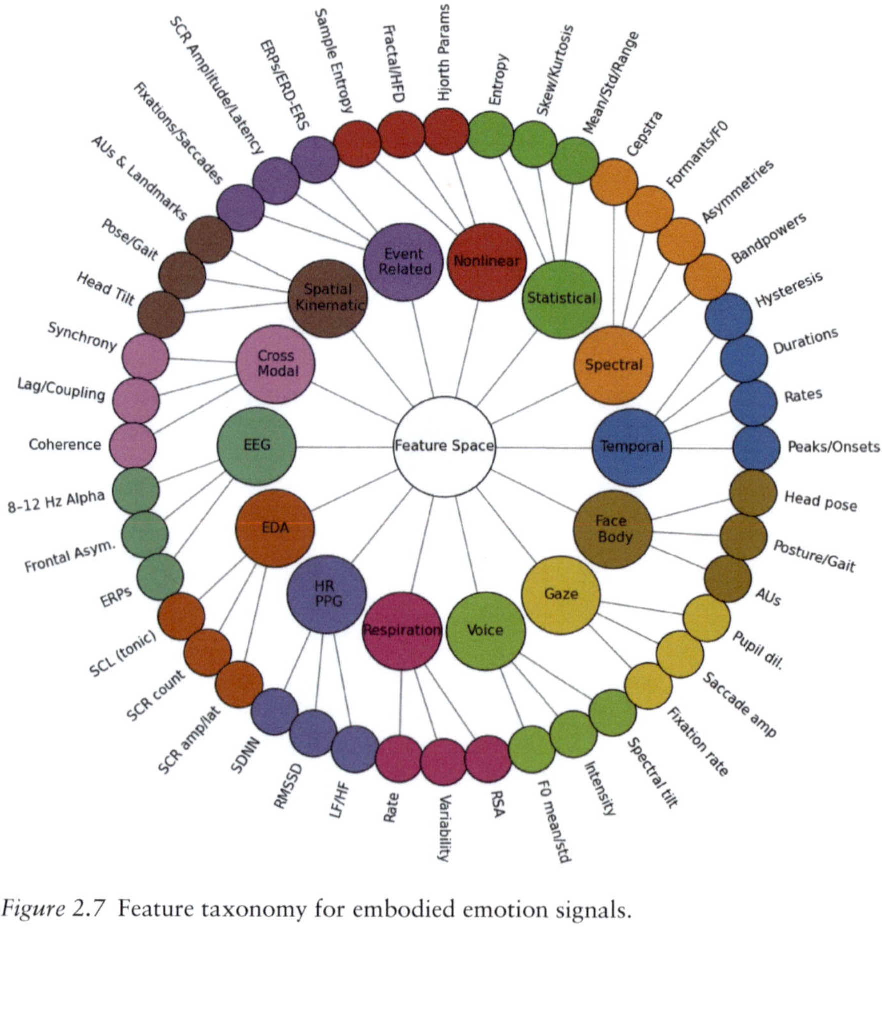

Figure 2.7 Feature taxonomy for embodied emotion signals.

where stimuli are mundane and irregular, sliding windows are more appropriate: you let the model learn *when* the signal changes without forcing it to align to an artificial timeline. The same logic governs window length. If you care about quick surges (think startle or social friction), you need short windows and generous overlap. If you are modelling mood drift over an hour, long windows that smooth local turbulence make more sense. Even the best feature can underperform if it inhabits the wrong timescale (Can et al., 2023).

There is also a humbler point: *redundancy is a feature, not a flaw, when it crosses modalities*. People regulate. Suppression flattens the face yet leaves EDA active; reappraisal can quiet autonomic arousal while leaving a fleeting frown. If you rely on a single channel, you are essentially trusting a single *witness*. Fusing voice with EDA, or head pose with HRV, makes the system resilient when one witness goes quiet (Gross, 2015). This is why, in practice, we often keep a small, interpretable set from each modality rather than eking out a marginal gain from an exotic transform in just one.

How do we check that a chosen vocabulary still matches the data we collected? Not by faith. A simple, revealing exercise is to look at the geometry of your feature table before you train anything heavy. In Figure 2.8, we project a windowed feature matrix into the first two principal components. Even though the example is didactic, the practice scales: a low-dimensional plot often exposes drift (e.g., early sessions vs. late sessions), confounds (e.g., motion vs. speaking), or the gratifying separation of conditions that tells you the representation is on the right track (see Figure 2.8). When the plot shows only a cloud, it is not a failure; it is an instruction: adjust windows, revisit normalisation, or prune features that are louder than they are helpful.

Pruning is its own craft. A common anti-pattern in our field is to hoard features *just in case* and then hide behind a regulariser. A more sensible approach is to ask each feature to justify its presence. We can do this with ablations in a baseline model or even with simple, transparent statistics. Figure 2.9 uses the latter method and ranks features by their absolute correlation with a synthetic target. In real projects, you will prefer permutation importance or ablations in a small, calibrated model (ridge or logistic regression plus Platt scaling), but the principle remains the same: demonstrate that a feature adds value. The benefits are twofold. First, you shed unnecessary weight and improve calibration under distribution shift (the real world is unpredictable). Second, you maintain an audit trail that a clinician, an IRB, or a sceptical colleague can understand without needing a decoder ring (Can et al., 2023).

All this sounds technical, and it is, but the through-line is psychological. Features are claims about processes. Tonic EDA asserts something different from SCR rate; frontal alpha asymmetry speaks to approach/withdrawal in a way that total alpha power does not; F0 variance and spectral tilt tell a different story about vocal effort and affect than raw intensity. When the model's output says *high arousal* and you can point to elevated SCRs, decreased

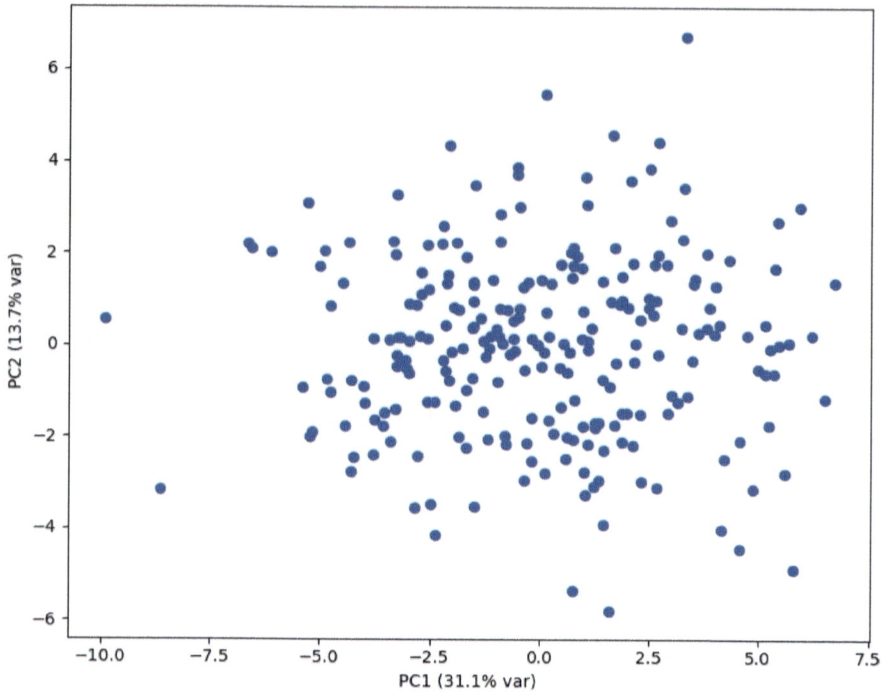

Figure 2.8 PCA of windowed multimodal features (first two components).

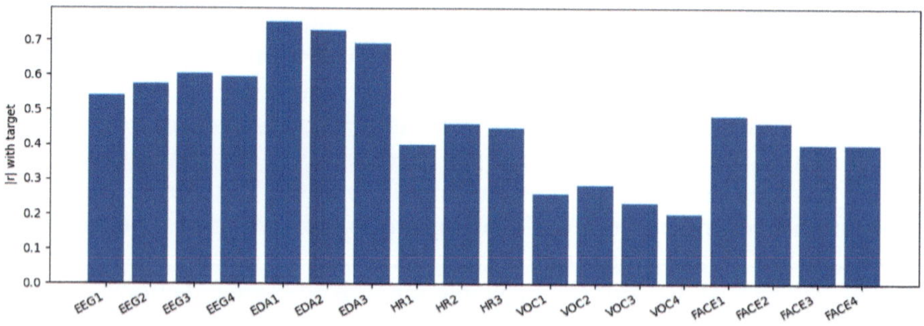

Figure 2.9 Simple feature importance via |correlation| with target.

RMSSD, and a livelier F0 contour, your explanation isn't a post-hoc story; it is the design working as intended (Russell, 1980; Gross, 2015; Can et al., 2023).

At some point, handcrafted descriptors meet their limits. If you collect a lot of data, or if your contexts change faster than you can curate features, *representation learning* becomes attractive. Self-supervised approaches can distil robust embeddings without dense labels. The trick is to preserve auditability.

We should not care only that the embedding predicts but that it behaves consistently across subgroups and doesn't smuggle in sensitive attributes. A pragmatic pattern is to learn a compact embedding and then pass it to a simple, well-calibrated head (ridge/GBDT) so you can still interrogate the system and publish a legible model card (Can et al., 2023).

Despite technical sophistication, the psychological validity of extracted features must remain central. Features must be theoretically grounded to reflect known emotional constructs. For instance, HRV metrics relate strongly to emotional regulation capacity (Thayer et al., 2012), while pupil dilation has been linked to emotional arousal and cognitive effort (Laeng et al., 2012). Hand-crafted features remain strong baselines because they carry *theoretical anchors* and are easy to audit. But when you have enough data, or when your domain shifts often, *representation learning* helps:

- *Self-supervised* objectives (e.g., predicting masked segments or future frames) learn compact embeddings that capture structure without dense labels, which are rare in affective data (Can et al., 2023).
- *Cross-modal contrastive* learning aligns, say, audio – physiology or face – EDA, so the embedding space encodes synchrony and lag relations; this can stabilise fusion when clocks drift.
- *Hybrid stacks* that feed learned embeddings into simple, calibrated models (ridge/logistic with Platt scaling) often beat deeper end-to-end systems in the wild, where missingness and context shifts dominate.

Even here, keep the *ethics* close: learned representations can smuggle sensitive attributes or dataset-specific quirks. Audit for subgroup performance, do feature-attribution sanity checks, and publish model cards (Can et al., 2023). The sensitive nature of emotional data necessitates ethical caution. Researchers must ensure data anonymisation, respect participant consent about inferred states, and maintain transparency regarding the emotional interpretations made through computational methods (WHO, 2024; Hanisch et al., 2021).

We can say that *features* are the vocabulary we use to retell the story to a model. The trap is to think of features as a shopping list. In embodied emotion, features are *commitments* to a theory of how appraisal unfolds, to a choice of time-scale, to a stance on regulation, and to a definition of context. A good feature set is therefore small, legible, and *explicitly tied* to the processes you care about (Can, Mahesh, & André, 2023). So, the main question is, *which features carry psychological meaning?* Here is the brief overview:

EEG: Bandpowers (delta–gamma), *frontal alpha asymmetry, event-related dynamics* (ERPs/ERD–ERS) capture attention and approach – withdrawal tendencies at millisecond resolution (Can et al., 2023). Keep features *window-consistent* with the phenomena you target (short windows for phasic reactivity, longer for sustained states);

EDA: Tonic level (SCL) indexes baseline arousal; *phasic SCR* count, amplitude, and latency index event-linked sympathetic bursts. Proper decomposition (tonic vs. phasic) is essential (Can et al., 2023);

Cardiac (HR/PPG/HRV): Time-domain HRV (SDNN, RMSSD) and *frequency-domain HRV* (LF, HF, LF/HF) reflect autonomic balance; combine with *respiratory* measures to contextualise respiratory sinus arrhythmia (RSA) (Can et al., 2023);

Voice: prosodic (F0 mean/variance, intensity), *spectral* (tilt, centroid), and *voice-quality* (jitter, shimmer) features often align with valence and arousal changes and remain robust in real-world audio, especially when the face is occluded;

Gaze, Face, Body: fixation rate, saccade amplitude, and *pupil dilation* (gaze) plus *AU intensities, head pose,* and *posture/gait* (face/body) externalise appraisal and action readiness; suppression can dampen visible cues, so pairing with physiology helps resolve ambiguity (Gross, 2015; Can et al., 2023).

2.5 Time Series Data Preprocessing

Time is an inherent dimension of emotions. Emotional states are rarely static. They evolve, intensify, diminish, and shift dynamically over time. Consequently, embodied emotion data frequently emerges in the form of a *time series*. These sequences of data points are collected at regular intervals. Preprocessing these temporal sequences for emotion analysis demands special considerations, significantly differing from approaches applicable to static data (Kuppens & Verduyn, 2017). Emotions naturally change and flow, responding to external events and internal cognitive appraisals (Scherer, 2009). Heartbeats speed up, skin conductance rises, EEG rhythms shift, and facial expressions change. All of these patterns carry essential emotional meaning. Thus, properly capturing, aligning, and interpreting emotional data requires treating time not as an afterthought but as a fundamental organising dimension.

Real-world emotion recordings are rarely perfect. Missing data can occur due to sensor malfunction, human movement, or environmental interference. We ensure that each stream has monotonic timestamps, a known sampling rate, and explicit units. Only then do we touch the signal itself. In physiology, the first enemy is *loss of continuity*. Real recordings drop packets, electrodes loosen, wearables shift on the skin, and people move. We identify missing segments and annotate their cause when known. For time series data, missing values are commonly addressed using interpolation methods (linear or spline) to maintain the continuity of emotional trajectories (Little & Rubin, 2019). Emotion data often includes noise from sensor fluctuations or external disturbances. Time series smoothing methods such as moving averages, median filters, or advanced methods like Gaussian smoothing help preserve the genuine emotional signals by reducing unwanted variability.

Multimodal emotion analysis commonly involves combining multiple sensor streams recorded at different sampling rates (e.g., EEG at 256 Hz, GSR at 20 Hz, video at 30 fps). Temporal alignment ensures that data streams represent the same emotional events simultaneously, preventing analytical confusion or false interpretations (Calvo & D'Mello, 2010). Feature extraction translates raw temporal signals into structured inputs suitable for machine learning. Commonly extracted features include statistical measures (mean, variance, skewness), frequency domain features (spectral bands in EEG), and event-related features (peak detection, latency).

The following script is a complete, ready-to-run pipeline for preparing real-time series data for analysis in emotion research. It reads your existing files for a primary signal and a secondary modality, infers the sampling rate, repairs only very short gaps, smooths noisy measurements, resamples everything to a common rate, and aligns both streams in time. It then cuts the data into short windows, extracts simple statistical and spectral features, removes low-quality windows, standardises features using training data only to avoid leakage, and saves both a feature table and clear diagnostic figures. You only need to point the configuration at the top to your files and, if needed, set the correct column names.

```
import numpy as np
import pandas as pd
import matplotlib.pyplot as plt
from scipy.ndimage import gaussian_filter1d
from scipy.signal import welch, resample_poly
from numpy.linalg import lstsq
from fractions import Fraction
from math import gcd
import json
import os

PRIMARY_CSV = "data_final.csv"          # your primary time-series file
PRIMARY_TIME_COL = None                 # e.g., "t", "time", "times-
tamp"; set None to auto-detect
PRIMARY_VALUE_COL = None                # e.g., "x", "value", "sig-
nal"; set None to auto-detect

SECONDARY_CSV = "speech_modality.csv"   # your secondary modality file
SECONDARY_TIME_COL = None               # set None to auto-detect
SECONDARY_VALUE_COL = None              # e.g., "speech_prob", "prob";
set None to auto-detect

FS_TARGET = 4.0                         # Hz target resample rate
GAP_INTERP_THRESHOLD_S = 2.0            # s; interpolate only gaps <=
this
SMOOTH_SIGMA_S = 0.5                    # s; Gaussian sigma in seconds
ALIGNMENT_TOL_S = 0.25                  # s; nearest-neighbor alignment
tolerance
WINDOW_S = 8.0
```

```
HOP_S = 4.0
TRAIN_FRACTION = 0.7

def pick_col(df, preferred, fallbacks):
    if preferred is not None and preferred in df.columns:
        return preferred
    for c in fallbacks:
        if c in df.columns:
           return c
   raise ValueError(f"None of the columns { [preferred] + fall-
backs if preferred else fallbacks } found in {list(df.columns)}")

def to_seconds(series):
      """Return (seconds_array, is_datetime). Tries datetime
first; falls back to numeric."""
    try:
        dt = pd.to_datetime(series, utc=True, errors="raise")
        secs = (dt.view("int64") / 1e9).to_numpy() # POSIX
seconds
        return secs, True
    except Exception:
        vals = pd.to_numeric(series, errors="coerce").
to_numpy(dtype=float)
        if not np.isfinite(vals).any():
            raise ValueError("Time column could not be parsed
as datetime or numeric seconds.")
        return vals, False

def normalize_time_for_alignment(t_primary, t_secondary, abs_
primary, abs_secondary):
    """
    If both are absolute timestamps, align on absolute seconds.
    Otherwise, shift both to start at zero and align relatively.
    """
    if abs_primary and abs_secondary:
        return t_primary, t_secondary
    return t_primary - np.nanmin(t_primary), t_secondary - np
.nanmin(t_secondary)

def interpolate_short_gaps(t, x, max_gap_seconds=2.0):
    """
    Interpolate linearly only across gaps with duration <=
max_gap_seconds.
    Longer gaps remain NaN.
    """
    t = np.asarray(t, dtype=float)
    x = np.asarray(x, dtype=float)
```

```
    isnan = ~np.isfinite(x)

    # Identify contiguous NaN runs
    runs = []
    in_run = False
    start = None
    for i, flag in enumerate(isnan):
        if flag and not in_run:
           in_run = True
           start = i
        elif not flag and in_run:
           runs.append((start, i - 1))
           in_run = False
    if in_run:
        runs.append((start, x.size - 1))

    x_interp = x.copy()
    for s, e in runs:
        gap_duration = t[e] - t[s] if e > s else 0.0
        if gap_duration <= max_gap_seconds:
            left = s - 1
            right = e + 1
            if left >= 0 and right < x.size and
np.isfinite(x[left]) and np.isfinite(x[right]):
                x_interp[s:e+1] = np.interp(t[s:e+1],
[t[left], t[right]], [x[left], x[right]])
    return x_interp

def bandpower_welch(x, fs, fmin, fmax):
    f, Pxx = welch(x, fs=fs, nperseg=min(len(x), int(fs * 8)))
    idx = (f >= fmin) & (f <= fmax)
    return np.trapz(Pxx[idx], f[idx]) if np.any(idx) else np.nan

def linear_trend(x):
    y = np.asarray(x)
    X = np.vstack([np.arange(y.size), np.ones(y.size)]).T
    beta, *_ = lstsq(X, y, rcond=None)
    return float(beta[0])

def infer_fs(t_seconds):
    dt = np.diff(t_seconds)
    dt = dt[np.isfinite(dt) & (dt > 0)]
    if dt.size == 0:
        raise ValueError("Cannot infer sampling rate (insuf-
ficient or invalid time data).")
    return 1.0 / np.median(dt)

p_df = pd.read_csv(PRIMARY_CSV)
```

```
t_col = pick_col(p_df, PRIMARY_TIME_COL, ["t", "time",
"timestamp", "datetime", "Time", "Timestamp"])
x_col = pick_col(p_df, PRIMARY_VALUE_COL, ["x", "value",
"signal", "y", "amp", "amplitude"])

t_primary_raw, primary_is_abs = to_seconds(p_df[t_col])
x_raw = pd.to_numeric(p_df[x_col], errors="coerce").
to_numpy(dtype=float)

# Sort by time and drop exact-duplicate time stamps if any
order = np.argsort(t_primary_raw)
t_primary_raw = t_primary_raw[order]
x_raw = x_raw[order]
keep = np.ones_like(t_primary_raw, dtype=bool)
keep[1:] = t_primary_raw[1:] > t_primary_raw[:-1]
t_primary_raw, x_raw = t_primary_raw[keep], x_raw[keep]

fs_raw = infer_fs(t_primary_raw)

# Normalize time for plotting convenience (relative seconds
from start)
t_primary_rel = t_primary_raw - np.nanmin(t_primary_raw)

# ------- 2) Short-gap interpolation; long-gap masking -------
x_interp = interpolate_short_gaps(t_primary_rel, x_raw,
max_gap_seconds=GAP_INTERP_THRESHOLD_S)
valid_mask = np.isfinite(x_interp).astype(float)

# ------- 3) Denoise / Smooth ----------
sigma_samples = max(1e-6, SMOOTH_SIGMA_S * fs_raw) # Gaussian
sigma in samples
x_fill = np.where(np.isfinite(x_interp), x_interp, np.nanmean
(x_interp))
x_smooth = gaussian_filter1d(x_fill, sigma=sigma_samples)

# ------- 4) Resample with anti-aliasing ----------
ratio = Fraction(FS_TARGET / fs_raw).limit_denominator(1000)
up, down = ratio.numerator, ratio.denominator

x_for_resample = np.where(np.isfinite(x_smooth), x_smooth,
np.nanmean(x_smooth))
x_resampled = resample_poly(x_for_resample, up, down)
mask_resampled = resample_poly(valid_mask, up, down)

# Resampled time vector (relative seconds)
n_res = x_resampled.size
t_resampled = np.arange(n_res) / FS_TARGET
mask_resampled = np.clip(mask_resampled, 0, 1)
```

```
# ---------- 5) Load and align second modality ----------
s_df = pd.read_csv(SECONDARY_CSV)

sb_t_col = pick_col(s_df, SECONDARY_TIME_COL, ["t", "time",
"timestamp", "datetime", "Time", "Timestamp"])
sb_v_col = pick_col(s_df, SECONDARY_VALUE_COL, ["speech_prob",
"prob", "probability", "value", "y"])

t_secondary_raw, secondary_is_abs = to_seconds(s_df[sb_t_col])
b_vals = pd.to_numeric(s_df[sb_v_col], errors="coerce").to_
numpy(dtype=float)

# Sort, deduplicate
order_b = np.argsort(t_secondary_raw)
t_secondary_raw = t_secondary_raw[order_b]
b_vals = b_vals[order_b]
keep_b = np.ones_like(t_secondary_raw, dtype=bool)
keep_b[1:] = t_secondary_raw[1:] > t_secondary_raw[:-1]
t_secondary_raw, b_vals = t_secondary_raw[keep_b], b_vals
[keep_b]

# Align time bases (absolute if both timestamped; else
relative)
t_primary_align, t_secondary_align = normalize_time_for_alignment(
    t_primary_raw, t_secondary_raw, primary_is_abs, secondary_
is_abs
)

# Build dataframes for merge_asof (use resampled primary
timeline)
series_df = pd.DataFrame({"t": t_resampled, "x": x_resampled,
"valid": mask_resampled})
speech_df = pd.DataFrame({"t": (t_secondary_align - np.nanm
in(t_primary_align)), "speech_prob": b_vals})
series_df.sort_values("t", inplace=True)
speech_df.sort_values("t", inplace=True)

aligned=pd.merge_asof(series_df, speech_df, on="t", direction=
"nearest", tolerance=ALIGNMENT_TOL_S)

# ---------- 6) Windowing & Feature Extraction ----------
starts = np.arange(0, float(series_df["t"].iloc[-1]) - WINDOW_S
+ 1e-9, HOP_S)

rows = []
for s in starts:
    e = s + WINDOW_S
    m = (aligned["t"] >= s) & (aligned["t"] < e)
    seg = aligned.loc[m]
```

```
    if seg.empty:
        continue
    xw = seg["x"].to_numpy()
    qw = seg["valid"].to_numpy()
    sw = seg["speech_prob"].to_numpy()
    coverage = float(np.mean(qw > 0.5))
    feats = {
        "t_start": float(s),
        "t_end": float(e),
        "n": int(xw.size),
        "coverage": coverage,
        "mean": float(np.mean(xw)),
        "std": float(np.std(xw)),
        "min": float(np.min(xw)),
        "max": float(np.max(xw)),
        "trend": linear_trend(xw),
        # Spectral bands relative to FS_TARGET = 4 Hz
        "bp_vlow": bandpower_welch(xw, FS_TARGET, 0.01, 0.08),
        "bp_low": bandpower_welch(xw, FS_TARGET, 0.08, 0.5),
        "bp_high": bandpower_welch(xw, FS_TARGET, 0.5, 1.5),
        "speech_mean": float(np.nanmean(sw)) if np.isfinite(sw).
any() else np.nan,
    }
    rows.append(feats)

features = pd.DataFrame(rows)

# 7) Quality filtering and train/test standardization
features_qc = features[features["coverage"] >= 0.8].reset_index
(drop=True)

cut_time = features_qc["t_end"].max() * TRAIN_FRACTION if not
features_qc.empty else 0.0
train_idx = features_qc["t_end"] <= cut_time
test_idx = ~train_idx

num_cols = ["mean", "std", "min", "max", "trend", "bp_vlow",
"bp_low", "bp_high", "speech_mean"]
train_means = features_qc.loc[train_idx, num_cols].mean()
train_stds  =  features_qc.loc[train_idx,  num_cols].std().
replace(0, 1.0)

features_scaled = features_qc.copy()
features_scaled[num_cols] = (features_qc[num_cols] - train_
means) / train_stds

# ---------- 8) Save artifacts ----------
out_csv = "ts_preprocessing_features.csv"
features_scaled.to_csv(out_csv, index=False)
```

```
params = {
    "fs_raw": float(fs_raw),
    "fs_target": FS_TARGET,
    "window_seconds": WINDOW_S,
    "hop_seconds": HOP_S,
    "gap_interpolation_threshold_s": GAP_INTERP_THRESHOLD_S,
    "alignment_tolerance_s": ALIGNMENT_TOL_S,
    "train_split_end_time": float(cut_time),
    "primary_csv": os.path.abspath(PRIMARY_CSV),
    "secondary_csv": os.path.abspath(SECONDARY_CSV),
    "primary_time_col": t_col,
    "primary_value_col": x_col,
    "secondary_time_col": sb_t_col,
    "secondary_value_col": sb_v_col,
}
with open("ts_preprocessing_params.json", "w") as f:
    json.dump(params, f, indent=2)
```

The goal of this pipeline is to turn raw sensor recordings into tidy, comparable numbers that a model or a human can understand. Real sensors sometimes stop briefly or lose contact, so the script first fills only very short gaps by drawing a straight line between the nearest valid points, and it leaves longer outages as missing in order not to invent data. Because sensors are also noisy, a gentle Gaussian smoothing is applied so that rapid jitters are reduced while the broader shape of the signal remains intact. Different devices often record at different speeds, which makes direct comparison difficult, so the script converts the primary signal to a common target rate using a method that prevents artificial distortion. It then lines up the primary signal with the second data stream in real time within a small tolerance, so values from the same moments can be compared.

Next, the data are sliced into short, partly overlapping windows. For each window, the script calculates simple summaries such as average level, variability, minimum and maximum, the overall upward or downward trend, and how much energy sits in slow, medium, or faster fluctuations. It also records the average value of the second modality over the same period. Each window carries a quality score based on how much real, non-missing data it contains, and windows below the threshold are excluded so that downstream analysis is not driven by gaps. To evaluate models fairly, the script separates the earlier portion of time as training and keeps the later portion for testing, then scales the features using only the training part so that future data is not allowed to influence the past. Finally, it writes a clean feature table to a CSV file and stores a small JSON file with the exact settings for reproducibility.

2.6 Preprocessing Visual Data for Emotion Analysis

When we work with video, the most helpful thing we can do is keep the picture simple and steady. A camera that records smoothly (around thirty frames per second), a face that is well lit from the front, and a view that shows the head and a bit of the shoulders usually give us clean signals. Heavy compression can also be misleading: blocky artefacts in a low-quality file sometimes look like real facial movements to an algorithm, so moderate, consistent compression is preferable (Das, 2023).

For analysis, specialised software is useful. It first finds the face in each frame and keeps following it as the person moves. Then it pinpoints a set of stable reference points, for example, the corners of the eyes and mouth, the tip of the nose, and the outline of the jaw (see Figure 2.10). *Find–follow–straighten* routine, implemented by widely used tools such as *RetinaFace* and *MediaPipe Face Mesh*, helps the later emotion models focus on meaningful changes in the face rather than on head pose or camera position (Bazarevsky et al., 2020; Deng et al., 2020; Li & Deng, 2020). If the person turns too far to the side or tilts their head a lot, the system simply marks those moments as less reliable instead of pretending it knows more than it does (Kollias, 2022).

Before we analyse anything, we adjust brightness and contrast so that faces look as if they were filmed under similar conditions. Gentle, local contrast methods (for example, adaptive histogram equalisation) tend to do this well (Li & Deng, 2020). Alongside these corrections, we should save a few simple quality notes for every frame. For example, it is useful to record how sharp the image is, how large the face is on screen, whether glasses or hands

Figure 2.10 Face detection and landmark extraction.

are covering key areas, and how much the head is turned. Those notes are later used to down-weight doubtful frames rather than to throw them away, which helps systems behave more robustly *in the wild* (Stappen et al., 2021).

Researchers often describe expressions in **action units**, which are small, named movements such as lifting the inner eyebrows or pulling the lip corners (Ekman & Rosenberg, 2005). In practice, the computer measures both shape (how far landmarks move) and appearance (how local texture changes) around these regions. These little time patterns can separate a deliberate smile from a relieved one or a fleeting frown from a sustained one, and they are especially helpful when we later combine vision with physiology and voice (Kossaifi et al., 2017; Can et al., 2023).

Faces are not the whole story. People also *speak* with their bodies. Modern pose estimators can track major joints and hands in real time, giving us simple yet informative measures such as upper-body expansion, sway, and blink or saccade rates. These cues are valuable when faces are partially covered, culturally restrained, or simply off camera (Bazarevsky et al., 2020; Davey et al., 2021; Pereira et al., 2024).

When we feed images to deep models, we keep things consistent and honest. All face crops are resized to the same dimensions and normalised in the same way so that the network does not learn accidental differences between cameras. We also imitate the noise that we expect in daily life (rotations, brightness, blur), so the model learns to ignore them. At the same time, we keep an *interpretable line* running next to the deep features: we continue to compute action-unit signals and landmark movements and check that the network's internal representation still lines up with those human-readable cues. If it does not, that is a warning that the model may be keying on identity, background or other shortcuts (Li & Deng, 2020; Minderer et al., 2021).

We must also remember that people do not feel in single frames. Frame-by-frame predictions jump around and can be noisy. We therefore smooth the evidence over short intervals and group them into meaningful segments, which can then be aligned with peaks in skin conductance, dips in heart-rate variability, or voice changes. The result is a timeline that reads like a story rather than a flicker book (Can et al., 2023; Ringeval et al., 2017).

2.7 Audio Signals for Embodied Emotion Analysis

When people speak, their voices often reveal more about their feelings than their words. A catch in the throat that appears only on certain topics, a brighter pitch when mentioning a friend, or a flattening of loudness after a long day are bodily traces of appraisal and arousal transmitted through the respiratory system, the larynx, and the vocal tract. Because emotion influences breathing patterns, laryngeal tension, and articulatory timing, the acoustic signal provides a practical window into autonomic shifts and regulatory efforts (MacIntyre, 2022; Schuller & Batliner, 2013). Voice is a non-intrusive, richly embodied channel that travels effectively across everyday contexts, from therapy rooms to cars and mobile phones (Latif et al., 2020; Haq & Jackson, 2011).

Listeners instinctively rely on four clusters of cues when they wish to discover what the voice conveys. *Prosody* (variations in pitch or fundamental frequency), *loudness*, and *rhythm* reflect arousal and urgency; rapid speech and rising pitch often indicate agitation or excitement, while slower, quieter speech is typical in sadness and fatigue (Cowen et al., 2019; Akçay & Oğuz, 2020). *Voice quality*, how *breathy* or *tense* the voice sounds, stems from vocal-fold vibration and glottal airflow, and frequently changes with stress or relief (Gobl & Chasaide, 2003; Hashem et al., 2023). *Spectral–timbral* patterns (described by MFCCs or similar features) mirror the shape of the vocal tract and articulatory accuracy, which can diminish under stress (Eyben & Schuller, 2015; Khalil et al., 2019). Lastly, *paralinguistic events* (sighs, laughs, hesitations) serve as emotional punctuation and are useful indicators when language is culturally restrained (Trigeorgis et al., 2016; Haq et al., 2011).

Same as in the case of other types of datasets, field recordings are rarely clean. They come with air-conditioning hum, traffic, room reverberation, and changing microphone distance. A well-documented front end, therefore, matters more than exotic models. When it comes to the recording of raw data, we start by *keeping capture simple and consistent*: a single channel at 16 kHz or 24 kHz, stable input gain that avoids clipping, and a short calibration phrase to check levels. On phones and wearables, it helps to log the device model so that later analyses can account for microphone differences (Latif et al., 2020). Proceed with *cleaning that preserves the meaning*. Light spectral gating or Wiener filtering can lower stationary background noise; mild dereverberation enhances intelligibility in reverberant spaces; and *voice-activity detection (VAD)* removes long silences so that subsequent statistics reflect the voice, not the room (Eyben et al., 2015; Tan et al., 2021). When multiple people speak, *speaker diarisation* separates streams so that features represent one speaker at a time (Park et al., 2022). We then normalise signals on a comparable scale (peak- or loudness-normalisation within safe limits) so that differences in microphone gain are not mistaken for differences in emotion (Schuller & Batliner, 2013).

Segmentation is used to cut the stream into small, overlapping windows (often 2–4 s) to capture the arc of an utterance, while keeping *episodes* (moments of clear rise and recovery) in view for later alignment with physiology or gaze. Fixed windows are convenient, but event-based windows (at breaths or pauses) often tell the cleaner story (Eyben et al., 2015; Ringeval et al., 2019). From each window, we compute *prosodic* features (F0 level and range, energy statistics, speaking rate), *voice-quality* measures (jitter, shimmer, harmonic-to-noise ratio; sometimes glottal parameters via COVAREP-style analysis), and *spectral* descriptors (MFCCs, spectral centroid and tilt). These are simple but effective markers of arousal and control when averaged, differenced, and smoothed over time (Eyben et al., 2015; Latif et al., 2020;

Khalil et al., 2019). We add *temporal derivatives* (how fast pitch or energy is changing) because emotion is often carried in the *movement* rather than the static value (Akçay & Oğuz, 2020).

Alongside handcrafted features, *self-supervised acoustic embeddings* have become the default backbone. Models such as *wav2vec 2.0, HuBERT, BYOL-S*, and large audio networks trained on spoken-word and sound events yield robust representations that transfer well to emotion tasks with minimal fine-tuning (Baevski et al., 2020; Hsu et al., 2021; Kong et al., 2020). These embeddings are not magic; we still stabilise them with per-speaker normalisation, small amounts of smoothing, and *data augmentation* (noise, reverberation, small pitch and tempo shifts, SpecAugment-style masking) to avoid overfitting to recording conditions (Park et al., 2019; Latif et al., 2020).

Two confounds deserve explicit treatment: (1) in the case of *content leakage*, models can cheat by learning *what was said* (lexical content) rather than *how it was said*. We mitigate this with phoneme-balanced prompts, adversarial training against transcripts, or evaluations that hold content constant (Poria et al., 2021); (2) it is important to take care about *speaker identity*, because many features are stable traits (average pitch, formant structure). We therefore evaluate across unseen speakers and, when possible, decorrelate identity using adversarial losses or embedding anonymisation (Champion, 2023; Stappen et al., 2021).

Reliable systems are *humble* about uncertainty. They attach quality indicators (VAD confidence, SNR, clipping rate) to each window, smooth predictions over short spans, and abstain when evidence is weak. They are tested beyond a single lab: cross-corpus and cross-device evaluations are the norm in community challenges such as *AVEC* and *MuSe*, which repeatedly show that careful preprocessing and calibration often matter more than one more model layer (Ringeval et al., 2019; Stappen et al., 2021). For continuous targets (arousal/valence), we report the *concordance correlation coefficient;* for imbalanced categories, the *unweighted average recall* avoids a misleading overall accuracy (Chamishka et al., 2022).

Audio rarely stands alone. Its greatest value appears when we align it with *physiology* (EDA peaks, HRV dips) and *vision* (micro-expressions, gaze shifts): subtle tremor in the voice that coincides with a skin-conductance surge is stronger evidence than either cue by itself (Can et al., 2023).

To demystify what *audio preprocessing* does, Figure 2.11 walks through the entire pipeline using *the same recording*. That matters: because the clip never changes, you can see exactly how each step clarifies the emotional traces in the voice rather than introducing new artefacts. Think of it as cleaning a lens, then switching between views that highlight different parts of the same scene.

In panel A, you're looking at the raw waveform. It's messy but alive: you can already glimpse the broad arc of the performance, with a gentler start, a brighter middle, and a softer ending. Panel B shows the denoised signal. The background haze is lifted just enough to make the speech stand out, without

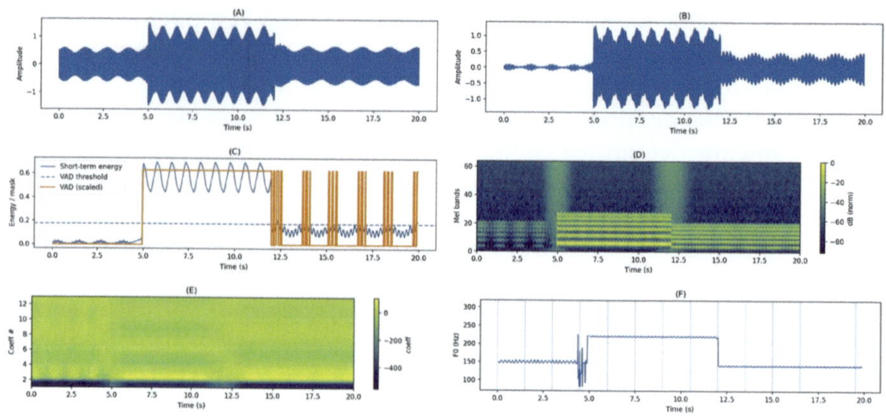

Figure 2.11 End-to-end audio preprocessing on a single recording. (A) Raw waveform with natural noise and breathing. (B) Denoised waveform after light spectral gating, preserving expressive dynamics. (C) Short-term energy with a simple VAD threshold; the mask indicates speech-dominant regions. (D) Log-mel spectrogram, revealing richer high-frequency energy during the central, higher-arousal segment. (E) MFCCs (13 coefficients) summarising timbre over time. (F) Pitch contour (F0) with fixed 3-second analysis windows used for episode-level modelling.

flattening the expressive rises and falls. This step doesn't *beautify* the speaker; it simply reduces distractions so later measurements describe the voice rather than the room. Panel C adds a practical layer: short-term energy (how strong the voice is at each moment) and a simple VAD. The dashed line is the operating point; the mask highlights where speech dominates. VAD stops long silences or rustling from sneaking into your summary statistics. In panel D, the same signal is shown as a log-mel spectrogram, i.e., a time–frequency map that gently resembles what the human ear pays attention to. Brighter bands in the middle of the clip reflect higher arousal: the voice becomes more energetic, richer in overtones, and therefore *brighter* on the page. Panel E condenses that picture into MFCCs, compact timbral descriptors that many emotion models use as inputs. You can see them drift and tighten across the three phases of the clip; it's a shorthand for how the vocal tract shapes the sound under different emotional loads. Panel F traces the pitch contour (F0) and draws the analysis windows used downstream. The contour rises and varies more in the central portion (exactly where the spectrogram and energy also looked more intense), giving a coherent multisided view of increased arousal. The vertical lines mark fixed windows that later models will treat as *mini-episodes*.

2.8 Preparing Text Data for Understanding Emotions in the Body

People *lean* on words to register how they feel. Unlike facial muscle activity or heart rate, text carries *appraisal* and *context*: who or what the feeling is about, why it matters, and how it unfolds over time. Decades of psycholinguistic work show that function words, pronoun use, tense, and affect terms correlate with mood, coping, and health outcomes (Pennebaker & Chung, 2011; Boyd et al., 2022). Modern NLP adds scale: large corpora and pretrained language models can surface subtle emotional signals beyond simple positive/negative labels (Acheampong et al., 2020; Buechel & Hahn, 2016; Demszky et al., 2020).

Text fills in what physiology and behaviour cannot say on their own. A spike in skin conductance tells you *that* something mattered; a sentence often tells you *what* and *why*. When synchronised with timestamps text makes it possible to link *appraisals* (*I felt cornered when the question came up*) with *bodily responses* (arousal peak + brief gaze aversion) (Zadeh et al., 2018; Tsai et al., 2019; Hazarika et al., 2020). Text also travels well: when cameras or wearables are impractical, reflective journals and brief check-ins can still capture shifts in affect and regulation strategies (Pennebaker & Chung, 2011; Boyd et al., 2022).

The goal is to make text *machine-readable without washing out affect.* Over-aggressive cleaning (stripping emojis, elongations, punctuation, casing) can erase cues that carry strong emotional meaning online (Barbieri et al., 2016; Mohammad, 2022). A practical rule:

- normalize obvious noise (HTML, boilerplate),
- standardize whitespace and Unicode,
- *preserve* emojis, repeated letters ("soooo"), exclamation marks, and laughter tokens because they are emotion features, not dirt (Novak et al., 2015; Mohammad, 2022).

Below is a Python illustration that keeps expressive cues intact while preparing tokens for analysis.

```
import re
def clean_keep_affect(text):
    text = re.sub(r'https?://\S+|www\.\S+', ' <URL> ', text)
# keep a marker
    text = re.sub(r'@\w+', ' <USER> ', text) # anonymize
mentions
   text = re.sub(r'#(\w+)', r'\1', text) # drop hash, keep tag
   text = text.replace('\u200d', '') # zero-width joiner
   text = re.sub(r'\s+', ' ', text).strip()
   return text

demo = Path("my_text_file.txt").read_text(encoding="utf-8")
print(clean_keep_affect(demo))

Output: Sooo happy!!! Thanks <USER> — yesterday was awful:
<URL>
```

There are two dependable ways to turn language into signals your models can read. The first is *lexicon-guided scoring,* where curated inventories map words to emotions (e.g., NRC Emotion Lexicon; LIWC-22 categories). They are transparent and useful for small datasets or clinical explainability (Mohammad & Turney, 2013; Boyd et al., 2022). A lexicon example in Python can be represented as:

```
from nrclex import NRCLex
text = "I feel relieved and proud today, but yesterday I was
anxious."
emo = NRCLex(text)
print(emo.top_emotions)

Output: [('anticipation', 0.2857142857142857)]
```

The second route uses *contextual embeddings.* Models like BERT/RoBERTa encode words in context and can be fine-tuned for multi-label emotion (e.g., GoEmotions' 27 classes), capturing irony, negation, and who-did-what-to-whom better than bag-of-words (Devlin et al., 2019; Liu et al., 2019; Demszky et al., 2020).

Emotion labels depend on the *unit of analysis*. Sentence-level labels work for short posts; therapy transcripts often need turn-level or episode-level summaries (Buechel & Hahn, 2016). For multimodal work, align text spans to time (utterance start/stop) so they can be compared with concurrent changes in voice or physiology (Zadeh et al., 2018; Tsai et al., 2019). When domains differ (clinical vs. social media), expect domain shift and fine-tuning or few-shot adaptation usually helps (Demszky et al., 2020; Acheampong et al., 2020).

2.9 Gaze Data Analysis in Embodied Emotion Recognition

We reveal a lot with our eyes even when we say nothing. People in a tense meeting glance repeatedly at the exit; a parent lingers on a child's face longer than on anyone else's; a student's pupils open a little wider during a hard problem and relax again when it's solved. These small movements are not random wanderings. They reflect shifts in *attention, motivation,* and *arousal,* linking cognition and physiology in real time (Holmqvist et al., 2015; Joshi & Gold, 2020). That is why gaze belongs in an embodied-emotion toolkit alongside physiology, speech, and facial behaviour: it lets us watch *where* the mind goes and *how strongly* the body is engaged.

Emotion changes what we look at and how we look. Threat cues pull the eyes quickly and often keep them there; curiosity broadens the search and produces more exploratory scanpaths; sadness slows the pace and shortens saccades (Carvalho et al., 2014; Orquin & Holmqvist, 2018; Wen et al., 2022). Pupil diameter adds a direct physiological handle: it tracks sympathetic arousal and mental effort, rising within a second of increased load or affect and falling with relief (Mathôt, 2018; Joshi & Gold, 2020). These properties make gaze especially powerful when faces are masked or speech is sparse: it provides a running marker of engagement that we can align with skin conductance, heart-rate variability, or vocal tremor.

Good gaze data starts with a *quiet, careful setup*. Whether you use a remote tracker or head-mounted glasses, brief calibration and a quick validation check pay off later; even small miscalibrations can bias conclusions about what attracted attention (Holmqvist et al., 2015; Orquin & Holmqvist, 2018). In the wild, you will encounter blinks, eyelashes, and brief tracking losses. Rather than discarding whole trials, we (i) *detect blinks,* (ii) *interpolate short gaps,* and (iii) apply *gentle smoothing* so that fixation detection is not driven by sensor jitter (Kret & Sjak-Shie, 2019). For *pupil size,* we remove blink-related spikes, correct for slow drift, and control or record *luminance*, because lighting changes can mimic emotion (Mathôt, 2018).

You can see the core idea in Figure 2.12. We convert the raw gaze path (x–y over time) into *velocity* (how fast the point of regard is moving), and then mark intervals that stay below a sensible, data-driven threshold as *fixations*. The shaded bands show those moments when the eyes truly rest on something rather than fluttering from noise. In affective contexts, longer or repeated fixations on threat- or loss-related areas are common in anxiety, while broader, more exploratory patterns appear with curiosity and interest (Armstrong & Olatunji, 2012; Kidd & Hayden, 2015). Practically, we smooth the velocity trace, set the threshold from a robust percentile of the distribution, and apply a *minimum-duration* rule so that blinks or micro-movements are not misread as fixations (Kret & Sjak-Shie, 2019; Holmqvist et al., 2015).

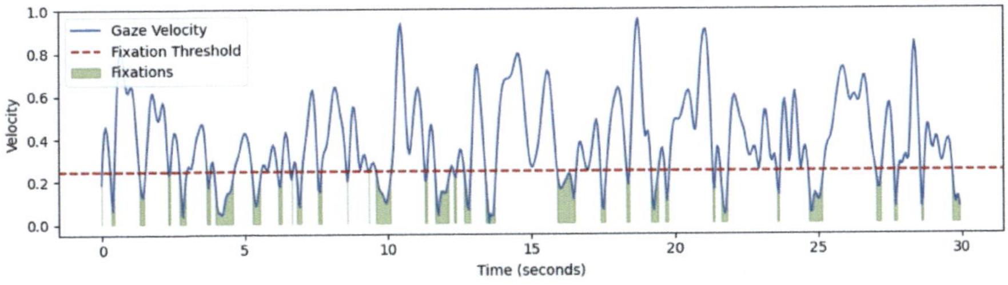

Figure 2.12 Fixation detection from gaze velocity.

From cleaned traces, we extract features that map neatly onto psychological processes:

- *Fixation metrics* (mean duration, total dwell time in Areas of Interest (AOIs), and transitions between AOIs), index *engagement* and *attentional bias* (Holmqvist et al., 2015; Orquin & Holmqvist, 2018).
- *Saccade metrics* (rate, amplitude, and peak velocity) reflect *search strategy* and arousal; anxious scanning often looks fast and shallow, whereas confident search is slower and more targeted (Armstrong & Olatunji, 2012; Kidd & Hayden, 2015).
- *Pupil metrics,* such as tonic level and phasic dilation (peak, latency, recovery), track *autonomic activation* and *effort* with good temporal fidelity (Mathôt, 2018; Joshi & Gold, 2020).
- *Scanpath structure* (entropy, sequence patterns, and AOI transition matrices) captures how organised the exploration is; high entropy can indicate either curiosity or distraction, depending on context (Holmqvist et al., 2015).

In experiments, fixation classification is often done with simple velocity- or dispersion-threshold rules (I-VT or I-DT). For mobile recordings, short-window Hidden Markov Models or Bayesian filters improve robustness to head motion and brief losses (Holmqvist et al., 2015).

Gaze is deeply personal. It reveals what attracts us and what we avoid, and it can serve as a biometric identifier. We therefore minimise raw storage (features instead of full streams), obtain *explicit consent* for any inference of emotion, and disclose the limits of what the system can say (WHO, 2024). On-device processing is preferred for mobile systems, where raw video must be stored, and access is tightly controlled. Gaze can also leak sensitive traits, which makes *privacy-preserving design* and simple user controls to pause logging non-negotiable (Kröger et al., 2020; Steil et al., 2019). Cultural variation matters: direct eye contact can signal attention in many Western settings but deference or politeness-avoidance in parts of East Asia; gaze scanning strategies also differ across cultures, so cross-population validation is essential (Senju et al., 2013; Uono & Hietanen, 2015; Pang et al., 2024).

2.10 Multimodal Data Fusion for Embodied Emotion

The promise of artificial psychology is not that one sensor will finally *see* emotion; it's that *multiple, imperfect witnesses,* such as EEG rhythms, EDA bursts, HRV balance, vocal prosody, facial micro-gestures, gaze, posture, and textual context, can be made to *agree enough* about what happened and for whom. Technically, that agreement is a fusion problem; scientifically, it is a commitment to the idea that emotion is distributed across body and setting rather than localised in a single channel (Poria et al., 2018; Can et al., 2023). The question for this section is practical: *how do we model the joint story in a way that survives the wild missing packets, clock drift, suppression, masks, noise, and still earns the trust of a clinician, a teacher, or a user?*

A first design choice is *when* to fuse (Figure 2.13). In *early fusion,* we concatenate features from synchronised windows and learn one model. This is attractive when clocks are tight and coverage is high; it lets the learner capture cross-modal covariance directly, such as a rise in EDA coinciding with a slight F0 increase and a head pitch change (Can et al., 2023). In *intermediate fusion*, we learn a shared representation that forces modalities to meet in a latent space while keeping their specifics nearby; this tends to be robust when sampling rates differ or when windows do not align perfectly (Hazarika et al., 2020; Lahat et al., 2015). In *late fusion*, each modality votes separately and a meta-learner or rule set reconciles them; it's the most modular and usually the most resilient to device failure or dropout (Poria et al., 2018; Can et al., 2023). There is no dogma here since it is well known that strong systems often mix styles: feature-level fusion for stable pairs (voice+face),

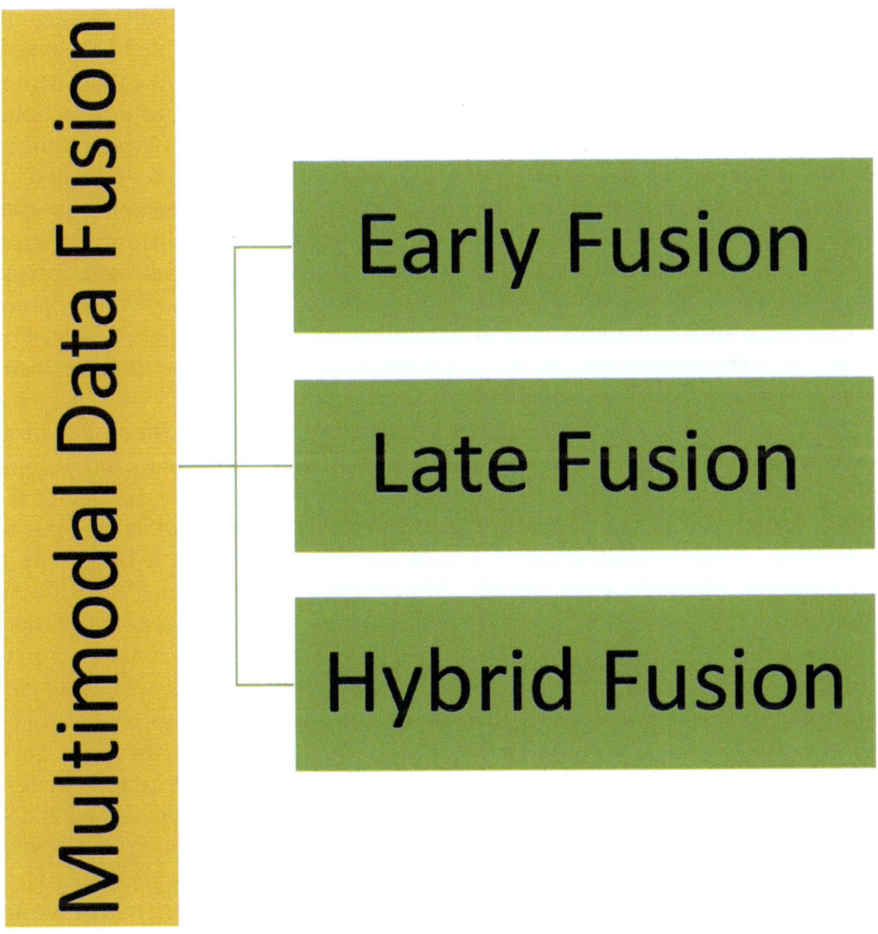

Figure 2.13 Multimodal data fusion approaches.

decision-level fusion to hedge against sensors that disappear mid-session (Mai et al., 2019).

Underneath the timing lies a *representation* problem. If one believes that physiology and behaviour share a small *semantic* core (arousal, valence, control), then it makes sense to learn *modality-invariant* embeddings while preserving *modality-specific* factors for cases where channels disagree (Hazarika et al., 2020). Recent multimodal transformers operationalise this by creating cross-attention pathways where audio can attend to face, face to text, and so on, letting the model soft-align *what* changes with *when* it changes (Tsai et al., 2019; Liang et al., 2024). Self-supervised pretraining has pushed this further: models trained to align raw video, audio, and text without labels learn representations that later adapt to emotion tasks with remarkably few annotations (Akbari et al., 2021; Alayrac et al., 2022). For embodied emotion, such pretraining tames data scarcity and reduces the pressure to over-label, which is ethically important when labels touch mental states (Can et al., 2023).

Physiological fusion presents its subtleties. Autonomic signals *diverge on purpose* under regulation: a person can keep a neutral face while EDA spikes, or slow their breathing and recover HRV while the voice still carries strain (Gross, 2015; Can et al., 2023). Good models treat divergence not as noise to be averaged out but as *evidence of strategy*. Intermediate fusion methods from neuroimaging (e.g., multi-set CCA and joint ICA) were designed to extract covarying brain–behaviour components and are increasingly used to bind physiology and behaviour as well (Sui et al., 2020). In our domain, mCCA–jICA has been used to link grey–white matter patterns with acceptance ability (high vs. low), highlighting how *shared* and *specific* structure can be separated and interpreted in human terms (Grecucci et al., 2023). The moral is straightforward: choose a fusion family that makes *disagreement interpretable* rather than invisible.

The recent wave of *multimodal sentiment/emotion* work offers a toolkit we can adapt rather than reinvent. Tensor-fusion and low-rank fusion decompositions keep interaction terms without exploding parameters (Zadeh et al., 2017; Liu et al., 2018). Modality-invariant/specific splits (MISA) regularise the latent space so that what is shared does not memorise a single channel's quirks (Hazarika et al., 2020). Multimodal transformers (MulT) learn directional cross-attention (e.g., how voice changes guide the reading of face) (Tsai et al., 2019). More recently, masked-prediction objectives over raw video–audio–text (VATT) reduce reliance on manual features, which is helpful in the wild where feature extraction can fail silently (Akbari et al., 2021). Survey work since 2020 converges on two lessons: pretrain broadly, then *fine-tune gently* with regularisation and calibration; and treat missingness as a first-class citizen rather than a preprocessing error (Poria et al., 2018; Mai et al., 2019; Ramaswamy & Palaniswamy, 2024; Can et al., 2023). Comparable machine-learning frameworks have also been applied to affect-linked constructs beyond core emotions, such as love addiction, where model features and explanations clarify predictive factors (Farahani et al., 2025).

There is also a *causal* question we must not duck. Predicting labels is not the same as understanding processes. When we deploy systems that will nudge learners or trigger clinical check-ins, stakeholders ask counterfactual questions such as *why?* and *what if?*. While deep fusion models are excellent pattern recognisers, their explanations can drift toward after-the-fact narratives. Two design moves help. First, anchor part of your representation in *human-meaningful features* (SCR rate, RMSSD, F0 variability, AU12 intensity) so the model can *speak* physiology when asked to justify a prediction (Mauss et al., 2005; Benedek & Kaernbach, 2010; Latif et al., 2021). Second, use *calibrated* outputs with risk bands and decision rules validated on held-out days and subgroups; a calibrated 0.8 must mean *8 out of 10 similar cases were like this*, or your deployment will quietly erode trust (Guo et al., 2017; Can et al., 2023). This is less glamorous than a state-of-the-art leaderboard result, but for artificial psychology, it is the difference between a demo and a system.

A persistent difficulty is *domain shift*: the model learns in quiet rooms and then meets backpacks, video calls, and dialects. We can do better than hope. Lightweight *personalisation* (subject-specific normalisation, a few minutes of fine-tuning, or a small adapter module) often restores performance cheaply (Ringeval et al., 2019; Gideon et al., 2019). *Semi-supervised* and *self-supervised* updates that continue to learn on-device without labels (e.g., predicting the next segment or aligning modalities that co-occur) reduce drift while keeping raw data private (Fang et al., 2022; Akbari et al., 2021). Recent work has also examined how language models trained with differential privacy can be compressed through knowledge distillation and pruning, potentially facilitating their deployment in resource-constrained environments.

What about *text* and *context*, given that Chapter 02 places language alongside the body? In real deployments, textual traces (journals, messages, brief EMA notes) act as a *semantics stabiliser*. When physiology is noisy and face is masked, a sentence fragment (I'm overwhelmed, but okay) can disambiguate arousal's *valence*. Modern language models fine-tuned for affect provide context embeddings that, fused with physiology, improve robustness, particularly when the world changes (Haq & Jackson, 2011; Poria et al., 2018). Care is needed to prevent leakage of sensitive attributes; model cards should report subgroup performance and any known shortcuts the system might exploit (Mitchell et al., 2019).

Evaluation for fusion systems must go beyond accuracy. We must report concordance or F1, but also *calibration, temporal stability, subgroup parity,* and *ablation* results showing that each modality contributes as intended. Held-out days, held-out devices, and held-out raters form the minimum stress tests for an embodied emotion model claiming to work in the wild (Can et al., 2023; Ringeval et al., 2019). If the model cannot answer, *what happens when the watch dies?* or *what if microphones are muted?*, it is not ready.

In short: choose when to fuse based on synchronisation reality; learn representations that separate what modalities share from what they keep to themselves; pretrain broadly, calibrate carefully, and personalise lightly; treat disagreement between channels as a *psychological* fact, not a modelling nuisance; and evaluate like you mean to deploy. This is how we turn a tangle of signals into a system that earns its keep in classrooms, clinics, and daily life.

References

Acheampong, F. A., Wenyu, C., & Nunoo-Mensah, H. (2020). Text-based emotion detection: Advances, challenges, and opportunities. *Engineering Reports*, *2*(7), e12189.

Aguilera, A., Mellado, D., & Rojas, F. (2023). An assessment of in-the-wild datasets for multimodal emotion recognition. *Sensors*, *23*(11), 5184.

Akbari, H., Yuan, L., Qian, R., Chuang, W. H., Chang, S. F., Cui, Y., & Gong, B. (2021). VATT: Transformers for multimodal self-supervised learning from raw video, audio and text. *Advances in Neural Information Processing Systems*, *34*, 24206–24221.

Akçay, M. B., & Oğuz, K. (2020). Speech emotion recognition: Emotional models, databases, features, preprocessing methods, supporting modalities, and classifiers. *Speech Communication*, *116*, 56–76.

Alayrac, J. B., Donahue, J., Luc, P., Miech, A., Barr, I., Hasson, Y., & Simonyan, K. (2022). Flamingo: A visual language model for few-shot learning. *Advances in Neural Information Processing Systems*, *35*, 23716–23736.

Armstrong, T., & Olatunji, B. O. (2012). Eye tracking of attention in the affective disorders: A meta-analytic review and synthesis. *Clinical Psychology Review*, *32*(8), 704–723.

Baevski, A., Zhou, Y., Mohamed, A., & Auli, M. (2020). wav2vec 2.0: A framework for self-supervised learning of speech representations. *Advances in Neural Information Processing Systems*, *33*, 12449–12460.

Barbieri, F., Ronzano, F., & Saggion, H. (2016). What does this emoji mean? A vector space skip-gram model for twitter emojis. In N. Calzolari, K. Choukri, T. Declerck, S. Goggi, M. Grobelnik, B. Maegaard, J. Mariani, H. Mazo, A. Moreno, J. Odijk, & S. Piperidis (Eds.), *Proceedings of the Tenth International Conference on Language Resources and Evaluation (LREC 2016)* (pp. 3967–3972). European Language Resources Association (ELRA).

Barker, D., Tippireddy, M. K. R., Farhan, A., & Ahmed, B. (2025). Ethical considerations in emotion recognition research. *Psychology International*, *7*(2), 43.

Bazarevsky, V., Grishchenko, I., Raveendran, K., Zhu, T., Zhang, F., & Grundmann, M. (2020). Blazepose: On-device real-time body pose tracking. *arXiv preprint arXiv:2006.10204*.

Benedek, M., & Kaernbach, C. (2010). Decomposition of skin conductance data by means of nonnegative deconvolution. *Psychophysiology*, *47*(4), 647–658.

Botes, M. (2025). Regulatory challenges of digital health: The case of mental health applications and personal data in South Africa. *Frontiers in Pharmacology*, *16*, 1498600.

Boucsein, W. (2012). *Electrodermal activity*. Springer.

Boyd, R. L., Ashokkumar, A., Seraj, S., & Pennebaker, J. W. (2022). The development and psychometric properties of LIWC-22. *Austin, TX: University of Texas at Austin*, *10*, 1–47.

Buechel, S., & Hahn, U. (2016, August). Emotion analysis as a regression problem—dimensional models and their implications on emotion representation and metrical evaluation. In *Proceedings of the twenty-second european conference on artificial intelligence* (pp. 1114–1122).

Calvo, R. A., & D'Mello, S. K. (2010). Affect detection: An interdisciplinary review of models, methods, and their applications. *IEEE Transactions on Affective Computing*, *1*(1), 18–37.

Can, Y. S., Mahesh, B., & André, E. (2023). Approaches, applications, and challenges in physiological emotion recognition—a tutorial overview. *Proceedings of the IEEE*, *111*(10), 1287–1313.
Carvalho, N., Noiret, N., Vandel, P., Monnin, J., Chopard, G., & Laurent, E. (2014). Saccadic eye movements in depressed elderly patients. *PLoS One*, *9*(8), e105355.
Chamishka, S., Madhavi, I., Nawaratne, R., Alahakoon, D., De Silva, D., Chilamkurti, N., & Nanayakkara, V. (2022). A voice-based real-time emotion detection technique using recurrent neural network empowered feature modelling. *Multimedia Tools and Applications*, *81*(24), 35173–35194.
Champion, P. (2023). Anonymizing speech: Evaluating and designing speaker anonymization techniques. *arXiv preprint arXiv:2308.04455*.
Coan, J. A., & Allen, J. J. (2004). Frontal EEG asymmetry as a moderator and mediator of emotion. *Biological Psychology*, *67*(1–2), 7–50.
Cowen, A. S., Elfenbein, H. A., Laukka, P., & Keltner, D. (2019). Mapping 24 emotions conveyed by brief human vocalization. *American Psychologist*, *74*(6), 698.
Dael, N., Mortillaro, M., & Scherer, K. R. (2012). Emotion expression in body action and posture. *Emotion*, *12*(5), 1085.
Das, R., & Singh, T. D. (2023). Multimodal sentiment analysis: A survey of methods, trends, and challenges. *ACM Computing Surveys*, *55*(13s), 1–38.
Davey, S., Halberstadt, J., & Bell, E. (2021). Where is emotional feeling felt in the body? An integrative review. *PLoS One*, *16*(12), e0261685.
Davidson, R. J. (2004). What does the prefrontal cortex "do" in affect: Perspectives on frontal EEG asymmetry research. *Biological Psychology*, *67*(1–2), 219–234.
Delorme, A., & Makeig, S. (2004). EEGLAB: an open source toolbox for analysis of single-trial EEG dynamics including independent component analysis. *Journal of Neuroscience Methods*, *134*(1), 9–21.
Demszky, D., Movshovitz-Attias, D., Ko, J., Cowen, A., Nemade, G., & Ravi, S. (2020). GoEmotions: A dataset of fine-grained emotions. *arXiv preprint arXiv:2005.00547*.
Deng, J., Guo, J., Ververas, E., Kotsia, I., & Zafeiriou, S. (2020). Retinaface: Single-shot multi-level face localisation in the wild. In *Proceedings of the IEEE/CVF conference on computer vision and pattern recognition* (pp. 5203–5212).
Devlin, J., Chang, M. W., Lee, K., & Toutanova, K. (2019, June). Bert: Pre-training of deep bidirectional transformers for language understanding. In *Proceedings of the 2019 conference of the North American chapter of the association for computational linguistics: human language technologies, volume 1 (long and short papers)* (pp. 4171–4186).
Ekman, P., & Friesen, W. V. (1978). *Facial action coding system: A technique for the measurement of facial movement*. Consulting Psychologists Press.
Ekman, P., & Rosenberg, E. L. (Eds.). (2005). *What the face reveals: Basic and applied studies of spontaneous expression using the Facial Action Coding System (FACS)* (2nd ed.). Oxford University Press.
Eyben, F., & Schuller, B. (2015). openSMILE:) The Munich open-source large-scale multimedia feature extractor. *ACM SIGMultimedia Records*, *6*(4), 4–13.
Fang, P. F., Li, X., Yan, Y., Zhang, S., Kang, Q. Y., Li, X. F., & Lan, Z. Z. (2022). Connecting the dots in self-supervised learning: a brief survey for beginners. *Journal of Computer Science and Technology*, *37*(3), 507–526.
Farahani, H., Watson, P., Bezan, T., Kovač, N., Winter, L. C., Blagojević, M., & Jiménez, P. (2024). PsAIchology: An Intelligent Direction in Psychological Sciences. In *10th international scientific conference Technics, Informatics and Education-TIE 2024*. Faculty of Technical Sciences Čačak, University of Kragujevac.
Farahani, H., Watson, P., Kovač, N., Sheykhangafshe, F. B., Azadfallah, P., Allahyari, A., & Chesli, R. R. (2025). Unraveling the complexity of love addiction

using machine learning algorithms: The influence of positive and negative affect, interpersonal needs, and self-hate. In *International handbook of love: Transcultural and transdisciplinary perspectives* (pp. 1–22). Springer Nature Switzerland.
Gendron, M., & Barrett, L. F. (2009). Reconstructing the past: A century of ideas about emotion in psychology. *Emotion Review, 1*(4), 316–339.
Gideon, J., McInnis, M. G., & Provost, E. M. (2019). Improving cross-corpus speech emotion recognition with adversarial discriminative domain generalization (ADDoG). *IEEE Transactions on Affective Computing, 12*(4), 1055–1068.
Gobl, C., & Chasaide, A. N. (2003). The role of voice quality in communicating emotion, mood and attitude. *Speech Communication, 40*(1–2), 189–212.
Grecucci, A., Dadomo, H., Salvato, G., Lapomarda, G., Sorella, S., & Messina, I. (2023). Abnormal brain circuits characterize borderline personality and mediate the relationship between childhood traumas and symptoms: a mCCA+ jICA and random forest approach. *Sensors, 23*(5), 2862.
Gross, J. J. (2015). Emotion regulation: Current status and future prospects. *Psychological Inquiry, 26*(1), 1–26.
Guo, C., Pleiss, G., Sun, Y., & Weinberger, K. Q. (2017, July). On calibration of modern neural networks. In *International conference on machine learning* (pp. 1321–1330). PMLR.
Hanisch, S., Arias-Cabarcos, P., Parra-Arnau, J., & Strufe, T. (2021). Privacy-protecting techniques for behavioral biometric data: A survey. *arXiv preprint arXiv:2109.04120.*
Haq, S., & Jackson, P. J. (2011). Multimodal emotion recognition. In W. Wang (Ed.), *Machine audition: Principles, algorithms and systems* (pp. 398–423). IGI Global Scientific Publishing.
Hashem, A., Arif, M., & Alghamdi, M. (2023). Speech emotion recognition approaches: A systematic review. *Speech Communication, 154*, 102974.
Hazarika, D., Zimmermann, R., & Poria, S. (2020, October). Misa: Modality-invariant and-specific representations for multimodal sentiment analysis. In *Proceedings of the 28th ACM international conference on multimedia* (pp. 1122–1131).
Holmqvist, K., Nyström, M., Andersson, R., Dewhurst, R., Jarodzka, H., & Van de Weijer, J. (2015). *Eye tracking: A comprehensive guide to methods and measures.* Oxford University Press.
Hsu, W. N., Bolte, B., Tsai, Y. H. H., Lakhotia, K., Salakhutdinov, R., & Mohamed, A. (2021). Hubert: Self-supervised speech representation learning by masked prediction of hidden units. *IEEE/ACM Transactions on Audio, Speech, and Language Processing, 29*, 3451–3460.
Jobin, A., Ienca, M., & Vayena, E. (2019). Artificial Intelligence: The global landscape of ethics guidelines. *Nature Machine Intelligence, 1*(9), 389–399.
Joshi, S., & Gold, J. I. (2020). Pupil size as a window on neural substrates of cognition. *Trends in Cognitive Sciences, 24*(6), 466–480.
Khalil, R. A., Jones, E., Babar, M. I., Jan, T., Zafar, M. H., & Alhussain, T. (2019). Speech emotion recognition using deep learning techniques: A review. *IEEE Access, 7*, 117327–117345.
Kidd, C., & Hayden, B. Y. (2015). The psychology and neuroscience of curiosity. *Neuron, 88*(3), 449–460.
Klein, M., Witthöft, M., & Jungmann, S. M. (2025). Interoception in individuals with autism spectrum disorders: A systematic literature review and meta-analysis. *Frontiers in Psychiatry, 16*, 1573263.
Kollias, D. (2022). Abaw: Valence-arousal estimation, expression recognition, action unit detection & multi-task learning challenges. In *Proceedings of the IEEE/CVF conference on computer vision and pattern recognition* (pp. 2328–2336).
Kong, Q., Cao, Y., Iqbal, T., Wang, Y., Wang, W., & Plumbley, M. D. (2020). Panns: Large-scale pretrained audio neural networks for audio pattern recognition. *IEEE/ACM Transactions on Audio, Speech, and Language Processing, 28*, 2880–2894.

Kossaifi, J., Tzimiropoulos, G., Todorovic, S., & Pantic, M. (2017). AFEW-VA database for valence and arousal estimation in-the-wild. *Image and Vision Computing*, *65*, 23–36.
Kovač, N., Ratković, K., Farahani, H., & Watson, P. (2024). A practical applications guide to machine learning regression models in psychology with Python. *Methods in Psychology*, *11*, 100156.
Kovač, N., Ratković, K., Watson, P., Farahani, H., & Bagheri Sheykhangafshe, F. (2025a). Machine learning classification models for predicting chronic pain. *Current Psychology*, 1–14. Advance online publication.
Kovač, N., Ratković, K., Farahani, H., & Watson, P. (2025b). Machine learning regression models for internal shame. *Acta Psychologica*, *260*, 105721.
Kret, M. E., & Sjak-Shie, E. E. (2019). Preprocessing pupil size data: Guidelines and code. *Behavior Research Methods*, *51*(3), 1336–1342.
Kröger, J. L., Lutz, O. H. M., & Müller, F. (2020). What does your gaze reveal about you? On the privacy implications of eye tracking. In *IFIP international summer school on privacy and identity management* (pp. 226–241). Springer.
Kuppens, P., & Verduyn, P. (2017). Emotion dynamics. *Current Opinion in Psychology*, *17*, 22–26.
Laeng, B., Sirois, S., & Gredebäck, G. (2012). Pupillometry: A window to the preconscious?. *Perspectives on Psychological Science*, *7*(1), 18–27.
Lahat, D., Adali, T., & Jutten, C. (2015). Multimodal data fusion: An overview of methods, challenges, and prospects. *Proceedings of the IEEE*, *103*(9), 1449–1477.
Latif, S., Qadir, J., Qayyum, A., Usama, M., & Younis, S. (2020). Speech technology for healthcare: Opportunities, challenges, and state of the art. *IEEE Reviews in Biomedical Engineering*, *14*, 342–356.
Latif, S., Rana, R., Khalifa, S., Jurdak, R., Qadir, J., & Schuller, B. (2021). Survey of deep representation learning for speech emotion recognition. *IEEE Transactions on Affective Computing*, *14*(2), 1634–1654.
Li, S., & Deng, W. (2020). Deep facial expression recognition: A survey. *IEEE Transactions on Affective Computing*, *13*(3), 1195–1215.
Liang, P. P., Zadeh, A., & Morency, L. P. (2024). Foundations & trends in multimodal machine learning: Principles, challenges, and open questions. *ACM Computing Surveys*, *56*(10), 1–42.
Lin, W., & Zhang, Y. (2022, July). Review of researches on the emotion recognition and affective computing based on HCI. In *2022 7th International Conference on Image, Vision and Computing (ICIVC)* (pp. 573–578). IEEE.
Little, R. J., & Rubin, D. B. (2019). *Statistical analysis with missing data*. John Wiley & Sons.
Liu, Y., Ott, M., Goyal, N., Du, J., Joshi, M., Chen, D., & Stoyanov, V. (2019). Roberta: A robustly optimized bert pretraining approach. *arXiv preprint arXiv:1907.11692*.
Liu, Z., Shen, Y., Lakshminarasimhan, V. B., Liang, P. P., Zadeh, A., & Morency, L. P. (2018). Efficient low-rank multimodal fusion with modality-specific factors. *arXiv preprint arXiv:1806.00064*.
MacIntyre, A. D. (2022). *The analysis of breathing and rhythm in speech*. University of London, University College London.
Mai, S., Hu, H., & Xing, S. (2019, July). Divide, conquer and combine: Hierarchical feature fusion network with local and global perspectives for multimodal affective computing. In *Proceedings of the 57th annual meeting of the association for computational linguistics* (pp. 481–492).
Mathôt, S. (2018). Pupillometry: Psychology, physiology, and function. *Journal of Cognition*, *1*(1), 16.
Mauss, I. B., Levenson, R. W., McCarter, L., Wilhelm, F. H., & Gross, J. J. (2005). The tie that binds? Coherence among emotion experience, behavior, and physiology. *Emotion*, *5*(2), 175.

Minderer, M., Djolonga, J., Romijnders, R., Hubis, F., Zhai, X., Houlsby, N., & Lucic, M. (2021). Revisiting the calibration of modern neural networks. *Advances in Neural Information Processing Systems*, *34*, 15682–15694.
Mitchell, M., Wu, S., Zaldivar, A., Barnes, P., Vasserman, L., Hutchinson, B., & Gebru, T. (2019, January). Model cards for model reporting. In *Proceedings of the conference on fairness, accountability, and transparency* (pp. 220–229).
Mohammad, S. M. (2022). Best practices in the creation and use of emotion lexicons. *arXiv preprint arXiv:2210.07206*.
Mohammad, S. M., & Turney, P. D. (2013). Crowdsourcing a word–emotion association lexicon. *Computational Intelligence*, *29*(3), 436–465.
Novak, P. K., Smailović, J., Sluban, B., & Mozetič, I. (2015). Sentiment of emojis. *PLoS One*, *10*(12), e0144296.
Orquin, J. L., & Holmqvist, K. (2018). Threats to the validity of eye-movement research in psychology. *Behavior Research Methods*, *50*(4), 1645–1656.
Pang, H. T., Zhou, X., & Chu, M. (2024). Cross-cultural differences in using nonverbal behaviors to identify indirect replies. *Journal of Nonverbal Behavior*, *48*(2), 323–344.
Park, D. S., Chan, W., Zhang, Y., Chiu, C. C., Zoph, B., Cubuk, E. D., & Le, Q. V. (2019). Specaugment: A simple data augmentation method for automatic speech recognition. *arXiv preprint arXiv:1904.08779*.
Park, T. J., Kanda, N., Dimitriadis, D., Han, K. J., Watanabe, S., & Narayanan, S. (2022). A review of speaker diarization: Recent advances with deep learning. *Computer Speech & Language*, *72*, 101317.
Pennebaker, J. W., & Chung, C. K. (2011). Expressive writing and its links to mental and physical health. In H. S. Friedman (Ed.), *Oxford handbook of health psychology* (pp. 417–437). OUP.
Pereira, R., Mendes, C., Ribeiro, J., Ribeiro, R., Miragaia, R., Rodrigues, N., & Pereira, A. (2024). Systematic review of emotion detection with computer vision and deep learning. *Sensors*, *24*(11), 3484.
Pinna, T., & Edwards, D. J. (2020). A systematic review of associations between interoception, vagal tone, and emotional regulation: Potential applications for mental health, wellbeing, psychological flexibility, and chronic conditions. *Frontiers in Psychology*, *11*, 1792.
Poria, S., Majumder, N., Hazarika, D., Cambria, E., Gelbukh, A., & Hussain, A. (2018). Multimodal sentiment analysis: Addressing key issues and setting up the baselines. *IEEE Intelligent Systems*, *33*(6), 17–25.
Poria, S., Majumder, N., Hazarika, D., Ghosal, D., Bhardwaj, R., Jian, S. Y. B., & Mihalcea, R. (2021). Recognizing emotion cause in conversations. *Cognitive Computation*, *13*(5), 1317–1332.
Ramaswamy, M. P. A., & Palaniswamy, S. (2024). Multimodal emotion recognition: A comprehensive review, trends, and challenges. *Wiley Interdisciplinary Reviews: Data Mining and Knowledge Discovery*, *14*(6), e1563.
Ringeval, F., Schuller, B., Valstar, M., Cummins, N., Cowie, R., Tavabi, L., & Pantic, M. (2019, October). AVEC 2019 workshop and challenge: state-of-mind, detecting depression with AI, and cross-cultural affect recognition. In *Proceedings of the 9th international on audio/visual emotion challenge and workshop* (pp. 3–12).
Ringeval, F., Schuller, B., Valstar, M., Gratch, J., Cowie, R., Scherer, S., & Pantic, M. (2017, October). Avec 2017: Real-life depression, and affect recognition workshop and challenge. In *Proceedings of the 7th annual workshop on audio/visual emotion challenge* (pp. 3–9).
Russell, J. A. (1980). A circumplex model of affect. *Journal of Personality and Social Psychology*, *39*(6), 1161.
Scherer, K. R. (2009). The dynamic architecture of emotion: Evidence for the component process model. *Cognition and Emotion*, *23*(7), 1307–1351.

Schuller, B., & Batliner, A. (2013). *Computational paralinguistics: Emotion, affect and personality in speech and language processing*. John Wiley & Sons.

Senju, A., Vernetti, A., Kikuchi, Y., Akechi, H., Hasegawa, T., & Johnson, M. H. (2013). Cultural background modulates how we look at other persons' gaze. *International Journal of Behavioral Development*, *37*(2), 131–136.

Soleymani, M., Garcia, D., Jou, B., Schuller, B., Chang, S. F., & Pantic, M. (2017). A survey of multimodal sentiment analysis. *Image and Vision Computing*, *65*, 3–14.

Sui, J., Jiang, R., Bustillo, J., & Calhoun, V. (2020). Neuroimaging-based individualized prediction of cognition and behavior for mental disorders and health: methods and promises. *Biological psychiatry*, *88*(11), 818-828.

Stappen, L., Baird, A., Christ, L., Schumann, L., Sertolli, B., Messner, E. M., & Schuller, B. W. (2021). The MuSe 2021 multimodal sentiment analysis challenge: sentiment, emotion, physiological-emotion, and stress. In *proceedings of the 2nd on multimodal sentiment analysis challenge* (pp. 5–14).

Steil, J., Koelle, M., Heuten, W., Boll, S., & Bulling, A. (2019, June). Privaceye: privacy-preserving head-mounted eye tracking using egocentric scene image and eye movement features. In *Proceedings of the 11th ACM symposium on eye tracking research & applications* (pp. 1–10).

Tan, X., & Zhang, X. L. (2021, June). Speech enhancement aided end-to-end multi-task learning for voice activity detection. In *ICASSP 2021–2021 IEEE International Conference on Acoustics, Speech and Signal Processing (ICASSP)* (pp. 6823–6827). IEEE.

Thayer, J. F., Åhs, F., Fredrikson, M., Sollers III, J. J., & Wager, T. D. (2012). A meta-analysis of heart rate variability and neuroimaging studies: implications for heart rate variability as a marker of stress and health. *Neuroscience & Biobehavioral Reviews*, *36*(2), 747–756.

Trigeorgis, G., Ringeval, F., Brueckner, R., Marchi, E., Nicolaou, M. A., Schuller, B., & Zafeiriou, S. (2016, March). Adieu features? end-to-end speech emotion recognition using a deep convolutional recurrent network. In *2016 IEEE international conference on acoustics, speech and signal processing (ICASSP)* (pp. 5200–5204). IEEE.

Tsai, Y. H. H., Bai, S., Liang, P. P., Kolter, J. Z., Morency, L. P., & Salakhutdinov, R. (2019, July). Multimodal transformer for unaligned multimodal language sequences. In *Proceedings of the conference. Association for computational linguistics. Meeting* (Vol. 2019, p. 6558).

Uono, S., & Hietanen, J. K. (2015). Eye contact perception in the west and east: A cross-cultural study. *PLoS One*, *10*(2), e0118094.

VanderPlas, J. (2016). *Python data science handbook: Essential tools for working with data*. O'Reilly Media.

Wen, M., Dong, Z., Zhang, L., Li, B., Zhang, Y., & Li, K. (2022). Depression and cognitive impairment: Current understanding of its neurobiology and diagnosis. *Neuropsychiatric Disease and Treatment*, *18*, 2783–2794.

World Health Organization. (2024). *Ethics and governance of artificial intelligence for health: Large multi-modal models. WHO guidance*. World Health Organization.

Wu, Y., Mi, Q., & Gao, T. (2025). A comprehensive review of multimodal emotion recognition: Techniques, challenges, and future directions. *Biomimetics*, *10*(7), 418.

Zadeh, A. B., Chen, M., Poria, S., Cambria, E., & Morency, L. P. (2017). Tensor fusion network for multimodal sentiment analysis. *arXiv preprint arXiv:1707.07250*.

Zadeh, A. B., Liang, P. P., Poria, S., Cambria, E., & Morency, L. P. (2018, July). Multimodal language analysis in the wild: Cmu-mosei dataset and interpretable dynamic fusion graph. In *Proceedings of the 56th annual meeting of the association for computational linguistics (Volume 1: Long Papers)* (pp. 2236–2246).

3 Language Subject and Body for Artificial Intelligence in Psychology

Dioneia Motta Monte-Serrat and Carlo Cattani

3.1 Introduction to Interdisciplinarity Among Computational Linguistics, Neurolinguistics and Cognitive Computing: Making the Interpretation of Intelligent Systems More Intuitive

This chapter is inspired by an interdisciplinary approach, which proves to be a field of excellence for interconnecting emotion and cognition – since the individual's linguistic cognitive process is compatible with the expression of emotions – with artificial intelligence, AI – which also presents the same foundations of the linguistic cognitive process when using language and classifying emotions (Monte-Serrat & Cattani, 2021). We investigate the connection between language, emotion and cognition carried out by intelligent systems (so-called in this book Artificial Intelligence Psychology, shortly AIP), based on the dynamics of the human cognitive linguistic process.

Human cognition, although not fully deciphered, is responsible for the articulation of two fronts: the logical front (if P, then Q) and the axiomatic or contextual field (Monte-Serrat & Cattani, 2021). These two fronts make up the unique or universal structure of language, whether from individuals or from machines (Monte-Serrat & Cattani, 2021, 2022). An understanding of the dynamics of the human cognitive linguistic process as integrative of the logical and axiomatic/contextual features of the linguistic cognitive process creates new possibilities in the assessment of emotions (Artificial Psychology). The perspective of approaching emotions according to the universal structure of language makes it possible to analyze emotions under a semantic dimension, linked to a subjective context, and under a logical dimension, with both emotional perspectives being able to give rise or not to decisions (Monte-Serrat & Cattani, 2021, 2022). In this way, intelligent systems can deal with previously categorized emotions, or process information under a dynamic aspect. To put it better, on the one hand, intelligent systems absorb pre-established values in a unified way (categorized emotions), or on the other hand, they deal with the fluid values of emotions (emotions captured according to contextual reality). In this chapter, therefore, we present computational linguistics strongly linked to neurolinguistics, psychology and cognitive computing, so that the system's interpretation will be more

DOI: 10.4324/9781003495123-3

intuitive as it learns to interpret better the appropriate context of the emotion at play (Monte-Serrat & Cattani, 2022).

This chapter articulates language, subject and body to assist in the development and use of intelligent systems aimed at AIP. Section 3.1 makes an interdisciplinary introduction showing the permeability of the universal structure of the cognitive linguistic process in the scientific branches of linguistics, neurolinguistics, computational linguistics, and cognitive computing, making it clearer how to achieve human intuition in the development of intelligent systems. The details of the elements of the cognitive linguistic process' unique structure and its connection with subjectivity are presented in Section 3.2. Section 3.3 discusses the concept of emotion and the role of symbolic mediation through language, distinguishing the concept of language from the concept of languages spoken in the world. Section 3.4 articulates language, cognition and subject, showing that the cognitive linguistic process is the seat of emotions, both in the central nervous system of individuals and in the configuration of the algorithmic core of intelligent systems. Section 3.5 shows how to predict and measure subjectivity through emotions. The suggestion of an Artificial Psychology structured not only in logical categories, but also in real-valued functions is offered in Section 3.6. Section 3.7 draws attention to the dynamic system characteristic of the cognitive linguistic process and the possibilities that this understanding brings to the development of more intuitive smart tools. Section 3.8 provides an overview of the chapter's content, concluding that emotions go beyond logical categorizations, also arising from values linked to the environment. In this case, Artificial Psychology systems need to articulate concepts from psychology, linguistics, neurolinguistics and psychoanalysis to computational cognition to encompass subjectivity. When dealing with subjects, developers and applicators of Artificial Psychology must be aware of ethical principles, since they are dealing with the core cognition and decision-making of intelligent systems' users.

3.2 The Unique Architecture of Language Combined With Subjectivity

Language (understood as a linguistic cognitive process, according to Monte-Serrat & Cattani, 2021), is a dynamical system that mediates between reality and mind, acting in the process of meaning construction, which, in turn, depends on a system of symbols and linguistic signs codified through rules of use (Araújo, 2011, pp. 9–10). A dynamical system is a mathematical–logical model that connects causes (forces) and effects (variations of the kinematical state, as a function of time). A linguistic cognitive process is a logical model that connects causes (stimuli-events) and effects, i.e. the variations of the psychological-cognitive state of our mind, as functions of time (this can be seen from the way our memory develops over time). It is important to highlight that the language sign system does not automatically assign meaning (although some linguistic theories consider it so); for this reason, language must be considered within its social context.

There is a diversity of views on what the human cognitive process is. Authors present a consensus that language is particularly complex; that it presents regularity (syntactic restrictions, semantic and pragmatic objectives, discourse etc.); that it can be modeled mathematically as a dynamic system (Elman, 1995; Kelso et al., 1988; Thelen, 1988). Elman states that dynamic system modeling does not operate on symbols, but it incorporates dynamics into the system, allowing movement from certain regions to others and making certain transitions difficult (Elman, 1995, p. 196): "internal representations of words are not symbols but locations in state space […] and processing rules are not symbolic specifications but the dynamics of the system".

We believe that there are two possibilities for working on language and emotion in AI: one possibility is to work with categorized emotions accompanied by syntactic and semantic restrictions; the other possibility is to model the dynamics of the system, making certain transitions in the construction of information difficult. This second possibility, contrary to what Elman suggests, may indeed interfere with the symbolization process, which is uniquely human, as the mental representation arises from the human experience exercised in each context of reality.

On the one hand, therefore, we have the "rules" of structural organization of language that link a repository of facts to individual words, adding restrictive regulations on how these links can be made so that these words are combined in the form of sentences (Elman, 1995, p. 197). Sentences, once subject to grammatical rules, can be constructed into higher-level structures or broken down into dimensions that reflect syntactic, orthographic or phonological properties (Elman, 1995, pp. 197–198).

The dynamics of the cognitive linguistic process, responsible for the construction of meaning, must be considered. The "movement" of language features is connected to the time element, which can be predictable, when provided by syntax, or unpredictable, when provided by context interference (Monte-Serrat & Belgacem, 2017; Monte-Serrat et al., 2017). The importance of identifying the time element in research into cognitive processes, be they human beings or intelligent systems, lies in the interference of time on the "value" of the word in the discursive chain, which is an aspect linked to the construction of meaning. In short: language symbols are intrinsically context-free; they are always the same regardless of their use (Elman, 1995, p. 198). However, the context can change the meaning, as seen in the following two examples: "The dream is over" (phrase said by John Lennon when the group The Beatles dissolved); "The dream is over" (Mr. José from the bakery, when referring to a sweet bread called "dream" in Brazil). The same sentence changes its meaning when we change its context.

The study of cognition requires interdisciplinary scientific investigation of the mind and intelligence. Among the disciplines most used in these investigations are linguistics, neurolinguistics, psychology, philosophy, anthropology, computer science and artificial intelligence (AI). The term Artificial Psychology to describe the investigation of psychological phenomena through artificial intelligence, AI, refers, in this chapter, to the fundamental structure of the cognitive linguistic process (dynamic relationship between the logical and axiomatic/contextual features of language, which can lead decision-making or not), including aspects involved in the perception of emotions. Psychology, therefore, which studies mental states and processes mixed with emotional perceptions, integrates the cognitive linguistic process (Monte-Serrat & Cattani, 2022). The basic human temperaments (melancholic, choleric and sanguine) are not detached from subjectivity. Therefore, there is no way to talk about a cognitive linguistic process without taking psychological or subjective aspects into account.

Neurolinguistics deals with the cognitive linguistic process as a physiological process (chemical, physical and mechanical functions of the body). Perlovsky (2007 p. 2) proposes the physical theory of mind relating cognition and language with thermodynamics and informational theories. He describes the mental model according to a functional hierarchy, which goes from sensory-motor activity (lower region of the hierarchy) to concepts of objects, contexts, and situations. According to the author (2007), language is seen as a system of different operators that help the brain translate the physical world into intelligible information for the biological body.

We know, however, that language cannot be reduced to sensory-motor activities, as individuals express themselves in different and unique ways. To Perlovsky's perspective we can add subjectivity. Subjectivism in language refers to the concept of language proposed by Lacan (2011[1957]), that is, language as a complex formation that involves the conscious and unconscious. In 1949, Lacan takes advantage of Bouasse's optical scheme to describe the role of language mediation (as a symbolic plane) that links the real body of individuals to their imaginary body (understood as subjectivity).

AIP cannot disregard that subjectivity is not limited to the simple approximation of concepts and psychological states but involves sensory or motor data that are integrated into the individual's psychic life, generating a different order of operations in which symbolic activity intervenes (Monte-Serrat, 2012). AIP must consider that subjectivity does not arise from emotions but has its origins in the human activity of representation (Le Gaufey, 1998).

3.3 Emotions and the Role of Symbolic Mediation Through Language

Scarantino (2021) highlights the importance of recognizable theories of emotions conceived as phenomenologically salient responses of a subject to events in the reality that surrounds them, triggering behavioral changes. He describes emotions as complex tasks and states that there is still uncertainty as to whether emotions are rational.

Considering that this chapter articulates computational linguistics with neurolinguistics and cognitive computing, it is not appropriate to approach emotion as isolated categories. Due to this complexity, we prefer to seek the foundations of the cognitive linguistic process to try to overcome aspects of emotions that can assist in the development of AIP tools, and that is why language (taken as a process and not as spoken languages around the world) is considered in its dynamic aspect that articulates logical reasoning to environmental stimuli, and whose functions and properties must be fully considered in the development of an AIP.

The French philosopher Michel Pêcheux (1975) explains that sense, meaning or information has a social, ideological and psychological trajectory that causes tension in the sedimentation of meanings. There is a "legal illusion" of what the individual is (Edelman, 1980, p. 14), that is, he is, namely, the "ideological representation of society as a set of distinct and free individuals" (Miaille, 1979, p. 111), endowed with an autonomous, entirely visible form (Pêcheux, 1975). From this perspective, subject and subjectivity are idealized and frozen in categories of "valuation of action" (Lagazzy, 1988, p. 20). According to Haroche (1984), "the subject of law, in bureaucracy, comes from the writings of the law and has nothing to say about himself". Bureaucratically speaking, we can categorize individuals and their emotions (Monte-Serrat, 2012), however, fuzzy logic, an extension of classical Boolean logic, shows that in addition to the two categories true/false or 0/1, there are also intermediate categories, that is, something can be true or false only up to a certain point, assuming a value between 0 and 1. The concept of fuzzy logic can provide ways to solve the problem of teaching a machine to categorize emotions in a less idealized and more realistic way.

Subjectivity and emotion have to do with the linguistic cognitive process and with the development of a Super AI. What we have in 2024 is AI still limited to specific tasks (e.g. image classification, audio transcription). For now, General AI that understands and learns any intellectual task does not reach the capacity of a graduate, engineer or researcher; on the contrary, it has produced alarming effects. While McCarthy, an American computer scientist, in 1956 first used "artificial intelligence" to refer to a computer that used mathematical logic, we, in this chapter, make it clear that, according to the foundations of the cognitive linguistic process, cognition is not restricted to logical characteristics. This question leads us to understand the paradox of AI: the more it automates data analysis, the more work is required of a human being to interpret edge cases, provide high-level scrutiny and give meaning to insights. An artificial intelligence that exploits only the logical characteristics of cognition will be increasingly dependent on the human element: AI lacks the development of algorithmic modeling strategies that also encompass the axiomatic (contextual) aspects of cognition.

Taking as a starting point the idea according to which the subject is neither born nor develops but is constituted in an articulated way at the social level (Elia, 2004, p. 36), we can understand that the subject is an "act of response" (Elia, 2004, p. 41), in relation to the environment (act of response corresponds to a symbolization process). Therefore, we propose that AIP promotes a hybridization of the concept of individual as "legal illusion", as defined by Edelman (1980, p. 14) with the concept of subjectivity arising from stimuli originating from the environment (symbolization process for humans which is replaced by the tokenization process in terms of artificial intelligence). This way makes it possible to circumvent cognition under its fundamental dynamic aspects that combine logical features with axiomatic features (resulting from impacts that arise from the individual's contextual reality).

The categories of emotions have important methodological implications to be considered from the perspective of both fronts of the cognitive linguistic process. Prescriptive definitions of emotions may not necessarily be homogeneous, differing in terms of the spoken language and the context from which they were taken for categorization (Monte-Serrat, 2021). This phenomenon is due to the intermediation of human beings who, when experiencing a certain situation, represent it (symbolic process). This experience of symbolization is uniquely human and can give rise to emotions that are different from the ideally categorized emotions (disconnected from the original context). Symbolization, being a uniquely human process, has been offset by the human work of tokenization and categorization, behind the scenes of creating intelligent systems.

The role of symbolic mediation through language, as a dynamic process, promotes a confluence of heterogeneous domains within a great complexity in which emotions come from a different order of subjective operations that are not limited to logical reasoning. For Scarantino (2021), emotions score low in terms of rationality and fail when rooted in both theoretical approaches and common sense: an adequate appreciation of emotions in terms of rationality requires a series of distinctions.

Research dedicated to emotions cannot disregard the human symbolization process. It comprises a subjective organization that is not of the order of visual perception but results from the fact that the subject is the object of the other's gaze (Le Gaufey, 1998, p. 75). The study of emotions, therefore, considers a relationship that comes from outside, from human or artificial support (Roudinesco, 1998, p. 371). In the process of symbolization there is an identification of the subject linked to the field of the Other (the Big Other, as Lacan names it) (Lacan, 1964, p. 253), the effect of which results in a unity (something external joins something internal under symbols) that is given externally. The subject experiences an invisible cohesion through something visible, better said, the subject experiences a contour, a circumscription (Ildefonse, 2012). This description of psychology and psychoanalysis for the symbolic process carried out through language (understood as a dynamic process) directs our attention to the value of emotion, which cannot be understood as being solely logical.

3.4 Language, Cognition and Subject: The Seat of Emotions Is the Brain

Scarantino (2021) clarifies that although the physical seat of emotions is the brain, there is no way to match neural circuits to individual types of emotion. The author states that the brain is embodied and inserted into environments that are essential for it to implement symbols of different types of emotions. He (Scarantino, 2021) adds that emotions such as anger, fear and shame vary in terms of behavioral and physiological expression characteristics, as well as duration and intensity, making it difficult to measure distinctive behavioral patterns of emotions.

The difficulty of pointing out empirical evidence to classify basic emotions, and the difficulty of articulating emotions to assessments of contextual meaning can serve as a warning to researchers on the topic. The complexity in approaching emotions in terms of information processing leads to the attempt to approach the topic of emotion from the perspective of the foundations of cognition. Cognition is dynamic and occurs in only one way and not another: it articulates logical features with contextual (axiomatic) features (Monte-Serrat & Cattani, 2021; Monte-Serrat, 2022). Exploring emotions at the fundamental level of the cognitive linguistic process brings advantages and insights that prevent the researcher from deviating from the focus of their research, which becomes even more complex when encompassing the area of artificial intelligence, AI. To explore emotions, we suggest adopting the bases of the cognitive process described by Monte-Serrat and Cattani (2021), which are the same, both in humans and machines, since the universal structure of language is axiomatic-logical.

Emotion refers to value and, according to Gernet in Detienne (1969), the notion presupposes the valorization of classical faculties such as: attitudes, mental and bodily aspects. Gernet (in Detenne, 1969, p. 127) assumes that in the different areas of value "we can recognize an 'intention'" which in turn presupposes a process of idealization. The linguistic use of the word "implies the notion of value [which] can relate to all kinds of 'objects – even, occasionally, to human beings as "precious"' (Gernet in Detienne, 1969), p. 127.

Considering that the foundations of the cognitive linguistic process mix logical reasoning and experience in relation to a contextual reality, when studying emotions, it is necessary to appreciate them according to "values". According to Gernet in Detienne, (1969, pp 121-122) the notion of value is "abstract par excellence" and presupposes the valorization of classical faculties such as: attitudes, mental and bodily. So, the appreciation of emotions through mental or bodily attitudes occurs in the final stretch of the cognitive linguistic process – which begins by collecting stimuli from the outside to transport them to the central nervous system and, at the end, organizing them in a logical way which will trigger decision-making or not (Perlovsky & Kozma, 2007). Given the different areas of value collected by the dynamics of the cognitive linguistic process, there may be the recognition or identification of an "intention", which, in the structure of the cognitive linguistic process presupposes a process of idealization (Gernet in Detenne, 1969, p. 127).

We may consider that if the linguistic use of the word (spoken or written discourse) "implies the notion of value [the word] can relate to all kinds of 'objects" – even, occasionally, to human beings as 'precious'" (Gernet in Detenne, 1969, p. 127). Thus, even on the surface of language (linguistic use of the word or written or spoken speech), when it is detected that an intention to relate something as "precious" (decision-making) was constituted, it can be inferred that, in the foundations of language (cognitive linguistic process), the axiomatic trait (relating to the subjective experience of contextual reality) goes through a process of idealization/representation, that is, it becomes logically organized as an action or intention to classify something as "precious". What we intend to clarify at this point is that, when an emotion stops being "abstract par excellence" and becomes "intention", the emotion under study becomes easier to identify and categorize.

3.5 Predictability and Measurability of the Subject Through Emotion

Intelligent systems can, on the one hand, work with previously categorized emotions, arising from a static (categorized) context, while, on the other hand, the systems can process information collected from a dynamic contextual reality (Monte-Serrat, 2021). In this section, the general and contemporary aspects of the status of subjectivity are articulated with the social and technical dimensions of discourse. If discourse is understood as effects of meaning between interlocutors in a socio-historical context (Pêcheux, 1975), we recognize the importance of studying emotions from a discursive perspective, since subjectivity depends on the dynamics of the cognitive linguistic process (as explained in previous sections) and is not something previously given. Subjectivity (and, consequently, the emotions that arise from it) is constituted in enunciation (Elia, 2004).

Articulating subjectivity and discourse leads us to the theory of Discourse Analysis (Pêcheux, 1975) which points to two possibilities for categorizing subjectivity: i) discourse (effects of meaning between interlocutors) can be something idealized (disconnected from contextual reality) interfering equally in the constitution of the individual's subjectivity (subjectivity considered to be disconnected from contextual reality); ii) discourse (meaning effects between interlocutors) is linked to the dynamic context of reality, reflecting this dynamic in the dynamic constitution of subjectivity. The first category of subjectivity (which is constituted from idealized discourse, that is, disconnected from reality) is predictable and measurable, as the ideology is previously placed so that the subject is constituted in accordance with it (Monte-Serrat, 2012; Pêcheux, 1975; Althusser, 2010). On the other hand, the subjectivity that is constituted from contextual dynamics is unpredictable and, for this reason, difficult to measure.

Sherry Turkle's (1984) ideas about the influence of technology on identity help us draw some conclusions about emotions under interactions with artificial intelligence. Subjectivity in contemporary times and identity issues are objects of scientific interest to enrich studies on emotion. Monte-Serrat's doctoral thesis (2012) explains the implications of materialism and ideology in the constitution of subjectivity (subjectivity that comes from idealized discourse versus subjectivity that comes from discourse based on contextual reality). These categories of subjectivity are due to the subject not as something previously given, but as constituted in the enunciation, that is, in the discursive and symbolic scope (Lacan, 1949; Pêcheux & Orlandi, 1995), related to the discursive linguistic process.

The theory of Discourse Analysis (Pêcheux & Orlandi, 1995) discerns ideological effects (such as the transparency of language, the universality of meanings, categorizations of meanings and emotions), as ways of discriminating between what is individual and universalizing or generalizing subjectivity through fluid discourses that give a liquid aspect to modernization (Bauman, 2000; Lee, 2005). Intelligent systems provide instantaneity and a collective memory, constructing the image (subjectivity) as something that goes beyond the experience lived by the subject.

Artificial intelligence presents individuals with knowledge that is not obtained through the subjects' direct perception (visually or by experiencing reality) (Lacan, 1966; Monte-Serrat & Tfouni, 2010, pp. 57–58). The "knowledge" offered by AI to the user is distant from the contextual reality experienced by the individual and the latter's decisions and emotions, therefore, are rooted in the information previously offered by AI. The users interacting with the AI support their emotions and decisions not from a knowledge of a reality experienced by the individuals themselves (Monte-Serrat & Cattani, 2023), but from a reality idealized and generalized given by the AI tool.

Predictability and measurability of subjectivity/emotion through artificial intelligence, AI, have made use of (frozen/generic) categories of emotions. The optimization of AI tools in the assessment of emotions will be achieved when intelligent systems are able to consider that the subject is not something previously given (frozen or idealized category), but the subject (along with his emotions) is an effect of the discourse between interlocutors. In this way, there is a "rupture" in the conception of subjectivity, as either it is seen as something idealized in categories, or it is seen as something that depends on the dynamics of the cognitive linguistic process.

This rupture in the conception of subjectivity for application in AI tools has an important effect on the discursive dimension. Through Machine Learning tools, systems assimilate data (frozen, ideally categorized) instead of assimilating the individual's emotional reactions in relation to their environment. From the perspective of the individual as a user of an AI tool, they will have their subjectivity/emotion or reaction influenced by a tool that offers "automatic" knowledge (processed by the machine) of a given reality.

The subject's decision-making, when reacting to knowledge idealized by the machine, can lead to worrying consequences, such as unethical, antisocial decision-making or can even lead the individual to the decision to eliminate their own life.

Another effect of the rupture in the conception of subjectivity for application in AI tools is related to the diversity of AI hallucinations. According to Mohit Sewak (2024), AI has no imagination but presents probabilistic errors that interfere with the cognition of the user who interacts with it. Intelligent systems disseminate information that is not based on received information or the real world, which is equivalent to human invention or imagination, which can generate disastrous human reactions such as depression, suicide, committing crimes, unethical attitudes and so on. Sewak (2024) lists some AI hallucinations: ignoring or contradicting data provided by the user, for example, memory failure or denial of basic facts; distorting input data; presenting a lack of fidelity to the source, adding facts; inventing facts or events out of thin air; and generating false information.

3.6 Artificial Intelligence in Psychology in a Constituent Structure of Real-Valued Functions: Language, Subject and Body

Considering the search for a structure of real-valued functions that brings consistency of human cognition to intelligent systems and corrects hallucinations (which cannot be confused with bugs to be fixed), we propose the understanding that language, subject and body are connected through the cognitive linguistic process (which has two fronts: the logical front and the axiomatic/contextual front) (Monte-Serrat & Cattani, 2021). The formation of subjectivity, emotions and decision-making has deep causes laid down in the foundations of language and cognition. It is from this structure of the cognitive linguistic process that we can build ethical and consistent intelligent systems. Although unraveling hallucinations is a complex task, we suggest discarding the surface complexities of language and cognition to consider a basic and simple path to improving technology – the path revealed by the fundamental and universal structure of the cognitive linguistic process with its logical and axiomatic fronts redefining the capabilities of AI and its impact on users' lives.

We seek to change the paradigm to reflect on the design of intelligent systems under the conception that language and cognition are a dynamic process and this needs to be present in the core algorithm of AI. It's about rethinking the conditions under which AI is designed and what can be achieved with this different approach. We suggest that the legitimization of the use of the dynamics of the cognitive linguistic process in AI comes from the structural relationship that its two fronts (axiomatic and logical) guarantee the consistency of human cognition and decision-making. How to describe this universal structure in the algorithmic core so that intelligent systems are successful in avoiding bugs and hallucinations?

Sadegh-Zadeh et al. (2024) suggest neural remodeling and investigation of plasticity of artificial neural networks with a focus on learning processes by examining regression and classification problems to improve performance through iterative learning and optimization. Monte-Serrat and Cattani (2024) describe some research related to the integration of physical and cybernetic systems aimed at introducing new functionalities to modify the configuration of autonomous driving vehicles, since it has been observed that the vehicle's driving behavior is subject to respond differently than the driver expects, causing accidents. The authors argue that knowledge of the structure of the cognitive linguistic process dispels uncertainties in the black box of new technologies, enabling coherence in decision-making carried out by cognitive computing.

Khan and Ishrat (2024), when describing challenges and suggesting solutions in embodied Artificial Intelligence, explain that this type of AI interacts with the environment, as it results from the conversion of advanced computing with physical robotics. The authors state that embodied AI differs from traditional AI, which focuses on autonomous tasks. Monte-Serrat and Cattani (2024), and Khan and Ishrat (2024) agree that the challenges of embodied AI lie in the integration of sensors into real-time data processing, highlighting that decision-making arising from the use of AI entails concerns regarding safety and ethics.

Shiv interviewed by Abrahams (Shiv & Abrahams, 2020) states that the emotional brain depends on the individual's mindset, which can tend towards risk-averse behaviors or risk-tolerant behaviors. Shiv assures that emotion and motivation shape the formation of decisions; that is, our decisions, our behaviors are unconsciously shaped by the emotional system of the brain, and this is the fundamental premise of neuroscience and communication. This perspective is important because it corroborates the idea that reason is not enough for decision-making but depends on other elements arising from the environment. The way the brain (cognitive linguistic process) works is linked to instinctive brain systems, shaping decisions in the end.

Intelligent systems are not restricted to performing repetitive tasks, as they are equipped with logical reasoning and decision-making capacity. In this case, their algorithms rely on predefined rules that represent reality to unite thought, perception and action so that they perform tasks or make decisions autonomously. This intelligence is something limited and specific to certain tasks, which cannot be confused with human consciousness, which involves language, subjectivity and the body. Consciousness is the state of being aware, especially of something within oneself or of an external object, state or fact. Conscious AI must consider an ethical and socially responsible approach because of its potential to transform the lives and decisions of individual users of intelligent systems (Monte-Serrat & Cattani, 2023). What was once treated as a black box can now be understood considering the cognitive linguistic process, whose structure is universal, permeating humans and machines.

These conjectures lead us to conclude that real-valued functions are not found in the logical feature of the cognitive linguistic process, but are found in the axiomatic feature, which is linked to the environment (Monte-Serrat, 2021; Monte-Serrat & Cattani, 2024). Palacios (2024) writes about "Intertheory Relations in Physics" to show that the idea of science that establishes a logical structure to reduce studied phenomena has not been sufficient and shows the need to use infinite limits to explain symmetry-breaking phenomena. The author argues that the subsumption of models to the field of experience correlates these models to structures that satisfy fundamental laws, encompassing the field of experience. She also argues that reductions in physics normally have a "local" character, that is, of models of a single system. The author suggests that there is a structural relationship between theories to be compared, but also between empirical facts on which theories can describe real systems. Mental states captured from physical states are represented differently in finite systems. This conception is in line with the conception that there may be an alternative position regarding the logical reduction of mental states. Nowadays, quantum mechanics is being applied to intelligent systems under the thesis that everything is, ultimately, made up of the same fundamental physical entities.

3.7 Linguistic Cognitive Process as a Dynamical System

Human language is linked to the human cognitive linguistic system, which is equipped with subsystems that carry stimuli to the central nervous system (Copstead & Banasik, 2013; Monte-Serrat & Cattani, 2021). Conway (2020) discusses the learning that occurs with visual-motor patterns; auditory language-like material; non-linguistic auditory input, such as tones or musical timbre sequences; letter sequences; visual forms and tactile input. As a dynamic system, the cognitive linguistic process undergoes changes over time. The stimulus captured by the subsystem (tactile, gustatory, auditory, visual), upon reaching the central nervous system, is organized rationally so that it becomes something intelligible. Considering that reality is not governed only by deterministic laws, at a quantum level the laws of physics are also considered probabilistic in relation to a given instant in time. Conway (2020) speculates how the brain learns environmental structure and suggests fundamental principles for understanding neurocognitive mechanisms. The author reviews research on this subject, showing two sets of associated neurocognitive mechanisms that underlie learning, one consisting of perceptual plasticity of the stimuli encountered and the other dependent on attention that integrates global patterns over time.

Understood as a dynamic system, the cognitive linguistic process allows for the possibility that the real value matrix can be represented by multiscale models. According to Palacios (2024), scientific modeling that requires the appeal to characteristics and properties of different mesoscale levels admits that the world is divided into distinct levels (microscopic and macroscopic), and that the higher level (phenomenological) can be derived from the next lower level (microscopic). Palacios states that multiscale models are useful in modeling interdisciplinary systems.

Other possibilities focus on the real-valued functions of intelligent systems optimized according to quantum theory. Quantum physics has its foundations in the study of energy at the most fundamental level (electrons and photons) that acts on all scales. Extremely small objects, according to physics, can simultaneously present characteristics of waves and particles (wave-particle duality). Quantum physics is intended to explain the reactions between particles, as well as the forces with which these particles interact. Once accepted that language, subject and body are connected through the cognitive linguistic process, and that subjectivity/consciousness, emotions and decision-making have their origin in the foundations of language and cognition, we discuss the question posed by Ferrie (2024) on whether quantum physics provides consciousness. As we explained in Section 3.3, subjectivity, consciousness and symbolic representation are essentially human. This does not prevent a new science of consciousness for AI from being developed to imitate human consciousness, even if it only superficially imitates the interaction between the two fronts of the cognitive linguistic process: the logical feature with the axiomatic (environment) feature.

3.8 Conclusion

In this chapter we exposed the universal structure of language according to the fundamental theory of neurolinguistics, showing that the human brain dynamics to form knowledge and lead to decision-making are structurally the same as those of intelligent systems. We also show that Artificial Intelligence in Psychology which works with categories of emotions can incur errors in its predictions, since human emotions depend not only on logical categorization, but also on value operations linked to the context of the individual's reality. The complexity of emotions is approached in the light of psychology, linguistics and psychoanalysis, clarifying that emotions are subjective and that the subject and body must be considered by Artificial Psychology. In this case, we propose an approach to language/cognition as a dynamic system with two fronts, one logical and the other axiomatic/contextual. The first consists of the logical organization of stimuli so that they can be understood. The second is linked to functions with values captured from the environment. This conception of the "core" of intelligence, whether human or machine, is intended to assist in the design and use of intelligent Artificial Psychology systems, making both developers and users aware that there may be interference in cognition, decision-making and emotions (addiction, emotional involvement, depression), which entails the primordial need to rethink Artificial Psychology considering ethical principles.

The application of Artificial Intelligence in Psychology to intelligent systems will probably increase user addiction and dependence on interacting with practically magical tools. The reason for the intensification of this user dependence on AI stems from the phenomenon that the user "feels seen". The algorithm trained to make suggestions according to the user's tastes awakens an enchantment in the individual and an obsession that ends up driving their choices and decision-making.

However perfected and like humans, both in decision-making and in the expression of emotions, intelligent systems must be framed in the warning that Nzongo (2024) makes: although technology is a primary element in many social issues, its factors cannot take precedence over AI's impacts on social, ethical and political issues. Recommender systems change the user's choices and decisions, which can lead them to become addicted to artificial intelligence technology, preventing them from interacting socially. This example given by Nzongo (2024) shows that intelligent tools cannot be developed only according to stakeholders' preferences, but rather according to what users want and need. Monte-Serrat and Cattani (2023) show that designers are those who translate human needs into the core of the intelligent system that, subsequently, will interfere with users' emotions and decision-making. What would the future of society be like if Artificial Psychology were not aligned with ethical principles? Chaos.

References

Althusser, L. (2010). Ideology and ideological state apparatuses (notes towards an investigation). In M. G. Durham & D. M. Kellner (Eds.), *Cultural theory: An anthology* (pp. 204–222). Wiley-Blackwell.

Araújo, I. L. (2004). Do signo ao discurso: introdução à filosofia da linguagem. Parábola.

Bauman, Z. (2000). *Liquid modernity*. Polity.

Conway, C. M. (2020). How does the brain learn environmental structure? Ten core principles for understanding the neurocognitive mechanisms of statistical learning. *Neuroscience & Biobehavioral Reviews, 111*, 139–149. https://doi.org/10.1016/j.neubiorev.2020.01.032

Copstead, L. E., & Banasik, J. (2013). *Pathophysiology* (5th ed.). Elsevier.

Detienne, M. (1969). Gernet (Louis) Anthropologie de la Grèce antique. *Archives de Sciences Sociales des Religions, 28*(1), 203-204.

Edelman, B. (1980). *La Practica Ideologica del Derecho*. Editorial Tecnos.

Elia, L. (2004). *O conceito de sujeito*. Jorge Zahar.

Elman, J. L. (1995). Language as a dynamical system. In R. F. Port & T. van Gelder (Eds.), *Mind as motion: Explorations in the dynamics of cognition* (pp. 195–223). MIT Press.

Ferrie, C. (2024, September 29). Does quantum physics give us consciousness? *Medium*. https://csferrie.medium.com/does-quantum-physics-give-us-consciousness-08a2ab965495

Haroche, C. (1984). *Faire dire, vouloir dire: la détermination et la désambiguïsation dans la grammaire* (Vol. 17). Presses Univ. Septentrion.(original book)

Ildefonse, F. (2012). L'agalma et le dieu. Retour sur le dossier platonicien. In C. M. Carastro (Ed.), *Agalma ou les figurations de l'invisible. Approches comparées* (Conference proceedings, 13–14 February 2012, Paris, INHA, EHESS).

Kelso, J. A. S., Mandell, A. J., & Shlesinger, M. F. (1988). *Dynamic patterns: The self-organization of brain and behavior*. World Scientific.

Khan, W., & Ishrat, M. (2024). Embracing the future: Navigating the challenges and solutions in embodied artificial intelligence. In P. Raj, A. Rocha, S. P. Singh, P. K. Dutta, & B. S. Vadivazhagan (Eds.), *Building embodied AI systems: The agents, the architecture principles, challenges, and application domains* (Lecture Notes in Networks and Systems, Vol. 14). Springer. https://doi.org/10.1007/978-3-031-68256-8_13

Lacan, J. (1949). Le stade du miroir comme formateur de la fonction du Je telle qu'elle nous est révélée dans l'expérience psychanalytique. *Revue Française de Psychanalyse*, *13*, 449–455.

Lacan, J. (1998). O sujeito e o outro (I): A alienação. In J. Lacan, *O seminário: Livro 11 – Os quatro conceitos fundamentais da psicanálise*. Jorge Zahar. (Original work published 1964)

Lacan, J. (1966). Propos sur la causalité psychique. In *Écrits* (Vol. 1). Éditions du Seuil.

Lacan, J. (2011). The seminar of Jacques Lacan: Book V: The formations of the unconscious: 1957-1958.

Lagazzy, S. (1988). *O desafio de dizer não*. Pontes.

Lee, R. (2005). Bauman, liquid modernity and dilemmas of development. *Thesis Eleven*, *83*(1), 61–77. https://doi.org/10.1177/0725513605050511

Le Gaufey, G. (1998). *El lazo especular: Un estudio traversero de la unidad imaginaria*. Edelp SA.

Miaille, M. (1979). *Uma introdução crítica ao direito*. Moraes Editores.

Monte-Serrat, D. (2012). *Literacy and legal discourse* (Doctoral dissertation, University of São Paulo). https://doi.org/10.11606/T.59.2013.tde-14032013-104350

Monte-Serrat, D., & Belgacem, F. B. (2017). Subject and time movement in virtual reality. *International Journal of Research & Methodology in Social Science*, *3*(3), 19. https://zenodo.org/record/1322579

Monte-Serrat, D., Belgacem, F., & Maldonato, M. (2017). Decision making: The complexity of choice processes. *International Journal of Research & Methodology in Social Science*, *3*(4), 22–30.

Monte-Serrat, D. (2021). Operating language value structures in intelligent systems. *Advanced Mathematical Models & Applications*, *6*(1). http://jomardpublishing.com/UploadFiles/Files/journals/AMMAV1N1/v6n1/Monte-Serrat.pdf

Monte-Serrat, D., & Cattani, C. (2021). *The natural language for artificial intelligence*. Elsevier Academic Press.

Monte-Serrat, D., & Cattani, C. (2022). Applicability of emotion to intelligent systems. *Information Sciences Letters*, *11*, 1121–1129.

Monte-Serrat, D., & Cattani, C. (2023). Towards ethical AI: Mathematics influences human behavior. *Journal of Humanistic Mathematics*, *13*(2), 469–493.

Monte-Serrat, D., & Cattani, C. (2024). Unraveling what is at stake in the intelligence of autonomous cars. In *Machine learning for cyber physical systems: Advances and challenges* (pp. 195–217). Springer Nature Switzerland.

Monte-Serrat, D., & Tfouni, L. (2010). A dimensão política do sujeito na cadeia discursiva. *Linguagem & Sociedade*, *32*. https://periodicos.unb.br/index.php/les/article/view/10470/9225

Nzongo, F. (2024, March 18). AI needs design consciousness: My thoughts on ethics and human-centric design in AI advancements. *UX Collective*. https://uxdesign.cc/ai-needs-design-consciousness-1ee50288a957

Palacios, P. (2024). Intertheory relations in physics. In E. N. Zalta & U. Nodelman (Eds.), *The Stanford Encyclopedia of Philosophy* (Spring 2024 ed.). https://plato.stanford.edu/archives/spr2024/entries/physics-interrelate/

Pêcheux, M. (1975). *Les vérités de La Palice: Linguistique, sémantique, philosophie.* Maspero.

Pêcheux, M., & Orlandi, E. P. (1995). *Semântica e discurso: uma crítica à afirmação do óbvio*. Editora da UNICAMP.

Perlovsky, L. I., & Kozma, R. (2007). Neurodynamics of cognition and consciousness. In *Neurodynamics of cognition and consciousness* (pp. 1-8). Berlin, Heidelberg: Springer Berlin Heidelberg.

Roudinesco, E. (1998). *Dicionário de psicanálise.* Jorge Zahar.

Sadegh-Zadeh, S. A., Bahrami, M., Soleimani, O., & Ahmadi, S. (2024). Neural reshaping: The plasticity of the human brain and artificial intelligence in the learning process. *American Journal of Neurodegenerative Disease*, *13*(5), 34.

Scarantino, A., & Sousa, R. (2021). Emotion. In E. N. Zalta (Ed.), *The Stanford Encyclopedia of Philosophy* (Summer 2021 ed.). https://plato.stanford.edu/archives/sum2021/entries/emotion/

Sewak, M. (2024, December 10). Unmasking the surprising diversity of AI hallucinations. *Medium*. https://levelup.gitconnected.com/types-of-ai-hallucinations-e733e7b208ac

Shiv, B., & Abrahams, M. (2020, November 20). Feelings first: How emotion shapes our communication, decisions, and experiences. *Stanford GSB Insights*. https://www.gsb.stanford.edu/insights/feelings-first-how-emotion-shapes-communication-decisions-experiences

Thelen, E. (1988). Dynamical approaches to the development of behavior. In J. A. S. Kelso, M. F. Mandell, & M. F. Shlesinger (Eds.), *Dynamic patterns in complex systems* (pp. 348–369). World Scientific.

Turkle, S. (1984). *The second self: Computers and the human spirit.* MIT Press.

4 Decoding Emotions through EEG Signals

Nataša Kovač, Hojjatollah Farahani, and Peter Watson

4.1 Introduction

The study of emotion has long transcended the confines of introspection and self-report, demanding methods that can observe and interpret emotional responses in real time, directly from the body and brain. Among the most powerful tools available for such investigations is electroencephalography (EEG). This is a non-invasive technique that captures the brain's electrical activity with millisecond precision. EEG opens a unique window into the dynamic, embodied processes underlying human emotion, enabling researchers and technologists to track affective responses as they unfold across time (Li et al., 2022a; Lim et al., 2024). This chapter explores how EEG signals can be decoded to infer emotional states, laying the groundwork for applications in clinical psychology, adaptive technologies, and human-computer interaction (Kukhilava et al., 2025).

Unlike structural neuroimaging modalities such as CT or MRI, which provide detailed snapshots of brain anatomy, EEG offers a real-time recording of neural oscillations, i.e., fluctuations in electrical potential produced by synchronised neuronal activity. These oscillations vary across frequency bands (e.g., alpha, beta, gamma), and each band is associated with distinct cognitive and emotional functions. For example, alpha suppression is commonly linked to attentional engagement and affective arousal, while frontal asymmetries in alpha or beta activity have been correlated with emotional valence and motivational direction (Chen et al., 2019; Reznik & Allen, 2018). These neural rhythms serve as physiological substrates of emotion and are accessible in naturalistic settings, making EEG especially valuable for embodied emotion research (Lim et al., 2024).

What sets EEG apart in the context of emotion detection is its ability to reflect *both conscious and preconscious affective states*. Emotional changes that may not be explicitly recognised or reported by the individual can nonetheless manifest in EEG features such as event-related potentials (ERPs) or changes in power spectral density. This capacity to capture subtle, dynamic shifts makes EEG a preferred modality for applications requiring immediate emotional awareness, ranging from mental health monitoring to adaptive

DOI: 10.4324/9781003495123-4

user interfaces and affect-sensitive robotics (Gkintoni et al., 2025; Lim et al., 2024).

Another strength of EEG lies in its affordability, portability, and accessibility. While MRI scanners are confined to hospital environments, EEG headsets are increasingly available as wearable or even consumer-grade devices, enabling emotion tracking in the home, workplace, or classroom (Riedl et al., 2020). This democratisation of brain data paves the way for large-scale, personalised emotion monitoring systems that are embedded in everyday life (Kukhilava et al., 2025).

Decoding emotion from EEG is far from trivial. Raw EEG signals are notoriously noisy, affected by muscle activity, eye blinks, and environmental artefacts. The mapping between EEG features and emotional states is not one-to-one. It requires sophisticated preprocessing, feature engineering, and machine learning models to uncover patterns that are meaningful, generalisable, and interpretable (Thottempudi et al., 2024; Islam et al., 2016). The variability of EEG across individuals and contexts further complicates analysis, underscoring the importance of flexible models and rigorous cross-subject evaluation (Li et al., 2022a).

In recent years, advances in computational modelling have markedly improved our ability to analyse and classify emotion-related EEG signals. Deep architectures now learn *spatiotemporal features* directly from multi-channel time series (e.g., TSception), while *multimodal* designs fuse EEG with peripheral physiology (e.g., EDA/HRV) to capture complementary aspects of arousal and valence (Ding et al., 2022; Soufineyestani et al., 2021). The field has also coalesced around *larger datasets*, clearer *elicitation protocols*, and *benchmarking practices* that enable fairer comparisons across studies and populations (Li et al., 2022a; Kukhilava et al., 2025).

The enduring challenge in psychological science is moving beyond subjective self-report to achieve an objective measure of human affect. Within this pursuit, EEG has emerged as an indispensable tool. Leveraging its capacity for high-quality temporal resolution, EEG provides a direct, non-invasive glimpse into the brain's rapid electrical responses, capturing the neural dynamics that define our emotional lives. This synthesis integrates findings across psychological, neurological, and cognitive sciences to detail the mechanisms and promise of EEG-based emotion recognition (ER).

To decode emotion, we must first agree on its architecture. Psychologists offer two principal frameworks. While the discrete emotion model (e.g., classifying fear or happiness) remains conceptually intuitive, the dimensional model, specifically the axes of valence (the feeling of pleasantness or unpleasantness) and arousal (the degree of physiological activation), has proven most effective for computational analysis (Ozdemir et al., 2021). By converting the richness of subjective experience into measurable coordinates, this model enables the rigorous testing required for machine learning applications. Crucially, EEG's electrical measures are less susceptible to conscious control than behavioural cues, offering a unique opportunity to access a more authentic, unmediated neural signature of internal affective states (Li et al., 2022b).

The efforts to decode emotion are fundamentally grounded in neurological findings that link specific brain wave activity to emotional processes. Among the most robust and highly cited features is the phenomenon of prefrontal alpha asymmetry:

- The electrical power within the alpha frequency band (8–13 Hz) over the prefrontal cortex reliably correlates with emotional approach and withdrawal tendencies. Greater relative alpha activity (or reduced power) in the left frontal region is associated with positive valence and approach-related emotions, while the same relative pattern over the right frontal region signals negative valence and withdrawal (Gkintoni et al., 2025). This asymmetry forms the neurophysiological cornerstone of valence decoding.
- The intensity, or arousal component, is typically reflected in the power of faster oscillations, such as beta (14–30 Hz) and especially gamma (>30 Hz) waves. Higher power in these faster bands is often interpreted as increased cortical activation corresponding to states like excitement or anxiety (Li et al., 2022b).

These key features are extracted using advanced signal processing techniques like the computation of Differential Entropy, preparing the brain's subtle signals for deep analysis.

The final step in this integrative process belongs to cognitive science, where we employ computational models to build functional decoders. The advent of deep learning has been transformative, allowing complex architectures, like convolutional neural networks (CNNs), to automatically learn the non-linear mappings between raw or extracted EEG features and the defined emotional dimensions (Gkintoni et al., 2025). This shift moves the burden of feature selection to the algorithm, significantly improving classification accuracy beyond what traditional statistical methods can achieve.

The implications of reliably decoding emotion are profound, driving innovation across various sectors:

- Adaptive Technologies: The development of affective computing creates interfaces that adjust dynamically to the user's mood, from educational software that detects frustration to cars that monitor driver stress (Li et al., 2022b).
- Clinical Objectivity: In mental health, ER offers the potential for objective biomarkers, augmenting or refining the diagnosis and monitoring of affective disorders like depression and anxiety.

- Human Factors: Integrating emotion detection into passive brain-computer interfaces (BCIs) enhances safety and performance in high-stakes operational environments (Gkintoni et al., 2025).

The combination of robust psychological frameworks, identifiable neurological signatures, and powerful cognitive computational tools has firmly established EEG as a leading modality for emotion recognition. The path forward requires establishing generalised, subject-independent models to ensure this exciting research translates into reliable, real-world technologies.

4.2 The Role of EEG in Emotion Detection

The human brain, in its continuous interplay of cognition and physiology, generates patterns of electrical activity that reflect not only thoughts and perceptions but also emotional states. EEG provides a direct and temporally precise window into this activity, making it one of the most effective tools for real-time emotion detection. Unlike neuroimaging methods that rely on metabolic changes (e.g., fMRI or PET), EEG captures electrical fluctuations on the scalp produced by postsynaptic potentials in cortical neurons. These signals, typically recorded across 16 to 128 channels, enable researchers to observe how the brain responds to emotional stimuli on a millisecond scale. This is a level of granularity unmatched by other non-invasive techniques (Li et al., 2022a; Lim et al., 2024).

The use of EEG in emotion detection relies on a fundamental assumption: emotional processes influence neural oscillations in a consistent and detectable way. Emotions are not abstract or solely located in the so-called *limbic system*; they are embodied in brain-wide neural activity that EEG can record with excellent temporal resolution. Emotional responses involve changes in attention, arousal, and motivational systems, all of which impact EEG spectral content. For example, heightened arousal often associates with reduced alpha power in posterior regions, while approach-related emotions (such as joy or anger) are frequently connected with increased left frontal activity. This is a phenomenon widely recognised as *frontal alpha asymmetry* (Harmon-Jones & Gable, 2018; Allen et al., 2018).

These spectral and spatial EEG patterns are not random; they follow organised trajectories that relate to the emotional valence (positive or negative), arousal (intensity), and sometimes even the specific category of the emotion (such as fear, disgust, or surprise). Researchers have consistently shown that particular frequency bands (delta: 1–4 Hz, theta: 4–8 Hz, alpha: 8–13 Hz, beta: 13–30 Hz, and gamma: >30 Hz) are differently affected during emotionally charged events. For instance, increased theta activity has been observed in frontal midline areas during the encoding of emotional memories, while beta and gamma activities tend to rise with emotional engagement and focused attention (Zheng & Lu, 2015; Hajcak & Foti, 2020).

Beyond spectral analysis, EEG is also highly sensitive to ERPs, i.e., brief voltage fluctuations in the EEG signal that occur in response to specific sensory, cognitive, or emotional events. Certain ERP components, such as the P300, N400, and late positive potential (LPP), are modulated by emotional content. The LPP, in particular, is robustly enhanced by emotionally salient stimuli, reflecting sustained attention and affective processing. These potentials serve as reliable temporal markers of when emotional processing occurs and how it unfolds in the brain (Hajcak & Foti, 2020; Li et al., 2022a), allowing researchers to build a chronological map of affective reactivity.

One of the major strengths of EEG is its *ecological compatibility* with real-world emotion research. Portable EEG systems now make it feasible to measure emotion in naturalistic settings, such as classrooms, workplaces, or therapeutic environments, without compromising signal fidelity (Sabio et al., 2024). This makes EEG an ideal modality for embodied emotion studies where emotional experience is situated in context and influenced by bodily interactions, social dynamics, and environmental cues (Kukhilava et al., 2025). In contrast to laboratory-constrained methods like fMRI, EEG supports mobile, continuous emotion tracking, aligning well with the embodied and dynamic nature of affect.

EEG is also particularly well-suited for affective computing applications. In human–computer interaction, adaptive systems rely on real-time affect detection to personalise feedback, adjust difficulty levels, or shift dialogue tone. EEG can supply these systems with continuous input about the user's emotional state, creating a feedback loop between brain and machine. Such applications are being explored in fields as diverse as gaming, education, neurofeedback, and mental health support (Lim et al., 2024; Li et al., 2022a). This trajectory aligns with Artificial Psychology ('PsAIchology') as a framing for integrating AI with psychological science (Farahani et al., 2024). For example, biofeedback tools can use EEG markers of emotional distress to trigger relaxation protocols, while emotion-aware virtual tutors can respond to signs of boredom or frustration by altering instructional pace.

Despite its many advantages, EEG-based emotion detection also faces key challenges. The EEG signal is highly susceptible to artefacts from eye movements, muscle contractions, and even cable noise. Isolating emotion-specific components from such noise requires sophisticated preprocessing techniques and domain expertise (Islam et al., 2016). The mapping between EEG features and emotions is not universally fixed; it varies between individuals due to anatomical, psychological, and cultural differences. This necessitates the use of *personalised models* or transfer learning techniques that adapt classifiers to individual neural profiles (Kukhilava et al., 2025).

Another consideration is the *ambiguity of affective labels*. Emotions are often multidimensional and context-dependent, and the labels used in emotion datasets (such as happy or sad) may not fully capture the nuanced emotional states participants experience. Some researchers have addressed this by adopting dimensional models of emotion, such as the *valence-arousal space*, which represent emotion as a point on a continuous 2D plane. EEG has shown promise in predicting these continuous values, especially when combining spectral, topographical, and temporal features (Li et al., 2022a; Lim et al., 2024).

In recent years, EEG research has also benefited from open datasets like DEAP, SEED, and DREAMER, which provide synchronised EEG recordings with validated emotional stimuli and ground-truth affect ratings (Koelstra et al., 2011; Zheng & Lu, 2015; Katsigiannis & Ramzan, 2017). These datasets have enabled researchers to benchmark algorithms, train deep learning models, and explore generalisability across users and sessions. Python libraries such as MNE-Python, PyEEG, and NeuroKit2 now allow seamless integration of EEG data processing, feature extraction, and machine learning pipelines, lowering the barrier for new researchers to enter the field (Gramfort et al., 2014; Makowski et al., 2021; Bao et al., 2011).

EEG stands at the forefront of emotion detection science, offering a powerful combination of *temporal precision, wearable accessibility,* and *neurophysiological richness*. By decoding emotional signatures embedded in electrical brain activity, EEG enables a deeply embodied view of emotion. As the field evolves, EEG will continue to play a central role in developing adaptive, responsive, and emotionally intelligent systems, while also deepening our scientific understanding of how emotions are encoded in the brain (Li et al., 2022a; Kukhilava et al., 2025).

4.3 EEG Data Acquisition and Preprocessing

The reliability of emotion detection through EEG hinges critically on the quality and consistency of data acquisition and preprocessing. EEG signals are inherently delicate, often buried under layers of noise, physiological artefacts, and environmental interferences. Thus, before any meaningful emotional patterns can be extracted or analysed, raw EEG recordings must undergo a rigorous and methodologically coherent preprocessing pipeline. This section delves into how EEG data are captured and the key steps required to prepare these data for emotion analysis, with a focus on reproducibility, transparency, and robustness in emotional computing applications (Keil et al., 2014; Picton et al., 2000).

EEG data acquisition begins with the placement of electrodes on the scalp, typically following the international 10–20 system or its high-density extensions like the 10–10 or 10–5 systems. These standardised placements ensure anatomical consistency across subjects, particularly over regions such as the prefrontal cortex, temporal lobes, and parietal areas, which are crucial in emotional processing (Alarcao & Fonseca, 2017; Coan & Allen, 2004; Davidson, 1998; Klem, 1999; Oostenveld & Praamstra, 2001; Jurcak et al., 2007). Emotionally salient activity is often found in frontal and temporal regions, making electrodes like F3, F4, F7, F8, and T7, T8 of particular interest. The number of electrodes used varies by study, ranging from 14 in portable consumer-grade headsets to 64 or even 128 channels in high-resolution research-grade systems.

Signal sampling rates typically range from 128 Hz in lightweight systems to 512 Hz or higher in clinical-grade setups. A higher sampling rate improves temporal resolution but increases the volume of data and computational complexity. To ensure clean recordings, electrode-skin impedance must be minimised, usually below 5 kΩ, which is achieved using conductive gels or saline-based electrodes. Subject preparation, including skin cleaning and minimising movement or blinking during recording, plays a substantial role in reducing contamination by artefacts (Hinrichs et al., 2020; Kappenman & Luck, 2010; Luca et al., 2021).

Once the raw EEG data are collected, the preprocessing phase begins. This step is crucial not only to remove noise but also to preserve emotion-relevant information embedded in subtle fluctuations of the signal. The first stage typically involves *bandpass filtering* to isolate frequencies of interest (commonly between 0.5 Hz and 45 Hz), removing slow drifts and high-frequency artefacts such as power line interference or muscle activity (EMG). Zero-phase Butterworth or FIR filters are often used to avoid phase distortions (Delorme & Makeig, 2004; Gramfort et al., 2013; Keil et al., 2014).

Artefact removal is another critical preprocessing step. Eye blinks, saccades, facial muscle activity, and body movements introduce strong artefacts into the EEG signal. Independent Component Analysis (ICA) is widely employed to separate these non-neural sources, allowing researchers to identify and remove components corresponding to artefacts without discarding entire epochs. In some cases, automated algorithms like artefact subspace reconstruction (ASR) or wavelet-based artefact detection are applied, especially in real-time or large-scale studies (Craik et al., 2019; Hyvärinen & Oja, 2000; Jung et al., 2000; Kothe & Makeig, 2013; Krishnaveni et al., 2006).

Epoching follows artefact rejection, where continuous EEG data are segmented into smaller time windows (e.g., 1 to 5 seconds) aligned with stimulus onset or participant response (Delorme & Makeig, 2004). These epochs are labelled based on emotional ground truth, which is often derived from standardised datasets (like DEAP or MAHNOB-HCI) or via real-time ratings using self-assessment manikins (SAM) or affective scales (Bradley & Lang, 1994; Koelstra et al., 2011; Soleymani et al., 2011). Epochs with residual noise or voltage fluctuations beyond physiological limits (e.g., $>\pm 100$ μV) are typically excluded from further analysis to maintain data integrity (Picton et al., 2000).

Baseline correction is also applied to each epoch, usually by subtracting the mean voltage in a pre-stimulus interval from the entire segment. This process eliminates slow voltage drifts and ensures that comparisons across trials reflect changes due to the emotional stimulus rather than background neural fluctuations. After baseline correction, signals may be re-referenced to improve signal-to-noise ratio and spatial resolution. Another essential step is *channel interpolation* for any bad electrodes identified during acquisition or cleaning. This ensures that spatial information is preserved across the scalp, especially when working with topographical mapping or spatially-aware machine learning models. Interpolation uses surrounding electrode values to estimate the signal at a faulty location without introducing bias (Perrin et al., 1989; Yao, 2001; Keil et al., 2014).

For studies involving *deep learning* or more computationally intensive pipelines, EEG signals are often transformed into frequency-domain or time-frequency representations. Techniques such as short-time Fourier transform (STFT), wavelet transform, or empirical mode decomposition (EMD) allow researchers to explore how emotional content modulates EEG activity across both time and frequency. These transformed features are particularly useful for capturing transient emotion dynamics that may not appear in raw time-domain signals (Cohen, 1995; Huang et al., 1998; Torrence & Compo, 1998; Craik et al., 2019).

Modern Python toolkits like MNE-Python (Gramfort et al., 2013), NeuroKit2, and PyEEG offer integrated functions for all these preprocessing steps. For example, with MNE, raw EEG data can be filtered, epoched, and cleaned using a few lines of code, enabling transparent and replicable pipelines. In real-world applications such as affective brain-computer interfaces (aBCIs) or mobile neurofeedback, real-time preprocessing is implemented using embedded signal processing routines and edge computing devices (Gramfort et al., 2013; Makowski et al., 2021; Bao et al, 2011).

Standardising preprocessing pipelines is crucial for replicability across emotion recognition studies. The growing availability of open preprocessing templates, such as those provided by the BIDS-EEG initiative, encourages methodological transparency and promotes reproducibility across labs and platforms. By publishing preprocessing code and metadata, researchers enable others to replicate findings, reanalyse datasets, or build upon existing work with confidence (Pernet et al., 2019).

In emotion research, preprocessing is more than a technical necessity. The emotions we seek to decode from EEG are embodied in complex, noisy, and transient brain activity. Preprocessing shapes how these signals are interpreted, which neural features are amplified or suppressed, and ultimately, which emotional insights emerge. Therefore, the preprocessing phase must be carried out with theoretical sensitivity, statistical rigour, and methodological transparency, ensuring that the neural echoes of emotion are heard as clearly and truthfully as possible (Keil et al., 2014; Suhaimi et al., 2020).

4.4 Feature Extraction from EEG Signals

The transition from raw EEG recordings to meaningful emotional interpretation is paved through the crucial stage of feature extraction. In essence, feature extraction distils the complex, multidimensional EEG signal into a manageable set of numerical representations that reflect the underlying neural patterns associated with different affective states. These features serve as the input for classifiers, neural networks, or other analytical models and profoundly influence the accuracy and interpretability of emotion detection systems. A well-structured feature extraction pipeline not only enhances predictive performance but also unveils neurophysiological insights into how emotions are embodied in brain activity (Jenke et al., 2014; Alarcão & Fonseca, 2017).

EEG signals are characterised by their rich temporal dynamics and frequency composition, making both time-domain and frequency-domain features valuable for emotion recognition. Time-domain features, such as mean amplitude, standard deviation, root mean square (RMS), zero-crossing rate, and Hjorth parameters (activity, mobility, and complexity), provide basic statistical summaries of the brain's electrical fluctuations. These features are relatively straightforward to compute and interpret (Hjorth, 1970), and often capture gross changes in arousal or attentional states. For example, higher standard deviation and RMS values have been associated with increased emotional arousal (Islam et al., 2021; Suhaimi et al., 2020).

More commonly, however, emotion recognition studies rely on frequency-domain features extracted through the Fourier Transform or more flexible approaches like wavelet decomposition. The EEG spectrum is traditionally divided into five bands: delta (0.5–4 Hz), theta (4–8 Hz), alpha (8–13 Hz), beta (13–30 Hz), and gamma (>30 Hz). Each band reflects distinct cognitive and emotional processes (Alarcão & Fonseca, 2017). For instance, increased alpha power is often associated with relaxed states, whereas beta and gamma activity are linked with emotional arousal and cognitive engagement. Emotional valence, particularly in frontal asymmetry paradigms, has been linked to differential alpha power between the left (F3) and right (F4) hemispheres (Davidson et al., 1990; Coan & Allen, 2004), where greater left frontal activation corresponds to positive emotions and right frontal activation to negative emotions.

In recent studies, power spectral density (PSD) values calculated for each frequency band and channel remain among the most widely used features for emotion detection. These values can be computed using Welch's method or multitaper spectral estimation, both offering robustness against noise and variability (Welch, 2003; Thomson, 1982). Features can be normalised per channel or expressed as relative power within each band to control for inter-subject variability.

Beyond these conventional spectral features, time-frequency representations have grown in popularity for capturing the dynamic nature of emotional responses. STFT, Continuous Wavelet Transform (CWT), and Hilbert-Huang Transform (HHT) are used to analyse how frequency content evolves (Cohen, 1995; Torrence & Compo, 1998; Huang et al., 1998). This approach is particularly powerful for detecting rapid shifts in emotional states triggered by stimuli, such as those found in real-time aBCIs. These time-frequency maps are often fed into convolutional neural networks (CNNs), where the network learns discriminative patterns without requiring explicit manual feature design (Schirrmeister et al., 2017; Bashivan et al., 2015).

Another promising set of features comes from nonlinear and entropy-based metrics that capture the complexity and irregularity of EEG signals. Features such as approximate entropy, sample entropy, permutation entropy, and fractal dimension have been used to differentiate between high and low arousal states, particularly in more spontaneous or naturalistic emotional settings (Pincus, 1991; Richman & Moorman, 2000; Bandt & Pompe, 2002; Higuchi, 1988; Katz, 1988). These measures are grounded in the idea that emotional experiences modulate the chaotic dynamics of neural activity and that emotional dysregulation, such as in anxiety or depression, often manifests in altered EEG complexity (Patel et al., 2021; Zuo et al., 2022).

Phase synchronisation and coherence features, particularly inter-hemispheric or cross-channel coherence, have also shown relevance. Emotional processing is often distributed across multiple brain regions, and these connectivity features capture how well different regions are communicating. High theta-band coherence between frontal and temporal lobes, for instance, has been linked to increased emotional intensity during video stimuli (Lachaux et al., 1999; Nolte et al., 2004; Jenke et al., 2014).

From a computational standpoint, feature selection is often performed to reduce dimensionality and prevent overfitting. Techniques such as mutual information analysis, recursive feature elimination, and principal component analysis (PCA) help identify the most informative features for classification (Guyon & Elisseeff, 2003; Peng et al., 2005; Jolliffe, 2005; Bishop, 2006). Dimensionality reduction also improves model generalisability, a key consideration when developing emotion recognition systems that must operate across individuals and contexts.

Python libraries like scipy.signal, pywt (for wavelets), mne-features, and NeuroKit2 facilitate robust feature extraction pipelines. For example, mne-features can generate dozens of statistical, spectral, and complexity-based features per channel with minimal coding. These libraries also support integration with machine learning frameworks such as scikit-learn, enabling seamless transitions from signal processing to model training (Virtanen et al., 2020; Lee et al., 2019; Gramfort et al., 2014; Makowski et al., 2021; Pedregosa et al., 2011).

It is important to note that feature extraction is not merely a mechanical step in the pipeline; it reflects theoretical assumptions about the neural underpinnings of emotion. For example, choosing to compute frontal alpha asymmetry as a key feature assumes that valence is localised in frontal circuits. Similarly, the use of wavelet-based features reflects an understanding of emotion as a time-evolving process (Davidson et al., 1990; Coan & Allen, 2004; Torrence & Compo, 1998). Thus, feature extraction should be theory-informed, empirically validated, and tailored to the specific emotion recognition context.

Extracting features from EEG signals for emotion detection is a delicate balance between signal fidelity, computational efficiency, and theoretical relevance. The extracted features serve as the neural signatures of emotion, enabling researchers and engineers to decode affective states with increasing accuracy and nuance. As the field advances, hybrid features combining spectral, temporal, spatial, and nonlinear dimensions are likely to become the standard, especially as machine learning algorithms grow more adept at handling multidimensional and multimodal data (Zheng & Lu, 2015; Craik et al., 2019; Suhaimi et al., 2020).

4.5 Machine Learning for EEG-Based Emotion Recognition

The integration of machine learning (ML) into EEG-based emotion recognition marks a pivotal advancement in affective computing and neuroscience. While traditional statistical techniques offered limited capabilities in deciphering the multifaceted and non-linear characteristics of brain signals, ML methods provide powerful tools capable of learning hidden patterns and generalising across subjects and emotional states. These models have catalysed progress in transforming EEG data from opaque waveforms into actionable emotional insights with practical applications in mental health monitoring, adaptive interfaces, and affect-sensitive systems (Torres et al., 2020). Comparable supervised pipelines are also used across psychological health domains, including prediction and classification of chronic pain outcomes (Kovač et al., 2025a). A complementary line of work uses calibrated regression to predict internal shame, with XGBoost performing best and distress tolerance emerging as the strongest predictor (Kovač et al., 2025b).

At the core of this process lies the transformation of EEG features into input vectors suitable for machine learning classifiers or regressors. The learning algorithms attempt to construct mappings from these feature vectors to emotional states, which are typically represented either categorically (e.g., happy, sad, angry, relaxed) or dimensionally (e.g., valence, arousal, dominance). Supervised learning remains the predominant paradigm, with models trained on labelled datasets such as DEAP, DREAMER, SEED, and AMIGOS (Koelstra et al., 2011; Katsigiannis & Ramzan, 2017; Zheng & Lu, 2015; Miranda-Correa et al., 2018). In these datasets, EEG recordings are synchronised with ground truth emotional labels derived from self-report questionnaires, facial expression analysis, or physiological markers. Classical ML algorithms such as Support Vector Machines (SVM), k-Nearest Neighbours (KNN), Random Forests (RF), and Logistic Regression (LR) have long served as reliable baselines due to their simplicity and interpretability (Zheng et al., 2017; Al-Nafjan et al., 2017). Among these, SVM is particularly effective in high-dimensional spaces and has shown consistent performance across binary and multiclass emotion classification tasks (Al-Nafjan et al., 2017). Related machine-learning frameworks have also been applied to affect-linked constructs beyond core emotions, such as love addiction, where features and explanations clarify predictive factors (Farahani et al., 2025).

With the exponential growth in EEG datasets and computational power, deep learning architectures have begun to outperform traditional models by autonomously learning feature hierarchies from raw or minimally processed signals. CNNs, originally designed for images, have been repurposed to handle time-frequency EEG representations such as spectrograms or wavelet transforms; compact architectures like EEGNet demonstrate strong performance while remaining lightweight (Lawhern et al., 2018). These networks excel at extracting spatial and temporal dependencies between EEG channels, particularly when fed 2D matrix inputs formed by stacking frequency bands across electrode locations (Topić & Russo, 2021).

Recurrent Neural Networks (RNNs) and their more stable variant, Long Short-Term Memory (LSTM) networks, are particularly well-suited for modelling temporal dynamics of emotional states. LSTMs capture long-range dependencies in EEG time series and have shown competitive results on valence/arousal recognition in DEAP and related corpora (Alhagry et al., 2017). For instance, LSTMs have demonstrated strong performance in modelling arousal fluctuations over several minutes, outperforming both CNNs and classical models in dynamic settings (Tripathi et al., 2017). Hybrid architectures combining CNN and LSTM layers are increasingly popular, offering a unified framework that captures both spatial and temporal patterns in EEG (Wang et al., 2022). These models are especially relevant for real-time emotion monitoring, such as in aBCIs, where accurate emotion decoding must occur continuously without delay.

Beyond supervised learning, unsupervised and semi-supervised approaches are gaining traction due to the inherent difficulty of acquiring large-scale, precisely labelled EEG data. Clustering algorithms like K-Means and Gaussian Mixture Models (GMMs) have been used to group EEG patterns without prior labelling, revealing latent affective structures. Autoencoders learn latent embeddings that can improve downstream classification or cross-modal fusion (Liu et al., 2016). More recently, autoencoders and generative adversarial networks (GANs) have been employed to learn latent feature embeddings and augment EEG datasets, addressing issues of class imbalance and data scarcity (Zhang et al., 2022; Kalashami et al., 2022).

An important consideration in EEG-based emotion recognition is the issue of individual variability. Brain responses to emotional stimuli vary significantly across individuals due to differences in personality, attention, fatigue, or even electrode placement. To address this, domain adaptation and transfer learning techniques are being introduced. Models trained on one subject or dataset are fine-tuned on a small portion of data from a new user, enabling better generalisation. Domain-adversarial training (DANN) encourages features that are discriminative for emotion yet invariant across subjects or sessions (Ganin et al., 2016), and EEG-specific variants such as BiDANN or contrastive alignment have shown cross-subject gains (Li et al., 2018; Shen et al., 2022).

Model evaluation is another key component of this workflow. Accuracy, precision, recall, F1-score, and Area Under the ROC Curve (AUC) are standard performance metrics. However, in emotion detection tasks involving imbalanced datasets (e.g., fewer instances of *disgust* or *fear*), metrics such as Matthews Correlation Coefficient (MCC) or Brier score offer more balanced assessments (Matthews, 1975; Brier, 1950; Chicco & Jurman, 2020). Cross-validation strategies, such as leave-one-subject-out (LOSO), are commonly used to ensure robust generalisation across individuals (Kunjan, 2021; Su et al., 2023).

From a Python implementation perspective, scikit-learn remains a widely used library for classical ML models (Pedregosa et al., 2011), while deep learning applications frequently rely on TensorFlow or PyTorch (Abadi et al., 2016; Paszke et al., 2019). For psychology-focused pipeline patterns and regression modelling in Python, see (Kovač et al., 2024). For EEG-specific tasks, libraries like MNE, braindecode, and DeepEEG provide streamlined functions for preprocessing, feature extraction, and training deep networks. For example, using braindecode, one can train a CNN to classify raw EEG trials with only a few lines of code, leveraging prebuilt architectures such as Deep4Net or EEGNet (Gramfort et al., 2013; Lawhern et al., 2018; Schirrmeister et al., 2017).

To illustrate this, consider a scenario where one aims to classify high vs. low arousal from EEG data recorded during emotional video viewing. After preprocessing (filtering, epoching), features such as alpha and beta band power are computed per channel. These features are then fed into an SVM or CNN classifier, which is trained using 10-fold cross-validation or LOSO. Accuracy scores and confusion matrices are computed, and misclassified trials are examined to refine feature selection or labelling strategies (Koelstra et al., 2011; Wang et al., 2022).

As emotion recognition systems mature, interpretability becomes increasingly critical, especially in clinical or high-stakes applications. Tools such as SHapley Additive exPlanations (SHAP) and Local Interpretable Model-Agnostic Explanations (LIME) are being adapted for EEG, helping researchers understand which features or channels contribute most to predictions (Lundberg & Lee, 2017; Ribeiro et al., 2016).

ML is a cornerstone of EEG-based emotion recognition, enabling the translation of neurophysiological signals into affective insights with ever-increasing fidelity. The field is rapidly advancing from static, offline classification to real-time, adaptive models embedded in wearable devices and interactive systems. As the datasets grow and methods evolve, the dream of emotionally intelligent machines interpreting our brainwaves in real-time edges closer to reality.

4.6 Case Studies and Experiments

In EEG-based emotion recognition, case studies and experimental applications provide the critical validation of theoretical models and technical advancements. These real-world scenarios bridge the gap between algorithmic potential and practical implementation, offering insights not only into the performance of machine learning pipelines but also into user variability, ecological validity, and system usability.

One illustrative case study centres around an experiment designed to classify emotional arousal levels during multimedia consumption. Participants were presented with a curated series of video clips, each standardised for emotional content based on valence and arousal scores from the DEAP dataset (Koelstra et al., 2011). While viewing these clips, EEG signals were captured using a 32-channel headset following the international 10–20 system. The goal was to distinguish between high-arousal and low-arousal responses using machine learning techniques.

We recreated a classic EEG-emotion experiment using our 32-channel, four-band dataset. Each 1-second EEG epoch was converted to power in theta (4–7 Hz), alpha (8–13 Hz), beta (14–30 Hz), and gamma (30–45 Hz). We then compared high-arousal vs. low-arousal moments, trained several models, and produced visualisations that make the results easy to read, even without a signal-processing background. The case study begins with a simple question: can we tell, from second-by-second EEG activity, whether a person is in a relatively calm or a relatively activated state while watching emotionally charged material? To make that question answerable, we reduced each 1-second EEG segment into four familiar frequency bands, theta, alpha, beta and gamma, over thirty-two electrodes laid out on the scalp. These band powers give us a compact picture of how strongly different rhythms were expressed at different locations. The rest of the analysis is an attempt to make that picture visible and trustworthy, and to show that the patterns it contains are not only statistically useful but also physiologically sensible.

A good place to start is with the overview of the data. The paired heatmaps in Figure 4.1 arrange channels on the horizontal axis and the four bands on the vertical axis, with colour representing power.

Panel A summarises low-arousal moments, while panel B summarises high-arousal moments. Even without learning any model, the contrast is striking. On the high-arousal side, alpha power darkens across many posterior channels, a signature of alpha suppression that often accompanies engagement and attention. At the same time, beta and gamma brighten, especially over frontal and central electrodes, hinting at increased sensorimotor and cognitive activity. These heatmaps set expectations for everything that follows: if a classifier succeeds later, it is not doing so by mysterious tricks; it is reading the same large-scale shifts your eye can already see in this summary. If you

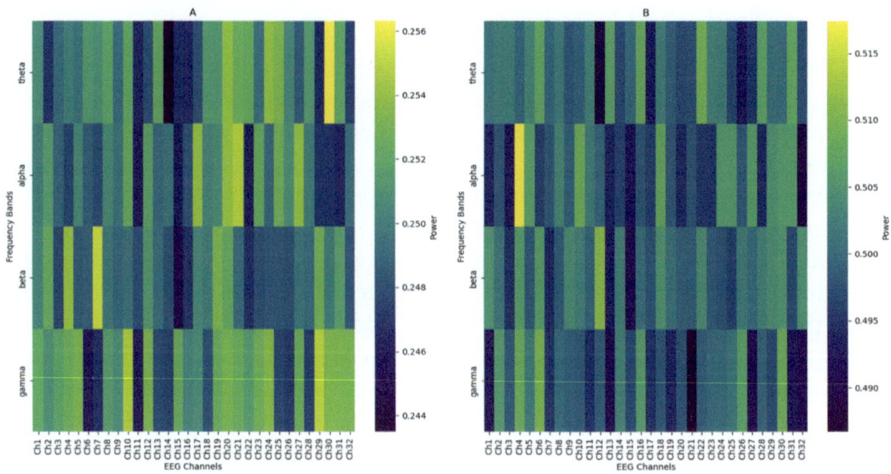

Figure 4.1 Channel-by-band power overview (low vs. high arousal).

want to compute those band-power summaries from raw epochs yourself, this tiny helper does it with Welch spectra and a clean interface:

```
import numpy as np
from scipy.signal import welch

BANDS = {"theta": (4, 7), "alpha": (8, 13), "beta": (14, 30),
"gamma": (30, 45)}

def bandpowers(epoch, sfreq, bands=BANDS):
    f, Pxx = welch(epoch, fs=sfreq, nperseg=min(256, epoch.sha
pe[-1]), axis=-1)
    out = {}
    for name, (lo, hi) in bands.items():
        idx = (f >= lo) & (f <= hi)
         out[name] = Pxx[..., idx].mean(-1) # mean power per
channel
    return out
```

Having a visual intuition is reassuring, but we still need to quantify how well band-power patterns separate the two states. The ROC curve in Figure 4.2 takes all test epochs and asks how confidently a standard SVM assigns them to high arousal as the decision threshold is swept from conservative to liberal.

The steadily rising blue curve and the area under it (AUC = 0.84) indicate that, across many thresholds, the model is able to rank genuine high-arousal epochs above low-arousal ones much more often than by chance.

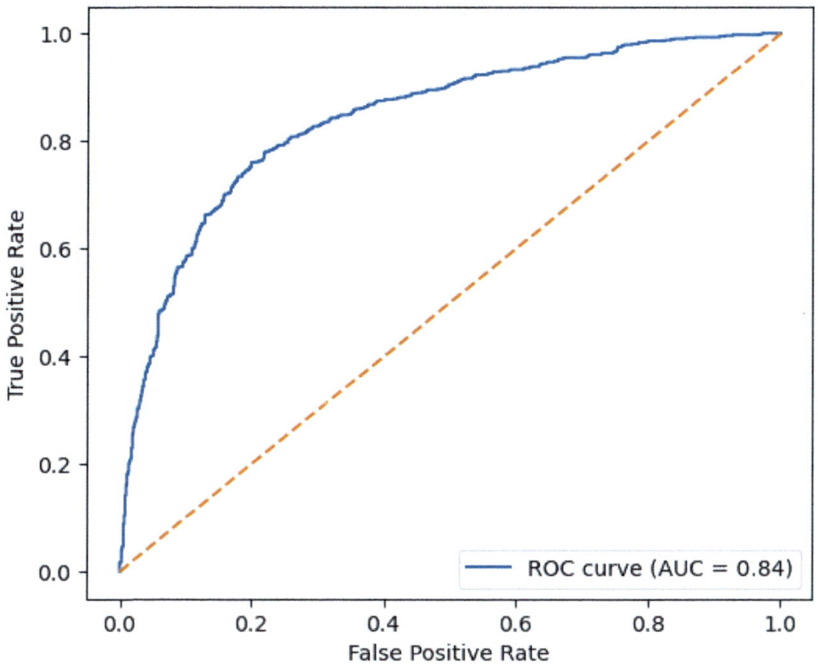

Figure 4.2 ROC curve of the SVM arousal classifier.

In practical terms, if we had to choose a single operating point, most errors would likely occur near the decision boundary rather than through gross misclassifications. Below is the minimal evaluation setup we used to obtain that ROC/AUC and the confusion counts; it accepts any scikit-learn classifier and ensures the bookkeeping remains streamlined.

```
from sklearn.metrics import roc_curve, auc, confusion_matrix

def evaluate_classifier(clf, X_test, y_test):
    scores = clf.predict_proba(X_test)[:, 1] if hasattr(clf,
"predict_proba") else clf.decision_function(X_test)
    fpr, tpr, _ = roc_curve(y_test, scores)
    cm = confusion_matrix(y_test, (scores >= 0.5).astype(int))
    return (fpr, tpr, auc(fpr, tpr)), cm
```

The confusion matrix in Figure 4.3 makes this concrete. Each cell counts how many test epochs fall into that true–predicted pairing.

The diagonal cells dominate, which reflects what accuracy looks like, but the off-diagonal cells are still informative: there are marginally more low-arousal epochs mistaken as high than the other way round. This asymmetry

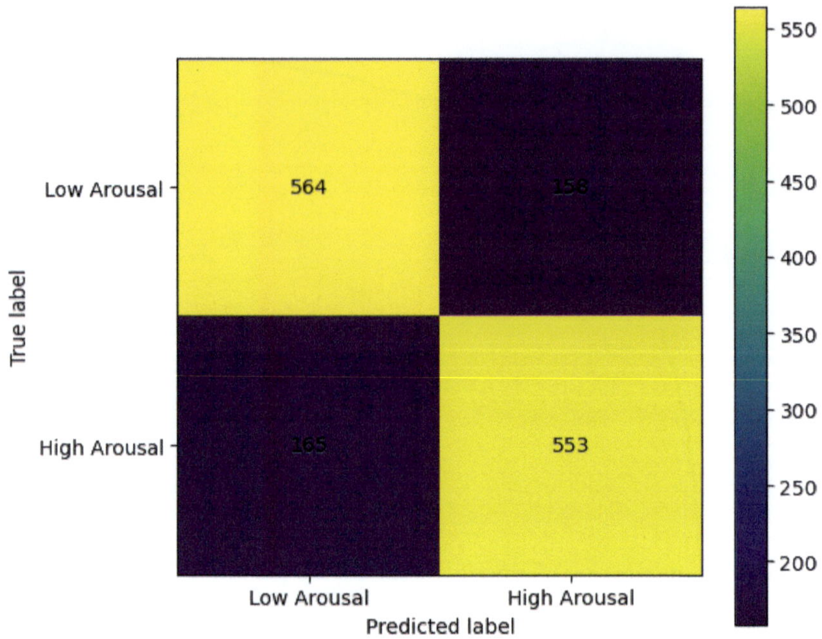

Figure 4.3 Confusion matrix at 0.5 decision threshold.

aligns with the physiology. High arousal has a distinct, stereotyped signature (lower alpha, higher beta/gamma), so the classifier tends to be fairly confident when it detects it. Low arousal is a wider, quieter category; some *calm* epochs still exhibit small bursts of frontal beta or residual occipital alpha suppression, and those can be pushed over the threshold. Readers seeking a rule of thumb can view this matrix as one: when features shift towards the *engaged* side, the model is likely to err by classing it as high arousal.

After establishing that classification is feasible, we can return to the question of *where* on the head these differences live. The band-by-region difference map in Figure 4.4 computes the mean power in each lobe-level region and then subtracts Low from High.

Negative values (blue) therefore indicate *less power in high arousal states*, while positive values (yellow) signify *more*. The pattern aligns with the heatmaps but emphasises an anatomical perspective. Alpha activity decreases notably in the parietal–occipital region during high arousal, reflecting reduced idling in visual areas, whereas beta and gamma increase fronto-centrally, consistent with motor preparation and executive control. This figure's aim is not to impress with colour but to anchor the machine-learning narrative in a map familiar to neuroscientists. The small utility below demonstrates how

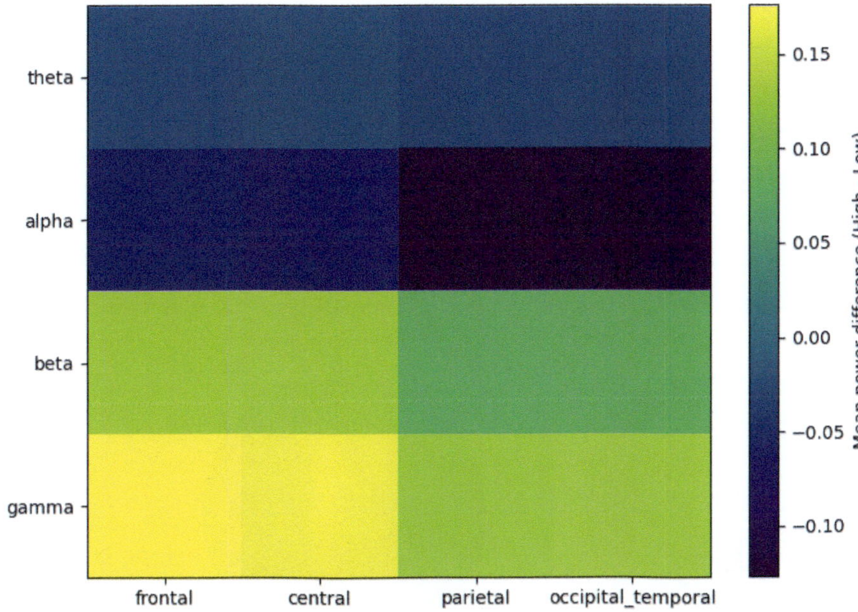

Figure 4.4 Band-by-region differences (High – Low).

these region averages are derived once you provide a mapping from channels to regions.

```
import pandas as pd

def regional_difference(df, region_map, bands=("theta","alpha",
"beta","gamma")):
    df = df.copy()
    df["Region"] = df["Channel"].map(region_map)
   means = df.groupby(["Label","Region","Band"])["Power"].mea
n().unstack("Label")
    # columns assumed {0: Low, 1: High}
    delta = (means[1] - means[0]).unstack("Region")
    return delta.loc[list(bands)]
```

Topographic plots offer the most immediate, intuitive view of those spatial shifts. In Figure 4.5, each scalp disk shows the interpolated distribution of alpha or beta power across electrodes for the two conditions.

When readers look first at the pair of alpha maps, they should notice how high-arousal alpha evacuates the back of the head relative to low arousal.

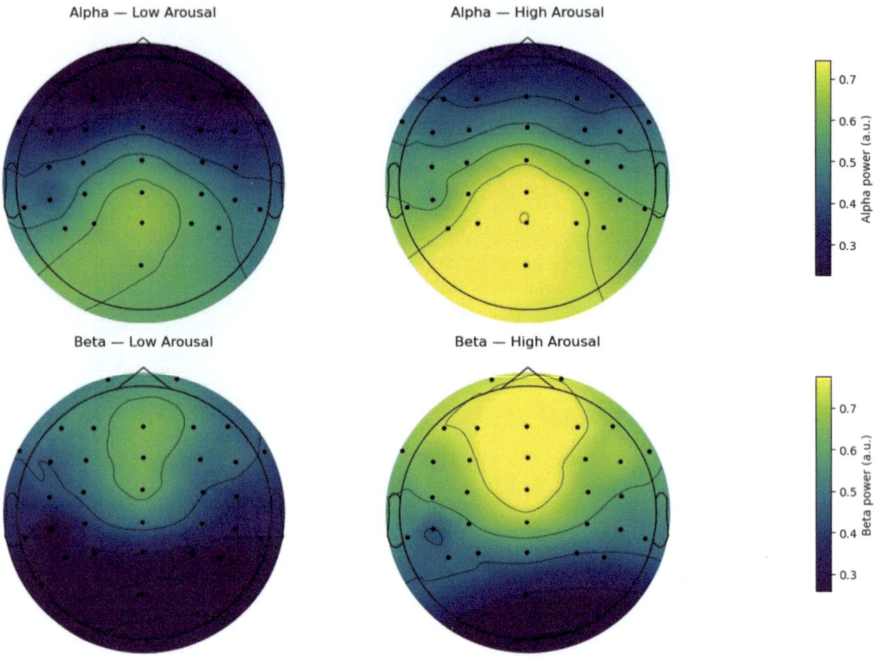

Figure 4.5 Topographic maps of band power by condition.

When they shift to the beta maps, they should see the opposite in the midline fronto-central zone: high arousal pulls the colours upward there. These plots let a non-technical reader verify with a glance that the classifier did not invent distinctions; it leaned on real, spatially coherent changes. Under the hood, we simply average per-condition band powers by channel; this helper prepares those arrays for plotting with MNE's plot_topomap:

```
def topomap_arrays(df, band):
    sub = df[df["Band"] == band]
    low = sub[sub["Label"] == 0].groupby("Channel")["Power"].
mean()
   high = sub[sub["Label"] == 1].groupby("Channel")["Power"].
mean()
    return {"low": low, "high": high}
```

Because deep networks are often used on image-like representations of EEG, it is fair to ask what a convolutional model *sees*. The panel in Figure 4.6 averages the first-layer feature maps of a small CNN separately for high- and low-arousal epochs.

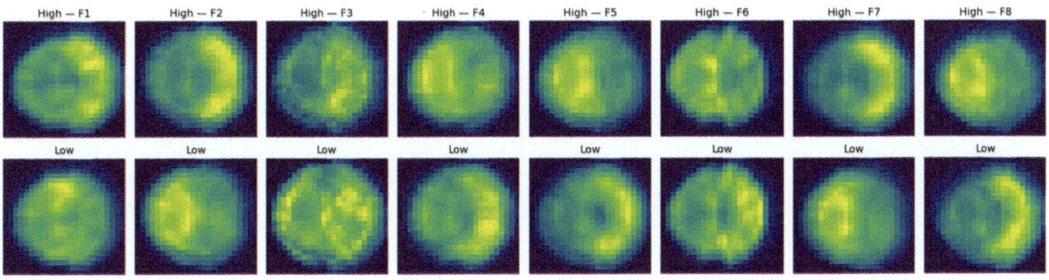

Figure 4.6 First-layer CNN feature maps (High vs. Low).

You can think of these maps as the network's primitive detectors. Several filters light up the back of the head in a way that echoes alpha suppression; others accentuate the anterior band-power texture that increases in high arousal. The point of the figure is not that readers should interpret every filter, but that the network's earliest computations are already aligned with the scalp physiology established above. When a model's internals rhyme with domain knowledge, confidence in its outputs grows. For that, we pull activations like this:

```
import tensorflow as tf

def first_layer_activations(model, X, y, layer_name="conv1"):
    probe = tf.keras.Model(model.input, model.get_layer(layer_
name).output)
    A = probe.predict(X, verbose=0)        # (N,H,W,C)
    A_high = A[y == 1].mean(axis=0)        # (H,W,C)
    A_low = A[y == 0].mean(axis=0)
    return A_low, A_high
```

Temporal behaviour is the next dimension a reader will care about. Real experiences are not random shuffles of calm and excitement; they have stretches and transitions. In Figure 4.7, we plot a simple, real-time tracker: a sliding-window logistic regression that updates every second.

The blue line shows the ground-truth label toggling between 0 and 1; the orange line shows the model's probability of high arousal. The eye should be drawn to the gentle, short delays when the blue step flips. Those lags are expected because the window needs a few samples of the new state before its average features tilt decisively; once it has them, the orange line hugs the plateau. This kind of behaviour is exactly what one wants from a feedback display or a biofeedback loop: calm, stable estimates that change decisively but not erratically. The behaviour is produced by a tiny online routine like this:

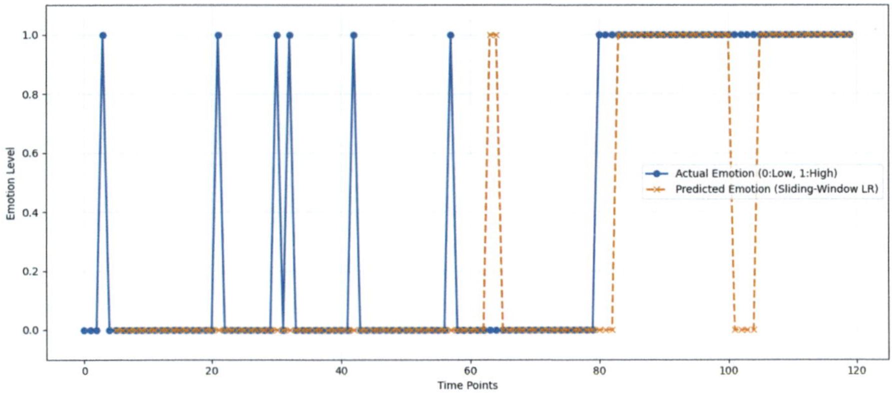

Figure 4.7 Within-subject real-time tracking (sliding-window LR).

```
from sklearn.linear_model import SGDClassifier

def sliding_tracker(X_seq, y_seq, win=8, lr=1e-3):
    clf = SGDClassifier(loss="log_loss", learning_rate="optimal",
eta0=lr, random_state=0)
    probs = []
    for t in range(len(X_seq)):
        start = max(0, t - win + 1)
        Xw, yw = X_seq[start:t+1], y_seq[start:t+1]
        if t == 0:          # initialize classes
          clf.partial_fit([X_seq[t]], [y_seq[t]], classes=[0,1])
        else:
          clf.partial_fit(Xw, yw) # refine with current window
        p = 1 / (1 + np.exp(-clf.decision_function([X_seq[t]]
)[0]))
        probs.append(0.7*probs[-1] + 0.3*p if probs else p)
    return np.array(probs)
```

A second tracking view, Figure 4.8, tells a different but equally important story. Here, the orange curve comes from an echo-state network trained to generalise across people, then applied to a new subject.

The curve floats between about 0.5 and 0.8 and only occasionally approaches the extremes. This does not mean the model has failed. It is signalling *uncertainty* born of domain shift: the new subject's power distributions and noise profile differ from those seen in training, so the network hedges. Interpreting this figure teaches a valuable practical lesson. When models trained on group data are deployed to a fresh user, they may require brief calibration, reduced smoothing, or a few minutes of fine-tuning to regain the crisp step-like behaviour of the simpler within-subject tracker. In a tutorial, this figure earns its place precisely because the orange line does *not*

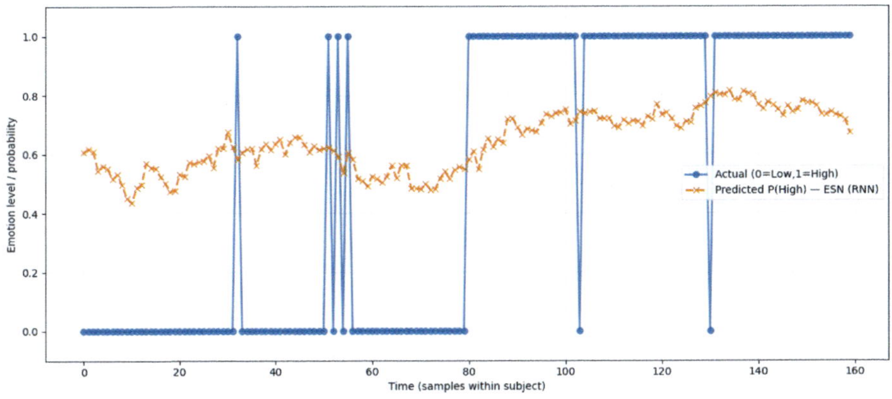

Figure 4.8 Cross-subject real-time tracking (echo-state network).

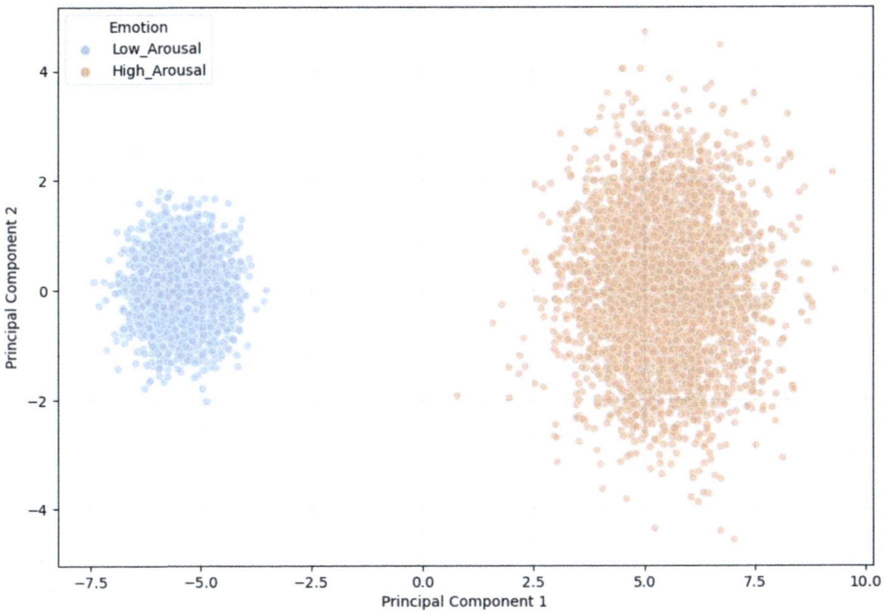

Figure 4.9 PCA projection of EEG features

follow the steps; it illustrates why probability outputs are meaningful and how to diagnose calibration issues.

Finally, the scatter plot in Figure 4.9 compresses the many band-power features into two principal components so we can see how the data cloud organises itself.

The two clusters corresponding to low and high arousal pull apart cleanly. A reader doesn't need to know the algebra to grasp the message: after all the preprocessing and feature extraction, the data occupy different neighbourhoods. This simple geometric picture closes the loop with the ROC and the confusion matrix: separable clouds are what make a high AUC and a strong diagonal possible. The projection itself is a one-liner, wrapped here so you can reuse it across subjects:

```
from sklearn.decomposition import PCA

def pca_2d(X):
    pca = PCA(n_components=2, random_state=0)
    Z = pca.fit_transform(X)
    return Z, pca
```

Taken together, these figures tell a coherent story. The heatmaps and topographies reveal physiologically plausible changes in rhythmic activity across the scalp as arousal rises. The band-by-region differences and the CNN feature maps show that hand-crafted features and learned filters are converging on the same spatial–spectral signatures. The ROC and confusion matrix translate those signatures into reliable decisions, and the two tracking plots demonstrate how those decisions behave when time and generalisation matter. The PCA view reassures us that the distinction is not a statistical mirage but a genuine separation in the feature space. For a reader new to EEG, this sequence is meant to function like a narrative walkthrough: first see the patterns; then measure them; then watch them unfold in time; finally, look under the hood to confirm the models are reading the same physiology you are.

Importantly, these experiments also exposed limitations. Cross-cultural variability, hardware differences (wet vs. dry electrodes), and inter-session inconsistencies remain persistent challenges. Addressing these through larger, more diverse datasets and robust preprocessing protocols remains an active area of research. The case studies demonstrate that EEG-based emotion recognition is not only technically viable but also interpretatively rich when accompanied by strong visual analytics and human-centred design. They affirm the promise of EEG as a window into affective states and establish a roadmap for future developments in real-time emotional computing, educational feedback systems, clinical monitoring, and human-computer interaction.

References

Abadi, M., Barham, P., Chen, J., Chen, Z., Davis, A., Dean, J., & Zheng, X. (2016). TensorFlow: a system for Large-Scale machine learning. In *12th USENIX symposium on operating systems design and implementation (OSDI 16)* (pp. 265–283).

Al-Nafjan, A., Hosny, M., Al-Ohali, Y., & Al-Wabil, A. (2017). Review and classification of emotion recognition based on EEG brain-computer interface system research: a systematic review. *Applied Sciences*, *7*(12), 1239.

Alarcão, S. M., & Fonseca, M. J. (2017). Emotions recognition using EEG signals: A survey. *IEEE Transactions on Affective Computing*, *10*(3), 374–393.

Alhagry, S., Fahmy, A. A., & El-Khoribi, R. A. (2017). Emotion recognition based on EEG using LSTM recurrent neural network. *International Journal of Advanced Computer Science and Applications*, *8*(10), 355–358. https://doi.org/10.14569/IJACSA.2017.081046.

Allen, J. J., Keune, P. M., Schönenberg, M., & Nusslock, R. (2018). Frontal EEG alpha asymmetry and emotion: From neural underpinnings and methodological considerations to psychopathology and social cognition. *Psychophysiology*, *55*(1), e13028.

Bandt, C., & Pompe, B. (2002). Permutation entropy: a natural complexity measure for time series. *Physical Review Letters*, *88*(17), 174102.

Bao, F. S., Liu, X., & Zhang, C. (2011). PyEEG: an open source Python module for EEG/MEG feature extraction. *Computational Intelligence and Neuroscience*, *2011*(1), 406391.

Bashivan, P., Rish, I., Yeasin, M., & Codella, N. (2015). Learning representations from EEG with deep recurrent-convolutional neural networks. *arXiv preprint arXiv:1511.06448*.

Bishop, C. M., & Nasrabadi, N. M. (2006). *Pattern recognition and machine learning* (Vol. 4, No. 4, p. 738). Springer.

Bradley, M. M., & Lang, P. J. (1994). Measuring emotion: The self-assessment manikin and the semantic differential. *Journal of Behavior Therapy and Experimental Psychiatry*, *25*(1), 49–59.

Brier, G. W. (1950). Verification of forecasts expressed in terms of probability. *Monthly Weather Review*, *78*(1), 1–3.

Chen, T. T., Wang, K. P., Cheng, M. Y., Chang, Y. T., Huang, C. J., & Hung, T. M. (2019). Impact of emotional and motivational regulation on putting performance: A frontal alpha asymmetry study. *PeerJ*, *7*, e6777.

Chicco, D., & Jurman, G. (2020). The advantages of the Matthews Correlation Coefficient (MCC) over F1 score and accuracy in binary classification evaluation. *BMC Genomics*, *21*(1), 6.

Coan, J. A., & Allen, J. J. (2004). Frontal EEG asymmetry as a moderator and mediator of emotion. *Biological Psychology*, *67*(1–2), 7–50.

Cohen, L. (1995). *Time-frequency analysis*. Prentice Hall.

Craik, A., He, Y., & Contreras-Vidal, J. L. (2019). Deep learning for electroencephalogram (EEG) classification tasks: a review. *Journal of Neural Engineering*, *16*(3), 031001.

Davidson, R. J. (1998). Anterior electrophysiological asymmetries, emotion, and depression: Conceptual and methodological conundrums. *Psychophysiology*, *35*(5), 607–614.

Davidson, R. J., Ekman, P., Saron, C. D., Senulis, J. A., & Friesen, W. V. (1990). Approach-withdrawal and cerebral asymmetry: Emotional expression and brain physiology: I. *Journal of Personality and Social Psychology*, *58*(2), 330.

Delorme, A., & Makeig, S. (2004). EEGLAB: An open source toolbox for analysis of single-trial EEG dynamics including independent component analysis. *Journal of Neuroscience Methods*, *134*(1), 9–21.

Ding, Y., Robinson, N., Zhang, S., Zeng, Q., & Guan, C. (2022). TSception: Capturing temporal dynamics and spatial asymmetry from EEG for emotion recognition. *IEEE Transactions on Affective Computing*, *14*(3), 2238–2250.

Farahani, H., Watson, P., Bezan, T., Kovač, N., Winter, L. C., Blagojević, M., & Jiménez, P. (2024). PsAIchology: An intelligent direction in psychological sciences. In *10th international scientific conference Technics, Informatics and Education-TIE 2024*. Faculty of Technical Sciences Čačak, University of Kragujevac.

Farahani, H., Watson, P., Kovač, N., Sheykhangafshe, F. B., Azadfallah, P., Allahyari, A., & Chesli, R. R. (2025). Unraveling the complexity of love addiction using machine learning algorithms: The influence of positive and negative affect, interpersonal needs, and self-hate. In C.-H. Mayer & E. Vanderheiden (Eds.), *International handbook of love: Transcultural and transdisciplinary perspectives* (pp. 1–22). Springer Nature.

Ganin, Y., Ustinova, E., Ajakan, H., Germain, P., Larochelle, H., Laviolette, F., & Lempitsky, V. (2016). Domain-adversarial training of neural networks. *Journal of Machine Learning Research*, *17*(59), 1–35.

Gkintoni, E., Aroutzidis, A., Antonopoulou, H., & Halkiopoulos, C. (2025). From neural networks to emotional networks: A systematic review of EEG-based emotion recognition in cognitive neuroscience and real-world applications. *Brain Sciences*, *15*(3), 220.

Gramfort, A., Luessi, M., Larson, E., Engemann, D. A., Strohmeier, D., Brodbeck, C., & Hämäläinen, M. (2013). MEG and EEG data analysis with MNE-Python. *Frontiers in Neuroinformatics*, *7*, 267.

Gramfort, A., Luessi, M., Larson, E., Engemann, D. A., Strohmeier, D., Brodbeck, C., & Hämäläinen, M. S. (2014). MNE software for processing MEG and EEG data. *Neuroimage*, *86*, 446–460.

Guyon, I., & Elisseeff, A. (2003). An introduction to variable and feature selection. *Journal of Machine Learning Research*, *3*(Mar), 1157–1182.

Hajcak, G., & Foti, D. (2020). Significance?... Significance! Empirical, methodological, and theoretical connections between the late positive potential and P300 as neural responses to stimulus significance: An integrative review. *Psychophysiology*, *57*(7), e13570.

Harmon-Jones, E., & Gable, P. A. (2018). On the role of asymmetric frontal cortical activity in approach and withdrawal motivation: An updated review of the evidence. *Psychophysiology*, *55*(1), e12879.

Higuchi, T. (1988). Approach to an irregular time series on the basis of the fractal theory. *Physica D: Nonlinear Phenomena*, *31*(2), 277–283.

Hinrichs, H., Scholz, M., Baum, A. K., Kam, J. W., Knight, R. T., & Heinze, H. J. (2020). Comparison between a wireless dry electrode EEG system with a conventional wired wet electrode EEG system for clinical applications. *Scientific Reports*, *10*(1), 5218.

Hjorth, B. (1970). EEG analysis based on time domain properties. *Electroencephalography and Clinical Neurophysiology*, *29*(3), 306–310.

Huang, N. E., Shen, Z., Long, S. R., Wu, M. C., Shih, H. H., Zheng, Q., & Liu, H. H. (1998). The empirical mode decomposition and the Hilbert spectrum for nonlinear and non-stationary time series analysis. *Proceedings of the Royal Society of London. Series A: Mathematical, Physical and Engineering Sciences*, *454*(1971), 903–995.

Hyvärinen, A., & Oja, E. (2000). Independent component analysis: Algorithms and applications. *Neural Networks*, *13*(4–5), 411–430.

Islam, M. K., Rastegarnia, A., & Yang, Z. (2016). Methods for artifact detection and removal from scalp EEG: A review. *Neurophysiologie Clinique/Clinical Neurophysiology*, *46*(4–5), 287–305.

Islam, M. R., Moni, M. A., Islam, M. M., Rashed-Al-Mahfuz, M., Islam, M. S., Hasan, M. K., & Lió, P. (2021). Emotion recognition from EEG signal focusing on deep learning and shallow learning techniques. *IEEe Access*, *9*, 94601–94624.

Jenke, R., Peer, A., & Buss, M. (2014). Feature extraction and selection for emotion recognition from EEG. *IEEE Transactions on Affective Computing*, *5*(3), 327–339.

Jolliffe, I. (2005). Principal component analysis. In B. S. Everitt & D. C. Howell (Eds.), *Encyclopedia of statistics in behavioral science* (Vols. 3, pp. 1581–1584). Wiley.

Jung, T. P., Makeig, S., Humphries, C., Lee, T. W., Mckeown, M. J., Iragui, V., & Sejnowski, T. J. (2000). Removing electroencephalographic artifacts by blind source separation. *Psychophysiology*, *37*(2), 163–178.

Jurcak, V., Tsuzuki, D., & Dan, I. (2007). 10/20, 10/10, and 10/5 systems revisited: their validity as relative head-surface-based positioning systems. *Neuroimage*, *34*(4), 1600–1611.

Kalashami, M. P., Pedram, M. M., & Sadr, H. (2022). EEG feature extraction and data augmentation in emotion recognition. *Computational Intelligence and Neuroscience*, *2022*(1), 7028517.

Kappenman, E. S., & Luck, S. J. (2010). The effects of electrode impedance on data quality and statistical significance in ERP recordings. *Psychophysiology*, *47*(5), 888–904.

Katsigiannis, S., & Ramzan, N. (2017). DREAMER: A database for emotion recognition through EEG and ECG signals from wireless low-cost off-the-shelf devices. *IEEE Journal of Biomedical and Health Informatics*, *22*(1), 98–107.

Katz, M. J. (1988). Fractals and the analysis of waveforms. *Computers in Biology and Medicine*, *18*(3), 145–156.

Keil, A., Debener, S., Gratton, G., Junghöfer, M., Kappenman, E. S., Luck, S. J., & Yee, C. M. (2014). Committee report: publication guidelines and recommendations for studies using electroencephalography and magnetoencephalography. *Psychophysiology*, *51*(1), 1–21.

Klem, G. H. (1999). The ten-twenty electrode system of the international federation. The international federation of clinical neurophysiology. *Electroencephalography and Clinical Neurophysiology*, *52*, 3–6.

Koelstra, S., Muhl, C., Soleymani, M., Lee, J. S., Yazdani, A., Ebrahimi, T., & Patras, I. (2011). Deap: A database for emotion analysis; Using physiological signals. *IEEE Transactions on Affective Computing*, *3*(1), 18–31.

Kothe, C. A., & Makeig, S. (2013). BCILAB: A platform for brain–computer interface development. *Journal of Neural Engineering*, *10*(5), 056014.

Kovač, N., Ratković, K., Farahani, H., & Watson, P. (2024). A practical applications guide to machine learning regression models in psychology with Python. *Methods in Psychology*, *11*, 100156.

Kovač, N., Ratković, K., Watson, P., Farahani, H., & Bagheri Sheykhangafshe, F. (2025a). Machine learning classification models for predicting chronic pain. *Current Psychology*, 1–14. Advance online publication.

Kovač, N., Ratković, K., Farahani, H., & Watson, P. (2025b). Machine learning regression models for internal shame. *Acta Psychologica*, *260*, 105721.

Krishnaveni, V., Jayaraman, S., Aravind, S., Hariharasudhan, V., & Ramadoss, K. (2006). Automatic identification and removal of ocular artifacts from EEG using wavelet transform. *Measurement Science Review*, *6*(4), 45–57.

Kukhilava, N., Tsmindashvili, T., Kalandadze, R., Gupta, A., Katamadze, S., Brémond, F., & Wirth, B. E. (2025). Evaluation in EEG Emotion Recognition: State-of-the-Art Review and Unified Framework. *arXiv preprint arXiv:2505.18175*.

Kunjan, S., Grummett, T. S., Pope, K. J., Powers, D. M., Fitzgibbon, S. P., Bastiampillai, T., & Lewis, T. W. (2021, September). The necessity of Leave One Subject Out (LOSO) cross validation for EEG disease diagnosis. In *International conference on brain informatics* (pp. 558–567). Springer International Publishing.

Lachaux, J. P., Rodriguez, E., Martinerie, J., & Varela, F. J. (1999). Measuring phase synchrony in brain signals. *Human Brain Mapping*, *8*(4), 194–208.

Lawhern, V. J., Solon, A. J., Waytowich, N. R., Gordon, S. M., Hung, C. P., & Lance, B. J. (2018). EEGNet: A compact convolutional neural network for EEG-based brain–computer interfaces. *Journal of Neural Engineering*, *15*(5), 056013.

Lee, G., Gommers, R., Waselewski, F., Wohlfahrt, K., & O'Leary, A. (2019). PyWavelets: A Python package for wavelet analysis. *Journal of Open Source Software*, *4*(36), 1237.

Li, G., Ouyang, D., Yuan, Y., Li, W., Guo, Z., Qu, X., & Green, P. (2022a). An EEG data processing approach for emotion recognition. *IEEE Sensors Journal*, *22*(11), 10751–10763.

Li, X., Zhang, Y., Tiwari, P., Song, D., Hu, B., Yang, M., & Marttinen, P. (2022b). EEG based emotion recognition: A tutorial and review. *ACM Computing Surveys*, *55*(4), 1–57.

Li, Y., Zheng, W., Cui, Z., Zhang, T., & Zong, Y. (2018, July). A novel neural network model based on cerebral hemispheric asymmetry for EEG emotion recognition. In *Proceedings of the Twenty-Seventh International Joint Conference on Artificial Intelligence (IJCAI-18)* (pp. 1561–1567). International Joint Conferences on Artificial Intelligence Organization. https://www.ijcai.org/proceedings/2018/217

Lim, R. Y., Lew, W. C. L., & Ang, K. K. (2024). Review of EEG affective recognition with a neuroscience perspective. *Brain Sciences*, *14*(4), 364.

Liu, W., Zheng, W. L., & Lu, B. L. (2016, September). Emotion recognition using multimodal deep learning. In *International conference on neural information processing* (pp. 521–529). Springer International Publishing.

Luca, J., Hazenfratz, M., Monteith, G., Sanchez, A., Gaitero, L., & James, F. (2021). Electrode scalp impedance differences between electroencephalography machines in healthy dogs. *Canadian Journal of Veterinary Research*, *85*(4), 309–311.

Lundberg, S. M., & Lee, S. I. (2017). A unified approach to interpreting model predictions. In *Advances in neural information processing systems* (Vol. 30). Curran Associates, Inc. https://proceedings.neurips.cc/paper/2017/hash/8a20a8621978632d76c43dfd28b67767-Abstract.html

Makowski, D., Pham, T., Lau, Z. J., Brammer, J. C., Lespinasse, F., Pham, H., & Chen, S. A. (2021). NeuroKit2: A Python toolbox for neurophysiological signal processing. *Behavior Research Methods*, *53*(4), 1689–1696.

Matthews, B. W. (1975). Comparison of the predicted and observed secondary structure of T4 phage lysozyme. *Biochimica et Biophysica Acta (BBA)-Protein Structure*, *405*(2), 442–451.

Miranda-Correa, J. A., Abadi, M. K., Sebe, N., & Patras, I. (2018). Amigos: A dataset for affect, personality and mood research on individuals and groups. *IEEE Transactions on Affective Computing*, *12*(2), 479–493.

Nolte, G., Bai, O., Wheaton, L., Mari, Z., Vorbach, S., & Hallett, M. (2004). Identifying true brain interaction from EEG data using the imaginary part of coherency. *Clinical Neurophysiology*, *115*(10), 2292–2307.

Oostenveld, R., & Praamstra, P. (2001). The five percent electrode system for high-resolution EEG and ERP measurements. *Clinical Neurophysiology*, *112*(4), 713–719.

Ozdemir, M. A., Degirmenci, M., Izci, E., & Akan, A. (2021). EEG-based emotion recognition with deep convolutional neural networks. *Biomedical Engineering/Biomedizinische Technik*, *66*(1), 43–57.

Paszke, A., Gross, S., Massa, F., Lerer, A., Bradbury, J., Chanan, G., & Chintala, S. (2019). Pytorch: An imperative style, high-performance deep learning library. In *Advances in neural information processing systems* (Vol. 30). Curran Associates,

Inc. https://proceedings.neurips.cc/paper/2017/hash/8a20a8621978632d76c43dfd28b67767-Abstract.html

Patel, P. R. R., & Annavarapu, R. N. (2021). EEG-based human emotion recognition using entropy as a feature extraction measure. *Brain Informatics*, *8*(1), 20.

Pedregosa, F., Varoquaux, G., Gramfort, A., Michel, V., Thirion, B., Grisel, O., & Duchesnay, É. (2011). Scikit-learn: Machine learning in Python. *The Journal of Machine Learning Research*, *12*, 2825–2830.

Peng, H., Long, F., & Ding, C. (2005). Feature selection based on mutual information criteria of max-dependency, max-relevance, and min-redundancy. *IEEE Transactions on Pattern Analysis and Machine Intelligence*, *27*(8), 1226–1238.

Pernet, C. R., Appelhoff, S., Gorgolewski, K. J., Flandin, G., Phillips, C., Delorme, A., & Oostenveld, R. (2019). EEG-BIDS, an extension to the brain imaging data structure for electroencephalography. *Scientific Data*, *6*(1), 103.

Perrin, F., Pernier, J., Bertrand, O., & Echallier, J. F. (1989). Spherical splines for scalp potential and current density mapping. *Electroencephalography and Clinical Neurophysiology*, *72*(2), 184–187.

Picton, T. W., Bentin, S., Berg, P., Donchin, E., Hillyard, S. A., Johnson, R., & Taylor, M. J. (2000). Guidelines for using human event-related potentials to study cognition: Recording standards and publication criteria. *Psychophysiology*, *37*(2), 127–152.

Pincus, S. M. (1991). Approximate entropy as a measure of system complexity. *Proceedings of the National Academy of Sciences*, *88*(6), 2297–2301.

Reznik, S. J., & Allen, J. J. (2018). Frontal asymmetry as a mediator and moderator of emotion: An updated review. *Psychophysiology*, *55*(1), e12965.

Ribeiro, M. T., Singh, S., & Guestrin, C. (2016, August). "Why should i trust you?" Explaining the predictions of any classifier. In *Proceedings of the 22nd ACM SIGKDD international conference on knowledge discovery and data mining* (pp. 1135–1144).

Richman, J. S., & Moorman, J. R. (2000). Physiological time-series analysis using approximate entropy and sample entropy. *American Journal of Physiology-Heart and Circulatory Physiology*, *278*(6), H2039–H2049.

Riedl, R., Minas, R. K., Dennis, A. R., & Müller-Putz, G. R. (2020). Consumer-grade EEG instruments: insights on the measurement quality based on a literature review and implications for NeuroIS research. In *NeuroIS Retreat 2020: Proceedings* (pp. 350–361). AIS Electronic Library. https://aisel.aisnet.org/neurois2020/24

Sabio, J., Williams, N. S., McArthur, G. M., & Badcock, N. A. (2024). A scoping review on the use of consumer-grade EEG devices for research. *PLoS One*, *19*(3), e0291186.

Schirrmeister, R. T., Springenberg, J. T., Fiederer, L. D. J., Glasstetter, M., Eggensperger, K., Tangermann, M., & Ball, T. (2017). Deep learning with convolutional neural networks for EEG decoding and visualization. *Human Brain Mapping*, *38*(11), 5391–5420.

Shen, X., Liu, X., Hu, X., Zhang, D., & Song, S. (2022). Contrastive learning of subject-invariant EEG representations for cross-subject emotion recognition. *IEEE Transactions on Affective Computing*, *14*(3), 2496–2511.

Soleymani, M., Lichtenauer, J., Pun, T., & Pantic, M. (2011). A multimodal database for affect recognition and implicit tagging. *IEEE Transactions on Affective Computing*, *3*(1), 42–55.

Soufineyestani, M., Khan, A., & Imtiaz, R. (2021). Physiological and psychological reactions to a musician, robot, or Boombox music player: Comparison between EDA, HRV, and EEG. *Neurological Research and Surgery*, *4*(1), 1–8.

Su, J., Zhu, J., Song, T., & Chang, H. (2023). Subject-independent eeg emotion recognition based on genetically optimized projection dictionary pair learning. *Brain Sciences*, *13*(7), 977.
Suhaimi, N. S., Mountstephens, J., & Teo, J. (2020). EEG-based emotion recognition: A state-of-the-art review of current trends and opportunities. *Computational Intelligence and Neuroscience*, *2020*(1), 8875426.
Thomson, D. J. (1982). Spectrum estimation and harmonic analysis. *Proceedings of the IEEE*, *70*(9), 1055–1096.
Thottempudi, P., Kumar, V., & Deevi, N. (2024). EEG artifact removal strategies for BCI applications: A survey. *Majlesi Journal of Electrical Engineering*, *18*(1), 187–197.
Topic, A., & Russo, M. (2021). Emotion recognition based on EEG feature maps through deep learning network. *Engineering Science and Technology, an International Journal*, *24*(6), 1442–1454.
Torrence, C., & Compo, G. P. (1998). A practical guide to wavelet analysis. *Bulletin of the American Meteorological Society*, *79*(1), 61–78.
Torres, E. P., Torres, E. A., Hernández-Álvarez, M., & Yoo, S. G. (2020). EEG-based BCI emotion recognition: A survey. *Sensors*, *20*(18), 5083.
Tripathi, S., Acharya, S., Sharma, R., Mittal, S., & Bhattacharya, S. (2017, February). Using deep and convolutional neural networks for accurate emotion classification on DEAP data. In *Proceedings of the AAAI conference on artificial intelligence* (Vol. 31, No. 2, pp. 4746–4752).
Virtanen, P., Gommers, R., Oliphant, T. E., Haberland, M., Reddy, T., Cournapeau, D., & Van Mulbregt, P. (2020). SciPy 1.0: Fundamental algorithms for scientific computing in Python. *Nature methods*, *17*(3), 261–272.
Wang, Y., Zhang, L., Xia, P., Wang, P., Chen, X., Du, L., & Du, M. (2022). EEG-based emotion recognition using a 2D CNN with different kernels. *Bioengineering*, *9*(6), 231.
Welch, P. (2003). The use of fast Fourier transform for the estimation of power spectra: A method based on time averaging over short, modified periodograms. *IEEE Transactions on Audio and Electroacoustics*, *15*(2), 70–73.
Yao, D. (2001). A method to standardize a reference of scalp EEG recordings to a point at infinity. *Physiological Measurement*, *22*(4), 693.
Zhang, Z., Liu, Y., & Zhong, S. H. (2022). GANSER: A self-supervised data augmentation framework for EEG-based emotion recognition. *IEEE Transactions on Affective Computing*, *14*(3), 2048–2063.
Zheng, W. L., & Lu, B. L. (2015). Investigating critical frequency bands and channels for EEG-based emotion recognition with deep neural networks. *IEEE Transactions on Autonomous Mental Development*, *7*(3), 162–175.
Zheng, W. L., Zhu, J. Y., & Lu, B. L. (2017). Identifying stable patterns over time for emotion recognition from EEG. *IEEE Transactions on Affective Computing*, *10*(3), 417–429.
Zuo, X., Zhang, C., Hämäläinen, T., Gao, H., Fu, Y., & Cong, F. (2022). Cross-subject emotion recognition using fused entropy features of EEG. *Entropy*, *24*(9), 1281.

5 Embodied Emotion from Medical Imaging

Nataša Kovač, Hojjatollah Farahani, and Peter Watson

5.1 Introduction

Emotions are not merely abstract states felt within the mind; they are deeply embodied processes rooted in the brain's structure and function. While psychological theories and behavioural models have long guided our understanding of emotion, modern neuroimaging has ushered in a new era, where emotional states can be visualised, localised, and quantified through high-resolution data captured by medical technologies such as computed tomography (CT) and magnetic resonance imaging (MRI). These imaging modalities provide unprecedented access to the neural substrates of affective experience, offering both structural and functional insights into how emotion is instantiated in the brain's architecture.

Medical imaging connects the subjective experience of emotion with its biological expressions. It enables researchers to observe changes in cortical thickness, subcortical volume, and neural activation patterns that relate to emotional processing, regulation, and memory. Regions such as the amygdala, insula, anterior cingulate cortex, and prefrontal areas are consistently identified across studies as key hubs in the affective brain. These structures do not function in isolation but operate within dynamic, distributed networks that encode valence, arousal, salience, and self-referential processing. Medical imaging has become a crucial tool for mapping these networks, fostering a more detailed understanding of emotion as an embodied, whole-brain phenomenon.

Emotions are not merely abstract psychological states; they are deeply embodied processes anchored in the structural and functional organisation of the brain (Damasio, 2021). Classic psychological models, such as physiological theories and cognitive appraisal frameworks, provide foundational perspectives, but the field has shifted significantly with the advent of high-resolution neuroimaging technologies. Methods such as CT, MRI, functional MRI (fMRI), and diffusion tensor imaging (DTI) allow researchers to visualise, localise, and quantify emotional processes in vivo (Pessoa, 2022; Barrett & Simmons, 2015). These technologies provide structural measures, like cortical thickness and subcortical volume, alongside functional measures of

DOI: 10.4324/9781003495123-5

neural activation and connectivity, mapping emotion within its neuroanatomical context.

Medical imaging serves as a bridge between the subjective experience of emotion and its objective biological markers. Consistent evidence points to the amygdala's role in detecting emotional salience (LeDoux, 2020), the insula's function in interoceptive awareness and disgust processing (Craig, 2009), the anterior cingulate cortex's involvement in regulation and conflict monitoring (Etkin et al., 2015), and the prefrontal cortex's engagement in appraisal and control of emotional states (Ochsner & Gross, 2005; Buhle et al., 2014). These regions do not act in isolation but as parts of large-scale, interconnected networks, such as the salience, default mode, and executive control networks, that encode affective dimensions of valence, arousal, and self-referential meaning (Menon, 2015; Feurer et al., 2021).

Advances in network neuroscience have reframed emotion as an emergent property of dynamic brain systems rather than as a product of static, modular structures. Resting-state fMRI and connectivity analyses reveal that affective states involve constantly shifting patterns of network activity contingent on environmental and bodily inputs (Feurer et al., 2021). Predictive coding theories suggest that the brain integrates sensory and interoceptive signals into top-down expectations, thereby shaping emotional experience in an ongoing loop of prediction and correction (Barrett & Simmons, 2015).

From a translational perspective, neuroimaging not only advances theoretical models but also informs clinical practice. Altered amygdala–prefrontal connectivity has been linked to anxiety disorders (Thomas et al., 2025), while reduced hippocampal volume correlates with depression (Schmaal et al., 2016). Such findings underscore the concept that emotional dysregulation is both a psychological and neurophysiological phenomenon, and highlight the potential of medical imaging to guide neuromodulatory interventions and psychotherapy tailored to individual neurobiological profiles (Koenigs & Grafman, 2009).

Modern neuroimaging positions emotion as a measurable, embodied experience supported by distributed neural networks. This integrative perspective enriches theoretical understanding and strengthens links to applied domains, including mental health treatment and artificial models of affect for psychology-driven AI systems. Beyond basic research, neuroimaging offers critical insights into emotional dysfunction and its neural correlates. In clinical populations, altered patterns in grey matter density or connectivity are often associated with disorders characterised by emotional dysregulation, such as depression, anxiety, post-traumatic stress disorder, and bipolar disorder. The ability to identify these neural markers provides both diagnostic potential and avenues for personalised intervention. Increasingly, researchers are exploring how emotion-specific neural patterns can inform not only treatment but also the prediction of emotional traits and states in healthy individuals.

Beyond basic research, neuroimaging has evolved into a cornerstone methodology for disentangling the complex neural architecture of emotional dysfunction. Its growing role in psychiatry reflects both its capacity to detect subtle circuit-level alterations that precede overt symptom expression and its utility in guiding targeted interventions. Multi-modal imaging approaches, combining structural MRI, functional MRI, diffusion imaging, and emerging neurochemical mapping, reveal patterns of abnormal connectivity and morphology that are remarkably consistent across diagnostic categories, suggesting transdiagnostic signatures of emotional dysregulation (Kaiser et al., 2015; Schmaal et al., 2016).

In major depressive disorder, volumetric reductions in the hippocampus and anterior cingulate cortex, alongside attenuated dorsolateral prefrontal activity, point towards impaired cognitive control over limbic driven affective responses (Disner et al., 2011). Anxiety disorders, including PTSD, frequently demonstrate hyper-responsivity of the amygdala during threat-related cues and persistent hypoactivity in regulatory prefrontal regions, consistent with a failure to disengage from perceived danger (Etkin & Wager, 2007; Zhu et al., 2012). Bipolar disorder exhibits a more dynamic pattern, with alternations between hyperconnectivity and hypoconnectivity in fronto-limbic circuits depending on mood state (Phillips & Swartz, 2014), reinforcing the view that emotional instability may arise from fluctuating network coordination rather than static structural deficits.

The prognostic potential of these findings lies in their capacity to identify individuals at heightened risk before clinical thresholds are crossed. Longitudinal imaging studies reveal that pre-existing anomalies in prefrontal–amygdala coupling can predict vulnerability to future mood or anxiety episodes, particularly under sustained stress exposure (Morawetz et al., 2017). This predictive dimension is now being operationalised in personalised intervention models, wherein neurobiological markers inform therapy choice, whether through cognitive-behavioural rehearsal targeting regulatory circuits, pharmacological modulation of neurotransmitter balance, or neuromodulatory techniques such as transcranial magnetic stimulation precisely aimed at disrupted cortical nodes.

Furthermore, neuroimaging is beginning to bridge the gap between research in healthy populations and clinical practice. Studies on non-clinical participants show that variations in amygdala–prefrontal dynamics not only correspond to stable emotional traits such as resilience and reactivity but also fluctuate in response to acute training in emotional regulation (Schweizer et al., 2013). Such plasticity underscores a hopeful prospect: that targeted neuromodulation or cognitive training could recalibrate dysfunctional circuits, a concept aligning with the principles of precision psychiatry and preventative mental healthcare (Adrián-Ventura et al., 2019).

In the broader context of affective neuroscience, these converging lines of evidence affirm that emotion is best understood as an emergent property of integrated neural systems, whose disruption manifests in both clinical symptoms and subtle shifts in everyday emotional life. The capacity to map and quantify these systems through neuroimaging not only advances theoretical models of emotion but also lays the foundation for interventions that are both scientifically grounded and individually tailored. As machine learning and computational modelling techniques evolve, CT and MRI data are being repurposed to train algorithms capable of recognising emotion-related brain signatures. These developments hold transformative implications for affective neuroscience and psychoradiology. We are approaching a threshold where it may be possible to infer emotional states not from self-report or observation, but from high-dimensional imaging data alone. Such progress raises not only technical but also philosophical and ethical questions: To what extent can emotion be reduced to a neural footprint? What does it mean for emotion to be legible to machines? The convergence of structural neuroanatomy, functional brain dynamics, and computational analysis offers a compelling lens through which to re-examine the nature of affect, not just as a psychological construct but as a measurable, embodied phenomenon etched into the architecture of the brain, consistent with the broader PsAIchology framing of integrating AI and psychological science (Farahani et al., 2024).

5.2 Emotional Insights From CT and MRI Data

Advancements in neuroimaging have fundamentally shifted the landscape of emotion research by rendering emotional processes visible, quantifiable, and spatially mappable within the human brain. Among the most powerful tools for this exploration are CT and MRI, both of which allow researchers to investigate the structural and functional substrates of affect. These technologies have enabled a growing body of work that treats emotion not merely as a psychological or behavioural output but as a biologically embodied phenomenon with distinct neural signatures. While CT imaging offers valuable information about brain structure, particularly in clinical populations where lesions or trauma may affect emotional regulation, MRI provides a more nuanced view into the dynamic, interconnected networks that support emotional processing in real time.

The ability to observe emotion-related brain activity has opened up new theoretical possibilities for understanding how emotions stem from the interaction of several neural systems. Instead of being confined to separate modules, current research indicates that emotional states emerge from networked interactions across cortical and subcortical regions. Studies using functional MRI (fMRI) have consistently highlighted areas such as the amygdala, insula, ventromedial prefrontal cortex (vmPFC), and anterior cingulate cortex (ACC) as involved in emotional reactivity, interoceptive awareness, and regulation (Craig, 2002, 2009; Etkin et al., 2015; Büchel, & Gross, 2015; Hiser & Koenigs, 2018; Phelps & LeDoux, 2005). These regions work together to produce affective responses that are appropriate to the context and socially adaptive, emphasising the embodied and integrative character of emotion.

For example, the amygdala's well-established role in fear detection and salience encoding is now understood to operate not in isolation but in reciprocal dialogue with the prefrontal cortex, which influences and interprets affective signals based on cognitive and social considerations (Etkin et al., 2015; Hiser & Koenigs, 2018; Phelps & LeDoux, 2005).

Structural MRI (sMRI) studies have further revealed that individual differences in emotional traits, such as trait anxiety, affective empathy, or emotional reactivity, are associated with measurable differences in brain morphology. Variations in grey matter volume or cortical thickness in emotion-relevant regions have been linked to stable patterns of emotional functioning. For example, increased volume in the anterior insula has been correlated with greater emotional awareness and empathy, while reductions in dorsolateral prefrontal cortex thickness are often observed in individuals with difficulties in emotion regulation or depression (van Dam et al., 2021). These findings contribute to a neuroanatomical grounding of emotional capacities, suggesting that the way individuals experience and manage their emotions is partly a function of their neural architecture.

CT imaging, although more limited in resolution compared to MRI, has been essential in revealing how structural brain abnormalities affect affective function, particularly in neurological injury. In cohorts with traumatic brain injury (TBI) and stroke, voxel-based lesion–symptom mapping has linked damage to the orbitofrontal and adjacent ventral prefrontal regions with behavioural disinhibition and socio-emotional disturbance, consistent with classic OFC roles in affective regulation (Knutson et al., 2015; Gläscher et al., 2012). For white-matter pathways, damage to the right uncinate fasciculus selectively impairs emotional empathy, highlighting tract-level influences on affective integration (Oishi et al., 2015; Herbet et al., 2015). In clinical pipelines, CT volumes are often co-registered to MRI-based or CT templates to improve normalisation for group analyses. This is an established practice facilitated by age-appropriate templates and toolboxes (Rorden et al., 2012).

Beyond structural findings, the real strength of MRI lies in its ability to capture the functional dynamics of emotional states as they unfold. Functional MRI studies using emotionally evocative tasks, such as viewing facial expressions, listening to emotionally charged sounds, or recalling autobiographical memories, have mapped activation patterns that correspond not only to general emotion categories (e.g., fear, joy) but also to specific dimensions of affect such as arousal and valence. These studies consistently report distinct yet overlapping activation clusters, suggesting that the brain represents emotions in a distributed and context-sensitive manner rather than through fixed, modular circuits. In particular, high arousal states tend to engage the anterior insula and amygdala more robustly, while positively valenced experiences show increased connectivity between the ventral striatum and medial prefrontal areas (Lindquist et al., 2012).

Moreover, the use of *resting-state functional connectivity* has opened a new frontier in understanding the intrinsic architecture of the emotional brain.

Researchers have begun to identify specific resting-state networks, such as the default mode network (DMN), salience network (SN), and central executive network (CEN), that exhibit characteristic patterns of connectivity associated with baseline emotional traits. Increased coupling between the amygdala and DMN, for example, has been linked to rumination and negative affect. At the same time, stronger connectivity between the CEN and the vmPFC correlates with better emotion regulation capacity. These resting-state findings emphasise the continuity between emotional traits and moment-to-moment emotional states, reinforcing the view that emotion is deeply embedded in the brain's baseline functional architecture (Kleckner et al., 2017).

Importantly, neuroimaging is beginning to bridge the gap between *subjective affective experience and objective neural data.* Using multivariate pattern analysis (MVPA), researchers can now classify emotional states based on distributed patterns of fMRI activity with increasing accuracy. These patterns extend across cortical and subcortical regions, suggesting that emotion is encoded through large-scale population codes rather than isolated loci. Some researchers have even proposed the existence of neural *signatures* for basic emotions. These are multiregional activation patterns that reliably predict states like sadness or fear across individuals and tasks. Although the universality and specificity of such signatures remain under debate, their emergence underscores the growing sophistication of MRI-based emotion decoding (Kragel & LaBar, 2015; Chang et al., 2015; Saarimäki et al., 2016; Zhou et al., 2021).

The integration of diffusion tensor imaging (DTI) has further expanded the anatomical resolution of emotion research. By mapping white-matter pathways, DTI reveals how information flows between regions involved in emotional generation and regulation. Integrity of the uncinate fasciculus, which connects the anterior temporal lobe/amygdala with orbitofrontal–vmPFC circuits, has been linked to individual differences in emotion regulation, emotional sensitivity, and related affective traits (Xu et al., 2022; Tromp et al., 2019; Xu et al., 2023; see also Granger et al., 2021). Such findings support the view that emotions depend on efficient communication between emotional and executive systems, not solely on isolated cortical loci.

As the field advances, a key question remains: to what extent can emotional profiles be inferred or predicted from neuroimaging data? While the current consensus is that such predictions are probabilistic and context-dependent, there is growing optimism that with the appropriate combination of anatomical, functional, and connectivity data, it may be possible to construct comprehensive neural models of emotion that reflect both transient states and enduring traits. These models hold promise not only for scientific understanding but also for clinical applications, such as early detection of affective disorders, personalised treatment planning, and the development of neurofeedback interventions based on real-time emotion tracking.

Taken together, CT and MRI have become indispensable tools for exploring the neural embodiment of emotion. They provide a means of anchoring affective experience within the biological substrate of the brain, offering insights that are at once structural, functional, and dynamic. As these technologies continue to evolve, their integration with computational modelling, artificial intelligence, and behavioural science will deepen our understanding of the emotional brain as a distributed system whose architecture both reflects and shapes the feelings we call our own.

5.3 Neuroimaging Data Preprocessing: Preparing CT and MRI Data for Emotion Analysis

The translation of raw neuroimaging data into meaningful emotional insights hinges on a meticulous and scientifically rigorous preprocessing pipeline. In studies of embodied emotion, where the goal is to identify subtle structural and functional correlates of affect, preprocessing is not merely a technical preamble but a foundational step that ensures both the validity and reproducibility of the findings. Whether derived from CT or MRI, neuroimaging data are subject to numerous sources of noise, artefact, and individual anatomical variability that must be accounted for before emotion-related analysis can proceed.

In the case of MRI, preprocessing typically begins with anatomical alignment and head motion correction. Even minimal head movements can distort voxel-based representations of emotional activation, leading to spurious findings or reduced statistical power. Algorithms such as FSL's MCFLIRT (Smith et al., 2004) or SPM's realignment module (Ashburner et al., 2014) are widely used to estimate and correct for motion by aligning each volume to a reference image. Motion artefacts are particularly problematic in emotional tasks, where stimuli may trigger involuntary reactions like facial expressions or body shifts. Therefore, studies involving affective elicitation often include motion parameters as covariates in subsequent statistical models to isolate genuine emotional activation from movement-induced signal changes (Esteban et al., 2019).

To screen for frame-wise intensity changes driven by head motion or rapid physiological shifts, we inspect temporal Derivative VARiance across voxels (DVARS). DVARS highlights sudden global changes in the BOLD volume from one frame to the next; large spikes are typical markers of motion or slice-to-slice corruption. DVARS are in Python, implemented as follows:

```
from nilearn.maskers import NiftiMasker
from nilearn import image
import numpy as np, matplotlib.pyplot as plt

bold = image.load_img("your.nii.gz")
masker = NiftiMasker(standardize=False, detrend=False).
fit(bold)
X = masker.transform(bold)          # shape: (n_scans,
n_voxels)
dX = np.diff(X, axis=0)
dvars = np.sqrt((dX**2).mean(axis=1)) * 1000 # scale for
visibility
```

```
m, s = dvars.mean(), dvars.std()
plt.figure(figsize=(16,4))
plt.plot(dvars); plt.axhline(m+2*s, color='orange', ls='--')
plt.axhline(m+3*s, color='red', ls='--')
plt.xlabel("Frame");  plt.ylabel("DVARS  (a.u.)");  plt.tit
le("DVARS (frame-wise)")
plt.tight_layout()
```

For our example shown in Figure 5.1, a single, pronounced spike aligns with the only obvious artefactual dip in the global signal. A clear outlier is visible around frame 176 (dashed lines show mean+2SD and mean+3SD alert levels). This simple check tells us where censoring or nuisance modelling (e.g., motion regressors) may be needed before any statistical analysis.

Alongside DVARS, we track the global mean signal as the average BOLD intensity inside the brain at each frame. This complements DVARS by showing slow drifts and abrupt drops on an absolute scale. In the same run, the global signal exhibits a single sharp deflection at the same time index as the DVARS spike, strengthening the case for targeted scrubbing or modelling of that frame and its neighbours. Python code for the global mean signal is:

```
bold = image.load_img("your.nii.gz")
masker = NiftiMasker(standardize=False, detrend=True).fit(bold)
X = masker.transform(bold)      # (n_scans, n_voxels)
global_ts = X.mean(axis=1)

plt.figure(figsize=(16,4))
plt.plot(global_ts); plt.xlabel("Frame"); plt.ylabel("Global
mean signal (a.u.)")
plt.title("Global mean fMRI signal"); plt.tight_layout()
```

The output of the previous code is shown in Figure 5.2. The deep transient around frame 176 mirrors the DVARS spike and is highly suggestive of head movement or brief acquisition instability.

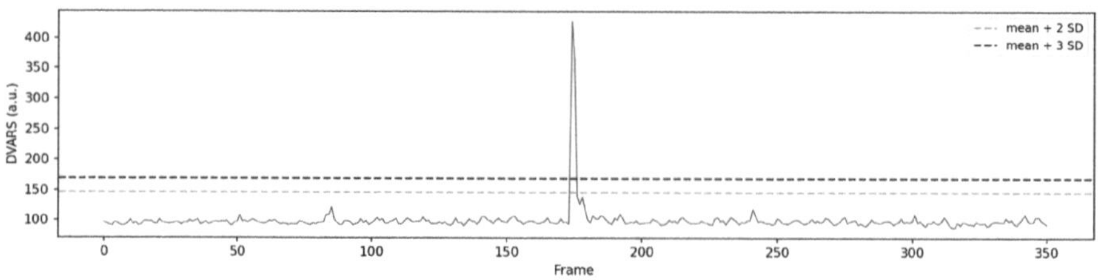

Figure 5.1 DVARS time-series.

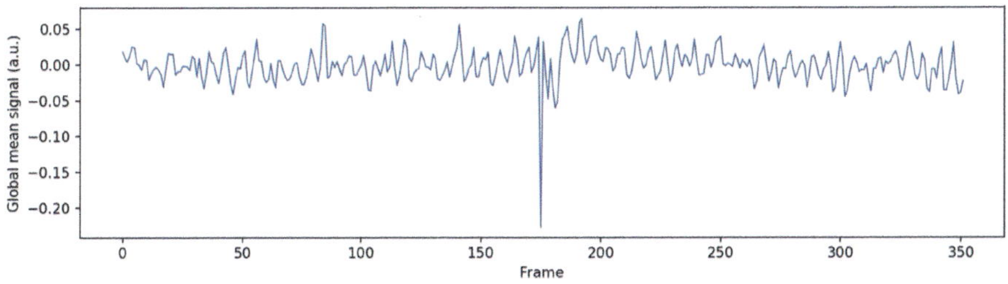

Figure 5.2 Global mean fMRI signal across time.

Following motion correction, anatomical normalisation ensures that each participant's brain is spatially aligned to a common reference template, such as the Montreal Neurological Institute Template-MNI152 (Fonov et al., 2011) or Talairach space (Collins et al., 1994). This step allows for group-level comparisons and voxel-wise analysis by transforming individual datasets into a shared neuroanatomical space. However, in emotion research, especially when exploring subcortical structures like the amygdala or hippocampus, misalignment during normalisation can blur the signal and reduce the specificity of regional findings. As such, high-resolution templates and nonlinear warping algorithms, such as those provided by ANTs (Madge, 2020), are often employed to preserve anatomical detail. Manual inspection and quality control are also essential to verify the fidelity of spatial normalisation, particularly when working with clinical or paediatric populations where brain morphology may deviate from standard templates.

Before coregistration and tissue segmentation, it helps to illustrate how common filters change anatomical contrast. The panel in Figure 5.3 compares a raw T1-weighted slice with Gaussian smoothing and edge-enhancing operators (Sobel, Frangi, Laplacian). Only modest smoothing is used in typical workflows; stronger edge filters are *diagnostic* visuals here, not steps we apply to the anatomical pipeline. Showing them reminds the reader why over-filtering can exaggerate edges and mislead registration or segmentation.

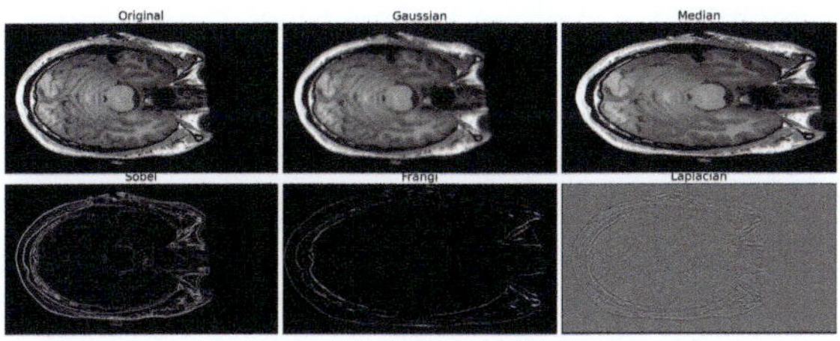

Figure 5.3 Effect of basic filters on the middle axial slice of T1w.

To produce the panel from Figure 5.3, we can use this code:

```
t1w = image.load_img("your.nii.gz")
sl = image.index_img(t1w, None).get_fdata()[:,:,t1w.shape[2]
//2]
sl = (sl - np.percentile(sl,2)) / (np.percentile(sl,98)-np.
percentile(sl,2)+1e-9)

panels = {
  "Original": sl, "Gaussian": gaussian_filter(sl,1),
  "Median": gaussian_filter(sl,0.01), "Sobel": sobel(sl),
  "Frangi": frangi(sl), "Laplacian": laplace(sl)
}
fig, axes = plt.subplots(2,3,figsize=(12,7))
for ax,(k,v) in zip(axes.ravel(), panels.items()): ax.imsh
ow(v,cmap='gray'); ax.set_title(k); ax.axis('off')
fig.tight_layout()
```

For functional MRI data, preprocessing continues with slice timing correction and spatial smoothing. Because different slices of the brain are acquired at slightly different times during each repetition time (TR), slice timing correction adjusts the data to a common temporal reference. While its necessity depends on the acquisition protocol (e.g., whether multi-band acceleration was used), the inclusion of this step is generally recommended in event-related emotional tasks to improve the temporal alignment of stimulus responses. Spatial smoothing, on the other hand, enhances signal-to-noise ratio by averaging voxel intensities within a defined kernel, typically around 6–8 mm of full-width half-maximum. Though this step can obscure fine-grained patterns, it increases the sensitivity to detect broader regional activation and compensates for inter-individual anatomical variability (Poldrack et al., 2020).

When decoding or classifying emotions, extra preprocessing steps are often used to prepare data for machine learning pipelines. These include temporal filtering to remove low-frequency drifts, z-scoring to standardise voxel intensities, and extracting region-of-interest (ROI) time series for feature creation. In studies aiming to predict emotional valence or arousal from fMRI data, denoising techniques such as Independent Component Analysis (ICA) based artefact removal (e.g., ICA-AROMA) and physiological noise correction (e.g., RETROICOR) are used to ensure predictions are not influenced by non-neural sources. The growing use of MVPA and deep learning in emotion research highlights the importance of careful preprocessing, as even small inconsistencies can reduce model generalisability and interpretability.

We summarise temporal reliability with $tSNR = mean / SD$ of the BOLD signal at each voxel. High tSNR implies stable time series and greater sensitivity to detect task-evoked changes; low tSNR flags susceptibility or motion-sensitive regions (e.g., orbitofrontal cortex, anterior temporal lobes). The tSNR map (Figure 5.4) shows broadly good coverage with expected drops near sinuses and inferior temporal regions. Warm colours indicate higher temporal stability, while cooler areas flag regions where effects may be harder to detect.

A *tSNR histogram* in Figure 5.5 complements the map by showing the overall quality of the run. Here, most brain voxels cluster around ~35–55,

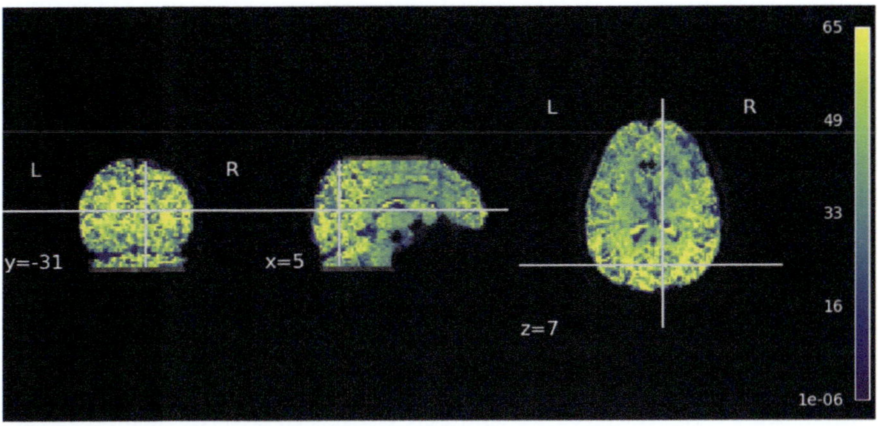

Figure 5.4 tSNR (mean/SD) over the run.

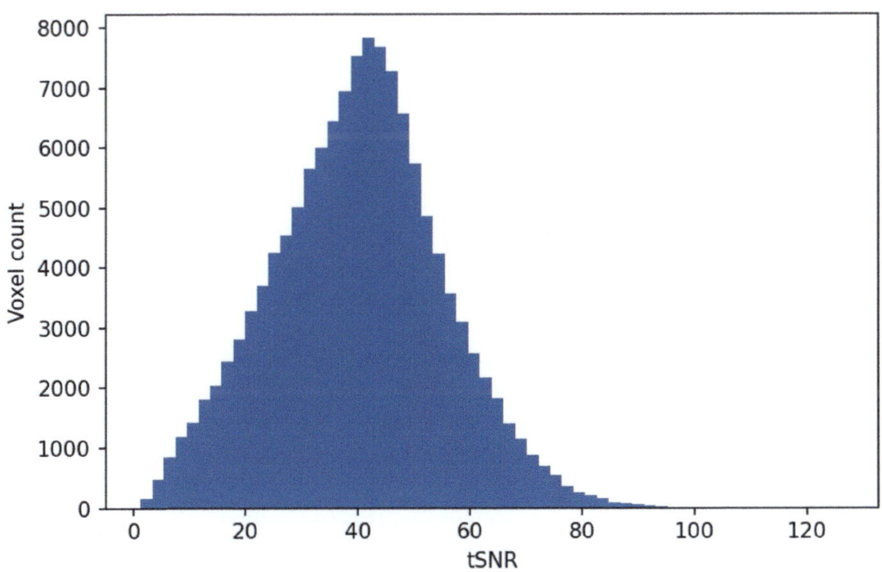

Figure 5.5 Distribution of within-brain tSNR values.

with a long upper tail. Such distributions are typical for 3 T fMRI at 2–3 mm isotropic resolution. If the bulk of voxels fell below ~20–25, we'd anticipate reduced sensitivity and would consider stricter denoising, more aggressive censoring, or excluding the run. Peak around ~40–50 suggests adequate data quality for first-level GLM in this subject.

Preprocessing of *structural MRI* data also involves several important steps. For grey matter morphometry analyses, tools like FreeSurfer (Fischl, 2012) and CAT12 are used to segment the brain into tissue classes (grey matter, white matter, cerebrospinal fluid), extract cortical thickness measures, and compute surface-based metrics such as gyrification and curvature. These morphological features are then statistically compared across individuals with different emotional profiles, such as high versus low trait anxiety or emotional dysregulation. Accurate segmentation is crucial, especially in emotion-relevant regions that have complex folding patterns or diverse tissue properties. Visual inspection of segmentations and following standardised preprocessing pipelines are essential to ensure reliability, particularly when analysing small subcortical structures that play significant roles in emotional processing.

When working with CT data, preprocessing tends to be more constrained due to lower spatial resolution and the absence of functional contrast. In clinical and lesion–symptom mapping studies, CT lesion masks are routinely normalised or co-registered to common MRI templates to facilitate group localisation and statistical mapping (Bates et al., 2003; Karnath et al., 2004; Rorden et al., 2012). Practical pipelines apply skull stripping and lesion segmentation to enhance anatomical clarity before analysis (Hu et al., 2023; Muschelli et al., 2015; Najm et al., 2019). Although MRI is generally more sensitive than CT for subtle pathology such as diffuse axonal injury and microstructural white-matter damage, CT remains valuable where MRI is unavailable or contraindicated and as part of retrospective cohorts (Dabas et al., 2024; Shenton et al., 2012; Vo et al., 2022).

Cross-modal preprocessing, which combines CT, structural MRI, functional MRI, and even DTI, is gaining popularity in integrative models of emotion. These pipelines involve advanced coregistration and fusion techniques to align datasets with differing resolutions and contrasts. When analysing emotional processing across modalities, preserving anatomical congruence is critical. For example, the structural connectivity derived from DTI must align precisely with the functional activations from fMRI to assess emotion-related network dynamics. Fusion methods such as joint independent component analysis (jICA) or canonical correlation analysis (CCA) are increasingly used to identify shared components across modalities that track with emotional traits or responses.

An emerging trend in neuroimaging preprocessing is the shift toward *automated, reproducible workflows* that combine best practices with open-source accessibility. Pipelines such as fMRIPrep (Esteban et al., 2019), MRIQC (Esteban et al., 2017), and Nipype (Gorgolewski et al., 2011) enable researchers to preprocess large datasets with minimal manual intervention while maintaining consistency and transparency. In emotion research, where data are often collected across multiple sessions, tasks, or sites, such standardised workflows are essential for harmonisation and scalability. The availability of Brain Imaging Data Structure (BIDS) formatting further facilitates dataset sharing and reuse, accelerating progress toward large-scale models of embodied emotion (Gorgolewski et al., 2016).

While preprocessing may appear as a technical backdrop to the more conceptual work of emotion analysis, it is, in fact, one of the most consequential stages in determining the success and credibility of neuroimaging-based emotion research. Errors or inconsistencies introduced at this stage can propagate through to final interpretations, potentially leading to invalid conclusions about the neural bases of affect. Conversely, careful, validated preprocessing unlocks the full potential of neuroimaging to reveal the embodied architecture of emotional life, setting the stage for accurate modelling, meaningful prediction, and responsible application.

5.4 Revealing Emotional Patterns in CT and MRI Scans

The growing convergence between affective neuroscience and neuroimaging has brought to light a critical realisation: emotional experiences are not abstract psychological states detached from the body but are physically encoded across multiple levels of brain architecture. As CT and MRI technologies become increasingly refined, they allow researchers to move beyond localisation of emotional processes and instead focus on identifying and characterising patterns with distributed, reproducible, and functionally meaningful configurations of neural activation, morphology, and connectivity that reflect the embodied nature of emotion. These patterns form the neurobiological substrate upon which subjective feeling states emerge and fluctuate, offering measurable indices of emotional function and dysfunction.

MRI, with its ability to capture both structural and functional information, has played a central role in this effort. fMRI studies often begin by isolating ROIs known to be involved in emotional processing, such as the amygdala, anterior insula, vmPFC, and ACC, and examining how these regions activate in response to emotional stimuli or tasks. However, more recent work has shown that single-region analyses are insufficient to capture the full complexity of emotional states. Emotional experiences are dynamic, multicomponent phenomena involving sensory processing, autonomic feedback, cognitive interpretation, and motor preparation. Therefore, researchers have turned to MVPA, dynamic causal modelling (DCM), and graph theoretical approaches to detect *distributed emotional patterns* that span across brain systems and time.

For example, studies using emotional film clips, facial expression tasks, or autobiographical memory recall have consistently revealed that specific emotional categories, such as fear, happiness, disgust, or sadness, are associated with unique but overlapping patterns of activation. Rather than being localised, these patterns typically involve synchronised activity across limbic regions, sensory cortices, and default mode network hubs. A fear-related pattern, for instance, may involve co-activation of the amygdala, periaqueductal grey, and right anterior insula, combined with suppression in the medial prefrontal cortex. In contrast, sadness may show stronger engagement of the subgenual ACC, posterior cingulate cortex, and precuneus, suggesting greater involvement of self-referential processing (Kragel & LaBar, 2016).

Such findings are strengthened by *pattern classification algorithms*, which can learn to distinguish emotional states based on fMRI voxel-level data. These classifiers, often employing support vector machines or neural networks, are trained on labelled data to predict unseen emotional states from brain activation patterns. The success of these models demonstrates that emotional information is not just detectable but *decodable* within neuroimaging data (Pereira et al., 2009; Haynes, 2015; Norman et al., 2006; Kragel & LaBar, 2015; Chang et al., 2015). This ability to infer emotional states from brain data opens new frontiers for emotion tracking in real time, particularly in clinical populations where self-report may be unreliable.

MRI-based structural analyses have also uncovered persistent morphological patterns linked to emotional traits and tendencies. Voxel-based morphometry and cortical thickness studies consistently associate regional brain anatomy with affective capacities. Regarding empathy, structural differences commonly found in the anterior insula and inferior frontal gyrus (IFG) reflect individual variability. Grey matter measures in the anterior insula correlate with trait empathy, while IFG morphology also varies with affective-empathy scores (Mutschler et al., 2013; Banissy et al., 2012). In mood and personality disorders, major depressive disorder shows significant hippocampal volume reductions, especially with early onset and recurrent episodes, along with widespread but modest cortical thinning, including prefrontal regions (Schmaal et al., 2016; Schmaal et al., 2017). Borderline personality disorder literature reports changes in limbic volumes (e.g., amygdala/hippocampus) and decreased prefrontal cortical thickness in several samples, consistent with impaired top-down regulation (Nunes et al., 2009; Giannoulis et al., 2025; Rossi et al., 2015).

These anatomical patterns are not static. Longitudinal imaging studies have documented *neuroplastic changes* in emotion-related structures in response to therapeutic interventions such as mindfulness training, cognitive-behavioural therapy, or pharmacological treatment. For example, patients with depression often show increases in hippocampal volume following successful treatment, while the normalisation of hyperactive amygdala responses to negative stimuli has been observed with exposure therapy in anxiety disorders. Such findings point to the potential of structural and functional patterns to serve not just as markers of emotional states but as *biomarkers of emotional change*.

CT is generally less sensitive than MRI for subtle lesions, but it can still be useful in lesion–symptom mapping pipelines; converging work shows orbitofrontal/anterior temporal damage and disruption of fronto-limbic white-matter tracts are linked to emotional flattening, disinhibition, and impaired social–affective judgement (Bechara et al., 2000; Koenigs & Tranel, 2007; Hiser & Koenigs, 2018; Operskalski et al., 2015). For sensitivity, MRI (including diffusion methods) consistently outperforms CT for many fine-grained pathologies (e.g., diffuse axonal injury, white-matter disease), but CT can complement MRI when triangulating structure–function relationships.

One promising development involves *connectivity-based pattern analysis*, where researchers examine how emotional experiences are shaped by communication between brain regions rather than isolated activity. Using DTI, which traces white matter tracts, and resting-state fMRI, researchers can construct emotional connectivity profiles for individuals. High emotional granularity is the ability to distinguish and label subtle emotional states. It has been linked to increased connectivity between the prefrontal cortex and the insula, suggesting enhanced top-down modulation of interoceptive signals. Conversely, emotional rigidity or impulsivity has been associated with stronger amygdala-subcortical coupling and reduced connectivity with regulatory cortical regions (Fan et al., 2016).

Recent innovations have pushed these analyses even further by employing *deep learning models* to automatically extract emotional features from imaging data. These models can identify latent representations of affect that are not easily visible through standard statistical techniques. For instance, convolutional neural networks (CNNs) trained on MRI slices have been used to predict anxiety or depression severity with considerable accuracy. While still in early stages, such approaches hold the potential to uncover hidden emotional patterns embedded in high-dimensional brain data, enabling more personalised and precise emotion science. Related machine-learning frameworks have also been applied to affect-linked constructs beyond core emotions, such as love addiction, where features and explanations clarify predictive factors (Farahani et al., 2025).

As researchers continue to refine these techniques, the goal is not merely to map emotion onto the brain but to understand the *embodied logic of affective experience*. Emotional patterns in neuroimaging data are shaped by a complex interplay of structural predispositions, situational demands, and internal states. They vary across individuals, evolve across time, and reflect both the universality and the individuality of emotional life. CT and MRI thus serve as more than diagnostic tools. They are *windows into the embodied architecture of human feeling,* offering a rare and powerful glimpse into the neural choreography of the emotional self.

5.5 Towards Automated Emotion Detection: Algorithms and Neuroimaging

The increasing convergence of neuroscience, artificial intelligence, and affective computing has paved the way for automated systems capable of detecting emotional states directly from neuroimaging data. With the rapid expansion of data availability and algorithmic sophistication, the field is witnessing a shift from descriptive and correlational brain-emotion studies towards predictive and diagnostic frameworks that leverage machine learning to decode emotion from MRI and CT scans. In this landscape, Python has emerged as the dominant programming language, enabling the integration of neuroimaging preprocessing tools, machine learning frameworks, and statistical modelling into unified, replicable pipelines (Kovač et al., 2024). This section explores the design and implementation of automated emotion detection systems based on neuroimaging, with an emphasis on Python-based practices and the role of computational models in transforming raw brain data into affective insights.

At the core of automated emotion detection is the representation of high-dimensional neuroimaging data in a form that is amenable to algorithmic learning. For MRI, this often involves voxel-wise data from functional scans or morphological features such as cortical thickness and regional volumes from structural scans. In Python, such features are typically extracted using libraries like nibabel, nilearn, or PySurfer, which provide interfaces to load, visualise, and manipulate neuroimaging data in NIfTI format. Once the imaging features are prepared, they can be combined with behavioural or physiological labels, such as emotion ratings or arousal indices, to form supervised datasets for model training.

The most common approach to emotion decoding involves the use of *machine learning classifiers* trained to predict discrete emotions (e.g., fear, happiness) or continuous affective dimensions (e.g., valence, arousal) from imaging data. Python's scikit-learn library offers a robust suite of algorithms for this purpose, including support vector machines (SVMs), random forests, and logistic regression, all of which have been widely applied in neuroimaging research. For example, a basic pipeline might include loading preprocessed fMRI activation maps, flattening voxel data into 1D feature vectors, and training an SVM to distinguish between high- and low-arousal states:

```
from sklearn.svm import SVC
from sklearn.model_selection import cross_val_score
from sklearn.preprocessing import StandardScaler
import numpy as np

# X: fMRI data (n_samples x n_voxels), y: arousal labels
scaler = StandardScaler()
X_scaled = scaler.fit_transform(X)
```

```
clf = SVC(kernel='linear', C=1)
scores = cross_val_score(clf, X_scaled, y, cv=5)

print(f"Mean classification accuracy: {np.mean(scores):.2f}")
```

This type of approach allows for the rapid evaluation of model performance across individuals, tasks, or emotional conditions. With proper validation and regularisation, it is possible to interpret model weights and identify the most predictive brain regions associated with emotional states, resulting in predictive and neuroscientific insight. Comparable supervised pipelines are also used in psychological health domains, for example, the classification of chronic pain outcomes (Kovač et al., 2025). A complementary line of work uses calibrated regression to predict internal shame, with XGBoost performing best and distress tolerance emerging as the strongest predictor (Kovač et al., 2025b).

In recent years, emotion detection has moved beyond classical machine learning toward *deep learning*, particularly when working with raw or minimally preprocessed imaging data (Avberšek et al., 2022). CNNs have been adapted to handle three-dimensional (3D) MRI volumes, allowing models to learn spatial features directly from imaging slices or volumes without the need for manual feature engineering. Python frameworks such as PyTorch and TensorFlow facilitate the development of these models, offering modules for 3D convolutions, data augmentation, and graphics processing unit acceleration. For instance, a simplified version of a 3D CNN for binary emotion classification might look like:

```
import torch
import torch.nn as nn

class Emotion3DCNN(nn.Module):
    def __init__(self):
        super(Emotion3DCNN, self).__init__()
        self.conv1 = nn.Conv3d(1, 16, kernel_size=3)
        self.pool = nn.MaxPool3d(2)
         self.fc1 = nn.Linear(16 * 13 * 13 * 13, 2) # Adjust
dimensions based on input shape

    def forward(self, x):
        x = self.pool(torch.relu(self.conv1(x)))
        x = x.view(-1, 16 * 13 * 13 * 13)
        x = self.fc1(x)
        return x
```

Such models have been used to classify emotional traits from structural MRI, detect affective disorders, or predict momentary affect from task-based fMRI. However, they require large datasets and careful regularisation to avoid overfitting. This represents a challenge given the limited sample sizes common in neuroimaging studies.

To address this, researchers have adopted *transfer learning* and *feature selection* strategies. For example, models pre-trained on large datasets like UK Biobank or the Human Connectome Project can be fine-tuned on smaller emotion-labelled datasets, improving performance and stability. Additionally, dimensionality reduction techniques like principal component analysis (PCA) or feature importance ranking (e.g., using sklearn.feature_selection.SelectKBest) are often used to reduce computational load and focus learning on the most informative regions.

Another important development is the application of *multimodal fusion* (He et al., 2020), where structural, functional, and diffusion data are integrated into unified models. Python-based pipelines using packages like MNE-Python, dipy, and nilearn allow for preprocessing and aligning different modalities. These fused models can capture more complex emotional dynamics. For instance, they are combining structural connectivity from DTI with task-based fMRI activation to predict how individuals will respond emotionally to a stressor or social cue.

Automated emotion detection systems have also begun to incorporate *temporal dynamics*, especially in studies using naturalistic stimuli such as films, narratives, or social interactions. Recurrent neural networks (RNNs) and transformers have been used to model how emotional responses evolve, based on dynamic fluctuations in brain activity. The PyTorch library, in particular, provides flexible modules for constructing such models, enabling time series classification and prediction from BOLD signal trajectories.

The ethical implications of automated emotion detection from brain data must also be acknowledged. While these systems offer the potential for emotion-aware technologies, personalised medicine, and affective monitoring, they raise questions about privacy, consent, and the interpretability of predictions. Misclassification of emotional states, especially in sensitive contexts like mental health or judicial settings, can have serious consequences. Therefore, the deployment of such systems requires rigorous validation, transparent reporting of limitations, and ethical safeguards that prioritise user autonomy and well-being.

Looking ahead, one of the most promising directions involves *real-time emotion decoding* using fMRI neurofeedback. In these setups, brain activity is analysed in real time to provide participants with feedback on their current emotional state, allowing them to learn to self-regulate affect through neural training. Python scripts leveraging NiTime, NeuroFeedback Suite, or real-time data streaming APIs are central to implementing these feedback loops. The combination of online detection and adaptive feedback introduces an entirely new interactive, embodied, and computationally mediated paradigm for emotion research.

Automated emotion detection from neuroimaging is thus not a distant aspiration but an increasingly operational reality. Python-based tools and algorithms offer a powerful foundation for this work, enabling reproducible, scalable, and interpretable systems that can decode the emotional self from the architecture and activity of the brain. As techniques continue to mature, these systems will play a critical role in reshaping how we understand, measure, and intervene in the emotional dimensions of human experience.

5.6 Case Studies and Experiments

To bridge the technical sophistication of neuroimaging-based emotion detection with practical application, this section presents an illustrative case study and simulated experiments that demonstrate how CT and MRI data can be harnessed, analysed, and interpreted in the context of emotion research. These examples are especially designed for readers who may not have a deep background in neuroimaging or machine learning but wish to understand how the integration of these tools reveals embodied emotional processes.

We analyse a public dataset *ds000201* from *OpenNeuro* (Nilsonne et al., 2018). The dataset is organised in BIDS format and includes multiple participants (e.g., sub-9001, sub-9002, ...), often with two sessions each (ses-1, ses-2). For each session, there is:

- a functional BOLD run named task-arrows (EPI time series), and
- a high-resolution T1-weighted anatomical image.

Each functional run is accompanied by an events.tsv file containing, at minimum, onset, duration, and trial_type per event. In this dataset, the events also include additional columns (e.g., *event_type*, *cue_to_participant*, *stimulus_type*, *time_until_response*, and *rated_success_of_regulation*). These reveal that participants viewed emotional pictures (e.g., IAPS images) and were periodically cued (e.g., "Maintain") on how to respond, making it an emotion-related task. To keep this case study focused and fully reproducible, we present a *single-subject* analysis (sub-9001, ses-1). The same steps apply to any subject/session pair. Keep in mind that you don't need to load the entire dataset, especially since these datasets may be very memory-intensive. A single subject can already demonstrate how emotion-related signals are modelled and interpreted.

Before any brain map is created, the timing of the task is turned into predictors in a *design matrix* (see Figure 5.6). Think of it as the storyboard of the experiment, frame by frame. Each column is a regressor (e.g., the task condition and slow *drift* terms that remove scanner trends); each row corresponds to one time point (one fMRI volume).

The leftmost column labelled **arrows** encodes when task events occurred (convolved with a hemodynamic response model so it matches brain physiology). The remaining columns (drift_1...drift_16 and constant) capture slow scanner drifts and the baseline. Figure 6 shows the *inputs* to the statistical model. A clear design matrix ensures we can later claim that *activity*

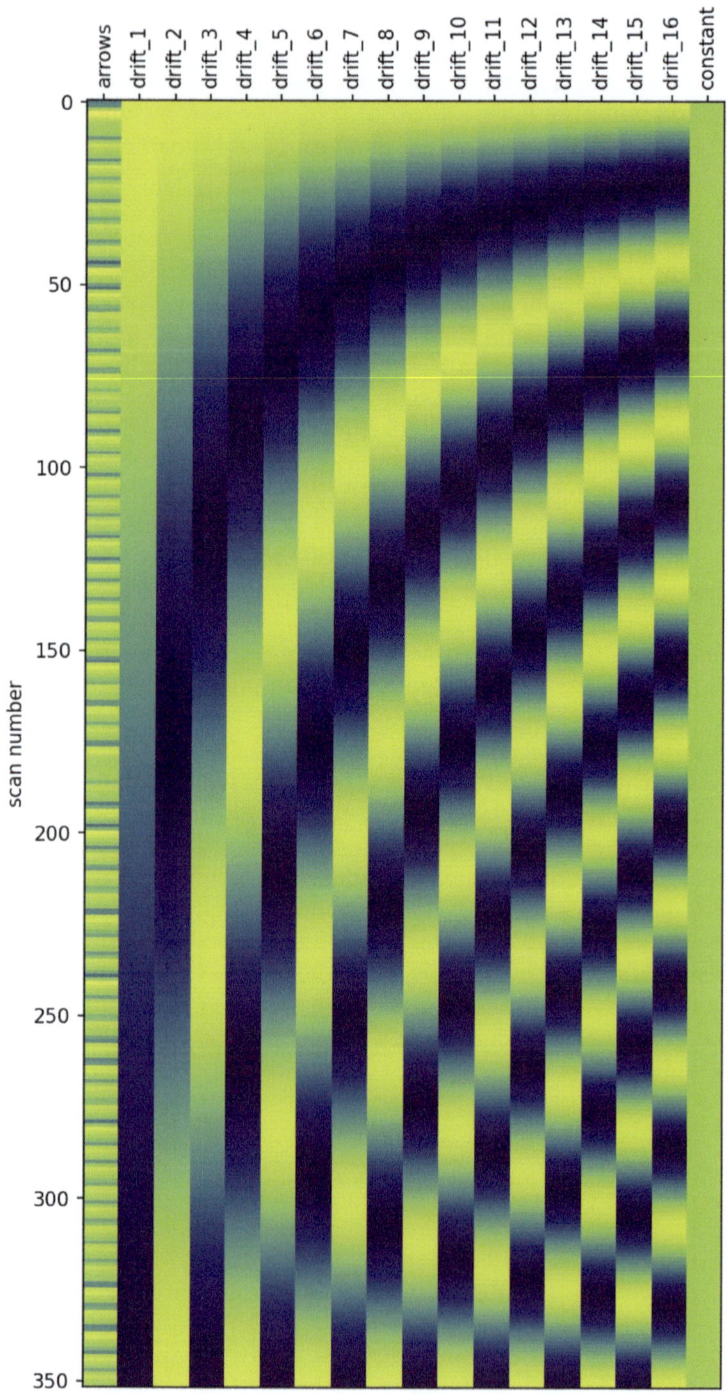

Figure 5.6 Design matrix forsub-9001/ses-1.

increased during the task rather than inadvertently modelling artefacts or idle periods. If the colours look like waves, that's expected. Those sinusoid-like *drift* columns remove slow fluctuations unrelated to emotion processing.

Before zooming into slices, we first show a *glass-brain* overview (Figure 5.7) of the whole z-map to give the reader an immediate sense of where the task leaves its footprint. This global view is helpful for non-technical readers: it reveals that effects are distributed across the cortex and not confined to a single spot, and it lets us check symmetry and gross alignment without committing to a specific slice. The unthresholded z-map for Task > baseline is projected through the brain in four canonical views (left sagittal, coronal, right sagittal, axial). Brighter voxels indicate stronger |z|. This *X-ray-style* view is ideal for a fast global orientation before we pick exact slices.

With the design matrix in place, we fit a *first-level* general linear model (GLM) to estimate where the BOLD signal increased or decreased during the task relative to the implicit baseline. We use a canonical haemodynamic response and standard nuisance terms (cosine drifts; AR(1) noise model). The result is a *z-map*: higher values mean a stronger task effect. We present the *unthresholded* statistical map in a slice series. Showing the continuous z-values before applying any threshold helps readers grasp the full spatial pattern (including subtle, subthreshold structure) and prevents the impression that activation is *all-or-nothing*. From inferior to superior, Figure 5.8 shows continuous effect sizes rather than a hard cutoff. This makes bilateral patterns and gradual changes with z-position visible and prepares the reader for the thresholded view that follows.

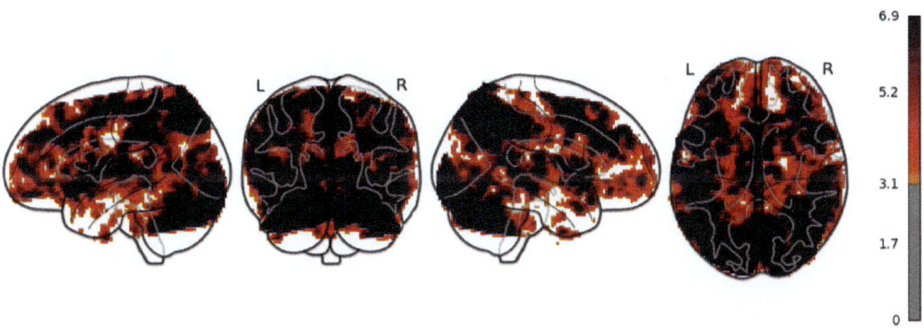

Figure 5.7 Glass-brain overview (MNI152 space, affine-aligned).

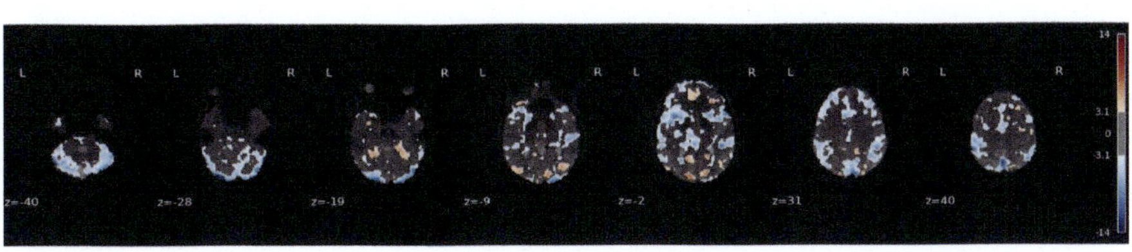

Figure 5.8 Axial slice series (unthresholded z for Task > baseline).

To anchor the effect in 3D coordinates, we add an unthresholded orthogonal cut (Figure 5.9) with crosshairs. This answers the practical question of *where the peak is* before we move to a cleaned, thresholded display. Sagittal, coronal, and axial planes with crosshairs provide world-coordinate context for the strongest cluster. Using the continuous map here avoids hiding near-threshold structure.

Having oriented the reader with unthresholded views, we now apply a conventional cluster-forming display threshold of $|z|>3.1$ (see Figures 5.10 and 5.11). The thresholded maps simplify interpretation for reports and tables while preserving the bilateral, fronto-parietal pattern seen above.

Multiple axial slices (bottom of the brain to the top) in Figure 5.10 show clusters where the task significantly modulated activity. Warm colours (red) indicate positive z-scores (activation > baseline), while cool colours (blue) indicate negative z-scores (deactivation < baseline). A slice series makes spatial patterns easy to spot (e.g., bilateral, posterior, or frontal effects) without getting lost in a single 3-D view.

Orthogonal cuts shown in Figure 5.11 (sagittal, coronal, axial) with crosshairs provide world coordinates of the peak shown. Readers often want to know where exactly a strong effect lies. This view provides precise coordinates for reporting or ROI definition. We use a two-tailed display ($|z|>3.1$),

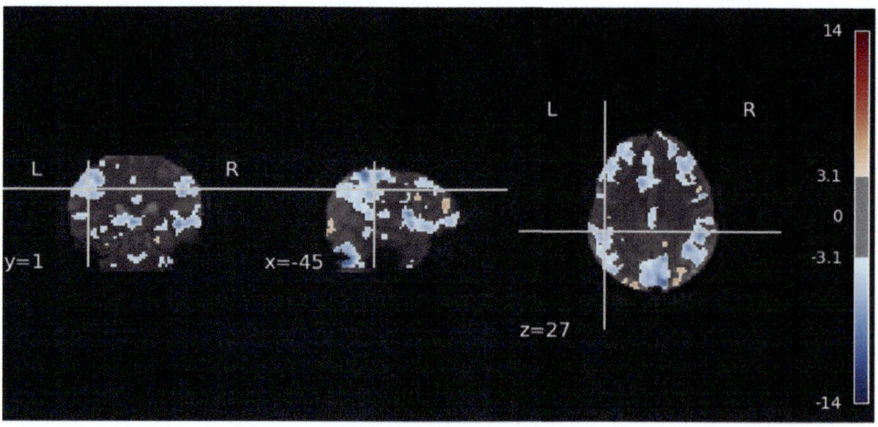

Figure 5.9 Orthogonal cuts (unthresholded z for Task > baseline).

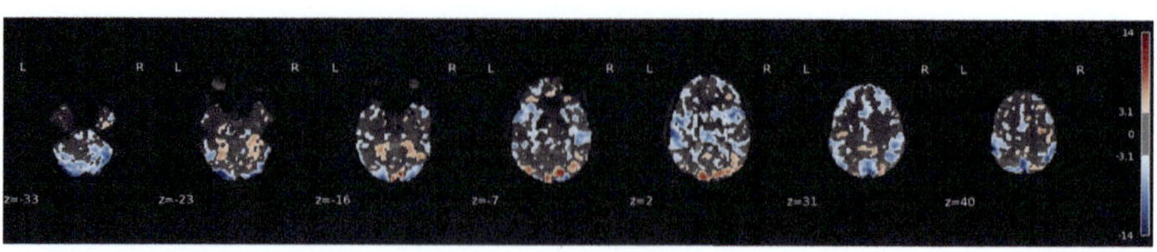

Figure 5.10 Task > baseline, axial cut-series, $|z|>3.1$.

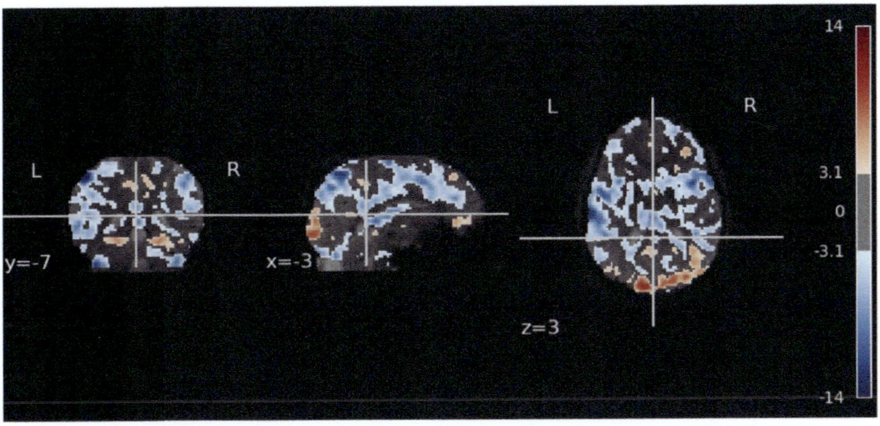

Figure 5.11 Task > baseline, orthogonal views, |z|>3.1.

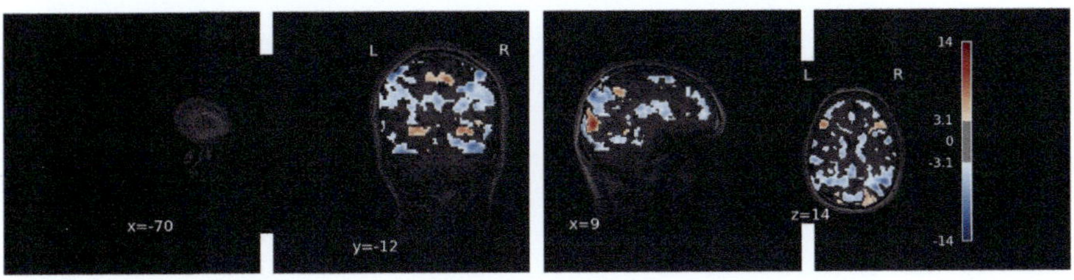

Figure 5.12 Task > baseline, overlaid on the subject's T1.

so both positive and negative effects are visible. This is why the colourbar ranges from negative to positive values. A negative value does *not* mean *bad*. It rather simply indicates a lower BOLD signal than baseline in that region during the task period.

Group templates are convenient, but many readers understand the anatomy best when effects are shown on the person's own T1 image.

Three orthogonal mosaics show how the thresholded z-map sits on the participant's high-resolution anatomy. It reassures the reader that the activations are not abstract blobs. They align with recognisable anatomical landmarks in this individual.

Emotion research often highlights the amygdala and vmPFC. To make the results accessible, we extract the mean z-value from small, predefined ROIs and present them as simple bars with a 95% bootstrap band in Figure 5.13. These summaries are not formal hypothesis tests here. They're intuitive summaries that help non-specialists relate the map to familiar emotion-related loci.

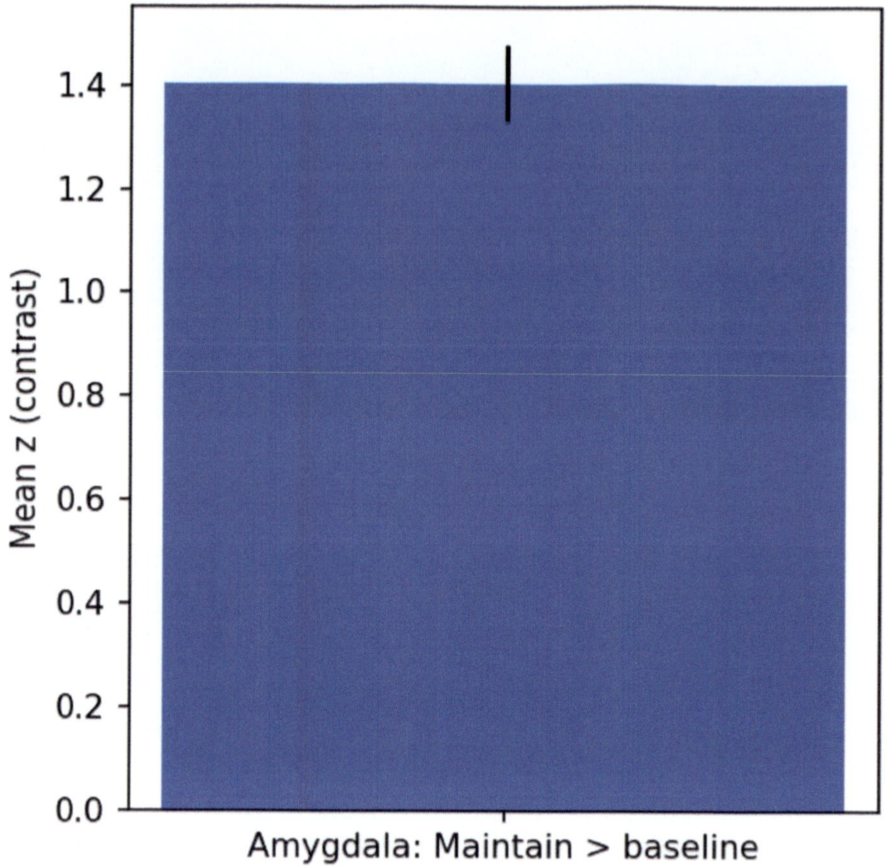

Figure 5.13 ROI summary: Amygdala, mean z for Task > baseline.

The bar shows the mean effect within a bilateral amygdala ROI. The thin line marks a 95% bootstrap interval around the mean. For emotion tasks that involve viewing affective images, amygdala engagement is a common expectation. A positive mean suggests the task period coincides with increased signal in this region (in this subject).

vmPFC is another canonical node in affect and regulation (Figure 5.14). Here, the mean is close to zero with a wide uncertainty band. Not all emotion-linked regions *light up* in every subject or task. Showing both amygdala and vmPFC side-by-side prevents cherry-picking and teaches that individual datasets differ.

We will now demonstrate how we computed ROI bars in Python. Define a small spherical ROI (e.g., radius 6 mm) using MNI coordinates or load a standard atlas mask; then average the GLM z-map within that ROI:

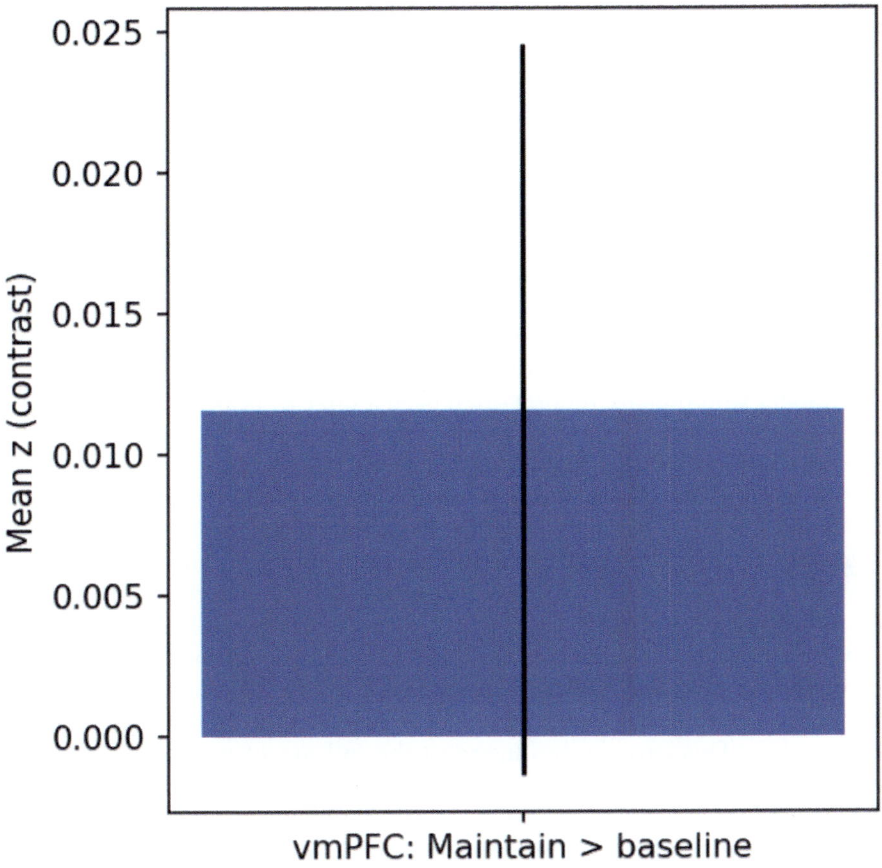

Figure 5.14 ROI summary: vmPFC, mean z for Task > baseline.

```
from nilearn.maskers import NiftiSpheresMasker
from nilearn import image

zmap_img = image.load_img("your.nii.gz") # your GLM contrast
# Example: left & right amygdala centers (approx MNI); replace
with your own
amygdala_seeds = [(-22, -4, -16), (22, -4, -16)]
masker = NiftiSpheresMasker(seeds=amygdala_seeds, radius=6,
standardize=False)
roi_vals = masker.fit_transform(zmap_img).ravel() # average
across seeds
mean = roi_vals.mean()
```

Beyond *where is stronger*, readers often ask how regions interact. A psychophysiological interaction (PPI) analysis probes whether the coupling between a seed region (here, amygdala) and the rest of the brain changes with the psychological context (the task events). We illustrate this with a single uncorrected exploratory map shown in Figure 5.15.

The blue points in Figure 5.15 indicate voxels where coupling with the amygdala is weaker during the task. Warm tones (if present) would indicate stronger coupling. Figure 15 introduces the idea that emotion is not just about local activation but also about network dynamics. For a single subject, this is illustrative; group-level replication is required for firm conclusions. PPI is sensitive to how we model events and noise. Treat single-subject PPI displays as *hypothesis-generating*, not as definitive evidence.

Readers who prepare reports often need a table of peaks and cluster sizes. We exported peaks above $|z|>3.1$ with a minimal extent (e.g., $k \geq 10$ voxels). We are showing only the first 8 rows in Table 5.1.

This single-subject case study demonstrates the complete path from task design to statistical maps, from maps to interpretable summaries, and from local activation to context-dependent interactions. The visual strategy (design matrix → glass-brain (global) → unthresholded slices → unthresholded ortho → thresholded axial/ortho → subject-space overlay → ROI bars → PPI → peak table) lets non-technical readers follow the logic without wrestling with code. We see how an emotion-evoking task leaves a measurable footprint in the brain and how that footprint can be explained clearly, reproducibly, and responsibly. This case study illustrates the full arc of neuroimaging-based emotion research using tools that are increasingly open, intuitive, and replicable. While the technical foundations are complex, the insights they generate can be visualised, explained, and appreciated even by those with limited programming or neuroscience expertise.

By embedding emotion in visible, measurable brain patterns, we foster a deeper public and scientific understanding of how the brain embodies emotional life. The integration of real-time monitoring, predictive modelling, and visually intuitive platforms promises a future in which neuroscience is not just the domain of specialists but a source of emotional self-understanding, clinical insight, and human connection.

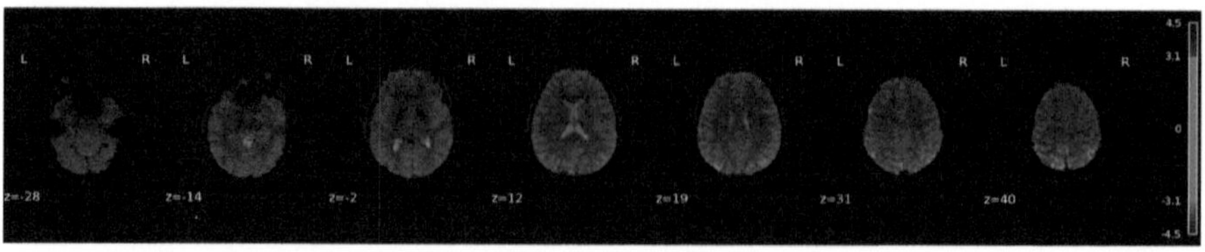

Figure 5.15 PPI map: Amygdala × task, thresholded.

Table 5.1 Peak/cluster summary,|z|>3.1, k≥10

Cluster ID	X	Y	Z	*Peak stat*	*Cluster size (mm3)*
1	5.61499786	–49.843994	–14.32048	11.993052	35285
1a	13.1149979	–44.218994	–2.3204727	11.6147929	
1b	24.3649979	–34.843994	–11.920479	11.4090705	
1c	–9.3850021	–51.718994	–2.3204727	10.632828	
2	–33.760002	–40.468994	–11.920479	9.77413744	3265
2a	–46.885002	–38.593994	–2.3204727	5.86542419	
2b	–50.635002	–31.093994	–7.1204758	3.55650637	
2c	–41.260002	–31.093994	2.47953033	3.26262283	

Columns include: Cluster ID (with sub-peaks 1a, 1b, …), MNI X/Y/Z (mm), Peak Stat (z-value), and Cluster Size (mm^3 for the main peak). The sign of Peak Stat indicates the direction (positive = activation; negative = deactivation). The Figure 5.12 colorbar shows both positive and negative ranges, as we used a two-tailed display. That's why you'll see negative values in figures even though the table caption says $z>3.1z > 3.1$. However, our Table 5.1 records |z|>3.1 (absolute value).

References

Adrián-Ventura, J., Costumero, V., Parcet, M. A., & Ávila, C. (2019). Linking personality and brain anatomy: a structural MRI approach to Reinforcement Sensitivity Theory. *Social Cognitive and Affective Neuroscience*, *14*(3), 329–338.

Ashburner, J., Barnes, G., Chen, C. C., Daunizeau, J., Flandin, G., Friston, K., & Penny, W. (2014). SPM12 manual. *Wellcome Trust Centre for Neuroimaging, London, UK*, *2464*(4), 53.

Avberšek, L. K., & Repovš, G. (2022). Deep learning in neuroimaging data analysis: Applications, challenges, and solutions. *Frontiers in Neuroimaging*, *1*, 981642.

Banissy, M. J., Kanai, R., Walsh, V., & Rees, G. (2012). Inter-individual differences in empathy are reflected in human brain structure. *Neuroimage*, *62*(3), 2034–2039.

Barrett, L. F., & Simmons, W. K. (2015). Interoceptive predictions in the brain. *Nature Reviews Neuroscience*, *16*(7), 419–429.

Bates, E., Wilson, S. M., Saygin, A. P., Dick, F., Sereno, M. I., Knight, R. T., & Dronkers, N. F. (2003). Voxel-based lesion–symptom mapping. *Nature Neuroscience*, *6*(5), 448–450.

Bechara, A., Damasio, H., & Damasio, A. R. (2000). Emotion, decision making and the orbitofrontal cortex. *Cerebral Cortex*, *10*(3), 295–307.

Buhle, J. T., Silvers, J. A., Wager, T. D., Lopez, R., Onyemekwu, C., Kober, H., & Ochsner, K. N. (2014). Cognitive reappraisal of emotion: a meta-analysis of human neuroimaging studies. *Cerebral Cortex*, *24*(11), 2981–2990.

Chang, L. J., Gianaros, P. J., Manuck, S. B., Krishnan, A., & Wager, T. D. (2015). A sensitive and specific neural signature for picture-induced negative affect. *PLoS Biology*, *13*(6), e1002180.

Collins, D. L., Neelin, P., Peters, T. M., & Evans, A. C. (1994). Automatic 3D intersubject registration of MR volumetric data in standardized Talairach space. *Journal of Computer Assisted Tomography*, *18*(2), 192–205.

Craig, A. D. (2002). How do you feel? Interoception: the sense of the physiological condition of the body. *Nature Reviews Neuroscience*, *3*(8), 655–666.

Craig, A. D. (2009). How do you feel—now? The anterior insula and human awareness. *Nature Reviews Neuroscience*, *10*(1), 59–70.

Dabas, M. M., Alameri, A. D., Mohamed, N. M., Mahmood, R., Kim, D. H., Samreen, M., & Khan, S. (2024). Comparative efficacy of MRI and CT in traumatic brain injury: A systematic review. *Cureus*, *16*(10), e72086.

Damasio, A. (2021). *Feeling & knowing: Making minds conscious*. Pantheon.

Disner, S. G., Beevers, C. G., Haigh, E. A., & Beck, A. T. (2011). Neural mechanisms of the cognitive model of depression. *Nature Reviews Neuroscience*, *12*(8), 467–477.

Esteban, O., Birman, D., Schaer, M., Koyejo, O. O., Poldrack, R. A., & Gorgolewski, K. J. (2017). MRIQC: Advancing the automatic prediction of image quality in MRI from unseen sites. *PLoS One*, *12*(9), e0184661.

Esteban, O., Markiewicz, C. J., Blair, R. W., Moodie, C. A., Isik, A. I., Erramuzpe, A., & Gorgolewski, K. J. (2019). fMRIPrep: a robust preprocessing pipeline for functional MRI. *Nature Methods*, *16*(1), 111–116.

Etkin, A., & Wager, T. D. (2007). Functional neuroimaging of anxiety: A meta-analysis of emotional processing in PTSD, social anxiety disorder, and specific phobia. *American Journal of Psychiatry*, *164*(10), 1476–1488.

Etkin, A., Büchel, C., & Gross, J. J. (2015). The neural bases of emotion regulation. *Nature Reviews Neuroscience*, *16*(11), 693–700.

Fan, L., Li, H., Zhuo, J., Zhang, Y., Wang, J., Chen, L., & Jiang, T. (2016). The human brainnetome atlas: A new brain atlas based on connectional architecture. *Cerebral Cortex*, *26*(8), 3508–3526.

Farahani, H., Watson, P., Bezan, T., Kovač, N., Winter, L. C., Blagojević, M., & Jiménez, P. (2024). PsAIchology: An intelligent direction in psychological sciences. In *10th international scientific conference Technics, Informatics and Education-TIE 2024*. Faculty of Technical Sciences Čačak, University of Kragujevac.

Farahani, H., Watson, P., Kovač, N., Sheykhangafshe, F. B., Azadfallah, P., Allahyari, A., & Chesli, R. R. (2025). Unraveling the complexity of love addiction using machine learning algorithms: The influence of positive and negative affect, interpersonal needs, and self-hate. In C.-H. Mayer & E. Vanderheiden (Eds.), *International handbook of love: Transcultural and transdisciplinary perspectives* (pp. 1–22). Springer Nature.

Feurer, C., Jimmy, J., Chang, F., Langenecker, S. A., Phan, K. L., Ajilore, O., & Klumpp, H. (2021). Resting state functional connectivity correlates of rumination and worry in internalizing psychopathologies. *Depression and Anxiety*, *38*(5), 488–497.

Fischl, B. (2012). FreeSurfer. *Neuroimage*, *62*(2), 774–781.

Fonov, V., Evans, A. C., Botteron, K., Almli, C. R., McKinstry, R. C., Collins, D. L., & Brain Development Cooperative Group. (2011). Unbiased average age-appropriate atlases for pediatric studies. *Neuroimage*, *54*(1), 313–327.

Giannoulis, E., Nousis, C., Sula, I. J., Georgitsi, M. E., & Malogiannis, I. (2025). Understanding the borderline brain: A review of neurobiological findings in Borderline Personality Disorder (BPD). *Biomedicines*, *13*(7), 1783.

Gläscher, J., Adolphs, R., Damasio, H., Bechara, A., Rudrauf, D., Calamia, M., & Tranel, D. (2012). Lesion mapping of cognitive control and value-based decision making in the prefrontal cortex. *Proceedings of the National Academy of Sciences*, *109*(36), 14681–14686.

Gorgolewski, K. J., Auer, T., Calhoun, V. D., Craddock, R. C., Das, S., Duff, E. P., & Poldrack, R. A. (2016). The brain imaging data structure, a format for organizing and describing outputs of neuroimaging experiments. *Scientific Data*, *3*(1), 1–9.

Gorgolewski, K., Burns, C. D., Madison, C., Clark, D., Halchenko, Y. O., Waskom, M. L., & Ghosh, S. S. (2011). Nipype: a flexible, lightweight and extensible neuroimaging data processing framework in python. *Frontiers in Neuroinformatics*, *5*, 13.

Granger, S. J., Leal, S. L., Larson, M. S., Janecek, J. T., McMillan, L., Stern, H., & Yassa, M. A. (2021). Integrity of the uncinate fasciculus is associated with emotional pattern separation-related fMRI signals in the hippocampal dentate and CA3. *Neurobiology of Learning and Memory*, *177*, 107359.

Haynes, J. D. (2015). A primer on pattern-based approaches to fMRI: Principles, pitfalls, and perspectives. *Neuron*, *87*(2), 257–270.

He, Z., Li, Z., Yang, F., Wang, L., Li, J., Zhou, C., & Pan, J. (2020). Advances in multimodal emotion recognition based on brain–computer interfaces. *Brain Sciences*, *10*(10), 687.

Herbet, G., Lafargue, G., Moritz-Gasser, S., de Champfleur, N. M., Costi, E., Bonnetblanc, F., & Duffau, H. (2015). A disconnection account of subjective empathy impairments in diffuse low-grade glioma patients. *Neuropsychologia*, *70*, 165–176.

Hiser, J., & Koenigs, M. (2018). The multifaceted role of the ventromedial prefrontal cortex in emotion, decision making, social cognition, and psychopathology. *Biological Psychiatry*, *83*(8), 638–647.

Hu, D., Liang, H., Qu, S., Han, C., & Jiang, Y. (2023). A fast and accurate brain extraction method for CT head images. *BMC Medical Imaging*, *23*(1), 124.

Kaiser, R. H., Andrews-Hanna, J. R., Wager, T. D., & Pizzagalli, D. A. (2015). Large-scale network dysfunction in major depressive disorder: A meta-analysis of resting-state functional connectivity. *JAMA Psychiatry*, *72*(6), 603–611.

Karnath, H. O., Fruhmann Berger, M., Zopf, R., & Küker, W. (2004). Using SPM normalization for lesion analysis in spatial neglect. *Brain*, *127*(4), e10–e10.

Kleckner, I. R., Zhang, J., Touroutoglou, A., Chanes, L., Xia, C., Simmons, W. K., & Feldman Barrett, L. (2017). Evidence for a large-scale brain system supporting allostasis and interoception in humans. *Nature -Human Behaviour*, *1*(5), 0069.

Knutson, K. M., Dal Monte, O., Schintu, S., Wassermann, E. M., Raymont, V., Grafman, J., & Krueger, F. (2015). Areas of brain damage underlying increased reports of behavioral disinhibition. *The Journal of Neuropsychiatry and Clinical Neurosciences*, *27*(3), 193–198.

Koenigs, M., & Grafman, J. (2009). The functional neuroanatomy of depression: Distinct roles for ventromedial and dorsolateral prefrontal cortex. *Behavioural Brain Research*, *201*(2), 239–243.

Koenigs, M., & Tranel, D. (2007). Irrational economic decision-making after ventromedial prefrontal damage: evidence from the Ultimatum Game. *Journal of Neuroscience*, *27*(4), 951–956.

Kovač, N., Ratković, K., Farahani, H., & Watson, P. (2024). A practical applications guide to machine learning regression models in psychology with Python. *Methods in Psychology*, *11*, 100156.

Kovač, N., Ratković, K., Watson, P., Farahani, H., & Bagheri Sheykhangafshe, F. (2025a). Machine learning classification models for predicting chronic pain. *Current Psychology*, 1–14. Advance online publication.

Kovač, N., Ratković, K., Farahani, H., & Watson, P. (2025b). Machine learning regression models for internal shame. *Acta Psychologica*, *260*, 105721.

Kragel, P. A., & LaBar, K. S. (2015). Multivariate neural biomarkers of emotional states are categorically distinct. *Social Cognitive and Affective Neuroscience*, *10*(11), 1437–1448.

Kragel, P. A., & LaBar, K. S. (2016). Decoding the nature of emotion in the brain. *Trends in Cognitive Sciences*, *20*(6), 444–455.

LeDoux, J. (2020). *The deep history of ourselves: The four-billion-year story of how we got conscious brains*. Penguin.

Lindquist, K. A., Wager, T. D., Kober, H., Bliss-Moreau, E., & Barrett, L. F. (2012). The brain basis of emotion: a meta-analytic review. *Behavioral and Brain Sciences*, *35*(3), 121–143.

Madge, V. (2020). *Evaluating Voxelmorph: A learning-based 3D non-linear registration algorithm, against the non-linear symmetric normalization technique from ANTs*. McGill University.

Menon, V., & Toga, A. W. (2015). *Brain mapping: An encyclopedic reference* (pp. 597–611). Academic Press.

Morawetz, C., Bode, S., Baudewig, J., & Heekeren, H. R. (2017). Effective amygdala-prefrontal connectivity predicts individual differences in successful emotion regulation. *Social Cognitive and Affective Neuroscience*, 12(4), 569–585.

Muschelli, J., Ullman, N. L., Mould, W. A., Vespa, P., Hanley, D. F., & Crainiceanu, C. M. (2015). Validated automatic brain extraction of head CT images. *Neuroimage*, *114*, 379–385.

Mutschler, I., Reinbold, C., Wankerl, J., Seifritz, E., & Ball, T. (2013). Structural basis of empathy and the domain general region in the anterior insular cortex. *Frontiers in human neuroscience*, 7, 177.

Najm, M., Kuang, H., Federico, A., Jogiat, U., Goyal, M., Hill, M. D., & Qiu, W. (2019). Automated brain extraction from head CT and CTA images using convex optimization with shape propagation. *Computer Methods and Programs in Biomedicine*, *176*, 1–8.

Nilsonne, G., Tamm, S., d'Onofrio, P., Thuné, H. Å., Schwarz, J., Lavebratt, C., Liu, J. J., Månsson, K. N. T., Sundelin, T., Axelsson, J., Fransson, P., Kecklund, G.,

Fischer, H., Lekander, M., & Åkerstedt, T. (2018). *ds000201* (Version R1.0.5) [Data set]. OpenNeuro.

Norman, K. A., Polyn, S. M., Detre, G. J., & Haxby, J. V. (2006). Beyond mind-reading: Multi-voxel pattern analysis of fMRI data. *Trends in Cognitive Sciences*, *10*(9), 424–430.

Nunes, P. M., Wenzel, A., Borges, K. T., Porto, C. R., Caminha, R. M., & De Oliveira, I. R. (2009). Volumes of the hippocampus and amygdala in patients with borderline personality disorder: A meta-analysis. *Journal of Personality Disorders*, *23*(4), 333–345.

Ochsner, K. N., & Gross, J. J. (2005). The cognitive control of emotion. *Trends in Cognitive Sciences*, *9*(5), 242–249.

Oishi, K., Faria, A. V., Hsu, J., Tippett, D., Mori, S., & Hillis, A. E. (2015). Critical role of the right uncinate fasciculus in emotional empathy. *Annals of Neurology*, *77*(1), 68–74.

Operskalski, J. T., Paul, E. J., Colom, R., Barbey, A. K., & Grafman, J. (2015). Lesion mapping the four-factor structure of emotional intelligence. *Frontiers in Human Neuroscience*, *9*, 649.

Pereira, F., Mitchell, T., & Botvinick, M. (2009). Machine learning classifiers and fMRI: A tutorial overview. *Neuroimage*, *45*(1), S199-S209.

Pessoa, L. (2022). *The entangled brain: How perception, cognition, and emotion are woven together*. MIT Press.

Phelps, E. A., & LeDoux, J. E. (2005). Contributions of the amygdala to emotion processing: From animal models to human behavior. *Neuron*, *48*(2), 175–187.

Phillips, M. L., & Swartz, H. A. (2014). A critical appraisal of neuroimaging studies of bipolar disorder: toward a new conceptualization of underlying neural circuitry and a road map for future research. *American Journal of Psychiatry*, *171*(8), 829–843.

Poldrack, R. A., Huckins, G., & Varoquaux, G. (2020). Establishment of best practices for evidence for prediction: a review. *JAMA Psychiatry*, *77*(5), 534–540.

Rorden, C., Bonilha, L., Fridriksson, J., Bender, B., & Karnath, H. O. (2012). Age-specific CT and MRI templates for spatial normalization. *Neuroimage*, *61*(4), 957–965.

Rossi, R., Lanfredi, M., Pievani, M., Boccardi, M., Rasser, P. E., Thompson, P. M., & Frisoni, G. B. (2015). Abnormalities in cortical gray matter density in borderline personality disorder. *European Psychiatry*, *30*(2), 221–227.

Saarimäki, H., Gotsopoulos, A., Jääskeläinen, I. P., Lampinen, J., Vuilleumier, P., Hari, R., & Nummenmaa, L. (2016). Discrete neural signatures of basic emotions. *Cerebral Cortex*, *26*(6), 2563–2573.

Schmaal, L., Hibar, D. P., Sämann, P. G., Hall, G. B., Baune, B. T., Jahanshad, N., & Veltman, D. J. (2017). Cortical abnormalities in adults and adolescents with major depression based on brain scans from 20 cohorts worldwide in the ENIGMA Major Depressive Disorder Working Group. *Molecular Psychiatry*, *22*(6), 900–909.

Schmaal, L., Veltman, D. J., van Erp, T. G., Sämann, P. G., Frodl, T., Jahanshad, N., & Hibar, D. P. (2016). Subcortical brain alterations in major depressive disorder: findings from the ENIGMA Major Depressive Disorder working group. *Molecular Psychiatry*, *21*(6), 806–812.

Schweizer, S., Grahn, J., Hampshire, A., Mobbs, D., & Dalgleish, T. (2013). Training the emotional brain: Improving affective control through emotional working memory training. *Journal of Neuroscience*, *33*(12), 5301–5311.

Shenton, M. E., Hamoda, H. M., Schneiderman, J. S., Bouix, S., Pasternak, O., Rathi, Y., & Zafonte, R. (2012). A review of magnetic resonance imaging and diffusion tensor imaging findings in mild traumatic brain injury. *Brain Imaging and Behavior*, *6*(2), 137–192.

Smith, S. M., Jenkinson, M., Woolrich, M. W., Beckmann, C. F., Behrens, T. E., Johansen-Berg, H., & Matthews, P. M. (2004). Advances in functional and structural MR image analysis and implementation as FSL. *Neuroimage*, *23*, S208–S219.

Thomas, K. S., Jones, C. R., Williams, M. O., & Vanderwert, R. E. (2025). Neural correlates of emotion regulation and associations with disordered eating during preadolescence. *Developmental Psychobiology*, *67*(1), e70009.

Tromp, D. P., Williams, L. E., Fox, A. S., Oler, J. A., Roseboom, P. H., Rogers, G. M., & Kalin, N. H. (2019). Altered uncinate fasciculus microstructure in childhood anxiety disorders in boys but not girls. *American Journal of Psychiatry*, *176*(3), 208–216.

van Dam, W. O., & Chrysikou, E. G. (2021). Effects of unilateral tDCS over left prefrontal cortex on emotion regulation in depression: evidence from concurrent functional magnetic resonance imaging. *Cognitive, Affective, & Behavioral Neuroscience*, *21*(1), 14–34.

Vo, D. T., Phan, C. C., Le, H. G. N., Vo, T. P., Mai, U. T. T., Le, H. K., & Ha, T. B. T. (2022). Diffuse axonal injury: a case report and MRI findings. *Radiology Case Reports*, *17*(1), 91–94.

Xu, E. P., Nguyen, L., Leibenluft, E., Stange, J. P., & Linke, J. O. (2023). A meta-analysis on the uncinate fasciculus in depression. *Psychological Medicine*, *53*(7), 2721–2731.

Xu, E., Nguyen, L., Hu, R., Stavish, C. M., Leibenluft, E., & Linke, J. O. (2022). The uncinate fasciculus in individuals with and at risk for bipolar disorder: A meta-analysis. *Journal of Affective Disorders*, *297*, 208–216.

Zhou, F., Zhao, W., Qi, Z., Geng, Y., Yao, S., Kendrick, K. M., & Becker, B. (2021). A distributed fMRI-based signature for the subjective experience of fear. *Nature Communications*, *12*(1), 6643.

Zhu, X., Wang, X., Xiao, J., Liao, J., Zhong, M., Wang, W., & Yao, S. (2012). Evidence of a dissociation pattern in resting-state default mode network connectivity in first-episode, treatment-naive major depression patients. *Biological Psychiatry*, *71*(7), 611–617.

6 Exploring Affective Images and Emotion Elicitation in Embodied Emotions

Nataša Kovač, Hojjatollah Farahani, and Peter Watson

6.1 Introduction

Human emotions do not exist in isolation; they manifest vividly through interactions between individuals and their environments. Central to these interactions are visual stimuli (faces, body postures, and contextual scenes) which powerfully evoke and shape emotional experiences. The processes of emotion elicitation, particularly through visual and embodied modalities, have profound implications for understanding emotional dynamics. This chapter explores how affective images and deliberate emotion elicitation techniques help uncover the intricate connections between visual perception, bodily responses, and emotional experience. By integrating historical insights, contemporary methodologies, computational advances, and ethical considerations, we establish a comprehensive understanding of how visual and emotional stimuli shape embodied emotional responses.

In recent decades, emotion research has progressively integrated the concept of embodiment, recognising that affective experience is deeply rooted in bodily processes that interact with neural and perceptual systems. This embodied perspective extends beyond viewing emotion as a cognitive appraisal of external stimuli, positioning it instead within dynamic, reciprocal loops between sensory input, interoceptive states, and motor expression (Niedenthal, 2007; Barrett, 2017). Affective images, whether photographic depictions, artistic renderings, or controlled laboratory scenes, serve as potent elicitors that engage these loops, influencing facial muscle activation, posture, heart rate variability, and respiratory patterns, which in turn modulate the appraisal and intensity of emotional responses (Critchley & Garfinkel, 2017).

Within experimental psychology, affective image-based paradigms are crucial both for standardisation and ecological validity. The International Affective Picture System offers reproducible stimuli with normative ratings, yet novel approaches have introduced immersive visual environments, dynamic stimuli, and culturally relevant imagery to elicit emotions that resonate more deeply with embodied states (Lang et al., 1997; Mikels et al., 2005). These developments allow researchers to examine how sensorimotor resonance, proprioceptive feedback, and interoceptive accuracy contribute to

DOI: 10.4324/9781003495123-6

the generation and regulation of emotion (Craig, 2009). Such methodologies not only clarify the mechanisms underpinning emotional experience but also illuminate individual and cultural differences in bodily involvement during affective processing.

Practical applications follow naturally from these insights. In clinical contexts, guided imagery incorporating bodily engagement, through posture adjustment, breath patterns, or weighted tactile feedback, has shown promise in modulating affective states for individuals with anxiety and mood disorders (Gross, 2015; Matsumoto et al., 2008). In resilience training and wellbeing interventions, carefully designed affective images can evoke adaptive bodily states that strengthen positive affect and reduce stress reactivity. These approaches bridge laboratory research and applied psychology, demonstrating that the systematic use of affective imagery in embodied contexts offers a scientifically grounded, versatile tool for both understanding and enhancing human emotional life.

6.2 Visual Stimuli and Embodied Emotions: Foundations and Importance

Visual stimuli have long played a pivotal role in emotion research, offering insights into the nuanced interplay between perception, cognition, and emotion. Historical investigations have revealed how visual imagery elicits diverse emotional reactions, demonstrating that images are potent tools for emotional engagement and research. Early psychological experiments by pioneers such as Ekman (1973) and Friesen (1972) underscored the universality of facial expressions, suggesting that basic emotions could be reliably elicited and recognised across cultures through visual means. These foundational studies established visual stimuli, especially facial imagery, as critical tools for investigating emotional processes.

The theoretical basis for using visual stimuli in emotion research emerges from the understanding of embodied cognition, where emotional states are not just psychological phenomena but are deeply connected to physical bodily states and environmental interactions. According to this framework, visual stimuli do not merely evoke emotional states; they actively shape bodily responses, physiological reactions, and subsequent emotional experiences. Figure 6.1 summarises this flow, emphasising the embodied link between what is seen and how the body reacts. For instance, viewing a fearful face can trigger autonomic nervous system responses such as increased heart rate or skin conductance, reflecting embodied emotional activation.

Contemporary research extends this theoretical framework by exploring complex interactions between visual cues and bodily expressions, highlighting how context modifies emotional perception. Studies involving dynamic interactions between visual stimuli (e.g., emotional scenes, facial expressions, and body postures) emphasise the importance of ecological validity in eliciting genuine emotional responses. These investigations reveal that emotional

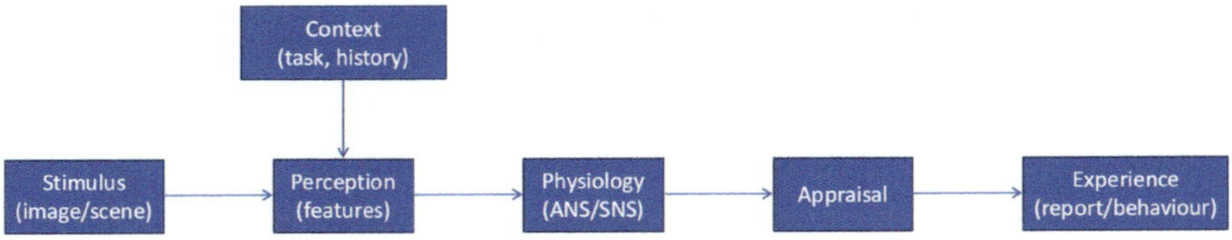

Figure 6.1 From visual stimulus to embodied emotion.

experiences are not static but contextually driven, dynamically influenced by the integration of facial, bodily, and environmental cues.

The significance of visual stimuli in eliciting embodied emotions lies in their ability to replicate naturalistic emotional contexts within controlled laboratory settings. This capability is invaluable for experimental rigour, providing researchers with precise control over stimulus parameters while capturing authentic emotional reactions. Consequently, visual stimuli have become indispensable in advancing our understanding of embodied emotional processes, forming the cornerstone of contemporary emotion research and practical applications in fields such as psychotherapy, affective computing, and media psychology.

6.3 Embodied Emotion Elicitation: Principles and Techniques

Emotion elicitation lies at the core of embodied emotion research, probing ways to provoke real, lived emotional reactions in the body, not merely in subjective self-report. Two key methods have emerged as complementary yet distinct: *priming* (a subtle preparatory exposure that implicitly influences subsequent emotional responses) and *provoking* (the deliberate presentation of emotionally charged stimuli to trigger robust bodily and psychological reactions). Figure 6.2A sketches a brief priming sequence, while Figure 6.2B shows a sustained provoking sequence.

Priming involves exposing individuals to brief cues (often outside of awareness) that subtly bias emotional responses later. Affective priming research illustrates how valenced stimuli (words, images, or odours) rapidly influence subsequent behaviour or perception even when not consciously perceived (Rohr et al., 2021). For example, masked emotional words can accelerate the recognition of congruent targets or reduce cognitive interference (Visalli et al., 2023). In contrast, *provoking* consists of direct exposure to emotionally intense stimuli, such as film clips, evocative scenes, or immersive virtual environments. Film-based induction, standardised image sets (International Affective Picture System, IAPS), and Virtual Reality (VR) scenarios reliably evoke strong emotional responses measurable via physiological and behavioural channels (Boğa et al., 2023). Each method serves different experimental goals: priming is ideal when subtle shifts or non-conscious modulation are

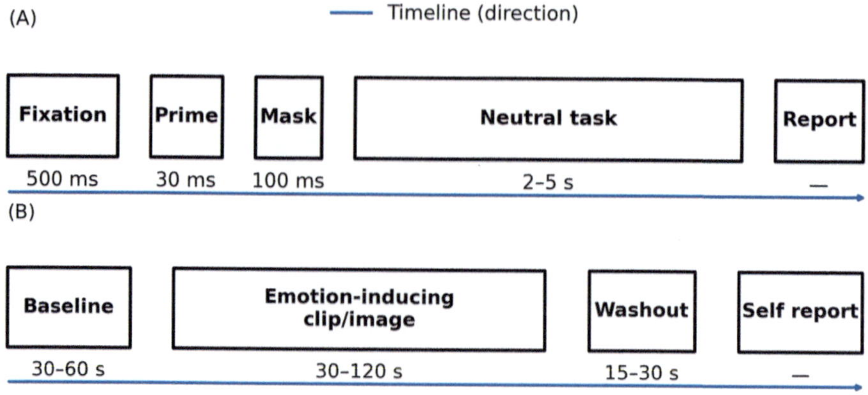

Figure 6.2 Families of elicitation designs: (A) Priming timeline; (B) Provoking timeline.

crucial; provoking suits investigations of full-bodied emotional states, high arousal responses, or ecological validity.

Embodied emotion theories propose that emotions are grounded in bodily states, sensorimotor simulations, and interoception (Barsalou, 2008; Reddan et al., 2024). The *embodied simulation framework* asserts that perceiving emotion triggers partial reenactments in somatosensory and motor cortices, providing a physiological pathway for emotion elicitation via bodily resonance (Reddan et al., 2024). Behavioural mimicry, such as facial muscle activation during perception, has been shown to facilitate emotional experience (Niedenthal, 2007).

Interoceptive priming also plays a key role since bodily signals like heartbeat, respiration, and visceral awareness modulate emotional readiness. Salamone et al. (2021) demonstrated that priming interoceptive sensations engages insular and anterior cingulate networks, influencing subsequent emotional interpretation (e.g., rating of images).

From a psychophysiological perspective, embodied elicitation relies on autonomic and somatic signatures: heart rate variability (HRV), electrodermal activity (EDA), facial electromyography (EMG), and pupillometry may all change in response to even implicit priming. As recognised in modern affective computing, these signals map bodily emotional responses central to both priming and provoking techniques.

Emotion elicitation methods are not merely academic. They underpin applications across multiple domains.

1. *Affective computing and artificial intelligence (AI) system training.* Emotion algorithms require rich, embodied emotional data. Using priming and provoking methods to elicit genuine emotion helps in building datasets like DECEiVeR (Aly et al., 2024) and VR-based platforms such as the Magic Xroom (Mousavi et al., 2023), where stimuli adapt in

real time to evoke flow-related emotional states. This trajectory aligns with the 'Artificial Psychology' (PsAIchology) framing that integrates AI methods within psychological science (Farahani et al., 2024).

2. *Clinical and therapeutic interventions.* Subtle priming techniques, such as odour-word priming or memory-based positivity primes, can modulate mood or reduce negative emotional biases, offering a gentle, potentially therapeutic route (Cereghetti et al., 2024; Bargh et al., 1996).
3. *Education and simulation training.* In simulation education, recognising emotional states via physiological feedback (heart rate, facial muscle activation) and elicitation through scenario priming enhances learners' emotional engagement and learning outcomes (LeBlanc et al., 2024).
4. *Cognitive and social psychology research.* Emotional priming influences cognitive control (e.g., emotional Stroop paradigms), decision-making, and social behaviour (Visalli et al., 2023; Dennison, 2024).

To clarify practical considerations, Table 6.1 shows a high-level comparison highlighting their respective strengths:

Priming is especially powerful in studies of personality or clinical styles: for example, depressed individuals show greater bias following negative primes and slower adjustment to positive primes (Rohr et al., 2021). Provoking, in contrast, enables immersive study of full-bodied emotional episodes using film, VR, or live scenarios (Boğa et al., 2023; Polo et al., 2025).

Eliciting emotion should always occur within an ethically guided framework. Priming often escapes conscious awareness, raising questions of consent. Thus, participants must be fully informed indirectly, without revealing prime content. Provoking may evoke intense psychological states; thus, debriefing, emotional support, and screening protocols are essential. Because emotion elicitation impacts physiological systems, measurement must be

Table 6.1 Comparative characteristics of priming and provoking methods for emotion elicitation.

Aspect	*Priming*	*Provoking*
Awareness	Often subliminal or implicit	Explicit and consciously perceived
Emotional Intensity	Subtle, low-arousal modulation	Strong, high-arousal emotions
Physiological Signature	Minimal but measurable (e.g., EDA fluctuations)	Robust autonomic response (HR, facial EMG, pupillometry)
Application Contexts	Mood modulation, non-conscious bias, social priming	Film stimuli, VR scenarios, IAPS images
Temporal Effects	Small shifts in baseline emotional readiness	Immediate emotional experience

conducted sensitively and respectfully. Robust protocols for data privacy, participant autonomy, and emotional risk minimisation are fundamental.

Embodied emotion elicitation rests on a principled integration of priming and provoking methods, grounded in physiology, somatosensory simulation, and interoceptive feedback. These methodologies enable researchers to evoke and study authentic emotional states across multiple contexts, from subtle mood shifts to immersive experiences, informing fields from affective computing to clinical intervention and education. With appropriate ethical safeguards and multimodal physiological measurement, emotion elicitation continues to drive forward our understanding of how emotional experiences are embodied, enacted, and measured in profound ways.

6.4 Facial Expressions, Body Language, and Contextual Influences on Emotional Experience

The perception and elicitation of emotion are deeply embodied processes, with facial expressions, body language, and contextual cues operating as essential components of the emotional communication system. Visual cues, especially those derived from the human face and posture, serve as crucial mediators in the embodied experience of emotion, influencing not only how emotions are conveyed but also how they are internally experienced by both the emitter and the observer. In this section, we examine the integrative role of these non-verbal modalities, highlighting the dynamic interplay between facial and bodily signals and the surrounding context in shaping emotional perception and elicitation.

Facial expressions are widely recognised as primary channels for non-verbal emotional communication. Rooted in Darwinian theories of evolution, facial expressions are often viewed as biologically hardwired signals designed to convey survival-relevant information (Darwin, 1872; Ekman, 1992). Classic research has long emphasised the universality of six basic emotions (happiness, sadness, anger, fear, surprise, and disgust), each associated with specific facial muscle configurations. However, recent evidence complicates this narrative by highlighting the variability and contextual dependency of these expressions.

Jack et al. (2012) used dynamic three-dimensional modelling and machine learning approaches to reveal that cross-cultural perception of facial emotion differs substantially, challenging the universality hypothesis. Research using deep learning facial recognition technologies has shown that micro-expressions (transient, involuntary facial movements) can offer rich insight into underlying affective states that may not align with overt emotional expressions (Yan et al., 2013). In the context of embodied emotion research, facial mimicry also emerges as a key mechanism. When individuals unconsciously imitate another's facial expression, it fosters affective resonance and emotional alignment. This is a process crucial for empathy and social bonding (Wood et al., 2016). This mimetic mirroring facilitates embodied simulation, a neural mechanism through which observers internalise the emotional states of others (Gallese & Sinigaglia, 2011).

Beyond the face, the body provides an expansive canvas for emotional signalling. Posture, gesture, and kinetic energy in movement all contribute to how emotions are perceived and felt. For example, open and expansive postures often indicate confidence or joy, while contracted or defensive postures can signal fear, shame, or anxiety (Carney et al., 2010; de Gelder, 2016). Even in the absence of facial information, observers can often accurately discern emotional states based solely on body configuration and motion (Atkinson et al., 2004; de Gelder et al., 2015; Blythe et al., 2023).

Recent embodied cognition models suggest that body posture not only reflects emotional states but also actively influences them. In one study, participants asked to adopt certain postures experienced congruent shifts in mood and self-appraisal, a phenomenon known as postural feedback (Stepper & Strack, 1993; Elkjær et al., 2022). While some recent replications have questioned the magnitude of these effects (Cesario, Jonas, & Carney, 2017), evidence continues to support the notion that posture contributes to emotional embodiment, particularly in high-stakes or socially evaluative situations.

Body expressions are crucial in situations of emotional ambiguity, where facial expressions alone are insufficient. For instance, de Gelder (2016) argues that whole-body expressions act as holistic emotional units that often override or reinterpret facial cues. In virtual agents, combining facial + vocal/body cues can shape trust and recognition (Torre et al., 2019; Tsiourti et al., 2019). While facial and bodily signals are vital, their interpretation is rarely isolated from contextual information. Context modulates the perception of emotional cues, refining or even inverting the affective message. In naturalistic settings, emotional expressions are interpreted within a complex web of social, cultural, spatial, and temporal variables. For example, Aviezer et al. (2012) demonstrated that observers often rely more on body posture than facial expression when faced with incongruent emotional cues (e.g., a smiling face on a defeated body). These findings suggest that bodily context not only colours emotional interpretation but can dominate the emotional appraisal process.

Cultural and situational norms also play a crucial role. Park and Han (2018) found that collectivist cultures tend to emphasise contextual cues over facial expressions when decoding emotions, whereas individualistic cultures prioritise facial cues. This has implications for designing AI-based emotion recognition systems in multicultural environments, where facial data alone may yield biased or misleading interpretations.

Temporal dynamics, including the timing and sequencing of expressions, also influence how emotions are perceived. Dynamic facial expressions, which unfold over time, tend to be more accurately recognised than static ones (Krumhuber et al., 2021). Similarly, the preceding emotional context of an interaction shapes anticipatory biases, where observers expect congruent emotional expressions and may misinterpret ambiguous signals to fit those expectations (Barrett, 2017).

Affective understanding is fundamentally multimodal. Rather than operating as discrete channels, facial expressions, body language, and contextual features are integrated into a cohesive perceptual experience. The embodied approach posits that this integration occurs not merely at a cognitive level, but within the perceptual-motor and visceral systems of the observer (Niedenthal et al., 2005). The perceiver's body plays a constitutive role in emotion perception, with sensorimotor resonance (i.e., bodily simulation of another's posture or expression) guiding emotional inferences.

Neuroimaging implicates interoceptive and premotor circuits during bodily emotion perception (Azzalini et al., 2019), consistent with predictive-processing accounts (Clark, 2013). These findings align with predictive processing models, which suggest that the brain uses embodied priors to anticipate and interpret emotional signals in a top-down manner (Clark, 2013).

6.5 Methods of Embodied Emotion Priming and Provoking

The scientific exploration of emotion necessitates methodologies that can reliably and ethically elicit affective responses in controlled environments. Among these, *priming* and *provoking* methods represent two foundational strategies that serve distinct psychological and neurobiological purposes in embodied emotion research. While both aim to evoke emotional states, they differ significantly in subtlety, intensity, and temporal dynamics. This section outlines the theoretical underpinnings, procedural approaches, and ethical considerations for both methods, emphasising their application in embodied emotional studies and affective computing.

Priming refers to the psychological technique of preparing an individual's emotional or cognitive system by exposing them to specific, often subtle cues that influence their subsequent affective experience or behaviour without conscious awareness. In the context of embodied emotion, priming is particularly useful for engaging pre-existing emotional schemas without overt stimulation, allowing researchers to explore how emotions arise from implicit cognitive-affective networks. Several paradigms have emerged to prime emotional states:

- *Semantic priming,* wherein participants are exposed to emotionally valenced words (e.g., death, joy) that bias their responses to subsequent stimuli (Elgendi et al., 2018).
- *Affective visual priming,* where briefly presented images (such as facial expressions, affective scenes, or symbolic cues) influence perception or judgment, even if presented subliminally (Elgendi et al., 2018; Nava & Turati, 2020).

- *Embodied priming,* which leverages bodily manipulations, such as facial muscle activation or posture, to bias affective experience and related physiology (Price & Harmon-Jones, 2015; Van Cappellen et al., 2022).

Recent findings suggest that priming not only influences affective judgments but can modulate physiological responses such as heart rate variability (Carlisle et al., 2012; Li et al., 2007) and skin conductance (Nava & Turati, 2020). These embodied correlates reveal that priming is not merely a cognitive effect but engages the broader nervous system, aligning with the principles of embodied cognition.

In contrast to priming, provoking methods are designed to *explicitly and robustly evoke emotional states,* often through multimedia stimuli that are rich in affective content. These methods are used when stronger, more observable emotional reactions are required, particularly in studies involving psychophysiological measurement, neuroimaging, or behavioural change. The most commonly used tools include:

- *Standardised image databases* such as IAPS and OASIS (Kurdi et al., 2017), which provide a range of affective scenes normed for valence and arousal.
- *Emotion-inducing film clips,* such as those from the Database for Emotional Movie Stimuli or the FilmStim (Schaefer et al., 2010), deliver continuous, multimodal emotional experiences.
- *Auditory stimuli,* including affective music and sound effects, have proven effective in eliciting sadness, fear, and joy, often used in immersive settings (Khalfa et al., 2005).
- *VR-based emotional scenarios,* which provide high ecological validity and embodiment, enable participants to engage emotionally through real-time, immersive interaction (Somarathna et al., 2022).

In embodied research, provoking methods are increasingly paired with *real-time physiological monitoring,* such as electroencephalography (EEG), EMG, heart rate variability, and galvanic skin response, to detect the embodied correlates of the elicited emotions (Shu et al., 2018). These measurable responses allow for objective validation of emotional states, enriching our understanding of how external stimuli translate into embodied emotional experiences.

Both priming and provoking techniques operate on shared but differently emphasised *cognitive-affective and sensorimotor pathways.*

- *Priming* functions primarily via *top-down* cognitive processes. It activates associative memory networks and predictive coding mechanisms that prepare the individual for an expected emotional context (Barrett, 2017). This anticipatory activation often remains below the threshold of awareness, influencing perception and interpretation.

- *Provoking,* by contrast, engages *bottom-up sensory integration* mechanisms. Emotional stimuli directly trigger autonomic and limbic responses, particularly involving the amygdala, insula, and brainstem nuclei, that manifest as observable physiological and affective reactions (Pessoa, 2013).

Importantly, the *embodiment hypothesis* suggests that both priming and provoking activate internal simulations of emotional experience via *sensorimotor re-enactment.* This aligns with theories of grounded cognition, wherein emotions are not only mental states but bodily states reactivated in perception and action (Niedenthal, 2007; Baumgartner et al., 2006).

Given the *potential vulnerability* of participants during emotion elicitation studies, ethical protocols must be rigorously followed. The following considerations are paramount:

1. *Informed consent* must explicitly state the possibility of emotional discomfort and detail the nature of the stimuli, especially when using provocative methods.
2. *Debriefing procedures* should be comprehensive, offering emotional support and the option to withdraw data if participants feel distressed.
3. *Use of trauma-sensitive design* is crucial when employing emotionally intense stimuli. Participants with a history of trauma or psychological conditions should be pre-screened or offered opt-outs.
4. *Minimising deception* is essential, particularly for priming techniques that may operate subliminally. While some degree of masking may be needed for methodological validity, it should never compromise participant safety.
5. *Institutional oversight,* such as approval from ethics committees or Institutional Review Boards, is mandatory for all studies involving emotional elicitation.

Recent guidelines from affective computing and human–computer interaction research emphasise *participant agency, emotional aftercare, and transparency* (Mohammad, 2022) in the use of AI-driven affective systems. For example, studies involving virtual agents designed to provoke emotional responses must be especially cautious to avoid manipulative interaction patterns or emotionally misleading cues. To ensure both scientific validity and ethical soundness, the following best practices are recommended:

- Use *multi-method validation,* combining self-report, behavioural, and physiological measures.
- *Calibrate stimuli* using normative databases to match participant demographics and cultural backgrounds.
- Employ *randomised controlled designs* to reduce bias and habituation.

- Pilot test all priming and provoking materials in smaller samples to assess tolerability and effect size.
- Incorporate *adaptive algorithms* in real-time systems that monitor participant distress and adjust stimuli intensity accordingly.

Figure 6.3 shows a calibration scatter in the valence–arousal space, which we use to verify balanced coverage and avoid clustering stimuli in one quadrant before running the study.

Figure 6.4 sketches the adaptive loop we use in practice: continuous measurement (e.g., EDA/HR) feeds a decision policy that either pauses or adjusts intensity, with clear stop criteria.

Priming and provoking are complementary methods of emotional elicitation that, when used ethically and precisely, can reveal the complex interplay between cognition, emotion, and embodiment. Their integration into affective science and applied technologies, such as therapeutic interfaces and emotionally aware AI, marks a significant step towards more nuanced and responsive emotional systems. As affective research becomes increasingly multimodal and personalised, these methods will remain foundational tools in our quest to understand and model the embodied human emotional experience.

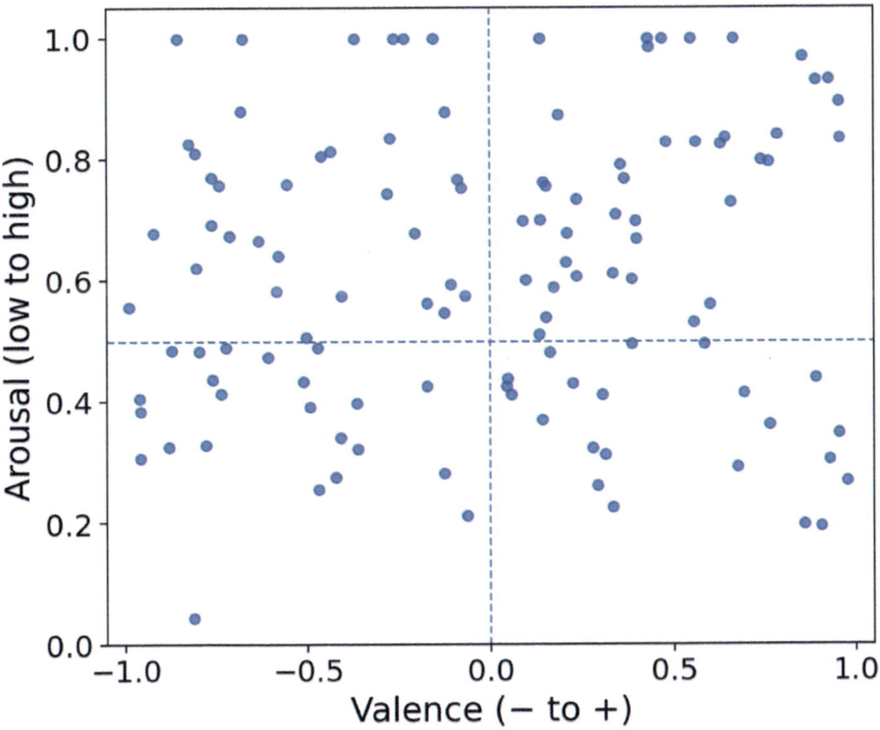

Figure 6.3 Stimulus calibration map (valence × arousal).

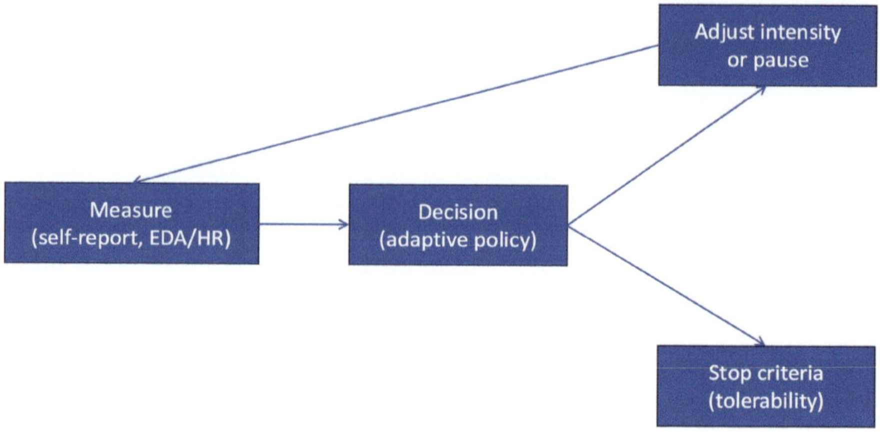

Figure 6.4 Adaptive elicitation loop (monitor → decide → adjust).

6.6 Computational Analysis of Affective Images and Emotional Elicitation

In the last decade, the field of emotion research has been transformed by advances in computational methods, especially those powered by artificial intelligence and machine learning. The capacity to automatically analyse and interpret affective visual stimuli has not only expanded the scale and efficiency of affective research but also deepened our understanding of embodied emotion. Rather than relying solely on subjective self-report or manual coding, researchers can now draw on sophisticated algorithms to extract and classify emotional information from facial expressions, bodily postures, and even contextual visual cues. These methods are particularly vital in complex experimental setups where continuous emotional monitoring is needed or where real-time emotion modelling is essential, such as in virtual agents, adaptive learning environments, or therapeutic interventions. For psychology-focused, Python-based modelling patterns and regression pipelines, see (Kovač et al., 2024).

At the core of this computational turn lies the development of emotion recognition systems that leverage deep learning architectures, particularly convolutional neural networks (CNNs), to identify subtle affective patterns within static images or video streams. Facial expression recognition (FER) has emerged as one of the most widely explored applications in this area. Using large annotated datasets like AffectNet (Mollahosseini et al., 2017), RAF-DB (Li et al., 2017), and FER2013, researchers train models that can predict basic and compound emotions based on the activation of facial landmarks, muscle dynamics, and temporal transitions.

The move towards real-time FER systems has further improved ecological validity in emotion elicitation studies, allowing researchers to monitor facial affect as participants engage with emotionally provocative stimuli. To make the processing steps concrete, Figure 6.5 shows a compact FER pipeline (preprocess → CNN encoder → classifier) alongside an illustrative saliency heatmap highlighting face regions that drive a predicted label.

Yet emotion is rarely confined to the face. Recent models increasingly emphasise the importance of full-body information in emotion understanding. These multimodal systems integrate facial features with body language cues, such as arm gestures, posture openness, and motion fluidity, to more

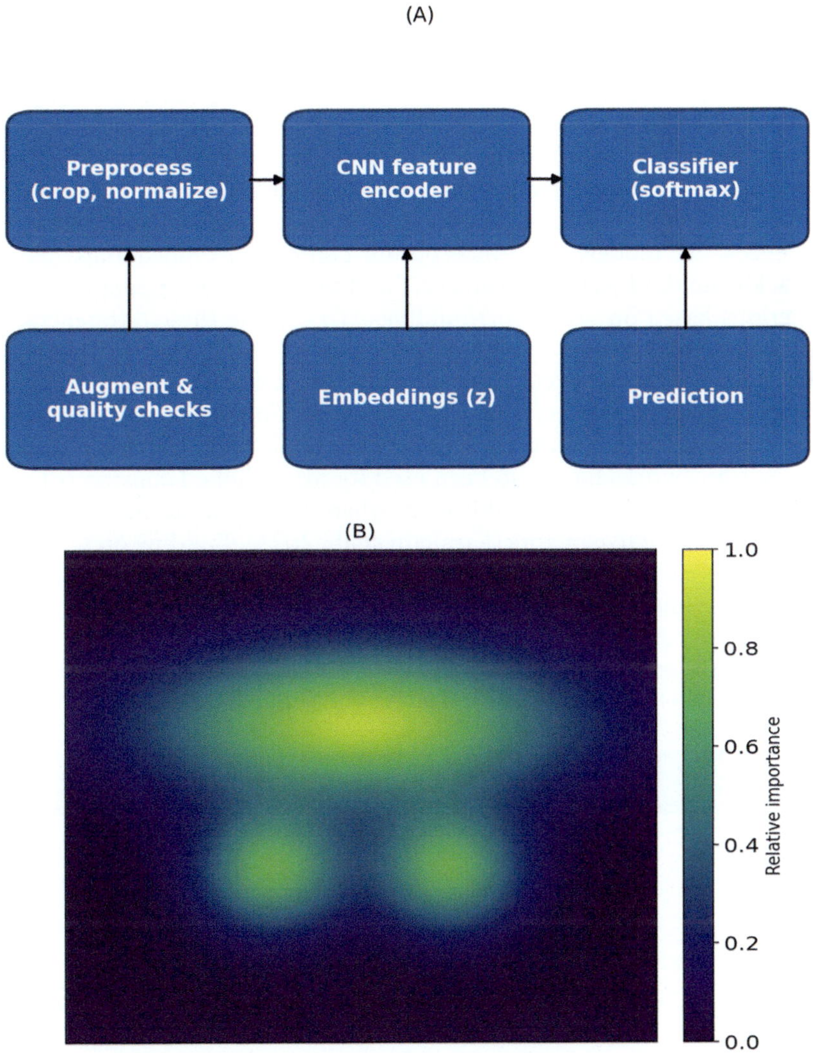

Figure 6.5 Facial emotion recognition overview: (A) FER pipeline; (B) saliency heatmap indicating image regions most influential for the prediction.

accurately decode affective states. Figure 6.6 connects this multimodal view to our conceptual model by showing how face, body, and scene jointly inform perceived emotion.

Temporal modelling techniques like Long Short-Term Memory networks and Transformer-based architectures allow these systems to maintain a memory of gesture progression, enabling better interpretation of dynamic emotional behaviour over time. This is particularly useful in contexts where the emotional response is not immediate but unfolds across several moments, such as during narrative-based video stimuli or in therapy simulations using avatars (Kosti et al., 2019; Mittal et al., 2020).

A crucial innovation in this space involves context-aware emotional modelling. While early systems assumed that emotions are universal and static, current trends recognise the layered nature of emotional experience, which is often shaped by surrounding environmental cues. For example, a smiling expression in a funeral scene may carry a completely different emotional meaning than the same expression in a birthday party. To capture these differences, AI models now incorporate contextual embeddings (extracting background, object co-occurrence, and temporal consistency) to modify predictions based on visual surroundings. To capture these differences, current models incorporate contextual cues, such as background, objects, and global scene, to refine predictions. Multi-branch CNNs and context-aware networks that fuse person and scene information consistently outperform person-only baselines (Kosti et al., 2019; Lee et al., 2019). Related machine-learning frameworks have also been used for affect-linked constructs beyond core emotions, such as love addiction, where feature patterns and explanations clarify predictive factors (Farahani et al., 2025). Building on this, Figure 6.7 contrasts early fusion (concatenate features, then classify) with late fusion (separate classifiers whose scores are fused), a practical choice when combining face, body, and scene/context streams.

Beyond recognition, computational techniques are also revolutionising how emotion is elicited. Generative AI tools like Generative Adversarial

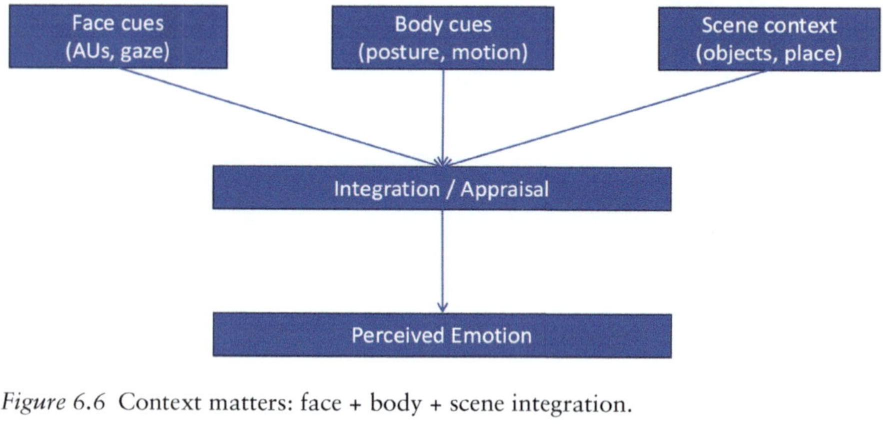

Figure 6.6 Context matters: face + body + scene integration.

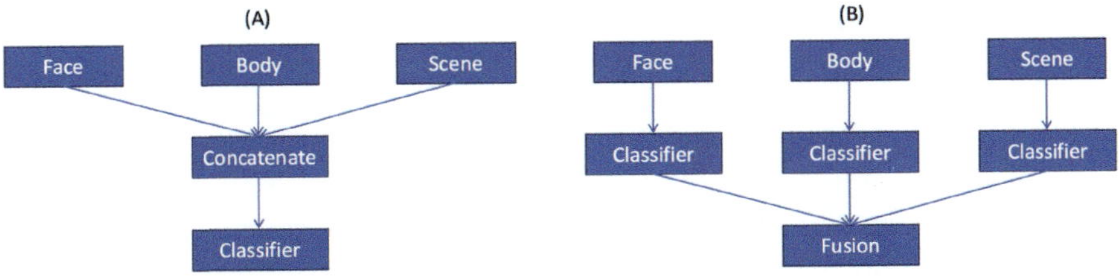

Figure 6.7 Strategies for combining face, body, and scene features in multimodal emotion recognition: (A) early fusion; (B) late fusion.

Networks and diffusion models are used to synthetically generate affective images tailored to specific emotional categories. These generated stimuli offer several advantages: they are controllable, ethically safe, and capable of spanning the full valence–arousal space with fine-grained precision. For instance, rather than sourcing distressing real-world images to provoke anxiety, researchers can create synthetic scenes that are sufficiently evocative without being ethically problematic. Emotion-generative agents are being tested in VR and Augmented Reality (AR) settings, where AI-driven virtual characters engage users in emotionally rich conversations, adjusting their expressions and gestures based on user feedback (Galanos et al., 2021).

The use of computational methods for emotional elicitation demands rigorous validation. While model accuracy remains a primary concern, embodiment researchers also investigate the degree to which AI-predicted emotions correspond with physiological signals, such as heart rate variability, pupil dilation, or galvanic skin response. In these studies, emotional predictions are considered valid not only when they match participant self-reports but also when they synchronise with autonomic nervous system responses. This dual benchmarking ensures that computational analyses are grounded in embodied emotional realities, not just visual classification heuristics. A number of case studies illustrate these methods in practice. Comparable supervised pipelines are also applied to psychological health outcomes, for example, the classification of chronic pain (Kovač et al., 2025a). A complementary line of work uses calibrated regression to predict internal shame, with XGBoost performing best and distress tolerance emerging as the strongest predictor (Kovač et al., 2025b). For example, end-to-end multimodal architectures combining facial video with other streams (e.g., audio, text, or gaze) improve recognition in naturalistic settings compared with facial-only models (Tzirakis et al., 2021; Gu et al., 2018). In another project, real-time EEG classification was used to monitor affect during video stimuli and could be integrated to adapt stimulus delivery on the fly (Nandi et al., 2021).

Such examples demonstrate that computational systems are not only observers of affect but can act as *interactive co-regulators* of emotional experience. This aligns closely with embodied theories of emotion, where affect is not a static label but a process dynamically co-constructed between agent and environment. The future of emotional elicitation lies in these intelligent, responsive systems that adapt to the user's embodied state in real time.

Yet challenges remain. Bias in training datasets, particularly in facial expression data across cultures and skin tones, continues to undermine the generalisability of many models. Ethical debates are also mounting regarding the manipulation of emotional states via automated systems, particularly in commercial applications where user consent and emotional safety may be compromised. To navigate this, emerging frameworks propose transparency, participant control, and real-time opt-out mechanisms in any system capable of emotional modulation.

As AI continues to evolve, the integration of computational methods into embodied emotion research opens new frontiers for inquiry and application. From designing personalised therapeutic interventions to enhancing the affective responsiveness of artificial agents, these tools offer powerful means of decoding and modulating human emotion. The key, however, lies in grounding these technologies in robust psychological theory and embodied ethics, ensuring that the machines we build recognise emotion not just as data, but as human experience.

6.7 Measuring and Quantifying Embodied Emotional Responses

Understanding embodied emotion requires not just the elicitation and recognition of emotional states, but also their rigorous measurement and quantification. Emotion, inherently multifaceted, manifests across multiple physiological, behavioural, and computational domains. While subjective self-report remains a valuable source of emotional insight, it is insufficient when investigating real-time, unconscious, or embodied affective processes. Therefore, contemporary emotion research employs a unified methodological framework that integrates physiological sensors, behavioural observations, and algorithmic quantification tools to provide a multilayered and objective understanding of emotional experience. This section synthesises core methods for measuring embodied emotion and discusses their complementarities, applications, and challenges in both lab-based and naturalistic settings.

Among the most established techniques in the physiological domain is HRV, a widely accepted index of autonomic nervous system function. HRV captures the variation in time intervals between successive heartbeats, offering insight into sympathetic and parasympathetic activity. Emotional states characterised by arousal, such as fear or excitement, often lead to reductions in HRV, while relaxed or positive affective states are associated with greater variability (Shaffer & Ginsberg, 2017). Tools like the Polar H10 and Empatica E4 wristband allow for non-invasive, continuous HRV monitoring (Umair et al., 2021), making them ideal for both lab-based emotion induction tasks and field studies. HRV is particularly well-suited for embodied research due to its close ties to vagal tone and the neurovisceral integration model, which positions bodily regulation at the centre of affective processing (Smith et al., 2017).

EEG provides a more direct window into the brain's electrical activity during emotional processing. It is especially useful for examining the temporal dynamics of emotion, capturing millisecond-level changes in cortical activation. Specific EEG markers, such as frontal alpha asymmetry, have been consistently associated with approach or avoidance motivational tendencies, thereby linking emotion to embodied action schemas (Coan & Allen, 2004; Harmon-Jones et al., 2010). In more advanced setups, source localisation techniques like sLORETA can be used to estimate the origin of emotional signals within cortical networks, enhancing the spatial interpretability of EEG data. Mobile EEG systems are increasingly deployed in ecologically valid settings, such as immersive VR or real-world social interactions, enabling the study of embodied emotion beyond the confines of the lab.

Another powerful physiological method is *skin conductance response (SCR)*, often used to measure sympathetic nervous system arousal. SCR detects changes in sweat gland activity driven by emotional arousal. Unlike HRV or EEG, which may reflect both valence and arousal, SCR is a relatively pure index of arousal intensity, regardless of whether the emotion is positive or negative. This makes it an excellent tool for measuring emotional responses to provocative stimuli, such as fear-inducing images or emotionally charged film scenes. Importantly, combining SCR with facial and behavioural measures enhances interpretative power, as high arousal alone does not distinguish between anger, fear, or excitement.

Beyond physiological signals, *behavioural and observational measures* provide critical insights into how emotions are embodied and expressed. *Eye-tracking*, for example, allows researchers to examine visual attention patterns and pupil dilation during emotional tasks. Participants tend to fixate more quickly and longer on emotionally salient regions, such as the eyes or mouth in faces, particularly when processing threat or socially relevant cues (Vetter et al., 2019; Capriola-Hall et al., 2021). Changes in *pupil size* have also been linked to affective arousal and cognitive effort, providing a dual index of embodied emotional engagement (Mathôt, 2018; van der Wel & van Steenbergen, 2018).

Perhaps one of the most influential tools in behavioural emotion research is the *Facial Action Coding System (FACS)*, originally developed by Ekman and Friesen (1978) and now often implemented with automated software such as OpenFace. FACS identifies distinct facial muscle movements (action units) and maps them onto specific emotional expressions. For example, the combination of AU6 (cheek raiser) and AU12 (lip corner puller) is strongly associated with genuine (Duchenne) smiling. Automated FACS systems offer a non-invasive and real-time means of capturing facial expressivity, which is particularly relevant in studies of emotion contagion, mimicry, or emotion regulation.

Postural and gesture analysis is another growing area of embodied emotion measurement. Advances in depth sensing and motion capture technologies, such as Microsoft Kinect (Zhang, 2012) and OpenPose (Kim et al., 2021), allow for real-time tracking of body configuration, movement fluidity, and gesture dynamics. These kinematic features can then be analysed to infer emotional states. For instance, slow, constricted movements may indicate sadness or fear, while expansive, energetic gestures are often linked to happiness or anger. Integrating posture data with facial and vocal cues creates a richer and more holistic model of embodied emotion.

On the computational front, emotion quantification has been significantly advanced by the use of *multimodal machine learning models*. These systems integrate data from physiological signals, facial expressions, and behavioural features to predict emotional states with high accuracy. Ensemble methods, recurrent neural networks, and attention-based architectures like Transformers are now employed to fuse temporal data streams and classify emotions dynamically. Emotion recognition challenges such as DEAP (Koelstra et al., 2011) and AMIGOS (Miranda-Correa et al., 2018) have provided benchmark datasets that pair EEG, SCR, HRV, and video data with self-reported emotional labels, enabling researchers to train models that learn the temporal and cross-modal dependencies inherent to emotional responses.

Quantifying embodied emotion also involves estimating *valence-arousal dimensions* rather than discrete emotion labels. Models like the circumplex model of affect (Russell, 1980) conceptualise emotions along continuous dimensions of pleasure and activation, which can be mapped using regression-based models on physiological and behavioural inputs. For example, a system may output a high arousal–low valence profile, suggesting a state of anxiety or anger. These dimensional outputs are especially useful in adaptive systems that need to respond to gradients of emotion rather than fixed categories.

Despite these advancements, challenges remain in aligning computational predictions with subjective experience. Embodied emotional responses are highly individual, shaped by personal history, cultural background, and context. Personalised calibration of emotion recognition systems, through baseline recordings, user-specific models, or adaptive learning, is crucial for achieving ecological validity and ethical sensitivity. As emotion measurement becomes more automated and multimodal, integrating these methods offers a more comprehensive and embodied view of affect. Physiological data captures internal states, behavioural observations reflect external expressions, and computational modelling provides the analytical link that connects these layers. Collectively, they enable a rich, multidimensional understanding of how emotion is not just felt or reported, but experienced through the body, expressed in movement, and interpreted by intelligent systems.

6.8 Embodied Emotion Elicitation in Digital and Virtual Environments

As digital interfaces become more immersive, the elicitation of emotion in virtual contexts has shifted from a passive process to one that is fundamentally embodied and interactive. VR, AR, and emotionally intelligent digital agents now offer unprecedented opportunities to simulate, modulate, and analyse emotional experiences with a level of ecological validity previously unattainable in traditional laboratory settings. These technologies not only improve the realism of emotional stimuli but also engage users' sensory, motor, and cognitive systems in ways that resemble real-world embodiment.

At the core of VR-based emotion elicitation lies the principle of immersion. Unlike static or two-dimensional emotional stimuli, immersive VR environments surround the user with multisensory cues that imitate real-world affective situations. When equipped with motion tracking, haptic feedback, and 360-degree visual rendering, VR scenarios can induce fear, joy, sadness, or awe with remarkable intensity and authenticity. A person walking across a narrow bridge suspended over a digital canyon will typically show the same autonomic responses (elevated heart rate, skin conductance spikes, postural adjustments) as they would in a similar physical environment. This immersive realism facilitates not just emotional induction but full-body affective engagement, making VR a uniquely embodied tool for emotion science (Carl et al., 2019).

Researchers have harnessed these affordances to create controlled yet emotionally immersive simulations. For example, VR platforms have been utilised to foster empathy by immersing participants in the embodied perspectives of marginalised groups, such as refugees or individuals with disabilities. These perspective-taking experiences evoke affective resonance and promote pro-social behaviour more effectively than written narratives or video presentations because users move, look, and act as the digital self (Herrera et al., 2018). The emotional engagement in such cases is not purely cognitive or representational; it arises from embodied simulation within a virtual environment.

AR technologies, although less immersive than VR, offer unique opportunities for contextualised emotional elicitation. AR overlays affective content, such as animated avatars, visual distortions or symbolic elements, onto real-world settings, enhancing emotional significance without disconnecting users from their surroundings. These have been employed in therapeutic contexts, such as exposure therapy for phobias, with augmented reality exposure therapy demonstrating clinical efficacy comparable to in-vivo exposure and a strong therapeutic alliance (Hasan et al., 2023; Eshuis et al., 2021). Because users retain access to their physical bodies and space, AR-based emotion elicitation maintains bodily orientation while seamlessly layering emotional stimuli in meaningful ways.

Another emerging domain is the use of *digital avatars and virtual agents*. These are animated characters capable of facial expressions, gestures, and emotional dialogue, capable of interacting with users in emotionally responsive manners. These agents are increasingly equipped with affect recognition systems that detect and respond to the user's emotions in real time, creating dynamic affective loops. For example, a virtual therapist may adjust their voice tone and facial expression based on the user's sadness cues, or a virtual classroom assistant may display encouragement when detecting signs of frustration. Such emotionally contingent responses foster the perception of empathy and relational presence, leading to deeper emotional engagement (Stock-Homburg, 2022; Abdollahi et al., 2022).

Critically, these virtual agents do not simply simulate emotion. They often *elicit* it. Users tend to form emotional bonds with virtual characters, experiencing trust, embarrassment, pride, or compassion depending on the scenario. This socio-emotional interactivity is a cornerstone of embodied digital emotion, as it reflects not just internal states but social dynamics mediated by digital bodies. The design of these agents (including their facial features, voice modulation, eye contact, and physical proximity) significantly shapes the perceived appropriateness and impact (Fischer et al., 2019; Numata et al., 2020).

Despite these promising developments, several challenges complicate the use of digital platforms for embodied emotion elicitation. *One concern is standardisation.* While immersive technologies enable personalisation and contextual richness, this very flexibility makes cross-study comparison and reproducibility more difficult. Unlike film clips or image sets, which have normative emotional ratings, VR environments are often bespoke, and their emotional impact can vary depending on the user's familiarity with digital media, susceptibility to immersion, or motion sickness.

Another limitation involves cultural and individual variability. Emotions elicited through virtual agents may differ across cultures due to varying norms around expression, social hierarchy, and technology interaction. Users with autism spectrum conditions or alexithymia may not respond to emotionally expressive avatars in the same way as neurotypical individuals, highlighting the need for adaptable and inclusive design sensitive to user traits and culture (Park & Whang, 2022; Su et al., 2023).

Ethical considerations are also paramount. The capacity to provoke intense emotional responses in virtual environments, especially fear, trauma, or shame, raises concerns about user safety, particularly when such responses are triggered unintentionally or without appropriate debriefing. Developers must ensure that emotion-inducing content includes clear warnings, exit mechanisms, and post-exposure emotional regulation tools. As these technologies become more integrated into everyday applications, the need for emotional safeguarding becomes urgent.

Latency and realism also remain technical hurdles. Subtle delays in avatar response, unnatural motion patterns, or mismatched vocal tone can produce uncanny valley effects, disrupting emotional immersion. To mitigate this, ongoing research focuses on improving real-time synchronisation between user affect and agent behaviour through predictive modelling and low-latency sensors.

Despite these challenges, the potential for embodied emotional elicitation in digital environments is vast. As sensor technologies, computational models, and immersive design principles evolve, the line between digital and physical emotion continues to blur. In the near future, it is plausible to imagine emotionally intelligent virtual companions that not only recognise our feelings but help us navigate them, while providing comfort, challenge, or motivation based on our embodied emotional profile in real time.

What distinguishes digital emotion elicitation from traditional methods is not just the medium but the nature of the interaction. It is no longer about observing static stimuli but about *inhabiting* a scene, *co-regulating* with digital others, and *embodying* emotion in a multisensory continuum. This shift represents more than a technological enhancement; it redefines how we study, simulate, and perhaps even feel emotion in the digital age.

6.9 Case Studies and Experiments

The theoretical and methodological developments discussed throughout this chapter culminate in a range of case studies and experimental investigations that illustrate how embodied emotion can be effectively elicited, measured, and interpreted using integrated visual and computational strategies. These examples bridge the gap between controlled laboratory protocols and applied emotional experiences in digital, clinical, or social contexts. By examining how priming and provoking stimuli, physiological and behavioural measurement tools, and immersive digital environments coalesce in real-world studies, we gain insight into the practical and scientific value of this multidimensional approach.

Participants were immersed in a virtual public-speaking scenario, a setup known to elicit anxiety and measurable physiological arousal (Pertaub et al., 2002) in VR audiences. Recent work also validates VR public-speaking training and reports good user acceptance, while multimodal VR studies combine psychophysiology with facial analysis to model affect in real time (Slater et al., 2006; Bachmann et al., 2023; Bastida et al., 2024)

An illustrative experiment manipulated posture to test causal effects on emotional responding. Leaning forward (approach-related) versus reclining altered both startle eyeblink magnitude and late positive potential while participants viewed appetitive pictures, indicating that posture can modulate reflexive and electrocortical responses to emotional stimuli (Price et al., 2012). Converging work shows that leaning forward increases relative left-frontal cortical activation to appetitive cues, consistent with approach motivation (Harmon-Jones et al., 2011). Recent posture experiments also report small but reliable effects of expansive/upward postures on positive affect and cardiac vagal reactivity (RSA) under controlled lab conditions (Van Cappellen et al., 2022).

In applied digital psychotherapy, conversational agents and affect-aware virtual systems have shown clinically meaningful reductions in depression or anxiety in randomised trials, and reviews now map their opportunities and limits (Fitzpatrick et al., 2017; Liu et al., 2022; He et al., 2022; Boucher et al., 2021). Systems increasingly fuse vocal/facial cues with wearable signals to adapt interaction in real time.

In education, affect-aware systems detect facial expressions and eye gaze to adapt content and questions. Classic work such as *Gaze Tutor* dynamically redirects attention using eye-tracking, and **Affective AutoTutor** adjusts strategies based on learners' affect, yielding engagement benefits and learning gains in certain cohorts. Recent surveys and studies continue to integrate gaze with real-time emotion recognition in learning environments (D'Mello et al., 2012; D'Mello & Graesser, 2013; Myers, 2021; Cisse, 2024).

Perhaps the most complex integration of visual, computational, and physiological tools is found in multimodal datasets designed specifically for embodied emotion research. The MAHNOB-HCI dataset, for example, was created through a series of experiments where participants watched emotional film clips while their facial expressions, gaze direction, electrocardiographic activity, respiration, and EEG were recorded simultaneously (Soleymani et al., 2011). This dataset allowed researchers to develop predictive models of emotion that combined both bottom-up and top-down inputs, including context-aware video modelling and affective memory cues. Models trained on such datasets have since been used in healthcare, assistive robotics, and adaptive gaming environments, further emphasising the practical value of multimodal embodied emotion elicitation research.

The WESAD dataset is a widely used benchmark for studying how wearable signals change under different affective states. Participants wore a *RespiBAN* device on the chest (high-rate recording) together with an *Empatica E4* wristband. WESAD provides synchronised streams such as respiration, ECG, EMG, and skin conductance (EDA) from the chest device, and EDA, blood-volume pulse (PPG/BVP), temperature, and 3-axis acceleration from the wristband. Sampling is high on the chest (≈700 Hz) and lower but sufficient for physiology on the wrist (e.g., BVP 64 Hz, EDA/TEMP 4 Hz, ACC 32 Hz). In the original protocol, each subject passes through blocks such as *baseline, stress (Trier Social Stress Test), amusement*, and *meditation*, which are distributed with canonical label codes. For this chapter, we focus on the three most common classes, *baseline, stress*, and *amusement*, because they appear in every subject and are the most frequently modelled across papers.

Figure 6.8 visualises what these wearable signals look like in practice. Panel A shows a short segment from the chest device: respiration (slow sinusoidal wave), ECG (sharp QRS spikes), EMG (brief muscle bursts), and EDA (slow tonic drift with small phasic responses). Panel B shows the wrist: BVP/

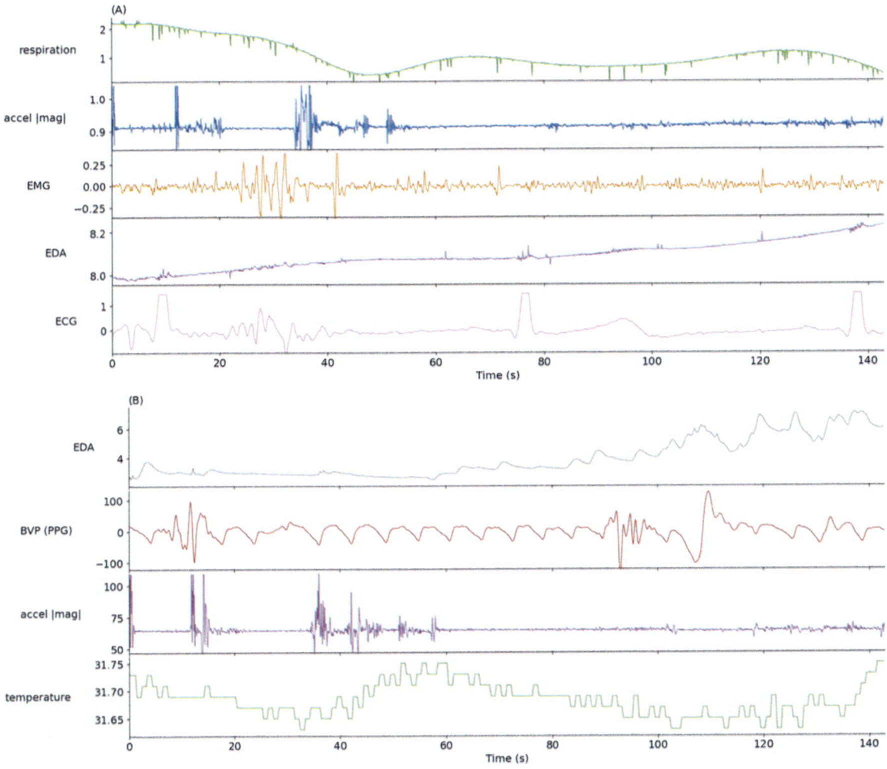

Figure 6.8 Wearable signals in WESAD: (A) chest channels; (B) wrist channels.

PPG (regular pulse peaks), EDA (tonic level), acceleration magnitude (movement), and temperature (slow drift). Together, the two devices provide a compact, multimodal view of physiology that responds to emotional context.

WESAD's structure makes it convenient for *windowed analysis*: we divide each recording into short overlapping windows (e.g., 10 s length, 5 s step), extract robust statistical and spectral features per window, and then learn to distinguish *baseline* vs. *stress* vs. *amusement* using models such as KNN, SVM-RBF, or Random Forest. The subject identifier is always used as a *group* during cross-validation to avoid leakage across people (details in the next subsections). This case study will use WESAD solely as an illustration of the end-to-end process: light preprocessing, quick EDA, subject-aware evaluation, and simple, interpretable diagnostics.

Wearable signals are messy. Wrist acceleration can spike during a gesture. EMG bursts can look like noise. BVP/PPG can momentarily drop. EDA drifts slowly over time. Instead of throwing data away, we apply *gentle*, per-feature cleanup that keeps the median behaviour intact while preventing extreme values from dominating the models.

We keep the preprocessing intentionally simple and leakage-proof. We start by working only with the engineered *numeric* features and leave identifiers such as *subject* and *label* untouched. Any infinities that appear from filtering are treated as missing values, so they do not spread through the pipeline. Missing data are then filled with the *median* of the respective feature, with that median calculated only on the *training subjects*. Because wearable streams sometimes produce sudden spikes (a wrist flick in ACC, a brief PPG dropout, a sudden EMG burst), we *winsorise* each feature by trimming its tails at the 1st and 99th percentiles. These cut points are again determined using the training set. Features that are essentially constant across training samples are removed, as near-zero variance provides no discriminative information and only introduces noise. We standardise each feature with *RobustScaler* (centring by the median and scaling by the interquartile range), so the spread is stabilised without being affected by outliers as a z-score would be. All these quantities (medians, percentile cut points, variance mask, scaling factors) are calculated on the training set and then applied unchanged to the held-out test subjects, ensuring a subject-aware pipeline with no information leakage.

To make the effect concrete, Figure 6.9 contrasts a representative feature before and after preprocessing: the raw histogram shows a long right tail due to motion bursts, whereas the winsorised-and-robust-scaled version preserves the central bulk of the distribution while taming the extremes.

Before we put any models to work, it helps to look at the shape of the data, and to detect what ranges the features live in, which ones are skewed or heavy-tailed, and where the three WESAD conditions might already separate. Figures 6.10–6.12 are designed for a fast but informative pass through the dataset. They are produced after the light preprocessing from the previous step, so you're looking at the same value space the models will see.

We will start with the marginal histograms in Figure 6.10. Each small axis shows the distribution of one engineered feature across all subjects and windows. Several sensors naturally produce skewed, long-tailed histograms (e.g., BVP and accelerometer variability), while others are tighter and closer to unimodal (e.g., respiratory percentiles in calm segments). These shapes justify the robust treatment we used: winsorization avoids rare spikes dominating the scale, and robust scaling keeps the bulk of values comparable without forcing strict normality. You'll also notice that many features have most of their mass near zero after scaling. That's expected because medians are roughly centred at zero, and the interquartile range defines the unit. This panel is useful for spotting features that still behave oddly (e.g., multimodal or near-constant), which are candidates for later pruning or careful interpretation.

Next, examine the class-conditioned view in Figure 6.11. Here, we display the top-K features selected by a straightforward ANOVA F-score (calculated solely on the training split), standardised to z-units, and separated by class. The width of the violin indicates density, while the dashed lines signify

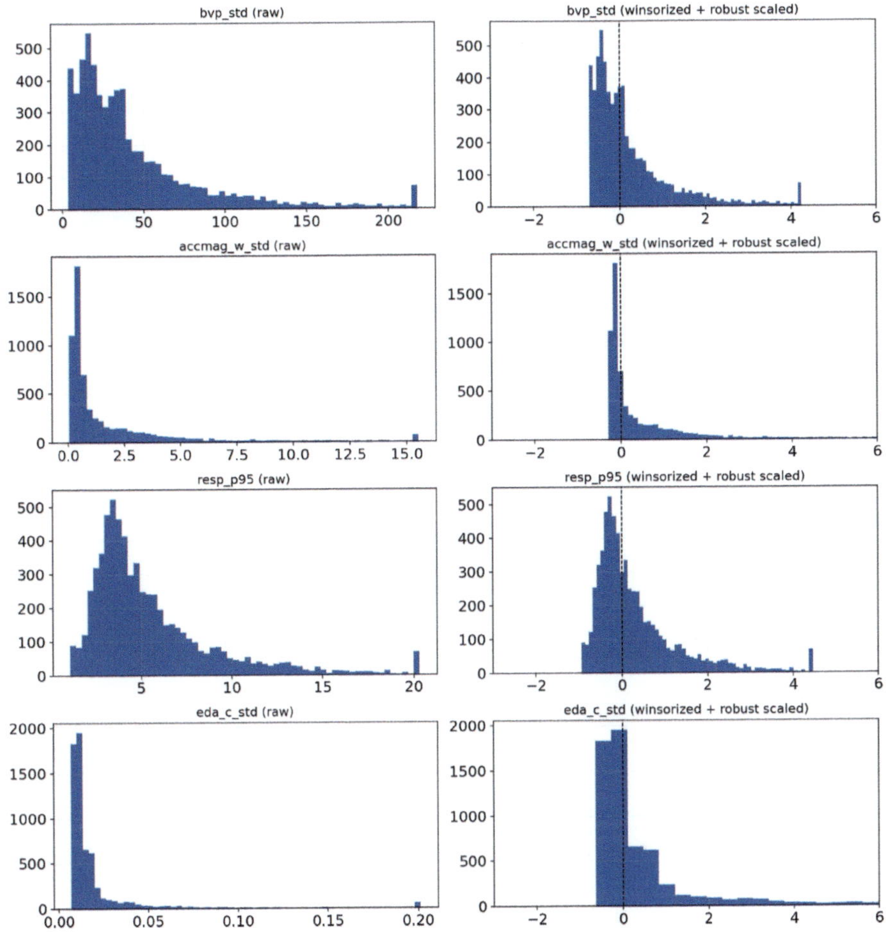

Figure 6.9 Gentle outlier handling across selected features: raw histograms in the left column and corresponding distributions after 1st–99th percentile clipping and robust scaling using the median and interquartile range in the right column.

the median and quartiles. Several well-known psychophysiological patterns emerge: chest and wrist EDA dispersion and upper percentiles tend to rise during *stress* compared to *baseline*, aligning with increased sympathetic activation. Respiration percentiles often increase during stress or active states, whereas *Baseline* shows lower and more compact values. Accelerometer summary statistics often become wider during *amusement* periods, as participants sometimes move or laugh, whereas *baseline* generally remains more contained. Not every feature distinguishes clearly. Overlapping violins serve as a helpful reminder that we are dealing with noisy, naturalistic signals.

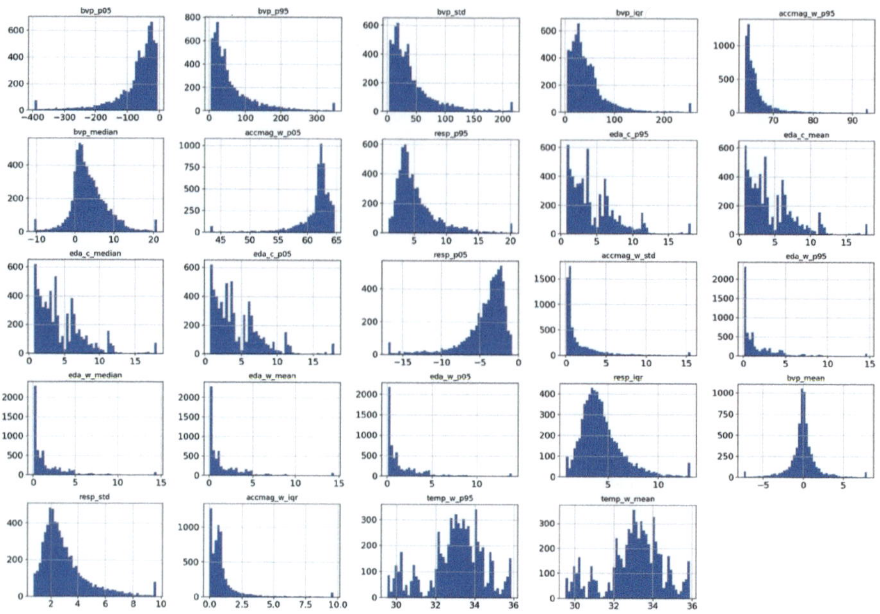

Figure 6.10 Distribution snapshots of representative engineered features.

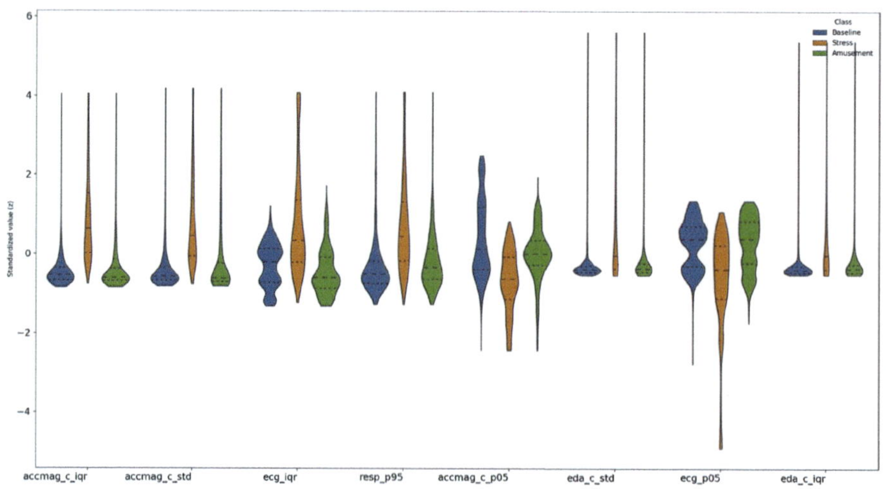

Figure 6.11 Class-conditioned violin plots for the top-K discriminative features (z-scaled).

Figure 6.12 offers the same top-K set with box plots, which emphasise nested quantiles deep into the tails. This view is handy when you want to confirm that apparent class differences are not driven only by a handful of extreme windows. For instance, if stress shows a consistently higher ladder of quantiles for an EDA statistic, that suggests a shift of the bulk, not just

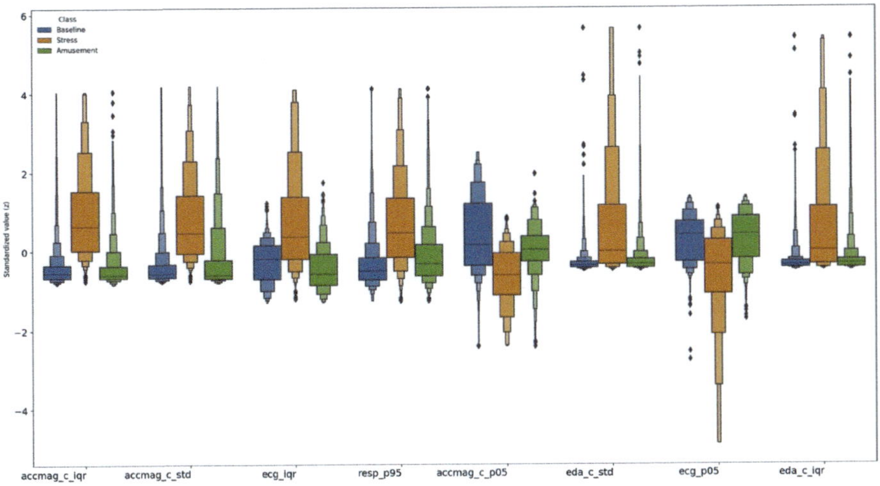

Figure 6.12 Box plots of the same top-K features, highlighting deep quantiles.

a few outliers. Conversely, if only the highest rungs separate, you may be looking at sporadic bursts (e.g., brief motion or sudden SCR flares) rather than a stable level shift. This is a useful diagnostic context when deciding how aggressively to regularise the model or whether to engineer additional robust features.

A few notes help when reading these panels. Each distribution combines windows from many participants. Baselines differ by person. To respect that, the modelling section always splits train and test by subject to avoid leakage. All axes use a common standardised scale so features can be compared side by side. The values show distance from the median measured in IQR units, not the original sensor units. When a feature looks bimodal or multimodal, the shape often reflects protocol phases (baseline versus task) and small differences in sensor placement rather than fundamentally different physiology. That is the kind of structure the classifiers will be asked to separate.

We evaluate three complementary classifiers, KNN, SVM with an RBF kernel, and a Random Forest, under a *subject-aware* split so that people the model sees at training time are never seen at test time. This is the right framing for wearables: generalisation must run across unseen users, not just unseen windows. In Figure 6.13, we summarise data efficiency with 5-fold cross-validation (CV), where each fold holds out entire subjects so that no subject appears in both training and validation. Each curve shows the mean macro-F1 across the five folds as we increase the number of training windows, and the shaded band is one standard deviation across folds. KNN climbs steadily yet plateaus well below the margin-based methods, which is a sign of underfitting with noisy, heterogeneous physiological features. SVM-RBF reaches a high cross-validated Macro-F1 quickly and then flattens.

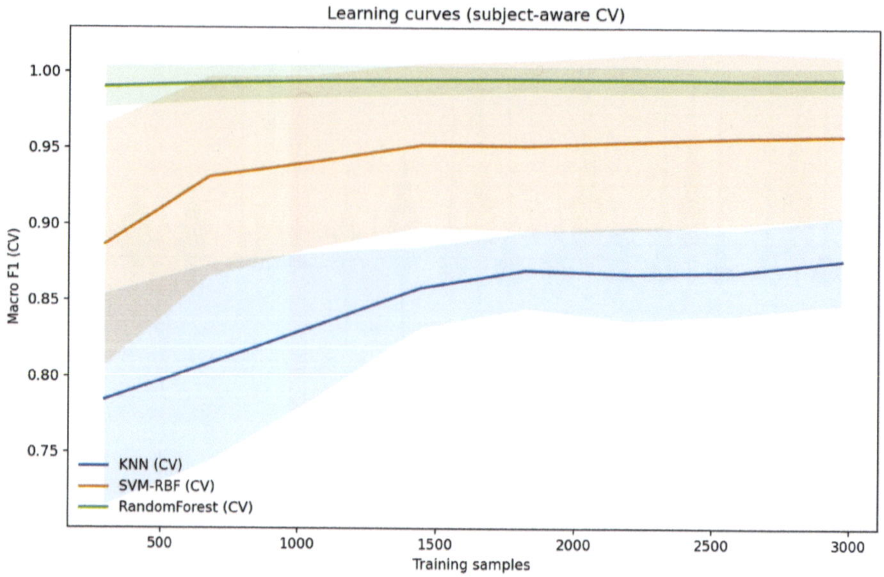

Figure 6.13 Learning curves.

Random Forest tracks a similar trend but with a consistently higher ceiling, suggesting that ensembles of trees capture nonlinear interactions among respiration, EDA, ECG and accelerometry that a local method like KNN misses. The gap between cross-validated curves and the final test number is expected because the test split represents a distinct set of people. The shape of the curve (rather than the absolute height) is what informs whether adding data is likely to help.

Aggregate scores across several metrics are compactly compared in Figure 6.14. We report a compact set of test-set metrics. Accuracy is the fraction of correct predictions. Balanced accuracy is the average of per-class recalls, which treats the three classes equally. Macro precision, macro recall, and macro F1 average the corresponding per-class scores with equal weight, so no single class dominates the summary. ROC-AUC is computed in a one-vs-rest fashion for each class and then averaged, and Average Precision is the area under the precision–recall curve averaged across classes. We also include two agreement measures that account for chance: Cohen's kappa and the Matthews correlation coefficient.

Random Forest leads on Accuracy, Macro F1, ROC-AUC (OvR) and Average Precision (macro), and posts the best agreement measures (Cohen's κ and MCC). SVM-RBF is a solid second: it edges close to RF on precision-oriented measures but lags on recall for the *stress* class. KNN is consistently last across metrics. With window-level features and subject variability, a simple neighbourhood rule struggles to separate *baseline* from the activated

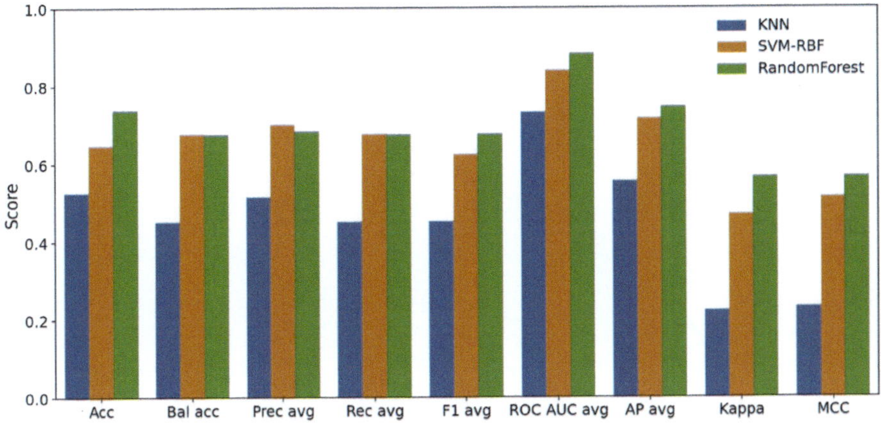

Figure 6.14 Aggregate metrics by model.

states. In practice, this means the ensemble not only makes more correct calls overall but also balances performance across *baseline*, *stress*, and *amusement*, whereas KNN struggles to separate the activated states from *baseline*.

Threshold-free comparisons reinforce this ranking. Figure 6.15 shows macro-averaged ROC curves: Random Forest achieves the highest area (AUC ≈ 0.883), SVM-RBF follows (≈ 0.840) and KNN trails (≈ 0.732).

Precision-recall, which is more sensitive to class prevalence, tells the same story in Figure 6.16. RF yields the best macro Average Precision (≈ 0.745), SVM-RBF is next (≈ 0.716), and KNN is far lower (≈ 0.557). Practically, this means RF not only ranks windows correctly more often but also keeps a higher precision at useful recall levels.

Where the models succeed and fail is clearest in the confusion matrices of Figure 6.17. Random Forest classifies *stress* most reliably (≈ 78% recall) and *Baseline* strongly (≈ 81%), but *amusement* remains the hardest condition, with ≈ 43% recall and a tendency to be absorbed by *baseline*. This is not unusual with natural laughter and motion overlapping low-arousal periods. SVM-RBF flips that pattern: it recognises *Amusement* very well (≈ 88% recall) but over-assigns other states to *amusement*, depressing recall for *stress* and *baseline*. KNN exhibits broad confusion, especially for *stress*, which is split almost evenly across the three classes. This matches its lower macro F1.

Finally, we look at *why* the models decide as they do. Figure 6.18 reports permutation importance on the test set for the best model (Random Forest): wrist temperature statistics dominate, followed by chest accelerometer variability (IQR) and a family of EDA features from both chest and wrist.

Figure 6.19 presents mean |SHAP| values computed with a tree explainer on the trained forest. Here, chest accelerometer features surface even more prominently, with EDA and ECG quantiles close behind. The two views provide complementary insights rather than identical ones. Permutation

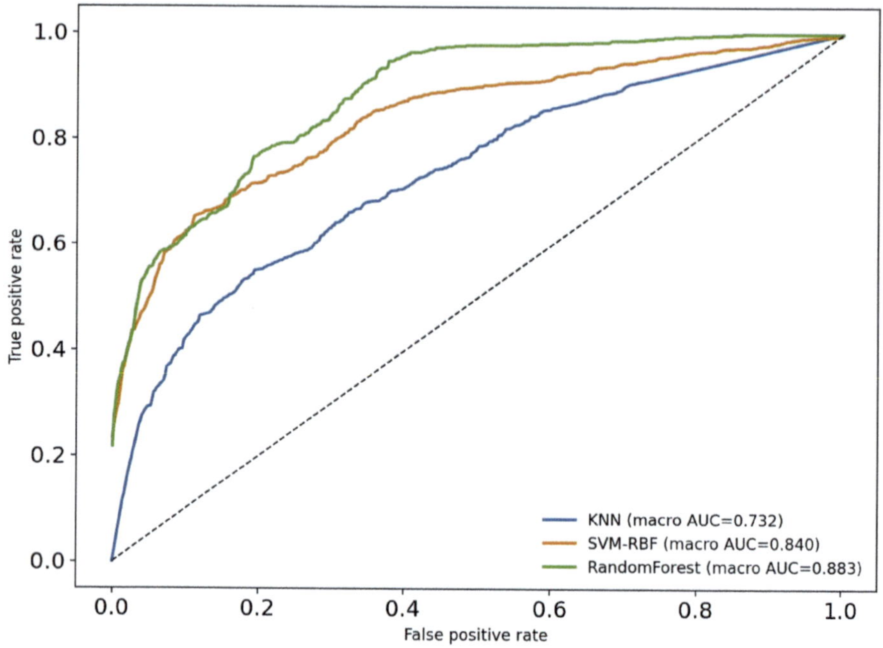

Figure 6.15 Macro ROC (one-vs-rest).

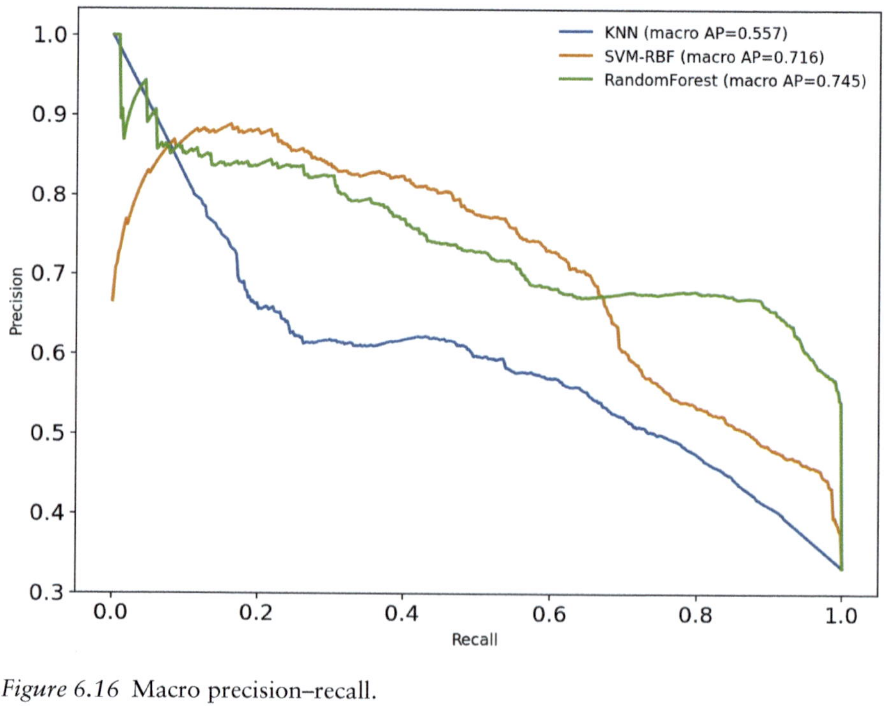

Figure 6.16 Macro precision–recall.

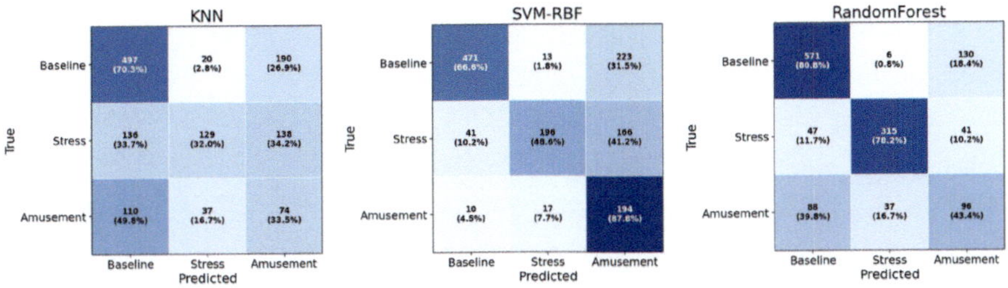

Figure 6.17 Confusion matrices.

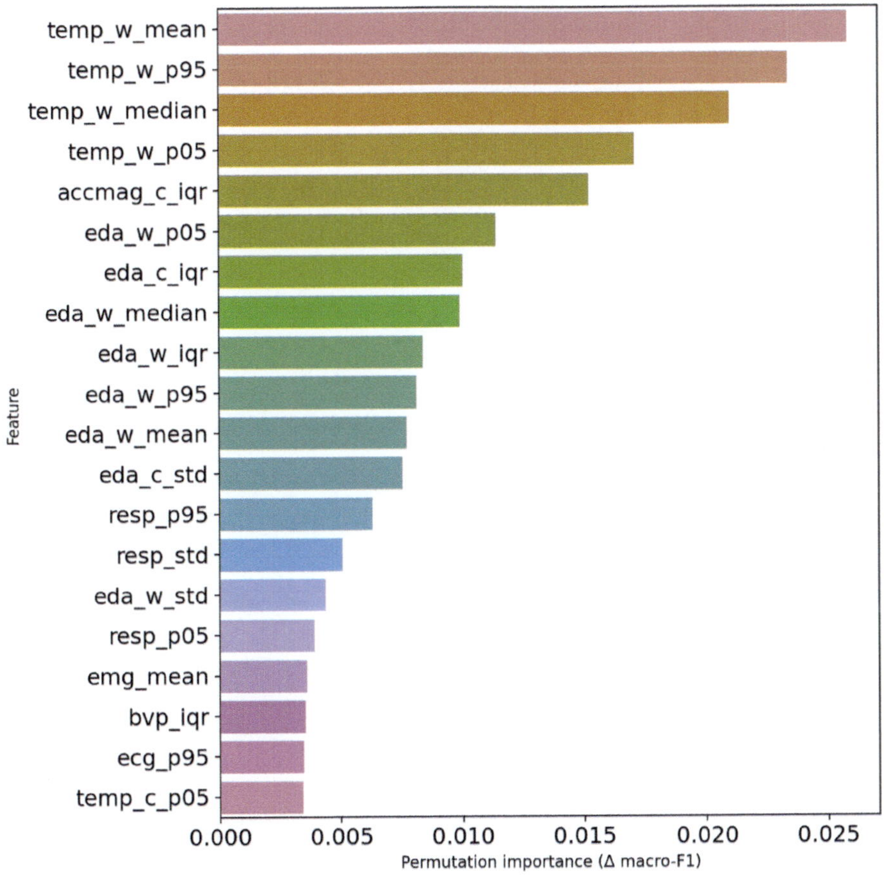

Figure 6.18 Permutation importance (Random Forest).

importance measures how much each feature affects predictive performance on held-out data. In contrast, SHAP values explain how the model internally attributes importance to its inputs. When features are correlated, such as multiple summaries from temperature or accelerometer channels, their

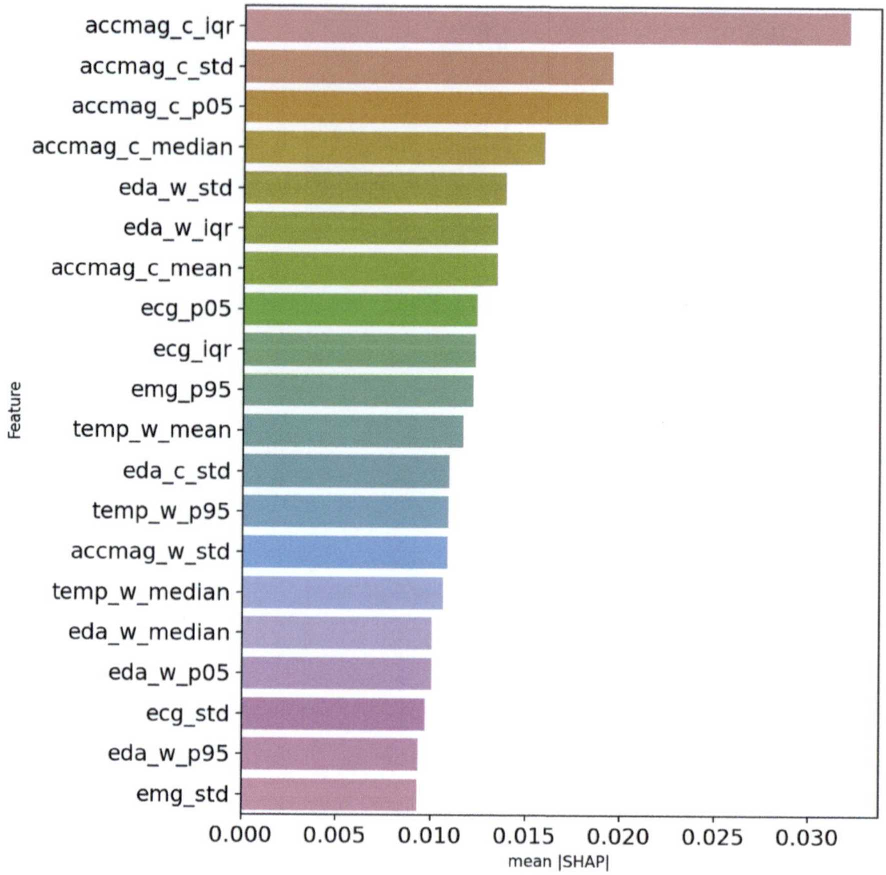

Figure 6.19 SHAP importance (Random Forest).

contributions may shift between the two approaches. The physiological story is consistent: motion intensity/variability, skin conductance level dynamics, and peripheral temperature shifts are key drivers separating baseline from aroused states, while ECG quantiles contribute to episodes with marked cardiovascular change.

Analysis revealed that on subject-held-out WESAD windows, Random Forest is the most reliable all-rounder across metrics and thresholds. SVM-RBF performs competitively and is often the better choice when you care most about recalling *amusement*. KNN lags on this feature set and is not recommended. The remaining confusion between *amusement* and *baseline* points to two practical extensions that are likely to help: add temporal context (either sequence models or features computed over longer horizons) and, where the use case allows it, apply light per-subject calibration. Both are aimed at lifting the *amusement* recall without giving up *stress* detection.

Looking beyond the numbers, the case study illustrates a broader shift in method: from isolated snapshots of emotion to a more embodied and context-aware view. The combination of elicitation design, wearable sensing, and subject-aware modelling lets us capture not only what people report but also how they feel, express, regulate, and respond as situations unfold. Emotion is treated less as a static label and more as a dynamic process that emerges from interactions among body, context, and technology.

As this direction develops, a few principles matter. Methods should be transparent and reproducible, especially when multiple data streams are fused. Ethical safeguards belong in the system from the start, particularly when using emotionally charged stimuli or lifelike avatars. And wherever possible, personalisation should guide both stimulus delivery and model interpretation to respect the individual nature of affective experience. With these guardrails in place, integrated approaches like the one shown here can shape how we study and use emotion across scientific, clinical, and social settings.

6.10 Ethical Perspectives and Future Directions

As embodied emotion research advances through increasingly sophisticated methods, ranging from immersive virtual environments and wearable biosensors to AI-driven affect recognition, the importance of grounding this progress in robust ethical frameworks becomes paramount. Emotion, by its very nature, lies at the core of personal identity and vulnerability. The ability to provoke, monitor, and interpret emotional states, especially through embodied and computational systems, raises fundamental questions about consent, autonomy, privacy, and the appropriate boundaries of scientific inquiry and technological design. This concluding section reflects on the ethical dimensions of embodied emotion research and proposes future directions that responsibly harness its potential across scientific and applied domains.

One of the primary ethical concerns arises from the *power asymmetry embedded in emotional technologies*. Unlike traditional experimental setups where participants voluntarily engage in controlled stimuli, many modern platforms, especially those embedded in daily-use devices, can track and respond to emotional signals without explicit awareness. Facial recognition algorithms, passive biometric sensors, and emotion-adaptive agents may infer affective states from micro-expressions or physiological changes that users themselves are not consciously aware of. This passive detection poses a profound risk of emotional surveillance, especially when deployed in educational, workplace, or consumer settings. In such contexts, users must retain clear and ongoing agency over what is collected, how it is interpreted, and to whom the data is accessible (Crawford & Paglen, 2021).

As computational systems are increasingly capable of *modulating emotion*, the line between emotional support and manipulation becomes blurred. While virtual therapists or learning assistants may adjust tone and pacing to reduce distress or improve engagement, these same mechanisms could be employed to nudge user behaviour in commercial or political contexts. The ethics of *emotional persuasion*, particularly through avatars that appear empathetic or human-like, must be critically evaluated. Transparency regarding system intentions, affective capabilities, and data flow should be central design principles in any emotionally responsive system.

Bias and representation also demand attention. Emotion recognition systems are often trained on datasets that lack cultural, racial, and neurodiversity. Facial expression data, in particular, has been shown to perform poorly on individuals with darker skin tones, non-Western affective styles, or conditions such as autism spectrum disorder. This not only leads to reduced accuracy but reinforces exclusionary emotional norms, implying that certain expressions are *standard* or *correct* while others are marginalised or misclassified. Future work must prioritise dataset inclusivity and model generalisability, ensuring that emotional systems are valid across diverse populations and do not inadvertently pathologise or ignore authentic emotional expressions (Rhue, 2018).

As emotion elicitation becomes more immersive, the potential for *emotional harm or dysregulation* increases. Provoking fear, shame, or sadness in tightly controlled lab settings may be justifiable for short-term insight, but reproducing these experiences in virtual environments with less supervision can overwhelm users or re-trigger past trauma. Ethical protocols must therefore adapt to account for the *intensity, realism, and duration* of digital affective stimuli. Measures such as emotional safety check-ins, post-session debriefing, and accessible opt-out features should be standard practice in both research and commercial applications.

Looking forward, the future of embodied emotion research lies in *responsible integration*. This means not simply fusing physiological, behavioural, and visual data streams, but doing so in a way that respects the user's emotional boundaries, preferences, and contexts. Emotion-aware systems should evolve towards personalisation, not only to improve accuracy but also to align with individual emotional goals and sensitivities. For example, affective technologies designed for neurodiverse users may need to accommodate reduced facial expressivity or unique sensory profiles without defaulting to deficit-based assumptions.

Interdisciplinary collaboration will be essential. Ethical frameworks must be co-developed by researchers, ethicists, technologists, designers, and users themselves. Participatory design methods can ensure that emotional systems are not only functional but empowering. This user-centred ethos is particularly important in clinical and educational contexts, where emotional tools should support regulation, growth, and resilience rather than impose normative emotional states.

Another critical direction is the *development of explainable emotional AI*. As models become more opaque and data-hungry, users must be able to understand how emotional predictions are made, on what basis, and with what level of certainty. Explainability is not merely a technical issue. It is a matter of emotional dignity. When systems suggest that someone is angry, anxious, or disengaged, those interpretations must be transparent and open to challenge, not treated as absolute truths.

The future also holds promise in *multisensory emotional modelling*, where touch, voice, motion, and even interoceptive signals (like gut feelings) are integrated into rich embodied models of affect. With wearable technology becoming more sophisticated, the ability to decode these subtle embodied cues will deepen our understanding of how emotions unfold and interact with cognition and behaviour. However, this progress must be guided by *data minimisation and user consent*, ensuring that the richness of emotion is not reduced to a commodity or surveillance metric.

As emotions become increasingly entangled with algorithmic systems, we must ask what kind of emotional future we want to build. Do we seek tools that optimise productivity and compliance, or systems that foster empathy, reflection, and authentic connection? The answer to this question will shape not only the trajectory of research but also the broader cultural meanings we assign to emotion in the digital age. Embodied emotion research, with its ability to trace affect across body, brain, and environment, holds tremendous promise. But its success will not be measured by technical precision alone. It will be defined by its ability to humanise emotion science, to respect the complexity of feeling, and to co-create technologies that serve rather than subvert our emotional lives.

References

Abdollahi, H., Mahoor, M. H., Zandie, R., Siewierski, J., & Qualls, S. H. (2022). Artificial emotional intelligence in socially assistive robots for older adults: A pilot study. *IEEE Transactions on Affective Computing*, *14*(3), 2020–2032.

Aly, L., Godinho, L., Bota, P., Bernardes, G., & da Silva, H. P. (2024). Acting emotions: A comprehensive dataset of elicited emotions. *Scientific Data*, *11*(1), 147.

Atkinson, A. P., Dittrich, W. H., Gemmell, A. J., & Young, A. W. (2004). Emotion perception from dynamic and static body expressions in point-light and full-light displays. *Perception*, *33*(6), 717–746.

Aviezer, H., Trope, Y., & Todorov, A. (2012). Body cues, not facial expressions, discriminate between intense positive and negative emotions. *Science*, *338*(6111), 1225–1229.

Azzalini, D., Rebollo, I., & Tallon-Baudry, C. (2019). Visceral signals shape brain dynamics and cognition. *Trends in Cognitive Sciences*, *23*(6), 488–509.

Bachmann, M., Subramaniam, A., Born, J., & Weibel, D. (2023). Virtual reality public speaking training: Effectiveness and user technology acceptance. *Frontiers in Virtual Reality*, *4*, 1242544.

Bargh, J. A., Chen, M., & Burrows, L. (1996). Automaticity of social behavior: Direct effects of trait construct and stereotype activation on action. *Journal of Personality and Social Psychology*, *71*(2), 230.

Barrett, L. F. (2017). *How emotions are made: The secret life of the brain*. Pan Macmillan.

Barsalou, L. W. (2008). Grounded cognition. *Annu. Rev. Psychol.*, *59*(1), 617–645.

Bastida, L., Sillaurren, S., Loizaga, E., Tomé, E., & Moya, A. (2024). Exploring human emotions: A virtual reality-based experimental approach integrating physiological and facial analysis. *Multimodal Technologies and Interaction*, *8*(6), 47.

Baumgartner, T., Esslen, M., & Jäncke, L. (2006). From emotion perception to emotion experience. Emotions evoked by pictures and classical music. *Brain Research*, *1078*(1), 68–76. https://doi.org/10.1016/j.brainres.2005.12.074

Blythe, E., Garrido, L., & Longo, M. R. (2023). Emotion is perceived accurately from isolated body parts, especially hands. *Cognition*, *230*, 105260.

Boğa, M., Koyuncu, M., Kaça, G., & Bayazıt, T. O. (2023). Comparison of emotion elicitation methods: 3 methods, 3 emotions, 3 measures. *Current Psychology*, *42*(22), 18670–18685.

Boucher, E. M., Harake, N. R., Ward, H. E., Stoeckl, S. E., Vargas, J., Minkel, J., & Zilca, R. (2021). Artificially intelligent chatbots in digital mental health interventions: a review. *Expert Review of Medical Devices*, *18*(sup1), 37–49.

Capriola-Hall, N. N., Ollendick, T. H., & White, S. W. (2021). Attention deployment to the eye region of emotional faces among adolescents with and without social anxiety disorder. *Cognitive Therapy and Research*, *45*(3), 456–467.

Carl, E., Stein, A. T., Levihn-Coon, A., Pogue, J. R., Rothbaum, B., Emmelkamp, P., & Powers, M. B. (2019). Virtual reality exposure therapy for anxiety and related disorders: A meta-analysis of randomized controlled trials. *Journal of Anxiety Disorders*, *61*, 27–36.

Carlisle, M., Uchino, B. N., Sanbonmatsu, D. M., Smith, T. W., Cribbet, M. R., Birmingham, W., & Vaughn, A. A. (2012). Subliminal activation of social ties moderates cardiovascular reactivity during acute stress. *Health Psychology*, *31*(2), 217.

Carney, D. R., Cuddy, A. J., & Yap, A. J. (2010). Power posing: Brief nonverbal displays affect neuroendocrine levels and risk tolerance. *Psychological Science*, *21*(10), 1363–1368.

Cereghetti, D., Coppin, G., Porcherot, C., Cayeux, I., Sander, D., & Delplanque, S. (2024). Beyond self-report measures of arousal: A new priming task to capture activation of relaxing and energizing feelings elicited by odors. *Food Quality and Preference*, *119*, 105227.

Cesario, J., Jonas, K. J., & Carney, D. R. (2017). CRSP special issue on power poses: What was the point and what did we learn?. *Comprehensive Results in Social Psychology*, *2*(1), 1–5.

Cisse, A. H. (2024, November). Real-time adaptive learning environments using gaze and emotion recognition engagement and learning outcomes. In *International conference on computers in education*.

Clark, A. (2013). Whatever next? Predictive brains, situated agents, and the future of cognitive science. *Behavioral and Brain Sciences*, *36*(3), 181–204.

Coan, J. A., & Allen, J. J. (2004). Frontal EEG asymmetry as a moderator and mediator of emotion. *Biological Psychology*, *67*(1–2), 7–50.

Craig, A. D. (2009). How do you feel—now? The anterior insula and human awareness. *Nature Reviews Neuroscience*, *10*(1), 59–70.

Crawford, K., & Paglen, T. (2021). Excavating AI: The politics of images in machine learning training sets. *Ai & Society*, *36*(4), 1105–1116.

Critchley, H. D., & Garfinkel, S. N. (2017). Interoception and emotion. *Current Opinion in Psychology*, *17*, 7–14.

D'Mello, S., & Graesser, A. (2013). AutoTutor and affective AutoTutor: Learning by talking with cognitively and emotionally intelligent computers that talk back. *ACM Transactions on Interactive Intelligent Systems (TiiS)*, *2*(4), 1–39.

D'Mello, S., Olney, A., Williams, C., & Hays, P. (2012). Gaze tutor: A gaze-reactive intelligent tutoring system. *International Journal of Human-Computer Studies*, *70*(5), 377–398.

Darwin, C. (1872). *The expression of the emotions in man and animals*. John Murray.

De Gelder, B. (2016). *Emotions and the body*. Oxford University Press.

De Gelder, B., de Borst, A. W., & Watson, R. (2015). The perception of emotion in body expressions. *Wiley Interdisciplinary Reviews: Cognitive Science*, *6*(2), 149–158.

Dennison, J. (2024). Emotions: Functions and significance for attitudes, behaviour, and communication. *Migration Studies*, *12*(1), 1–20.

Ekman, P. (1973). Cross-cultural studies of facial expression. *Darwin and Facial Expression: A Century of Research in Review*, *169222*(1), 45–60.

Ekman, P. (1992). An argument for basic emotions. *Cognition & Emotion*, *6*(3–4), 169–200.

Ekman, P., & Friesen, W. V. (1978). *Facial action coding system: A technique for the measurement of facial movement*. Consulting Psychologists Press.

Elgendi, M., Kumar, P., Barbic, S., Howard, N., Abbott, D., & Cichocki, A. (2018). Subliminal priming—state of the art and future perspectives. *Behavioral Sciences*, *8*(6), 54.

Elkjær, E., Mikkelsen, M. B., Michalak, J., Mennin, D. S., & O'Toole, M. S. (2022). Expansive and contractive postures and movement: A systematic review and meta-analysis of the effect of motor displays on affective and behavioral responses. *Perspectives on Psychological Science*, *17*(1), 276–304.

Eshuis, L. V., Van Gelderen, M. J., Van Zuiden, M., Nijdam, M. J., Vermetten, E., Olff, M., & Bakker, A. (2021). Efficacy of immersive PTSD treatments: A systematic review of virtual and augmented reality exposure therapy and a meta-analysis of virtual reality exposure therapy. *Journal of Psychiatric Research*, *143*, 516–527.

Farahani, H., Watson, P., Bezan, T., Kovač, N., Winter, L. C., Blagojević, M., & Jiménez, P. (2024). PsAIchology: An Intelligent Direction in Psychological Sciences. In *10th international scientific conference Technics, Informatics and Education-TIE 2024*. Faculty of Technical Sciences Čačak, University of Kragujevac.

Farahani, H., Watson, P., Kovač, N., Sheykhangafshe, F. B., Azadfallah, P., Allahyari, A., & Chesli, R. R. (2025). Unraveling the complexity of love addiction using machine learning algorithms: The influence of positive and negative affect, interpersonal needs, and self-hate. In C.-H. Mayer & E. Vanderheiden (Eds.), *International handbook of love: Transcultural and transdisciplinary perspectives* (pp. 1–22). Springer Nature.

Fischer, K., Jung, M., Jensen, L. C., & Aus der Wieschen, M. V. (2019, March). Emotion expression in HRI–when and why. In *2019 14th ACM/IEEE international conference on Human-Robot Interaction (HRI)* (pp. 29–38). IEEE.

Fitzpatrick, K. K., Darcy, A., & Vierhile, M. (2017). Delivering cognitive behavior therapy to young adults with symptoms of depression and anxiety using a fully automated conversational agent (Woebot): a randomized controlled trial. *JMIR Mental Health*, *4*(2), e7785.

Friesen, W. V. (1972). *Cultural differences in facial expressions in a social situation: An experimental test of the concept of display rules*. University of California.

Galanos, T., Liapis, A., & Yannakakis, G. N. (2021, September). AffectGAN: Affect-based generative art driven by semantics. In *2021 9th international conference on Affective Computing and Intelligent Interaction Workshops and Demos (ACIIW)* (pp. 1–7). IEEE.

Gallese, V., & Sinigaglia, C. (2011). What is so special about embodied simulation? *Trends in Cognitive Sciences*, *15*(11), 512–519.

Gross, J. J. (2015). Emotion regulation: Current status and future prospects. *Psychological Inquiry*, *26*(1), 1–26.

Gu, Y., Yang, K., Fu, S., Chen, S., Li, X., & Marsic, I. (2018, July). Multimodal affective analysis using hierarchical attention strategy with word-level alignment. In *Proceedings of the conference. Association for Computational Linguistics. Meeting* (Vol. 2018, p. 2225).

Harmon-Jones, E., Gable, P. A., & Peterson, C. K. (2010). The role of asymmetric frontal cortical activity in emotion-related phenomena: A review and update. *Biological Psychology*, *84*(3), 451–462.

Harmon-Jones, E., Gable, P. A., & Price, T. F. (2011). Leaning embodies desire: Evidence that leaning forward increases relative left frontal cortical activation to appetitive stimuli. *Biological Psychology*, *87*(2), 311–313.

Hasan, S., Alhaj, H., & Hassoulas, A. (2023). The efficacy and therapeutic alliance of augmented reality exposure therapy in treating adults with phobic disorders: Systematic review. *JMIR Mental Health*, *10*(1), e51318.

He, Y., Yang, L., Zhu, X., Wu, B., Zhang, S., Qian, C., & Tian, T. (2022). Mental health chatbot for young adults with depressive symptoms: A single-blind, three-arm randomized controlled trial. *Journal of Medical Internet Research*, *24*(11), e40719. https://doi.org/10.2196/40719

Herrera, F., Bailenson, J., Weisz, E., Ogle, E., & Zaki, J. (2018). Building long-term empathy: A large-scale comparison of traditional and virtual reality perspective-taking. *PLoS One*, *13*(10), e0204494.

Jack, R. E., Caldara, R., & Schyns, P. G. (2012). Internal representations reveal cultural diversity in expectations of facial expressions of emotion. *Journal of Experimental Psychology: General*, *141*(1), 19.

Khalfa, S., Schon, D., Anton, J. L., & Liégeois-Chauvel, C. (2005). Brain regions involved in the recognition of happiness and sadness in music. *Neuroreport*, *16*(18), 1981–1984.

Kim, W., Sung, J., Saakes, D., Huang, C., & Xiong, S. (2021). Ergonomic postural assessment using a new open-source human pose estimation technology (OpenPose). *International Journal of Industrial Ergonomics*, *84*, 103164.

Koelstra, S., Muhl, C., Soleymani, M., Lee, J. S., Yazdani, A., Ebrahimi, T., & Patras, I. (2011). Deap: A database for emotion analysis; using physiological signals. *IEEE Transactions on Affective Computing*, *3*(1), 18–31.

Kosti, R., Alvarez, J. M., Recasens, A., & Lapedriza, A. (2019). Context based emotion recognition using emotic dataset. *IEEE Transactions on Pattern Analysis and Machine Intelligence*, *42*(11), 2755–2766.

Kovač, N., Ratković, K., Farahani, H., & Watson, P. (2024). A practical applications guide to machine learning regression models in psychology with Python. *Methods in Psychology*, *11*, 100156.

Kovač, N., Ratković, K., Watson, P., Farahani, H., & Bagheri Sheykhangafshe, F. (2025a). Machine learning classification models for predicting chronic pain. *Current Psychology*, 1–14. Advance online publication.

Kovač, N., Ratković, K., Farahani, H., & Watson, P. (2025b). Machine learning regression models for internal shame. *Acta Psychologica*, *260*, 105721.

Krumhuber, E. G., Küster, D., Namba, S., & Skora, L. (2021). Human and machine validation of 14 databases of dynamic facial expressions. *Behavior Research Methods*, *53*(2), 686–701.

Kurdi, B., Lozano, S., & Banaji, M. R. (2017). Introducing the open affective standardized image set (OASIS). *Behavior Research Methods*, *49*(2), 457–470.

Lang, P. J., Bradley, M. M., & Cuthbert, B. N. (1997). International Affective Picture System (IAPS): Technical manual and affective ratings. *NIMH Center for the Study of Emotion and Attention*, *1*(39–58), 3.

LeBlanc, V. R., Brazil, V., & Posner, G. D. (2024). More than a feeling: Emotional regulation strategies for simulation-based education. *Advances in Simulation*, *9*(1), 53.
Lee, J., Kim, S., Kim, S., Park, J., & Sohn, K. (2019). Context-aware emotion recognition networks. In *Proceedings of the IEEE/CVF international conference on computer vision* (pp. 10143–10152).
Li, S., Deng, W., & Du, J. (2017). Reliable crowdsourcing and deep locality-preserving learning for expression recognition in the wild. In *Proceedings of the IEEE conference on computer vision and pattern recognition* (pp. 2852–2861).
Li, W., Moallem, I., Paller, K. A., & Gottfried, J. A. (2007). Subliminal smells can guide social preferences. *Psychological Science*, *18*(12), 1044–1049.
Liu, H., Peng, H., Song, X., Xu, C., & Zhang, M. (2022). Using AI chatbots to provide self-help depression interventions for university students: A randomized trial of effectiveness. *Internet Interventions*, *27*, 100495.
Mathôt, S. (2018). Pupillometry: Psychology, physiology, and function. *Journal of Cognition*, *1*(1), 16.
Matsumoto, D., Keltner, D., Shiota, M. N., O'Sullivan, M. A. U. R. E. E. N., & Frank, M. (2008). Facial expressions of emotion. *Handbook of Emotions*, *3*, 211–234.
Mikels, J. A., Fredrickson, B. L., Larkin, G. R., Lindberg, C. M., Maglio, S. J., & Reuter-Lorenz, P. A. (2005). Emotional category data on images from the international affective picture system. *Behavior Research Methods*, *37*(4), 626–630.
Miranda-Correa, J. A., Abadi, M. K., Sebe, N., & Patras, I. (2018). Amigos: A dataset for affect, personality and mood research on individuals and groups. *IEEE Transactions on Affective Computing*, *12*(2), 479–493.
Mittal, T., Bhattacharya, U., Chandra, R., Bera, A., & Manocha, D. (2020, April). M3er: Multiplicative multimodal emotion recognition using facial, textual, and speech cues. In *Proceedings of the AAAI conference on artificial intelligence* (Vol. 34, No. 2, pp. 1359–1367).
Mohammad, S. M. (2022). Ethics sheet for automatic emotion recognition and sentiment analysis. *Computational Linguistics*, *48*(2), 239–278.
Mollahosseini, A., Hasani, B., & Mahoor, M. H. (2017). Affectnet: A database for facial expression, valence, and arousal computing in the wild. *IEEE Transactions on Affective Computing*, *10*(1), 18–31.
Mousavi, S. M. H., Besenzoni, M., Andreoletti, D., Peternier, A., & Giordano, S. (2023, September). The Magic XRoom: A flexible VR platform for controlled emotion elicitation and recognition. In *Proceedings of the 25th international conference on mobile human-computer interaction* (pp. 1–5).
Myers, M. H. (2021). Automatic detection of a student's affective states for intelligent teaching systems. *Brain Sciences*, *11*(3), 331.
Nandi, A., Xhafa, F., Subirats, L., & Fort, S. (2021). Real-time emotion classification using EEG data stream in e-learning contexts. *Sensors*, *21*(5), 1589.
Nava, E., & Turati, C. (2020). Subliminal affective priming changes the 'feeling' towards neutral objects in infancy. *Social Neuroscience*, *15*(4), 447–457.
Niedenthal, P. M. (2007). Embodying emotion. *Science*, *316*(5827), 1002–1005.
Niedenthal, P. M., Barsalou, L. W., Winkielman, P., Krauth-Gruber, S., & Ric, F. (2005). Embodiment in attitudes, social perception, and emotion. *Personality and Social Psychology Review*, *9*(3), 184–211.
Numata, T., Sato, H., Asa, Y., Koike, T., Miyata, K., Nakagawa, E., & Sadato, N. (2020). Achieving affective human–virtual agent communication by enabling virtual agents to imitate positive expressions. *Scientific Reports*, *10*(1), 5977.
Park, J., & Han, G. (2018). Collectivism and the development of indigenous psychology in South Korea. In W. W. Li, D. Hodgetts, & K. H. Foo (Eds.), *Asia-Pacific perspectives on intercultural psychology* (pp. 53–74). Routledge.

Park, S., & Whang, M. (2022). Empathy in human–robot interaction: Designing for social robots. *International Journal of Environmental Research and Public Health*, *19*(3), 1889.

Pertaub, D. P., Slater, M., & Barker, C. (2002). An experiment on public speaking anxiety in response to three different types of virtual audience. *Presence*, *11*(1), 68–78.

Pessoa, L. (2013). *The cognitive-emotional brain: From interactions to integration*. MIT Press.

Polo, E. M., Iacomi, F., Rey, A. V., Ferraris, D., Paglialonga, A., & Barbieri, R. (2025). Advancing emotion recognition with Virtual Reality: A multimodal approach using physiological signals and machine learning. *Computers in Biology and Medicine*, *193*, 110310.

Price, T. F., & Harmon-Jones, E. (2015). Embodied emotion: The influence of manipulated facial and bodily states on emotive responses. *Wiley Interdisciplinary Reviews: Cognitive Science*, *6*(6), 461–473.

Price, T. F., Dieckman, L. W., & Harmon-Jones, E. (2012). Embodying approach motivation: Body posture influences startle eyeblink and event-related potential responses to appetitive stimuli. *Biological Psychology*, *90*(3), 211–217.

Reddan, M. C., Chang, L., Kragel, P., & Wager, T. D. (2024). Somatosensory and motor contributions to emotion representation. *arXiv preprint arXiv:2411.08973*.

Rhue, L. (2018). Racial influence on automated perceptions of emotions. *SSRN 3281765*.

Rohr, M., & Wentura, D. (2021). Degree and complexity of non-conscious emotional information processing–a review of masked priming studies. *Frontiers in Human Neuroscience*, *15*, 689369.

Russell, J. A. (1980). A circumplex model of affect. *Journal of Personality and Social Psychology*, *39*(6), 1161.

Salamone, P. C., Legaz, A., Sedeño, L., Moguilner, S., Fraile-Vazquez, M., Campo, C. G., & Ibañez, A. (2021). Interoception primes emotional processing: Multimodal evidence from neurodegeneration. *Journal of Neuroscience*, *41*(19), 4276–4292.

Schaefer, A., Nils, F., Sanchez, X., & Philippot, P. (2010). Assessing the effectiveness of a large database of emotion-eliciting films: A new tool for emotion researchers. *Cognition and Emotion*, *24*(7), 1153–1172.

Shaffer, F., & Ginsberg, J. P. (2017). An overview of heart rate variability metrics and norms. *Frontiers in Public Health*, *5*, 258.

Shu, L., Xie, J., Yang, M., Li, Z., Li, Z., Liao, D., & Yang, X. (2018). A review of emotion recognition using physiological signals. *Sensors*, *18*(7), 2074.

Slater, M., Pertaub, D. P., Barker, C., & Clark, D. M. (2006). An experimental study on fear of public speaking using a virtual environment. *CyberPsychology & Behavior*, *9*(5), 627–633.

Smith, R., Thayer, J. F., Khalsa, S. S., & Lane, R. D. (2017). The hierarchical basis of neurovisceral integration. *Neuroscience & Biobehavioral Reviews*, *75*, 274–296.

Soleymani, M., Lichtenauer, J., Pun, T., & Pantic, M. (2011). A multimodal database for affect recognition and implicit tagging. *IEEE Transactions on Affective Computing*, *3*(1), 42–55.

Somarathna, R., Bednarz, T., & Mohammadi, G. (2022). Virtual reality for emotion elicitation–a review. *IEEE Transactions on Affective Computing*, *14*(4), 2626–2645.

Stepper, S., & Strack, F. (1993). Proprioceptive determinants of emotional and nonemotional feelings. *Journal of Personality and Social Psychology*, *64*(2), 211.

Stock-Homburg, R. (2022). Survey of emotions in human–robot interactions: Perspectives from robotic psychology on 20 years of research. *International Journal of Social Robotics*, *14*(2), 389–411.

Su, H., Qi, W., Chen, J., Yang, C., Sandoval, J., & Laribi, M. A. (2023). Recent advancements in multimodal human–robot interaction. *Frontiers in Neurorobotics*, *17*, 1084000.

Torre, I., Carrigan, E., McDonnell, R., Domijan, K., McCabe, K., & Harte, N. (2019, October). The effect of multimodal emotional expression and agent appearance on trust in human-agent interaction. In *Proceedings of the 12th ACM SIGGRAPH conference on motion, interaction and games* (pp. 1–6).

Tsiourti, C., Weiss, A., Wac, K., & Vincze, M. (2019). Multimodal integration of emotional signals from voice, body, and context: Effects of (in) congruence on emotion recognition and attitudes towards robots. *International Journal of Social Robotics*, *11*(4), 555–573.

Tzirakis, P., Chen, J., Zafeiriou, S., & Schuller, B. (2021). End-to-end multimodal affect recognition in real-world environments. *Information Fusion*, *68*, 46–53.

Umair, M., Chalabianloo, N., Sas, C., & Ersoy, C. (2021). HRV and stress: A mixed-methods approach for comparison of wearable heart rate sensors for biofeedback. *IEEe Access*, *9*, 14005–14024.

Van Cappellen, P., Ladd, K. L., Cassidy, S., Edwards, M. E., & Fredrickson, B. L. (2022). Bodily feedback: expansive and upward posture facilitates the experience of positive affect. *Cognition and Emotion*, *36*(7), 1327–1342.

Van der Wel, P., & Van Steenbergen, H. (2018). Pupil dilation as an index of effort in cognitive control tasks: A review. *Psychonomic Bulletin & Review*, *25*(6), 2005–2015.

Vetter, P., Badde, S., Phelps, E. A., & Carrasco, M. (2019). Emotional faces guide the eyes in the absence of awareness. *ELife*, *8*, e43467.

Visalli, A., Ambrosini, E., Viviani, G., Sambataro, F., Tenconi, E., & Vallesi, A. (2023). On the relationship between emotions and cognitive control: Evidence from an observational study on emotional priming Stroop task. *PLoS One*, *18*(11), e0294957.

Wood, A., Rychlowska, M., Korb, S., & Niedenthal, P. (2016). Fashioning the face: Sensorimotor simulation contributes to facial expression recognition. *Trends in Cognitive Sciences*, *20*(3), 227–240.

Yan, W. J., Wu, Q., Liang, J., Chen, Y. H., & Fu, X. (2013). How fast are the leaked facial expressions: The duration of micro-expressions. *Journal of Nonverbal Behavior*, *37*(4), 217–230.

Zhang, Z. (2012). Microsoft kinect sensor and its effect. *IEEE Multimedia*, *19*(2), 4–10.

7 Text-Based Emotion Recognition and Detection

Mining Sentiments and Feelings

Nataša Kovač, Hojjatollah Farahani, and Peter Watson

Emotions shape human experiences deeply, influencing decisions, relationships, health, and overall well-being. Among various ways to express emotions, textual data uniquely captures complex emotional differences through words and language structures. With the rapid growth of digital communication platforms, social media, and online interactions, analysing text has become an essential method for emotion recognition, significantly impacting psychology, health informatics, marketing, and artificial intelligence (AI). This integration aligns with the Artificial Psychology (PsAIchology) framing that connects AI methods and psychological science (Farahani et al., 2024). Textual data naturally contain emotional information, which can be explicit, through clearly stated emotional words (e.g., *happy*, *anxious*, *angry*), or implicit, conveyed through tone, context, metaphor, or sentiment. Emotional analysis of text requires robust computational methods to decode these intricate emotional expressions accurately. The rise of Natural Language Processing (NLP) techniques has greatly improved our ability to interpret and analyse emotional content in textual data.

Historically, text-based emotion recognition was mainly manual, with psychologists relying on qualitative analysis of diaries, interviews, and written correspondence. In contemporary psychological research, the integration of advanced computational techniques such as text mining and sentiment analysis has opened new methodological frontiers for understanding the nuances of human emotional expression within therapeutic and clinical contexts. The spoken words of patients captured during interviews are more than narrative data; they are psycholinguistic structures that encode affective states, cognitive patterns, and interpersonal dynamics. By applying text mining to transcribed interviews, psychologists can systematically detect latent themes, relational markers, and shifts in language usage that may remain elusive through traditional qualitative coding alone (Tausczik & Pennebaker, 2010). Such computational augmentation does not replace human interpretation but rather enriches it, enabling a multi-layered analysis of emotional tone, self-referential language, and the evolution of linguistic markers that correlate with psychological change.

DOI: 10.4324/9781003495123-7

Sentiment analysis extends this potential by quantifying emotional valence in patient discourse, thus transforming subjective narratives into measurable indicators of affective states. When integrated into a longitudinal therapeutic framework, sentiment analysis allows clinicians to observe whether emotional polarity (in terms of positivity, negativity, or ambivalence) shifts across treatment sessions (Mohammad, 2021). This quantitative insight aligns closely with the psychodynamic principle that language serves as an externalised expression of internal affective regulation (Ricardi, 2025). As patients progress through therapy, their lexical patterns often become less dominated by catastrophic or self-blaming terms and more characterised by agentic, hopeful expressions, phenomena that can be captured empirically through affective lexical modelling. This analytic complement to clinical intuition supports the growing call for data-informed clinical practice in psychotherapy research (Ingram & Siegle, 2009).

Beyond individual analysis, text mining methods facilitate the identification of collective response patterns across patient populations. Through natural language processing pipelines, large corpora of therapeutic session transcripts can be coded for thematic density, metaphorical content, or even markers of therapeutic alliance, offering psychologists a scalable means to test psychological theory against naturally occurring discourse (Pennebaker & Chung, 2011). Importantly, this approach underscores the ethical imperative of maintaining confidentiality while harnessing anonymised linguistic data to drive precision in clinical psychology (Alm, 2012). The fusion of computational and interpretative paradigms thus represents an epistemological evolution: the movement from purely hermeneutic understanding towards an integrative model where human empathy and machine learning together construct deeper insights into mental healing. By systematically analysing how language embodies transformation, psychologists can trace therapeutic progress in a more transparent and scientifically rigorous manner, transforming qualitative narratives into bridges between subjective experience and measurable change. The development of computational linguistics introduced quantitative approaches, enabling researchers to systematically evaluate large textual datasets. Early works by Pennebaker and Chung (2011) established linguistic markers linked to psychological states and health outcomes, forming a foundational knowledge that informs modern NLP-based emotional analysis.

Contemporary methods employ sophisticated NLP techniques, including sentiment analysis, emotion lexicons, and machine learning models. Sentiment analysis typically categorises text into positive, negative, or neutral sentiments, providing a foundational but coarse-grained approach to emotional analysis (Liu, 2022). Emotion lexicons such as NRC Emotion Lexicon (Mohammad & Turney, 2013), Linguistic Inquiry and Word Count (LIWC)

(Pennebaker et al., 2001), and Affective Norms for English Words (ANEW) (Bradley & Lang, 1999) provide comprehensive word-emotion mappings, enabling more detailed emotional insights. Machine learning and deep learning further advance this analysis by extracting emotional context from semantic embeddings, achieving unparalleled accuracy in emotional classification tasks (Devlin et al., 2019). For psychology-focused, Python-based pipeline patterns and regression modelling, see (Kovač et al., 2024).

Text-based emotion recognition has proven particularly insightful in clinical settings. Analysis of patient narratives, social media posts, or therapeutic dialogues reveals emotional patterns essential for mental health diagnostics and interventions. Recent studies demonstrate the efficacy of textual emotion detection in identifying early indicators of depression, anxiety, or suicidal ideation, underscoring its critical role in proactive mental health care (De Choudhury et al., 2013a). Integrating textual emotional data with physiological and behavioural measures further enriches emotional analysis, providing a comprehensive understanding of embodied emotional experiences. Multimodal approaches leverage synchronised text, voice, facial expressions, and physiological data, significantly enhancing emotion recognition accuracy (D'Mello & Kory, 2015).

Ethical considerations remain paramount in text-based emotional analysis. Text data often reveals deeply personal and sensitive emotional states, raising privacy concerns. Researchers must uphold stringent ethical standards, including participant consent, data anonymisation, transparency of data usage, and secure data handling practices (Jobin et al., 2019).

To facilitate readers' hands-on exploration, public datasets like the Emotion Intensity in Tweets dataset (EmoInt) (Mohammad & Bravo-Marquez, 2017), the SemEval Sentiment Analysis datasets (Dimitrov et al., 2024), or publicly available tweets and Reddit discussions offer valuable resources for practical emotional analysis. These datasets enable robust methodological exploration, supporting reproducible and transparent research.

7.1 The Power of Words: Exploring Emotion in Text

Words are more than mere symbols arranged on a page or a screen; they carry emotional resonance, capture human experiences, and reveal deep psychological truths. Through words, we narrate our joys and sadness, express fears and hopes, and communicate frustrations and desires. The emotional power embedded in language provides a window into the human psyche, making text a rich source for understanding not just what we say, but how we feel. Emotion embedded in language is central to our identity, social interactions, and psychological health (Pennebaker & Chung, 2011).

Humans inherently use language as an expressive tool, instinctively encoding emotions within words. The process of writing or speaking involves not only cognitive but also emotional processes, linking internal emotional states with external linguistic expressions. Research demonstrates that linguistic choices, such as specific word usage, sentence structure, and narrative style, reflect underlying emotional and psychological states (Tausczik & Pennebaker, 2010). For example, a person experiencing anxiety might subconsciously use more tentative words like *maybe* or *perhaps*, while someone expressing sadness may use more first-person singular pronouns (*I*, *me*, *myself*) and negative emotion words like *loss*, *sad*, and *alone*. Through the systematic analysis of these language patterns, researchers can identify emotional states that may not be immediately obvious through other modes of communication. Emotions embedded in text can often be subtle, concealed in linguistic cues rather than being explicitly stated. Words carry emotional weight not only in their literal meaning but also in their connotations and contextual usage. For instance, the phrase *I'm fine* can either communicate genuine well-being or mask deeper emotional distress, depending on the broader linguistic setting. Likewise, metaphors and idiomatic expressions (*feeling blue*, *broken-hearted*, *on cloud nine*) show how language creatively captures complex emotional states.

Language patterns not only reflect immediate emotional reactions but can also reveal long-term psychological states and personality traits. Linguistic analysis has demonstrated potential in detecting depression, anxiety, stress, and even signs of suicidal ideation through textual data such as social media posts, therapy transcripts, or personal diaries (De Choudhury et al., 2013b). James Pennebaker's foundational work on expressive writing reveals the therapeutic power of emotional expression through text. He found that individuals who wrote openly about traumatic events experienced significant improvements in mental and physical health compared to those who wrote neutrally about mundane topics (Pennebaker, 1997). Writing about emotions, even without direct feedback, seems to organise and clarify thoughts, reducing stress and fostering emotional regulation.

Thus, the emotional significance of text has implications beyond mere analysis. It directly impacts psychological well-being. This connection between emotion, language, and health forms the theoretical foundation for numerous applications in clinical psychology, digital health interventions, and emotional AI. To systematically explore emotional content in language, researchers rely on frameworks categorising emotions along key dimensions or discrete categories:

- *Dimensional Models* classify emotions according to continuous dimensions, primarily valence (pleasantness vs. unpleasantness), arousal (intensity), and dominance (control or power). Russell's Circumplex Model is a prime example, placing emotions in a two-dimensional circular space defined by valence and arousal (Russell, 1980).
- *Categorical Models* are found in discrete emotional theories, which identify specific emotions such as joy, sadness, anger, fear, surprise, and disgust. Theories by Ekman (1992) or Plutchik (1980a) are well-known categorical models used extensively in text emotion analysis.

Below is an illustrative Python example for quickly exploring emotional dimensions using the NRCLex package (Mohammad & Turney, 2013), providing an intuitive bar plot visualisation of emotional word distribution:

```
from nrclex import NRCLex
import matplotlib.pyplot as plt

text = "Today, I'm thrilled about the upcoming vacation but slightly anxious about flying."

# Analyze emotional content
emotion_analysis = NRCLex(text)
emotion_freq = emotion_analysis.raw_emotion_scores

# Plot emotional distribution
plt.figure(figsize=(8, 4))
plt.bar(emotion_freq.keys(), emotion_freq.values())
plt.title("Distribution of emotions")
plt.xlabel("Emotion")
plt.ylabel("Frequency")
plt.tight_layout()
plt.show()
```

Visualising textual emotion via word clouds helps uncover dominant emotional themes intuitively. Below is an example illustrating this method:

```
from wordcloud import WordCloud

text = "I felt joyful, inspired, and motivated after talking to my friend, though still slightly worried."

wordcloud = WordCloud(width=800, height=400, background_color='white').generate(text)

plt.figure(figsize=(10, 5))
plt.imshow(wordcloud, interpolation='bilinear')
plt.axis("off")
plt.title("Word Cloud-emotions")
plt.tight_layout()
plt.show()
```

A word cloud (Figure 7.1) produced by the previous code instantly communicates the emotional landscape, capturing dominant emotions (e.g., joyful, motivated, inspired) that vividly portray a complex emotional moment.

While text emotion analysis offers profound insights, ethical considerations must guide its practice. Analysing emotional content in text data must

Figure 7.1 Word cloud example.

always respect privacy, consent, and confidentiality. Text data can reveal deeply personal psychological states, making anonymisation and ethical oversight non-negotiable components of research and practical applications (Jobin et al., 2019).

7.2 Natural Language Processing for Emotion Analysis

NLP is the set of methods that lets computers work with human language. In the context of emotion, NLP helps us move from unstructured text to structured evidence about what people may feel. A post, a review, or a line of dialogue becomes a set of clues. By combining linguistics with statistical learning, NLP turns those clues into interpretable signals about affect and mood (Jurafsky & Martin, 2025; Cambria et al., 2015).

Most projects follow a simple flow. We begin by tidying the text so that later steps do not get distracted by noise. Lowercasing, splitting into words, and reducing words to a base form prevent us from counting the same idea in many ways (Bird et al., 2009). Common words such as *the* or *and* are often removed because they rarely carry emotion. This stage does not detect feelings on its own. It prepares the ground so later methods can focus on meaningful content.

A straightforward way to estimate emotions is to look up words in a curated dictionary. Resources such as the NRC Emotion Lexicon map words to categories like joy, anger, fear, sadness, disgust, surprise, trust, and anticipation. If a text contains many joy words and very few anger words, we can say the balance of evidence points towards joy. Lexicons are transparent and easy to explain to non-specialists, and they work even when there is little training data. Their weakness is context. *Great* is usually positive, yet in *great, just perfect*, it can be sarcastic. Lexicons are best used as baselines and as tools for auditing what more complex models might be picking up (Mohammad & Turney, 2013). Many systems start with sentiment polarity because it tells us whether the overall tone is positive or negative. Rule-based tools like VADER work well on short informal texts and require no training data (Hutto & Gilbert, 2014). Polarity is useful, but emotions are richer than a single scale. A sentence can carry both excitement and fear at the same time. For that, we need models that read words in context.

The biggest advance in the last few years came from Transformer models that learn how words behave in many contexts during pretraining, then adapt to a specific task with a small amount of labelled data (Vaswani et al., 2017; Devlin et al., 2019; Rogers et al., 2021). These models are good at separating close feelings, for example, anger versus annoyance, because they consider the surrounding words and the way expressions are used together. In practice, many teams start with a public model and fine-tune it on their domain. The short snippet below sends a sentence to a pre-trained emotion classifier and returns label scores. It is meant to show the idea rather than to teach coding.

```
from transformers import pipeline
clf = pipeline("text-classification",
       model="j-hartmann/emotion-english-distilroberta-base",
       return_all_scores=True)
clf("I am excited about the launch but a little nervous")
```

Output:

```
[[{'label': 'anger', 'score': 0.0006416769465431571},
  {'label': 'disgust', 'score': 0.00023304736532736557},
  {'label': 'fear', 'score': 0.9930770397186279},
  {'label': 'joy', 'score': 0.0027830556500703096},
  {'label': 'neutral', 'score': 0.0005855631898157299},
  {'label': 'sadness', 'score': 0.0017977369716390967},
  {'label': 'surprise', 'score': 0.0008818271453492343}]]
```

The output lists emotions with probabilities that sum to one. You can read it as a distribution of plausible feelings expressed by the sentence.

Because emotion datasets are often unbalanced, accuracy alone can be misleading. We prefer macro-averaged F1, which treats each emotion equally, and per-class precision and recall, which reveal where a model confuses classes. When the system outputs probabilities, curves such as ROC and precision-recall help us understand performance at different decision thresholds. Visual tools like confusion matrices and label frequency plots make these ideas easy to read at a glance.

Words shift meaning with context. *Fine* can be contentment or sarcasm. Irony and humour often require knowledge that spans several sentences or a shared background. Domain shift is common. A model trained on tweets may not work well on clinical notes or customer support chat without additional tuning. Annotation is also noisy because people sometimes disagree about what a text conveys. These challenges are active research topics, and they are the reason we combine simple, explainable methods with stronger learned models.

Inferring feelings from language touches on privacy and dignity. Good practice includes clear consent for data use, minimal collection, transparency about how the model was trained, and regular checks for bias in both data and outputs (Hovy & Spruit, 2016; Blodgett et al., 2020; Jobin et al., 2019). In sensitive settings, we recommend human oversight and aggregate reporting rather than individual classification.

7.3 EmText: Analysing Sentiments in Embodied Emotion

We use the term Emotionally embodied Text (EmText) to emphasise that textual expressions can reflect not only appraisals but also bodily and affective states, an approach grounded in theories of embodied/grounded cognition and embodied emotion (Barsalou, 2008; Niedenthal, 2007; Niedenthal & Maringer, 2009). Evidence linking emotional language to neural and bodily processes further motivates this view (Saxbe et al., 2013; Giraud et al., 2023), alongside multimodal datasets and reviews that connect physiology with emotion recognition (Park et al., 2020; Larradet et al., 2020).

EmText is a methodological approach designed to integrate linguistic analysis with embodied emotion frameworks. Rather than viewing text as simply informational or expressive, EmText views linguistic output as inherently tied to emotional bodily states, such as anxiety manifesting in stomach discomfort, happiness felt as warmth, or sadness experienced as heaviness in the chest. It bridges psychology, neuroscience, and linguistics, leveraging computational tools to identify deeper emotional experiences in textual data (Barsalou, 2008). Related machine-learning frameworks have been applied to affect-linked constructs beyond core emotions, such as love addiction, where features and explanations clarify predictive factors (Farahani et al., 2025). EmText relies heavily on the theory of embodied cognition, proposing that language and thought processes are deeply grounded in sensory-motor experiences. According to this framework, emotional words (*hurt*, *warm*, *heavy*) evoke corresponding physical sensations and motor responses in the reader or listener, facilitating richer emotional understanding beyond purely cognitive interpretation (Barsalou, 2008; Niedenthal et al., 2005).

For instance, reading *she felt crushed by sadness* activates neural patterns associated with physical heaviness, making emotion perception embodied rather than purely conceptual. Recognising these embodied metaphors and expressions through computational text analysis enhances the interpretive power of emotional AI applications. To analyse embodied sentiments in text, EmText methodologies typically involve:

- *Identifying Embodied Metaphors*: Detecting metaphorical language explicitly connected to bodily sensations.
- *Emotion-Sensation Lexicons:* Leveraging specialised lexicons linking emotions to physiological sensations (e.g., heat for anger, heaviness for sadness).
- *Contextual Embodied Emotion Modelling*: Using advanced NLP tools (e.g., transformers) to model emotional context and capture embodied emotional states.

Here's a practical Python example demonstrating how to detect embodied emotional metaphors using simple keyword matching:

```
import re


text = "I felt heavy with grief but her smile warmed my heart."
# Define basic embodied metaphor patterns
embodied_patterns = {
    'sadness': ['heavy', 'crushed', 'weight'],
    'happiness': ['warm', 'light', 'bright'],
    'anger': ['hot', 'burning', 'fuming'],
    'fear': ['cold', 'chilled', 'frozen']
}

embodied_emotions = {}
for emotion, keywords in embodied_patterns.items():
    for kw in keywords:
        if re.search(r'\b' + kw + r'\b', text.lower()):
            embodied_emotions[emotion] = embodied_emotions.
get(emotion, 0) + 1

print("Detected embodied emotions:", embodied_emotions)
```

Output:

```
Detected embodied emotions: {'sadness': 1}
```

This simple method effectively identifies embodied emotional expressions, highlighting different emotional experiences embedded in linguistic metaphors (*heavy* for sadness, *warm* for happiness). Visualisation greatly aids in understanding how embodied emotions appear in text. Figure 7.2 presents one example implemented with PyPlutchik (Semeraro et al., 2021). Panel (A) displays the relative frequency of the eight primary emotions arranged on Plutchik's wheel (Plutchik, 1980b). Each petal's length is proportional to that emotion's share (neutral is omitted). Panel (B) shows the primary dyads, i.e., pairs such as *love* (joy + trust), *optimism* (anticipation + joy),

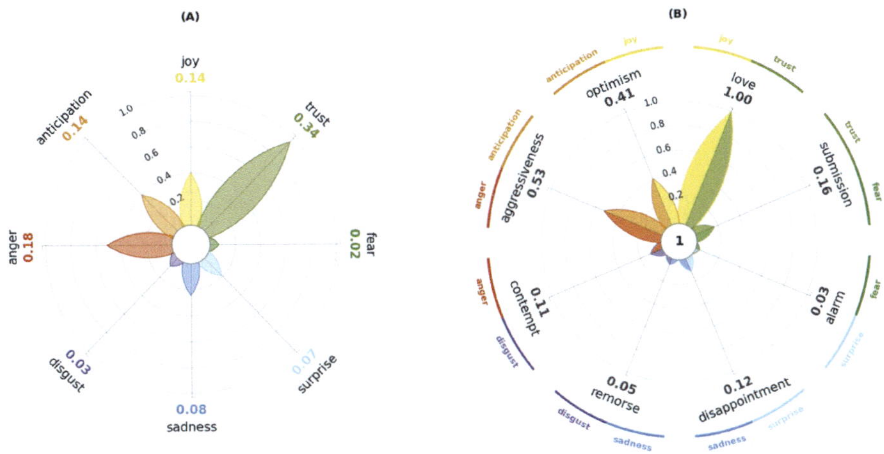

Figure 7.2 Embodied emotion profiles in text: (A) distribution of primary emotions on Plutchik's wheel; (B) intensities of Plutchik's primary dyads derived from those primaries.

and *aggressiveness* (anger + anticipation), computed from the primaries and rescaled so the largest dyad reaches the outer ring. Together, these views make it easy to read both the dominant feelings in the corpus and the blended, embodied states that co-occur in language.

Clinical psychology increasingly recognises the value of EmText methods. Analysis of therapy session transcripts can reveal embodied emotions associated with psychological conditions (e.g., anxiety manifesting as physical tension, sadness as heaviness). An EmText analysis might look for embodied emotional cues in clinical dialogues, highlighting critical therapeutic insights, as it is shown in Table 7.1.

Clinical psychology increasingly recognises the value of EmText methods for reading embodied emotions in language. Short phrases in therapy transcripts often carry bodily metaphors that point to affective states. *Heavy* tends to co-occur with sadness, *tight* with anxiety, and *warm* with happiness. Table 7.1 shows how a simple EmText pass can surface these cues and present them in a compact form that a clinician can scan during or after a session. The goal is not diagnosis but faster noticing. When a transcript highlights repeated references to tightness, weight, or warmth, the therapist gains a structured view of how the client's body enters the narrative.

Modern transformer models help with this task because they read words in context and learn how metaphors behave across many examples. The transformer architecture builds a representation of each token while attending to the rest of the sentence, which lets the model connect *heavy* with *sadness* in *my heart feels heavy*, and ignore it in unrelated uses (Vaswani et al., 2017). BERT introduced bidirectional pretraining that predicts masked words from

Table 7.1 Illustrative EmText cues in short clinical utterances: detected emotion and salient embodied expression

Text excerpt	*Detected emotion*	*Embodied expression*
I feel completely drained and heavy.	Sadness	heavy
My chest feels tight whenever worried	Anxiety	tight
Happiness feels warm, like sunlight.	Happiness	warm

both left and right context and improved many classification tasks, including emotion recognition (Devlin et al., 2019). RoBERTa refined this recipe through longer training and dynamic masking and often yields stronger results on downstream text classification (Liu et al., 2019). DistilBERT keeps most of BERT's language understanding while being smaller and faster, which makes it practical for real-time assistance in clinics or call centres (Sanh et al., 2019). The Hugging Face ecosystem wraps these models in a single function call, which is why the short code example below returns a label and a confidence score for a clinical sentence (Wolf et al., 2020). Below is a simple demonstration of emotion classification using HuggingFace transformers:

```
from transformers import pipeline

classifier = pipeline("text-classification", model="bhadresh
-savani/distilbert-base-uncased-emotion")
text = "My heart feels heavy with sadness."
result = classifier(text)
print("Emotion classification:", result)
```

Output:

```
config.json: 100% 768/768 [00:00<00:00, 73.9kB/s]
model.safetensors: 100% 268M/268M [00:23<00:00, 16.7MB/s]
tokenizer_config.json: 100% 291/291 [00:00<00:00, 29.0kB/s]
vocab.txt: 232k/? [00:00<00:00, 4.78MB/s]
special_tokens_map.json: 100% 112/112 [00:00<00:00, 7.59kB/s]

Device set to use mps:0
Emotion classification: [{'label': 'sadness', 'score':
0.947920560836792}]
```

When you see {'label': 'sadness', 'score': 0.95}, read it as the model's current best guess and its confidence. In practice, you would calibrate thresholds, evaluate per emotion, and fine-tune on domain text such as therapy notes before deployment.

Analysing embodied emotions from text carries ethical responsibilities. Emotional expressions, particularly those tied to embodied experiences, are deeply personal. Ethical guidelines must ensure sensitive handling, informed consent, anonymisation, and strict confidentiality when applying EmText analyses in research or practical applications (Jobin et al., 2019).

7.4 Emsemitext for Clinical Insights

This section introduces *Emsemitext*, our term for a practical approach that reads clinical language through the lens of the body. The idea is simple. People often describe feelings as bodily states. A client says *my chest feels tight*, *grief is heavy*, or *I feel warm and light again*. Emsemitext treats those phrases as signals, links them to established emotion categories, and then tracks how they change over time. The method draws on research in embodied cognition, metaphor, and clinical language, and it packages those lines of work into a workflow that a health team can adopt with modest technical support. The label is new in this book. The building blocks are not. Comparable supervised pipelines are also used across psychological health domains, including the classification of chronic pain outcomes (Kovač et al., 2025a). A complementary line of work uses calibrated regression to predict internal shame, with XGBoost performing best and distress tolerance emerging as the strongest predictor (Kovač et al., 2025b). Prior work shows that emotions are grounded in perception and action, that metaphors map bodily sensations to affective meaning, and that clinical text contains reliable markers of mental health status (Barsalou, 2008; Lakoff & Johnson, 2008; Mohammad & Turney, 2013; Cohn et al., 2004; Rumshisky et al., 2016; De Choudhury et al., 2013a).

Clinicians already listen for language that points to the body. A therapist notes repeated references to weight, tightness, heat, cold, or emptiness. A psychiatrist reads *numb* and *frozen* and wonders about dissociation. These cues are not diagnoses. They are patterns that help structure a conversation. Embodied expressions are common across languages and cultures, which means they can support cross-setting work when combined with local knowledge about idioms (Kövecses, 2003; Gibbs, 2005). Cognitive science offers a reason for their stability. When people talk about feelings, they recruit the same sensory and motor systems that help them navigate the world, so the vocabulary of the body becomes the vocabulary of emotion (Niedenthal, 2007; Barsalou, 2008).

Clinical text concentrates these signals. Therapy notes, patient journals, and peer support forums contain first-person narratives that mix symptoms, events, and feelings. Large-scale studies find that language use changes with depression and anxiety, including shifts in pronoun use, negations, and affect lexicon frequency (Rude et al., 2004; Coppersmith et al., 2014; Guntuku et al., 2017). When we add embodied phrases to this picture, we get a complementary channel that is intuitive for clinicians and easy to explain to patients. Emsemitext makes this channel explicit. Emsemitext is a *workflow* that links clinical language to embodied emotion cues and then aggregates those cues for monitoring and reflection. It is not a single algorithm. It is not a diagnostic tool. It is a way to organise textual evidence so that a team can ask better questions. The workflow rests on three pillars.

1. A *compact mapping between words and embodied cues.* For example, *heavy* tends to align with sadness, *tight* with anxiety or fear, *warm* with happiness or relief. The mapping is derived from published lexicons, clinical annotations, and small domain-specific extensions (Mohammad & Turney, 2013; Pennebaker et al., 2015).
2. Contextual *disambiguation.* The same word can be literal or metaphorical. *Carrying this heavy bag* is not the same as *my heart feels heavy.* Modern Transformer models help decide which sense is active, and they do so by reading the surrounding words and the speaker's prior statements (Devlin et al., 2019; Liu et al., 2019; Rogers et al., 2021).
3. Longitudinal *aggregation.* A single session can be noisy. Patterns across several sessions are more informative. Emsemitext counts and normalises embodied cues per visit, then visualises trends so a clinician can see whether heaviness is fading or tightness is spiking after a medication change. This builds on work that tracks sentiment and symptom language over time in mental health records and social media (De Choudhury et al., 2013a; Rumshisky et al., 2016; Chancellor & De Choudhury, 2020).

Consider two short vignettes built from common patterns in the literature. A client in grief therapy repeatedly uses *heavy*, *weighed down*, and *drained.* Across eight sessions, the total frequency of heaviness words drops, while words of warmth and lightness begin to appear. Even without a probability model, the pattern supports the client's report that activities feel less effortful. In a different case, a client with panic symptoms uses *tight*, *pressure*, and *grip* around the chest. The language spikes after a stressful work event, then recedes after a breathing protocol and schedule changes. Neither pattern proves recovery or relapse. Each gives the team a shared set of observations to discuss. These vignettes echo findings that bodily metaphors are stable markers of affect, that therapy progress can be read in narrative texture, and that text-based monitoring can complement clinical judgement when used with care (Kövecses, 2003; Angus et al., 1999; Cohn et al., 2004).

The core of Emsemitext is the mapping from expressions to embodied cues and then to emotion categories. The safest way to build it is to start from established resources and adapt. The NRC Emotion Lexicon links words to eight basic emotions and has been validated across tasks and languages (Mohammad & Turney, 2013). LIWC provides psychologically grounded dictionaries that have seen decades of use in clinical and health research, including categories for body and sensation (Pennebaker et al., 2015). These resources do not focus on embodied phrases, but they cover many affective expressions and provide a template for annotation guidelines.

A practical annotation protocol looks like this. Begin with a seed list of candidate phrases such as *heavy*, *light*, *tight*, *open*, *warm*, *cold*, *numb*, *empty*, *shaky*, and *grounded*. Collect short spans from your own corpus that contain these words. Ask two or more annotators with clinical knowledge to judge whether the span uses the word metaphorically to describe feeling states or literally to describe the physical world. When the usage is metaphorical, ask the annotators to link the span to one or more emotions. Measure agreement with Cohen's kappa or Krippendorff's alpha and resolve disagreements in discussion. Keep the label set small. The goal is to capture robust signals rather than all details. This process follows well-tested practice in clinical NLP and metaphor annotation (Neumann et al., 2019; Shutova, 2010; Demner-Fushman et al., 2009).

Two safeguards help maintain quality. First, separate detection from interpretation. Mark that a phrase is an embodied cue, then record the emotion label, and keep notes on context. Second, revalidate the mapping on a new sample every few months, since vocabulary shifts with time and with the population you serve. Drift monitoring is a standard requirement in clinical prediction models and applies here as well (Saria et al., 2018).

When the same word can be literal or metaphorical, context decides. Transformer models learn context during pretraining and have strong results on metaphor detection, emotion classification, and clinical note tasks after fine-tuning (Devlin et al., 2019; Liu et al., 2019; Chalkidis et al., 2020; Neumann et al., 2019). For Emsemitext, we use them for two tasks. First, we filter out literal uses that would inflate counts. Second, we recover emotion when the cue word is absent but the pattern is clear. A sentence like *it takes everything to get out of bed* often conveys heaviness even if the word *heavy* never appears. Model outputs are not facts. They are hypotheses that guide attention. Team members should spot-check a small sample every cycle and confirm that the reasoning still makes sense.

Model choice depends on constraints. DistilBERT is small and works on a laptop. RoBERTa is stronger in many classification tasks. ClinicalBERT style models learn from notes and can pick up domain phrasing more quickly, although they require careful governance because of the data used to pretrain them (Alsentzer et al., 2019; Sanh et al., 2019; Liu et al., 2019). Regardless of the model, calibration and per-class metrics matter because embodied cues are sparse and imbalanced. Reports should include macro-F1 and per emotion precision and recall rather than only overall accuracy, echoing recommendations in clinical NLP evaluation (Roberts et al., 2022).

Emsemitext aims to provide views that fit into a clinical hour. Three summaries tend to work well:

1. A one-page view that lists the most frequent embodied cues for the session, a brief selection of supporting quotes, and a small bar showing change since the last visit. This mirrors common practice in psychotherapy notes and supports reflective supervision.
2. A line plot for each cue, normalised per thousand words, with markers for significant events, for example, a medication change or a life stressor. This type of timeline appears in prior work on symptom tracking in notes and helps detect sudden shifts that warrant a conversation (Rumshisky et al., 2016).
3. A compact summary of co-occurrence between cues, for example, heaviness with numbness or tightness with racing thoughts. The goal is to reveal patterns across sessions that match known clinical constellations such as anxious depression or grief with anger. Co-occurrence analysis is standard in corpus linguistics and public health text mining, and it adapts well here (Berry & Kogan, 2010).

All displays must flag uncertainty. If the model is not confident that *tight* is metaphorical, the card should mark it as tentative or exclude it from counts. This keeps trust high and fosters a culture of cautious interpretation.

Emsemitext is a complement to clinical practice, not a replacement. It is most useful in four settings:

- When caseloads are large, a weekly scan for sudden increases in heaviness or tightness can prompt a check-in. Prior work shows that such text-based alerts are feasible in health systems when combined with clinician oversight (Rumshisky et al., 2016).
- Many therapies invite clients to write between sessions in order to monitor progress. Aggregating embodied cues in those entries can reveal improvement that is not yet visible in standard scales. Narrative transformation has long been used as evidence of change, and Emsemitext provides a quantitative mirror for that tradition (Angus et al., 1999).
- A card that displays a client's own words next to a simple trend line can support collaborative planning. People often find it easier to discuss their language than a raw score, which improves engagement.
- Teams can ask population questions, such as which embodied cues are common in patients who drop out early, or how seasonal stressors shift the mix of heaviness and tightness. Population analysis has already improved service design in digital mental health, and the same approach applies here when data governance is strong (Chancellor & De Choudhury, 2020).

Inferring internal states from text is sensitive. Clinical text includes personal stories and protected health information. Responsible use requires attention to governance at each step. Data should be minimised, stored securely, and de-identified whenever possible. Access should be logged and limited to the care team. Outputs should never be used to deny services or benefits. They should be used to structure conversations and to suggest that a clinician take a closer look. These recommendations align with guidance for digital mental health analytics and clinical NLP deployments (Benton et al., 2017; Chen et al., 2022; Roberts et al., 2022).

Bias is a practical risk. If a mapping is built from one group's language, it may not capture the metaphors used by other groups. Teams should test for differential performance across demographic slices and invite local stakeholders to review the cue list. Community involvement improves construct validity and has become standard in ethical AI projects in health (Gebru et al., 2021; Chen et al., 2022). Transparency is equally important. A short public document that describes what is collected, why it is collected, and how it is used allows clients to give informed consent. For research, institutional review and clear protocols are mandatory.

Emsemitext focuses on language. Many patients show emotion with posture, breath, or silence. Text cannot capture all of that, and it should not try. Future work will link text with other low-burden signals, for example, heart rate variability or simple ecological momentary assessments, always with explicit consent and clear opt-out options. Another direction is multilingual support. Idioms vary, and so do metaphors, but cross-linguistic work suggests that basic mappings such as weight for sadness and warmth for happiness are widespread. Careful local validation will still be needed (Kövecses, 2003; Mohammad, 2012).

Finally, models drift. Vocabulary changes. Service delivery changes. The safest way to keep Emsemitext useful is to build a habit of regular review. Set a reminder every quarter to sample a few dozen outputs and ask whether the reasoning still makes sense. If not, retrain, revise the cue list, and document the change. This is ordinary model stewardship, and it belongs in any clinical AI project (Saria et al., 2018; Roberts et al., 2022).

7.5 Case Studies in Text-Based Emotion Analysis

Emotion in text is rarely explicit. It surfaces in word choice, in the balance of positive and negative cues, and when people talk to each other, in how one turn responds to the last. This section examines three widely used corpora that capture these facets at different levels of complexity: short single-label posts from the Twitter Emotion dataset (Saravia et al., 2018), multi-label comments with overlapping feelings from the GoEmotions dataset (Demszky et al., 2020), and conversational utterances where emotions evolve over turns found in the MELD dataset (Poria et al., 2018). MELD is used here as a text-only stand-in for EmotionLines.

Across all three, the unit of analysis is a short span of language stored as text. What differs is how emotion is annotated and what additional structure is available. Twitter Emotion assigns exactly one label per instance drawn from a small set of basic emotions. This makes it a clean testbed for single-label classification and for inspecting which categories are easily separated by surface cues. GoEmotions allows multiple labels to co-occur on the same text (for example, admiration and joy), expanding the label space and requiring evaluation to account for overlap and class imbalance. MELD preserves the utterance-level label but adds two integers, dialog_id and turn_id, that place each line inside a conversation. Those fields enable a second kind of inference: not only *what emotion is expressed here?* but also, *given the current state, what tends to come next?*

The goals in this section are accordingly threefold: (1) to quantify how much signal simple lexical features carry for emotion recognition in short texts, and to make the resulting error patterns legible; (2) to handle multi-label annotation properly by treating prediction as a set decision rather than a single choice, and to use metrics that reflect both common and rare emotions; (3) to read emotion in context by estimating transition tendencies across dialogue turns and illustrating how local dynamics shape short emotional arcs.

Methods are kept deliberately comparable. A classical baseline uses TF-IDF features and a linear classifier (Logistic Regression as the mainline, with LinearSVC as a margin-based contrast). A compact transformer baseline (DistilBERT) is fine-tuned on the same splits to show what contextual representations add without changing anything else. For single-label tasks, performance is summarised with accuracy and macro-F1 and interpreted through confusion matrices and ROC analyses. For multi-label data, evaluation shifts to micro- and macro-averaged F1 and precision–recall behaviour. For conversations, a row-normalised transition matrix summarises how emotions flow from one turn to the next; a short timeline from a single dialogue makes those flows concrete.

Preprocessing is minimal and transparent. Text is used as provided, with Unicode normalisation and standard tokenisation inside the vectorisers or tokeniser. Where label vocabularies differ by name but not meaning, they are unified (e.g., MELD's *neutral* is treated as *no_emotion*, and *joy* as *happiness*), so comparisons remain consistent. All experiments are seeded for reproducibility and rely on the datasets library, which downloads and caches corpora locally. The following Python snippet shows only the structural idea: each dataset is mapped into a consistent dataframe with the fields needed for its task. Additionally, this code shows the exact schema used in the analysis.

```
# unified schema examples (illustrative)
from datasets import load_dataset
import pandas as pd

# Twitter Emotion: single-label
tw = load_dataset("dair-ai/emotion")
twitter_train  =  pd.DataFrame({"text":  tw["train"]["text"],
"label": tw["train"]["label"]})
```

```
# GoEmotions: multi-label (binarized later)
go = load_dataset("go_emotions", "simplified") # or a prefil-
tered split you selected
go_train    =    pd.DataFrame({"text":    go["train"]["text"],
"labels": go["train"]["labels"]})

# MELD (text-only): single-label + dialogue structure
meld_urls = {
     "train": "https://raw.githubusercontent.com/declare-lab/
MELD/master/data/MELD/train_sent_emo.csv",
     "dev": "https://raw.githubusercontent.com/declare-lab/
MELD/master/data/MELD/dev_sent_emo.csv",
     "test": "https://raw.githubusercontent.com/declare-lab/
MELD/master/data/MELD/test_sent_emo.csv",
}
meld = load_dataset("csv", data_files=meld_urls)
def norm_emotion(s):
    s = str(s).lower().strip()
    return {"neutral":"no_emotion","joy":"happiness"}.get(s, s)
meld_train = pd.DataFrame({
    "dialog_id": meld["train"]["Dialogue_ID"],
    "turn_id": meld["train"]["Utterance_ID"],
    "text": meld["train"]["Utterance"],
      "label_name":pd.Series(meld["train"]["Emotion"]).map(no
rm_emotion)
})
```

The Twitter corpus contains short, self-contained posts labelled with a single emotion from a small vocabulary (sadness, joy, love, anger, fear, surprise). Because each tweet receives exactly one label, the task is a classic single-label classification problem; results are easy to interpret, and the errors are often intuitive.

The first thing to notice is the class balance. Figure 7.3 shows a long tail: *joy* is the most common category, followed by *sadness*; *surprise* is rare. This matters for how we read all subsequent results. With few examples, a model will see fewer lexical patterns for *surprise* during training, and evaluation metrics that average over classes (e.g., macro-F1) are more informative than plain accuracy.

Trained on bag-of-words features with TF-IDF, the model produces an almost diagonal confusion matrix (Figure 7.4). The rows are normalised to 100%, so each percentage shows how a true class is distributed across predictions. Joy is the easiest class, with ≈ 96% correct. Sadness is also high at ≈ 91%. Mid-tier performance appears for anger (≈ 75%) and fear (≈ 71%). Love splits across love (≈ 48%) and joy (≈ 43%), reflecting lexical overlap between affectionate and joyful wording. Surprise is the hardest label, with only ≈ 27% correct and substantial spillover into joy (≈ 39%) and fear (≈ 20%), which is consistent with its contextual and low-frequency nature.

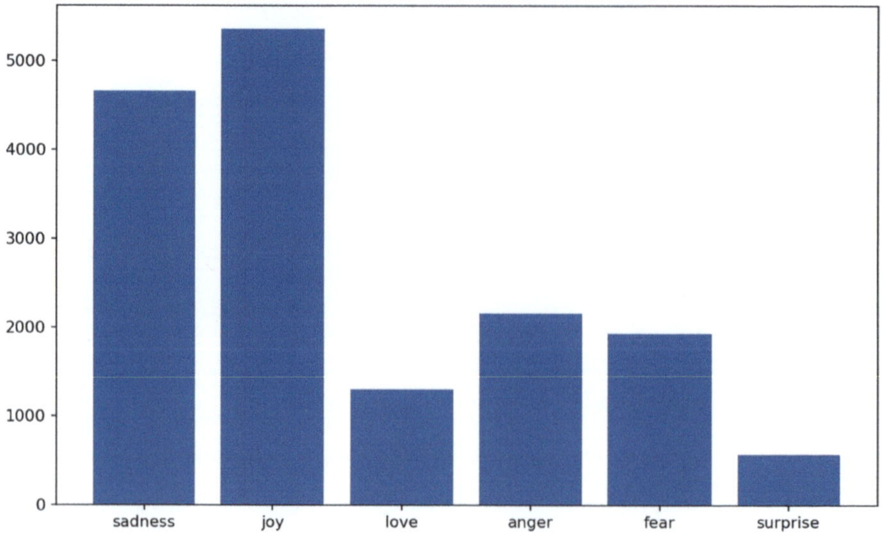

Figure 7.3 Twitter Emotion label distribution in the training split.

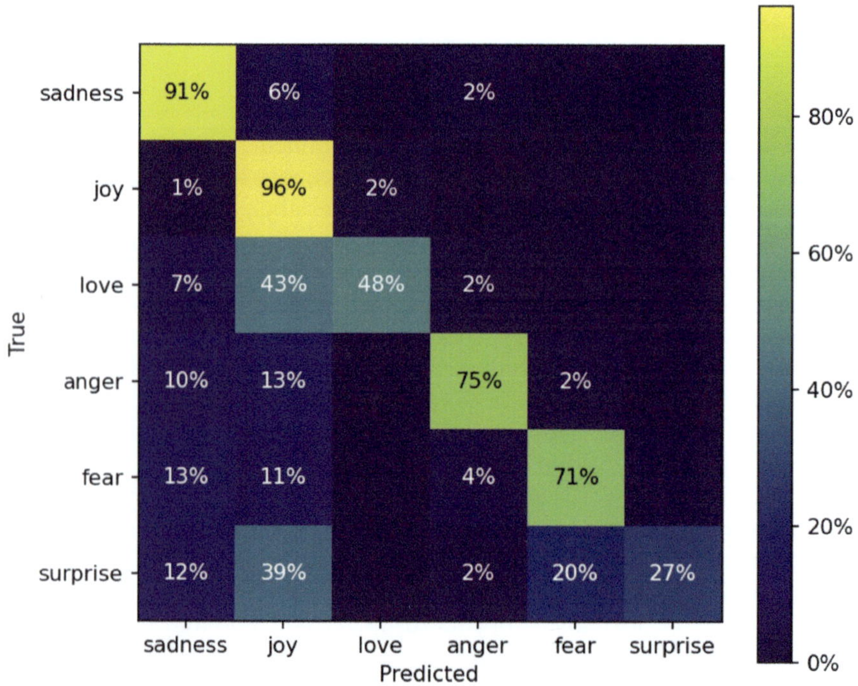

Figure 7.4 Row-normalised confusion matrix for a TF-IDF + logistic regression classifier for Twitter emotion.

Threshold-free separability tells the same story. The ROC overlay in Figure 7.5 plots each emotion against the rest; curves crowd the top-left, and the macro-AUC is ≈ 0.985. High AUC means that, for most classes, a simple linear model can rank true positives above negatives with few trade-offs. In practice, this confirms that much of Twitter's emotional signal lives in easily learned lexical patterns (hashtags, intensifiers, sentiment words) rather than long-range context.

A lightweight transformer fine-tune provides an instructive counterpoint. Figure 7.6 shows the row-normalised confusion matrix after a short DistilBERT training run on the same split. The model produces a confusion matrix that is almost entirely diagonal. This means that each row answers the question: *Given all actual instances of this emotion, how did the model classify them?* The diagonal cells for *sadness* (≈ 96%), *joy* (≈ 95%), and *anger* (≈ 94%) are very high. This indicates that these categories are effectively captured by surface cues such as keywords, intensifiers, and sentiment-bearing expressions. *Fear* is slightly lower (≈ 90%), and two systematic confusions appear: *love* is sometimes predicted as *joy* (≈ 14%), and *surprise* splits between *fear* (≈ 21%) and *joy* (≈ 12%), with only ≈ 62% correct. Both patterns make linguistic sense. *Love* and *joy* share positive valence and overlapping vocabularies; short tweets often lack enough context to separate *I love this* from *this makes me happy*. *Surprise* frequently arrives via punctuation and interjections that can also accompany alarm, so *fear* and *surprise* are not cleanly separable in short text.

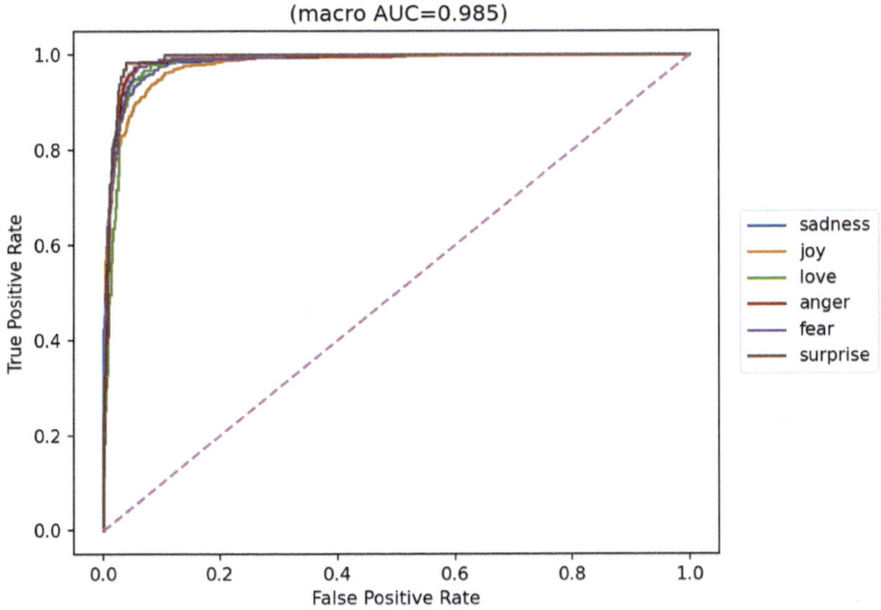

Figure 7.5 Twitter emotion ROC curves for a TF-IDF plus logistic regression baseline.

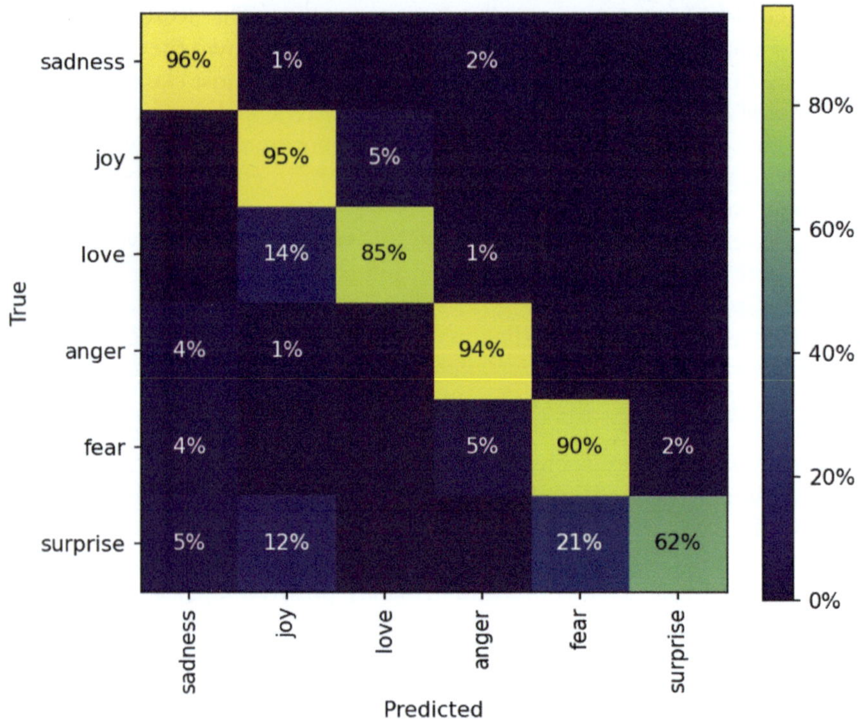

Figure 7.6 Twitter emotion transformer confusion matrix row normalised.

TF-IDF is a strong baseline, but in our runs, a small fine-tuned transformer surpasses it (compare Figure 4 and Figure 6). Accuracy along the diagonal rises for anger (≈ 75% → 94%), fear (≈ 71% → 90%), love (≈ 48% → 85%), and sadness (≈ 91% → 96%), while joy stays high (≈ 96%). Surprise remains the hardest class because it is rare (see Figure 3), yet performance more than doubles (≈ 27% → 62%). Residual confusion still flows from *surprise* into joy (~12%) and fear (~21%), reflecting lexical ambiguity and class imbalance rather than a lack of contextual capacity. The transformer's contextual representations disambiguate overlaps such as *love* vs. *joy* and pick up cues that TF-IDF misses, while imbalance keeps *surprise* fragile; class-weighted training or rebalanced sampling would likely trim the remaining spillover.

Taken together, these four figures sketch a coherent picture of emotion in short social posts. Imbalance shapes the problem; lexical features already separate most classes extremely well; *love* versus *joy* and *surprise* versus *fear* mark the natural fault lines; and transformer gains are not automatic at a small scale. This establishes a clear baseline before we turn to settings where the task itself is harder. These include cases with multiple overlapping labels and the presence of conversational context.

GoEmotions widens the lens from a single, mutually exclusive label to overlapping emotions. A single comment can be tagged with several feelings (e.g., *admiration* and *joy*), plus a frequent *neutral* tag. This small change in annotation reshapes both modelling and evaluation: instead of choosing one class, a model must decide a set of labels; instead of accuracy, we read precision–recall behaviour and class-balanced F-scores.

The first constraint is the label landscape itself. Figure 7.7 illustrates the uneven distribution of examples across the 28 categories. *Neutral* dominates the corpus. Positive social signals such as *admiration*, *approval*, and *gratitude* are common. Many others, such as *pride*, *nervousness*, and *embarrassment,* are tiny. This long tail creates two pressures: the model learns very sharp detectors for frequent categories, and it is tempted to default to *neutral* when evidence is thin.

Because a comment can carry multiple labels, a standard confusion matrix is not entirely suitable. We include one nonetheless as a top-1 visualisation, selecting each example's most confident predicted label to produce Figure 7.8. Interpret it as a qualitative map rather than a strict scorecard. The bright diagonal for *neutral* reflects its scale and lexical distinctiveness; *gratitude* and *optimism* also display relatively clear diagonals, likely influenced by formulaic phrases (*thank you, I hope*...). Off-diagonal smears indicate natural ambiguities: *admiration* merges with *approval* and *joy*; *annoyance* with *anger* and *disapproval*; *sadness* with *disappointment*, *grief*, and *remorse*. Rare, psychologically specific categories (*embarrassment*, *nervousness*, *pride*) have minimal signal and spread broadly into neighbours or revert to *neutral*. The

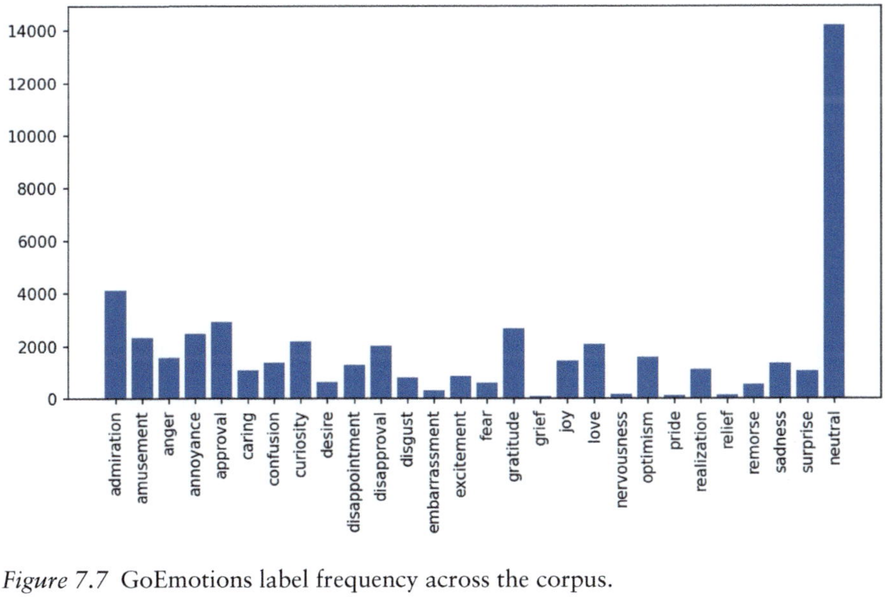

Figure 7.7 GoEmotions label frequency across the corpus.

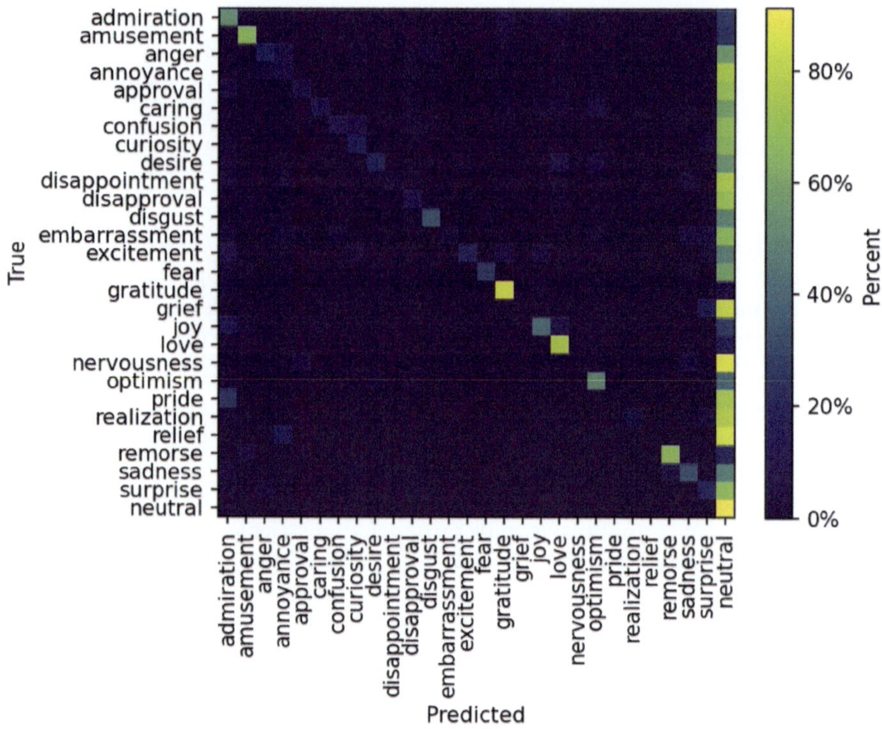

Figure 7.8 GoEmotions confusion matrix after projecting the multi-label task to a single top-1 label and row normalizing.

inventory is comprehensive, but much of it exists within a low-data regime where surface cues are subtle and context is important.

For evaluation that respects multi-label reality, we collapse all one-vs-rest decisions into a micro-averaged precision–recall curve. Figure 7.9 climbs near the top-left at small recall (the model's highest-confidence detections are usually correct) and then falls steadily as recall increases, reflecting the cost of retrieving rarer, harder labels. The title reports a macro average precision ≈ 0.408, which treats every emotion equally. This reveals how the long tail lowers the overall average, exactly the behaviour observed in the top-1 heatmap.

A minimal schematic of what we compute looks like this (the point is the evaluation, not the particular model):

```
# Y_test: (n_samples, n_labels) binary matrix
# decision_function -> scores; sigmoid -> probabilities per
label
from scipy.special import expit
Y_score = expit(ovr_logreg.decision_function(X_test))
```

```
# micro-PR for the multi-label task
from sklearn.metrics import precision_recall_curve,
average_precision_score
p, r, _ = precision_recall_curve(Y_test.ravel(), Y_score.ra
vel())
macro_ap = average_precision_score(Y_test, Y_score,
average="macro")
```

Interpreting the three figures together gives a clear picture of the dataset rather than just the model. The frequency profile (Figure 7.7) explains why *neutral* and a handful of social-approval emotions are easy and why specificity is hard. The top-1 confusion (Figure 7.8) let us see *which* categories blur together when we force a single choice. The micro-PR curve (Figure 7.9) then quantifies the set-prediction task itself: strong precision at low recall, steady degradation as we chase the tail. Improvements, therefore, hinge on better thresholding per label (not a single 0.5 cut), reweighting or focal losses to lift rare classes, and models that can borrow context beyond the sentence when the wording alone is too polite, too brief, or too subtle to carry the feeling.

MELD adds structure that the previous corpora lack: each utterance belongs to a dialogue (dialog_id) and has an order (turn_id). The label inventory is compact, *no_emotion*, *anger*, *disgust*, *fear*, *happiness*, *sadness*, *surprise*, but the distribution is not. Figure 7.10 shows a heavy skew toward *no_emotion*, with *happiness* the next most frequent and the rest far smaller.

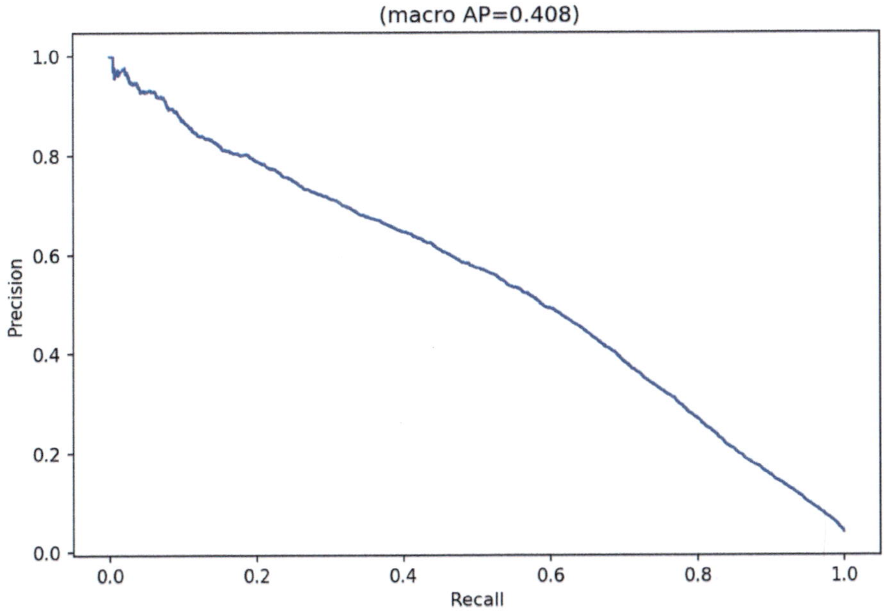

Figure 7.9 GoEmotions precision–recall curve aggregated across labels for a TF-IDF plus one-vs-rest logistic regression model.

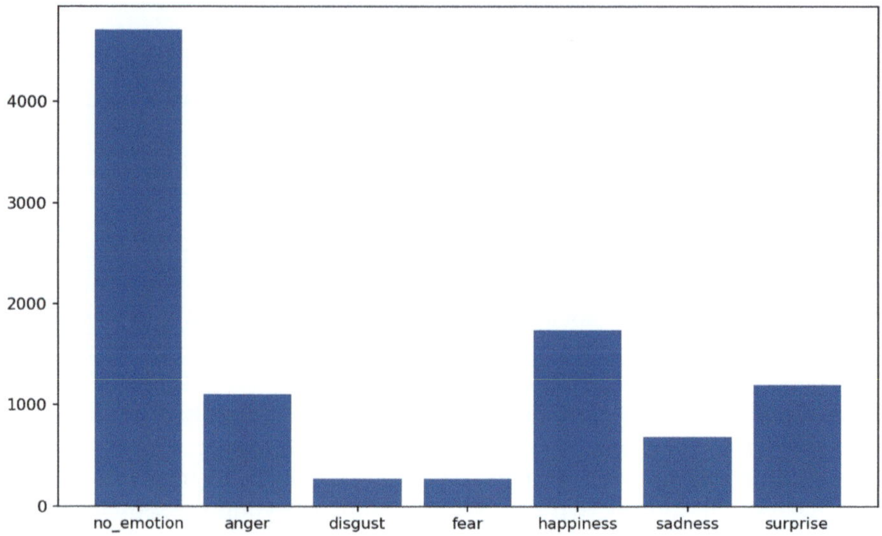

Figure 7.10 MELD label distribution in the training split.

This imbalance sets the baseline expectation: the model will see ample neutral language and relatively little evidence for the rarer negative states.

Two plots make the conversational setting tangible. The short trajectory in Figure 7.11 traces one dialogue turn by turn: long neutral stretches punctuated by brief spikes to *happiness* or *surprise*.

Aggregating across all conversations, the row-normalised transition matrix in Figure 7.12 summarises *what tends to come next*. Rows are current emotion, and columns are next emotion with percentages per row. From *no_emotion*, the most likely next step is to remain neutral (≈ 57%), with non-trivial flows into *happiness* (~13%) and *surprise* (~10%). Negative emotions show persistence but also leakage toward neutrality; for example, *sadness* → *sadness* is about 30%, but *sadness* → *no_emotion* is even more common (~39%). These flows are exactly what a turn-by-turn system must model if it is to use context rather than treat utterances in isolation.

On single-utterance classification, the TF-IDF + Logistic Regression baseline (Figure 7.13) yields overall accuracy around 0.54 and macro-F1 around 0.26. Class recall is highly uneven. Performance is highly skewed toward no_emotion (92% recall) while most other classes are frequently mapped to neutral (anger 77%, disgust 79%, fear 82%, happiness 75%, sadness 81%, surprise 53% to neutral), with true class recalls on the diagonal of 11%, 3%, 4%, 19%, 7%, and 40% respectively. This is consistent with short, context-poor turns and strong label imbalance.

Threshold-free separability is modest. The ROC overlay in Figure 7.14 clusters well below the perfect top-left corner; the macro-AUC of ≈ 0.723

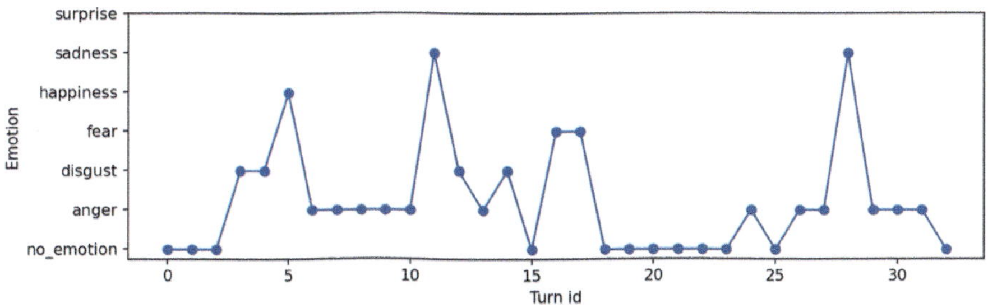

Figure 7.11 Example dialogue timeline in MELD.

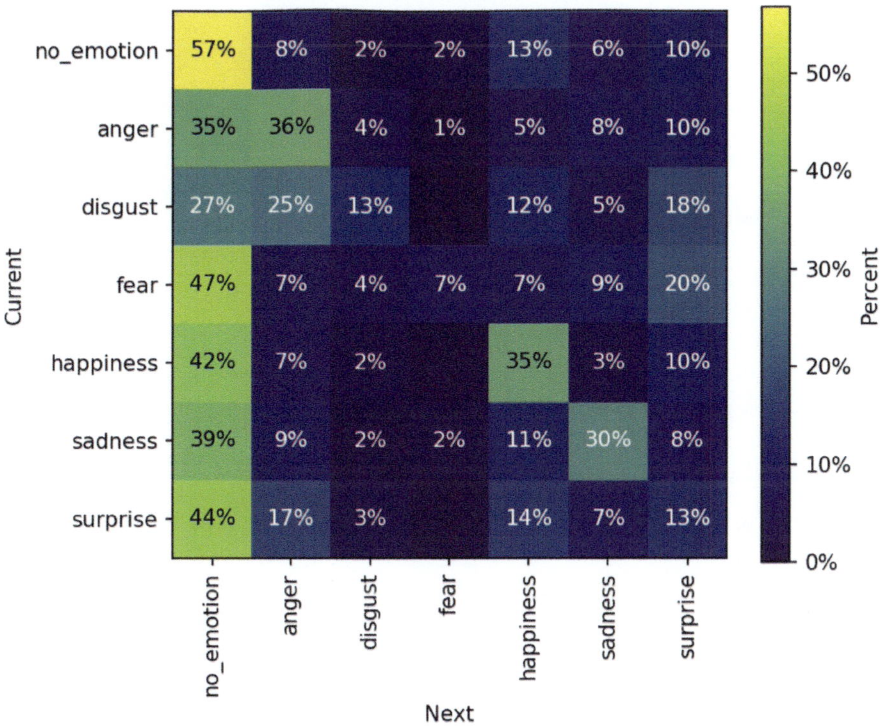

Figure 7.12 Dialogue emotion transition matrix in MELD.

is respectable for broad categories but far from the near-separation seen on Twitter. In other words, lexical cues alone only partly separate emotions once we move into dialogue.

A small transformer (DistilBERT) trained on the same split changed coverage (compare Figure 7.13 and Figure 7.15) for most classes but leaves clear asymmetries. Neutral drops to ~85% compared with the TF-IDF baseline, while happiness rises to ~60% and surprise improves to ~63%. Anger sits near ~44%, fear remains low at ~10%, and disgust is rarely recovered

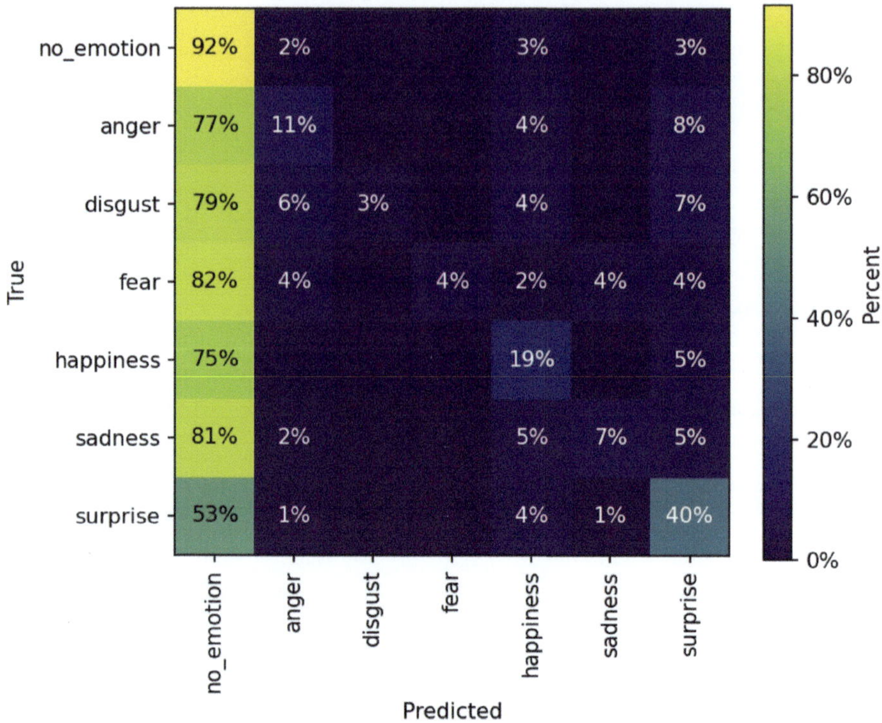

Figure 7.13 Confusion matrix for the TF-IDF logistic regression baseline on MELD.

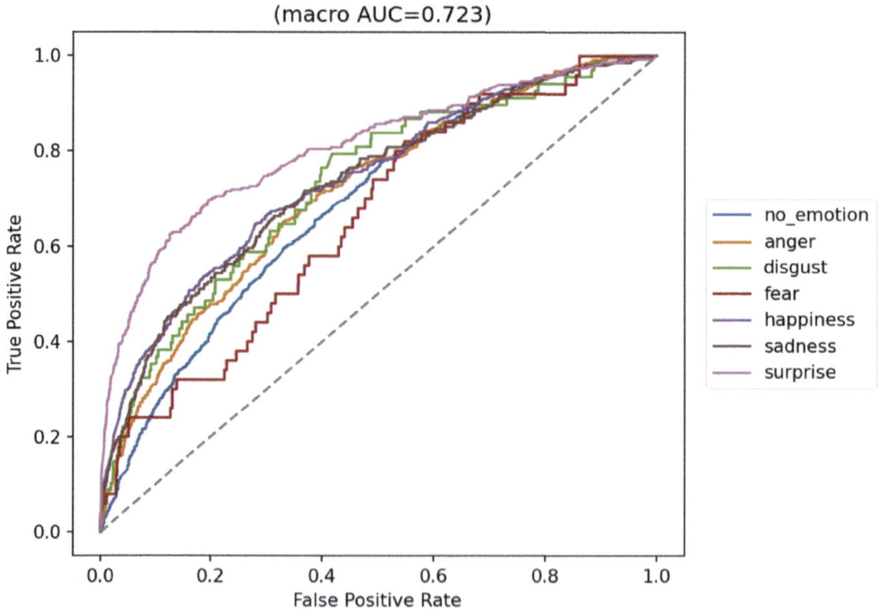

Figure 7.14 ROC curves by class for MELD with a logistic regression baseline.

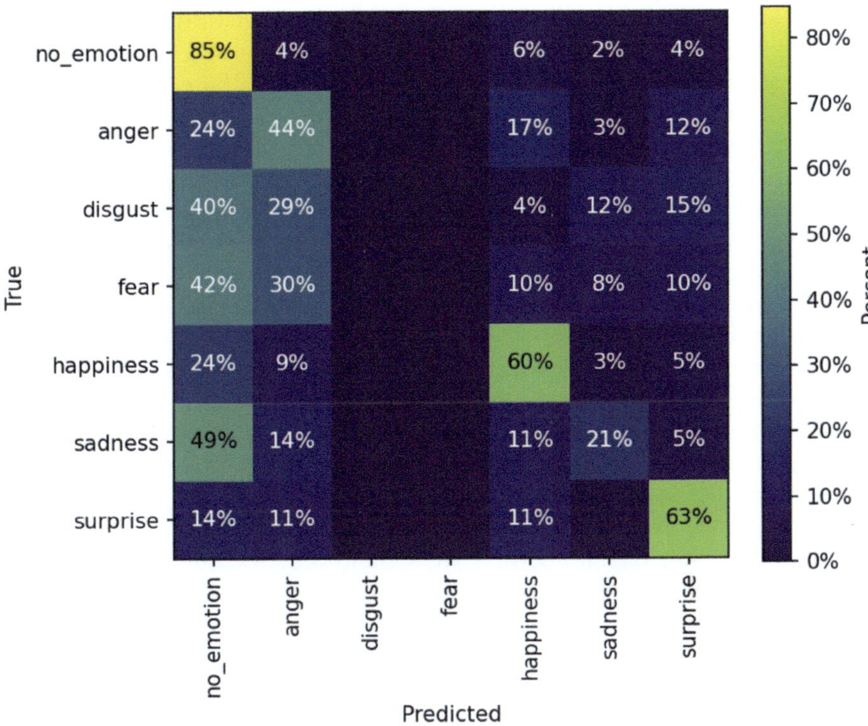

Figure 7.15 Confusion matrix for a small DistilBERT fine-tune on MELD.

(~3–4%), with many instances drifting into *no_emotion* or neighbouring negatives. The net effect is a sharper diagonal for happiness and surprise, little relief for the rarer negatives, and a modest reduction for neutral. This is evidence that context helps some positive states, but the class imbalance and short utterances still drive confusion.

Taken together, the six figures outline the challenge that conversation brings. Label skew and brevity bias models toward neutrality; negative states require more context to distinguish; and even when a model scores well overall, macro-averaged metrics and the transition view reveal where it struggles. The practical implication is clear: dialogue-aware systems need both better representations and sequence-level objectives that reward getting the *flow* right, not just the next label in isolation.

The three case studies trace a gradient in difficulty. On short, single-label tweets, the signal is overwhelmingly lexical and simple linear models soak it up. Macro-F1 is high for Twitter (Figure 16 shows ≈ 0.73 for Logistic Regression and ≈ 0.83 for LinearSVC), and the ROC overlay is close to the top-left corner (Figure 7.5). The row-normalised confusion (Figure 7.4) is nearly diagonal, with two recurrent fault lines: love frequently bleeds into joy, and surprise often drifts toward fear and joy. A small transformer fine-tune improves rather than hurts in this regime, sharpening most diagonals and boosting the hardest class: surprise rises to ≈ 62% recall while fear reaches ≈ 90% (Figure 6).

GoEmotions changes the evaluation lens rather than the domain. Many comments carry several emotions, so any single-label summary understates the difficulty. The frequency plot in Figure 7.7 shows why this matters. Neutral dominates, and several positive labels, such as admiration and approval, are common, while many others live in the long tail. The top-1 confusion in Figure 7.8 is therefore a proxy, not a verdict. It still helps us see where boundaries blur. Admiration often appears near approval, annoyance often sits near anger, and several rare categories scatter into neutral when the signal is faint. For an overall picture, the precision–recall curve in Figure 7.9 is the most honest summary. The curve is macro-averaged with an area of about 0.408, which means high precision at very small recall, followed by a smooth decline as the model tries to retrieve low-frequency labels. This behaviour is exactly what the long-tail distribution in Figure 7.7 would suggest. The macro-F1 bar in Figure 7.16, around 0.22 for our baseline, is low by design. Macro-averaging gives every emotion the same weight as neutral and gratitude, so it exposes how imbalance, label overlap, and subtle cues govern this dataset.

MELD pushes the problem into context. Utterances are short, the label distribution is skewed toward no_emotion (Figure 7.10), and identical words can map to different states depending on the previous turn. Macro-F1 falls accordingly (≈ 0.26–0.29 in Figure 7.16), and threshold-free separability

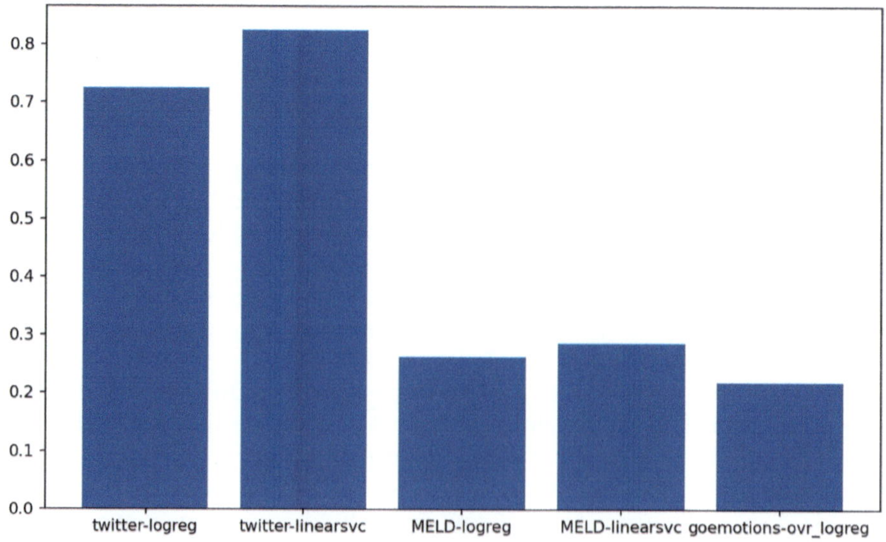

Figure 7.16 Macro-F1 summary across datasets and models.

settles near a macro-AUC of ≈ 0.723 (Figure 7.14). The transition matrix (Figure 7.12) shows why: conversations often remain in, or revert to, neutral; many negative states flow into no_emotion on the next turn. Both the classical baseline (Figure 7.13) and the small transformer (Figure 7.15) reflect that inertia. No_emotion drops from ≈ 92% on the diagonal in the TF-IDF baseline (Figure 7.13) to ≈ 85% with the transformer (Figure 7.15). Happiness, surprise and anger improved their performance. The single-dialogue timeline (Figure 7.11) is a micro-view of the same story, with long, calm stretches punctuated by short spikes.

A few practical implications follow naturally: (1) match your evaluation to the task and remember that confusion matrices and ROC overlays tell most of the truth for single-label data while micro/macro-PR and per-label thresholds matter in multi-label settings; (2) lexical baselines remain strong for short posts and transformers help most when you either scale training or give them context they can use; (3) class imbalance is not just a minor issue. It directly influences what the model learns and what readers may misunderstand if only accuracy is reported; (4) in dialogue, sequence matters: the transition view is not cosmetic; it is the target for systems that need to understand how emotions move across turns.

This chapter's figures give a compact map of those realities. Twitter shows how far simple features go. GoEmotions shows why evaluation must change when feelings overlap. MELD shows why context and dynamics belong in the objective. The next steps can incorporate whether intensity-aware corpora, such as DENS, or mental-health contexts like Vent. This would make those themes sharper rather than overturn them: better thresholds for the tail, better calibration, and models that reward getting the flow of emotion right, not just the next label in isolation.

References

Alm, C. O. (2012). The role of affect in the computational modeling of natural language. *Language and Linguistics Compass*, 6(7), 416–430.

Alsentzer, E., Murphy, J. R., Boag, W., Weng, W. H., Jin, D., Naumann, T., & McDermott, M. (2019). Publicly available clinical BERT embeddings. *arXiv preprint arXiv:1904.03323*.

Angus, L., Levitt, H., & Hardtke, K. (1999). The narrative processes coding system: Research applications and implications for psychotherapy practice. *Journal of Clinical Psychology*, 55(10), 1255–1270.

Barsalou, L. W. (2008). Grounded cognition. *Annual Review of Psychology*, 59(1), 617–645.

Benton, A., Coppersmith, G., & Dredze, M. (2017, April). Ethical research protocols for social media health research. In *Proceedings of the first ACL workshop on ethics in natural language processing* (pp. 94–102).

Berry, M. W., & Kogan, J. (Eds.). (2010). *Text mining: Applications and theory*. John Wiley & Sons.

Bird, S., Klein, E., & Loper, E. (2009). *Natural language processing with Python: Analyzing text with the natural language toolkit*. O'Reilly Media, Inc.

Blodgett, S. L., Barocas, S., Daumé Iii, H., & Wallach, H. (2020). Language (technology) is power: A critical survey of" bias" in nlp. *arXiv preprint arXiv:2005.14050.*

Bradley, M. M., & Lang, P. J. (1999). *Affective norms for English words (ANEW): Instruction manual and affective ratings* (Vol. 30, No. 1, pp. 25–36). Technical report C-1, the center for research in psychophysiology, University of Florida.

Cambria, E., & Hussain, A. (2015). Sentic computing. *Cognitive Computation*, *7*(2), 183–185.

Chalkidis, I., Fergadiotis, M., Malakasiotis, P., Aletras, N., & Androutsopoulos, I. (2020). LEGAL-BERT: The muppets straight out of law school. *arXiv preprint arXiv:2010.02559.*

Chancellor, S., & De Choudhury, M. (2020). Methods in predictive techniques for mental health status on social media: A critical review. *NPJ Digital Medicine*, *3*(1), 43.

Chen, H., Gomez, C., Huang, C. M., & Unberath, M. (2022). Explainable medical imaging AI needs human-centered design: guidelines and evidence from a systematic review. *NPJ Digital Medicine*, *5*(1), 156.

Cohn, M. A., Mehl, M. R., & Pennebaker, J. W. (2004). Linguistic markers of psychological change surrounding September 11, 2001. *Psychological Science*, *15*(10), 687–693.

Coppersmith, G., Dredze, M., & Harman, C. (2014, June). Quantifying mental health signals in Twitter. In *Proceedings of the workshop on computational linguistics and clinical psychology: From linguistic signal to clinical reality* (pp. 51–60).

D'mello, S. K., & Kory, J. (2015). A review and meta-analysis of multimodal affect detection systems. *ACM Computing Surveys (CSUR)*, *47*(3), 1–36.

De Choudhury, M., Counts, S., & Horvitz, E. (2013b, April). Predicting postpartum changes in emotion and behavior via social media. In *Proceedings of the SIGCHI conference on human factors in computing systems* (pp. 3267–3276).

De Choudhury, M., Gamon, M., Counts, S., & Horvitz, E. (2013a). Predicting depression via social media. In *Proceedings of the international AAAI conference on web and social media* (Vol. 7, No. 1, pp. 128–137).

Demner-Fushman, D., Chapman, W. W., & McDonald, C. J. (2009). What can natural language processing do for clinical decision support? *Journal of biomedical informatics*, *42*(5), 760–772.

Demszky, D., Movshovitz-Attias, D., Ko, J., Cowen, A., Nemade, G., & Ravi, S. (2020). GoEmotions: A dataset of fine-grained emotions. *arXiv preprint arXiv:2005.00547.*

Devlin, J., Chang, M. W., Lee, K., & Toutanova, K. (2019, June). Bert: Pre-training of deep bidirectional transformers for language understanding. In *Proceedings of the 2019 conference of the North American chapter of the association for computational linguistics: human language technologies, volume 1 (long and short papers)* (pp. 4171–4186).

Dimitrov, D., Alam, F., Hasanain, M., Hasnat, A., Silvestri, F., Nakov, P., & Da San Martino, G. (2024, June). Semeval-2024 task 4: Multilingual detection of persuasion techniques in memes. In *Proceedings of the 18th international workshop on Semantic Evaluation (SemEval-2024)* (pp. 2009–2026).

Ekman, P. (1992). An argument for basic emotions. *Cognition & Emotion*, *6*(3–4), 169–200.

Farahani, H., Watson, P., Bezan, T., Kovač, N., Winter, L. C., Blagojević, M., & Jiménez, P. (2024). PsAIchology: An intelligent direction in psychological sciences. In *10th international scientific conference Technics, Informatics and Education-TIE 2024.* Faculty of Technical Sciences Čačak, University of Kragujevac.

Farahani, H., Watson, P., Kovač, N., Sheykhangafshe, F. B., Azadfallah, P., Allahyari, A., & Chesli, R. R. (2025). Unraveling the complexity of love addiction using machine learning algorithms: The influence of positive and negative affect, interpersonal needs, and self-hate. In C.-H. Mayer & E. Vanderheiden (Eds.), *International handbook of love: Transcultural and transdisciplinary perspectives* (pp. 1–22). Springer Nature.

Gebru, T., Morgenstern, J., Vecchione, B., Vaughan, J. W., Wallach, H., Iii, H. D., & Crawford, K. (2021). Datasheets for datasets. *Communications of the ACM*, *64*(12), 86–92.

Gibbs Jr, R. W. (2005). *Embodiment and cognitive science*. Cambridge University Press.

Giraud, M., Marelli, M., & Nava, E. (2023). Embodied language of emotions: Predicting human intuitions with linguistic distributions in blind and sighted individuals. *Heliyon*, *9*(7), e17892.

Guntuku, S. C., Yaden, D. B., Kern, M. L., Ungar, L. H., & Eichstaedt, J. C. (2017). Detecting depression and mental illness on social media: An integrative review. *Current Opinion in Behavioral Sciences*, *18*, 43–49.

Hovy, D., & Spruit, S. L. (2016). The social impact of natural language processing. In *The 54th annual meeting of the association for computational linguistics proceedings of the conference, Vol. 2 (Short Papers)*. Association for Computational Linguistics.

Hutto, C., & Gilbert, E. (2014, May). Vader: A parsimonious rule-based model for sentiment analysis of social media text. In *Proceedings of the international AAAI conference on web and social media* (Vol. 8, No. 1, pp. 216–225).

Ingram, R. E., Siegle, G. J., & Steidtmann, D. (2009). Methodological issues in the study of depression. *Handbook of Depression*, *2*, 69–92.

Jobin, A., Ienca, M., & Vayena, E. (2019). The global landscape of AI ethics guidelines. *Nature Machine Intelligence*, *1*(9), 389–399.

Jurafsky, D., & Martin, J. H. (2025, August 24). *Speech and language processing: An introduction to natural language processing, computational linguistics, and speech recognition, with language models* (3rd ed.) [Online manuscript].

Kovač, N., Ratković, K., Farahani, H., & Watson, P. (2024). A practical applications guide to machine learning regression models in psychology with Python. *Methods in Psychology*, *11*, 100156.

Kovač, N., Ratković, K., Watson, P., Farahani, H., & Bagheri Sheykhangafshe, F. (2025a). Machine learning classification models for predicting chronic pain. *Current Psychology*, 1–14. Advance online publication.

Kovač, N., Ratković, K., Farahani, H., & Watson, P. (2025b). Machine learning regression models for internal shame. *Acta Psychologica*, *260*, 105721.

Kövecses, Z. (2003). *Metaphor and emotion: Language, culture, and body in human feeling*. Cambridge University Press.

Lakoff, G., & Johnson, M. (2008). *Metaphors we live by*. University of Chicago press.

Larradet, F., Niewiadomski, R., Barresi, G., Caldwell, D. G., & Mattos, L. S. (2020). Toward emotion recognition from physiological signals in the wild: Approaching the methodological issues in real-life data collection. *Frontiers in Psychology*, *11*, 1111.

Liu, B. (2022). *Sentiment analysis and opinion mining*. Springer Nature.

Liu, Y., Ott, M., Goyal, N., Du, J., Joshi, M., Chen, D., & Stoyanov, V. (2019). Roberta: A robustly optimized bert pretraining approach. *arXiv preprint arXiv:1907.11692*.

Mohammad, S. (2012). # Emotional tweets. In * *SEM 2012: The First Joint Conference on Lexical and Computational Semantics–Volume 1: Proceedings of the main conference and the shared task, and Volume 2: Proceedings of the Sixth International Workshop on Semantic Evaluation (SemEval 2012)* (pp. 246–255).

Mohammad, S. M. (2021). Sentiment analysis: Automatically detecting valence, emotions, and other affectual states from text. In H. L. Meiselman (Ed.), *Emotion measurement* (pp. 323–379). Woodhead Publishing.
Mohammad, S. M., & Bravo-Marquez, F. (2017). WASSA-2017 shared task on emotion intensity. *arXiv preprint arXiv:1708.03700*.
Mohammad, S. M., & Turney, P. D. (2013). Crowdsourcing a word–emotion association lexicon. *Computational Intelligence*, *29*(3), 436–465.
Neumann, M., King, D., Beltagy, I., & Ammar, W. (2019). ScispaCy: Fast and robust models for biomedical natural language processing. *arXiv preprint arXiv:1902.07669*.
Niedenthal, P. M. (2007). Embodying emotion. *Science*, *316*(5827), 1002–1005.
Niedenthal, P. M., & Maringer, M. (2009). Embodied emotion considered. *Emotion Review*, *1*(2), 122–128.
Niedenthal, P. M., Barsalou, L. W., Winkielman, P., Krauth-Gruber, S., & Ric, F. (2005). Embodiment in attitudes, social perception, and emotion. *Personality and Social Psychology Review*, *9*(3), 184–211.
Park, C. Y., Cha, N., Kang, S., Kim, A., Khandoker, A. H., Hadjileontiadis, L., & Lee, U. (2020). K-EmoCon, a multimodal sensor dataset for continuous emotion recognition in naturalistic conversations. *Scientific Data*, *7*(1), 293.
Pennebaker, J. W. (1997). Writing about emotional experiences as a therapeutic process. *Psychological Science*, *8*(3), 162–166.
Pennebaker, J. W., & Chung, C. K. (2011). Expressive writing: Connections to physical and mental health. In H. S. Friedman (Ed.), *The Oxford handbook of health psychology* (pp. 417–437). Oxford University Press.
Pennebaker, J. W., Boyd, R. L., Jordan, K., & Blackburn, K. (2015). *The development and psychometric properties of LIWC2015*. University of Texas.
Pennebaker, J. W., Francis, M. E., & Booth, R. J. (2001). Linguistic inquiry and word count: LIWC 2001. *Mahway: Lawrence Erlbaum Associates*, *71*(2001), 2001.
Plutchik, R. (1980a). A general psychoevolutionary theory of emotion. In R. Plutchik & H. Kellerman (Eds.), *Theories of emotion* (pp. 3–33). Academic Press.
Plutchik, R. (1980b). *Emotion: Theory, research, and experience* (Vol. 1). Theories of emotion.
Poria, S., Hazarika, D., Majumder, N., Naik, G., Cambria, E., & Mihalcea, R. (2018). Meld: A multimodal multi-party dataset for emotion recognition in conversations. *arXiv preprint arXiv:1810.02508*.
Ricardi, F. (2025). From symptom to symbol. Language in psychotherapy. *Medical Research Archives*, *13*(2). https://doi.org/10.18103/mra.v13i2.6225
Roberts, K., Demner-Fushman, D., Voorhees, E. M., Bedrick, S., & Hersh, W. R. (2022). Overview of the TREC 2022 clinical trials track. In *Proceedings of the Thirty-First Text REtrieval Conference (TREC 2022)*. National Institute of Standards and Technology. https://doi.org/10.6028/NIST.SP.500–338.trials-overview
Rogers, A., Kovaleva, O., & Rumshisky, A. (2021). A primer in BERTology: What we know about how BERT works. *Transactions of the Association for Computational Linguistics*, *8*, 842–866.
Rude, S., Gortner, E. M., & Pennebaker, J. (2004). Language use of depressed and depression-vulnerable college students. *Cognition & Emotion*, *18*(8), 1121–1133.
Rumshisky, A., Ghassemi, M., Naumann, T., Szolovits, P., Castro, V. M., McCoy, T. H., & Perlis, R. H. (2016). Predicting early psychiatric readmission with natural language processing of narrative discharge summaries. *Translational Psychiatry*, *6*(10), e921–e921.
Russell, J. A. (1980). A circumplex model of affect. *Journal of Personality and Social Psychology*, *39*(6), 1161.

Sanh, V., Debut, L., Chaumond, J., & Wolf, T. (2019). DistilBERT, a distilled version of BERT: Smaller, faster, cheaper and lighter. *arXiv preprint arXiv:1910.01108*.
Saravia, E., Liu, H. C. T., Huang, Y. H., Wu, J., & Chen, Y. S. (2018). CARER: Contextualized affect representations for emotion recognition. In *Proceedings of the 2018 conference on empirical methods in natural language processing* (pp. 3687–3697).
Saria, S., Butte, A., & Sheikh, A. (2018). Better medicine through machine learning: What's real, and what's artificial?. *PLoS Medicine*, *15*(12), e1002721.
Saxbe, D. E., Yang, X. F., Borofsky, L. A., & Immordino-Yang, M. H. (2013). The embodiment of emotion: Language use during the feeling of social emotions predicts cortical somatosensory activity. *Social Cognitive and Affective Neuroscience*, *8*(7), 806–812.
Semeraro, A., Vilella, S., & Ruffo, G. (2021). PyPlutchik: Visualising and comparing emotion-annotated corpora. *PLoS One*, *16*(9), e0256503.
Shutova, E. (2010, June). Automatic metaphor interpretation as a paraphrasing task. In *Human language technologies: The 2010 annual conference of the North American chapter of the association for computational linguistics* (pp. 1029–1037).
Tausczik, Y. R., & Pennebaker, J. W. (2010). The psychological meaning of words: LIWC and computerized text analysis methods. *Journal of Language and Social Psychology*, *29*(1), 24–54.
Vaswani, A., Shazeer, N., Parmar, N., Uszkoreit, J., Jones, L., Gomez, A. N., & Polosukhin, I. (2017). Attention is all you need. In *Advances in neural information processing systems* (Vol. 30). Curran Associates, Inc. https://proceedings.neurips.cc/paper/2017/hash/3f5ee243547dee91fbd053c1c4a845aa-Abstract.html
Wolf, T., Debut, L., Sanh, V., Chaumond, J., Delangue, C., Moi, A., & Rush, A. M. (2020, October). Transformers: State-of-the-art natural language processing. In *Proceedings of the 2020 conference on empirical methods in natural language processing: System demonstrations* (pp. 38–45).

8 Integrating Multimodal Data for Comprehensive Understanding of Embodied Emotions

Nataša Kovač, Hojjatollah Farahani, and Peter Watson

8.1 Introduction

Emotions rarely unfold in isolation within a single channel of human experience; rather, they dynamically evolve through coordinated changes in voice, facial expression, autonomic physiology, and cognitive appraisals that are continuously shaped by temporal, contextual, and cultural factors. Each modality, be it vocal prosody, micro facial movements, or cardiac variability, offers a distinct yet complementary vantage point into the underlying affective process (Scherer, 2009). The meaning of emotion thus emerges from the integration of these expressive and physiological modalities, where cross-channel synchrony provides more diagnostic value than any single signal alone (Kragel & LaBar, 2016). Through this multimodal lens, emotion becomes a temporally extended, embodied event rather than a transient, discrete reaction, unfolding across milliseconds in neural and physiological shifts and across minutes or hours in expressive and cognitive alignment.

Recent advancements in affective neuroscience and computational modelling have deepened understanding of this multimodal nature by linking dynamic emotion patterns to both neural circuitry and behavioural expression. For instance, synchronised analyses of facial electromyography, vocal tone, and autonomic signals reveal latent structures of emotional complexity not captured by self-report or single modality observation (Harrison et al., 2013; Celeghin et al., 2017). These integrative approaches enable the discovery of emotion signatures that distinguish adaptive from maladaptive affect regulation, bridging laboratory measures with ecologically valid human experience (Mauss & Robinson, 2009). Importantly, multimodal frameworks recognise that emotional expression and perception are not universal constants but culturally encoded patterns shaped by language, display rules, and social context (Mesquita, 2017). Understanding emotion through these converging modalities provides psychologists and neuroscientists with a more holistic and temporally precise depiction of how affect arises, transforms, and influences behaviour.

As computational and physiological recording tools continue to expand, multimodal data analysis offers a transformative paradigm for both basic and applied psychology. By synthesising cross-temporal records of voice,

DOI: 10.4324/9781003495123-8

facial dynamics, neurophysiology, and cognition, researchers can construct multidimensional trajectories that trace the unfolding of emotion in real time. This integration is not simply technical; it represents a conceptual shift towards embracing emotional life as an emergent phenomenon grounded in the complex interaction of brain, body, and social environment. Within clinical and therapeutic settings, such multimodal perspectives promise to reveal early markers of emotional dysregulation, support patient-specific formulations, and extend emotion research from laboratories into the rich temporal texture of everyday human experience.

This interplay is precisely why a multimodal approach has become essential in the empirical study of embodied emotion. Audio and visual streams capture expressive behaviour, while biosignals such as electroencephalography (EEG) and electromyography (EMG) record concurrent changes in neural and peripheral activity. Together, these channels offer complementary perspectives on the same underlying episode, and their integration has consistently been shown to enhance recognition performance compared to single streams, both in laboratory settings and in real-world data. Recent reviews summarise these improvements and attribute them to cross-modal complementarity and error compensation between asynchronous cues, especially when speech prosody and facial actions are combined with physiological signals. This convergence is now extensively documented across benchmark corpora and application contexts (Koromilas & Giannakopoulos, 2021; Pillalamarri & Shanmugam, 2025).

As research has expanded beyond acted dialogues to include spontaneous and web-based sources, four common recording regimes have emerged: covert recordings of spontaneous interactions, acted performances, elicitation through carefully designed tasks, and annotation of public media. Each regime balances control with ecological validity, resulting in different distributional shifts in language, scene dynamics, and emotional intensity. A widely referenced taxonomy maps this landscape and advocates for using diverse datasets to enhance generalisation beyond laboratory environments (Koromilas & Giannakopoulos, 2021).

Within this framework, corpora vary significantly in what they reveal about embodiment. For example, CMU-MOSEI (Zadeh et al., 2018) offers broad-scale diversity and naturalistic speech, making it an ideal testbed for cross-speaker modelling. Conversely, IEMOCAP (Busso et al., 2008) provides carefully recorded audio and motion imagery with strong ground truth from acted dyads. These datasets exemplify the tension between ecological validity and annotation control that underpins multimodal affect research, influencing which models perform best in specific studies (Koromilas & Giannakopoulos, 2021). Methodologically, the field has shifted from rule-based pipelines to representation learning. Deep models can learn the coupled structure across audio, text, and vision, and focus attention on the most informative stream amid noisy data. Recent reviews emphasise that advances in attention mechanisms and representation learning have been crucial for practical performance, though they also increase the demands for data and computation (Hosseini et al., 2024; Ramaswamy & Palaniswamy, 2024; Chandraumakantham et al., 2024).

Fusion remains a key design choice when integrating modalities. Classical taxonomies distinguish early or feature-level fusion, decision-level fusion, and intermediate approaches that combine representations learned from each stream. Comparative reviews show that no single strategy is superior. Feature-level fusion performs well when signals are well aligned and low-dimensional; decision fusion is more robust when channels are missing; and intermediate fusion often outperforms when cross-modal interactions are complex or alignment is weak. Guidance from EEG-focused multimodal reviews suggests choosing feature fusion when timing is critical and cues are complementary, and weighting features by their relative informativeness. Decision fusion is preferable when sensors may fail or drift at different times, and exploring cross-modal attention is advised when interactions are inherently predictive (Pillalamarri & Shanmugam, 2025).

Alignment itself presents a primary challenge. Speech prosody develops over hundreds of milliseconds, facial actions occur at video rates, and neural signatures can lag behind behaviour. Recent work tackles these mismatches with temporal alignment architectures and graph-based fusion that reason jointly about interactions across time and between streams. These techniques lessen reliance on strict synchronisation and have achieved state-of-the-art results on unaligned benchmarks using far fewer parameters than earlier transformers (Koromilas & Giannakopoulos, 2021).

The embodied perspective also underscores the role and limitations of physiology. Physiological signals often provide genuinely complementary information about arousal and regulatory effort, yet they are non-stationary and person-specific. Variability both between and within subjects remains a key obstacle for cross-subject generalisation and has driven a wave of domain adaptation and generalisation techniques. The latest systematic reviews catalogue sources of uncertainty, from measurement to instrumentation and environment, and recommend explicit cross-subject and cross-session evaluation designs (Pillalamarri & Shanmugam, 2025). Evaluation practices in multimodal emotion research reflect this complexity. Class-based metrics such as macro F1 measure balance across categories, while aggregated metrics like accuracy and weighted accuracy track overall performance. Many studies now include agreement-oriented metrics when continuous affect is predicted. The broader recommendation is to adopt speaker-independent splits and report both per-class and overall metrics to avoid overly optimistic estimates due to overfitting on speakers or contexts (Koromilas & Giannakopoulos, 2021; Hosseini et al., 2024).

A final theme in contemporary literature is the shift from benchmarking to deployment. Multimodal systems are entering health education and customer service, where continuous monitoring, adaptation, and empathy are valued. Surveys emphasise that the benefits of multimodal integration come with obligations, including the need for larger and more diverse datasets, careful handling of bias and missing data, and transparent modelling to ensure users and clinicians can trust predictions about sensitive internal states (Chandraumakantham et al., 2024; Hosseini et al., 2024; Pillalamarri & Shanmugam, 2025).

This chapter begins with these themes. The goal is to show how integrating heterogeneous signals produces a more comprehensive view of embodied emotion while being honest about the scientific and engineering trade-offs involved. The subsequent discussion treats fusion as a modelling choice inherently linked to data realities such as alignment, missing data, and subject variability. It considers evaluation as a design decision that must account for both category balance and person independence. Most importantly, it views embodiment not merely as a slogan but as a practical premise. If emotion is spread across voice, face, and body, a science of emotion should be distributed accordingly, employing methods that learn from the strengths and blind spots of each stream together (Ramaswamy & Palaniswamy, 2024; Koromilas & Giannakopoulos, 2021; Pillalamarri & Shanmugam, 2025). This integration aligns with the 'Artificial Psychology' (PsAIchology) framing that connects AI methods with psychological science (Farahani et al., 2024).

8.2 Understanding Embodied Emotion Across Modalities

Emotion is not confined to one organ or one output channel. It unfolds as coordinated change across brain, body, and behaviour that can be sensed through movement of the face and body, modulations of the voice, patterns of words, and cascades of neural and peripheral physiology. A modern view treats these concurrent changes as complementary windows into an underlying embodied process rather than competitors for a single correct signal. Evidence for this view spans psychology and affective neuroscience, where vocal prosody, facial action, posture, autonomic physiology, and central electrophysiology are all shown to covary with shifts in affect, and where interoceptive mechanisms link bodily state to subjective feeling. Reviews that survey these response systems emphasise the value of reading emotion through multiple channels in parallel and summarise how text, audio, visual behaviour, and physiology each contribute distinct but interacting information about the same episode of experience (Ramaswamy & Palaniswamy, 2024; Cai et al., 2023). Interoception provides a mechanistic bridge by which cardiac and respiratory rhythms, electrodermal activity, and muscle activation inform perception and action, and contemporary syntheses highlight manipulations of interoception as a route to changing affective state and its readouts across modalities (Weng et al., 2021).

In practice, each modality samples a different projection of this latent process. Visual analysis resolves the configuration and dynamics of the face and body, where systems based on action units, landmarks, optical flow, and spatiotemporal deep encoders capture both static morphology and rapid micromovements. Large surveys document steady gains of such models in the wild and their sensitivity to context, lighting, and occlusion. They also underline that body gestures and head pose complement facial cues when expression is subtle or constrained, which motivates joint visual encodings that respond to whole-person behaviour rather than isolated faces (Leong et al., 2023; Du et al., 2019; Canal et al., 2022). Audio carries spectral and temporal correlates of arousal and valence through pitch, intensity, spectral tilt, and rhythmicity. Meta-analyses show that prosody discriminates emotions above chance across languages and that deep models operating on spectrograms exceed classical prosodic baselines, but they also show sensitivity to speaker identity and recording conditions, which motivates domain-aware or self-supervised pretraining before fusion (Juslin et al., 2018; Kakuba et al., 2023).

Physiology contributes a complementary slice of the state space. Electrodermal activity indexes sympathetic drive, electrocardiography and photoplethysmography report chronotropic and inotropic control, respiration patterns reflect metabolic and regulatory shifts, and facial electromyography records covert action in zygomatic and corrugator systems that often escape the camera. Electroencephalography resolves oscillatory and event-related dynamics associated with appraisal and attention. Reviews across physiology summarise characteristic signatures at the level of features and their typical reliability, while also warning that single channels are often ambiguous because many non-emotional factors can elicit similar changes. This motivates simultaneous sampling of several peripheral and central channels and model families that can learn the joint structure of their trajectories (Egger et al., 2019; Shu et al., 2018; Ramaswamy & Palaniswamy, 2024). A recent critical review of multimodal datasets catalogues how these physiological channels are increasingly paired with audio and video so that emotional episodes can be studied through both behaviour and bodily state on the same time base (Al-Azani & El-Alfy, 2025).

This multimodal orientation is not only theoretical. It is now the practical default in affective computing because no single signal captures the breadth of an episode and because different channels fail in different ways. Large surveys that span more than two hundred papers converge on the same point. Vision excels at specific expression categories but degrades under pose changes. Audio generalises better to distance and partial occlusion but is brittle to noise and dialect. Physiology can be recorded without visible behaviour and is difficult to fake, yet it requires instrumentation and careful artefact control. Text reveals appraisal and goals when available, but is sparse in many interactive settings. The advantage of fusing channels is strongest when the signals bear complementary error patterns and when training data refreshes each channel under the same elicitation and label scheme (Cai et al., 2023; Ramaswamy & Palaniswamy, 2024; Pan et al., 2023; Wu et al., 2025).

Understanding how these channels align in time is essential. Emotional responses recruit systems with different latencies. Facial muscle activity can precede visible expression. Electrodermal responses build more slowly than changes in fundamental frequency. EEG dynamics can move on the order of tens of milliseconds. Dataset builders, therefore, stress synchronised acquisition and careful alignment across devices, since timebase mismatch can inflate apparent discordance among channels and confuse fusion architectures. Public corpora such as MAHNOB-HCI (Soleymani et al., 2011) and RECOLA (Ringeval et al., 2013) have become reference points because they provide audio, video, and physiology recorded in lockstep with consistent annotation scales, and they have catalysed a generation of multimodal benchmarks (Cai et al., 2023). Recent surveys underline that collecting such corpora is costly and that many teams still rely on bespoke data, which limits comparability and external validity (Al-Azani & El-Alfy, 2025).

A second axis of understanding concerns representation. Classical pipelines derived hand-crafted features such as mel-frequency cepstral coefficients for audio, action units for video, power in canonical EEG bands, or time-domain statistics for heart rate variability. These features still serve as strong baselines and, when carefully engineered, encode domain insight that helps when data are scarce or labels are noisy. The field has nevertheless shifted toward deep encoders that learn hierarchical representations directly from raw or lightly processed streams. On the visual side, this includes three-dimensional convolutional encoders and attention models that summarise facial dynamics. On the audio side, convolutional transformers operating on spectrograms or learnable filterbanks provide state-of-the-art performance. For physiology, temporal convolutional networks and transformers learn patterns in multichannel signals with fewer assumptions about stationarity. Comparative studies show that deep encoders, when trained or adapted with self-supervised objectives, generally outperform classical features and reduce the need for manual signal processing, although they may be more brittle under distribution shift (Rouast et al., 2021; García-Hernández et al., 2024; Montero Quispe et al., 2022; Zhang et al., 2024).

These representational advances matter most when channels are combined. Fusion can occur at the feature level, the decision level, or through joint sequence models that pass attention across streams. Surveys and benchmarks chronicle steady gains from moving beyond naive concatenation toward architectures that explicitly model cross-modal influence. Examples include cross-modal attention, where audio cues steer the model towards high-motion parts of the face, and conditioning, where physiological signals adjust the visual encoder to highlight features linked to arousal. Graph-based and transformer frameworks now dominate, and head-to-head comparisons report that hybrid designs that mix early and late fusion often offer the best trade-off between flexibility and robustness to missing modalities (Jiang et al., 2020; Liu et al., 2021; Wu et al., 2025; Cai et al., 2023). The most recent overviews echo the same conclusion and locate the next frontier in self-supervised pretraining, weak supervision from large but noisy web corpora, and robust handling of missing or asynchronous streams (Ramaswamy & Palaniswamy, 2024; Zhang et al., 2024; Pan et al., 2023).

Understanding embodied emotion also requires attention to the structure of labels. Discrete schemes such as the seven basic categories are widely used for interpretability and have driven progress in video- and audio-based recognition. Dimensional schemes in arousal and valence align more naturally to physiology and allow continuous annotation. Contemporary surveys recommend treating labels as complementary and, where possible, learning shared representations that support both category and dimension outputs to encourage generalisation across contexts and datasets (Ramaswamy & Palaniswamy, 2024; Cai et al., 2023). The choice of label space also shapes evaluation. Macro-averaged metrics are preferred when class priors are balanced, while the area under the Receiver Operating Characteristic (ROC) curve and average precision reveal discrimination beyond a single threshold and are essential when the task is imbalanced or when calibrated probabilities are required for decision support. Reviews of benchmarking practice call for reporting both accuracy and probabilistic quality measures, such as the Brier score, to capture overconfidence and for auditing subgroup performance to surface cultural and demographic sensitivity (Ahmed et al., 2023; Al-Azani & El-Alfy, 2025).

Reviews identify three recurring ethical risks for emotion recognition. Katirai argues that systems can yield inequitable outcomes when built on questionable assumptions, that they process sensitive emotional data with attendant privacy risks, and that deployment in domains such as employment or healthcare can produce harm (Katirai, 2024). A recent analysis of multimodal emotion datasets echoes these points, noting how consent and licensing restrictions limit dataset distribution and reproducibility and underscoring the importance of explicit informed consent for multimodal recordings (Al-Azani & El-Alfy, 2025). These concerns are not an afterthought. They shape data collection protocols and motivate the multimodal route because it allows selective emphasis on less identifying channels, such as peripheral physiology, when visual or audio capture is inappropriate.

Taken together, these strands outline a coherent picture of embodied emotion across modalities. Visual, vocal, textual, and physiological views each provide a partial but meaningful slice of the same latent process. Their temporal dynamics and error profiles differ in ways that make them natural partners. Public datasets and modern deep sequence models have made it practical to align and learn from them jointly. As the surveys repeatedly note, progress now depends on synchronised and diverse corpora, on architectures that model cross-modal influence while tolerating missing data, and on evaluation that values calibrated probabilities and fairness alongside headline accuracy (Cai et al., 2023; Ramaswamy & Palaniswamy, 2024). This integrative perspective frames the rest of the chapter, where methods for sensing, representing, and fusing these signals are developed with the goal of a more faithful account of affect as it is enacted by the whole person.

8.3 Fusing Sensors for Holistic Embodied Emotion Analysis

The promise of multimodal emotion science rests on a simple observation. No single sensor captures the breadth of how bodies register and express affect. Speech carries prosodic contours that mark arousal and valence. Faces and posture reveal rapid motoric adjustments that accompany appraisal. Brain and peripheral physiology index covert regulation and autonomic change. When these streams are analysed in concert, the result is often more accurate and more robust than any one channel alone. Reviews across affective computing consistently document this complementarity and show that fusion is the organising principle that turns heterogeneous signals into a coherent account of embodied emotion (Ramaswamy & Palaniswamy, 2024). Related machine-learning frameworks have also been applied to affect-linked constructs beyond core emotions, such as love addiction, where features and explanations clarify predictive factors (Farahani et al., 2025).

Fusing sensors begins with a design choice about representation. Early fusion concatenates features from each modality to form a single joint vector, which is then fed to a classifier. This strategy gives the learner maximal access to cross-modal interactions, but it is sensitive to scale, missing values, and the curse of dimensionality effects. Late fusion trains a specialist per modality and combines their outputs by averaging, stacking, or learned gating. This strategy is robust to sensor dropouts and allows per-modality calibration at the expense of modelling rich cross-terms. Hybrid or intermediate fusion blends both by learning modality-specific encoders and then integrating them through attention, tensor factorisation, or graph message passing in a mid-level space. Contemporary surveys in affective and multimodal sentiment analysis trace these patterns and catalogue their strengths and limits with numerous exemplars across audio, vision, language, and physiology (Lian et al., 2023a; Gandhi et al., 2023; Zhao et al., 2025).

The theoretical rationale for fusion follows two complementary arguments: (1) the information argument holds that modalities carry partly non-overlapping cues. Acoustic energy in higher frequency bands is sensitive to breathy or tense phonation, while corrugator activity and frontalis activity in facial electromyography track subtle negative and surprise-related dynamics, even when faces are partially occluded. When these cues are pooled, the joint representation increases mutual information with the latent emotion; (2) the reliability argument holds that when noise or occlusion affects one channel, others can stabilise inference. Evidence theory and decision level combination frameworks formalise this idea through rules that weight sources by credibility and consistency, and these ideas have informed multimodal inference for decades and continue to appear in modern deep fusion systems (Lian et al., 2023a).

In practice, embodied emotion fusion is shaped by temporal structure. Emotion unfolds over hundreds of milliseconds to many seconds, and different sensors sample at different rates. For a concrete illustration, one public multimodal corpus records audio at 44.1 kHz while video is captured at ten frames per second, alongside high-frequency biosignals, which immediately creates heterogeneous time bases that a model must reconcile (Chen et al., 2022b). Surface electromyography in the same corpus is sampled at ten kilohertz with a fifty to one thousand hertz bandpass, and electroencephalography is sampled at five kilohertz and then downsampled to one kilohertz for analysis, which underscores the need to align fast neural or muscular activity with much slower facial and vocal streams (Chen et al., 2022b). Temporal encoders, therefore, need to summarise and align information across scales either before fusion or inside the network. Surveyed architectures caution that forcing strict word-level or frame-level synchrony can be brittle and instead advocate learning correspondences directly from data, a view that motivates cross-modal attention over loosely aligned sequences and avoids spurious matches introduced by naive resampling (Zhao et al., 2025). In practice, modality-specific temporal embeddings are learned with one-dimensional convolutions for local dynamics, recurrent units for longer dependencies, and self-attention for global context, after which cross-modal attention layers exchange information on a shared time base (Zhao et al., 2025). Contemporary reviews of multimodal emotion recognition further document transformer-based fusion that learns inter- and intra-modal relations without explicit hard alignment, consolidating evidence that careful temporal modelling is central to reliable fusion in affect analysis (Ramaswamy & Palaniswamy, 2024).

Attention-based fusion has become a dominant pattern because it allows the model to learn when to listen to which sensor. Cross-modal attention can project audio keys and queries into a space where visual values are retrieved or the inverse, which yields localised correspondences between prosodic bursts and micro facial actions. Hierarchical attention can first weight features within each modality, then integrate across modalities. Recent transformer architectures extend this idea with shared or alternating attention blocks that pass information among streams while preserving modality identity. Reviews of affective modelling and multimodal sentiment analysis document strong performance gains from such attention mechanisms across laboratory and in the wild settings (Ramaswamy & Palaniswamy, 2024; Gandhi et al., 2023; Zhao et al., 2025).

The choice among early, late, and hybrid fusion depends on data scale, annotation quality, and application constraints. Early fusion shines when there is adequate data to learn cross-terms and when modalities are reliably present for most trials. Late fusion is preferred when sensors are unevenly available, when calibration and interpretability at the decision level matter, or when one wishes to swap modalities without retraining the entire stack. Hybrid fusion becomes attractive when we expect sparse but important interactions, such as moments when a short vocal burst aligns with a brief brow raise. Comprehensive surveys recommend matching the fusion strategy to the error structure of the modalities and to the target deployment setting rather than adopting a single recipe (Lian et al., 2023a; Le et al., 2023).

Handling missing or asynchronous inputs is central in embodied emotion projects. In real environments, a camera may be occluded or a microphone may clip while physiological sensors drift or disconnect. Robust pipelines, therefore, include imputation at the feature level, a mixture of experts with a learned gating network that downweights missing experts, or architectures explicitly trained with random modality dropout so that the network learns to operate with any subset of inputs. Reviews report that such techniques reduce failure rates and allow graceful degradation when sensors are unreliable, which is essential in mobile or clinical contexts (Le et al., 2023; Ramaswamy & Palaniswamy, 2024).

A second practical axis concerns the feature space. Handcrafted features remain competitive for physiological channels where domain knowledge encodes meaningful spectral bands and summary statistics. For example, discrete cosine or band power features in electroencephalography and amplitude dispersion in facial electromyography are standard and are often concatenated with learned embeddings from audio or vision encoders. On the learned side, consistency and specificity objectives encourage networks to retain a unique modality structure while aligning shared emotion-relevant factors. Information bottleneck formulations likewise force intermediate representations to preserve cross-modal signals that predict affect while discarding nuisance variation. Recent work in multimodal fusion for affect leverages these principles to improve generalisation and reduce overfitting to superficial cues such as illumination, identity, or background noise (Zhao et al., 2025; Ramaswamy & Palaniswamy, 2024).

Embodied emotion often requires integration of physiology with behaviour. Classic affective corpora such as DEAP (Koelstra et al., 2011), DECAF (Donahue et al., 2014), and AMIGOS (Miranda-Correa et al., 2018) illustrate how electroencephalography and peripheral signals complement vision and audio, and they continue to motivate fusion strategies that respect both slow autonomic trends and fast motoric expressions. Surveys of datasets underscore that these collections differ in sampling rates, annotation granularity, and synchronisation fidelity, which again shapes fusion designs. Models that first regularise within modality, then combine decisions or mid-level embeddings have proven to be reliable choices across such varied conditions (Cai et al., 2023).

Interpretability is not optional in health, education, or safety applications. Decision-level fusion supports modality attribution, which helps analysts see whether a classification leaned primarily on voice prosody, facial motion, or physiological changes. Mid-level fusion can be probed with attention maps and sensitivity analysis to reveal cross-modal interactions; for example, a case where the model attends jointly to a sharp rise in pitch and a transient frontalis activation when labelling surprise (Ramaswamy & Palaniswamy, 2024). Recent reviews recommend reporting per-modality contributions and explanation diagnostics alongside accuracy to catch spurious correlations and demographic shortcuts and to promote trust in multimodal affect systems (Udahemuka et al., 2024).

Evaluation practices must reflect both accuracy and reliability. When fusion is successful, macro-averaged F1 and area under precision-recall curves typically improve because minority classes benefit from signals that are salient in only some channels. Yet probability, quality and calibration remain important because practitioners act on model confidence as well as labels. Many fusion pipelines, therefore, calibrate per modality posteriors before combination or calibrate the fused output after stacking. Reviews recommend reporting discrimination and calibration together to give a complete picture of utility in downstream decisions that affect people (Ramaswamy & Palaniswamy, 2024).

Finally, embodied emotion work benefits from a disciplined engineering perspective. Data preprocessing should harmonise sampling rates and apply sensor-specific denoising before any joint modelling. Feature spaces should be standardised so that early fusion is not dominated by a single high-variance stream. When late or hybrid fusion is used, per-modality validation ensures that the integrated system does not hide a failing sensor behind a strong counterpart. Across recent literature, one sees a convergence toward modular pipelines in which each stream has its own encoder and diagnostics, and a fusion block learns when and how to combine them, a view that aligns with the natural division of embodied signals into articulatory, visual motor, and physiological families (Gandhi et al., 2023; Le et al., 2023).

Figure 8.1 depicts the behaviour of a two-expert late-fusion scheme across mixing weights and shows a clear maximum near equal weighting, a pattern consistent with complementary signals whose errors are not fully shared. When the weight moves from either extreme toward an even split, performance first rises and then levels, peaking near the middle. If the two experts make mistakes independently often enough, averaging their probabilities suppresses idiosyncratic noise and reduces variance, so the fused decision achieves a higher macro F1 than either expert alone. If the experts are made more similar or their errors become tightly coupled, the curve flattens and the gain disappears. That contrast is the essence of useful multimodal fusion. The benefit does not come from stacking models for its own sake. It comes from combining signals that carry complementary evidence about the same underlying emotional state.

This intuition links directly to the practice guidelines that close this section. Embodied emotion work benefits from a disciplined engineering perspective. Data preprocessing should harmonise sampling rates and apply sensor-specific denoising before any joint modelling. Feature spaces should be standardised so that early fusion is not dominated by a single high-variance stream. When late or hybrid fusion is used, per-modality validation ensures that the integrated system does not hide a failing sensor behind a

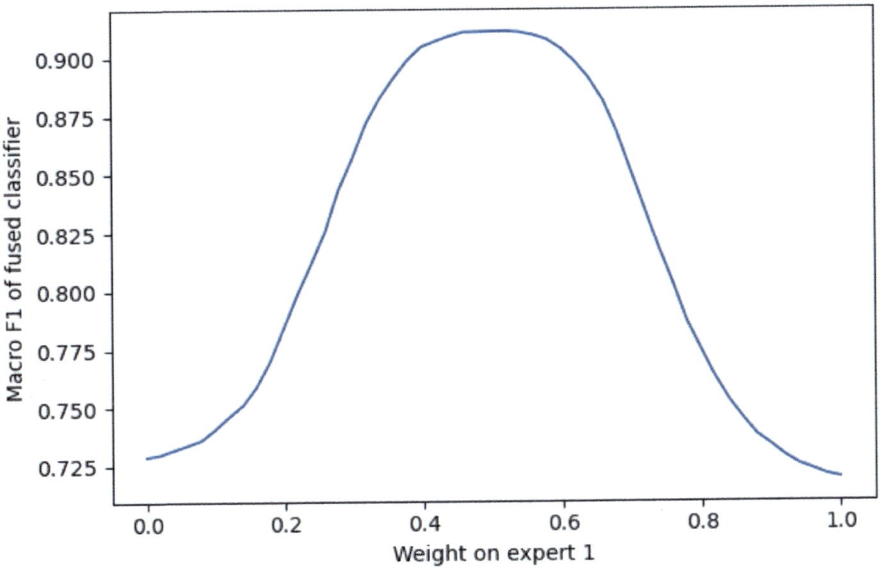

Figure 8.1 Weighted late fusion of two calibrated experts.

Note: The x-axis shows the weight assigned to expert 1, while expert 2 receives the complementary weight.

strong counterpart. Across recent literature there is a convergence towards modular pipelines in which each stream is processed by its own encoder with per-modality diagnostics, and a dedicated fusion block learns how and when to combine these representations (Zhao et al., 2024; Udahemuka et al., 2024), a view that aligns with the standard grouping of embodied signals into behavioural articulatory and visual-motor channels such as facial and vocal cues, and physiological channels both central and peripheral such as EEG, electrodermal, and cardiovascular measures (Ramaswamy & Palaniswamy, 2024). Taken together, these principles define fusion as the central act in multimodal emotion inference. When we respect the temporal character of each sensor, choose fusion mechanisms that match the data regime, plan for missing inputs, and audit interpretation and calibration, integrated systems yield a richer and more trustworthy view of embodied affect than any single stream. This is not simply a performance claim. It reflects the fact that emotions are embodied in distributed and partially independent physiological and behavioural processes. Fusion aligns our analytical tools with that biological reality and is therefore the cornerstone of a comprehensive science of embodied emotions (Ramaswamy & Palaniswamy, 2024; Lian et al., 2023a).

8.4 Machine Learning Approaches for Integrating Multimodal Emotion Data

A learning system that integrates audio, vision, language, and physiology must cope with signals that differ in sampling rate, statistical structure, and noise profile, yet still produce a single coherent estimate of an underlying affective state. This integration problem is not only about adding more features. It is a modelling task that addresses alignment across time, representation within each sensor, and principled fusion under uncertainty. Contemporary research converges on three building blocks: (1) modality-specific encoders transform raw streams such as spectrograms, facial landmarks, or band power from EEG into compact embeddings; (2) a fusion mechanism exchanges information across embeddings while preserving modality-specific cues; (3) the output head produces calibrated class probabilities or continuous affect scores and is evaluated with discrimination and reliability metrics. Surveys across affective computing consistently show that performance gains emerge when these elements are designed together rather than in isolation, particularly when physiological and behavioural channels are combined in a single learning objective (Ramaswamy & Palaniswamy, 2024; García-Hernández et al., 2024). For psychology-focused, Python-based pipeline patterns and regression modelling, see (Kovač et al., 2024).

A first layer of design concerns representation learning inside each modality. In speech, mel frequency cepstral coefficients, prosodic contours, and log-mel filterbank features remain strong inputs for classical learners and are also used as front ends for convolutional and transformer encoders that model long-range temporal patterns through self-attention (Lian et al., 2023b; García-Hernández et al., 2024). In the visual stream, modern pipelines start from face detection and landmark tracking, then pass frames or short clips through spatiotemporal networks that capture action units and micro-movements predictive of emotion, with attention replacing hand-crafted temporal pooling in many recent systems (Lian et al., 2023b). Physiological channels require different preprocessing. For EEG, short windows are transformed into spectral power over canonical bands delta, theta, alpha, beta, and gamma or into entropy and asymmetry indices, then aggregated across regions before classification. Reviews in sensing and biomedical engineering emphasise that band power and entropy families are the most reproducible correlates for affect classification, especially when combined with robust normalisation and artefact rejection (García-Hernández et al., 2024).

Fusion is the second design layer. Early fusion concatenates features across modalities before learning and is effective when streams are well aligned. Late fusion trains a separate model per modality and combines their outputs with a meta-learner or with probability rules. Hybrid fusion inserts cross-modal interactions between modality-specific encoders and the final decision, enabling both local and global integration. Standard taxonomies define these three families and document their trade-offs in alignment sensitivity, parameter efficiency, and robustness to missing data, with hybrid strategies often achieving the best balance on modern corpora (Lian et al., 2023b; Zhao et al., 2025; Al-Azani & El-Alfy, 2025).

Classical learning remains a strong baseline for integrated emotion analysis. Comparable supervised pipelines are also used across psychological health domains, for example, the classification of chronic pain outcomes (Kovač et al., 2025b). Support vector machines, logistic regression, random forests, and gradient boosting perform well when paired with careful feature scaling and cross-validation. In a late fusion setting, a stacked generaliser trained on out-of-fold predictions from modality-specific base models can exploit complementary strengths without demanding time alignment at the feature level. Stacking has a long history as an error-reducing meta-learning device and fits naturally when modalities differ in dimensionality and sampling rate (Wolpert, 1992). For probabilistic outputs, Platt scaling and isotonic regression convert raw scores to calibrated probabilities so that a fused system can weight modalities on a common scale and reason about confidence (Platt, 1999; Zadrozny & Elkan, 2002; Guo et al., 2017).

Deep learning has shifted the frontier by learning both representation and fusion end-to-end. Tensor-based fusion layers preserve unimodal signals while modelling multiplicative interactions, as in the Tensor Fusion Network (Zadeh et al., 2017), which factorizes cross-modal dynamics without manual feature design and has influenced subsequent affect models (Zadeh et al., 2017). Cross-modal transformers learn to align asynchronous streams by attending from one modality to another, replacing explicit alignment with data-driven correspondences. In multimodal sequence learning, attention blocks handle different sampling rates and variable lag, which is essential in emotion, where physiological responses trail facial or vocal cues. This approach is now widely cited for unaligned language-vision-audio sequences and has been adapted to affective computing tasks (Tsai et al., 2019; Lian et al., 2023b). Recent reviews document a rising use of attention and transformer families in emotion recognition, reflecting their ability to capture long-range dependencies and cross-modal context (García-Hernández et al., 2024).

Representation learning increasingly benefits from pretraining and self-supervision. Contrastive objectives align audio embeddings with visuo-facial or textual embeddings drawn from the same event, while pushing apart mismatched pairs. The goal is a modality-invariant yet content-sensitive space that supports transfer to downstream emotion labels with few annotations. Surveyed evidence shows that such objectives improve generalisation and robustness, particularly when paired with augmentations that mimic real recording conditions, for example, reverberation in speech or occlusion in faces (Gandhi et al., 2023; Ramaswamy & Palaniswamy, 2024).

A practical challenge in deployed systems is missing or degraded modalities. Cameras occlude, microphones saturate, electrodes drift. Late fusion can simply drop a base model at test time, yet hybrid and end-to-end systems must be trained to handle absence. Two strategies recur in the literature. The first is modality dropout, which randomly removes streams during training so the network learns to rely on whichever channels are present (Li, 2025). The second is teacher-student distillation (Touvron et al., 2021), where a full model teaches a reduced model through soft targets so that the student can operate with fewer inputs at inference. Reviews emphasise that robustness to missing channels is not automatic and should be validated explicitly with controlled ablations (Yoon & Kim, 2025; Lian et al., 2023b).

Learning targets and evaluation deserve equal attention. Categorical labels such as anger or joy can be complemented with dimensional targets such as valence and arousal, and multitask heads enable a model to share information across these views of affect. Performance should include macro-averaged discrimination metrics that respect class balance and explicit measures of probability quality. In emotion applications where decisions guide feedback to users, calibrated probabilities matter as much as raw accuracy. The Brier score (Brier, 1950) summarises overall probabilistic accuracy, while reliability diagrams and expected calibration error quantify systematic bias in confidence. Modern neural networks are often miscalibrated out of the box, yet simple post-hoc calibration improves decision quality without changing classification, which aligns with best practice for safety-critical or user-facing affect systems (Guo et al., 2017). Comparable psychology-focused pipelines using calibrated regression have been applied to predict internal shame, providing an example of explainable, probability-aware modelling in an affect domain (Kovač et al., 2025a).

The effect of post-hoc calibration on late-fusion reliability is illustrated in Figure 8.2. The dashed diagonal marks perfect calibration. Figure 8.2 (A) plots predicted confidence against observed accuracy for the uncalibrated classifier. The curve sits above the diagonal at mid to high confidence, which indicates overconfidence and yields an Expected Calibration Error (ECE) of 0.099 and a Maximum Calibration Error (MCE) of 0.230. Figure 8.2 (B) shows the same model after isotonic calibration. Points now align with the diagonal across the confidence range, and summary errors fall to ECE of 0.009 and MCE of 0.019 while discrimination is unchanged. This is the intended outcome of post-hoc calibration, where probabilities are adjusted

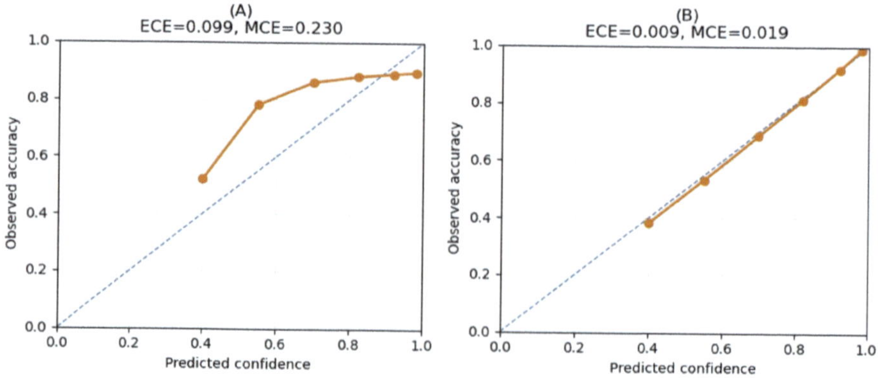

Figure 8.2 Reliability before and after calibration: (A) uncalibrated late-fusion reliability curve; (B) the same classifier after isotonic calibration.

without altering class decisions or macro F1, consistent with best practice in probabilistic evaluation for classification (Brier, 1950; Guo et al., 2017).

Interpretability closes the loop between sensors and models. Permutation importance and SHapley Additive exPlanations (SHAP) values expose which variables drive decisions and whether these align with intended psychophysiological theory. Attention maps localise the temporal segments or facial regions that contribute most to predictions. Surveys in multimodal sentiment and emotion analysis encourage reporting these diagnostics alongside accuracy to ensure that gains from fusion do not arise from artefacts, for example, speaker identity or background music, and to support fair comparisons across datasets and populations (Lian et al., 2023b; García-Hernández et al., 2024).

Finally, there is growing interest in responsible machine learning for affect (Baltrušaitis et al., 2018). This includes bias assessment across gender, age, and culture, uncertainty reporting, and clear provenance of training data. Reviews stress that multimodal systems amplify the risk of shortcut learning because multiple channels can entangle spurious cues. Robust pipelines therefore include stratified evaluation, cross-subject validation when appropriate, and transparent release of code and preprocessing steps to support replication (García-Hernández et al., 2024; Ramaswamy & Palaniswamy, 2024).

8.5 Case Studies in Multimodal Embodied Emotion

Here, we translate the chapter's ideas into practice by examining a specific case study based on a carefully selected multimodal dataset. The dataset used is PME4 (Chen et al., 2022a), collected to investigate how discrete emotions are expressed through coordinated streams of behaviour and physiological responses. Eleven adult participants with acting experience produced seven labelled expressions, following Ekman's basic set plus neutral. The labels include anger, fear, disgust, sadness, happiness, surprise, and neutral. Each trial lasted five seconds, with brief pauses in between, and the sessions were divided into five blocks to ensure each participant contributed multiple repetitions per emotion. Data collection is genuinely multimodal. When a participant spoke the sentence, *The sky is green*, four synchronised sensors recorded data simultaneously. A Universal Serial Bus (USB) webcam captured facial video at ten frames per second with 960 by 720 resolution. The laptop microphone recorded audio at 44.1 kHz. Eight scalp EEG electrodes at F3, Fz, F4, Cz, P3, Pz, P4, and O2 measured brain activity, bandpass filtered within the standard low-frequency range for cognitive research. Six facial EMG channels captured muscle activity from muscles involved in visible facial actions related to expression. After basic quality checks, the public dataset contains 3829 valid trials (Chen et al., 2022b). This design provides closely aligned audio, visual, neural, and muscular evidence for the same emotional state, making it ideal for exploring how different channels complement each other and testing whether combining them enhances recognition beyond any single stream.

The PME4 collection was developed to fill a gap in existing benchmarks. Many emotion datasets depend on spontaneous reactions to films or music and then rely on subjective ratings. PME4 uses posed expressions given by trained actors, which reduces ambiguity in labels and results in better alignment between what the subject intends to express and what the sensors detect. The protocol also maintains a useful structure within each trial. There is a short interval before speech begins, then the utterance itself, followed by a brief tail, allowing researchers to analyse pre-speech, during-speech, and post-speech dynamics if desired. The hardware choices keep the setup straightforward enough to be replicated while still capturing the essential data. Audio and video display the overt performance that people tend to interpret naturally. EEG and EMG record internal timing and muscle activation patterns that can be subtle but informative, especially when faces are partially obscured by electrodes. Collectively, these streams enable us to explore not only which modality performs best on its own but also how they interact.

In this section, the PME4 dataset acts as a testbed for an end-to-end multimodal analysis of embodied emotion. We create a unified trial-level table that combines features from audio, video, EEG, and EMG, along with the emotion label and the subject identifier. From this foundation, we develop interpretable baselines for each modality and a late fusion model that merges the streams. Generalisation is tested using a conventional train and test split, as well as a leave-one-subject-out (LOSO) protocol to assess robustness across individuals. Reliability is evaluated alongside accuracy through probability calibration, confidence distributions, and class-specific behaviour, making the quality of predicted probabilities transparent. The case study aims to show, within a single reproducible pipeline, how modelling emotion as a joint phenomenon across coordinated channels can lead to measurable improvements in predictive power and trustworthiness when tested on a public and well-documented resource.

We analyse the PME4 corpus of synchronised audio, video, EEG and EMG trials, reshaped into a single trial-level table with subject identifiers and one of seven emotion labels (anger, disgust, fear, happiness, neutral, sadness, surprise). Figure 8.3 (A) summarises the label distribution. The seven bars are nearly identical in height, with counts between about 545 and 548 per class, which confirms that the dataset is effectively balanced and that macro-averaged metrics are appropriate. Figure 8.3 (B) reports the headline result. The best single stream in this run is audio with a macro F1 of 0.439, whereas the late-fusion model reaches 0.466. The absolute gain is $\Delta \approx 0.026$, a modest but meaningful improvement that supports the claim that combining modalities corrects a portion of the errors each stream makes on its own.

For tables, we use abbreviated column names: *Acc* is accuracy, *F1m* is macro F1, *Prec_m* and *Rec_m* are macro precision and recall, *AUC_m* is the macro one-versus-rest ROC Area Under the Curve (AUC), *AP_m* is macro average precision, *Brier* is the mean squared error of the probability assigned

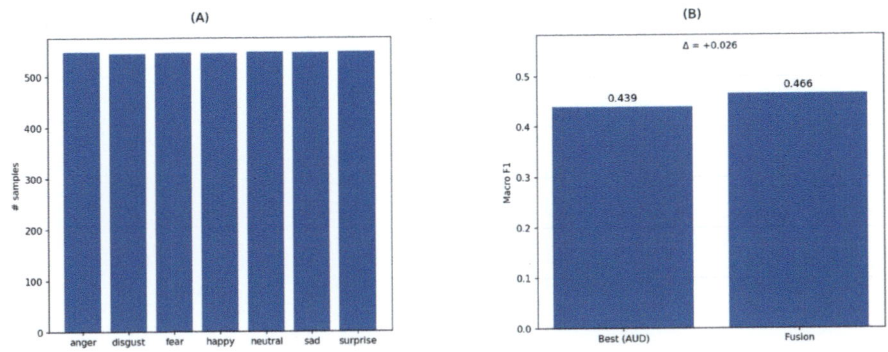

Figure 8.3 Dataset overview and headline fusion result: (A) class counts in the trial-level table; (B) macro F1 for the best single modality and the late-fusion model.

to the true class, and *LogLoss* is the cross-entropy on the full probability vector. The quantitative headline is summarised in Table 8.1. The table reports all the mentioned metrics. Consistent with Figure 8.3 (B), the late-fusion model edges the best single modality on macro F1 by about +0.026 and shows comparable or better probabilistic quality in the Brier and log-loss measures, where lower is better. This gives a compact view of both classification accuracy and calibration for the two headline systems.

Taken together, the balanced label distribution in Figure 8.3 (A) and the fusion advantage in Figure 8.3 (B) motivate the rest of the case study. The data offer a fair test of multimodal learning, and the initial comparison shows that integrating audio, video, EEG, and EMG pays off at evaluation time.

Figure 8.4 examines the structure of mistakes and shows when combining streams pays off. Figure 8.4 (A) presents the row-normalised confusion matrix for the late-fusion model. The diagonal cells sit in the mid-forties to low fifties for most classes, which is expected in a seven-way task with subtle boundaries. The off-diagonal pattern is not random. Fear and sadness are frequently confused in both directions, and neutral often drifts toward sadness. Surprise leaks into fear and happiness, while anger and disgust are mixed more than other pairs. These confusions cluster along affective similarity, which suggests that unimodal cues are sometimes insufficient to separate neighbours in valence or arousal.

Figure 8.4 (B) compares error counts for the two strongest single streams and for fusion using the same test split. Audio makes 643 mistakes and EMG makes 906. The overlap where both are wrong is 510, which marks the hardcore of cases that neither stream can resolve on its own. The fusion model makes 614 mistakes, fewer than EMG by about thirty-two per cent and slightly fewer than audio by 29 errors. This indicates that many errors are complementary. When audio is uncertain but EMG carries discriminative muscle activity, the fusion learner can follow the reliable cue, and vice versa.

Table 8.1 Headline test metrics for the best single modality and the late-fusion model.

Model	*Acc*	*F1_m*	*Prec_m*	*Rec_m*	*AUC_ovr_m*	*AP_m*	*LogLoss*	*Brier (true-class)*	*Brier (multiclass)*
LateFusion_Stacking	0.466	0.466	0.467	0.466	0.819	0.488	1.446	0.508	0.096
AllFeatures_HGB	0.615	0.615	0.618	0.615	0.902	0.69	1.445	0.331	0.082
LateFusion_Stacking+Cal	0.465	0.464	0.466	0.465	0.814	0.486	1.574	0.531	0.097
AllFeatures_HGB+Cal	0.621	0.621	0.627	0.621	0.897	0.687	1.131	0.4	0.076

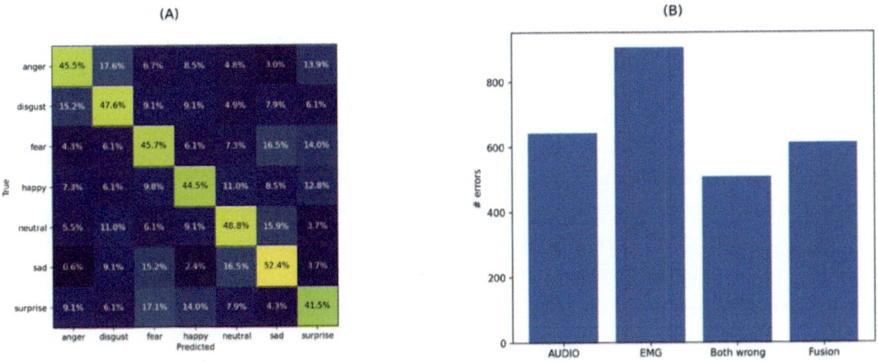

Figure 8.4 Error structure and fusion gains: (A) confusion matrix for the late-fusion model with rows normalised to percent per true class; (B) error counts for audio and EMG single-stream models, the overlap where both are wrong, and the late-fusion model.

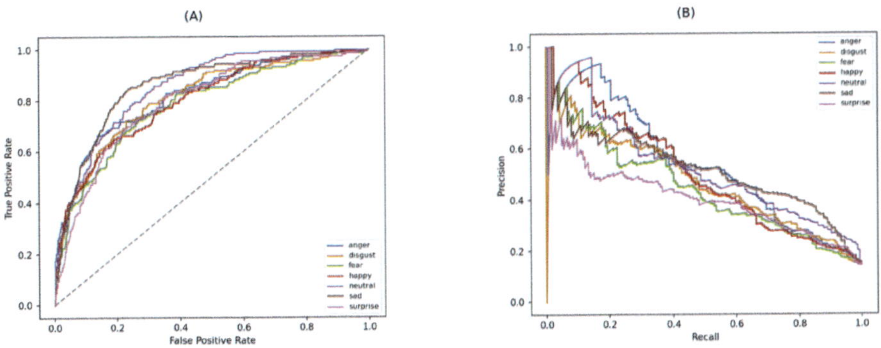

Figure 8.5 Discrimination of the late fusion model: (A) one-vs-rest ROC by class; (B) one-vs-rest precision–recall by class.

The residual 510 errors align with the densest off-diagonal bands in Figure 8.4 (A), such as fear versus sadness and neutral versus sadness, where both streams often point the wrong way. Those pairs are candidates for additional information from EEG or facial video or for more tailored features.

To understand how well the late-fusion model separates each emotion from the rest across decision thresholds, we examine receiver–operator behaviour and the associated precision–recall trade-offs on the held-out test set. Figure 8.5 (A) plots one-vs-rest ROC curves for all seven categories. The traces arch well above the diagonal reference, which indicates that the fused signal carries discriminative structure for every class. The spacing between curves is informative. Emotions with more stereotyped vocal or facial patterns tend to trace higher true-positive rates at the same false-positive rate, reflecting clearer separation in the fused feature space. Classes with broader acoustic and physiological expression display shallower segments of the curve, which signals that additional context or features may be needed to push the operating point further towards the top left.

Figure 8.5 (B) shifts the lens to precision–recall. Because each curve treats one class as *positive* against all others, precision falls as recall rises, revealing how quickly false alarms accumulate when we try to recover more positives. Several classes maintain relatively high precision over a wide recall range, which is consistent with the ROC view that their positive instances are well clustered. Others show a steeper decline, telling us that raising recall will require accepting more ambiguous cases. Together, these panels give a threshold-free picture of separability. They also guide the choice of operating points for applications that favour precision or recall, and they complement the macro F1 summaries in Table 1 by revealing where the score is earned along the full trade-off curve rather than at a single threshold.

The first question is how confident the fusion model is when it makes a prediction. Figure 8.6 (A) places the maximum predicted probability for each test instance into a histogram. Most cases cluster between roughly 0.30 and 0.60 with a taper toward very high confidence. This shape tells us the model rarely declares extreme certainty and spends much of its probability mass in mid-range values, which is typical when classes overlap and sensors provide partially redundant evidence. Most predictions sit in the mid-range, with relatively few at very high confidence. That distribution already hints that the model is cautious rather than over-certain.

The second question is whether those reported probabilities are trustworthy. Figure 8.6 (B) plots a reliability curve for the uncalibrated fusion model by binning predictions and comparing the bin's average confidence to the bin's empirical accuracy. The curve tracks the diagonal reasonably well through the middle of the range, then deviates near the extremes. The accompanying summary on the plot reports an expected calibration error close to 0.051 and a maximum calibration error around 0.316, indicating small but noticeable miscalibration in some bins.

Figure 8.6 (C) repeats the reliability analysis after isotonic calibration. The curve straightens in the mid-probability regime while the extremes remain data-limited, so the maximum error can fluctuate. In our run, the expected calibration error is about 0.062, and the maximum calibration error is about 0.381. Together with Figure 8.6 (A), these plots suggest that calibrating probabilities can refine trust in the score scale without materially altering class ranking or the overall discrimination reported earlier. In practical terms, the fusion system's probabilities are already usable, and post-hoc calibration mainly refines the middle of the scale without altering which examples rank above which.

Table 8.2 places these findings next to those from the all-features gradient-boosting model. Across both models, the calibrated variants keep accuracy and macro-F1 essentially unchanged while adjusting the probability quality measures. The fusion model maintains very low expected miscalibration, suggesting its scores can be interpreted directly as chances of being correct

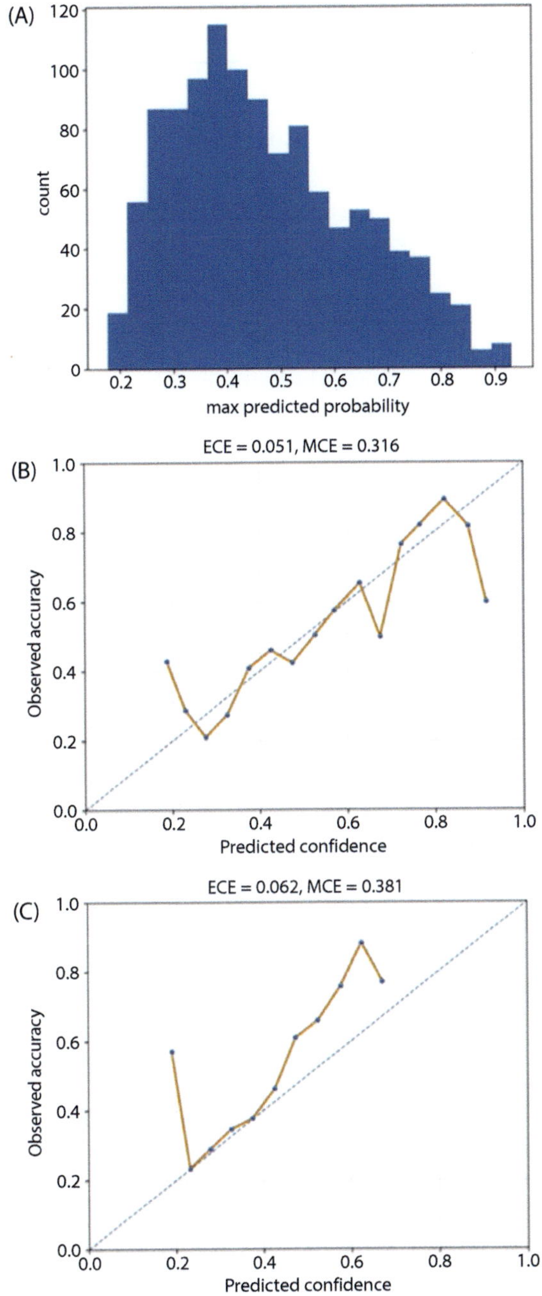

Figure 8.6 Confidence and reliability of the fusion model: (A) distribution of the maximum predicted probability on the test set; (B) reliability curve before calibration with ECE and MCE; (C) reliability curve after isotonic calibration with ECE and MCE.

Table 8.2 Calibration summary for late-fusion stacking and all-features gradient boosting, before and after isotonic calibration

Model	*Calibrated*	*ECE*	*MCE*	*Bins*
Fusion	FALSE	0.051	0.316	16
HGB	FALSE	0.212	0.314	15
Fusion	TRUE	0.062	0.381	11
HGB	TRUE	0.127	0.223	15

for most of the range. The larger maximum error reminds us to be cautious with the most confident outputs, where bins can be small and noisy. The gradient-boosting model follows the same pattern, reinforcing the view that probability calibration is a complementary step that improves interpretability rather than raw discrimination.

Figure 8.7 (A) traces how the late-fusion model improves as we give it more training trials. The cross-validation curve climbs steadily from roughly the low twenties to the mid-forties in accuracy as the sample count grows, while the training curve sits higher and slowly declines towards 60 percent. This pattern is typical for a model whose capacity is fixed while data volume increases. The widening data supply reduces variance and raises out-of-fold performance, yet there remains a stable gap between train and validation that signals headroom either for more expressive fusion or for stronger regularisation tuned to the larger regime. The key message is that additional multimodal data continues to improve accuracy and that fusion benefits predictably from scale.

Figure 8.7 (B) turns to person-level robustness by counting, subject by subject, which approach achieves the best macro F1 when each individual is held out during training. No single strategy dominates. A simple audio baseline often tops the chart, and fusion is a close second with several wins of its own. EEG alone rarely wins, and the all-features gradient boosting baseline only occasionally does. This distribution hints at real heterogeneity across participants. For some speakers, voice carries most of the discriminative signal. For others, the combination of streams gives the model complementary cues that a single modality misses.

Figure 8.7 (C) summarises those LOSO results more systematically by averaging macro F1 across people and adding standard deviation bars. Audio has the highest mean with modest spread, which is consistent with its many wins in Figure 8.7 (B) and suggests a relatively stable unimodal signal. Fusion comes next with a slightly lower mean but a wider error bar. Those wider spreads match the intuition from Figure 8.7 (B). Fusion helps some subjects a lot and others less, which is what we expect when different individuals lean on different channels. The gradient boosting baseline lags and shows high variability, which indicates that stacking calibrated per-modality models is the more reliable way to integrate streams in this dataset.

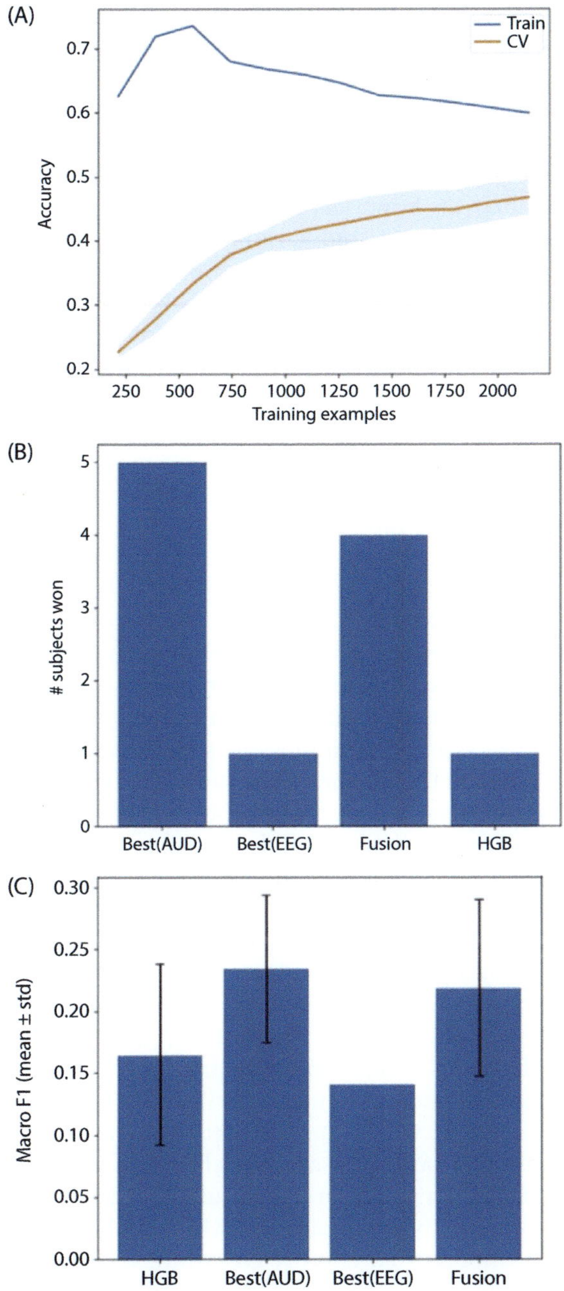

Figure 8.7 Learning and cross-subject generalisation: (A) learning curve for the late-fusion model with accuracy on the training set and in cross-validation as the number of training trials increases; (B) LOSO winners by subject counted across approaches; (C) LOSO macro F1 averaged over subjects with standard deviation bars for each approach.

Taken together, these learning and LOSO views convey two practical lessons: (1) multimodal fusion keeps improving with more data, so future collections that expand the number of trials should translate directly into better accuracy; (2) across-person generalisation is uneven, which argues for techniques that adapt the fusion weights or calibrate features at the subject level when deployment allows it.

Figure 8.8 summarises how the all-features gradient-boosting model distributes weight across streams and variables. Figure 8.8 (A) aggregates permutation importance by modality. Almost all positive contributions come from audio, with a total importance of about 0.114. EEG sits near zero, and EMG is slightly negative at roughly –0.150. Negative values can arise when a feature block is weak or redundant, so that randomising it occasionally helps the model on the test set. The takeaway is that in this tabular representation, the classifier leans primarily on acoustic cues while the physiological channels add little to this particular model.

Figure 8.8 (B) ranks individual variables. The list is dominated by summary statistics from the audio stream. The single most influential variable is *AUDIO_sd_000* with importance near 0.097, which is far ahead of the next features, such as *AUDIO_sd_001* around 0.019, and the audio median *AUDIO_p50_000* near 0.015. A few EMG dispersion terms and one EEG mean appear, but their effects are an order of magnitude smaller. Because these variables are time-aggregate descriptors of the MFCC trajectories, the pattern suggests that temporal variability in a small set of spectral bands is the primary driver of separation among the seven emotions in PME4.

Figure 8.8 (C) uses SHAP to check directionality on the top audio predictors for one representative class. For several variables, the red points have high feature values clustered on one side of the vertical zero line, while the blue points have low values clustered on the other. That consistent separation indicates monotonic influence rather than incidental correlation. In practical terms, higher short-term spectral variability for the leading MFCCs tends to push the score towards the class, and lower variability tends to pull it away, while the different percentiles, medians and quartiles modulate the effect.

These results align with earlier performance findings. Audio alone is a strong unimodal baseline, and much of the predictive mass in the all-features model resides there. At the same time, late fusion still outperforms the best single stream on average, which implies that other modalities provide complementary information once they are modelled separately and combined at the score level rather than mixed in one tabular learner. This contrast points to a concrete avenue for future work on PME4. Richer feature learning for EEG and EMG or models that capture cross-modal interactions could raise the non-audio contributions without sacrificing the strong acoustic signal.

This case study turned the chapter's ideas into a complete multimodal workflow on PME4, moving from a unified trial table to unimodal baselines, late fusion, discrimination analyses, calibration, and cross-subject tests. A good reading path starts broad and then narrows. Figure 8.3 establishes that

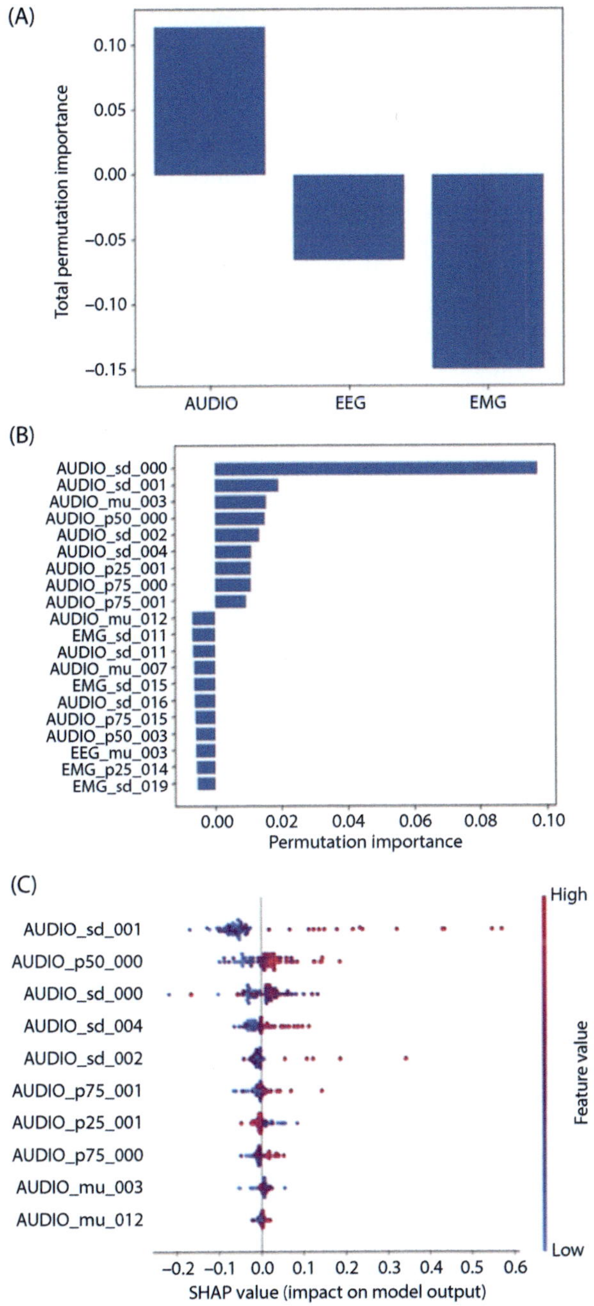

Figure 8.8 What drives decisions: (A) modality-level permutation importance for the all-features gradient-boosting model; (B) top 20 variables ranked by permutation importance; (C) SHAP summary for the top audio variables showing the direction and spread of their impact on one class score.

the labels are balanced and shows a small but consistent improvement when scores from different streams are fused. Figure 8.4 explains where that gain comes from by contrasting the confusion structure with the overlap of errors across strong single streams. Figure 8.5 then looks at class-wise separability across thresholds, so the reader is not tied to one decision point. Figure 8.6 focuses on probability quality. Confidence is compared with observed accuracy, and the calibrated variant nudges probabilities into better agreement without changing headline accuracy. Figure 8.7 addresses generalisation across people and shows that more data are likely to help. Figure 8.8 ends with model evidence about what drives decisions, with acoustic features contributing most in this tabular representation and other streams adding complementary signals that fusion can exploit.

Three conclusions follow: (1) embodied emotion benefits from combining sensors. Even when one stream is strongest, complementary errors mean that careful fusion does better than any single source; (2) the quality of probabilities matters for scientific use and for downstream systems. Reporting AUC and average precision together with Brier score, log loss, and calibration errors gives a truer picture than accuracy alone; (3) across-person robustness is the key challenge. LOSO remains an essential test and should guide future data collection and modelling choices.

The pipeline shown here is intentionally simple so that readers who are not specialists can reproduce it. Start from a clean trial table, compare fair baselines for each stream, fuse only at the score level, and always check both what improves and why. This provides a practical template for building trustworthy multimodal models of embodied emotion.

References

Ahmed, N., Al Aghbari, Z., & Girija, S. (2023). A systematic survey on multimodal emotion recognition using learning algorithms. *Intelligent Systems with Applications*, *17*, 200171.

Al-Azani, S., & El-Alfy, E. S. M. (2025). A review and critical analysis of multimodal datasets for emotional AI. *Artificial Intelligence Review*, *58*(10), 334.

Baltrušaitis, T., Ahuja, C., & Morency, L. P. (2018). Multimodal machine learning: A survey and taxonomy. *IEEE Transactions on Pattern Analysis and Machine Intelligence*, *41*(2), 423–443.

Brier, G. W. (1950). Verification of forecasts expressed in terms of probability. *Monthly Weather Review*, *78*(1), 1–3.

Busso, C., Bulut, M., Lee, C. C., Kazemzadeh, A., Mower, E., Kim, S., & Narayanan, S. S. (2008). IEMOCAP: Interactive emotional dyadic motion capture database. *Language Resources and Evaluation*, *42*(4), 335–359.

Cai, Y., Li, X., & Li, J. (2023). Emotion recognition using different sensors, emotion models, methods and datasets: A comprehensive review. *Sensors*, *23*(5), 2455.

Canal, F. Z., Müller, T. R., Matias, J. C., Scotton, G. G., de Sa Junior, A. R., Pozzebon, E., & Sobieranski, A. C. (2022). A survey on facial emotion recognition techniques: A state-of-the-art literature review. *Information Sciences*, *582*, 593–617.

Celeghin, A., Diano, M., Bagnis, A., Viola, M., & Tamietto, M. (2017). Basic emotions in human neuroscience: neuroimaging and beyond. *Frontiers in Psychology*, *8*, 1432.

Chandraumakantham, O., Gowtham, N., Zakariah, M., & Almazyad, A. (2024). Multimodal emotion recognition using feature fusion: An LLM-based approach. *IEEE Access*, *12*, 108052–108071.

Chen, J., Zhu, Z., & Ro, T. (2022a). *PME4: Emotion recognition with audio, video, EEG, and EMG* (Version 1) [Data set]. figshare.

Chen, J., Ro, T., & Zhu, Z. (2022b). Emotion recognition with audio, video, EEG, and EMG: A dataset and baseline approaches. *IEEE Access, 10*, 13229–13242.

Donahue, J., Jia, Y., Vinyals, O., Hoffman, J., Zhang, N., Tzeng, E., & Darrell, T. (2014, January). Decaf: A deep convolutional activation feature for generic visual recognition. In *International conference on machine learning* (pp. 647–655). PMLR.

Du, Z., Wu, S., Huang, D., Li, W., & Wang, Y. (2019). Spatio-temporal encoder-decoder fully convolutional network for video-based dimensional emotion recognition. *IEEE Transactions on Affective Computing*, *12*(3), 565–578.

Egger, M., Ley, M., & Hanke, S. (2019). Emotion recognition from physiological signal analysis: A review. *Electronic Notes in Theoretical Computer Science*, *343*, 35–55.

Farahani, H., Watson, P., Bezan, T., Kovač, N., Winter, L. C., Blagojević, M., & Jiménez, P. (2024). PsAIchology: An Intelligent Direction in Psychological Sciences. In *10th international scientific conference Technics, Informatics and Education-TIE 2024*. Faculty of Technical Sciences Čačak, University of Kragujevac.

Farahani, H., Watson, P., Kovač, N., Sheykhangafshe, F. B., Azadfallah, P., Allahyari, A., & Chesli, R. R. (2025). Unraveling the complexity of love addiction using machine learning algorithms: The influence of positive and negative affect, interpersonal needs, and self-hate. In C.-H. Mayer & E. Vanderheiden (Eds.), *International handbook of love: Transcultural and transdisciplinary perspectives* (pp. 1–22). Springer Nature.

Gandhi, A., Adhvaryu, K., Poria, S., Cambria, E., & Hussain, A. (2023). Multimodal sentiment analysis: A systematic review of history, datasets, multimodal fusion methods, applications, challenges and future directions. *Information Fusion*, *91*, 424–444.

García-Hernández, R. A., Luna-García, H., Celaya-Padilla, J. M., García-Hernández, A., Reveles-Gómez, L. C., Flores-Chaires, L. A., & Villalba-Condori, K. O. (2024). A systematic literature review of modalities, trends, and limitations in emotion recognition, affective computing, and sentiment analysis. *Applied Sciences*, *14*(16), 7165.

Guo, C., Pleiss, G., Sun, Y., & Weinberger, K. Q. (2017, July). On calibration of modern neural networks. In *International conference on machine learning* (pp. 1321–1330). PMLR.

Harrison, N. A., Kreibig, S. D., & Critchley, H. D. (2013). A two-way road. In J. Armony & P. Vuilleumier (Eds.), *The Cambridge handbook of human affective neuroscience* (pp. 82–106). Cambridge University Press.

Hosseini, S., Yamaghani, M. R., & Poorzaker Arabani, S. (2024). A review of the methods of recognition multimodal emotions in sound, image and text. *International Journal of Applied Operational Research-An Open Access Journal*, *12*(1), 29–41.

Jiang, Y., Li, W., Hossain, M. S., Chen, M., Alelaiwi, A., & Al-Hammadi, M. (2020). A snapshot research and implementation of multimodal information fusion for data-driven emotion recognition. *Information Fusion*, *53*, 209–221.

Juslin, P. N., Laukka, P., & Bänziger, T. (2018). The mirror to our soul? Comparisons of spontaneous and posed vocal expression of emotion. *Journal of Nonverbal Behavior*, *42*(1), 1–40.

Kakuba, S., Poulose, A., & Han, D. S. (2023). Deep learning approaches for bimodal speech emotion recognition: Advancements, challenges, and a multi-learning model. *IEEE Access*, *11*, 113769–113789.

Katirai, A. (2024). Ethical considerations in emotion recognition technologies: a review of the literature. *AI and Ethics*, *4*(4), 927–948.

Koelstra, S., Muhl, C., Soleymani, M., Lee, J. S., Yazdani, A., Ebrahimi, T., & Patras, I. (2011). Deap: A database for emotion analysis; Using physiological signals. *IEEE Transactions on Affective Computing*, *3*(1), 18–31.

Koromilas, P., & Giannakopoulos, T. (2021). Deep multimodal emotion recognition on human speech: A review. *Applied Sciences*, *11*(17), 7962.

Kovač, N., Ratković, K., Farahani, H., & Watson, P. (2024). A practical applications guide to machine learning regression models in psychology with Python. *Methods in Psychology*, *11*, 100156.

Kovač, N., Ratković, K., Farahani, H., & Watson, P. (2025a). Machine learning regression models for internal shame. *Acta Psychologica*, *260*, 105721.

Kovač, N., Ratković, K., Watson, P., Farahani, H., & Bagheri Sheykhangafshe, F. (2025b). Machine learning classification models for predicting chronic pain. *Current Psychology*, 1–14. Advance online publication.

Kragel, P. A., & LaBar, K. S. (2016). Decoding the nature of emotion in the brain. *Trends in Cognitive Sciences*, *20*(6), 444–455.

Le, H. D., Lee, G. S., Kim, S. H., Kim, S., & Yang, H. J. (2023). Multi-label multimodal emotion recognition with transformer-based fusion and emotion-level representation learning. *IEEE Access*, *11*, 14742–14751.

Leong, S. C., Tang, Y. M., Lai, C. H., & Lee, C. K. M. (2023). Facial expression and body gesture emotion recognition: A systematic review on the use of visual data in affective computing. *Computer Science Review*, *48*, 100545.

Li, X. (2025, March). Enhancing Video Based Emotion Recognition with Multi-Head Attention and Modality Dropout. In *CONF-MLA 2024: Proceedings of the 2nd International Conference on Machine Learning and Automation, CONF-MLA 2024, November 21, 2024, Adana, Turkey* (p. 133). European Alliance for Innovation.

Lian, H., Lu, C., Li, S., Zhao, Y., Tang, C., & Zong, Y. (2023a). A survey of deep learning-based multimodal emotion recognition: Speech, text, and face. *Entropy*, *25*(10), 1440.

Lian, H., Lu, C., Li, S., Zhao, Y., Tang, C., & Zong, Y. (2023b). A survey of deep learning-based multimodal emotion recognition: Speech, text, and face. *Entropy*, *25*(10), 1440.

Liu, W., Qiu, J. L., Zheng, W. L., & Lu, B. L. (2021). Comparing recognition performance and robustness of multimodal deep learning models for multimodal emotion recognition. *IEEE Transactions on Cognitive and Developmental Systems*, *14*(2), 715–729.

Mauss, I. B., & Robinson, M. D. (2009). Measures of emotion: A review. *Cognition and Emotion*, *23*(2), 209–237.

Mesquita, B., Boiger, M., & De Leersnyder, J. (2017). Doing emotions: The role of culture in everyday emotions. *European Review of Social Psychology*, *28*(1), 95–133.

Miranda-Correa, J. A., Abadi, M. K., Sebe, N., & Patras, I. (2018). Amigos: A dataset for affect, personality and mood research on individuals and groups. *IEEE Transactions on Affective Computing*, *12*(2), 479–493.

Montero Quispe, K. G., Utyiama, D. M., Dos Santos, E. M., Oliveira, H. A., & Souto, E. J. (2022). Applying self-supervised representation learning for emotion recognition using physiological signals. *Sensors*, *22*(23), 9102.

Pan, B., Hirota, K., Jia, Z., & Dai, Y. (2023). A review of multimodal emotion recognition from datasets, preprocessing, features, and fusion methods. *Neurocomputing*, *561*, 126866.

Pillalamarri, R., & Shanmugam, U. (2025). A review on EEG-based multimodal learning for emotion recognition. *Artificial Intelligence Review*, *58*(5), 131.

Platt, J. (1999). Probabilistic outputs for support vector machines and comparisons to regularized likelihood methods. *Advances in Large Margin Classifiers*, *10*(3), 61–74.

Ramaswamy, M. P. A., & Palaniswamy, S. (2024). Multimodal emotion recognition: A comprehensive review, trends, and challenges. *Wiley Interdisciplinary Reviews: Data Mining and Knowledge Discovery*, *14*(6), e1563.

Ringeval, F., Sonderegger, A., Sauer, J., & Lalanne, D. (2013, April). Introducing the RECOLA multimodal corpus of remote collaborative and affective interactions. In *2013 10th IEEE international conference and workshops on automatic face and gesture recognition (FG)* (pp. 1–8). IEEE.

Rouast, P. V., Adam, M. T., & Chiong, R. (2019). Deep learning for human affect recognition: Insights and new developments. *IEEE Transactions on Affective Computing*, *12*(2), 524–543.

Scherer, K. R. (2009). The dynamic architecture of emotion: Evidence for the component process model. *Cognition and Emotion*, *23*(7), 1307–1351.

Shu, L., Xie, J., Yang, M., Li, Z., Li, Z., Liao, D., & Yang, X. (2018). A review of emotion recognition using physiological signals. *Sensors*, *18*(7), 2074.

Soleymani, M., Lichtenauer, J., Pun, T., & Pantic, M. (2011). A multimodal database for affect recognition and implicit tagging. *IEEE Transactions on Affective Computing*, *3*(1), 42–55.

Touvron, H., Cord, M., Douze, M., Massa, F., Sablayrolles, A., & Jégou, H. (2021, July). Training data-efficient image transformers & distillation through attention. In *International conference on machine learning* (pp. 10347–10357). PMLR.

Tsai, Y. H. H., Bai, S., Liang, P. P., Kolter, J. Z., Morency, L. P., & Salakhutdinov, R. (2019, July). Multimodal transformer for unaligned multimodal language sequences. In *Proceedings of the conference. Association for computational linguistics. Meeting* (Vol. 2019, p. 6558).

Udahemuka, G., Djouani, K., & Kurien, A. M. (2024). Multimodal Emotion Recognition using visual, vocal and Physiological Signals: a review. *Applied Sciences*, *14*(17), 8071.

Weng, H. Y., Feldman, J. L., Leggio, L., Napadow, V., Park, J., & Price, C. J. (2021). Interventions and manipulations of interoception. *Trends in Neurosciences*, *44*(1), 52–62.

Wolpert, D. H. (1992). Stacked generalization. *Neural Networks*, *5*(2), 241–259.

Wu, Y., Mi, Q., & Gao, T. (2025). A comprehensive review of multimodal emotion recognition: Techniques, challenges, and future directions. *Biomimetics*, *10*(7), 418.

Yoon, S., & Kim, B. (2025). Multi-scale temporal fusion network for real-time multimodal emotion recognition in IoT environments. *Sensors*, *25*(16), 5066.

Zadeh, A. B., Liang, P. P., Poria, S., Cambria, E., & Morency, L. P. (2018, July). Multimodal language analysis in the wild: Cmu-mosei dataset and interpretable dynamic fusion graph. In *Proceedings of the 56th Annual Meeting of the Association for Computational Linguistics (Volume 1: Long Papers)* (pp. 2236–2246).

Zadeh, A., Chen, M., Poria, S., Cambria, E., & Morency, L. P. (2017). Tensor fusion network for multimodal sentiment analysis. *arXiv preprint arXiv:1707.07250*.

Zadrozny, B., & Elkan, C. (2002, July). Transforming classifier scores into accurate multiclass probability estimates. In *Proceedings of the eighth ACM*

SIGKDD international conference on Knowledge discovery and data mining (pp. 694–699).

Zhang, S., Yang, Y., Chen, C., Zhang, X., Leng, Q., & Zhao, X. (2024). Deep learning-based multimodal emotion recognition from audio, visual, and text modalities: A systematic review of recent advancements and future prospects. *Expert Systems with Applications*, *237*, 121692.

Zhao, F., Zhang, C., & Geng, B. (2024). Deep multimodal data fusion. *ACM Computing Surveys*, *56*(9), 1–36.

Zhao, K., Zheng, M., Li, Q., & Liu, J. (2025). Multimodal sentiment analysis: A comprehensive survey from a fusion methods perspective. *IEEE Access*, *13*, 64556–64583.

9 Unsupervised Learning for Embodied Emotion Discovery

Nataša Kovač, Hojjatollah Farahani, and Peter Watson

9.1 Introduction

Understanding human emotion is inherently complex. Emotional expressions emerge through intricate physiological patterns, subtle behavioural changes, nuanced textual expressions, and dynamic voice variations. As explored in previous chapters, supervised machine learning methods (algorithms trained explicitly on labelled emotional data) are powerful yet limited by the inherent need for extensive and accurately labelled datasets (Calvo & D'Mello, 2010). However, the process of labelling emotional states is subjective, labour-intensive, and sometimes inaccurate due to cultural variations, subjective judgements, and ambiguous emotional boundaries.

Unsupervised learning, in contrast, offers a novel avenue for embodied emotion discovery, bypassing the constraints of labelled datasets by enabling algorithms to explore and uncover hidden emotional structures directly from the raw data itself. Unlike supervised learning, unsupervised methods allow researchers to reveal natural groupings, subtle emotional distinctions, and unique physiological signatures without predefined emotion categories or labels (Hastie et al., 2009).

Unsupervised learning has emerged as an essential methodological paradigm in the exploration of embodied emotional phenomena, allowing researchers to uncover latent patterns within multimodal behavioural and physiological data without relying on predefined emotional labels. In the context of affective science and computational psychology, *embodied emotion* refers to the dynamic coupling between bodily states, perceptual feedback, and internal affective experiences. Traditional supervised machine learning paradigms, which depend heavily on labelled datasets reflecting subjective human annotation schemes, often impose rigid categorical frameworks, such as discrete emotions or continuous affective dimensions, that may obscure the complex, context-dependent nature of emotional embodiment. Conversely, unsupervised learning algorithms enable the discovery of emergent emotional structures by directly engaging with high-dimensional sensor data, including posture, movement dynamics, muscle activation patterns, facial micro-expressions, heart rate variability, and electrodermal activity. Through clustering, dimensionality reduction, and manifold learning approaches, unsupervised

DOI: 10.4324/9781003495123-9

systems can infer latent affective topologies that correspond to embodied states of arousal, valence, and motivational orientation, for example, techniques such as Gaussian mixture modelling, t-distributed stochastic neighbour embedding, and autoencoder networks, which allow the extraction of compact, interpretable representations of multimodal emotion-related data. The resulting low-dimensional embeddings capture relational patterns among bodily signals and afford the identification of implicit emotional prototypes that are not bound to preexisting psychological taxonomies. Additionally, more recent advances in deep unsupervised learning, e.g., variational autoencoders, contrastive learning frameworks, and diffusion-based generative models, further enhance the capacity to model nonlinear temporal dependencies and subtle intersubject variations in embodied expression. These models offer the possibility of formulating a data-driven cartography of emotional embodiment, where emotions are conceptualised as dynamic attractor states within sensorimotor and interoceptive spaces rather than as static categorical entities (Kingma & Welling, 2013; van der Maaten & Hinton, 2008). Integrating unsupervised learning with embodied emotion research also necessitates a shift in epistemological stance. Rather than treating emotion as an internal variable to be inferred from external behaviour, unsupervised algorithms approach emotion as an emergent property of coordinated bodily and contextual processes. This view aligns with inactivist and constructivist perspectives in affective neuroscience, which argue that emotions are enacted through bodily regulation and environmental engagement (Seth & Tsakiris, 2018; Barrett, 2017). When embodied data, such as motion capture trajectories or physiological oscillations, are subjected to unsupervised feature extraction, the emergent dimensions often map onto psychophysiological processes that underlie affective experience, such as autonomic synchrony, reactive motor readiness, or interoceptive awareness. Revealing these latent organisational principles, unsupervised learning provides a computational bridge between neural, bodily, and experiential components of emotion (Levenson, 2014). Moreover, the integration of unsupervised methods into embodied emotion holds significant implications for cross-cultural and developmental research. These models can identify population-specific or context-dependent structures of affective embodiment because they don't presuppose culturally biased emotion categories. In developmental contexts, unsupervised analysis of infants' or children's movement and physiological data can uncover prelinguistic affective patterns that precede the acquisition of explicit emotional concepts (Zhang et al., 2023). Similarly, in clinical applications, unsupervised learning can detect atypical emotional coordination patterns in disorders of affect regulation, such as depression, anxiety, or autism spectrum conditions, thus offering diagnostic and therapeutic insights grounded in embodied signal dynamics rather than subjective report (Kragel et al., 2016). Ultimately, unsupervised learning for embodied emotion represents an epistemic and methodological convergence between data-driven modelling and embodied cognition theory. By relinquishing the dependence on human-labelled emotion corpora, this approach opens a pathway towards understanding emotion as a distributed, emergent, and adaptive phenomenon, one that can be quantitatively described yet remains deeply grounded in bodily action and perception. The challenge moving forward lies in developing interpretability frameworks that translate the abstract representations generated by unsupervised models into psychologically meaningful constructs, thereby maintaining empirical rigour while respecting the complexity of embodied emotional life (Barsade & Gibson, 2012; Seth & Tsakiris, 2018).

This chapter focuses deeply on exploring unsupervised methods, demonstrating how these techniques powerfully enhance emotional AI research, offering fresh insights and uncovering new emotional phenomena previously undetectable through traditional methods. By learning directly from the inherent structure and patterns in physiological, behavioural, and textual signals, unsupervised algorithms can identify natural clusters of emotional experiences, delineate subtle emotional distinctions, and help generate entirely new emotional taxonomies aligned closely with actual human emotional experiences (Mehta et al., 2019).

In the forthcoming sections, readers will navigate step-by-step through essential preparations for unsupervised emotional discovery, delve into powerful unsupervised learning algorithms, and apply these methods practically across key emotional modalities such as EEG signals, image analysis, text data, and audio signals. By embracing unsupervised learning methodologies, researchers and practitioners can more fully uncover and understand the embodied nature of emotional experience, shedding new light on the intricate emotional landscape inherent to human cognition, physiology, and social interaction.

The journey begins by carefully preparing the ground for unsupervised analysis, identifying optimal preprocessing techniques, and laying a robust methodological foundation, before advancing into diverse applications that illustrate the power and versatility of unsupervised emotion exploration. Throughout this exploration, practical Python examples, clear visualisations, methodological insights, and careful ethical considerations will guide readers to confidently apply unsupervised techniques to their research and applications.

9.2 Preparing the Ground for Unsupervised Embodied Emotion Exploration

Unsupervised embodied–emotion analysis starts with stable, label-free representations that already encode affective regularities in speech, vision, text, and physiology. Self-supervised encoders are the practical backbone here:

emotion2vec for speech, DINOv2 for images, SBERT for text, and MNE-centric pipelines for EEG (Gramfort et al., 2013) that preserve physiologically meaningful variance before any clustering. These choices reduce reliance on annotation and improve generalisation across speakers, cameras, and sessions (Ma et al., 2023).

Benchmark datasets help align discovery with human judgements without driving the learning step itself. IEMOCAP (Busso et al., 2008) is widely used for speech and dyadic interaction. RAVDESS (Livingstone & Russo, 2018) provides carefully controlled audio-visual expressions, AffectNet (Mollahosseini et al., 2017) brings large-scale in-the-wild faces with both categorical and dimensional labels, and DEAP (Koelstra et al., 2011) integrates EEG with peripheral physiology under controlled stimuli. Using these sets for evaluation only keeps the exploration label-agnostic while enabling later triangulation.

EEG preparation benefits from standardised routines. The PREP pipeline (Bigdely-Shamlo et al., 2015) automates referencing and line-noise handling at scale, and independent component analysis remains a reliable method for ocular (Jung et al., 2000) and muscle artefact separation. Open tools in MNE-Python make these steps reproducible and transparent in research reports. Multimodal studies need accurate timing. When audio, video, and EEG are recorded on different devices, clock drift can mask true relations between channels. The Lab Streaming Layer provides per-sample timestamps, offset correction, and low-jitter synchronisation, which preserves the temporal structure that unsupervised discovery uses (Kothe et al., 2025).

Feature backbones should be compact and consistent across modalities. Wav2vec 2.0 and HuBERT (Hsu et al., 2021) remain strong general speech encoders, while emotion2vec focuses directly on affect transfer. DINOv2 (Oquab et al, 2023) yields robust visual features for frames or clips without labels, and SBERT (Reimers & Gurevych, 2019) provides sentence-level vectors that support topic and affect discovery in text. Standardising these representations and concatenating them into a single table prepares the ground for geometry and density analysis (Baevski et al., 2020).

Geometry and density must match the data. If the embedding space already separates affective neighbourhoods, partitions such as K-means are adequate and easy to report. When states are interleaved and uneven, HDBSCAN (Campello et al., 2020) identifies dense cores and flags noise instead of forcing every sample into a group. For visualisation without labels, UMAP preserves local neighbourhoods and often reveals smooth affective trajectories (McInnes et al., 2018). Multi-site or mixed-device studies can introduce batch effects that dominate unsupervised patterns. Recent EEG work demonstrates that ComBat-style harmonisation can reduce between-site artefacts in spectral features while preserving biological associations, thereby allowing clusters to reflect behaviour rather than hardware (Jaramillo-Jimenez et al., 2024).

Ethical preparation is part of the method. Contemporary analyses document demographic and domain biases in facial and speech emotion systems and call for fairness-aware evaluation, especially when models are trained or assessed with unbalanced datasets. In parallel, privacy-preserving strategies for affect recognition are moving forward with federated and differentially private methods for physiological and audio-visual signals (Sajjad et al., 2023).

Methodologically, the documentation standards you use in supervised psychology carry over directly to the unsupervised stage. Clear data preparation, diagnostics, and artefact sharing keep the subsequent interpretation of latent states defensible when linked to constructs such as internal shame or chronic pain (Kovač et al., 2024, 2025a, 2025b). This continuity supports transparent pipelines from discovery to inference.

Figure 9.1 illustrates the first visual check researchers typically perform. A two-component PCA projection of standardised multimodal features is coloured by K-means assignments, which reveals whether compact neighbourhoods exist before any sophisticated manifold analysis. When clusters appear in this view, analysts gain confidence that later density or graph-based methods will refine structure rather than create it.

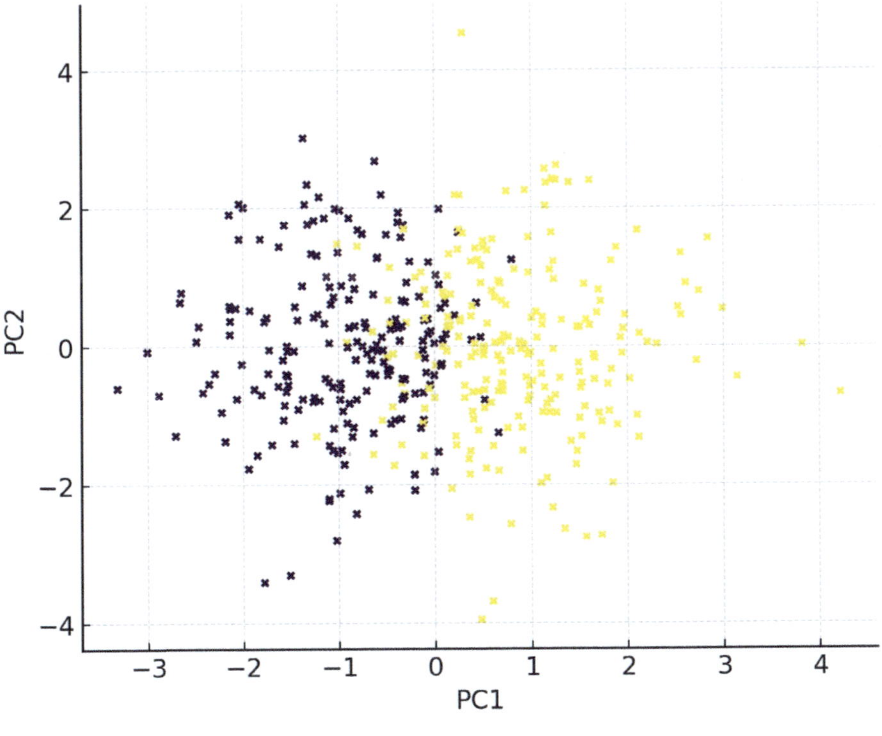

Figure 9.1 PCA projection of multimodal features with K-means clusters.

Model parsimony follows next. Figure 9.2 shows the elbow curve of within-cluster sum of squares as K increases. The bend indicates diminishing returns, which is useful when the goal is to keep the affect map interpretable for clinical or behavioural reporting. Selecting the smallest K near the elbow keeps the representation compact without sacrificing major structure.

Separation and cohesion should also be quantified. Figure 9.3 plots the silhouette across K, summarising how well samples match their own cluster compared to the nearest alternative. This diagnostic is quick to compute and helps guard against overly fine partitions that appear neat visually but have weak internal consistency (Rousseeuw, 1987).

Preparation choices by modality are summarised in Table 9.1 The emphasis is on compact features and encoders that are stable across datasets, which reduces the risk that unsupervised structure reflects device quirks rather than behaviour. For EEG, the table highlights a practical sequence that many teams adopt before clustering. For speech and vision, the listed encoders have shown strong transfer even without labels. For text, sentence-level vectors remain the most dependable starting point.

Reproducibility is helped by a concise checklist, presented in Table 9.2, that you can attach to preregistrations or method appendices. The steps run from standardisation and visualisation to model selection and device

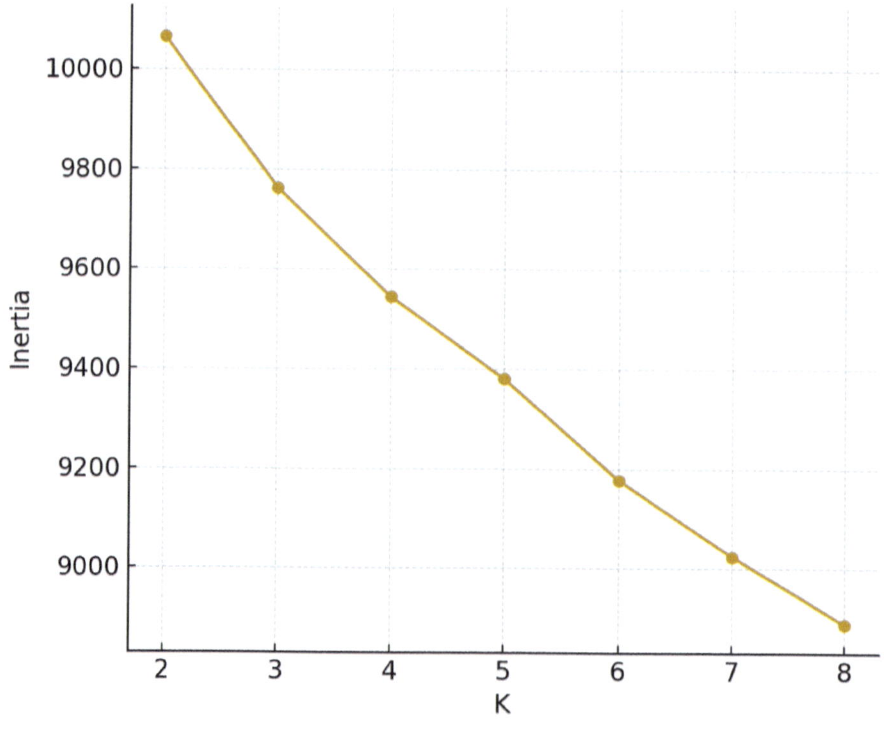

Figure 9.2 Elbow curve of the within-cluster sum of squares across K.

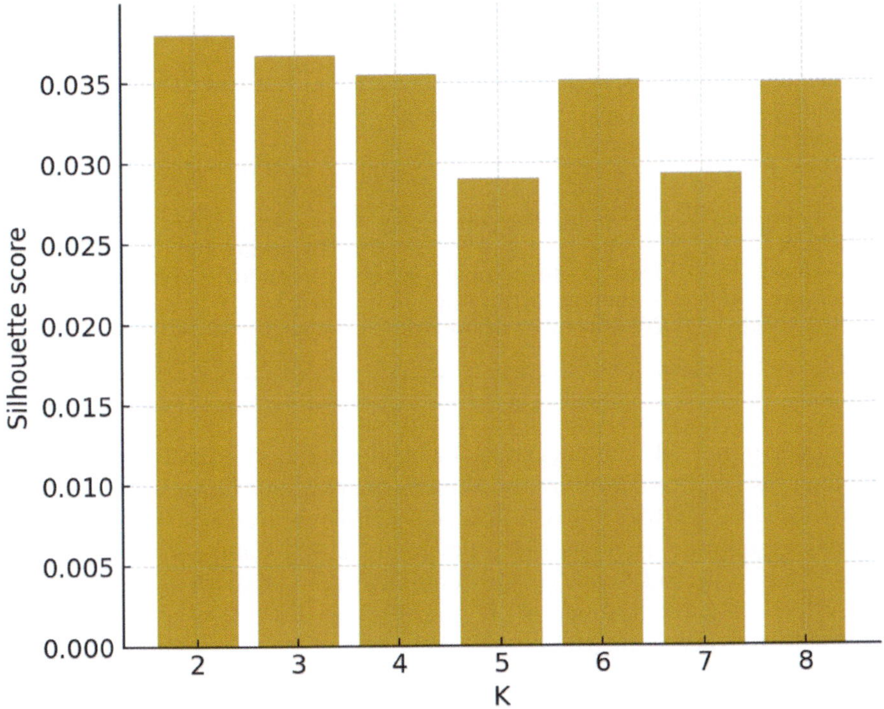

Figure 9.3 Silhouette scores across K for quick partition diagnostics.

Table 9.1 Modalities, compact feature choices, and encoder suggestions.

Modality	*Compact features in practice*	*Encoder or recipe*
Speech	Utterance embeddings pooled from frames	emotion2vec for affect transfer (Ma et al., 2023); wav2vec-2.0 or HuBERT for general features (Hsu et al., 2021).
EEG	Band powers, connectivity, and short spatiotemporal blocks	PREP → ICA → features in MNE-Python; consider self-supervised learning (SSL) pretraining before clustering (Bigdely-Shamlo et al., 2015).
Faces	Frame or clip features with identity suppression	DINOv2 for universal visual embeddings that cluster well without labels (Oquab et al, 2023).
Text	Sentence vectors and topic footprints	SBERT embeddings with topic discovery when needed (Reimers & Gurevych, 2019).

Table 9.2 Quick checklist for reproducible preparation.

Step	*Rationale*	*Typical tool*
Standardize features	Comparable scales across modalities	StandardScaler
Visualize geometry	Early neighbourhood sanity check	PCA or UMAP (McInnes et al., 2018)
Pick K or choose density	Match model to shape of data	K-means vs. HDBSCAN (Campello et al., 2020)
Synchronize streams	Preserve cross-modal timing	Lab Streaming Layer (Kothe et al., 2025)
Control batch effects	Prevent site or device drift	ComBat for EEG features (Jaramillo-Jimenez et al., 2024)

harmonisation. UMAP is suggested for neighbourhood visualisation because it preserves local structure in two dimensions without imposing linear constraints, while HDBSCAN is a practical density option when data contain sparse episodes or artefacts (McInnes et al., 2018; Campello et al., 2020). Synchronisation and batch control complete the list so that temporal and site effects do not masquerade as emotion structure (Kothe et al., 2025; Jaramillo-Jimenez et al., 2024).

9.3 Learning Algorithms in Embodied Emotion Detection

Partitioning methods are often the first stop once multimodal embeddings are reasonably well separated, because compact regions in a standardised space map cleanly to affective *neighbourhoods* that practitioners can inspect and name (McQueen, 1967). Gaussian mixtures extend this idea with probabilistic membership, which handles gradual transitions between states that are common in spontaneous affective behaviour and psychotherapy sessions (Dempster, Laird, & Rubin, 1977; Bishop & Nasrabadi, 2006). Model selection can remain parsimonious by using penalised criteria when deciding the number of components so that clusters convey structure without overfitting (Schwarz, 1978).

This geometric picture is visible in Figure 9.4, where K-means partitions a dataset into three compact groups while ignoring subtle curvature. The same experiment, summarised by the silhouette curve in Figure 9.5, shows how a quick validity check can guide the number of partitions before any interpretation with domain experts (Rousseeuw, 1987; Caliński & Harabasz, 1974; Davies & Bouldin, 2009).

When embodied states are uneven or interleaved, density-based discovery is usually more faithful to the data. DBSCAN identifies dense cores and leaves ambiguous points unlabelled, which is practical in in-the-wild logs where artefacts and rare episodes coexist (Ester et al., 1996). HDBSCAN

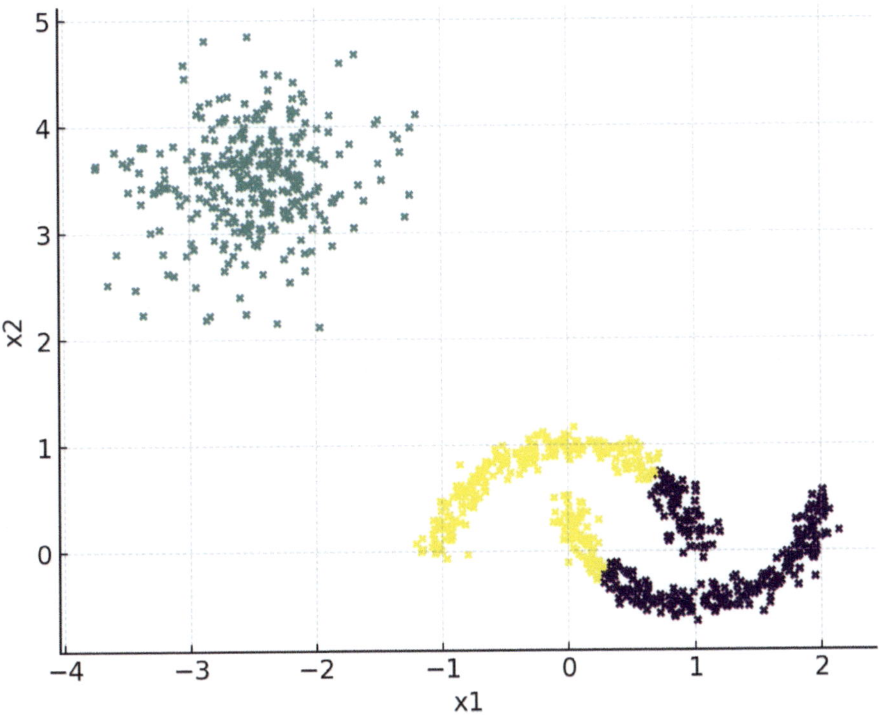

Figure 9.4 K-means on a mixed-geometry synthetic dataset (K=3): compact partitions despite non-convex structure.

generalises to variable densities and selects clusters that are stable across scales, which tends to produce more consistent segments for speech prosody, micro-expressions, or EEG bursts (Campello et al., 2013; McInnes et al., 2017). The contrast is visible in Figure 9.6, where the non-convex moon-shaped structure emerges naturally under DBSCAN while noise points remain isolated.

Graph-based perspectives are useful when latent affect lies on a manifold shaped by articulation, facial dynamics, or neural synchrony. Spectral clustering discovers communities from the Laplacian of a similarity graph and is known to recover non-linear boundaries that partitioning cannot capture (Ng et al., 2001; von Luxburg, 2007). Closely related constructions turn neighbourhoods into coordinates. Laplacian Eigenmaps and Diffusion Maps embed samples along smooth trajectories, which often align with arousal ramps, regulation cycles, or appraisal shifts (Belkin & Niyogi, 2003; Coifman & Lafon, 2006). Kernel PCA remains a classical alternative when feature maps are easier to encode than explicit graphs (Schölkopf et al., 1998). Modern practice frequently uses UMAP to visualise these neighbourhoods

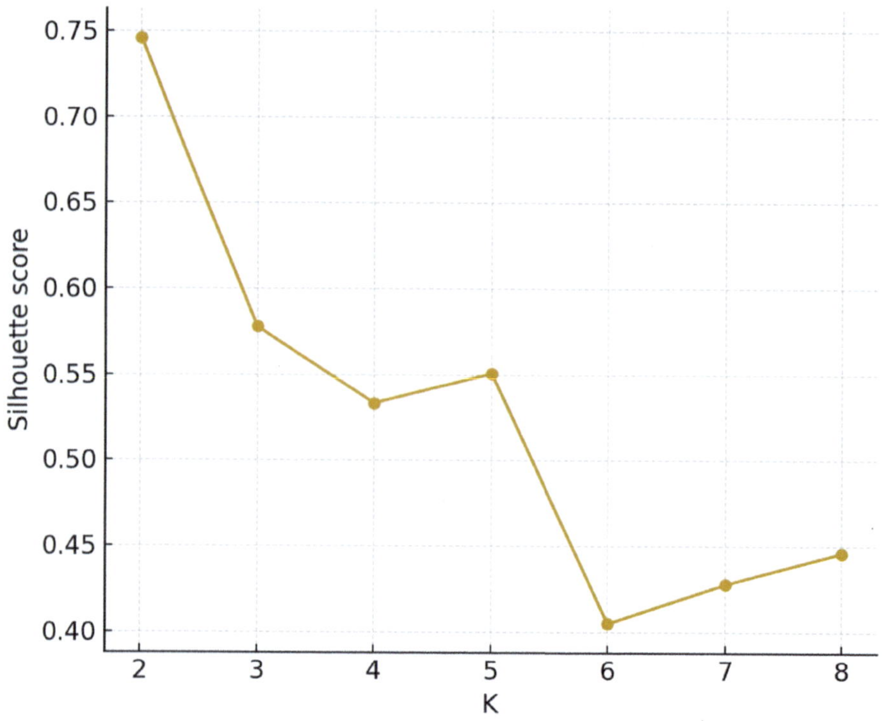

Figure 9.5 Silhouette score across K (2–8): a quick diagnostic for selecting the number of partitions.

while delegating clustering to a separate step to avoid confounding geometry with grouping (McInnes et al., 2018).

Deep clustering couples representation learning with grouping so that the feature space itself becomes more cluster-friendly. Deep Embedded Clustering refines an encoder using a soft assignment objective that pulls similar samples together and spreads clusters apart (Xie et al., 2016). Variational Deep Embedding combines a variational autoencoder with a mixture model to produce latent variables that are both generative and cluster-aware, an advantage when analysts later need counterfactual samples or uncertainty assessments (Jiang et al., 2016). In computer vision, self-labelling approaches use clusters as supervision to iteratively improve the backbone, which has proven effective for expression-like features in large, unlabelled corpora (Caron et al., 2018; Caron et al., 2020).

Temporal structure should be acknowledged because embodied emotion unfolds as episodes. A practical approach separates dynamics from geometry by detecting changepoints first and then clustering within segments, which reduces the burden on any single algorithm to capture both time and shape

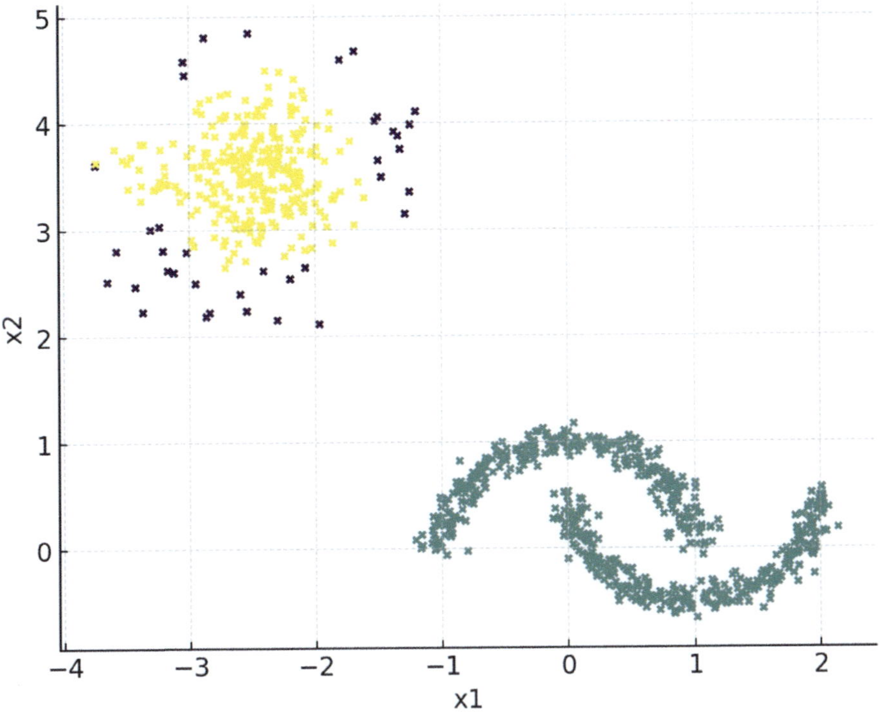

Figure 9.6 DBSCAN on the same dataset: recovery of non-convex clusters with explicit noise isolation.

(Truong et al., 2020). Bayesian online schemes or optimal partitioning methods provide additional options when near real-time decisions are required (Adams & MacKay, 2007; Killick et al., 2012). It has become central when data are sensitive or interventions must not degrade user well-being, since segmentation allows the system to abstain or defer decisions in ambiguous intervals (Farahani et al., 2024). Taken together, the families below serve complementary roles. Table 9.3 positions each algorithm in terms of assumptions, strengths, and caveats, which facilitates transparent preregistration. Table 9.4 lists internal indices that help select models without labels.

Table 9.5 distils pragmatic heuristics that align with real constraints in psychology labs and clinics. In translational settings, these choices can be integrated with supervised outcomes and theory, as demonstrated by recent cross-domain applications linking latent structure to complex constructs in mental health and interpersonal functioning (Farahani et al., 2025) and by methodologically careful pipelines used in predictive modelling (Kovač et al., 2025a).

Table 9.3 Algorithm families for embodied emotion discovery.

Family	*Core assumption*	*Typical use in affect data*	*Strengths*	*Caveats*
K-means	Globular clusters in Euclidean space	Clean, well-separated SSL embeddings	Fast and readable	Needs K and standardization (McQueen, 1967)
Gaussian mixtures (EM)	Mixture densities with soft membership	Overlapping states with gradual transitions	Uncertainty and flexible shapes	Risk of spurious components, select K with BIC (Dempster et al., 1977; Schwarz, 1978; Bishop & Nasrabadi)
DBSCAN	Dense regions separated by sparse areas	In-the-wild episodes with artefacts	No K, handles noise	Parameter sensitivity to scale (Ester et al., 1996)
HDBSCAN	Variable densities across clusters	Multimodal logs with rare states	Stable clusters across scales	Requires similarity choices (Campello et al., 2013; McInnes et al., 2017)
Spectral clustering	Manifold communities via Laplacian	Smooth affect trajectories	Non-linear boundaries	Graph construction is critical (Ng et al., 2001; von Luxburg, 2007)
Diffusion geometry	Heat-kernel neighbourhoods	Gradual affective progressions	Interpretable coordinates	Kernel and scale choices matter (Coifman & Lafon, 2006)
Deep clustering (DEC, VaDE)	Features and clusters co-learned	Large multimodal sets with weak labels	State-of-the-art transfer	Training stability and compute (Xie et al., 2016; Jiang et al., 2016)
Self-labelling vision (DeepCluster, SwAV)	Clusters drive backbone training	Expression features without labels	Scales to millions of samples	Careful augmentation design (Caron et al., 2018; Caron et al., 2020)

Table 9.4 Internal validity indices commonly used during method selection.

Index	*What it measures*	*When it shines*
Silhouette	Cohesion versus separation per point	Quick triage of K in partitions (Rousseeuw, 1987)
Calinski–Harabasz	Between to within dispersion ratio	Comparing many K on standardized features (Caliński & Harabasz, 1974)
Davies–Bouldin	Average similarity between clusters	Penalizing overlapping, diffuse clusters (Davies & Bouldin, 2009)

Table 9.5 Pragmatic selection heuristics.

Situation	*Prefer*	*Rationale*
SSL embeddings already separate well	K-means or GMM	Simpler models suffice; soft labels enable graded states
Many outliers and rare episodes	HDBSCAN	Labels noise explicitly and adapts to variable density
Non-linear boundaries and smooth progressions	Spectral or diffusion geometry	Captures manifold structure and temporal continuity
Very large unlabelled corpora	DeepCluster or SwAV	Use clusters as supervision to shape the encoder
Long sequences with regime shifts	Changepoint plus within-segment clustering	Factors dynamics from geometry for clearer interpretation (Truong et al., 2020)

9.4 Embodied Emotion Detection by Unsupervised EEG Signal Analysis

Unsupervised discovery with EEG starts long before clustering: the physics of the sensor, the low SNR, and cross-subject variability make early, standardised preprocessing a scientific necessity. A practical baseline is to combine automated referencing and line-noise handling with artefact separation, keeping every step reproducible and reportable (Bigdely-Shamlo et al., 2015; Gramfort et al., 2013). In practice, this means PREP-style early processing, then common average reference (or a robust variant), notch and band-pass filtering, and ICA for ocular and myogenic components, all logged in a pipeline that can be re-run on future cohorts.

The following Python code illustrates the minimal MNE-centric preprocessing for unsupervised learning. This code captures a reproducible baseline, filtering, average referencing, ICA cleanup, and short overlapping epochs, without entangling discovery with labels (Bigdely-Shamlo et al., 2015; Gramfort et al., 2013).

```
# Goal: produce clean epochs ready for unsupervised features.
import mne

raw = mne.io.read_raw_fif("subject_raw.fif", preload=True)
raw.notch_filter([50, 100])          # or 60 Hz depending on locale
raw.filter(1., 45., phase="zero-double")      # affect-friendly passband
raw.set_eeg_reference("average")          # robust CAR

ica = mne.preprocessing.ICA(n_components=20, random_state=97)
ica.fit(raw.copy().filter(1., None))
ica.detect_artifacts(raw, eog_ch=["HEO","VEO"]) # or use correlation templates
raw_clean = ica.apply(raw)

events = mne.make_fixed_length_events(raw_clean, duration=2.0, overlap=1.0)
epochs = mne.Epochs(raw_clean, events, tmin=0.0, tmax=2.0, baseline=None, preload=True)

# 'epochs' is now ready for spectral, covariance, or SSL embeddings.
```

After cleaning, the aim is a representation that respects EEG's spatial structure while remaining friendly to unsupervised geometry and density. Two families dominate. The first summarises spectral content to capture arousal-like and engagement-like variation without labels. The second summarises spatial structure via channel covariance: symmetric positive definite (SPD) matrices that encode how sensors co-fluctuate; mapping these matrices to a Riemannian tangent space yields Euclidean features amenable to clustering and manifold learning (Barachant et al., 2012; Yger et al., 2016). Tooling such as *pyRiemann* standardises this SPD-to-tangent workflow so you can reuse it across studies with minimal code (Barachant et al., 2022).

Connectivity features add a complementary lens when you expect coordinated network behaviour during emotion induction. Phase-based measures such as the phase-locking value (PLV) or phase slope index summarise frequency-specific synchrony; coherence variants capture magnitude-phase relations. These tools are powerful but require careful interpretation because volume conduction, filtering, and reference choices can bias apparent coupling (Bastos & Schoffelen, 2016; Chiarion et al., 2023). For unsupervised discovery, a pragmatic approach is to compute a compact panel, e.g., PLV in theta/alpha between a handful of regions of interest, and concatenate with bandpower or tangent-space features before clustering. A small panel (log-bandpower per channel and a targeted PLV) is shown in the Python code below. It offers an interpretable structure that plays well with unsupervised algorithms, while acknowledging the interpretational caveats of connectivity in EEG (Bastos & Schoffelen, 2016; Chiarion et al., 2023).

```
# Goal: compute per-epoch bandpower and a small PLV panel
between ROIs.
import numpy as np
from scipy.signal import welch, hilbert

sfreq = epochs.info["sfreq"]
data = epochs.get_data() # (n_epochs, n_channels, n_times)

# 1) Log-bandpower (theta 4-8 Hz, alpha 8-12 Hz, beta 13-30 Hz)
def bandpower(x, fs, fmin, fmax):
    f, Pxx = welch(x, fs=fs, nperseg=int(fs*1.0))
    idx = (f >= fmin) & (f <= fmax)
    return np.log(Pxx[..., idx].mean())


bp = []
for ep in data:
    bp.append([
        bandpower(ep[ch], sfreq, 4, 8),
        bandpower(ep[ch], sfreq, 8, 12),
        bandpower(ep[ch], sfreq, 13, 30)
    ] for ch in range(ep.shape[0]))
bp = np.array([np.ravel(x) for x in bp])

# 2) Simple PLV between two ROI averages in alpha band
roi1, roi2 = [0,1,2,3], [20,21,22,23]
def band_hilbert(ep, fs, fmin, fmax):
    # narrowband via FFT or IIR (omitted for brevity), then
analytic signal
    x = ep # assume prefiltered
    return hilbert(x, axis=-1)


plvs = []
for ep in data:
    s1 = ep[roi1].mean(axis=0)
    s2 = ep[roi2].mean(axis=0)
    a1 = band_hilbert(s1, sfreq, 8, 12)
    a2 = band_hilbert(s2, sfreq, 8, 12)
    phase_diff = np.angle(a1) - np.angle(a2)
    plv = np.abs(np.exp(1j*phase_diff)).mean()
    plvs.append(plv)

# Concatenate bandpower and PLV into a compact feature vector
per epoch.
features = np.column_stack([bp, np.array(plvs)[:, None]])
```

A second, intrinsically unsupervised tradition in EEG, microstate analysis, segments continuous data into brief, quasi-stable topographic patterns and studies their sequence statistics. Microstates act like a symbolic alphabet for the brain's ongoing dynamics and can be related, post hoc, to affective conditions or regulation episodes without ever using labels during discovery (Michel & Koenig, 2018; Haydock et al., 2025). While microstate modelling is not a drop-in replacement for feature-space clustering, it offers a complementary viewpoint when the temporal grammar of states is central.

Recent advances show that self-supervised learning (SSL) can pretrain EEG encoders on large unlabelled recordings using masked prediction or contrastive tasks, then expose low-dimensional embeddings for clustering. The effect is practical: cleaner separations and better cross-subject transfer before any labels are introduced (Zhang et al., 2024; see also newer spatial–temporal SSL variants). In effect, these studies allow you to discover latent EEG states, then relate them to behavioural markers, questionnaires, or physiological covariates in a second stage.

Algorithm choice should match the EEG geometry. When tangent-space or SSL embeddings already look well separated, K-means or Gaussian mixtures are adequate and easy to report. When the state space contains rare bursts, artefacts, or uneven dwell times, HDBSCAN excels by finding dense cores while leaving ambiguous samples unlabelled. This is crucial when you prefer abstention over forced assignment in sensitive applications (McInnes et al., 2017). In all cases, cluster in the full feature space; use 2-D projections only for inspection.

Covariance lives on an SPD manifold, while tangent-space mapping preserves geometry while enabling standard clustering. HDBSCAN labels dense EEG states and leaves borderline epochs as noise, which is desirable when you'd rather defer decisions than over-commit (Barachant et al., 2012; McInnes et al., 2017). Illustrative Python code for mapping epoch covariance to tangent space, embedding, then clustering without labels by HDBSCAN is as follows:

```
import numpy as np
from pyriemann.estimation import Covariances
from pyriemann.tangentspace import TangentSpace
from sklearn.preprocessing import StandardScaler
from sklearn.manifold import TSNE
import hdbscan


# epochs.get_data() -> shape (n_epochs, n_channels, n_times)
X = epochs.get_data()
covs = Covariances(estimator="oas").transform(X)


TS   =   TangentSpace().fit(covs).transform(covs)   #   Euclidean
features
Z = StandardScaler().fit_transform(TS)
```

```
# 2-D inspection only (cluster in full Z ideally)
Z2 = TSNE(n_components=2, perplexity=30, random_state=7).
fit_transform(Z)

labels = hdbscan.HDBSCAN(min_cluster_size=25).fit_predict(Z) #
abstains on ambiguous points (-1)
```

Finally, keep the bridge to downstream psychology explicit. Latent EEG states, cluster posteriors, distances to centroids, or dwell-time summaries can enter regression or classification models as structured covariates. This mirrors transparent modelling practices already used in supervised work, while keeping discovery label-agnostic at the outset (Kovač et al., 2025a).

9.5 Embodied Emotion Detection by Unsupervised Image Analysis

Unsupervised image analysis seeks affective structure directly from frames, without relying on expression labels, and then links the discovered states to behaviour or context. The practical starting point is a label-free visual backbone whose embeddings already emphasise content over nuisance factors like pose or lighting. In recent practice, DINOv2 offers robust, out-of-the-box image features that transfer well across datasets and can be clustered with minimal tuning (Oquab et al., 2024).

A persistent challenge is identity leakage: when the embedding space inadvertently clusters by who the person is rather than how they feel. Expression-specific self-supervision helps reduce this problem by shaping features so that local neighbourhoods reflect facial actions and not identity style (Shu et al., 2022). In that spirit, a pragmatic recipe is to extract general features with a strong universal backbone and then adapt with a light, expression-focused self-supervised objective if identity cues dominate (Shu et al., 2022).

Discovery should be divorced from evaluation. For images *in the wild*, AffectNet is a natural target for validation because it spans both categorical labels and continuous valence–arousal ratings at scale (Mollahosseini et al., 2017). For broader diversity and spontaneous footage, Aff-Wild2 adds long, unconstrained videos annotated in continuous space, and it is routinely used for cross-database tests after discovery (Kollias & Zafeiriou, 2018, 2019). RAF-DB complements these with curated, real-world faces and well-documented splits (Li et al., 2017). Using these corpora for *evaluation only* keeps the unsupervised stage clean while offering rigorous checks once clusters are found.

When analysts need interpretable anchors, action units (AUs) remain valuable because they provide a mechanistic lens on facial muscle activations. OpenFace 2.0 exposes AUs, landmarks, and head pose with a transparent pipeline; these signals can be summarised per cluster to name states post hoc without turning the discovery step into supervised learning (Baltrušaitis et al., 2016).

Clustering choices follow geometry. If embeddings already separate well, compact partitions are defensible and easy to report; when data contain rare episodes or ambiguous frames, HDBSCAN tends to recover stable cores and abstain elsewhere, which is often preferable in sensitive applications (McInnes et al., 2017). For visualisation only, UMAP reveals neighbourhoods without imposing linearity; the clustering itself should occur in the full embedding space to avoid projection artefacts (McInnes et al., 2018).

Fairness and privacy belong in the design loop. Facial datasets are not demographically neutral, and model performance can vary by age, gender, or ethnoracial group. Balanced attribute datasets such as FairFace can be used to *assess* representational balance of discovered states or to audit downstream classifiers trained on pseudo-labels (Karkkainen & Joo, 2021). Recent studies document bias patterns specifically in facial expression recognition and provide templates for measurement and mitigation. These steps should be acknowledged even in unsupervised workflows (Sajjad et al., 2023; Domínguez-Catena et al., 2024).

Methodologically, the reporting discipline you apply in supervised psychology (clear preprocessing, explicit hyperparameters, and transparent diagnostics) transfers directly to this unsupervised image setting. That consistency keeps the path from latent image states to psychological interpretation defensible (Kovač et al., 2024). The following code implements a label-free pipeline. DINOv2 extracts features from sampled video frames, and HDBSCAN groups them while leaving ambiguous frames unassigned. UMAP is used only for two-dimensional visualisation, which keeps clustering separate from possible projection distortions (Oquab et al., 2024; McInnes et al., 2017, 2018).

```
# Goal: extract frame embeddings with a universal backbone,
cluster without labels,
# and inspect neighborhoods in 2-D (clustering should happen
in full space).
# Requires: pip install timm umap-learn hdbscan opencv-python
import cv2, glob, numpy as np, torch, timm
from sklearn.preprocessing import StandardScaler
import hdbscan
import umap


# 1) Load frames (e.g., one every 8-10 frames to reduce
redundancy)
def sample_frames(video_path, stride=10, max_frames=512):
    cap, frames = cv2.VideoCapture(video_path), []
    i = 0
    while cap.isOpened() and len(frames) < max_frames:
        ret, frame = cap.read()
        if not ret: break
        if i % stride == 0:
        frames.append(cv2.cvtColor(frame, cv2.COLOR_BGR2RGB))
```

```
        i += 1
    cap.release()
    return frames

frames = sample_frames("session.mp4", stride=10)

# 2) Create DINOv2 model from timm (choose a small/medium ViT
for speed)
device = "cuda" if torch.cuda.is_available() else "cpu"
model = timm.create_model("vit_small_patch14_dinov2.lvd142m",
pretrained=True).to(device).eval()
transform = timm.data.transforms_factory.create_transform(
    input_size=model.default_cfg["input_size"][1],
is_training=False
)

# 3) Compute L2-normalized embeddings
with torch.inference_mode():
    feats = []
    for img in frames:
        x = transform(img).unsqueeze(0).to(device)
        z = model.forward_features(x)
        z = torch.nn.functional.normalize(z.mean(dim=1),
dim=1) # global average
        feats.append(z.squeeze(0).cpu().numpy())
X = np.vstack(feats)

# 4) Unsupervised clustering (density-friendly; abstains on
noise)
Z = StandardScaler().fit_transform(X)
labels = hdbscan.HDBSCAN(min_cluster_size=30).fit_predict(Z)

# 5) 2-D view for inspection only (do not cluster in 2-D)
U = umap.UMAP(n_neighbors=20, min_dist=0.05, random_state=7).
fit_transform(Z)
# Use U[:,0], U[:,1] to make a scatter plot colored by 'labels'.
```

To use this code, replace session.mp4 with your clip or folder of images. The clustering result labels give an integer per frame (with -1 for ambiguous frames), which you can map back to timestamps to visualise episodes. The UMAP coordinates are for sanity-check plots only.

Identity cues can dominate unsupervised image embeddings. Thus, it helps to neutralise static, person-specific style before discovery. The next listing implements a simple within-subject centring step: subtract each individual's mean embedding from their frames, preserving relative expression dynamics while dampening identity and background signatures. In practice, this reduces *who you are* variance and sharpens *how you feel* structure, improving density-based discovery in multi-person corpora; afterwards, you can recover interpretability by summarising cluster-wise action units (AUs) rather than reintroducing labels (Shu et al., 2022; Baltrušaitis et al., 2016). Because demographic imbalance can still imprint on representation quality, auditing clusters across balanced attribute benchmarks remains advisable even with centring (Karkkainen & Joo, 2021; Sajjad et al., 2023).

```
# Goal: reduce identity leakage by removing each person's
embedding mean before clustering.
# Assumes you have person IDs per frame (e.g., from a tracker
or face re-ID).
import numpy as np
from sklearn.preprocessing import StandardScaler
import hdbscan

# X: (n_frames, d) embeddings; person_id: (n_frames,) integers
def within_subject_centering(X, person_id):
    Xc = X.copy()
    for pid in np.unique(person_id):
        idx = np.where(person_id == pid)[0]
        Xc[idx] -= X[idx].mean(axis=0, keepdims=True)
    return Xc

Xc = within_subject_centering(X, person_id) # identity-mean
removed
Z = StandardScaler().fit_transform(Xc)
labels = hdbscan.HDBSCAN(min_cluster_size=30).fit_predict(Z)
```

When you have multiple people in the same recording, subtracting the per-person mean neutralises static identity style while preserving relative expression changes. If AUs are available (e.g., via OpenFace 2.0), compute AU rates per cluster to name the states afterwards without injecting labels into discovery (Baltrušaitis et al., 2016).

9.6 Embodied Emotion Detection by Unsupervised Text Data Analysis

Text offers a rich substrate for embodied emotion because language co-occurs with behaviour, physiology, and context; yet labels are costly and inconsistent. An unsupervised route is therefore attractive: build semantically faithful sentence embeddings, let geometry or density reveal latent themes, and only then map those themes into affective space (e.g., valence–arousal–dominance) for interpretation. In practice, sentence-level encoders such as Sentence-BERT, SimCSE, INSTRUCTOR, and E5 produce robust vectors that transfer across domains without task-specific labels. This is an essential property for diaries, counselling transcripts, or social streams (Reimers & Gurevych, 2019; Gao et al., 2021; Su et al., 2022; Wang et al., 2022).

Once embedded, discovery typically proceeds with modern topic models that **do not** require a preset number of topics and work directly in the continuous space. BERTopic clusters embeddings (often with HDBSCAN/UMAP under the hood) and then uses class-based TF–IDF to label topics; Top2Vec jointly organises words, documents, and topic vectors, letting the corpus determine topic counts automatically (Grootendorst, 2022; Angelov, 2020). Parameter choices (e.g., HDBSCAN min_cluster_size, UMAP n_neighbors) control granularity and interpretability; small adjustments can turn *too many micro-topics* into *stable, nameable themes* (Grootendorst, 2022).

To relate unlabelled themes to affect without turning the pipeline into supervision, a practical step is to project topics into the VAD space. Word-level norms such as Warriner–Kuperman–Brysbaert (2013) and the NRC VAD lexicon provide continuous scores for large vocabularies. Aggregating those over each topic's salient terms yields a rough affective fingerprint useful for naming or ordering topics, e.g., *high arousal / low valence* (Warriner et al., 2013; Mohammad, 2025). This post hoc mapping does not supply labels during discovery; it only guides interpretation and reporting.

When sequences matter, dynamic topic modelling supplies temporal structure, tracking how themes drift, split, or merge over time. Classical Dynamic Topic Models (DTM) handle discrete time slices; continuous-time variants and neural extensions incorporate word embeddings or networks to model smooth semantic evolution (Blei & Lafferty, 2006; Wang et al., 2012; Dieng et al., 2020; Zhang et al., 2022). In practice, many studies obtain a strong baseline by estimating static topics on a rolling window, then plotting topic prevalence as a function of time for exploratory inspection.

Fairness and privacy obligations remain, even when labels are absent. Surveys in NLP caution that *bias* is multidimensional and demands explicit normative framing; unsupervised clusters can still encode or amplify representational harms if sources are skewed (Blodgett et al., 2020). Broader critiques of large-scale text modelling emphasise documentation, dataset governance, and harm-aware evaluation, and other considerations that apply equally when topics become pseudo-labels for downstream prediction (Bender et al., 2021; Gallegos et al., 2024; Hovy & Prabhumoye, 2021). It has become central when data are sensitive or interventions must not degrade user well-being, so abstention, aggregation, and conservative naming are good defaults (Blodgett et al., 2020). Finally, keep the bridge to outcomes explicit: topic memberships, distances to topic centroids, and VAD fingerprints become structured predictors in transparent psychological analyses, aligning with reporting practices your group already uses for supervised models (Kovač et al., 2024). This continuity lets latent text structure inform theory without retrofitting labels post hoc.

To make the text pipeline concrete, the following code assembles a fully label-free workflow: it first encodes each utterance with a domain-robust sentence transformer (e.g., SBERT) to preserve semantics without supervision (Reimers & Gurevych, 2019), then induces topics using BERTopic, which couples density clustering and neighbourhood preservation via HDBSCAN and UMAP for stable, nameable themes (Grootendorst, 2022; McInnes et al., 2017, 2018). Finally, it assigns each discovered topic an affective fingerprint by projecting its salient terms into valence–arousal–dominance space using lexicons such as Warriner–Kuperman–Brysbaert or NRC-VAD; crucially, this VAD step is post hoc and guides interpretation without supplying labels during discovery (Warriner, Kuperman, & Brysbaert, 2013; Mohammad, 2025).

```
# pip install sentence-transformers bertopic umap-learn hdb-
scan pandas
from sentence_transformers import SentenceTransformer
from bertopic import BERTopic
from sklearn.metrics.pairwise import cosine_distances
import pandas as pd

# 1) Load texts: one row per message/utterance/entry (with
optional timestamp)
df = pd.read_csv("corpus.csv") # columns: ["text", "timestamp"]
texts = df["text"].fillna("").tolist()

# 2) Embed with a strong general-purpose model (swap for
SimCSE/INSTRUCTOR/E5 as needed)
embedder = SentenceTransformer("all-MiniLM-L6-v2")
X = embedder.encode(texts, batch_size=64, show_progress_
bar=True, normalize_embeddings=True)

# 3) Unsupervised topics (automatic count). For coarser themes:
increase min_cluster_size
topic_model = BERTopic(min_topic_size=40, calculate_
probabilities=True, verbose=True)
topics, probs = topic_model.fit_transform(texts, X)

# 4) Get representative words per topic
topic_info = topic_model.get_topic_info() # topic sizes and
names
topic_words = {t: [w for w, _ in topic_model.get_topic(t)
[:20]] # top-20 words
               for t in topic_info["Topic"] if t != -1}

# 5) Post hoc VAD mapping: merge topic words with a VAD lexicon
(Warriner or NRC VAD)
vad = pd.read_csv("vad_lexicon.csv") # columns:
word,valence,arousal,dominance
vad["word"] = vad["word"].str.lower()
```

```
def topic_vad(words):
    m = vad[vad["word"].isin([w.lower() for w in words])]
return m[["valence","arousal","dominance"]].mean()

topic_vads = {t: topic_vad(ws) for t, ws in topic_words.it
ems()}
topic_vads = pd.DataFrame(topic_vads).T # index=topic,
columns=V/A/D

# 6) (Optional) distance-to-topic-centroids as features for
downstream models
centroids = topic_model.c_tf_idf_ # or compute mean embedding
per topic
```

Sentence embeddings preserve semantics without labels; BERTopic groups them and generates interpretable descriptors; VAD projection provides an affective *fingerprint* for each latent theme without supervising discovery (Reimers & Gurevych, 2019; Grootendorst, 2022; Warriner et al., 2013).

To trace how unlabelled themes ebb and flow in real data, the following Python code turns static topics into a time series: it bins documents by period (e.g., weeks), normalises within each bin to obtain topic prevalence, and optionally joins these trajectories with each topic's valence–arousal–dominance fingerprint from the code for affect-aware plots. This rolling, label-free view is a transparent baseline that often suffices before fitting full dynamic topic models, which introduce temporal priors to capture smooth evolution or regime shifts (Blei & Lafferty, 2006; Wang et al., 2012). When abrupt changes are suspected (e.g., around interventions), the same prevalence series can be paired with standard changepoint analyses for exploratory checks before confirmatory modelling (Truong et al., 2020).

```
# Assume you have 'topics' from Listing 9.5.1 and a datetime
column 'timestamp'
df["topic"] = topics
df["date"] = pd.to_datetime(df["timestamp"]).dt.to_period(
"W") # weekly bins

# 1) Topic prevalence timeline
timeline = (df[df["topic"]!=-1]
           .groupby(["date","topic"])
           .size()
           .groupby(level=0)
           .apply(lambda x: x / x.sum()) # normalize per period
           .reset_index(name="prevalence"))
```

```
# 2) Merge with topic VAD for annotated plots or regime-change
analysis
timeline = timeline.merge(topic_vads.reset_index().rename(col
umns={"index":"topic"}),
                          on="topic", how="left")

# Now plot prevalence vs. time per topic, or summarize high-
arousal themes across weeks.
```

While full DTM provides principled temporal priors, a rolling-window prevalence view offers a strong, transparent baseline; it often suffices for exploratory analyses before fitting dynamic models (Blei & Lafferty, 2006; Zhang et al., 2022).

9.7 Embodied Emotion Detection by Unsupervised Audio Signal Analysis

Unsupervised audio analysis targets structure in vocal behaviour without relying on rater-provided emotion tags, which is essential in naturalistic settings where labels are sparse, subjective, or ethically sensitive. The modern recipe is straightforward: ensure signal hygiene, extract embeddings that capture paralinguistic cues, let geometry or density expose latent states, and only then examine how those states relate to context or outcomes. Self-supervised encoders trained on large unlabelled corpora, such as *wav2vec 2.0*, *HuBERT*, and *WavLM*, supply rich utterance-level representations that transfer to affect with minimal adaptation, while emotion-specific pretraining such as *emotion2vec* can sharpen separation among arousal- and valence-related acoustics (Baevski et al., 2020; Hsu et al., 2021; Chen et al., 2022; Zhang et al., 2024). Classic acoustic summaries (e.g., MFCCs, energy, and pitch trajectories) remain valuable for interpretability and complement neural embeddings during discovery (Eyben et al., 2015).

Before discovery, the research should resample to a consistent rate (e.g., 16 kHz), normalise loudness, remove long silences with voice activity detection, and diarise when multiple speakers are present. Unsupervised segmentation helps disentangle state changes from speaker turns: spectral-clustering diarisation and offline changepoint detection frequently suffice to carve the stream into interpretable units without labels (Park et al., 2019; Truong et al., 2020). In settings involving sensitive populations, abstaining from decisions in ambiguous segments (e.g., by labelling them as *noise* in density clustering) reduces the risk of spurious inferences from poor signal quality.

Embeddings from *WavLM*, *HuBERT*, or *wav2vec 2.0* summarise timbre, articulation, and prosodic contours; they are robust to lexical content and often cluster by speaking style or state even before fine-tuning (Baevski et al., 2020; Hsu et al., 2021; Chen et al., 2022). For broader non-speech affect (e.g., laughter, sighs, crying), audio-tagging backbones such as PANNs, BYOL-A, and OpenL3 provide complementary cues that capture non-verbal events absent from ASR-focused encoders (Kong et al., 2020; Niizumi et al., 2021; Cramer et al., 2019). Pooling choices matter: mean–std pooling is a strong default; attention pooling can emphasise high-energy or high-F0 regions typical of heightened arousal.

If SSL embeddings already separate cleanly, K-means or Gaussian mixtures provide simple, reportable partitions. Where recordings contain rare vocalisations, overlaps, or artefacts, HDBSCAN isolates dense cores and marks ambiguous segments as noise. This is a desirable behaviour when abstention is safer than forced assignment (Rousseeuw, 1987; McInnes et al., 2017). Two-dimensional projections (e.g., UMAP) are useful for sanity checks, but clusters should be computed in the full space to avoid projection artefacts. After unsupervised states are found, posterior memberships, dwell times, and transition statistics can enter transparent outcome models (Kovač et al., 2024, 2025a). This separation (discovery first, linkage later) keeps the pipeline label-agnostic at the representation stage while preserving interpretability at the analysis stage.

To operationalise the audio workflow, the following code implements a compact, label-free pipeline: it first segments the waveform into short, overlapping windows; then extracts self-supervised speech embeddings (illustrated with WavLM, but wav2vec 2.0 or HuBERT are drop-in alternatives) so paralinguistic cues are captured without transcripts (Chen et al., 2022; Baevski et al., 2020; Hsu et al., 2021). The embeddings are standardised and passed to HDBSCAN, which uncovers stable affective episodes while abstaining on ambiguous segments rather than forcing assignments (McInnes et al., 2017). A UMAP map is generated only for neighbourhood inspection and produces a visualisation that remains strictly separate from clustering to avoid projection artefacts (McInnes et al., 2018).

```
# pip install librosa torch torchaudio transformers hdbscan
umap-learn
import librosa, numpy as np
from transformers import WavLMModel, WavLMConfig, WavLMProcessor
from sklearn.preprocessing import StandardScaler
import hdbscan, umap

# 1) Load audio and segment (short fixed windows with overlap
work well)
y, sr = librosa.load("session.wav", sr=16000, mono=True)
frames = librosa.util.frame(y, frame_length=int(1.6*sr), hop_
length=int(0.8*sr)).T # 1.6s windows, 50% overlap

# 2) SSL embeddings (WavLM Base as an example)
processor = WavLMProcessor.from_pretrained("microsoft/wav
lm-base")
model = WavLMModel.from_pretrained("microsoft/wavlm-base")
.eval()
```

```
def embed(wave):
    inputs = processor(wave, sampling_rate=16000, return_
tensors="pt", padding=True)
    with torch.inference_mode():
        h = model(**inputs).last_hidden_state # (1, T, D)
        # Mean pooling over time for an utterance-level
embedding
        return h.mean(dim=1).squeeze(0).numpy()

X = np.vstack([embed(f) for f in frames])

# 3) Standardize and cluster (density; abstains on ambiguous
segments with label -1)
Z = StandardScaler().fit_transform(X)
labels = hdbscan.HDBSCAN(min_cluster_size=25).fit_predict(Z)

# 4) Optional 2-D map for inspection (do not cluster in 2-D)
U = umap.UMAP(n_neighbors=20, min_dist=0.05, random_state=7).
fit_transform(Z)
# Plot U[:,0], U[:,1] colored by 'labels' to inspect
neighborhoods.
```

SSL embeddings summarise paralinguistic cues without transcript labels; HDBSCAN surfaces stable affective *episodes* and leaves the rest unlabelled, which is safer in noisy or clinical audio (Chen et al., 2022; McInnes et al., 2017).

To emphasise prosodic structure before any representation learning, the next Python code builds episodes directly from low-level acoustics: it extracts frame-level fundamental frequency (F0) and loudness (RMS), detects change-points in the 2-D prosody stream to carve the audio into coherent segments, then pools simple statistics (mean, variance) per segment and clusters them (e.g., with K-means). This prosody-first route is intentionally transparent: F0 tracks tension and vocal effort while RMS indexes energy, giving segments that map naturally onto arousal-related interpretations without relying on transcripts or labels (Eyben et al., 2015). Using a principled F0 estimator such as YIN stabilises pitch in noisy, spontaneous speech (De Cheveigné & Kawahara, 2002), and offline changepoint detection separates regime shifts (e.g., calm → excited) from mere local fluctuations (Truong et al., 2020). By decoupling segmentation from clustering, the method avoids asking one model to learn both dynamics and geometry at once, and it supports cautious inference, so segments with ambiguous prosody can be left unclustered or flagged for review.

```
# pip install librosa ruptures scikit-learn
import librosa, numpy as np, ruptures as rpt
from sklearn.cluster import KMeans
from sklearn.preprocessing import StandardScaler
```

```
y, sr = librosa.load("session.wav", sr=16000, mono=True)
# 1) Frame-level prosody: pitch (F0) and loudness proxy
f0 = librosa.yin(y, fmin=50, fmax=400, sr=sr, frame_length=2048,
hop_length=160) # ~10 ms hop
rms   =   librosa.feature.rms(y=y,   frame_length=2048,   hop_
length=160).squeeze()

# 2) Changepoints on a compact 2-D prosody series
X   =   np.vstack([librosa.util.normalize(np.nan_to_num(f0)),
librosa.util.normalize(rms)]).T
algo = rpt.KernelCPD(kernel="rbf").fit(X)
bps = algo.predict(pen=10) # breakpoints (indices in frames)

# 3) Pool features within segments, then cluster
segs  =  [  (0,  bps[0])  ]  +  [  (bps[i],  bps[i+1])  for  i  in
range(len(bps)-1) ]
feat = []
for s, e in segs:
    fseg = X[s:e]
    feat.append(np.hstack([fseg.mean(axis=0), fseg
.std(axis=0)])) # mean/std of F0, RMS
feat = np.vstack(feat)

Z = StandardScaler().fit_transform(feat)
labels   =   KMeans(n_clusters=3,   n_init=20,   random_state=0).
fit_predict(Z)
# 'labels' marks prosody-defined episodes that you can align
with time, context, or physiology.
```

A prosody-first approach makes the segmentation step explicit, reducing pressure on clustering to capture both dynamics and geometry (Truong et al., 2020). It also yields interpretable features (pitch/energy) that map naturally to arousal-related constructs.

To capture non-speech affect (laughter, sobs, gasps, sighs, breathiness) next listing swaps ASR-oriented SSL encoders for audio-tagging backbones that are pre-trained to recognise diverse acoustic events. The pipeline extracts event-aware embeddings from models such as PANNs, BYOL-A, or OpenL3, pools them at the segment level, standardises, and then applies HDBSCAN so dense, recurrent vocal events emerge as unsupervised states while ambiguous segments are left unlabelled. This complements speech encoders by highlighting affective paralinguistic cues that carry a strong emotional signal even in the absence of words (Kong et al., 2020; Niizumi et al., 2021; Cramer et al., 2019).

```
# pip install torchlibrosa pytorch-lightning
# Example with PANNs-like features (pseudocode; replace with
an actual pretrained tagger)
```

```
import torch, numpy as np
from sklearn.preprocessing import StandardScaler
import hdbscan

class TaggerBackbone(torch.nn.Module):
    def __init__(self): ...
    def forward(self, x): ... # returns (batch, time, d)

model = TaggerBackbone().eval()
# Assume 'spec' is a log-mel spectrogram of shape (time, mel)
with torch.inference_mode():
    h = model(torch.from_numpy(spec)[None, None, ...]) # (
1, T, D)
    X = h.mean(dim=1).squeeze(0).numpy()       # event-aware
embedding

Z = StandardScaler().fit_transform(X)
labels = hdbscan.HDBSCAN(min_cluster_size=20).fit_predict(Z)
```

Audio-tagging backbones capture non-speech events (e.g., laughter, sobs, gasps) that are central to embodied emotion yet underrepresented in ASR-focused SSL features (Kong et al., 2020; Niizumi et al., 2021; Cramer et al., 2019). These findings indicate that the selection of model backbone functions is not a neutral engineering decision but is rather an implicit theoretical stance regarding which acoustic phenomena are treated as meaningful signals in human audio. Audio-tagging encoders, typically trained on broad sound ontologies such as AudioSet (Gemmeke et al., 2017), allocate substantial representational capacity to short, high-arousal non-verbal human vocalisations. As a result, embodied affective cues, including laughter, sobbing, gasping, and sighing, tend to be preserved within their latent spaces (Cramer et al., 2019; Kong et al., 2020). In contrast, ASR-oriented SSL encoders are optimised primarily for lexical robustness. Non-speech intervals are frequently collapsed into generic silence or background noise categories and thus contribute minimally to the self-supervised objective (Baevski et al., 2020; Hsu et al., 2021). Consequently, emotionally salient non-lexical vocal events are systematically underrepresented. For downstream emotion-recognition tasks, this pattern implies that systems relying exclusively on ASR-derived SSL features may inherit a structural linguistic bias and overlook embodied, non-verbal affective information, whereas audio-tagging backbones provide a more appropriate computational substrate for capturing the broader spectrum of human emotional expression.

References

Adams, R. P., & MacKay, D. J. (2007). Bayesian online changepoint detection. *arXiv preprint arXiv:0710.3742*.

Angelov, D. (2020). Top2vec: Distributed representations of topics. *arXiv preprint arXiv:2008.09470*.

Baevski, A., Zhou, Y., Mohamed, A., & Auli, M. (2020). wav2vec 2.0: A framework for self-supervised learning of speech representations. *Advances in Neural Information Processing Systems*, *33*, 12449–12460.

Baltrušaitis, T., Robinson, P., & Morency, L. P. (2016, March). Openface: an open source facial behavior analysis toolkit. In *2016 IEEE winter conference on applications of computer vision (WACV)* (pp. 1–10). IEEE.

Barachant, A., Barthélemy, Q., King, J. R., Gramfort, A., Chevallier, S., Rodrigues, P. L. C., & Corsi, M. C. (2022). pyRiemann/pyRiemann: v0. 5. *Zenodo*.

Barachant, A., Bonnet, S., Congedo, M., & Jutten, C. (2012). Multiclass brain–computer interface classification by Riemannian geometry. *IEEE Transactions on Biomedical Engineering*, *59*(4), 920–928.

Barrett, L. F. (2017). *How emotions are made: The secret life of the brain*. Pan Macmillan.

Barsade, S. G., & Gibson, D. E. (2012). Group affect: Its influence on individual and group outcomes. *Current Directions in Psychological Science*, *21*(2), 119–123.

Bastos, A. M., & Schoffelen, J. M. (2016). A tutorial review of functional connectivity analysis methods and their interpretational pitfalls. *Frontiers in Systems Neuroscience*, *9*, 175.

Belkin, M., & Niyogi, P. (2003). Laplacian eigenmaps for dimensionality reduction and data representation. *Neural Computation*, *15*(6), 1373–1396.

Bender, E. M., Gebru, T., McMillan-Major, A., & Shmitchell, S. (2021, March). On the dangers of stochastic parrots: Can language models be too big?. In *Proceedings of the 2021 ACM conference on fairness, accountability, and transparency* (pp. 610–623).

Bigdely-Shamlo, N., Mullen, T., Kothe, C., Su, K. M., & Robbins, K. A. (2015). The PREP pipeline: Standardized preprocessing for large-scale EEG analysis. *Frontiers in Neuroinformatics*, *9*, 16.

Bishop, C. M., & Nasrabadi, N. M. (2006). *Pattern recognition and machine learning* (Vol. 4, No. 4, p. 738). Springer.

Blei, D. M., & Lafferty, J. D. (2006, June). Dynamic topic models. In *Proceedings of the 23rd international conference on machine learning* (pp. 113–120).

Blodgett, S. L., Barocas, S., Daumé Iii, H., & Wallach, H. (2020). Language (technology) is power: A critical survey of" bias" in nlp. *arXiv preprint arXiv:2005.14050*.

Busso, C., Bulut, M., Lee, C. C., Kazemzadeh, A., Mower, E., Kim, S., & Narayanan, S. S. (2008). IEMOCAP: Interactive emotional dyadic motion capture database. *Language Resources and Evaluation*, *42*(4), 335–359.

Caliński, T., & Harabasz, J. (1974). A dendrite method for cluster analysis. *Communications in Statistics-Theory and Methods*, *3*(1), 1–27.

Calvo, R. A., & D'Mello, S. (2010). Affect detection: An interdisciplinary review of models, methods, and their applications. *IEEE Transactions on Affective Computing*, *1*(1), 18–37.

Campello, R. J., Kröger, P., Sander, J., & Zimek, A. (2020). Density-based clustering. *Wiley Interdisciplinary Reviews: Data Mining and Knowledge Discovery*, *10*(2), e1343.

Campello, R. J., Moulavi, D., & Sander, J. (2013, April). Density-based clustering based on hierarchical density estimates. In *Pacific-Asia conference on knowledge discovery and data mining* (pp. 160–172). Springer.

Caron, M., Bojanowski, P., Joulin, A., & Douze, M. (2018). Deep clustering for unsupervised learning of visual features. In *Proceedings of the European conference on computer vision (ECCV)* (pp. 132–149).

Caron, M., Misra, I., Mairal, J., Goyal, P., Bojanowski, P., & Joulin, A. (2020). Unsupervised learning of visual features by contrasting cluster assignments. *Advances in Neural Information Processing Systems*, *33*, 9912–9924.

Chen, S., Wang, C., Chen, Z., Wu, Y., Liu, S., Chen, Z., & Wei, F. (2022). Wavlm: Large-scale self-supervised pre-training for full stack speech processing. *IEEE Journal of Selected Topics in Signal Processing*, *16*(6), 1505–1518.

Chiarion, G., Sparacino, L., Antonacci, Y., Faes, L., & Mesin, L. (2023). Connectivity analysis in EEG data: a tutorial review of the state of the art and emerging trends. *Bioengineering*, *10*(3), 372.

Coifman, R. R., & Lafon, S. (2006). Diffusion maps. *Applied and Computational Harmonic Analysis*, *21*(1), 5–30.

Cramer, A. L., Wu, H. H., Salamon, J., & Bello, J. P. (2019, May). Look, listen, and learn more: Design choices for deep audio embeddings. In *ICASSP 2019–2019 IEEE International Conference on Acoustics, Speech and Signal Processing (ICASSP)* (pp. 3852–3856). IEEE.

Davies, D. L., & Bouldin, D. W. (2009). A cluster separation measure. *IEEE Transactions on Pattern Analysis and Machine Intelligence*, (2), 224–227.

De Cheveigné, A., & Kawahara, H. (2002). YIN, a fundamental frequency estimator for speech and music. *The Journal of the Acoustical Society of America*, *111*(4), 1917–1930.

Dempster, A. P., Laird, N. M., & Rubin, D. B. (1977). Maximum likelihood from incomplete data via the EM algorithm. *Journal of the Royal Statistical Society: Series B (Methodological)*, *39*(1), 1–22.

Dieng, A. B., Ruiz, F. J., & Blei, D. M. (2020). Topic modeling in embedding spaces. *Transactions of the Association for Computational Linguistics*, *8*, 439–453.

Domínguez-Catena, I., Paternain, D., Jurio, A., & Galar, M. (2024). Less can be more: Representational vs. stereotypical gender bias in facial expression recognition. *Progress in Artificial Intelligence*, *14*(1), 11–31.

Ester, M., Kriegel, H. P., Sander, J., & Xu, X. (1996, August). A density-based algorithm for discovering clusters in large spatial databases with noise. *kdd*, *96*(34), 226–231.

Eyben, F., Scherer, K. R., Schuller, B. W., Sundberg, J., André, E., Busso, C., & Truong, K. P. (2015). The Geneva Minimalistic Acoustic Parameter Set (GeMAPS) for voice research and affective computing. *IEEE Transactions on Affective Computing*, *7*(2), 190–202.

Farahani, H., Watson, P., Bezan, T., Kovač, N., Winter, L. C., Blagojević, M., … Jiménez, P. (2024). PsAIchology: An intelligent direction in psychological sciences. In *10th international scientific conference Technics, Informatics and Education—TIE 2024*. Faculty of Technical Sciences Čačak, University of Kragujevac.

Farahani, H., Watson, P., Kovač, N., Sheykhangafshe, F. B., Azadfallah, P., Allahyari, A., … Chesli, R. R. (2025). Unraveling the complexity of love addiction using machine learning algorithms: The influence of positive and negative affect, interpersonal needs, and self-hate. In C.-H. Mayer & E. Vanderheiden (Eds.), *International handbook of love: Transcultural and transdisciplinary perspectives* (pp. 1–22). Springer Nature.

Gallegos, I. O., Rossi, R. A., Barrow, J., Tanjim, M. M., Kim, S., Dernoncourt, F., & Ahmed, N. K. (2024). Bias and fairness in large language models: A survey. *Computational Linguistics*, *50*(3), 1097–1179.

Gao, T., Yao, X., & Chen, D. (2021). Simcse: Simple contrastive learning of sentence embeddings. *arXiv preprint arXiv:2104.08821*.

Gemmeke, J. F., Ellis, D. P., Freedman, D., Jansen, A., Lawrence, W., Moore, R. C., & Ritter, M. (2017, March). Audio set: An ontology and human-labeled dataset for audio events. In *2017 IEEE International Conference on Acoustics, Speech and Signal Processing (ICASSP)* (pp. 776–780). IEEE.

Gramfort, A., Luessi, M., Larson, E., Engemann, D. A., Strohmeier, D., Brodbeck, C., & Hämäläinen, M. (2013). MEG and EEG data analysis with MNE-Python. *Frontiers in Neuroinformatics*, 7, 267.

Grootendorst, M. (2022). BERTopic: Neural topic modeling with a class-based TF-IDF procedure. *arXiv preprint arXiv:2203.05794*.

Hastie, T., Tibshirani, R., & Friedman, J. (2009). *The elements of statistical learning: Data mining, inference, and prediction* (2nd ed.). Springer.

Haydock, D., Kadir, S., Leech, R., Nehaniv, C. L., & Antonova, E. (2025). EEG microstate syntax analysis: A review of methodological challenges and advances. *NeuroImage*, *309*, 121090.

Hovy, D., & Prabhumoye, S. (2021). Five sources of bias in natural language processing. *Language and Linguistics Compass*, *15*(8), e12432.

Hsu, W. N., Bolte, B., Tsai, Y. H. H., Lakhotia, K., Salakhutdinov, R., & Mohamed, A. (2021). HuBERT: Self-supervised speech representation learning by masked prediction of hidden units. *IEEE/ACM Transactions on Audio, Speech, and Language Processing*, *29*, 3451–3460.

Jaramillo-Jimenez, A., Tovar-Rios, D. A., Mantilla-Ramos, Y. J., Ochoa-Gomez, J. F., Bonanni, L., & Brønnick, K. (2024). ComBat models for harmonization of resting-state EEG features in multisite studies. *Clinical Neurophysiology*, *167*, 241–253.

Jiang, Z., Zheng, Y., Tan, H., Tang, B., & Zhou, H. (2016). Variational deep embedding: An unsupervised and generative approach to clustering. *arXiv preprint arXiv:1611.05148*.

Jung, T. P., Makeig, S., Humphries, C., Lee, T. W., Mckeown, M. J., Iragui, V., & Sejnowski, T. J. (2000). Removing electroencephalographic artifacts by blind source separation. *Psychophysiology*, *37*(2), 163–178.

Karkkainen, K., & Joo, J. (2021). Fairface: Face attribute dataset for balanced race, gender, and age for bias measurement and mitigation. In *Proceedings of the IEEE/CVF winter conference on applications of computer vision* (pp. 1548–1558).

Killick, R., Fearnhead, P., & Eckley, I. A. (2012). Optimal detection of changepoints with a linear computational cost. *Journal of the American Statistical Association*, *107*(500), 1590–1598.

Kingma, D. P., & Welling, M. (2013). Auto-encoding variational bayes. *arXiv preprint arXiv:1312.6114*.

Koelstra, S., Muhl, C., Soleymani, M., Lee, J. S., Yazdani, A., Ebrahimi, T., & Patras, I. (2011). Deap: A database for emotion analysis; Using physiological signals. *IEEE Transactions on Affective Computing*, *3*(1), 18–31.

Kollias, D., & Zafeiriou, S. (2018). Aff-wild2: Extending the aff-wild database for affect recognition. *arXiv preprint arXiv:1811.07770*.

Kollias, D., & Zafeiriou, S. (2019). Expression, affect, action unit recognition: Aff-wild2, multi-task learning and arcface. *arXiv preprint arXiv:1910.04855*.

Kong, Q., Cao, Y., Iqbal, T., Wang, Y., Wang, W., & Plumbley, M. D. (2020). PANNSs: Large-scale pretrained audio neural networks for audio pattern recognition. *IEEE/ACM Transactions on Audio, Speech, and Language Processing*, *28*, 2880–2894.

Kothe, C., Shirazi, S. Y., Stenner, T., Medine, D., Boulay, C., Grivich, M. I., & Makeig, S. (2025). The lab streaming layer for synchronized multimodal recording. *Imaging Neuroscience*, *3*, IMAG-a.

Kovač, N., Ratković, K., Farahani, H., & Watson, P. (2024). A practical applications guide to machine learning regression models in psychology with Python. *Methods in Psychology*, *11*, 100156.

Kovač, N., Ratković, K., Farahani, H., & Watson, P. (2025a). Machine learning regression models for internal shame. *Acta Psychologica*, *260*, 105721.

Kovač, N., Ratković, K., Watson, P., Farahani, H., & Bagheri Sheykhangafshe, F. (2025b). Machine learning classification models for predicting chronic pain. *Current Psychology*, 1–14. Advance online publication.

Kragel, P. A., & LaBar, K. S. (2016). Decoding the nature of emotion in the brain. *Trends in Cognitive Sciences*, *20*(6), 444–455.

Levenson, R. W. (2014). The autonomic nervous system and emotion. *Emotion Review*, *6*(2), 100–112.

Li, S., Deng, W., & Du, J. (2017). Reliable crowdsourcing and deep locality-preserving learning for expression recognition in the wild. In *Proceedings of the IEEE conference on computer vision and pattern recognition* (pp. 2852–2861).

Livingstone, S. R., & Russo, F. A. (2018). The Ryerson Audio-Visual Database of Emotional Speech and Song (RAVDESS): A dynamic, multimodal set of facial and vocal expressions in North American English. *PLoS One*, *13*(5), e0196391.

Ma, Z., Zheng, Z., Ye, J., Li, J., Gao, Z., Zhang, S., & Chen, X. (2023). emotion2vec: Self-supervised pre-training for speech emotion representation. *arXiv preprint arXiv:2312.15185*.

McInnes, L., Healy, J., & Astels, S. (2017). hdbscan: Hierarchical density-based clustering. *Journal of Open Source Software*, *2*(11), 205.

McInnes, L., Healy, J., & Melville, J. (2018). UMAP: Uniform manifold approximation and projection for dimension reduction. *arXiv preprint arXiv:1802.03426*.

McQueen, J. B. (1967). Some methods of classification and analysis of multivariate observations. In *Proceedings of the fifth Berkeley symposium on mathematical statistics and probability, Volume 1: Statistics* (pp. 281–297).

Mehta, D., Siddiqui, M. F. H., & Javaid, A. Y. (2019). Recognition of emotion intensities using machine learning algorithms: A comparative study. *Sensors*, *19*(8), 1897.

Michel, C. M., & Koenig, T. (2018). EEG microstates as a tool for studying the temporal dynamics of whole-brain neuronal networks: A review. *Neuroimage*, *180*, 577–593.

Mohammad, S. M. (2025). NRC VAD Lexicon v2: Norms for valence, arousal, and dominance for over 55k English terms. *arXiv preprint arXiv:2503.23547*.

Mollahosseini, A., Hasani, B., & Mahoor, M. H. (2017). AffectNet: A database for facial expression, valence, and arousal computing in the wild. *IEEE Transactions on Affective Computing*, *10*(1), 18–31.

Ng, A., Jordan, M., & Weiss, Y. (2001). On spectral clustering: Analysis and an algorithm. In T. Dietterich, S. Becker, & Z. Ghahramani (Eds.), *Advances in neural information processing systems*. MIT Press.

Niizumi, D., Takeuchi, D., Ohishi, Y., Harada, N., & Kashino, K. (2021, July). Byol for audio: Self-supervised learning for general-purpose audio representation. In *2021 International Joint Conference on Neural Networks (IJCNN)* (pp. 1–8). IEEE.

Oquab, M., Darcet, T., Moutakanni, T., Vo, H., Szafraniec, M., Khalidov, V., & Bojanowski, P. (2023). DINOv2: Learning robust visual features without supervision. *arXiv preprint arXiv:2304.07193*.

Oquab, M., Darcet, T., Moutakanni, T., Vo, H., Szafraniec, M., Khalidov, V., & Bojanowski, P. (2024). Dinov2: Learning robust visual features without supervision. *arXiv preprint arXiv:2304.07193*.

Park, T. J., Han, K. J., Kumar, M., & Narayanan, S. (2019). Auto-tuning spectral clustering for speaker diarization using normalized maximum eigengap. *IEEE Signal Processing Letters*, *27*, 381–385.

Reimers, N., & Gurevych, I. (2019). Sentence-BERT: Sentence embeddings using siamese bert-networks. *arXiv preprint arXiv:1908.10084*.

Rousseeuw, P. J. (1987). Silhouettes: a graphical aid to the interpretation and validation of cluster analysis. *Journal of Computational and Applied Mathematics*, *20*, 53–65.

Sajjad, M., Ullah, F. U. M., Ullah, M., Christodoulou, G., Cheikh, F. A., Hijji, M., & Rodrigues, J. J. (2023). A comprehensive survey on deep facial expression recognition: challenges, applications, and future guidelines. *Alexandria Engineering Journal*, *68*, 817–840.

Schölkopf, B., Smola, A., & Müller, K. R. (1998). Nonlinear component analysis as a kernel eigenvalue problem. *Neural Computation*, *10*(5), 1299–1319.

Schwarz, G. (1978). Estimating the dimension of a model. *The Annals of Statistics*, 461–464.

Seth, A. K., & Tsakiris, M. (2018). Being a beast machine: The somatic basis of selfhood. *Trends in Cognitive Sciences*, *22*(11), 969–981.

Shu, Y., Gu, X., Yang, G. Z., & Lo, B. (2022). Revisiting self-supervised contrastive learning for facial expression recognition. *arXiv preprint arXiv:2210.03853*.

Su, H., Shi, W., Kasai, J., Wang, Y., Hu, Y., Ostendorf, M., & Yu, T. (2022). One embedder, any task: Instruction-finetuned text embeddings. *arXiv preprint arXiv:2212.09741*.

Truong, C., Oudre, L., & Vayatis, N. (2020). Selective review of offline change point detection methods. *Signal Processing*, *167*, 107299.

van der Maaten, L., & Hinton, G. (2008). Visualizing data using t-SNE. *Journal of Machine Learning Research*, *9*(Nov), 2579–2605.

Von Luxburg, U. (2007). A tutorial on spectral clustering. *Statistics and Computing*, *17*(4), 395–416.

Wang, C., Blei, D., & Heckerman, D. (2012). Continuous time dynamic topic models. *arXiv preprint arXiv:1206.3298*.

Wang, L., Yang, N., Huang, X., Jiao, B., Yang, L., Jiang, D., & Wei, F. (2022). Text embeddings by weakly-supervised contrastive pre-training. *arXiv preprint arXiv:2212.03533*.

Warriner, A. B., Kuperman, V., & Brysbaert, M. (2013). Norms of valence, arousal, and dominance for 13,915 English lemmas. *Behavior Research Methods*, *45*(4), 1191–1207.

Xie, J., Girshick, R., & Farhadi, A. (2016, June). Unsupervised deep embedding for clustering analysis. In *International conference on machine learning* (pp. 478–487). PMLR.

Yger, F., Berar, M., & Lotte, F. (2016). Riemannian approaches in brain-computer interfaces: A review. *IEEE Transactions on Neural Systems and Rehabilitation Engineering*, *25*(10), 1753–1762.

Zhang, D. C., & Lauw, H. (2022, June). Dynamic topic models for temporal document networks. In *International conference on machine learning* (pp. 26281–26292). PMLR.

Zhang, M., Ma, B., Xiao, C., & Wang, C. (2024). Self-supervised learning-based emotion recognition using EEG. *Frontiers in Human Neuroscience*, *18*, 1334721.

Zhang, Z., Wang, L., & Yang, J. (2023). Weakly supervised video emotion detection and prediction via cross-modal temporal erasing network. In *Proceedings of the IEEE/CVF conference on computer vision and pattern recognition* (pp. 18888–18897).

10 Reinforcement Learning in the Realm of Embodied Emotion

Nataša Kovač, Hojjatollah Farahani, and Peter Watson

10.1 Introduction

For decades, psychologists, neuroscientists, and artificial intelligence researchers have sought to decode human emotions, not merely as abstract psychological states but as adaptive responses deeply embedded within dynamic interactions between humans and their environments. Emotions influence behaviour, shape decisions, and significantly affect learning processes through a complex interplay of reward systems, motivation, and behavioural adaptation (Rolls, 2014). However, when emotions are scrutinised through the joint lens of psychological science and computational learning, a far more uncomfortable truth is revealed: many prevailing theories underestimate the ruthlessness of emotional dynamics. Human emotion is not a gentle signalling system; it is an evolved mechanism engineered by natural selection to bias cognition in favour of survival and resource acquisition. Behavioural economics has repeatedly demonstrated that emotional biases systematically distort human judgement, often in predictable, maladaptive ways that deviate from rational-choice principles (Kahneman & Tversky, 2013). From loss aversion to threat amplification, emotional systems operate as diagnostic shortcuts, fast, efficient, and frequently brutal in their overriding of deliberative thought.

In recent years, reinforcement learning (RL), a robust computational paradigm inspired by how biological agents learn from rewards and punishments, has emerged as a persuasive framework for modelling, analysing, and ultimately improving human emotional interactions and experiences (Sutton & Barto, 2018).

RL-based models reinforce this insight, indicating that negative reinforcement, reward prediction errors, and unexpected outcomes produce disproportionately large shifts in behavioural policy updates, mirroring the human tendency to weight aversive information more heavily than positive feedback (Schultz, 2016). At the neural level, emotions are expressed through continuous prediction, evaluation, and error-correction loops that are functionally indistinguishable from RL mechanisms. The dopaminergic system, critical for signalling reward prediction errors, does not merely support learning but also shapes the intensity, duration, and direction of emotional responses

DOI: 10.4324/9781003495123-10

(Schultz, 2017). Emotional valence itself can be conceptualised as a dynamic estimate of expected value relative to shifting internal and external contexts. Psychological research demonstrates that chronic stress, trauma, and affect dysregulation distort value-estimation processes, resulting in maladaptive behavioural policies that persist long after environmental contingencies have changed (Pessoa, 2013). In essence, emotional disorders can be understood as pathological reinforcement schedules, overlearning of threat, underlearning of safety, and dysfunctional reward prediction mechanisms that confine individuals to rigid behavioural loops.

Contemporary affective neuroscience has increasingly abandoned the assumption that emotions are static, modular entities. Instead, emotional states are seen as emerging from distributed, context-sensitive appraisal processes integrating sensory cues, bodily states, memory, and social inference (Barrett, 2017). When RL models are applied to such multidimensional psychological processes, they expose a stark mismatch between how humans assume emotion's function and how they in fact operate. The emotional system is biased, noisy, and strategically tuned to optimise survival rather than well-being. It prioritises rapid threat detection over accuracy, social conformity over autonomy, and energy conservation over psychological flourishing. These computational and psychological insights necessitate a critical reassessment of long-held assumptions in clinical psychology, educational psychology, and behavioural intervention design.

If emotional learning mirrors RL mechanisms, therapeutic change must involve genuine policy updating, not gentle persuasion or reflective insight, but the systematic restructuring of reward contingencies, exposure patterns, and decision landscapes. Indeed, some of the most effective psychological interventions already rely implicitly on RL principles. Cognitive-behavioural exposure therapies modify avoidance policies through controlled prediction-error signalling; behavioural activation reshapes reward schedules to counter depressive withdrawal, and dialectical behaviour therapy manipulates contingencies to stabilise emotional responses. Such approaches function not because they align with comforting clinical narratives but because they force the emotional system to relearn through experience. RL therefore clarifies why human emotion is stubborn, why insight alone rarely transforms behaviour, and why deeply ingrained patterns of fear, attachment, or avoidance resist change until the underlying reinforcement architecture is dismantled and rebuilt. No romanticised or filtered interpretation of human emotional life withstands this computational scrutiny: emotions operate as learning systems, and learning systems are indifferent to human ideals of rationality, morality, or coherence. They follow the mathematics.

Unlike traditional supervised or unsupervised learning approaches, RL explicitly incorporates a temporal dimension of experience. Agents learn sequentially through trial-and-error interactions, adapting continuously based on received feedback signals. This interaction-based learning closely resembles how human emotional systems shape adaptive behaviours over time, often unconsciously guiding our decisions based on perceived emotional outcomes and expectations of future emotional rewards or costs (Damasio, 1996).

Emotional interaction can be framed as an RL control problem with explicit temporal credit assignment: an agent chooses actions, observes their consequences, and updates its policy to maximise long-run return (Sutton & Barto, 2018). To make this safe and useful in human-facing contexts, the learning loop is coupled to evaluation mechanisms and governance constraints. Figure 10.1 depicts this arrangement: experience is generated online, stored, and then used by a learner/optimiser to update the policy, while value/critic estimates stabilise learning and off-policy evaluation gates deployment. This separation is often termed *offline* or *batch* RL. It has become central when data are sensitive or interventions must not degrade user well-being (Levine et al., 2020).

Observations s_t are encoded by a state estimator and passed to the policy $\pi_\theta(a|s)$, which selects an action a_t. The environment (here, the human–computer setting with its world dynamics) returns a reward r_t and the next state s_{t+1}. Every interaction tuple is logged in a replay buffer, forming a dataset for learning. On the far right, the learner/optimiser performs gradient updates using this logged experience (off-policy), and the stacked value/critic module estimates future returns to reduce variance and improve stability.

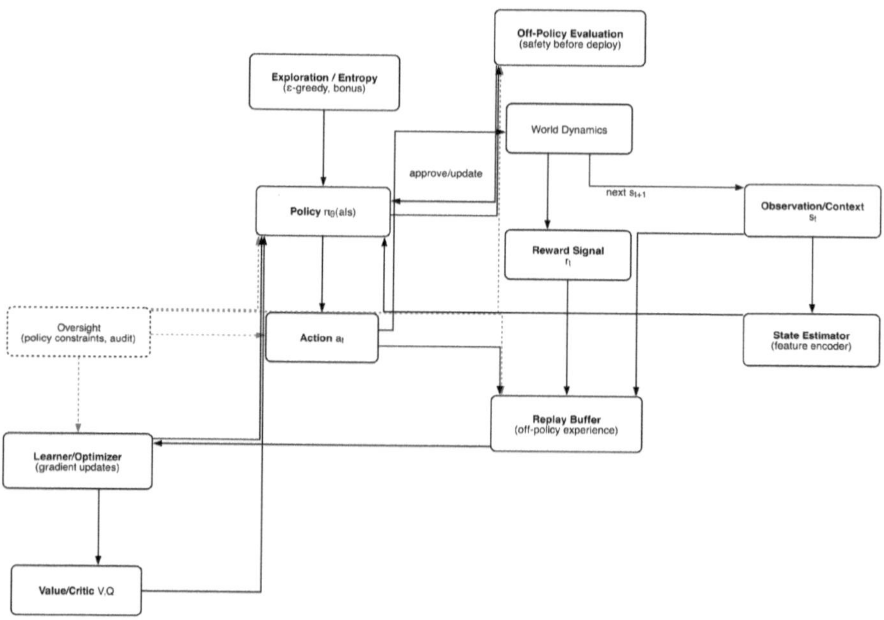

Figure 10.1 Core reinforcement learning loop with governance constraints and off-policy evaluation.

An exploration/entropy mechanism regularises the policy so it does not collapse prematurely on narrow behaviours, while off-policy evaluation tests candidate policies against the logged data before any change is approved for deployment. Dotted lines indicate governance and safety constraints that *constrain* optimisation rather than being added post hoc (Achiam et al., 2017; Thomas & Brunskill, 2016). Practically, this architecture lets us (i) gather interaction data conservatively, (ii) improve policies offline under explicit constraints, and (iii) deploy only after high-confidence evaluation. This approach is particularly important for emotion-sensitive applications.

By connecting RL with human emotion, we open a new topic for exploration, one that allows intelligent systems not just to recognise emotional states but to actively respond to, learn from, and even influence emotional experiences in context-aware, personalised ways. The state-of-the-art landscape of emotion-informed RL reveals a promising yet emerging field. Early efforts often viewed emotions simply as additional signals to enhance computational decision-making. However, recent advances have marked a paradigm shift, recognising emotions as essential states that influence entire decision processes within interactive settings. Cutting-edge algorithms now utilise emotional signals to adapt the behaviour of intelligent agents in real time. Related machine-learning frameworks have also been applied to affect-linked constructs beyond core emotions, such as love addiction, where feature patterns and explanations clarify predictive factors (Farahani et al., 2025). These agents develop policies that optimise not only traditional task performance but also emotional well-being, engagement, mental health outcomes, and educational effectiveness (Paiva et al., 2017).

A growing body of research highlights that integrating emotional signals into RL significantly enhances the human-computer interaction experience. Emotionally intelligent RL agents have begun to transform key areas such as mental health monitoring, personalised education, assistive robotics, and adaptive human-machine communication. For instance, in mental health, RL models adjust therapeutic interactions in real-time based on subtle emotional feedback, leading to more effective and empathetic mental health interventions (Jaques et al., 2016). In education, personalised learning agents harness emotional feedback to adapt difficulty, pacing, and motivational strategies, significantly improving learner engagement and educational outcomes (D'Mello & Graesser, 2013).

Despite these promising advancements, several challenges remain at the frontier of RL and emotional computing. Complexities inherent to emotional states pose critical questions for computational modelling. RL algorithms must handle noisy, sparse, delayed, and occasionally contradictory emotional feedback. Emotional adaptation through RL must align with stringent ethical guidelines, protecting the privacy, autonomy, and psychological safety of human participants. Thus, the field stands at a compelling intersection, balancing technological sophistication with careful consideration of ethical responsibility and psychological validity.

This chapter embarks on a profound exploration into this emerging landscape, aiming to provide readers with in-depth insights into how RL can effectively model and leverage human emotional dynamics. Through carefully selected case studies, recent developments, critical theoretical discussions, and thoughtful ethical considerations, we delve into how emotion-driven RL is redefining the relationships between humans and intelligent systems, shaping the future of interactive technology and enhancing our understanding of human emotional life.

10.2 Emotion-Driven Reinforcement Learning: A New Frontier in Human-Computer Interaction

In recent years, human-computer interaction (HCI) has experienced a significant paradigm shift, moving beyond task-driven exchanges to emotional and socially aware interactions. This integration aligns with the 'Artificial Psychology' (PsAIchology) framing that connects AI methods with psychological science (Farahani et al., 2024). Contemporary systems not only respond to explicit user commands but also actively sense, interpret, and adapt dynamically to the emotional states of users. At the heart of this transformation lies emotion-driven RL. This powerful computational framework enables intelligent agents to learn from emotional signals as intrinsic rewards, guiding adaptive, personalised, and context-sensitive interactions (Jaques et al., 2015).

Traditional RL algorithms operate by optimising numerical reward signals, typically aimed at maximising performance in well-defined tasks. However, such conventional approaches fail to reflect the complexity, nuance, and subjectivity of human emotional experiences. Emotion-driven RL fills this critical gap by integrating affective feedback, such as emotional valence, arousal, or psychological engagement, directly into the RL process. This approach fundamentally transforms how artificial agents interact with humans, ensuring responses and adaptations resonate emotionally, leading to deeper engagement and more meaningful interactions (Gratch & Marsella, 2014). For psychology-focused, Python-based modelling and pipeline patterns that complement these designs, see (Kovač et al., 2024). In practice, we map sensed affect to rewards and keep policies sufficiently exploratory to avoid brittle behaviour, as shown below:

```
import numpy as np
from typing import Mapping

def  affect_reward(valence:  float,  arousal:  float,  goals:
Mapping[str, float]) -> float:
    dv = valence - goals.get("valence", 0.0)
    da = arousal - goals.get("arousal", 0.0)
    towards = - (dv**2 + da**2)         # closer is better
```

```
    saturate = - 0.2 * (max(0, abs(valence)-1)**2 + max(0,
abs(arousal)-1)**2)
    return float(towards + saturate)
def exploration_schedule(t: int, eps0: float = 0.2, eps_min:
float = 0.02, half_life: int = 50_000) -> float:
    import math
    return max(eps_min, eps0 * math.exp(-t / half_life))
```

This code shows a mapping from affect to scalar reward, including the fact that agents should optimise engagement and well-being, not proxy clicks. The second function shows how to keep the agent curious. It represents an implementation detail behind the *Exploration/Entropy* box in Figure 10.1.

Emotion-driven RL marks a significant advancement in the realm of interactive technologies because emotions often implicitly guide human decision-making, behaviours, and social interactions. Capturing and incorporating these emotional dynamics into machine learning enhances not only the technical performance of HCI systems but also their psychological appropriateness and emotional intelligence, leading to interactions that feel more natural, empathetic, and responsive (Schuller & Schuller, 2018). At its core, emotion-driven RL treats emotional signals as feedback mechanisms or intrinsic rewards. For instance, an intelligent tutoring system can interpret students' emotional states, such as frustration, boredom, engagement, or delight, and adjust its instructional strategies in real-time. Similarly, assistive robots can sense user stress or discomfort, modifying their behaviour proactively to foster comfort and trust (Broekens et al., 2015).

These emotional reward signals may originate from multiple modalities, including physiological sensors (e.g., heart rate variability, electroencephalogram), facial expression recognition, voice analysis, or textual sentiment analysis. By interpreting these rich emotional inputs, RL algorithms learn policies that are explicitly shaped by human affective responses rather than solely task-based outcomes. Thus, emotion-driven RL agents effectively bridge the gap between computational effectiveness and human psychological needs, preferences, and well-being. Emotion-driven RL has demonstrated substantial promise across diverse interactive domains, including:

- *Affective Computing and Virtual Agents:* Virtual companions and conversational agents now integrate emotional feedback to enhance realism, empathy, and user bonding, leading to higher satisfaction and sustained user engagement (McDuff & Czerwinski, 2018).
- *Adaptive Gaming Experiences:* Games employ real-time emotional adaptation, dynamically adjusting difficulty, narratives, or interactive elements based on detected emotional states, thereby maximising enjoyment and engagement (Yannakakis & Togelius, 2011).
- *Robotics and Socially Assistive Robots:* Robots in caregiving contexts or therapeutic interventions increasingly utilise emotional reinforcement

signals to provide personalised emotional support, ensuring interactions remain sensitive, empathetic, and psychologically supportive (Breazeal et al., 2016).

Despite its transformative potential, emotion-driven RL faces unique methodological and practical challenges. Emotional signals are often noisy, ambiguous, context-dependent, and temporally dynamic, complicating their integration into RL frameworks. Key methodological issues include:

- *Temporal Credit Assignment:* Emotional responses can be delayed or ambiguous, complicating accurate attribution of emotional feedback to specific agent actions.
- *Individual Differences and Adaptation:* Emotional patterns and reactions vary significantly among individuals, requiring agents to learn rapidly and generalise robustly across diverse emotional profiles.
- *Ethical and Privacy Concerns*: Leveraging emotional signals necessitates stringent safeguards to respect user privacy, psychological safety, informed consent, and emotional autonomy.

These challenges are balanced by considerable opportunities: emotion-driven RL opens unprecedented possibilities to humanise technology, deepen user engagement, foster emotional well-being, and provide personalised support.

As RL moves deeply into emotional interactions, ethical responsibilities multiply. Systems must not exploit or manipulate emotions, nor compromise user autonomy and privacy. Ethical principles must include:

- *Transparency*: Users should be explicitly informed of how emotional data is collected, interpreted, and utilised.
- *Consent and Autonomy*: Emotional interactions must respect individual autonomy, offering clear mechanisms for users to manage or withdraw emotional data use.
- *Psychological Safety*: Emotion-driven interactions must prioritise emotional safety, ensuring interventions remain supportive rather than intrusive or coercive.

Figure 10.2 facilitates a deeper conceptual understanding of RL. This integrated conceptual representation illustrates the sophisticated interaction among emotional sensing, RL agent adaptation, user interaction, and ethical oversight.

This conceptual framework elucidates the complex, dynamic interactions in emotion-driven RL systems, highlighting how emotional sensing and ethical oversight comprehensively shape interactive and adaptive processes. Solid arrows show the fast control loop from user expression to sensing, analysis, interpretation, RL adaptation, and back to the user. Dashed arrows show cross-cutting ethical oversight that constrains data capture, feature use,

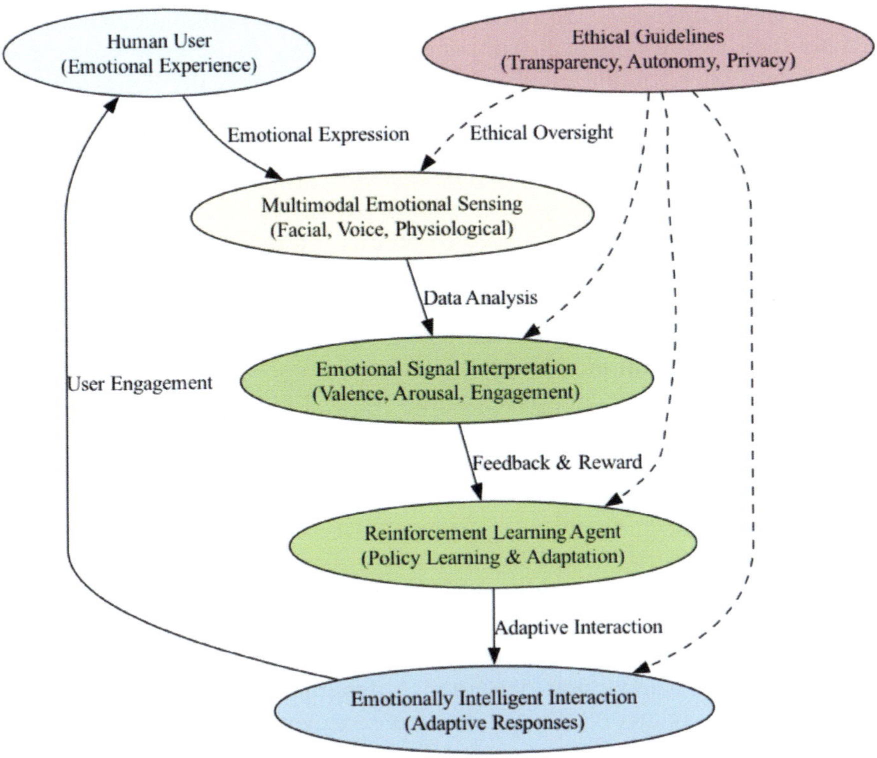

Figure 10.2 Emotion-driven reinforcement learning framework.

reward design, and allowable system actions, ensuring transparency, autonomy, and privacy throughout the loop.

10.3 Monitoring Mental Health with Reinforcement Learning

Mental health represents one of society's most pressing challenges, profoundly impacting quality of life, productivity, and well-being globally. Traditional approaches to monitoring and treating mental health issues rely largely on periodic assessments and self-reported measures, typically captured through clinical consultations, structured questionnaires, or interviews. However, these methods often lack granularity, timeliness, and ecological validity, failing to capture subtle day-to-day emotional fluctuations crucial for proactive intervention (Mohr et al., 2017).

The emergence of RL as a powerful computational paradigm in healthcare and mental health management has introduced transformative possibilities, shifting from reactive or periodic care towards proactive, continuous, and contextually sensitive mental health monitoring and support (Luo et al., 2022). RL methods, particularly when informed by embodied emotional signals such as physiological data, speech patterns, facial expressions, and behavioural cues, enable intelligent systems to dynamically adapt interactions, interventions, and monitoring strategies in real-time based on the user's mental and emotional states (Jaques et al., 2016). Comparable supervised pipelines are also used across psychological health domains, for example, the classification of chronic pain outcomes (Kovač et al., 2025b). Relatedly, regression pipelines have been used to predict internal shame from psychological predictors, demonstrating explainable ML in affect-linked constructs (Kovač et al., 2025a).

In conventional mental health monitoring, assessment intervals often span weeks or even months, limiting responsiveness and adaptive intervention. In contrast, RL agents continuously interact with individuals, learning from subtle emotional and behavioural signals, allowing early detection of emotional distress or mental health deterioration, and proactively adapting interventions to support mental health more effectively. This continuous adaptation approach significantly improves treatment personalisation and timeliness, directly addressing fluctuations in mental health conditions such as depression, anxiety, and stress disorders (Alasmrai et al., 2025).

RL-based monitoring systems leverage real-time multimodal emotional data (including speech analysis, wearable sensor data, facial emotion analysis, and digital behavioural patterns) to dynamically adjust their actions. These actions may involve alerting human caregivers, modifying therapeutic exercises, initiating supportive conversations through virtual agents, or recommending personalised self-care strategies. Importantly, the adaptability inherent to RL allows these interventions to evolve continuously, maximising emotional support and psychological benefit while minimising intrusiveness or discomfort.

Several pioneering applications of RL for mental health monitoring highlight the powerful potential of this approach:

- *Adaptive Digital Interventions*: RL systems have been integrated into smartphone-based mental health apps, dynamically adjusting intervention types and frequencies based on real-time assessments of emotional well-being (Liao et al., 2020).
- *Intelligent Conversational Agents and Chatbots*: Virtual mental health assistants utilise RL algorithms to adapt their conversational style, therapeutic strategies, and content dynamically, effectively responding to user emotional states and promoting emotional comfort and engagement (Fitzpatrick et al., 2017).
- *Wearable-Based Stress and Anxiety Management*: Wearable devices combined with RL-driven apps interpret continuous physiological data, such as heart rate variability and skin conductance, to personalise stress-reduction interventions in real-time, helping users maintain emotional balance and psychological well-being proactively (Rohani et al., 2018).

Implementing RL in mental health monitoring involves specific methodological considerations unique to this domain:

- *Sparse and Ambiguous Emotional Rewards*: Emotional and mental health signals are inherently complex, noisy, and ambiguous, making accurate reward interpretation challenging for RL agents.
- *Delayed and Long-Term Outcomes*: Emotional and mental health improvements often manifest gradually, posing significant temporal credit-assignment challenges for RL algorithms.
- *Personalisation and Generalisation*: Mental health states vary dramatically among individuals, necessitating RL models capable of personalised adaptation and rapid generalisation across diverse user profiles.

These challenges, however, provide significant opportunities for methodological innovation, such as sophisticated hierarchical RL architectures, contextual bandit algorithms, and advanced reward modelling techniques tailored specifically for mental health contexts.

RL applications in mental health raise critical ethical questions. Mental health data, by its very nature, are extremely sensitive, demanding strict adherence to ethical principles, including:

- *Privacy and Data Security*: Continuous emotional monitoring must rigorously ensure user confidentiality, informed consent, and secure data handling, preventing unauthorised access or unintended use.
- *Transparency and Explainability*: Users should clearly understand how their emotional data is collected, interpreted, and used for RL-driven adaptations, maintaining transparency and trust.
- *Psychological Safety and Autonomy*: RL-driven interventions should respect user autonomy, ensuring that proactive support remains non-intrusive, emotionally safe, and genuinely supportive rather than coercive or manipulative.

Those three principles aren't an afterthought. They are shaping the whole system. A rigorous design treats ethics as architectural constraints, not post-hoc add-ons. Privacy and security, transparency and explainability, and psychological safety and autonomy are specified a priori and enforced across sensing, inference, learning, and action. Figure 10.3 operationalises this approach by placing a governance layer that constrains data capture, feature use, policy optimisation, and escalation pathways throughout the system.

The dashed band across the top (Governance & Ethics) is a reminder that every layer beneath operates under explicit constraints: what can be sensed (consent), how it is stored (privacy and security), how inferences are reported (transparency and explainability), and what actions are allowed (psychological safety and user autonomy). The dashed connectors are not data pipes; they are *oversight links* showing that governance continuously limits and guides sensing, feature use, learning, and escalation.

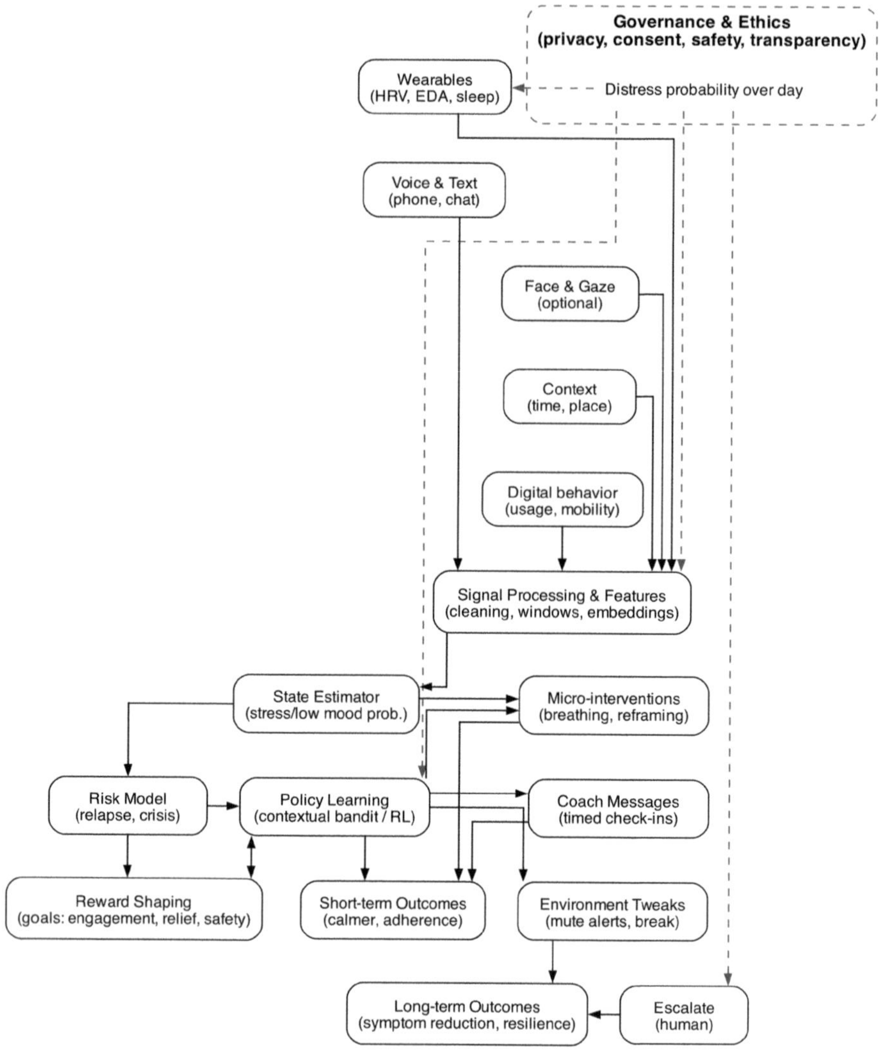

Figure 10.3 Monitoring mental health with reinforcement learning.

Beneath that, the signals row shows the kinds of input we might collect with consent: wearables (HRV, EDA, sleep), voice and text, optional face and gaze, simple context (time/place), and digital behaviour (e.g., phone-use rhythms). These raw streams are not yet emotions. They flow into Signal Processing & Features, where they're cleaned, synchronised, and summarised without discarding affect-laden cues. From there, two kinds of inferences are made. A State Estimator produces moment-to-moment probabilities (e.g., *low mood likely*), while a Risk Model looks ahead to estimate relapse or crisis risk. Keeping state and risk separate helps with explainability: one tells you *how things look now*, the other *what seems likely next*.

The following functions show a minimal contextual bandit for micro-interventions, risk-aware shaping, and a safe escalation rule that mirrors the graded actions in Figure 10.3:

```
import numpy as np

def softmax(x: np.ndarray, temp: float = 0.5) -> np.ndarray:
    z = x / max(1e-6, temp)
    z -= z.max()
    e = np.exp(z)
    return e / e.sum()

def choose_intervention(context_phi: np.ndarray, W: np.ndarray,
temp: float = 0.5) -> int:
    scores = W @ context_phi
    probs = softmax(scores, temp=temp)
    return int(np.random.choice(len(scores), p=probs))
def risk_shaped_reward(relief: float, engagement: float, risk_
prob: float,
            w_relief=0.6, w_eng=0.4, risk_penalty=2.0) -> float:
    base = w_relief * relief + w_eng * engagement
    return float(base - risk_penalty * max(0.0, risk_prob))

from dataclasses import dataclass

@dataclass
class EscalationPolicy:
    hi: float = 0.7 # high risk threshold
    lo: float = 0.4 # de-escalation threshold
    min_cooldown: int = 3 # interactions between escalations

def should_escalate(risk_now: float, last_escalation_steps_
ago: int, policy: EscalationPolicy) -> bool:
    return (risk_now >= policy.hi) and (last_escalation_
steps_ago >= policy.min_cooldown)
```

Decisions live in the next row. Policy learning (the RL component) selects actions, but it does so alongside reward shaping, where goals are set in human terms (*relief, engagement, safety*), not raw screen time. That's the practical expression of autonomy and safety from the bullet list above: the agent learns, but only within guardrails that favour well-being. Actions are graded. The system starts with micro-interventions (a breathing cue, a brief reframing), then coach messages (timed, light-touch check-ins), then environment tweaks (quieting notifications or suggesting a break). Only when risk warrants it does the system escalate to a human. This tiered design keeps help supportive, not intrusive, and it leaves room for human judgement when it matters most. Short-term (calmer now? adhered?) and long-term (symptom reduction, resilience) outcomes flow back to update the estimator and the learning policy. That feedback loop is how the system becomes more personal over time *without* relaxing its ethical boundaries.

10.4 Emotion-Driven Education

Education has traditionally emphasised cognitive dimensions, such as knowledge acquisition, logical reasoning, and skill development. Yet, decades of educational and psychological research underscore that learning is fundamentally intertwined with emotion. Emotional states, such as curiosity, frustration, boredom, and enjoyment, critically influence learners' motivation, engagement, retention, and overall academic achievement (Pekrun & Linnenbrink-Garcia, 2014). Despite this understanding, conventional educational systems often lack the flexibility and responsiveness required to address dynamic emotional experiences, relying instead on static instructional designs and uniform learning strategies.

Emotion-driven education, empowered by RL, represents a transformative shift toward responsive, personalised, and emotionally sensitive educational experiences. RL methodologies enable educational systems to continuously monitor learners' emotional states and dynamically adapt educational content, interactions, and strategies accordingly, optimising both learning outcomes and emotional well-being (D'Mello & Graesser, 2012).

At the heart of emotion-driven education lies the recognition that emotions are not mere secondary variables in the learning process but central drivers of educational success. RL uniquely addresses this perspective by treating emotional signals as key feedback mechanisms guiding instructional adaptation. Unlike traditional rule-based or predetermined interventions, RL-driven educational systems learn continuously from students' emotional responses, adapting in real-time to individual emotional profiles, preferences, and needs (Calvo & D'Mello, 2010). Figure 10.4 visualises a simple emotion-aware *policy surface*. It shows how an RL tutor can map combinations of learner arousal and task challenge to pedagogical actions, and how a learner's state moves through this space during a session (Pekrun, 2018; Baker et al., 2010).

Rows represent learner arousal (low–high) and columns task challenge (low–high). Each cell names the *recommended action* (e.g., *Maintain Flow*, *Micro-break*, *Scaffold & Pace*). The polyline traces a synthetic session: the learner starts under-engaged, enters a productive *flow* region (moderate arousal, moderate challenge), then spikes toward overload, prompting actions that de-escalate and re-scaffold. The goal is not to push difficulty relentlessly, but to stabilise around flow while preserving motivation and affective safety (Pekrun, 2018). Seen this way, affect becomes part of the state the tutor optimises: low arousal + low challenge calls for energising prompts; medium + medium favours holding pace; high arousal + high challenge triggers step-back or soothing actions before learning resumes. Empirically,

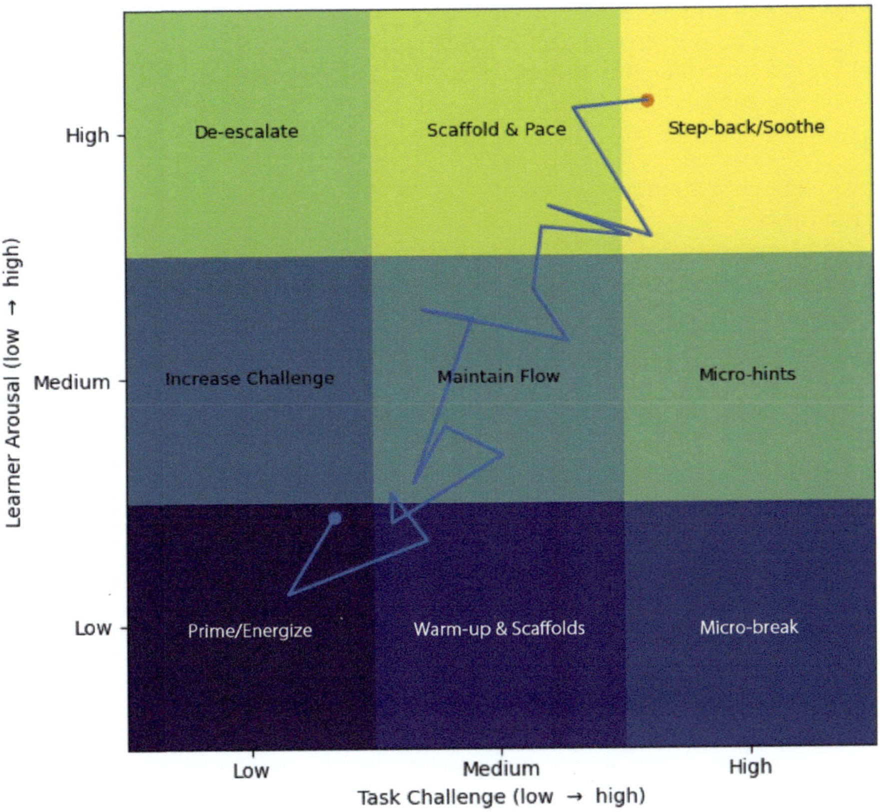

Figure 10.4 Emotion-aware policy surface with session trajectory.

keeping learners near that middle band is associated with better persistence, deeper processing, and fewer unproductive episodes of boredom or frustration (Baker et al., 2010). The policy surface is thus a compact picture of *how* an emotion-sensitive RL system operationalises the theories you cite. The next function encodes the policy surface from Figure 10.4, and a small utility turns sensed arousal–challenge into an action label:

```
from typing import Literal

Action = Literal["Energise", "Maintain Flow", "Micro-break",
"Scaffold & Pace", "De-escalate"]

def tutor_policy_surface(arousal: float, challenge: float) ->
Action:
    a, c = float(arousal), float(challenge)
    if a < 0.33 and c < 0.33:        # bored & easy
        return "Energise"
```

```
    if 0.33 <= a <= 0.66 and 0.33 <= c <= 0.66:
        return "Maintain Flow"
    if a > 0.66 and c > 0.66:        # overload
        return "De-escalate"
    if a > 0.66 and c <= 0.66:        # anxious, moderate task
        return "Micro-break"
    return "Scaffold & Pace"      # low arousal, high challenge
or mixed
```

Emotion-driven educational systems employ multimodal emotional sensing methods to detect learners' emotional states through facial expressions, gaze patterns, physiological responses (e.g., heart rate, skin conductance), voice dynamics, and interaction patterns (e.g., mouse movements, task completion times). By interpreting these emotional signals as intrinsic rewards or penalties, RL algorithms dynamically adjust learning difficulty, pacing, instructional style, content presentation, and motivational strategies to sustain engagement and support positive emotional experiences (Baker et al., 2010).

RL has already shown notable potential in emotion-driven education, with diverse applications illustrating its transformative possibilities:

- *Intelligent Tutoring Systems (ITS)*: Advanced ITS integrate RL-based emotion sensing to adjust instructional interventions dynamically, recognising frustration or disengagement and responding with personalised scaffolding, hints, or encouragement, thereby maintaining learner motivation and engagement (Arroyo et al., 2011).
- *Adaptive Educational Games:* Educational gaming environments leveraging RL can identify emotional states in real time, adapting gameplay difficulty and providing emotional support through tailored feedback, maintaining optimal challenge levels, and maximising enjoyment and learning efficacy (Conati & Maclaren, 2009).
- *Virtual Learning Environments (VLEs)*: Emotion-aware VLEs utilise RL to proactively manage learner emotions, adjusting content and interactions dynamically to reduce stress and anxiety, thereby improving overall learning experiences and outcomes, especially in remote or virtual educational contexts (Shute & Ke, 2012).

Integrating RL into emotion-driven educational systems presents several methodological challenges and opportunities:

- *Complexity of Emotional Signals*: Accurately interpreting subtle emotional indicators in educational settings requires sophisticated, multimodal data integration techniques to handle noisy, ambiguous, and context-dependent signals.

- *Delayed and Ambiguous Emotional Rewards*: Learner emotions can fluctuate rapidly, often delayed or influenced by external factors, making RL credit assignment particularly challenging.
- *Personalisation at Scale*: Effective RL-driven educational systems must rapidly adapt to diverse emotional profiles across a large student population, balancing individualised adaptation with scalability and generalisability.

These challenges present significant research opportunities, inviting the development of advanced hierarchical RL architectures, robust emotional signal interpretation methods, and innovative personalised learning strategies. Because students change over time, a simple *affect-stabilising curriculum* helps the tutor stay near the flow region while still progressing content. The next function implements the *keep near flow* principle (gentle push when calm, stronger pullback when arousal spikes):

```
def curriculum_step(difficulty: float, arousal: float, target_
arousal: float = 0.5,
                     k_up: float = 0.05, k_down: float = 0.08)
-> float:
    if arousal <= target_arousal:
        difficulty += k_up
    else:
        difficulty -= k_down
    return float(min(1.0, max(0.0, difficulty)))
```

As educational systems delve deeper into emotional monitoring and adaptive interactions, critical ethical responsibilities emerge:

- *Privacy and Data Protection*: Monitoring emotional states requires strict data privacy protocols, ensuring emotional data remains confidential, secure, and used exclusively for educational enhancement.
- *Transparency and Explainability*: Students, parents, and educators must fully understand how emotional data informs adaptive educational strategies, ensuring transparency, consent, and trustworthiness.
- *Autonomy and Emotional Safety*: RL-driven adaptations must carefully preserve student autonomy and emotional safety, avoiding manipulative practices and always prioritising emotional well-being alongside academic success.

References

Achiam, J., Held, D., Tamar, A., & Abbeel, P. (2017, July). Constrained policy optimization. In *International conference on machine learning* (pp. 22–31). PMLR.

Alasmrai, M. A., Ismail, R. M., & Ali Al-Abyadh, M. H. (2025). Personalized cognitive behavioral therapy for adults using machine learning: A multi-factor, reinforcement-based approach. *Fusion: Practice & Applications*, *20*(2), 53–64.

Arroyo, I., Woolf, B. P., Cooper, D. G., Burleson, W., & Muldner, K. (2011, July). The impact of animated pedagogical agents on girls' and boys' emotions, attitudes, behaviors and learning. In *2011 IEEE 11th international conference on Advanced learning technologies* (pp. 506–510). IEEE.

Baker, R., D'Mello, S., Rodrigo, M., & Graesser, A. (2010). Better to be frustrated than bored: The incidence and persistence of affect during interactions with three different computer-based learning environments. *International Journal of Human-Computer Studies*, *68*(4), 223–241.

Barrett, L. F. (2017). *How emotions are made: The secret life of the brain*. Pan Macmillan.

Breazeal, C., Dautenhahn, K., & Kanda, T. (2016). Social robotics. In B. Siciliano & O. Khatib (Eds.), *Springer handbook of robotics* (pp. 1935–1972). Springer.

Broekens, J., Jacobs, E., & Jonker, C. M. (2015). A reinforcement learning model of joy, distress, hope and fear. *Connection Science*, *27*(3), 215–233.

Calvo, R. A., & D'Mello, S. (2010). Affect detection: An interdisciplinary review of models, methods, and their applications. *IEEE Transactions on Affective Computing*, *1*(1), 18–37.

Conati, C., & Maclaren, H. (2009). Empirically building and evaluating a probabilistic model of user affect. *User Modeling and User-Adapted Interaction*, *19*(3), 267–303.

D'Mello, S., & Graesser, A. (2012). Dynamics of affective states during complex learning. *Learning and Instruction*, *22*(2), 145–157.

D'Mello, S., & Graesser, A. (2013). AutoTutor and affective AutoTutor: Learning by talking with cognitively and emotionally intelligent computers that talk back. *ACM Transactions on Interactive Intelligent Systems (TiiS)*, *2*(4), 1–39.

Damasio, A. R. (1996). *El error de Descartes*. Andrés Bello.

Farahani, H., Watson, P., Bezan, T., Kovač, N., Winter, L. C., Blagojević, M., & Jiménez, P. (2024). PsAIchology: An intelligent direction in psychological sciences. In *10th international scientific conference Technics, Informatics and Education-TIE 2024*. Faculty of Technical Sciences Čačak, University of Kragujevac.

Farahani, H., Watson, P., Kovač, N., Sheykhangafshe, F. B., Azadfallah, P., Allahyari, A., & Chesli, R. R. (2025). Unraveling the complexity of love addiction using machine learning algorithms: The influence of positive and negative affect, interpersonal needs, and self-hate. In C.-H. Mayer & E. Vanderheiden (Eds.), *International handbook of love: Transcultural and transdisciplinary perspectives* (pp. 1–22). Springer Nature.

Fitzpatrick, K. K., Darcy, A., & Vierhile, M. (2017). Delivering cognitive behavior therapy to young adults with symptoms of depression and anxiety using a fully automated conversational agent (Woebot): A randomized controlled trial. *JMIR Mental Health*, *4*(2), e7785.

Gratch, J., & Marsella, S. (2014). *Appraisal models* (pp. 54–67). Oxford University Press.

Jaques, N., McDuff, D., Kim, Y. L., & Picard, R. (2016, September). Understanding and predicting bonding in conversations using thin slices of facial expressions and body language. In *International conference on intelligent virtual agents* (pp. 64–74). Springer International Publishing.

Jaques, N., Taylor, S., Sano, A., & Picard, R. (2015, December). Multi-task, multi-kernel learning for estimating individual wellbeing. In *Proceedings of NIPS workshop on multimodal machine learning, Montreal, Quebec* (Vol. 898, p. 3).

Kahneman, D., & Tversky, A. (2013). Prospect theory: An analysis of decision under risk. InL. C. MacLean & W. T. Ziemba (Eds.), *Handbook of the fundamentals of financial decision making: Part I* (pp. 99–127). World Scientific Publishing.

Kovač, N., Ratković, K., Farahani, H., & Watson, P. (2024). A practical applications guide to machine learning regression models in psychology with Python. *Methods in Psychology*, *11*, 100156.

Kovač, N., Ratković, K., Farahani, H., & Watson, P. (2025a). Machine learning regression models for internal shame. *Acta Psychologica*, *260*, 105721.

Kovač, N., Ratković, K., Watson, P., Farahani, H., & Bagheri Sheykhangafshe, F. (2025b). Machine learning classification models for predicting chronic pain. *Current Psychology*, *44*, 15409–15422.

Levine, S., Kumar, A., Tucker, G., & Fu, J. (2020). Offline reinforcement learning: Tutorial, review, and perspectives on open problems. *arXiv preprint arXiv:2005.01643*.

Liao, P., Greenewald, K., Klasnja, P., & Murphy, S. (2020). Personalized heartsteps: A reinforcement learning algorithm for optimizing physical activity. *Proceedings of the ACM on Interactive, Mobile, Wearable and Ubiquitous Technologies*, *4*(1), 1–22.

Luo, Y., Wunderink, R. G., & Lloyd-Jones, D. (2022). Proactive vs reactive machine learning in health care: lessons from the COVID-19 pandemic. *Jama*, *327*(7), 623–624.

McDuff, D., & Czerwinski, M. (2018). Designing emotionally sentient agents. *Communications of the ACM*, *61*(12), 74–83.

Mohr, D. C., Zhang, M., & Schueller, S. M. (2017). Personal sensing: Understanding mental health using ubiquitous sensors and machine learning. *Annual Review of Clinical Psychology*, *13*(1), 23–47.

Paiva, A., Leite, I., Boukricha, H., & Wachsmuth, I. (2017). Empathy in virtual agents and robots: A survey. *ACM Transactions on Interactive Intelligent Systems (TiiS)*, *7*(3), 1–40.

Pekrun, R. (2018). Control-value theory: A social-cognitive approach to achievement emotions. *Big Theories Revisited*, *2*, 162–190.

Pekrun, R., & Linnenbrink-Garcia, L. (2014). Introduction to emotions in education. In L. Linnenbrink-Garcia & R. Pekrun (Eds.), *International handbook of emotions in education* (pp. 1–10). Routledge.

Pessoa, L. (2013). *The cognitive-emotional brain: From interactions to integration*. MIT Press.

Rohani, D. A., Faurholt-Jepsen, M., Kessing, L. V., & Bardram, J. E. (2018). Correlations between objective behavioral features collected from mobile and wearable devices and depressive mood symptoms in patients with affective disorders: Systematic review. *JMIR mHealth and uHealth*, *6*(8), e9691.

Rolls, E. T. (2014). *Emotion and decision making explained*. OUP.

Schuller, D., & Schuller, B. W. (2018). The age of artificial emotional intelligence. *Computer*, *51*(9), 38–46.

Schultz, W. (2016). Dopamine reward prediction-error signalling: A two-component response. *Nature Reviews Neuroscience*, *17*(3), 183–195.

Schultz, W. (2017). Reward prediction error. *Current Biology*, *27*(10), R369-R371.

Shute, V. J., & Ke, F. (2012). Games, learning, and assessment. In D. Ifenthaler, D. Eseryel, & X. Ge (Eds.), *Assessment in game-based learning: Foundations, innovations, and perspectives* (pp. 43–58). Springer.

Sutton, R. S., & Barto, A. G. (2018). *Reinforcement learning: An introduction* (2nd ed.). MIT Press.

Thomas, P., & Brunskill, E. (2016, June). Data-efficient off-policy policy evaluation for reinforcement learning. In *International conference on machine learning* (pp. 2139–2148). PMLR.

Yannakakis, G. N., & Togelius, J. (2011). Experience-driven procedural content generation. *IEEE Transactions on Affective Computing*, 2(3), 147–161.

11 Predicting Personality and Emotional Abilities from Brain Features Using Machine Learning

Alessandro Grecucci, Rodolfo Rizzi, Richard Bakiaj, Parisa Ahmadi Ghomroudi, Teresa Baggio, Khanitin Jornkokgoud, Miriam Langerbeck, and Irene Messina

11.1 The Brain Is a Mathematical Object

Molly: Our profile says you're doing everything you can to kill you...
Case: Profile?
Molly: We have developed a very detailed model.
We have broken down your personality into various
behavioral modules, with related standard analysis,
then recombined everything thanks to military software.
You're suicidal, Case. The model gives you a maximum of one month of life.
And our medical projection is that you will
need a new pancreas within a year.

William Gibson, Neuromancer, 1984

From a biological standpoint, the brain consists of neurons, glial cells, tissues, blood vessels, and various other anatomical components. However, for a cognitive neuroscientist seeking to comprehend how these structures contribute to mental abilities, solely relying on the biological perspective is inadequate. While anatomy and physiology serve as the foundation, they do not directly explain the unfolding of cognitive processes. To gain a comprehensive understanding of the brain, multiple perspectives are required, ranging from biological to cognitive, and even computational approaches. The present chapter begins with the concept of considering the brain as a mathematical object. This perspective allows for the application of mathematical and computational methods to understand and model brain functions. With a mathematical object we intend to have a structure made of mathematical relationships between the subparts. The subparts refer to a large number of dimensions. If we consider the approximate number of synapses, the brain can be described as an N-dimensional space of ~10^{15} dimensions (the state of every synapse contributes to the structure, and as such it is a dimension with a given range of values). If we consider the neurons, there are 10^{12} dimensions. Usually, in a cognitive neuroscience perspective, we rely on voxels as

DOI: 10.4324/9781003495123-11

the minimum unit of analysis, ending up to ~10^5 dimensions. Voxels can be clustered in brain regions leading to a much lower number of dimensions. Regardless of the level of analysis employed, the brain can be conceptualized as a mathematical structure composed of N dimensions.

What does this complex mathematical structure do? In a computational perspective, this structure performs operations that can be described as computations of functions (Churchland & Sejnowski, 2016). A function can be described as a mapping between elements of one set (the domain) and another set (the range). In other words, a computable function can be specified by a rule that indicates how to transform the first element into the second. In this framework, the brain's states and their transitions represent a system capable of complex computations (Churchland & Sejnowski, 2016), making it a powerful computational entity. To model brain states computationally, neuroscientists use vectors. A vector is an ordered set of numbers that can describe various parameters, such as neuronal firing rates, the gray matter density in voxels, or the connectivity between regions (Churchland & Sejnowski, 2016). A vector represents a brain state in an N-dimensional space (the whole brain). Brain states are points within this space[1]. Brain states can be conceptualized as specific arrangements within a part, or the entire, N-dimensional space. These states are associated with, or correspond to, specific psychological functions we perform. This conceptualization is useful for both understanding the brain itself and the machine learning (ML) analyses when they are applied to the brain. This perspective is indeed coherent with what we do when we analyze brain data with ML methods. In standard frequentist approaches, such as for example the generalized linear model (GLM), we typically begin by examining experimental manipulations (such as stimuli of different categories) and seek to identify corresponding variations in brain signals. Conversely, in ML approaches, we take the opposite approach: we begin with brain states and attempt to predict psychological variables from them. This flow of analysis aligns with the arguments we have presented thus far on brain functioning from a mathematical-computational perspective[2]. When we apply machine learning methods to the brain, we aim to predict cognitive states from brain states (intended as specific rearrangements of part of, or the entire, brain)[3]. If we denote cognitive states with the Greek letter "Ψ" and brain state with "σ", then when we apply machine learning methods, we aim to predict Ψ from σ[4]. See Figure 11.1 for a graphical representation. Going back to the computational perspective, the goal is to derive a function "f" that maps brain states (σ) into cognitive states (Ψ)[5]. This approach enables the predicting of psychological functions from neural data. The advantage of machine learning is that f can be used to predict new cases. In other words, f can be used to know which psychological operation is performed in a brain in a given state. This opens up the possibility of creating predictive models of psychological functions, as we will explore in the following sections. Before discussing these results, in the next section we introduce some useful machine learning concepts.

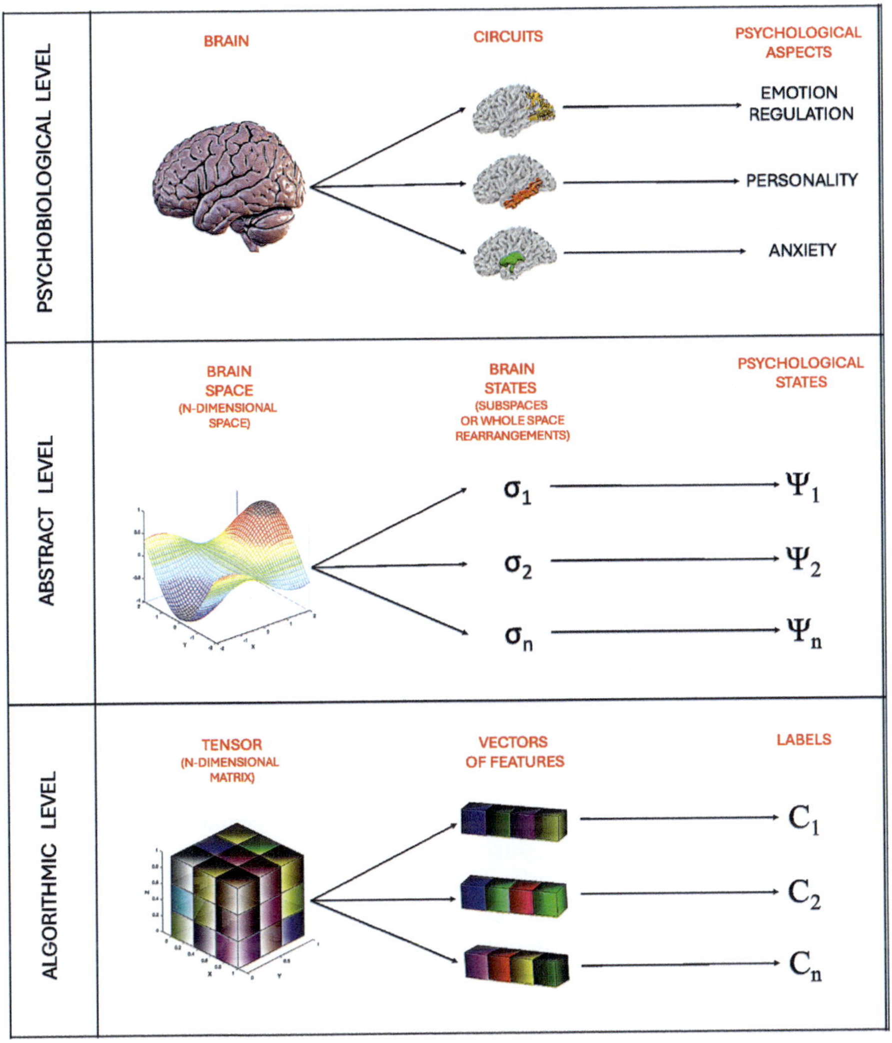

Figure 11.1 Levels of analysis.

11.2 Machine Learning Approaches to Predict Emotions and Personality

Over the past few decades, the field of neuroscience has made substantial strides in unveiling the complex neurobiological mechanisms underlying psychiatric and neurological disorders. However, the translation of research findings into clinical practice remains considerably limited (Prata et al., 2014; Woo et al., 2017). One possible reason for this gap is that traditional research methodologies often produce insights at the group level, which, while valuable, do not directly support individual-level clinical decision-making nor prediction of new cases (Arbabshirani et al., 2017; Mechelli & Viera, 2019). This discrepancy highlights the growing importance of machine learning in healthcare research (Yahata et al., 2017). Machine learning, a subfield of artificial intelligence (AI), has significantly evolved as a discipline aimed at developing intelligent systems capable of autonomously acquiring knowledge and making decisions. This domain focuses on extracting patterns from datasets and leveraging these patterns to forecast outcomes on novel, unseen data (Mitchell, 1997). Central to machine learning is the concept of generalizability, which pertains to the model's ability to apply learned rules from previous data to accurately predict outcomes in new datasets (Domingos, 2012; Mechelli & Viera, 2019). Generalizability serves as a cornerstone in evaluating the efficacy of machine learning models, emphasizing their potential in making reliable predictions across varying scenarios. Machine learning, with its multivariate nature, addresses the limitations of standard statistical approaches by considering variable interrelationships within a unified model, providing a more robust link between neurobiological underpinnings and the phenomenology of the disorder (Wolfers et al., 2018). More importantly, ML tests for generalization to new cases without assuming it as in standard statistical approaches. Indeed, one advantage of such methods relies on their power to extract predictive models from the data. These predictive models can be used to classify patients versus controls, or to predict clinical variables (relapse, treatment responses, symptomatic severity, etc.). In this way, ML's ability to extract predictive models holds promise for enhancing diagnostic accuracy and personalizing treatment strategies (Mechelli & Viera, 2019.

ML methods can be broadly categorized into supervised learning and unsupervised learning. Specifically, supervised learning involves training a model on labeled data, where the desired output is known. For example, a model might be trained to discriminate patients that suffer from personality disorders based on the underlying neural features (Gao et al., 2017). On the other hand, unsupervised learning deals with unlabeled data, aiming to uncover hidden patterns or structures. For instance, clustering algorithms can group patients with similar symptom profiles or brain activity patterns, potentially revealing subtypes of psychiatric disorders (Drysdale et al., 2017). However, supervised methods are often preferred for creating predictive models, especially when the goal is to predict a diagnosis (classification problem), predict a personality trait, or investigate a specific emotional ability (regression problem) (Grecucci et al., 2023). One of the most used classes of supervised machine learning is support vector machines (SVM), which are particularly effective in high-dimensional spaces, such as neuroimaging data (Mechelli & Viera, 2019). SVMs work by finding a hyperplane that best separates the data into different classes. The use of kernel functions, such as polynomial, radial-basis function (RBF), and sigmoid, allows SVMs to handle non-linear relationships by transforming the input data into a higher-dimensional space where a linear separator can be applied. One of the key advantages of SVMs is their ability to highlight which features (variables) are most important in distinguishing between classes. This feature's importance is crucial in neuroimaging, where understanding which brain regions are most predictive of a condition can provide insights into the underlying neurobiology (Orru et al., 2012)

To further enhance the insights gained from neuroimaging data, data-driven multimodal fusion approaches integrate information from features from different neuroimaging modalities (e.g., MRI, fMRI, EEG) as well as genetic data (Mechelli & Viera, 2019). These methods, such as canonical correlation analysis (CCA), joint independent component analysis (jICA), and parallel ICA (pICA), enable the combination of complementary data features to enhance the detection of disease-related patterns or psychological construct (Sui et al., 2020). By combining the information of each modality, fusion methods improve the robustness and reliability of neuroimaging biomarkers, facilitating more accurate diagnoses and treatment plans (Baggio et al., 2023; Grecucci et al., 2023, 2024; Jornkokgoud et al., 2024).

In the upcoming sections, we delve into recent neuro-predictive models of emotional abilities and personality traits that leverage machine learning methods.

11.3 Predicting Emotional Abilities

Emotions are multi-dimensional psycho-biological responses elicited by significant environmental triggers that produce changes in our subjective feelings, physiological responses, and behavioral manifestations (Grecucci et al., 2023; Mauss et al., 2005). Central to our understanding of the emotional response is the concept that in normal conditions, the emotional intensity correlates with the magnitude of the emotionality conveyed by the stimulus that elicited the response (Frederickson et al., 2018; Grecucci et al., 2020). Following Fechner's law describing the psychophysical response to sensory input, we can model the emotional response (y_e) as a function of the stimulus relevance (x_s) with the formula:

$$ye = \log(xs)$$

This model suggests that low-intensity stimuli trigger mild emotional reactions, whereas high-intensity stimuli induce intense emotional reactions (Grecucci et al., 2020). The response pattern aligns with the logarithmic scaling of sensory perception. Specifically, the response curve steeply ascends at lower stimulus values and flattens at higher levels, agreeing well with the laws of psychophysics discovered by Fechner. However, the dynamics of emotional response in daily life and in clinical settings show much more complexity than this simplified model (Grecucci et al., 2020). Variability in responses may therefore not only index proportionality to the stimulus objective intensity, but also intrinsic individual differences (Dadomo et al., 2016). Such deviations can be modeled by modifying the original equation to include several factors (see Grecucci et al., 2020 for a complete discussion of this model). We start by considering the "intensity" factor η, resulting in the modified equation:

$$ye = \log(xs) + \eta$$

where η denotes a variation of intensity that can either affect y_e in a positive or negative way, indicating an enhanced or diminished emotional response's intensity relative to the stimulus (see Figure 11.2 A). Another relevant aspect is the temporal dynamics of the emotional response. Indeed, responses can either be almost immediate, or precede the stimulus, or be largely delayed. To integrate these temporal disparities, the model can be broadened as follows:

$$ye = \log(xs + \tau) + \eta$$

where τ represents the time shift, with negative values indicating anticipatory responses ($\tau < 0$) and positive values reflecting delayed responses ($\tau > 0$) (see Figure 11.2 B).

Another important aspect that must be considered is the speed at which emotional responses escalate to their peak. This variability in the emotional response requires further modification in the equation:

$$ye = \omega * log(xs + \tau) + \eta (11.1)$$

Here, ω indicates the growth rate of the response, with values less than one indicating a rapid escalation and values greater than one a slower ascent (see Grecucci et al., 2020 for a graphical representation of this equation) (see Figure 11.2 C). Equation (11.1) describes a range of variations that we can observe in the clinical settings. Significant variation of the variables η, τ, and ω collectively define what we indicate by the term "emotional dysregulation". These factors may individually or collectively contribute to pathological emotional responses, such as those that are prematurely triggered, excessively intense, or rapidly peaking, necessitating targeted clinical attention (Dadomo et al., 2018). Indeed, challenges in managing emotions are linked to various psychological disorders (Kring & Sloan, 2009; Sheppes et al., 2015; Dadomo et al., 2018; Frederickson et al., 2018; Grecucci et al., 2020). Given the widespread emotion regulation challenges across psychological disorders, clinicians have begun to incorporate a range of emotion regulation strategies into their therapeutic methods (Leahy et al., 2011; Messina et al., 2013; Dadomo et al., 2016, 2018; Frederickson et al., 2018). From a translational research perspective, the ability to predict emotion regulation abilities holds promise for improving the diagnosis and treatment of

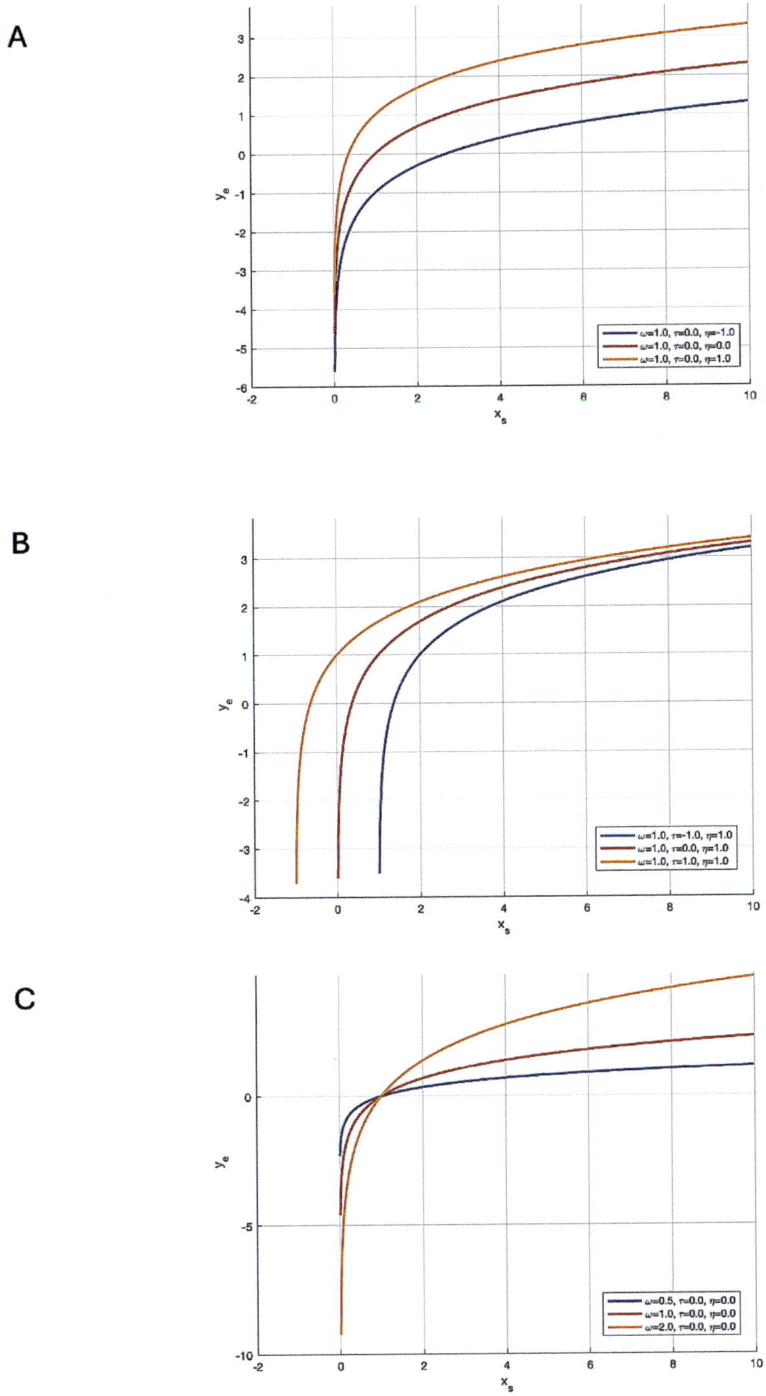

Figure 11.2 Family of equations to graphically represent the variations in emotional response according to the η(A) , τ(B) , and ω(C) factors.

individuals facing emotion regulation challenges. Machine learning can serve as a valuable tool in this endeavor, offering sophisticated algorithms capable of analyzing complex brain data to identify patterns and predict emotion regulation abilities. By leveraging machine learning techniques, researchers can develop predictive models that aid clinicians in identifying individuals at risk of emotional dysregulation and tailor interventions to meet their specific needs. This approach enhances the precision and effectiveness of clinical interventions, ultimately improving outcomes for individuals struggling with emotion regulation difficulties.

Before discussing these studies, we provide an introduction to the main strategies used in the following studies.

Reappraisal is referred to as "construing a potentially emotion-eliciting situation in non-emotional terms" (Gross, 1998, 2002). It is an antecedent-focused regulation strategy, modifying the emotion before it fully develops. Research has shown that reappraisal effectively reduces the intensity of negative emotional reactions and lowers the respiration rate. It also reduces the behavioral expressions associated with negative emotions, moderates physiological responses, and enhances well-being (Gross, 2002, 2015; Wolgast et al., 2011; Goldin et al., 2019).

Suppression is categorized as a response-focused emotion regulation strategy, involving modifying emotional responses after they have fully emerged. It is defined as an effort to inhibit the behavioral display of current emotions (Gross & Levenson, 1993). Several studies reveal that suppression leads to a reduction in positive emotional experiences while leaving negative emotions unaffected. Additionally, it has a negative physiological impact (Gross & Levenson, 1993; Gross, 2002; Mauss et al., 2005; Brans et al., 2013).

Acceptance is defined as "the active and ware embrace of private experiences without unnecessary attempts to change their frequency or form" (Hayes et al., 2012). It is an attitude of openness and curiosity towards the ongoing stream of thoughts and sensory experiences (Grecucci et al., 2015; Goldin et al., 2019). Acceptance is considered an adaptive emotion regulation strategy, positively linked to well-being (Aldao et al., 2010).

For what concerns the application of machine learning methods to predict emotional regulation abilities from neural features, one of the first attempts was made by Pappaianni and colleagues who used an unsupervised machine learning approach, known as source-based morphometry (SBM, Xu et al., 2009), based on Independent Component Analysis (ICA), to explore individual differences in structural brain characteristics associated with reappraisal usage. In their study, 37 participants were categorized into low and high reappraisal groups based on their scores from the Emotion Regulation Questionnaire (ERQ; Gross & John, 2003a, 2003b). The findings indicated a greater concentration of gray matter in a network encompassing the frontal, temporal, and parietal regions in low reappraisers compared to high reappraisers.

More recently, a pioneering study by Ghomroudi and colleagues (2023) developed a neuro-predictive model of both reappraisal and suppression usage able to successfully predict new cases. This study applied a combination of unsupervised and supervised machine learning algorithms to the structural MRI scans of 128 individuals. Initially, unsupervised machine learning in the form of group ICA was used to segment the brain into naturally occurring gray matter networks. Subsequently, supervised machine learning in the form of boosted trees was applied to predict individual differences in reappraisal and suppression. Two predictive models were extracted. The first model included a temporo-parahippocampal-orbitofrontal network (Independent component IC13) that correctly predicted individual differences in reappraisal use. The second model included insular and fronto-temporo-cerebellar networks (Independent component IC8) that successfully predicted suppression usage. Of note, psychological factors such as the level of anxiety, the opposite strategy usage, and specific emotional intelligence indicators contributed to the predictive models.

In another study, Grecucci and colleagues (Grecucci et al., under review) used a data fusion machine learning technique (mCCA-jICA) to identify combined gray and white matter networks associated with high and low acceptance ability. This study revealed that two covarying GM-WM networks distinguish high accepters from low accepters. The first network demonstrated decreased GM-WM concentration in a fronto-temporal-parietal circuit that overlaps significantly with the Default Mode Network. The second network showed increased GM-WM concentration in the orbitofrontal, temporal, and parietal regions associated with the Central Executive Network. Psychologically, high accepters showed greater openness to experience compared to low accepters. These results suggest that high accepters and low accepters differ in their neural and psychological mechanisms, supporting and extending previous research on the significance of acceptance as a strategy linked to well-being.

Besides structural evidence, the contribution of functional networks (resting state macro-networks) to emotion regulation has been recently investigated. Ghoumroudi and colleagues (under review) conducted a functional connectivity analysis on resting-state data from 134 individuals. Employing group-ICA an unsupervised machine learning approach, and regression analyses, the authors identified resting-state networks that predicted acceptance and reappraisal abilities. Acceptance was associated with the Executive, Affective (including subcortical emotion-related areas), and Sensorimotor networks, while Reappraisal was linked to the Sensorimotor network.

In summary, machine learning methods have proven successful in predicting emotional abilities such as emotion regulation strategies usage. Table 11.1

Table 11.1 Emotion regulation.

Authors	*Main findings*	*Year of publication*
Ghomroudi et al.	Combined unsupervised and supervised machine learning algorithms on structural MRI scans of 128 individuals was applied. Initially, group ICA segmented the brain into gray matter networks. Then, boosted trees predicted individual differences in reappraisal and suppression. Two models emerged: one involving a temporo-parahippocampal-orbitofrontal network (IC13) for reappraisal prediction, and another involving insular and fronto-temporo-cerebellar networks (IC8) for suppression prediction. Psychological factors, including anxiety levels, opposite strategy usage, and specific emotional intelligence indicators, contributed to these models	2023
Grecucci et al.	The mCCA-jICA data fusion technique was applied to 128 MRI scans of healthy individuals to identify combined grey and white matter networks associated with acceptance ability. Two covarying GM-WM networks differentiated high accepters from low accepters. The first network showed decreased GM-WM concentration in a fronto-temporal-parietal circuit, overlapping significantly with the default mode network. The second network showed increased GM-WM concentration in the orbito-frontal, temporal, and parietal regions, linked to the central executive network. High accepters also demonstrated greater openness to experience. These findings highlight distinct neural and psychological mechanisms between high and low accepters, emphasizing the importance of acceptance in well-being	2025
Ghomroudi, et al.	A functional connectivity analysis was conducted on resting-state data from 134 individuals. Using group-ICA, and regression analyses, resting-state networks were identified that predicted acceptance and reappraisal abilities. Acceptance was associated with the executive, affective, and sensorimotor networks, while reappraisal was linked to the sensorimotor network.	2024

11.4 Predicting Personality Traits

In this section, we delve into recent developments within personality neuroscience that have harnessed the power of machine learning methodologies to construct neuro-predictive models of personality traits. Specifically, we focus on abnormal personality traits, a domain that has garnered increasing attention due to its clinical relevance and impact on individuals' well-being (Langerbeck et al., 2023). By employing machine learning techniques, researchers have been able to analyze complex patterns in neurobiological data and identify neural signatures associated with various personality traits, including those considered atypical or pathological (Grecucci et al., 2023, 2024; Jornkokgoud et al., 2023, 2024). Such neuro-predictive models offer valuable insights into the underlying neural mechanisms of abnormal personality traits, shedding light on the neurobiological basis of conditions such as personality disorders. Furthermore, the application of machine learning in personality neuroscience opens up new avenues for personalized medicine and targeted interventions. By leveraging neuro-predictive models of personality, clinicians may be better equipped to identify at an early stage individuals at risk of developing personality disorders. Individuals with personality pathologies exhibit an enduring pattern of internal experiences and behaviors that significantly diverge from the societal norms within their culture (American Psychiatric Association, 2013). Notably, those diagnosed with borderline personality disorder (BPD) often show problems in emotion expression and mood regulation (Mendez-Miller et al., 2022). This is characterized by an unstable pattern of impulsive control, manifesting in both interpersonal relationships and behavior, that includes impulsive aggressive outbursts and engagement in health-sabotaging activities (i.e., cutting) (Dadomo et al., 2016; De Panfilis et al., 2019; Mendez-Miller et al., 2022). A precise and psychiatric diagnosis is often complex and difficult due to several issues (Grecucci et al., 2022; Rao et al., 2020). First, the presented symptoms are strongly fluctuating within patients, increasing their psychiatric vulnerability (Choi-Kain et al., 2020). Second, the currently used classification manuals use a categorical approach to classify personality disorders. In contrast, personality is usually identified on a spectrum, using five domains of personality (Ashton, 2017). Another issue with the classification problem is the immense overlap in symptoms between the different categories of personality disorder (Siefert et al., 2022). Lastly, the diagnosis of BPD relies on observable behavior. Affective neuroscience has emerged as a method to identify neurobiological markers which serve as an objective tool to diagnose a PD via machine learning methods (Grecucci et al., 2022). Previous studies suffered from many limitations such as the use of mass univariate analysis, which can only look at each voxel separately, ignoring statistical relationships between voxels (Lapomarda et al., 2021; Sorella et al., 2019). Another disadvantage is the consideration of the average of individuals within each group, ignoring individual variances. Finally, in the mentioned studies the results have not been tested on new cases, thus no conclusion about generalizability can be made. Machine learning is a promising tool to overcome these limitations. Three studies have used machine learning to investigate the neural correlates of BPD. Grecucci et al. (2022) constructed a predictive model of BPD by using multiple kernel learning, a form of support vector machine for classification. This approach identifies brain areas that contribute to the model as the most relevant source for classification by using whole-brain pattern-based information (Mourao-Miranda et al., 2012). The authors were able to outline a specific neuronal circuit, including the right putamen, the left thalamus, the right fusiform gyrus, the right amygdala, the lingual gyrus, the right middle, and superior orbitofrontal cortex (OFC), the left pallidum, the left fusiform gyrus, and portions of the cerebellum, supporting previous findings. In another study, Grecucci et al. (2023) provided further strength and insight into these findings. By applying a combination of supervised (Random Forest) and unsupervised ML (mCCA+jICA), the brain was parceled into networks of covarying grey and white matter concentration. Second, the authors were able to build from this a predictive model which was able to classify individuals with BPD. The use of machine learning in this study had the advantage that it was able to clearly unravel any potential ambiguity and that the found networks were able to correctly classify new unobserved cases. A more recent study by Langerbeck et al. (2023) investigated the neural correlates of borderline personality trait (BPT) using a subclinical sample. By applying kernel ridge regression (KRR), a form of support vector regression (SVR), the authors were able to provide a distinctive circuit, based on a whole brain level, including the frontal and parietal regions, as well as the Heschl's area, the thalamus, the cingulum, and the insula. Furthermore, BPT predictions increase when only the regions limited to the brain circuit derived from the BPD model (Grecucci et al., 2022) are considered, thereby confirming a certain overlap in brain structure between subclinical and clinical samples. This study shows that ML is able to classify new cases when using dimensional scales, like personality traits. See Table 11.2.

Another line of research tried to develop neuro-predictive models of narcissistic personality traits. Narcissism is a complex personality trait characterized by various facets, including impaired relationship functioning, inflated self-perceptions, and intrapersonal and interpersonal mechanisms aimed at preserving these perceptions (Campbell et al., 2011; Twenge & Campbell, 2003). The term narcissism encompasses a broad spectrum of personality functioning that impacts self-worth, coherence, uniqueness, attachment in relationships, and empathy (Ronningstam, 2011). Pathologically, narcissism can manifest as grandiose or vulnerable subtypes, each with distinct characteristics (Miller et al., 2011). Neuroscientific exploration of narcissism is a burgeoning field aiming to understand the neural underpinnings of this personality trait and disorder. For instance, recently, Jornkokgoud and colleagues (2023) developed a predictive model of narcissism based on neural and psychological features underlying individual differences in narcissistic personality traits among 135 healthy participants. They used KRR and SVR that successfully associated certain brain regions, including the lateral and middle frontal gyrus, angular gyrus, Rolandic operculum, and Heschl's gyrus, with individual differences in narcissistic traits. In another

Table 11.2 Borderline personality.

Authors	*Main findings*	*Year of publication*
Grecucci et al.	20 patients with BPD, 30 patients with bipolar disorder (BD), and 45 healthy controls, structural MRI, were analyzed with Multiple Kernel Learning (MKL). BPD was correctly classified (80% accuracy) against HC by a circuit, including the basal ganglia, amygdala, portions of the temporal lobes and of the orbitofrontal cortex. By contrasting BPD with BD a more specific circuit for BPD could be outlined. The authors suggest that BPD can be characterized by anomalies in a cortico-subcortical circuit related to affective instability.	2022
Grecucci et al.	20 patients with BPD and 45 healthy control participants HC), structural MRI (grey and white matter), were analyzed with multimodal canonical correlation analysis, random forest. Two GM-WM covarying circuits, including the basal ganglia, amygdala, portions of the temporal lobes and of the orbitofrontal cortex, correctly classified BPD against HC. These circuits are affected by child traumatic experiences (e.g. emotional and physical neglect, physical abuse) and were predictive of symptoms severity (interpersonal and impulsivity domains). The authors suggested that these results show that BPD is characterized by anomalies in GM and WM circuits that are related to early traumatic experiences.	2023
Langerbeck, et al.	Strucutural scans of 135 participants were analyzed with Kernel Ridge Regression. At a whole brain level, a circuit including frontal and parietal regions, the Heschl's area, thalamus, cingulum, and insula, is predictive of borderline traits. BPT predictions increased when only a BPD circuit was considered. The authors confirmed a certain overlap in brain structure between subclinical and clinical samples. The default-mode network predicts BPT, confirming previous observations on its role in the BPD.	2023

study, Jornkokgoud and colleagues (2024) capitalized on a combination of unsupervised and supervised machine learning methods to investigate the joint contributions of gray matter (GM) and white matter (WM) to narcissistic personality traits (NPT). Brain scans from 135 participants were first decomposed into eight independent networks of covarying GM and WM using parallel ICA. Stepwise regression and Random Forest algorithms were then employed to predict NPT. Results revealed a distributed network with GM alterations in fronto-temporal regions, the insula, and the cingulate cortex, along with WM alterations in cerebellar and thalamic regions. Of note this network was specific for narcissistic traits and did not predict other personality traits used as controls (histrionic, paranoid, and avoidant). These findings hold promise for advancing our understanding of personality traits and potentially identifying brain biomarkers to predict narcissistic personality traits. See Table 11.3.

Another recent line of research tested the hypothesis that personality disorders could be predicted from the brain patterns of therapists interacting with their patients. Tanzilli et al. (2022) demonstrated that subjective feelings and cortical responses (EEG) of therapists could predict the personality disorders of their clients. Fourteen therapists observed videos of patients with narcissistic, histrionic/borderline, and depressive personality disorders.

Table 11.3 Narcissistic personality.

Authors	*Method and main findings*	*Year of publication*
Jornkokgoud, et al.	Structural scans of 135 healthy individuals were considered. Brain regions such as the orbitofrontal cortex, Rolandic operculum, angular gyrus, rectus, and Heschl's gyrus were significant predictors of narcissistic traits. The study employed two supervised machine learning methods: Kernel Ridge Regression (KRR) and Support Vector Regression (SVR). Personality traits such as Borderline, Antisocial, Addicted, Negativistic, and Insecure (from PSSI), Machiavellianism and Narcissism (from SD3), and Openness, Agreeableness, and Conscientiousness (from NEO-PI-R) were significant predictors.	2023
Jornkokgoud, et al.	Structural scans of 135 healthy individuals were taken into consideration. This study used a combination of unsupervised and supervised machine learning methods to analyze the contributions of gray matter (GM) and white matter (WM) to narcissistic personality traits (NPT). Parallel Independent Component Analysis (p-ICA) was used to decompose brain scans into networks of covarying GM and WM. Stepwise regression and Random Forest regression were employed to predict NPT. A distributed network including GM alterations in fronto-temporal regions, insula, and cingulate cortex, and WM alterations in cerebellar and thalamic regions predicted NPT but not other personality traits (histrionic, paranoid, avoidant).	2024

They then completed assessments and underwent high-density EEG while viewing images of the patients' faces. Decision trees successfully predicted the patients' personality disorders with high accuracy (80% to 100%) based on therapists' subjective responses and EEG data. For example, criticized/devalued reactions identified narcissistic patients, while sexualized reactions predicted histrionic/borderline disorders. From a neural perspective, a key finding of this investigation was the ability of the late positive potential amplitude (LPP) within the hippocampus to effectively differentiate between personality disorders. Specifically, the initial LPP sub-component (Late Component 1, LC1) was triggered by the visual presentation of narcissistic versus depressive patients. The intermediate sub-component (LC2) differentiated between narcissistic and histrionic/borderline patients. The most durable LPP sub-component (LC3) was significant in distinguishing between depressive and histrionic/borderline patients. These results highlight the potential of ML methods to assist clinicians in diagnosing their clients based on their own subjective and neural responses.

Anxiety represents a highly diversified condition that includes intense adverse feelings of tension, apprehension, and worried thoughts, with additional physiological changes such as increased blood pressure and heart rate, dizziness, sweating, and nausea (Byrne & Rosenman, 1990; Yang et al., 2021). From a clinical point of view, anxiety diagnosis is mainly based on the structured clinical interview for DSM (SCID), a semi-structured interview that is able to assess different anxiety disorders, i.e., generalized anxiety disorder (GAD), panic disorder, social anxiety disorder (SAD), agoraphobia, specific phobia, selective mutism, separation anxiety disorder, substance/medication-induced anxiety disorder, anxiety disorder due to another medical condition, and other specified/unspecified anxiety disorder (American Psychiatric Association, 2013). In non-clinical settings anxiety is instead studied through self-report questionnaires and can be categorized both as a state, intended as a transient feeling, and a trait, intended as a stable predisposition to experience negative apprehensive affections (Spielberger et al., 1983). Anxiety trait can be considered a stable personality trait. Besides studies applying machine learning methods to fully diagnosed anxiety disorders, some recent studies have tried to develop neuro-predictive models of the anxious personality. For example, Saviola and colleagues have recently applied an unsupervised machine learning method based on group ICA on both structural and functional resting state MRI to a sample of 42 healthy individuals to investigate the relation between anxiety and brain macro-networks. They found that trait anxiety correlates with gray matter structural covariance of the default mode network and salience network, and correlates with resting-state functional connectivity of the frontal default mode network frontal regions, while state anxiety is associated only with resting-state functional connectivity of the default and salience networks (Saviola et al., 2020). Chavanne and colleagues investigated structural correlates of future anxiety symptoms during adolescence, using a voting classifier with Random Forest, support vector machine, and logistic regression algorithms. In a sample of 878 subjects they found that the caudate and pallidum gray matter volume at age 14 contributes to the prediction of GAD at age 18–23, with larger volumes associated with future GAD diagnosis (Chavanne et al., 2023). Most recently, Baggio et al. used a data fusion ML approach by combining gray and white matter data identifying covarying networks crucial for trait anxiety prediction through Parallel ICA and decision trees, which included the parietal, temporal, and frontal regions such as the postcentral gyrus, the precuneus, the anterior cingulate, and the middle temporal gyrus (Baggio et al., 2023). This study marks a significant departure from earlier single-modality studies, emphasizing the importance of integrating multiple brain modalities in understanding anxiety. A further investigation of trait anxiety individual differences has been done examining a larger sample of 554 individuals, particularly focusing on late adolescents and young adults, with the use of Parallel ICA (Baggio et al., under review). This study represents a great advancement not only because of the large sample size used, but also because it offers critical insights into anxiety's unique characteristics of a particular developmental phase, essential for creating accurate predictive models in non-clinical populations.

In another study, Wen et al. (2022) integrated white and gray matter network data for functional connectivity analysis in SAD patients, finding a disrupted connection in many areas such as the limbic regions, prefrontal and temporal areas (Wen et al., 2022).

Focusing only on white matter, Yoo and colleagues analyzed DTI data from 148 healthy participants, performing a connectome-based predictive modeling (CPM), using a younger adult group (n = 94) and an older adult group (n = 54) (Yoo et al., 2022). The connectome-wide data-driven CPM analysis identified several regions to predict trait anxiety levels; specifically there was a decreased structural connectivity among the lateral orbitofrontal cortex, the amygdala, the parahippocampal gyrus, the pallidum, and the temporal pole in highly anxious younger adults. When older adults were included in the analysis, an increased structural connectivity of frontotemporal and frontolimbic circuits was predictive of higher trait anxiety. No networks significantly predicted trait anxiety scores when only older adults were considered.

For studies focusing on task-related functional MRI, Portugal and colleagues (2019) predicted trait anxiety from brain activation during a dynamic face task, identifying regions like the rectus, inferior occipital cortex, cerebellum, and inferior and orbital frontal cortex as predictive of anxiety scores (Portugal et al., 2019).

Finally, Baggio et al.'s recent study (2023) focused on triple network functional connectivity in young adults, emphasizing the importance of a differential analysis of non-clinical anxiety in this distinct sensitive developmental phase. Notably, the authors identified increased connectivity of all the triple network sub-components (salience, default, and central executive networks) in high-anxious individuals. See Table 11.4.

Table 11.4 Trait anxiety.

Authors	*Method and main findings*	*Year of publication*
Portugal, et al.	Functional MRI scans of 82 patients and 72 healthy controls were taken into consideration. Whole-brain neural activity related to dynamic emotional face processing was able to predict self-report anxiety	2019
Saviola, et al.	Structural and functional MRI scans of 42 subjects. Trait anxiety was associated to structural covariance of the DMN and resting-state functional (rs-FC) connectivity of the DMN within frontal regions. State anxiety instead was associated only to rs-FC of SN and DMN	2020
Wen, et al.	Structural and functional MRI scans of 48 SAD patients, and 48 healthy controls were analyzed. SAD patients displayed a disrupted connection between the limbic and dorsal prefrontal, lateral temporal, and sensorimotor networks, and between the visual and sensorimotor networks. Moreover, there were negative correlations between HAMD scores and limbic-dorsal prefrontal and limbic-sensorimotor networks, and between illness duration and sensorimotor-visual networks	2022
Yoo, et al.	Diffusion weighted imaging scans of 148 subjects. Networks that predicted trait anxiety differ across age groups. Specifically, a negative network, which shares overlapping features with the amygdala-prefrontal circuitry, was present in 20–30 years of age young adults, whereas a positive network highlighted by frontotemporal and frontolimbic connectivity was present when both younger and older adults (20–80 years of age) are considered	2022
Chavanne, et al.	Structural MRI scans of 156 patients with clinical anxiety, and 424 healthy controls. MRI regional volumes of caudate and pallidum improved prediction performance of GAD	2023
Baggio et al.	Structural MRI scans of 158 subjects. Two covarying grey and white matter networks predicted trait anxiety levels, including precuneus, postcentral gyrus, anterior cingulate and superior temporal gyrus	2023
Baggio, et al	Structural MRI scans of 554 subjects. Higher anxious individuals exhibited a fronto-parieto-cerebellar network with decreased gray matter concentration, linked to bodily awareness and threat modulation, and a parieto-temporal network with increased white matter concentration, emphasizing insula and precuneus role	2024 (under review)

11.5 Conclusion

Integrating AI and computational methods into neuroscience provides a powerful framework for understanding the brain and extracting predictive models of psychological functions. By viewing the brain as a mathematical object that performs computational operations, we can develop predictive models that bridge the gap between biological structures and cognitive functions. This approach not only advances scientific knowledge but also opens new avenues for treating neurological and psychological disorders. These methods enhance the ability to identify robust biomarkers, improve diagnostic accuracy, and personalize treatment strategies. In conclusion, the integration of machine learning techniques into the investigation of neural features of personality traits holds the promise to revolutionize our comprehension of personality and opens up the possibility of making predictive models. By elucidating the neural correlates of these traits, researchers can gain a deeper understanding of their etiology and pathophysiology, which is crucial for informing diagnostic and therapeutic strategies.

Notes

1. Whether this N-dimensional space can be described mathematically as a Hilbert space (H), e.g., a generalization of Euclidean space to infinite dimensions, or any other mathematical space, is beyond the scope of this chapter. However, if we assume that H is a good approximation of the N-dimensional space that describes the brain, the following considerations apply. H is a vector space that allows for geometric calculations in multidimensional spaces. Brain states can be represented as subspaces within the Hilbert space. The elements of H are denoted as $|u\rangle$ a "ket" vector in Dirac notation.
2. This perspective is coherent with the Bayesian approaches and predictive coding theories to the brain.
3. Again, this perspective differs from the standard brain analyses for which we start from cognitive stimuli to see how they affect the brain signal (GLM analysis).
4. In Hilbert terminology, we predict Ψ from $|u\rangle$, part of H.
5. In Hilbert space terminology this is equivalent to finding the operator "O" that, when applied to $|u\rangle$ returns Ψ. Formally, $O \mid u\rangle = \Psi$.

References

Aldao, A., Nolen-Hoeksema, S., & Schweizer, S. (2010). Emotion-regulation strategies across psychopathology: A meta-analytic review. *Clinical Psychology Review*, *30*(2), 217–237. https://doi.org/10.1016/j.cpr.2009.11.004

Arbabshirani, M. R., Plis, S., Sui, J., & Calhoun, V. D. (2017). Single subject prediction of brain disorders in neuroimaging: promises and pitfalls. *Neuroimage*, *145*, 137e165. https://doi.org/10.1016/j.neuroimage.2016.02.079

Ashton, M. C. (2017). *Individual differences and personality* (3rd. ed.). Academic Press. http://www.sciencedirect.com/science/book/9780128098455

Asselmann, E., & Beesdo-Baum, K. (2015). Predictors of the course of anxiety disorders in adolescents and young adults. *Current Psychiatry Reports*, *17*(2), 7. https://doi.org/10.1007/s11920-014-0543-z

Baggio, T., Grecucci, A., Crivello, F., Joliot, M., Tzourio, C. (under review). Fronto-parietal and cerebellar circuits characterise individuals with high trait anxiety.

Baggio, T., Grecucci, A., Meconi, F., & Messina, I. (2023). Anxious brains: A combined data fusion machine learning approach to predict trait anxiety from morphometric features. *Sensors*, *23*(2), Article 2. https://doi.org/10.3390/s23020610

Brans, K., Koval, P., Verduyn, P., Lim, Y. L., & Kuppens, P. (2013). The regulation of negative and positive affect in daily life. *Emotion*, *13*(5), 926–939. https://doi.org/10.1037/a0032400

Byrne, D. G., & Rosenman, R. H. (1990). *Anxiety and the heart*. Taylor & Francis.

Campbell, W. K., Hoffman, B. J., Campbell, S. M., & Marchisio, G. (2011). Narcissism in organizational contexts. *Human Resource Management Review*, *21*(4), 268–284. https://doi.org/10.1016/j.hrmr.2010.10.007

Chavanne, A. V., Paillère Martinot, M. L., Penttilä, J., Grimmer, Y., Conrod, P., Stringaris, A., van Noort, B., Isensee, C., Becker, A., Banaschewski, T., Bokde, A. L. W., Desrivières, S., Flor, H., Grigis, A., Garavan, H., Gowland, P., Heinz, A., Brühl, R., Nees, F., … Artiges, E. (2023). Anxiety onset in adolescents: A machine-learning prediction. *Molecular Psychiatry*, *28*(2), Article 2. https://doi.org/10.1038/s41380-022-01840-z

Choi-Kain, L. W., Reich, D. B., Masland, S. R., Iliakis, E. A., & Ilagan, G. S. (2020). Longitudinal course of borderline personality disorder: What every clinician needs to know. *Current Treatment Options in Psychiatry*, *7*(3), 429–445.

Churchland, P.S., Sejnowski, T.J. (2016). The Computational Brain.The MIT Press. https://doi.org/10.7551/mitpress/11207.001.0001

Dadomo, H., Grecucci, A., Giardini, I., Ugolini, E., Carmelita, A., & Panzeri, M. (2016). Schema therapy for emotional dysregulation: Theoretical implication and clinical applications. *Frontiers in psychology*, 7, 1987.

Dadomo, H., Panzeri, M., Caponcello, D., Carmelita, A., & Grecucci, A. (2018). Schema therapy for emotional dysregulation in personality disorders: A review. In *Current opinion in psychiatry* (Vol. 31, Issue 1, pp. 43–49). Lippincott Williams and Wilkins. https://doi.org/10.1097/YCO.0000000000000380

De Panfilis, C., Schito, G., Generali, I., Ossola, P., Marchesi, C., Grecucci, A., & Gozzi, L. A. (2019). Emotions at the border: Increased punishment behavior during fair interpersonal exchanges in borderline personality disorder. *Journal of Abnormal Psychology*, *128*(2), 162–172. https://doi.org/10.1037/abn0000404

Domingos, P. (2012). A few useful things to know about machine learning. *Communications of the ACM*, *55*(10), 78e87. https://doi.org/10.1145/2347736.2347755

Drysdale, A. T., Grosenick, L., Downar, J., Dunlop, K., Mansouri, F., Meng, Y., & Liston, C. (2017). Resting-state connectivity biomarkers define neurophysiological subtypes of depression. *Nature Medicine*, *23*(1), 28–38.

Frederickson, J. J., Messina, I., & Grecucci, A. (2018). Dysregulated anxiety and dysregulating defenses: Toward an emotion regulation informed dynamic psychotherapy. *Frontiers in Psychology*, *9*. https://doi.org/10.3389/fpsyg.2018.02054

Gao, S., Osuch, E. A., Wammes, M., Théberge, J., Jiang, T. Z., & Colleagues. (2017). Discriminating bipolar disorder from major depression based on kernel svm using functional independent components. In *2017 IEEE 27th international workshop on Machine Learning for Signal Processing (MLSP)* (pp. 1–6). IEEE.

Grecucci, A., Monachesi, B., Messina, I. (2024). Reduced GM-WM concentration inside the Default Mode Network in individuals with high emotional intelligence and low anxiety: A data fusion mCCA+jICA approach. Soc Cogn Affect Neurosci. 2024 Mar 4;19(1):nsae018. 10.1093/scan/nsae018. PMID: 38451879; PMCID: PMC10919484.

Ghomroudi, P. A., Scaltritti, M., & Grecucci, A. (2023). Decoding reappraisal and suppression from neural circuits: A combined supervised and unsupervised machine learning approach. *Cognitive, Affective and Behavioral Neuroscience*. https://doi.org/10.3758/s13415-023-01076-6

Ghomroudi, P. A., Siugzdaite, R, Messina, I, & Grecucci, A. (2024). Decoding acceptance and reappraisal strategies from resting state macro networks. *Scientific Reports*. 14(1):19232. doi: 10.1038/s41598-024-68490-9.

Goldin, P. R., McRae, K., Ramel, W., & Gross, J. J. (2008). The neural bases of emotion regulation: Reappraisal and suppression of negative emotion. *Biological Psychiatry*, *63*(6), 577–586. https://doi.org/10.1016/j.biopsych.2007.05.031

Goldin, P. R., Moodie, C. A., & Gross, J. J. (2019). Acceptance versus reappraisal: Behavioral, autonomic, and neural effects. *Cognitive, Affective and Behavioral Neuroscience*, *19*(4), 927–944. https://doi.org/10.3758/s13415-019-00690-7

Grecucci, A., De Pisapia, N., Thero, D. K., Paladino, M. P., Venuti, P., & Job, R. (2015). Baseline and strategic effects behind mindful emotion regulation: Behavioral and physiological investigation. PLoS ONE, 10(1), Article e0116541. https://doi.org/10.1371/journal.pone.0116541

Grecucci, A., Dadomo, H., Salvato, G., Lapomarda, G., Sorella, S., & Messina, I. (2023). Abnormal brain circuits characterize borderline personality and mediate the relationship between childhood traumas and symptoms: A mCCA+jICA and Random Forest approach. *Sensors*, *23*(5), 2862. https://www.mdpi.com/1424-8220/23/5/2862

Grecucci, A., Ghomroudi, P. A., Monachesi, B., Messina, I., (2025). The neural signature of inner peace: morphometric differences between high and low accepters. *Mindfulness*, *16*, 42-59.

Grecucci, A., Lapomarda, G., Messina, I., Monachesi, B., Sorella, S., & Siugzdaite, R. (2022). Structural features related to affective instability correctly classify patients with borderline personality disorder. A supervised machine learning approach. *Frontiers in Psychiatry*, *13*, Article 804440.

Grecucci, A., Messina, I., Amodeo, L., Lapomarda, G., Crescentini, C., Dadomo, H., Panzeri, M., Theuninck, A., & Frederickson, J. (2020). A dual route model for regulating emotions: Comparing models, techniques and biological mechanisms. *Frontiers in Psychology*, *11*, 1–13. https://doi.org/10.3389/fpsyg.2020.00930

Grecucci, A., Sorella, S., & Consolini, J. (2023). Decoding individual differences in expressing and suppressing anger from structural brain networks: A supervised machine learning approach. *Behavioural Brain Research*, *439*, 114245.

Gross, J. J. (1998). The emerging field of emotion regulation: An integrative review. *Review of General Psychology*, *2*, 271–299.

Gross, J. J. (2002). Emotion regulation: Affective, cognitive, and social consequences. *Psychophysiology*, *39*(3), 281–291.

Gross, J. J. (2015). Emotion regulation: Current status and future prospects. *Psychological Inquiry*, *26*(1), 1–26. https://doi.org/10.1080/1047840X.2014.940781

Gross, J. J., & John, O. P. (2003a). Individual differences in two emotion regulation processes: Implications for affect, relationships, and well-being. *Journal of Personality and Social Psychology*, *85*(2), 348–362. https://doi.org/10.1037/0022-3514.85.2.348

Gross, J. J., & John, O. P. (2003b). Self report measures for love and compassion research: Personal growth and positive emotions. http://psychology.stanford.edu/~psyphy/resources.html

Gross, J. J., & Levenson, R. W. (1993). Emotional suppression: Physiology, self-report, and expressive behavior. *Journal of Personality and Social Psychology*, *64*(6), 970–986.

Hayes, S. C., Pistorello, J., & Levin, M. E. (2012). Acceptance and commitment therapy as a unified model of behavior change. *The Counseling Psychologist*, *40*(7), 976–1002. https://doi.org/10.1177/0011000012460836

Jornkokgoud, K., Baggio, T., Bakiaj, R., Wongupparaj, P., Job, R., & Grecucci, A. (2024). Narcissus reflected: Grey and White matter features joint contribution to the default mode network in predicting narcissistic personality traits. *European Journal of Neuroscience*, *59*(12), 3273–3291.

Jornkokgoud, K., Baggio, T., Faysal, M., Bakiaj, R., Wongupparaj, P., Job, R., & Grecucci, A. (2023). Predicting narcissistic personality traits from brain and psychological features: A supervised machine learning approach. *Social Neuroscience*, 1–14. https://doi.org/10.1080/17470919.2023.2242094

Kring, A. M., & Sloan, D. M. (2009). *Emotion regulation and psychopathology: A transdiagnostic approach to etiology and treatment*. Guliford.

Langerbeck, L., Baggio, T., Messina, I., Bhat, S., & Grecucci, A. (2023). Borderline shades: Morphometric features predict borderline personality traits but not histrionic traits. *NeuroImage: Clinical*, *40*, 103530.

Lapomarda, G., Grecucci, A., Messina, I., Pappaianni, E., & Dadomo, H. (2021). Common and different grey and white matter alterations in bipolar and borderline personality disorder: A source-based morphometry study. *Brain Research*, 1762. https://doi.org/10.1016/j.brainres.2021.147401

Leahy, R. L., Tirch, D., & Napolitano, L. A. (2011). *Emotion regulation in psychotherapy: A practitioner's guide*. Guilford.

Mauss, I. B., Levenson, R. W., McCarter, L., Wilhelm, F. H., & Gross, J. J. (2005). The tie that binds? Coherence among emotion experience, behavior, and physiology. *Emotion*, *5*(2), 175–190.

Mechelli, A., & Viera, S. (2019). *Machine learning: Methods and applications to brain disorders*. Academic Press.

Mendez-Miller, M., Naccarato, J., & Radico, J. A. (2022). Borderline personality disorder. *American Family Physician*, *105*(2), 156–161.

Messina, I., Sambin, M., Palmieri, A., & Viviani, R. (2013). Neural correlates of psychotherapy in anxiety and depression: A meta-analysis. *PLoS One*, *8*(9). https://doi.org/10.1371/journal.pone.0074657

Miller, J. D., Hoffman, B. J., Gaughan, E. T., Gentile, B., Maples, J., & Keith Campbell, W. (2011). Grandiose and vulnerable narcissism: A nomological network analysis. *Journal of Personality*, *79*(5), 1013–1042. https://doi.org/10.1111/j.1467-6494.2010.00711.x

Mitchell, T. M. (1997). *Machine learning*. McGraw Hill.

Mourao-Miranda, J., Portual, L., Rondina, J., & Shawe-Taylor, J. (2012). *Elastic-net Multiple Kernel Learning for multi-region neuroimaging-based diagnosis*. Proceedings of the 2nd NIPS Workshop on Machine Learning and Interpretation in Neuroimaging.

Orru, G., Pettersson-Yeo, W., Marquand, A. F., Sartori, G., & Mechelli, A. (2012). Using support vector machine to identify imaging biomarkers of neurological and psychiatric disease: A critical review. *Neuroscience & Biobehavioral Reviews*, *36*(4), 1140–1152.

Portugal, L. C. L., Schrouff, J., Stiffler, R., Bertocci, M., Bebko, G., Chase, H., Lockovitch, J., Aslam, H., Graur, S., Greenberg, T., Pereira, M., Oliveira, L., Phillips, M., & Mourão-Miranda, J. (2019). Predicting anxiety from wholebrain activity patterns to emotional faces in young adults: A machine learning approach. *NeuroImage: Clinical*, *23*, 101813. https://doi.org/10.1016/j.nicl.2019.101813

Pourramzani, A., & Monajemi, E. (2021). Prevalence of adaptive narcissism and its demographic correlations among the interns of guilan university of medical sciences, medical faculty: A cross-sectional study. *Iranian Journal of Psychiatry and Behavioral Sciences*, *15*(1), e101094. https://doi.org/10.5812/ijpbs.101094

Prata, D., Mechelli, A., & Kapur, S. (2014). Clinically meaningful biomarkers for psychosis: A systematic and quantitative review. *Neuroscience & Biobehavioral Reviews*, *45*, 134e141.

Rao, S., Heidari, P., & Broadbear, J. H. (2020). Developments in diagnosis and treatment of people with borderline personality disorder. *Current Opinion in Psychiatry*, *33*(5), 441–446. https://doi.org/10.1097/YCO.0000000000000625

Ronningstam, E. (2011). Narcissistic personality disorder in DSM-V--in support of retaining a significant diagnosis. *Journal of Personality Disorders*, *25*(2), 248. https://doi.org/10.3928/00485713-20090301-09

Saviola, F., Pappaianni, E., Monti, A., Grecucci, A., Jovicich, J., & De Pisapia, N. (2020). Trait and state anxiety are mapped differently in the human brain. *Scientific Reports*, *10*(1). https://doi.org/10.1038/s41598-020-68008-z

Sheppes, G., Suri, G., & Gross, J. J. (2015). Emotion regulation and psychopathology. *Annual Review of Clinical Psychology*, *11*, 379–405. https://doi.org/10.1146/annurev-clinpsy-032814-112739

Siefert, C. J., Porcerelli, J., Meehan, K. B., & Dauphin, B. (2022). Clinical utility of proposed dimensional personality disorder models: Considerations and opportunities. In *Personality disorders and pathology: Integrating clinical assessment and practice in the DSM-5 and ICD-11 era*. American Psychological Association.

Sorella, S., Lapomarda, G., Messina, I., Frederickson, J. J., Siugzdaite, R., Job, R., & Grecucci, A. (2019). Testing the expanded continuum hypothesis of schizophrenia and bipolar disorder. Neural and psychological evidence for shared and distinct mechanisms. *NeuroImage: Clinical*, *23*. https://doi.org/10.1016/j.nicl.2019.101854

Spielberger, C. D., Gorsuch, R. L., Lushene, Vagg, P. R., & Jacobs, G. A. (1983). *Manual for the state-trait anxiety inventory*. Consulting Psychologists Press.

Sui, J., Jiang, R., Bustillo, J., & Calhoun, V. D. (2020). Neuroimaging-based individualized prediction of cognition and behavior for mental disorders and health: Methods and promises. *Biological Psychiatry*, *88*(11), 818–828. https://doi.org/10.1016/j.biopsych.2020.04.037

Tanzilli, A., Trentini, C., Grecucci, A., Carone, N., Ciacchella, C., Lai, C., Sabogal-Rueda, M. D., Lingiardi, V. (2022). Therapist reactions to patient personality: A Pilot study of clinicians' emotional and neural responses using three clinical vignettes from in treatment series. *Frontiers in Human Neuroscience*, *16*, 1037486.

Twenge, J. M., & Campbell, W. K. (2003). "Isn't it fun to get the respect that we're going to deserve?" Narcissism, social rejection, and aggression. *Personality and Social Psychology Bulletin*, *29*(2), 261–272. https://doi.org/10.1177/0146167202239051

Wen, K., Zhao, Y., Zhang, F., Lui, S., Kemp, G. J., & Gong, Q. (2022). Large-scale dysfunctional white matter and grey matter networks in patients with social anxiety disorder. *iScience*, *25*(10), 105094. https://doi.org/10.1016/j.isci.2022.105094

Wolfers, T., Doan, N. T., Kaufmann, T., Alnæs, D., Moberget, T., Agartz, I., et al. (2018). Map- ping the heterogeneous phenotype of schizophrenia and bipolar disorder using norma- tive models. *JAMA Psychiatry*, *75*(11), 1146e1155. https://doi.org/10.1001/jamapsy chiatry.2018.2467

Wolgast, M., Lundh, L. G., & Viborg, G. (2011). Cognitive reappraisal and acceptance: An experimental comparison of two emotion regulation strategies. *Behaviour Research and Therapy*, *49*(12), 858–866. https://doi.org/10.1016/j.brat.2011.09.011

Woo, C.-W., Chang, L. J., Lindquist, M. A., & Wager, T. D. (2017). Building better biomarkers: Brain models in translational neuroimaging. *Nature Neuroscience*, *20*(3), 365e377. https://doi.org/10.1038/nn.4478

Xu, L., Groth, K. M., Pearlson, G., Schretlen, D. J., & Calhoun, V. D. (2009). Source-based morphometry: The use of independent component analysis to identify grey matter differences with application to schizophrenia. *Human Brain Mapping*, *30*(3), 711–724. https://doi.org/10.1002/hbm.20540

Yahata, N., Kasai, K., & Kawato, M. (2017). Computational neuroscience approach to biomarkers and treatments for mental disorders. *Psychiatry and Clinical Neurosciences*, *71*(4), 215–237.

Yang, X., Fang, Y., Chen, H., Zhang, T., Yin, X., Man, J., Yang, L., & Lu, M. (2021). Global, regional and national burden of anxiety disorders from 1990 to 2019: Results from the global burden of disease study 2019. *Epidemiology and Psychiatric Sciences*, *30*, e36. https://doi.org/10.1017/S2045796021000275

Yoo, C., Park, S., & Kim, M. J. (2022). Structural connectome-based prediction of trait anxiety. *Brain Imaging and Behavior*, *16*(6), 2467–2476. https://doi.org/10.1007/s11682-022-00700-2

12 An Explainable Fuzzy Cognition Methodology for CAD Diagnosis in Nuclear Medicine

Nikolaos I. Papandrianos, Anna Feleki, Ioannis Apostolopoulos, Elpiniki Papageorgiou, Nikolaos Papathanasiou, and Dimitrios J. Apostolopoulos

12.1 Introduction

Coronary artery disease (CAD) is the leading cause of death from heart disease. The term implies the buildup of blood in a segment of the heart that has died or was injured because of a blockage in the coronary artery. CAD is a significant, life-threatening disease, and medical attention should be sought immediately. Conventional methods are often invasive and time-consuming, utilizing a process that is prolonged and less convenient for patients (Papandrianos et al., 2022c).

Based on a literature review, convolutional neural networks (CNNs) have been developed for effective diagnosis of CAD, employing a range of methodologies, including both pre-trained architectures and models built from scratch. Papandrianos et al., (2022c) developed the red, green, blue (RGB)-CNN model for three-class classification in the diagnosis of CAD. There were 647 instances, with 134 cases referring to infarction, 251 cases to ischemia, and 262 to normal. Data augmentation techniques included rescaling, rotation, width shift range, height shift range, shear transformation, zooming, horizontal flip, and vertical flip. The RGB-CNN model obtained an accuracy of 91.86%, outperforming the pretrained networks, which scored an accuracy of 88.54%, 86.11% for VGG-16 and DenseNet-121, respectively. Apostolopoulos et al. (2020)developed the pre-trained network VGG-16. A total of 216 patients were included in attenuation correction (AC) and non-attenuation (NAC) correction in stress and rest conditions. The AC and NAC images were rescaled to 150x150. Data augmentation was applied with the rotation technique by a maximum of 45 degrees. VGG-16 yielded an accuracy of 74.53%, sensitivity of 75%, and specificity of 73.43%. Bansal et al. (2024) developed various pre-trained networks for the CAD classification. A total of 192 SPECT-MPI cases were included from an open dataset. The images were rescaled to a 256×256 pixel size. Data augmentation was applied, with the employment of shear transformations,

DOI: 10.4324/9781003495123-12

horizontal flip, rotation, zoom, shift in width, height and fill mode. Early stopping was applied to stop the training process and prevent the model from overtraining. InceptionV3 outperformed all models with an accuracy of 96.88%, with the rest of the models attaining the following accuracy values, DenseNet201 (93.75%), Xception (90.63%), EfficientNetB5 (90.63%), and ResNet101V2 (84.38%). Chen et al. (2021) analyzed CZT SPECT myocardial perfusion images with a three-dimensional CNN to classify whether the patient had CAD or not. A total of 979 gray-scale instances were included, which were rescaled to 70x70, where 601 instances correspond to healthy, and 378 instances to unhealthy. The proposed model attained accuracy, sensitivity, and specificity of 87.64%, 81.58%, and 92.16% accordingly, where five-fold cross-validation was applied. To interpret CNN results and identify the areas contributing to the respective prediction, Grad-CAM was utilized.

Furthermore, FCMs have been applied to a variety of CAD classification problems. Khodadadi et al. (2019) constructed FCM for the effective diagnosis of ischemic stroke. A total of 110 instances were included, where 12 characteristics served as input concepts (age, blood pressure, LDL cholesterol, HDL cholesterol, diabetes, heart disease, family history, smoking, BMI, exercise, sex, stroke history) with 1 output (risk of stroke). For the FCM training process and the initialization of the weights, the non-linear Hebbian method was employed. The proposed model achieved an accuracy of 93.6% ± 4.5%, outperforming traditional machine learning methods, including support vector machines (86.0% ± 5.27%) and K-nearest neighbors (80.2% ± 5.33%). Apostolopoulos et al. (2021), developed a State Space Advanced Fuzzy Cognitive Map (AFCM) model for the CAD diagnosis. The dataset included 303 instances, including 116 healthy cases and 187 diseased cases. Nuclear medicine experts defined the system's concepts and assigned linguistic values between them, and also established specific rules to enhance the model's knowledge. Thirty input characteristics were included, such as typical angina pectoris, atypical angina pectoris, atypical thoracic pain, dyspnea on exertion, asymptomatic status, gender (male and female), and age categories (e.g., age < 40), among others. The experts also designated state concepts, which were grouped into Predisposing Factors, Recurrent Disease, Demographic Characteristics, and Diagnostic Tests. The AFCM model included a single output node with three states, utilizing a SigmoidN activation function, along with an activator concept. The proposed model AFCM achieved 85.47% accuracy, 89.3% sensitivity, and 79.31% specificity, and it outperformed various machine learning models, where Chirp yielded 76.89% accuracy, and both AdaBoostM1 and Random Forest attained 74.58% accuracy.

Existing works on CAD do not employ explainability techniques and often employ single-modality data imaging or clinical data as their input data. This restricted feature set limited the ability of the model to represent the multiplicity of nature of coronary pathology and also limited its ability to be used in clinical practice. In this work, we attempt to tackle these limitations by applying the multimodal framework, named DeepFCM, that combines anatomical information from Polar maps, along with clinical data, while employing explainability techniques.

DeepFCM was first presented in (Feleki et al., 2023a) for diagnosing Non-Small Cell Lung Cancer (NSCLC). Clinical data, along with PET scans, were used as input concepts. RGB-CNN, a CNN developed from scratch, was trained on the PET images. For every instance, RGB-CNN generated a prediction, where these predictions and clinical data (SUVmax, tumor diameter) formed the input concepts. As an explanation technique, a concept graph demonstrated the relationships between input and output concepts. This method yielded an accuracy of 94.71%. In (Feleki et al., 2023c) DeepFCM was used for CAD diagnosis with clinical data and Polar Maps. It achieved an accuracy of 77.95%. The explainability framework was improved by comparing the inferred concept connections with both expert-initialized and randomly initialized weight structures. In (Feleki et al., 2023b) a subset of the most informative clinical features was selected and combined with Polar Maps, which reached an accuracy of 83.07%. Grad-CAM was used to interpret CNN outputs by highlighting important image areas. GPT-API was integrated to create human-readable explanations of the DeepFCM outputs. In (Feleki et al., 2024), the DeepFCM-PSO variant included the full set of clinical characteristics and PET images, which achieved 88.14% accuracy. Grad-CAM was used to identify malignant regions from RGB-CNN feature maps. GPT-API generated natural language explanations. In (Papageorgiou et al., 2025) DeepFCM-ELM was introduced by adding an Extreme Learning Machine (ELM) to the learning framework. The generated interconnections were demonstrated through the concept graph. Grad-CAM explained the CNN outputs, and GPT-API turned model predictions into clear language. DeepFCM-ELM reached an accuracy of 90.57%. A MDSS has also been developed by the EMERALD team (Samaras et al., 2024), which includes ML and FCM-based classification algorithms regarding CAD and NSCLC diagnosis, with various explainability techniques like graphical visualizations, textual explanations, Grad-CAM, SHapley Additive exPlanations (SHAP), and ablation heatmaps.

The current study experimented with the DeepFCM learning mechanism and developed important improvements to the PSO framework. These changes aim to navigate the solution space better and facilitate more accurate and stable solutions for CAD diagnosis. A significant innovation is the introduction of LLaMA 3.2-Vision, an open-source NLG model that does not depend on a limited number of tokens. The prompt for the NLG model was adjusted to generate clearer and more useful output for diagnosing CAD. This adjustment enables LLaMA 3.2-Vision to provide more precise and actionable insights that support the diagnostic process.

12.2 Materials and Methods

The dataset for this study was collected from the Clinical Sector of the Department of Nuclear Medicine at the University Hospital of Patras. The dataset includes 571 instances, with 248 cases classified as CAD-diseased and 323 as normal by nuclear experts. Participants underwent gated-Single Photon Emission Computed Tomography – Myocardial Perfusion Imaging (SPECT-MPI) and Invasive Coronary Angiography (ICA) within 60 days of the MPI procedure, determining their CAD diagnosis, which serves as the ground truth. The dataset included information on various patient attributes, which are binary normalized and used as input features for the FCM classification model and number 22: (1) Sex, (2) Age, (3) Body Mass Index (BMI), (4) CAD,(5) previous Acute Myocardial Infarction (AMI), (6) previous Percutaneous Coronary Intervention (PCI), (7) previous Coronary Artery Bypass Grafting (CABG), (8) previous STROKE, (9) Diabetes, (10) Smoking, (11) Hypertension, (12) Dyslipidemia, (13) Peripheral Angiopathy, (14) Chronic Kidney Disease, (15) Family History of CAD, (16) Asymptomatic, (17) Atypical Symptoms, (18) Angina-like, (19) Dyspnea on Exertion, (20) Incident of precordial pain, (21) Electrocardiogram (ECG), and (22) Preliminary Expert Diagnosis.

In addition to clinical data, imaging data in the form of Polar Maps was also included. These images provide a visual representation of myocardial perfusion. We present an example, showcasing a normal instance alongside a pathological case in Figure 12.1.

12.3 DeepFCM Methodology

The clinical data are processed with normalization techniques and are processed as input concepts by a FCM. A CNN trained from scratch, named RGB-CNN, is trained on the Polar Map images and generates a prediction for each image instance. These CNN predictions are incorporated as an additional input concept, forming the proposed multimodal model DeepFCM. For the initialization of interconnections among input-output concepts, expert knowledge is utilized in the form of fuzzy sets. PSO is included in

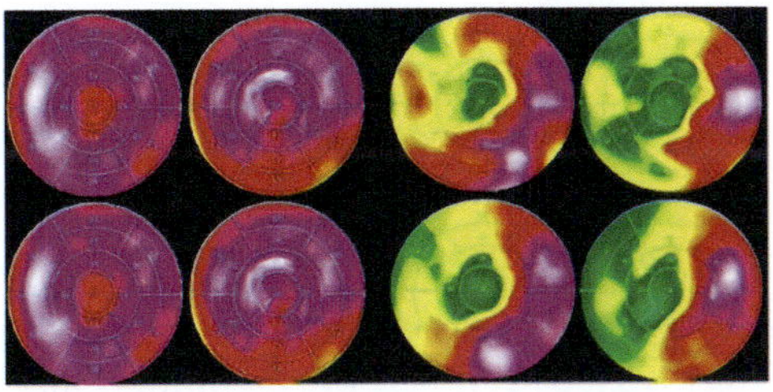

Figure 12.1 Representation of two Polar Maps instances (left), Normal (right), Pathological.

the DeepFCM training process to calculate the interconnections of concepts based on historical and expert knowledge, treating each weight matrix as a possible solution by minimizing the error function. A 10-fold cross-validation approach is applied to ensure the generalizability of DeepFCM-PSO results. By using the weight matrix attained in the training process, on the testing set, and comparing the DeepFCM-PSO predicted values to the actual dataset, performance metrics are calculated to evaluate the model's accuracy and effectiveness. The proposed model, DeepFCM-PSO, encapsulates transparent and understandable results, with the application of the following XAI methodologies: Grad-CAM and NLG with the Llama3.2-vision model, which can offer insights into the decision-making process.

In Figure 12.2, the methodological pipeline of the DeepFCM-PSO is demonstrated.

The steps of the proposed methodology are analyzed below:

12.3.1 *Clinical Dataset*

Step 1: Loading Clinical Dataset

The clinical data are loaded into the system through an external file, presenting an overview of the patient's status. The clinical dataset involves 22 diverse parameters, including demographic information and CAD diagnostic features.

Step 2: Data Preprocessing

- **Data normalization**: Regarding the clinical data of our research, we applied a normalization technique to the Age and BMI characteristics using the Min-Max technique (Papandrianos et al., 2022a) to rescale their values into the spectrum [0, 1].
- **Data shuffle**: To improve generalization, the data were inserted into the model in a random order to reduce any bias (Papandrianos et al., 2022b).

12.3.2 *Imaging Dataset*

Step 3: Loading Imaging Dataset

The Polar Map images are two-dimensional (2D) circular representations summarizing the results of the three-dimensional (3D) tomographic slices.

Step 4: Image Data Preprocessing

- Data normalization: Rescaling of pixel values was applied to fit them into the range of [0, 1], to simplify the computational process.
- Data shuffle: Shuffling of the imaging dataset was applied to randomize the order of the instances.

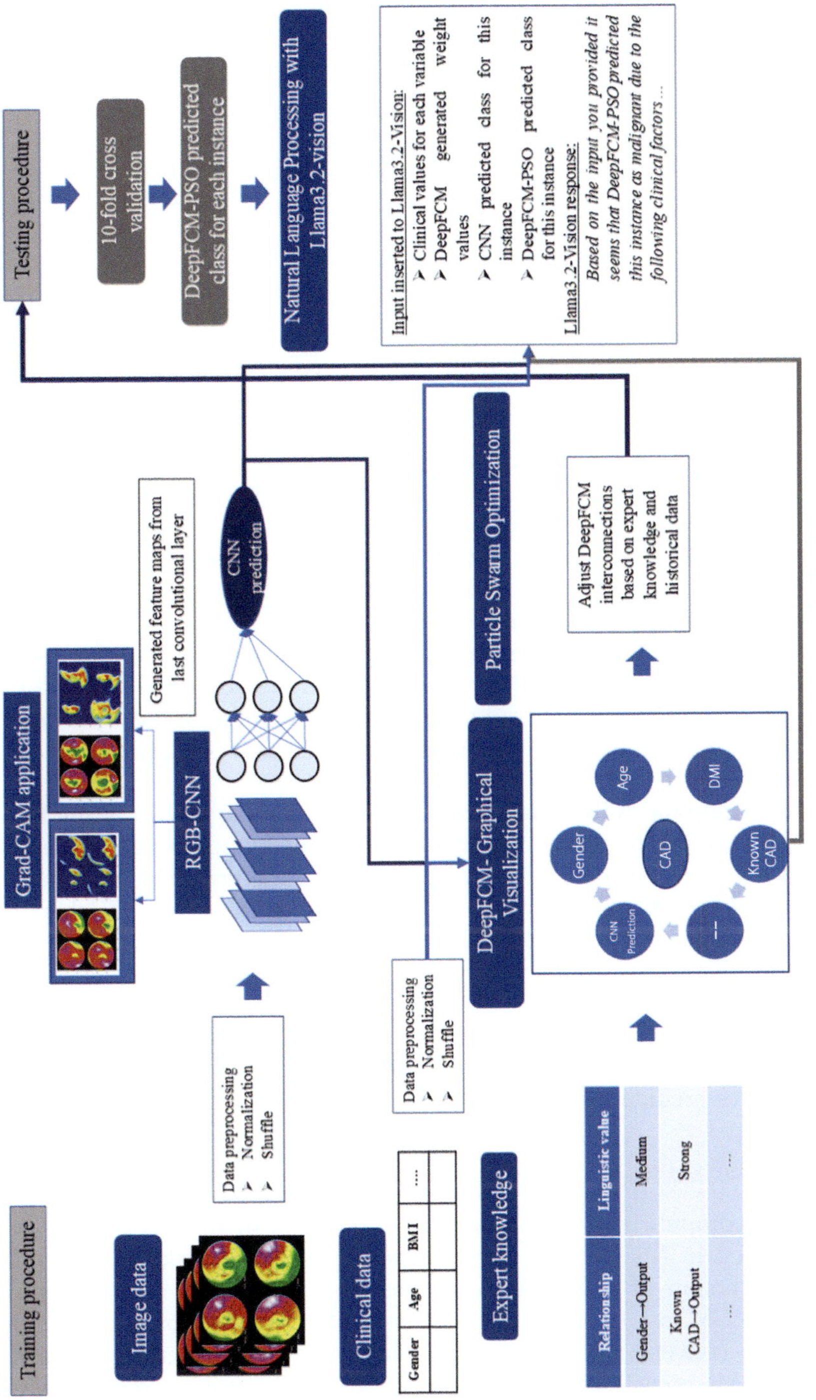

Figure 12.2 Demonstration of the methodological framework of the DeepFCM-PSO pipeline.

Step 5: RGB-CNN Training

A CNN represents an algorithm that includes input, hidden, and output layers. By employing diverse filters on input images, a CNN can automatically extract features. Through an intricate learning process, it retains the most salient pixel values (Papandrianos et al., 2022a).

RGB-CNN was implemented from scratch and trained on Polar maps images and generated a prediction for each instance. The following steps were applied.

- **Data augmentation**: Data augmentation was applied to increase the size of the dataset, achieve generalization of instances, and handle overfitting (Shijie et al., 2017). The techniques that were utilized are the following: a width shift range with a value of 0.1, a height shift range with a value of 0.1, and a zoom range with a value of 0.1.
- **Define CNN architecture**: An exploration was conducted with diverse architectures, varying the number of nodes in both convolutional and fully connected layers. Experimentation was conducted with different batch sizes, where a batch size of 16 yielded the best results. Moreover, the images were resized to a dimension of 300x300 pixels. The developed RGB-CNN model was constructed with three convolutional layers with 16, 32, and 64 nodes and two fully connected layers with 64 and 32 nodes, respectively. All layers included Rectified Linear Unit (ReLU) as an activation function, and the final fully connected layer included a sigmoid activation function. Adam optimizer was selected, along with binary cross-entropy as a loss function.
- **Early Stopping**: Additionally, early stopping was employed during RGB-CNN training to reduce redundant iterations by stopping the training process when the change between the validation error among consecutive epochs has a smaller value than a predefined threshold (Feleki et al., 2023b) (Heckel & Yilmaz, 2020). The maximum number of epochs was set to 300.
- **Extract CNN predictions**: The final fully connected layer of the RGB-CNN model consists of a single node, whose binary output (1 or 0) indicates the presence or absence of CAD. For each instance, RGB-CNN generates predictions.

Step 6: FCM-Based Classifier

FCMs are computing tools that are a combination of fuzzy logic and neural networks. FCMs have been introduced by Kosko (Kosko, 1986) as an advanced version of cognitive maps with the application of fuzzy causal functions. FCM is a fuzzy diagram that transforms a system into concepts, where each concept represents a variable, a state, or a characteristic of a system. FCMs consist of several nodes that demonstrate variables, where relationships among the nodes rely on the range [−1, 1]. The value of an interconnection expresses the strength of the relation (Feleki et al., 2023b, 2023c; Papageorgiou et al., 2005). In our study, a FCM is initially constructed using the 22 previously described clinical characteristics as input concepts.

Step 7: Integration of Clinical Data Along with CNN Predictions

The predicted values for each image instance derived from the RGB-CNN model along with the clinical data formed the input concepts for the proposed model DeepFCM.

Step 8: Validation Process

To ensure the reliability of our proposed model and prevent overfitting (Brownlee, 2018; Papandrianos et al., 2022a) K-fold cross-validation was employed, where *k* represents the number of batches used to divide the dataset. In our study, *k* was set to 10, where nine folds were employed for training and one fold for testing in each iteration. This process was repeated until every fold had been used once as the testing set.

Step 9: Initialization of Interconnections by Nuclear Experts

In our study, we utilize clinical characteristics along with CNN predictions as input concepts to the proposed model, DeepFCM. When an FCM is applied for decision-making, it can be effectively constructed either by leveraging expert domain knowledge or by employing a random initialization of concept weights. In our study, experts assigned linguistic values for each input-output interconnection, in the form of fuzzy sets. Fuzzy sets have a degree of uncertainty, in contrast to traditional binary logic, where statements are strictly true or false (Zadeh, 1965). Membership Functions (MFs) define fuzziness within a fuzzy set. The triangular MF was selected by the nuclear experts to represent linguistic values (Kreinovich et al. 2020). Nuclear experts assigned linguistic values (Very Weak, Weak, Medium, Strong, Very Strong) to define the impact of each input concept on the presence of CAD. These values were transferred to numerical values within the range [–1, 1], following the main aspects of fuzzy logic as defined in (Papageorgiou et al., 2005; Papageorgiou & Salmeron, 2013). When expert-defined values were not provided, interconnections were randomly initialized within the range [–1, 1].

The calculation of the weights in the FCM model, which constitutes causal relationships among concepts, is a crucial step in FCM learning. To enhance the dynamic capabilities of FCMs and update the weights based on the available data, learning algorithms were proposed and have been used in previous studies (Papageorgiou & Salmeron, 2013). Based on the literature on FCM learning algorithms, the most commonly used are evolutionary and population-based algorithms, which find great applicability in various disciplines, including medicine.

Step 10: Integration of PSO as a Learning Technique for the DeepFCM Training Process

In this study, Particle Swarm Optimization (PSO) was employed for the calculation of the weight matrix, which includes the total set of interconnections among concepts. PSO is known for its application to various optimization problems (Papageorgiou et al., 2005; Chen et al., 2020). It emulates the collective behavior observed in swarms, where a group of particles, each representing a potential solution, is randomly initialized within the search space. These particles then move through space, adapting their positions based on both their own experiences and the successes of their neighbors, converging toward a collective solution.

The PSO approach enables DeepFCM to effectively learn the interconnections among concepts by exploring the solution space starting from initial weighted values initially defined by nuclear experts. This guides the model toward semantically meaningful relationships but also allows refining of these connections based on the historical data, resulting in a more accurate and interpretable representation of the decision-making process.

Application of XAI Techniques

For transforming the DeepFCM into an interpretable tool, several approaches were applied. Firstly, through the DeepFCM graph, the relationships among input and output concepts are demonstrated, highlighting the most impactful factors for the diagnosis (Feleki et al., 2024).

Also, Grad-CAM is employed to understand the decision-making process of CNNs (Selvaraju et al., 2020). It identifies the most influential pixel regions in an input image that contribute to the classification outcome. Grad-CAM utilizes the generated feature maps from the last convolutional layer of the CNN, since these layers maintain important spatial information. By calculating the gradient of the target class, Grad-CAM assigns importance weights, allowing it to highlight the regions of the image that most influenced the model's prediction.

Application of Natural Language Generation Method to Interpret DeepFCM and RGB-CNN Results into Human-Understandable Language

As an additional technique, Natural Language Generation (NLG) was employed to translate the numerical results of the DeepFCM-PSO framework into clear, human-readable textual explanations. This was accomplished using the open-source language model Llama 3.2-Vision (Chi et al., 2024; Fedorov et al., 2024). Leveraging its multimodal capabilities, Llama 3.2-Vision processed the weight values produced by DeepFCM, the clinical characteristics, and the predictions from both the DeepFCM and CNN models in order to provide insights into the DeepFCM and RGB-CNN predictions.

12.4 Results

In this section, we demonstrate the DeepFCM-PSO classification performance and its integration into the developed MDSS (Feleki et al., 2024; Samaras et al., 2024) for the diagnosis of CAD, along with the provided XAI techniques. Table 12.1 presents a comparison across various models, with DeepFCM-PSO, both with randomly initialized weights and expert-guided initialization, and FCM-PSO, which is based solely on clinical data, also under the same initialization strategies for the interconnection among concepts. We also include the performance metrics attained from RGB-CNN, which relied exclusively on Polar Map imaging data.

The following evaluation metrics were included: accuracy, loss, sensitivity, specificity, and precision. DeepFCM-PSO was also evaluated using 10-fold cross-validation to ensure generalization of the performance estimation. We also computed the standard deviation of each performance metric across the ten folds.

Table 12.1 demonstrates that DeepFCM-PSO achieves higher classification performance when expert knowledge is used to initialize the interconnections among concepts, compared to relying on random initialization. Moreover, the results demonstrate that combining clinical and imaging data leads to more accurate and reliable CAD diagnosis, reinforcing the value of a multimodal approach in medical decision support systems, since FCM-PSO and RGB-CNN, which are based on clinical data and imaging data, respectively, attained lower performance metrics.

Table 12.2 presents an analysis of the relationships between clinical characteristics associated with CAD and the model output, as captured by the DeepFCM-PSO framework. The first column lists each input–output

Table 12.1 Comparison of performance metrics between DeepFCM-PSO models initialized with expert knowledge and random initialization, alongside single-modality models based solely on clinical and imaging data.

Model	*Accuracy*	*Loss*	*Sensitivity*	*Specificity*	*Precision*
FCM-PSO (random weights)	72.65% ± 3.86%	0.25% ± 0.04	70.71% ± 6.41%	78.51% ± 9.76%	72.94% ± 4.46%
FCM-PSO (expert knowledge)	73.24% ± 3.22%	0.28% ± 0.03	70.96% ± 9.19%	77.84% ± 9.67%	70.65% ± 4.86
RGB-CNN	74.58% ± 5.25%	0.45 ± 0.04	81.71% ± 5.59%	70.48% ± 9.51%	72% ± 7.85%
DeepFCM-PSO (random initialization)	75.49% ± 6.3%	0.24 ± 0.06	71.75% ± 10.95%	77.58% ± 10.04%	70.69% ± 9.76%
DeepFCM-PSO (expert knowledge)	**77.59% ± 4.34%**	**0.22 ± 0.04**	**78.05% ± 9.55%**	**76.29% ± 8.31%**	**74.05% ± 7.68%**

Table 12.2 Generated interconnections among input–output concepts with and without expert knowledge.

Relationship	*Suggested linguistic value*	*Transformed to a range of values*	*DeepFCM-PSO (expert knowledge)*	*DeepFCM-PSO (random initialization)*
Sex→Output	Very Weak	[0, 0.3]	0.25 ± 0.09	−0.46 ± 0.22
Age→Output	Very Weak	[0, 0.3]	0.28 ± 0.11	−0.2 ± 0.29
BMI→Output	Weak	[0.15, 0.5]	0.31 ± 0.08	−0.22 ± 0.31
known CAD→Output	Strong	[0.5, 0.85]	0.66 ± 0.12	0.37 ± 0.17
previous AMI→Output	Very Weak	[0, 0.3]	0.17 ± 0.12	0.19 ± 0.3
previous PCI→Output	Weak	[0.15, 0.5]	0.38 ± 0.09	0.14 ± 0.2
previous CABG→Output	Weak	[0.15, 0.5]	0.33±0.11	0.13 ± 0.24
previous STROKE→Output	Medium	[0.35, 0.65]	0.4 ± 0.08	0.02 ± 0.34
Diabetes→Output	Strong	[0.5, 0.85]	0.7 ± 0.09	0.21 ± 0.25
Smoking→Output	Medium	[0.35, 0.65]	0.47 ± 0.06	−0.02 ± 0.28
Hypertension→Output	Medium	[0.35, 0.65]	0.38 ± 0.06	−0.15 ± 0.22
Dyslipidemia→Output	Medium	[0.35, 0.65]	0.44 ± 0.1	−0.21 ± 0.19
Angiopathy→Output	Medium	[0.35, 0.65]	0.51 ± 0.09	0.16 ± 0.26
Chronic Kidney Disease→Output	Weak	[0.15, 0.5]	0.32 ± 0.09	0.12 ± 0.28
Family History of CAD→Output	Weak	[0.15, 0.5]	0.26 ± 0.06	−0.11 ± 0.24
Asymptomatic→Output	-Strong	[-0.85, -0.5]	−0.79 ± 0.06	−0.17 ± 0.23
Atypical Symptoms→Output	Very Strong	[0.7, 1]	0.75 ± 0.05	−0.18 ± 0.16
Angina Like→Output	Strong	[0.5, 0.85]	0.63 ± 0.04	0.05 ± 0.23
Dyspnea on Exertion→Output	Medium	[0.35, 0.65]	0.48 ± 0.09	−0.01 ± 0.26
Incident of Precordial Pain→Output	Strong	[0.5, 0.85]	0.61 ± 0.1	0.05 ± 0.34
ECG→Output	Medium	[0.35, 0.65]	0.29 ± 0.4	0.17 ± 0.28
Expert_Diagnosis_Binary→Output	Very Strong	[0.7, 1]	0.86 ± 0.09	0.34 ± 0.26
CNN_prediction→Output	Strong	[0.5, 0.85]	0.64 ±0.1	0.25 ± 0.16

relationship. The second column displays the corresponding linguistic value, as defined by expert nuclear cardiologists. These linguistic terms were transformed into numerical ranges using the triangular membership function, as shown in the third column. The fourth column includes the interconnection weights generated by DeepFCM-PSO when initialized with expert knowledge, while the fifth column provides the weights obtained through random initialization within the interval [−1, 1]. This comparative structure allows for the evaluation of the effect of expert-guided initialization on the interpretability and consistency of the resulting fuzzy cognitive map.

Table 12.2 demonstrates that the interconnection weights generated by the model closely match the initial relationships suggested by nuclear medicine experts, with only minor differences noted. These small differences are seen as reasonable adjustments based on the data. In contrast, when the interconnection weights were initialized randomly, without incorporating expert knowledge, the resulting values showed considerable deviation from expert-defined ranges. The absence of domain-specific priors caused the training process to explore the solution space without constraints, increasing the risk of convergence to local minima and producing suboptimal and less interpretable outcomes. Although the development of DeepFCM-PSO, with and without expert knowledge, achieved similar overall performance, the DeepFCM initialized by expert knowledge developed more meaningful and clinically interpretable weight structures. This result highlights DeepFCM's ability to incorporate domain expertise in its learning process, resulting in clearer and more understandable decision-making.

For the application of DeepFCM-PSO, through the developed MDSS, we refer to a patient with a medical history of known CAD, diabetes, smoking, hypertension, and dyspnea on exertion, where the expert predicted that this patient is pathological. Given these risk factors, both DeepFCM-PSO as a multimodal approach and the CNN based solely on image prediction classified this instance as pathological. As illustrated in Figure 12.3 DeepFCM-PSO predicted the instance as pathological with a high probability score of 98.55%, while the CNN, based solely on imaging data, predicted it as pathological with a probability score of 55.47%.

The DeepFCM-PSO graph further demonstrates the key contributing factors influencing the CAD diagnosis. The most impactful clinical indicators regarding CAD multimodal diagnosis include known CAD (weight: 0.51), diabetes (0.62), smoking (0.34), hypertension (0.68), dyspnea on exertion (0.58), expert diagnosis (0.51), and the CNN prediction (0.56).

For the interpretation of the RGB-CNN predictions, the Grad-CAM technique was employed. The JET colormap from the OpenCV library was utilized, where red represents the most influential pixel areas, and blue regions indicate pixel regions with lower impact.

In Figure 12.4, we present the Grad-CAM application, where the left panel displays the original Polar Map image of the patient, which provides a

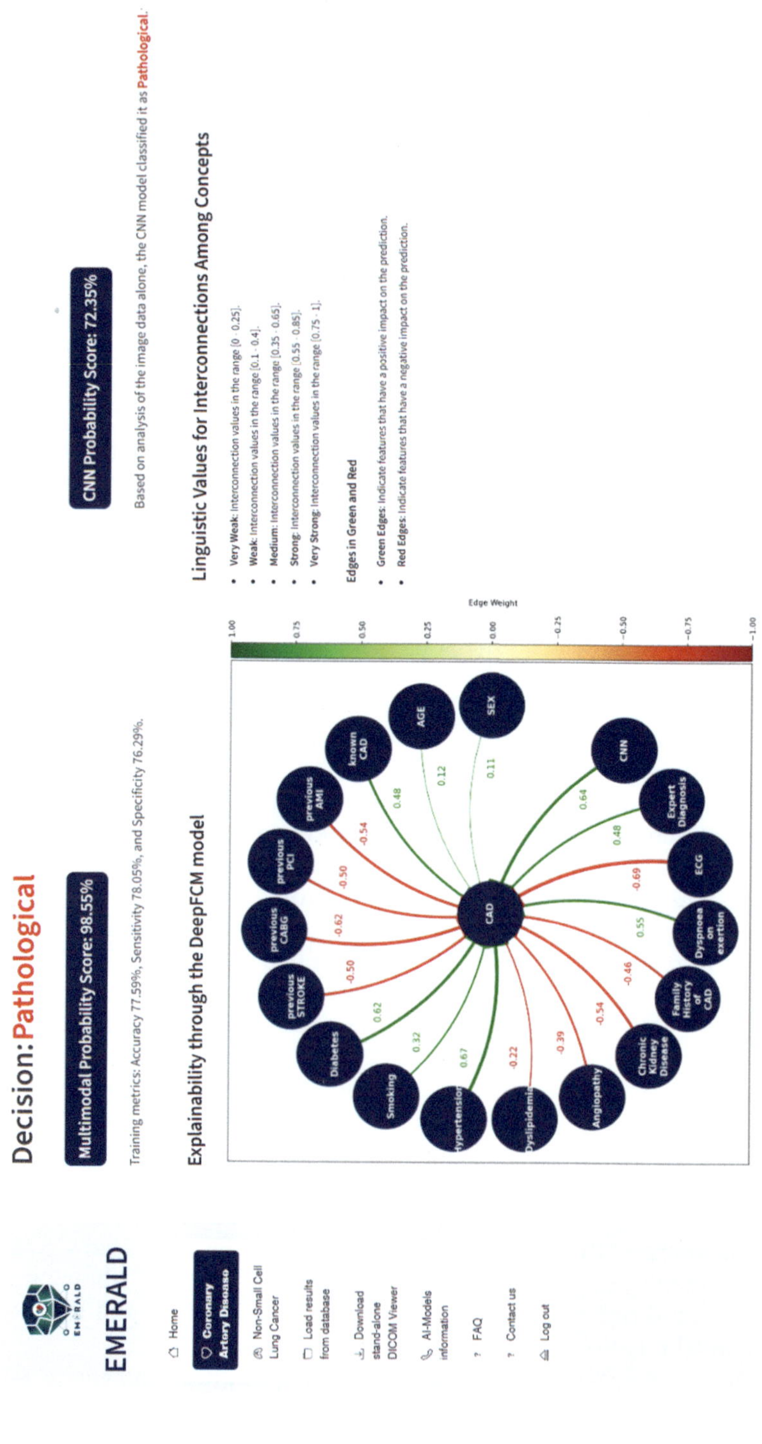

Figure 12.3 DeepFCM-PSO prediction for CAD multimodal diagnosis.

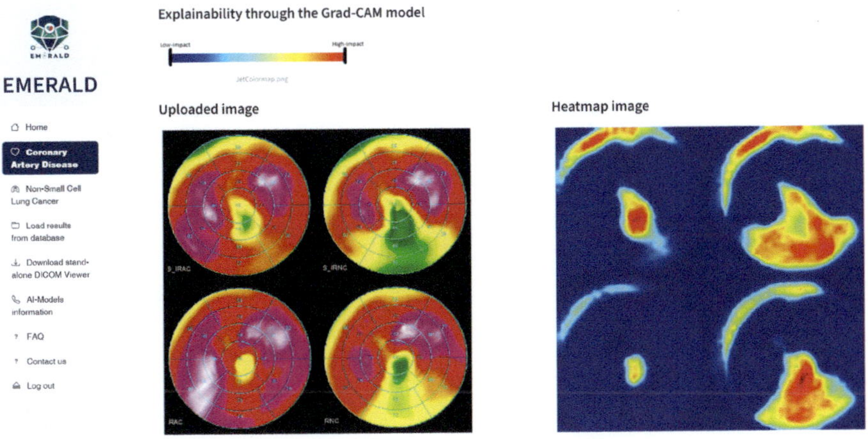

Figure 12.4 Grad-CAM application to the Polar map image.

visual representation of myocardial perfusion in both AC and NAC formats for stress and rest conditions.

The Grad-CAM heatmap effectively identified the most critical areas in the original image that contributed to the model's decision, where red represents high-impact pixel regions, and blue defines low-impact.

To further enhance explainability, we integrated NLG using the open-source Llama 3.2-vision model to translate DeepFCM's numerical outputs into human-understandable textual explanations. We constructed a prompt that includes the clinical variables, the Polar image of the specific instance, the generated weight values, the RGB-CNN prediction based on the image, and the DeepFCM-PSO multimodal predicted output, along with specific guidelines for the structure of the response.

The constructed prompt is utilized as input to the open-source model Llama 3.2-Vision, enabling it to translate the reasoning behind DeepFCM-PSO's decision-making process. In Figure 12.5, we present the Llama 3.2-Vision's response for this instance. The response effectively detects and analyzes the most influential clinical features, leveraging the weight values from the DeepFCM-PSO graph. Additionally, it provides a detailed analysis of the pathological regions detected in the uploaded polar map image.

12.5 Conclusions

The proposed model, DeepFCM-PSO, has proven to be a reliable and interpretable multimodal diagnostic model for CAD diagnosis. By incorporating expert-driven interconnections and explainable AI methodologies, DeepFCM-PSO enhances prediction accuracy and also provides transparency

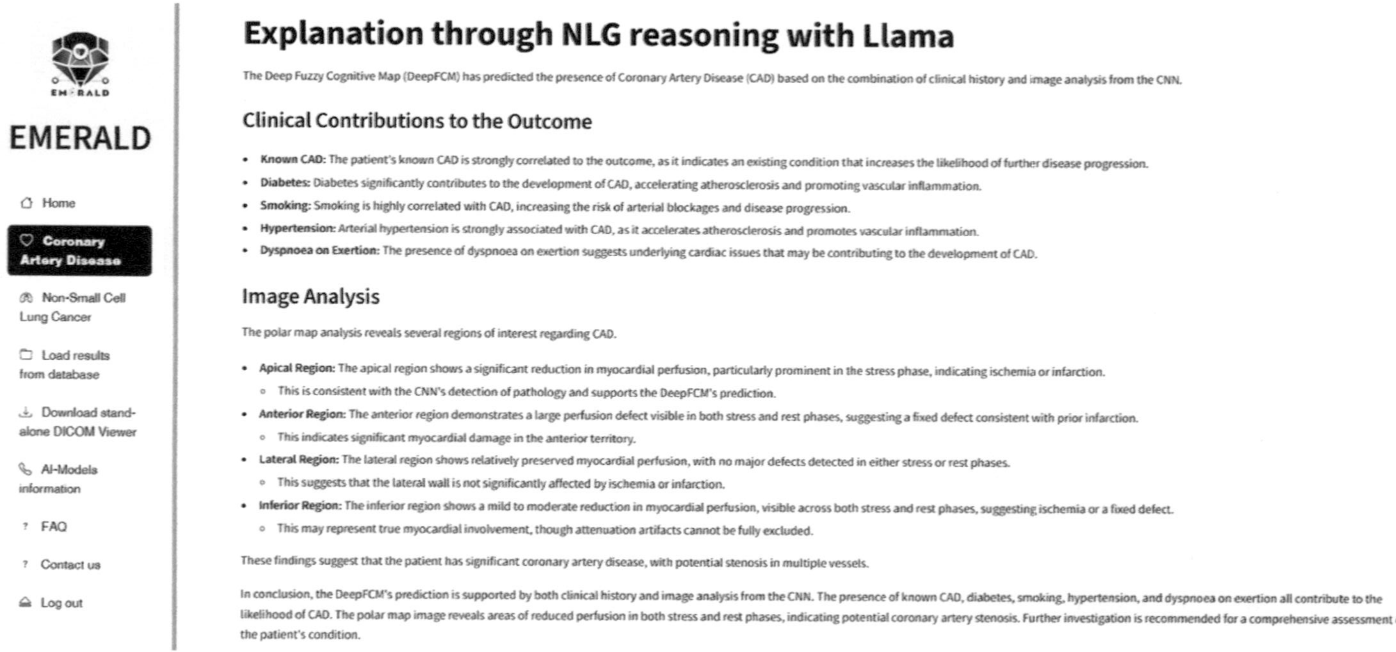

Figure 12.5 Llama3.2-Vision response for a CAD multimodal instance.

of the decision-making process. The model attained high performance metrics, with an accuracy of 77.59%, a loss of 0.22, a sensitivity of 78.05%, a specificity of 76.29%, and a precision of 74.05%, validated through a 10-fold cross-validation process. Furthermore, a comparative evaluation highlights that DeepFCM-PSO, particularly with expert-guided initialization, outperforms random weights initialization and achieves superior classification performance compared to single-modality methods such as FCM-PSO and RGB-CNN, which rely on clinical and imaging data, respectively. These results highlight the effectiveness of incorporating multimodal models in critical domains such as healthcare, where integrating diverse data sources can enhance diagnostic accuracy and decision-making reliability.

The proposed DeepFCM-PSO system demonstrated effectiveness and interpretability in diagnosing CAD. To ensure transparency, several XAI techniques were included in the MDSS. Graphical visualizations demonstrated the weighted influence of each feature on the CAD diagnosis. Grad-CAM also highlighted the most important areas in the Polar map images, which helped explain the RGB-CNN's predictions. Additionally, Llama3.2-Vision, an open-source language model, was used to translate the DeepFCM and RGB-CNN predictions into textual explanations. With these XAI techniques, DeepFCM-PSO provides a data-driven and transparent decision support system that builds trust in AI-assisted medical evaluations.

For future work, we aim to employ alternative learning methods in the DeepFCM training process and enhance the XAI techniques to further enhance the explainability of the results, while preserving high diagnostic accuracy. By advancing explainability methodologies, DeepFCM will contribute to a more interpretable and trustworthy AI-assisted decision-making framework in medical applications.

References

Apostolopoulos, I. D., Groumpos, P. P., & Apostolopoulos, D. I. (2021). State space advanced fuzzy cognitive map approach for automatic and non-invasive diagnosis of coronary artery disease. *Biomedical Physics & Engineering Express*, 7(4), 045007. https://doi.org/10.1088/2057-1976/abfd83

Apostolopoulos, I. D., Papathanasiou, N. D., Spyridonidis, T., & Apostolopoulos, D. J. (2020). Automatic characterization of myocardial perfusion imaging polar maps employing deep learning and data augmentation. *Hellenic Journal of Nuclear Medicine*, *23*(2), 125–132.

Bansal, M., Madan, P., Vishnoi, A., Srivastava, P., Choudhury, T., & Bansal, A. (2024). Detection of coronary artery disease using transfer learning. In *2024 International Conference on Artificial Intelligence and Emerging Technology (Global AI Summit)* (pp. 1242–1247). IEEE. https://doi.org/10.1109/GlobalAISummit62156.2024.10947935

Brownlee, J. (2018, May 22). A gentle introduction to K-fold cross-validation. *Machine Learning Mastery*. https://machinelearningmastery.com/k-fold-cross-validation/

Chen, H., Fan, D. L., Fang, L., Huang, W., Huang, J., Cao, C., Yang, L., He, Y., & Zeng, L. (2020). Particle swarm optimization algorithm with mutation operator for particle filter noise reduction in mechanical fault diagnosis. *International Journal of Pattern Recognition and Artificial Intelligence*, *34*(10), 2058012. https://doi.org/10.1142/S0218001420580124

Chen, J. J., Su, T. Y., Chen, W. S., Chang, Y. H., & Lu, H. H. S. (2021). Convolutional neural network in the evaluation of myocardial ischemia from CZT SPECT myocardial perfusion imaging: Comparison to automated quantification. *Applied Sciences*, *11*(2), 514. https://doi.org/10.3390/app11020514

Chi, J., Karn, U., Zhan, H., Smith, E., Rando, J., Zhang, Y., Plawiak, K., Delpierre Coudert, Z., Upasani, K., & Pasupuleti, M. (2024). *Llama Guard 3 vision: Safeguarding human-AI image understanding conversations* [Preprint]. arXiv. https://doi.org/10.48550/arXiv.2411.10414

Fedorov, I., Plawiak, K., Wu, L., Elgamal, T., Suda, N., Smith, E., Zhan, H., et al. (2024). *Llama Guard 3-1B-INT4: Compact and efficient safeguard for human-AI conversations* [Preprint]. arXiv. https://doi.org/10.48550/arXiv.2411.17713

Feleki, A., Apostolopoulos, I. D., Papageorgiou, E., Moustakidis, S., Papathanasiou, N. D., Apostolopoulos, D. J., Kokkinos, K., & Papandrianos, N. (2023a). Deep fuzzy cognitive map methodology for non-small cell lung cancer diagnosis based on positron emission tomography imaging. In *2023 14th International Conference on Information, Intelligence, Systems & Applications (IISA)* (pp. 1–6). IEEE. https://doi.org/10.1109/IISA59645.2023.10345912

Feleki, A., Apostolopoulos, I., Moustakidis, S., Papageorgiou, E., Papathanasiou, N., Apostolopoulos, D., & Papandrianos, N. (2023b). Explainable deep fuzzy cognitive map diagnosis of coronary artery disease: Integrating myocardial perfusion imaging, clinical data, and natural language insights. *Applied Sciences*, *13*(21), 11953. https://doi.org/10.3390/app132111953

Feleki, A., Apostolopoulos, I., Papageorgiou, K., Papageorgiou, E., Apostolopoulos, D., & Papandrianos, N. (2023c). A fuzzy cognitive map learning approach for coronary artery disease diagnosis in nuclear medicine. In *Artificial Intelligence Applications and Innovations* (pp. 14–25). Springer. https://doi.org/10.1007/978-3-031-39965-7_2

Feleki, A., Papandrianos, N., Apostolopoulos, I., Papageorgiou, E., Papathanasiou, N., Apostolopoulos, D., Alonso Moral, J. M., & Andreu-Perez, J. (2024). A medical decision support system for explainable multimodal detection of non-small cell lung cancer using clinical and PET data. In *Proceedings of EXPLAINABILITY 2024* (pp. 27–32). https://www.thinkmind.org/library/EXPLAINABILITY/EXPLAINABILITY_2024/explainability_2024_1_60_10032.html

Heckel, R., & Yilmaz, F. F. (2020). *Early stopping in deep networks: Double descent and how to eliminate it* [Preprint]. arXiv. https://doi.org/10.48550/arXiv.2007.10099

Khodadadi, M., Shayanfar, H., Maghooli, K., & Mazinan, A. H. (2019). Fuzzy cognitive map based approach for determining the risk of ischemic stroke. *IET Systems Biology*, *13*(6), 297–304. https://doi.org/10.1049/iet-syb.2018.5128

Kosko, B. (1986). Fuzzy cognitive maps. *International Journal of Man-Machine Studies*, *24*(1), 65–75. https://doi.org/10.1016/S0020-7373(86)80040-2

Kreinovich, V., Kosheleva, O., & Shahbazova, S. (2020). Why triangular and trapezoid membership functions: A simple explanation. In *Recent developments and the new direction in soft-computing foundations and applications* (pp. 25–31). Springer. https://doi.org/10.1007/978-3-030-38893-5_2

Papageorgiou, E., Feleki, A., Papandrianos, N., Apostolopoulos, I., Papageorgiou, K., Papathanasiou, N., & Apostolopoulos, D. (2025). Multimodal diagnosis using deep fuzzy cognitive map with extreme learning machine integrated into a medical decision support system for coronary artery disease and non-small cell lung cancer detection. In *Proceedings of the 28th Pan-Hellenic Conference on Progress in*

Computing and Informatics (PCI '24) (pp. 400–406). Association for Computing Machinery. https://doi.org/10.1145/3716554.3716615

Papageorgiou, E. I., Parsopoulos, K. E., Stylios, C. S., Groumpos, P. P., & Vrahatis, M. N. (2005). Fuzzy cognitive maps learning using particle swarm optimization. *Journal of Intelligent Information Systems*, *25*(1), 95–121. https://doi.org/10.1007/s10844-005-0864-9

Papageorgiou, E. I., & Salmeron, J. L. (2013). A review of fuzzy cognitive maps research during the last decade. *IEEE Transactions on Fuzzy Systems*, *21*(1), 66–79. https://doi.org/10.1109/TFUZZ.2012.2201727

Papandrianos, N. I., Apostolopoulos, I. D., Feleki, A., Apostolopoulos, D. J., & Papageorgiou, E. I. (2022a). Deep learning exploration for SPECT MPI polar map images classification in coronary artery disease. *Annals of Nuclear Medicine*, *36*(9), 823–833. https://doi.org/10.1007/s12149-022-01762-4

Papandrianos, N. I., Feleki, A., Moustakidis, S., Papageorgiou, E. I., Apostolopoulos, I. D., & Apostolopoulos, D. J. (2022b). An explainable classification method of SPECT myocardial perfusion images in nuclear cardiology using deep learning and Grad-CAM. *Applied Sciences*, *12*(15), 7592. https://doi.org/10.3390/app12157592

Papandrianos, N. I., Feleki, A., Papageorgiou, E. I., & Martini, C. (2022c). Deep learning-based automated diagnosis for coronary artery disease using SPECT-MPI images. *Journal of Clinical Medicine*, *11*(13), 3918. https://doi.org/10.3390/jcm11133918

Samaras, A.-D., Feleki, A., Apostolopoulos, I. D., Moustakidis, S., Papageorgiou, E., Kokkinos, K., & Papandrianos, N. (2024). Medical decision support system in nuclear medicine diagnosis for non-small cell lung cancer and coronary artery disease: A first stage prototype. In *2024 15th International Conference on Information, Intelligence, Systems & Applications (IISA)* (pp. 1–8). IEEE. https://doi.org/10.1109/IISA62523.2024.10786612

Selvaraju, R. R., Cogswell, M., Das, A., Vedantam, R., Parikh, D., & Batra, D. (2020). Grad-CAM: Visual explanations from deep networks via gradient-based localization. *International Journal of Computer Vision*, *128*(2), 336–359. https://doi.org/10.1007/s11263-019-01228-7

Shijie, J., Wang, P., Jia, P., & Hu, S. (2017). Research on data augmentation for image classification based on convolution neural networks. In *2017 Chinese Automation Congress (CAC)* (pp. 4165–4170). IEEE. https://doi.org/10.1109/CAC.2017.8243510

Zadeh, L. A. (1965). Fuzzy sets. *Information and Control*, *8*(3), 338–353. https://doi.org/10.1016/S0019-9958(65)90241-X

Index

Note: Page number in *Italics* refers to figures; page number in **Bold** refers to tables.

For Product Safety Concerns and Information please contact our
EU representative GPSR@taylorandfrancis.com Taylor & Francis
Verlag GmbH, Kaufingerstraße 24, 80331 München, Germany